SENECA

A PHILOSOPHER IN POLITICS

SENECA

A PHILOSOPHER IN POLITICS

BY

MIRIAM T. GRIFFIN

OXFORD
AT THE CLARENDON PRESS
1976

Oxford University Press, Ely House, London W. 1

GLASGOW NEW YORK TORONTO MELBOURNE WELLINGTON
CAPE TOWN IBADAN NAIROBI DAR ES SALAAM LUSAKA ADDIS ABABA
DELHI BOMBAY CALCUTTA MADRAS KARACHI DACCA
KUALA LUMPUR SINGAPORE HONG KONG TOKYO

ISBN 0 19 814365 6

*Printed in Great Britain
at the University Press, Oxford
by Vivian Ridler
Printer to the University*

PARENTIBUS OPTIMIS

PREFACE

RECENT Senecan scholarship concentrates on his methods of literary composition and moral instruction. That is as it should be, for Seneca's works were higher in quality and proved more potent in influence than his life. But the historian of the Early Empire and the literary biographer have an interest in Seneca as well. Their task is more difficult in one respect, for they cannot proceed without relating what Seneca wrote to what he did, and Seneca is a most uncooperative author for such a venture. This book, a revised version of an Oxford doctoral thesis submitted in the summer of 1968, is neither a biography of Seneca nor a history of the period of his political influence, but an example of the kind of study that is a necessary preliminary to both. It represents an attempt to confront directly the problem of how to relate Seneca's works to his life.

My first debt of gratitude is to Sir Ronald Syme. *Homines amplius oculis quam auribus credunt*: I am only one of many research students to profit as much from his personal inspiration and practical help from draft to proof as from his *Tacitus*. I also owe an incalculable debt to Miss Margaret Hubbard of St. Anne's College who supervised my work and well-being as under-graduate and Fulford Research Fellow at that generous institu-tion, and who gave up time she could not spare to read the greater part of the thesis in draft, making many suggestions that were then incorporated. The late Mrs. M. I. Henderson of Somerville College, who, as my tutor, first awakened my interest in Roman History and in Seneca, discussed the central problems with me and read an earlier version of Chapter 4. Professor P. A. Brunt, whose lectures on Stoicism and Politics in Michaelmas Term 1963 sug-gested many fruitful subjects for investigation, read the completed thesis. The extremely detailed and helpful comments supplied by him and by Professor Z. Stewart of Harvard University have been invaluable to me in improving the structure and balance of this study. Professor A. Momigliano very kindly drew my attention to evidence I would otherwise have missed, and Mr. C. D. N. Costa improved the accuracy of several chapters in proof. As for the errors that remain, I can only say that they would have been far greater in number were it not for the persistent meticulousness of the readers of the Clarendon Press.

Finally, I must record my gratitude to my former pupil, Mrs. E. G. Clark, for selfless and substantial assistance with the proof and *index locorum*; to my father, Mr. Leo Dressler, who spent many hours checking a difficult typescript; to my daughter Julia who proof-read the Indexes; and to my husband Jasper, whose help in reading several portions in draft has been more than equalled by his sacrifices in terms of domestic calm and comfort.

M. T. G.

Somerville College
December 1974

CONTENTS

ABBREVIATIONS

AE	*L'Année épigraphique.*
AJ	F. Abbott and A. C. Johnson, *Municipal Administration in the Roman Empire*, Princeton, N.J., 1926.
AJP	*American Journal of Philology.*
BMC I	*Coins of the Roman Empire in the British Museum*, vol. I, ed. H. Mattingly (1923).
CAH	*Cambridge Ancient History.*
CIL	*Corpus Inscriptionum Latinarum.*
CJ	*Classical Journal.*
Coll. Lat.	*Collection Latomus.*
CP	*Classical Philology.*
CPJ	*Corpus Papyrorum Judaicarum*, 3 vols., Cambridge, Mass., 1957–64.
CQ	*Classical Quarterly.*
CR	*Classical Review.*
CW	*Classical World.*
ESAR	*Economic Survey of Ancient Rome*, 5 vols., ed. T. Frank, Baltimore, Md., 1933–40.
FGH	F. Jacoby, *Die Fragmente der griechischen Historiker.*
Gym.	*Gymnasium.*
Haase	F. Haase, *L. Annaei Senecae Opera*, vol. III (containing fragments), Leipzig, 1852.
HRR	H. Peter, *Historicorum Romanorum Reliquiae.*
HSCP	*Harvard Studies in Classical Philology.*
ILS	H. Dessau, *Inscriptiones Latinae Selectae.*
JRS	*Journal of Roman Studies.*
JTS	*Journal of Theological Studies.*
MAAR	*Memoirs of the American Academy in Rome.*
MH	*Museum Helveticum.*
NC	*Numismatic Chronicle.*
NGG	*Nachrichten von der Gesellschaft der Wissenschaften zu Göttingen.*
N.J.f.d.kl.Alt.	*Neue Jahrbücher für das klassische Altertum.*
Not. Scav.	*Notizie degli scavi di antichità.*

ORF²	H. Malcovati, *Oratorum Romanorum Fragmenta*².
PBA	*Proceedings of the British Academy.*
PBSR	*Papers of the British School at Rome.*
PIR	*Prosopographia Imperii Romani.*
RAL	*Rendiconti della Classe di Scienze morali, storiche e filologiche dell'Academia dei Lincei.*
R-E	*Real-Encyclopädie der classischen Altertumswissenschaft.*
REA	*Revue des études anciennes.*
REG	*Revue des études grecques.*
REL	*Revue des études latines.*
RhM	*Rheinisches Museum für Philologie.*
RIC	H. Mattingly, E. A. Sydenham, *The Roman Imperial Coinage*, 5 vols., London, 1923–38.
RIL	*Rendiconti dell'Istituto Lombardo, Classe di Lettere, Scienze morali e storiche.*
Riv. di fil.	*Rivista di filologia.*
RPh	*Revue de philologie.*
SEG	*Supplementum Epigraphicum Graecum.*
SEHRE²	M. Rostovtzeff, *Social and Economic History of the Roman Empire*², ed. P. M. Fraser, 2 vols., Oxford, 1957.
SIG³	W. Dittenberger, *Sylloge Inscriptionum Graecarum* (3rd edition).
SVF	H. von Arnim, *Stoicorum Veterum Fragmenta*, 4 vols., Stuttgart, 1905.
TAPA	*Transactions of the American Philological Association.*
WJA	*Würzburger Jahrbücher für die Altertumswissenschaft.*

I

INTRODUCTION

The Seneca Problem

'Without the testimony of Tacitus, Seneca the statesman could hardly exist.'[1] Syme's tribute to the historian contains a remarkable fact about the statesman: he did not discuss his political career or his policies, though he wrote voluminously and in the first person. Only the *Apocolocyntosis* and *De Clementia* appear to betray directly his preoccupations as *amicus principis*. Are the rest of his works simply irrelevant to his political career? This problem is part of a wider one, for it is not merely Seneca the statesman that his works fail to reveal—it is Seneca the man. The surviving prose works, though addressed to contemporaries and concerned with practical moral problems, tell us little about Seneca's external life or about the people and events that formed its setting.[2]

One important result of this situation is our inability to date most of his works with certainty or precision. Those that can be placed definitely are attached to their dates by only one or two references: *Ad Polybium* to 43 by a reference to Claudius' imminent triumph;[3] *De Clementia* to late 55 or 56 by a statement of Nero's

---

[1] R. Syme, *Tacitus*, Oxford, 1958, p. 552.

[2] W. Trillitzsch, *Seneca im literarischen Urteil der Antike*, Amsterdam, 1971, II, pp. 301–24, has now assembled the autobiographical references, but since he is only interested in their contribution to the judgement of later writers on Seneca, he omits items about Seneca's friends and slaves while including Seneca's descriptions of his moods, moral failings, and aims as a philosopher which cannot be taken without question as keys to his real personality (see pp. 5–6), and passages from *De Vita Beata* which are only dubiously autobiographical (see p. 19). Apart from these two doubtful categories and passages of the epigrams which are not certainly Seneca's, Trillitzsch collects only about eighty references by Seneca to himself, many of them repetitions of the same facts.

[3] *Cons. Polyb.* 13. 2. See the Chronological Table in Appendix A1 for all these works.

age;[1] the *Naturales Quaestiones* to 62 or 63 by a report of the
Campanian earthquake.[2] The dating of the twenty-two books
of the *Epistulae Morales* hangs on one reference to a historical
event: the fire at Lugdunum.[3] Fortunately, we need not here
review the chronological difficulties of the dialogues. This has
been done for most of them in great detail by F. Giancotti, and
the problem is frequently discussed.[4]

What leaves these works suspended in the air is Seneca's
reluctance to mention his current public position, to allude to
current events, or to refer to contemporaries by name,[5] except
for the Emperor and the addressees of his various works.[6] Even
the domestic details are few:[7] we have only one certain allusion
to Seneca's wife Pompeia Paulina;[8] three references by name to
his older brother.[9] In the Consolation addressed to his mother
Helvia, Seneca reviews the members of his family that she has
mourned and those that remain to console her: Seneca's son
and three other grandchildren have died; she has lost her mother,
her uncle, and her husband; there remain her sister, her sons,
and two grandchildren, Marcus and Novatilla.[10] This work comes
the closest to offering us a description of Seneca's family, but,
even here, only two are actually named. Seneca did write a
biography of his father that has been lost:[11] presumably he had
to give some details there. The Letters contain a few details

---

[1] *Clem.* 1. 9, 1.   [2] *NQ* 6. 1.   [3] *Ep.* 91.

[4] F. Giancotti, *Cronologia dei 'Dialoghi' di Seneca*, Turin, 1957. The other
main works are noted in the summary preceding the Chronological Table in
Appendix A1.

[5] See, in Appendix D1, a list of the small number of contemporaries named
by Seneca.

[6] See the convenient summary of methods of dating Seneca's works by
B. Hambüchen, in *Die Datierung von Senecas Schrift Ad Paulinum De Brevitate
Vitae*, Diss., Köln, 1966, pp. 9–22. He eschews all but three of which the best
(references to events otherwise dated and references to events of his own life
dated by historical sources) are the ones noted here, and emphasizes how rarely
they can be used.

[7] A. J. M. Diepenbrock, *L. Annaei Senecae philosophi . . . vita*, Amsterdam,
1888, p. 42, was over-optimistic in describing Seneca's works as good sources
for his private life, despite their deficiencies as sources for his public life.

[8] *Ep.* 104.   [9] See Appendix D1.

[10] *Cons. Helv.* 2. 4–5; 18–19.

[11] Haase, frag. XV (98–9): *De Vita Patris*.

about his past: his poor health,[1] his philosophical education,[2] and the loss of his friend Serenus.[3] Of his life at the time of writing he tells us about his properties and travels, his ascetic habits and illnesses, and he also mentions a few friends.

The reasons for the paucity of concrete detail are no doubt various: a natural reserve may play some part; the emphasis on the inner life in Seneca's philosophy probably more. Finally, there is the role in which Seneca cast himself: a teacher of morals and a healer of minds. The effect of this standpoint is most striking in the Letters to Lucilius. This work is richer in personal detail and in allusions to contemporary life than any other. Yet we are a long way from Cicero's revealing letters to Atticus, one of Seneca's models.[4] The difference is not explained by Seneca's intention to publish them, clear as that intention is from Letter 21. 4. For Pliny's Letters, though intended for publication, are rich in details about Pliny's career, his friends, and his ambitions. It is true that Pliny's collection contains many letters based on genuine ones,[5] but even the entirely or almost entirely fictional character of Seneca's correspondence does not fully account for its lack of personal revelation: even Horace's poetic Epistles—which Seneca knew well and had in mind when writing[6]—give us more autobiographical detail.[7] Seneca, in fact, explicitly contrasts his rigid limitation of subject-matter with Cicero's advice to Atticus to write 'quod in buccam venerit', claiming a more important theme: 'sua satius est mala quam aliena tractare, se excutere, et videre quam multarum rerum candidatus sit, et non suffragari.'[8] Like political gossip, references

---

[1] See pp. 42 ff.   [2] Ep. 108.   [3] Ep. 63.

[4] Ep. 21. 4. Seneca's efforts to make the Letters appear to be a real correspondence are probably due to the influence of this model. The character of the Letters is further discussed on pp. 349–53 and in Appendix B4.

[5] For the literary models and genuine basis of Pliny's correspondence see A. N. Sherwin-White, The Letters of Pliny, Oxford, 1966, pp. 1–16.

[6] They are quoted in Ep. 119 and 120. Ep. 28 paraphrases Horace, Ep. 1. 11, 27.

[7] Horace describes his appearance in Ep. 1. 4, 15; 1. 7, 26. There is no such avowed self-portrait in Seneca. For a comparison of Horace's Epistles and Seneca's, pointing out that Horace's autobiographical information covers a wider range than Seneca's, see R. Heinze, N.J.f.d.kl.Alt. 43 (1919), especially pp. 313–14.

[8] Ep. 118. 1–2.

to the weather are branded as 'ineptiae', except when they are
used to introduce philosophical reflections.[1]

The philosophical letters of Epicurus were clearly in the
forefront of Seneca's mind when he wrote.[2] An advanced aspirant
to *sapientia*, Seneca advises, exhorts, and encourages his friend
Lucilius along the path to virtue (27; 38). Despite Seneca's
comparison of the Letters to intimate conversations between
friends (38; 75; cf. 40. 1), personal details are given only, at least
in theory, to further this end. They provide material for analysis
(e.g. 57; 63. 14) or lead to philosophical conclusions (e.g. 53. 5;
76). For this purpose, incidents from Lucilius' life (e.g. 28; 47)
or other lives (e.g. 27. 5; 30; 55. 2–7; 101) will do as well. The
fact that we are dealing with *exempla* and not with news is
especially clear from the fact that most of the people mentioned
are dead. Of the living, Seneca himself is the main *exemplum*
(6. 5). Lucilius is told to listen in on the author's private dialogue
with himself (27) or to imitate Seneca's practice, as illustrated
in the Letters, of abstracting a thought for meditation from his
daily reading (2. 4). Some of Seneca's stories about himself are
certainly spun out to add amusement or colour (e.g. 53; 108)
and once a technical discussion of olives and vines is pursued for
its own sake (86); but these exceptions do not remove the
reader's general impression that he is not really being brought close
to the author, that he is being told only what Seneca regards as
philosophically interesting and no more. There is no pattern in the
incidents recounted, no references back and forth to events. They
are pieces of a mosaic whose total shape we are not meant to see.

How then is Seneca's life to be uncovered? The concrete details
that Seneca gives in the Letters can be trusted: several of them
can be checked by outside information.[3] But the standpoint

---

[1] *Ep.* 23. 1; 67.

[2] *Ep.* 21. 5. Seneca even admired his style (*Ep.* 46. 1). The Letters are rich in
quotations from Epicurus. For their influence on the form of the early letters
see p. 352.

[3] See the list in K. Abel, *Bauformen in Senecas Dialogen*, Heidelberg, 1967, p. 105.
Add: Seneca's wife Paulina (Appendix D1); his suburban villa of *Ep.* 12 and
Tacitus, *Ann.* 15. 60, 4; his villa at Nomentum in *Epp.* 104; 110, cf. Pliny, *NH*
14. 51.

indicated above may make us wonder if some of the incidents described in the Letters have not been exaggerated or slanted to make the moral point sharper: did Seneca really stay in the bath-house at Baiae more than five minutes (56)? Did he really swim to shore (53)? Even if we are not inclined to such a trivial type of scepticism, we must admit that Seneca's picture of his personality in the Letters lacks plausibility and consistency: he is more concerned to offer the public examples of the moral preacher, the pedagogue, the struggling student, the zealous convert, than to portray his real relationship with his addressee Lucilius, or record his own moods.[1] Seneca's avowed interests should also make us wary of the great temptation to increase the information he supplies by assuming, as we scrutinize his works, that he alludes to the contemporary scene covertly or reveals the very ideas he implemented as *amicus principis*. His period of power, for which we have the greatest outside information about his position, his friends, and his possessions, presents the greatest temptation: can we not find allusions and ideas that fit and augment the precious data?

There are clear indications that the venture is hazardous. Thus, some passages seem to allude to events which, as we happen to know, occurred only after the composition of the works in question.[2] Again, the account of Seneca's frame of mind in exile, and of the truth of the charge on which he was exiled, varies noticeably between what he says in the Consolation to his mother and what he says in the Consolation to Polybius, though both works date from his exile.[3] We must also reckon with the

---

[1] G. Misch, *A History of Autobiography in Antiquity*, Eng. trans., 1950, II, pp. 419 ff.

[2] See the warning of P. Grimal, 'Est-il possible de dater un traité de Sénèque?', *REL* 27 (1949), 178 ff. I append a few examples of my own: *Cons. Helv.* 14. 2 (during Seneca's exile, A.D. 41-9) might well seem a reference to Agrippina's behaviour as the Emperor's mother; *Clem.* 1. 21, 2 (late 55 or 56) might seem a splendid justification of Corbulo's settlement in 63 (*Ann.* 15. 29); ibid. 1. 26, 1 might seem an allusion to the murder of Pedanius Secundus in 61 (*Ann.* 14. 42 ff.); *Ira* 3. 35 (before mid-52): 'deinde idem de re publica libertatem sublatam quereris quam domi sustulisti'—surely a hit at the speech of Cassius Longinus after Pedanius' murder in 61 (*Ann.* 14. 43-4; cf. 16. 7, 2)!

[3] See now the discussion of both works by Abel in *Bauformen*. He shows

fact that in antiquity Seneca was often accused of hypocrisy.[1] Such considerations warn the biographer to be careful not to beg the question of how Seneca the writer is related to Seneca the man.

Recent Senecan scholarship has shown an acute awareness of the problem outlined above. The chronology of the dialogues has been pruned of inconclusive and misleading arguments.[2] The emphasis in the study of the dialogues and letters has moved from biography to structure.[3] The main object of study is how the structure carries out the philosopher's avowed purpose of spiritual comfort and persuasion,[4] though peculiarities in argument and design are allowed to suggest other purposes as well.[5] If biographical and historical studies do not always show similar caution, the reason is that the work of the author can be studied profitably even apart from the man, but the life of the man cannot be studied without consideration of his works. For the biographer, some conception of the relation of Seneca's work to his life is absolutely essential.

Perhaps the answer is simple and negative: the essays and letters are pure products of Seneca's literary talent and energy, sharply dissociated from his other activities. This answer looks plausible when we consider how Seneca came to write philosophy.

---

that the *Ad Helviam* presupposes a claim of innocence, while chapter 13. 4 of *Ad Polybium* allows for the possibility, or even probability, of his guilt. For the difference in mood cf. *Cons. Helv.* 20 with *Cons. Polyb.* 18. 9. It cannot be established that the works date from different periods of Seneca's exile: see Appendix A1.

[1] Tacitus, *Ann.* 13. 42, cf. Dio 61. 10, 3; *Ann.* 14. 52–3.

[2] Giancotti's *Cronologia dei 'Dialoghi' di Seneca* is the most substantial contribution in this field. Grimal (above, p. 5 n. 2) aided the approach, as had E. Albertini before him in the first chapter of his *La composition dans les ouvrages philosophiques de Sénèque*, Paris, 1923. The discussion of chronology at the end of Abel's *Bauformen* is written mostly in the same cautious spirit. It may be that the researches being made by A. Delatte and E. Evrard with the use of a computer will reveal modulations in Seneca's stylistic habits that will help to determine the chronology of the doubtful works.

[3] For a clear discussion of the change see G. Maurach, *Der Bau von Senecas Epistulae Morales*, Heidelberg, 1970, pp. 20–4.

[4] P. Grimal, *REA* 51 (1949), 246 ff.; Abel, *Bauformen*.

[5] See Appendix B1.

Seneca's talents were first applied to oratory, but ill health (and perhaps an emperor's displeasure) led him to abandon speaking in public before his exile. Most, perhaps all, of his philosophical works were composed after that date.[1] Now Cicero had defended philosophy, as a legitimate activity for the Roman statesman in the intervals or at the close of his public duties.[2] If Seneca wrote philosophy even at the height of his ministerial duties, it may have been because for him these *inertia studia* (and the writing of Nero's speeches) were a substitute for *forensis eloquentia*.[3] Philosophy would not be an odd choice for a man with literary talent and ambition. Rome's greatest writer had proposed and answered the challenge of presenting the doctrines of the Greeks in elegant Latin. Of those who made the attempt at the same time as Cicero or or later, Quintilian could find few worthy even of mention, let alone praise.[4] Seneca himself names Livy and Papirius Fabianus as writers worthy of comparison with Cicero,[5] but there was clearly room for improvement. Seneca's choice of Latin as a medium is a sure sign that his interest in writing was at least as great as his interest in philosophy: serious philosophers in his time and immediately after wrote in Greek.[6] Cicero had tried to answer the objections of the educated who scorned the idea of reading philosophy in Latin when it was available in

[1] For the extant works see Appendix A1. Of the lost works, only *De Motu Terrarum* need be dated before the reign of Gaius on the evidence we have and even that early date has been disputed. (See p. 47 n. 2.)

[2] For example in *Off.* 2. 3–5. Plutarch, *Cato Minor* 20, describes Cato's adherence to this principle.

[3] Compare the scathing remarks attributed to Suillius Rufus by Tacitus in *Ann.* 13. 42, 3.

[4] Note the judgement of Cicero's contemporary, Cornelius Nepos: 'philosophiam ante eum incomptam Latinam sua conformarit oratione' (Frag. 3). In Quintilian 10. 1, 123–4, the only Stoic writer mentioned besides Seneca is Sergius Plautus, a man who may also have combined philosophical writing with a public career, cf. *PIR*[1] S 378. But the existence of other Stoic writers is implied in the phrase: 'Plautus in Stoicis rerum cognitioni utilis.'

[5] *Ep.* 100. 9 ff. Fabianus in this Letter is also compared with Asinius Pollio, but it is not clear whether Pollio is mentioned as a writer of philosophy or merely represents the opposite stylistic pole from Cicero. See the discussion by J. André in *La vie et l'œuvre d'Asinius Pollion*, Paris, 1949, p. 82.

[6] Brutus had written in both languages. Though they were not of Greek origin, the Sextii, Annaeus Cornutus, and Marcus Aurelius all wrote in Greek,

Greek,[1] but the persistence of this attitude probably goes some
way towards explaining why Seneca is not quoted or mentioned
as a standard philosophical authority until the Christian fathers.[2]

Philosophy in Latin then was a challenge, and moral philosophy
in particular allowed full scope to the talents of an orator turned
vitiorum insectator. Nevertheless, that cannot be the whole story.
The life of the moral philosopher, especially if he offered one
doctrine as the means to salvation and did not merely describe
different views, was expected to conform to what he wrote.
Seneca accepted that obligation: 'concordet sermo cum vita',
he promised.[3] The philosophy he wrote was meant for application
by his readers and himself. But since the advice Seneca gives in
his works is concerned with the state of the human soul and the
behaviour of men in their relations as individuals with each other
and the deity, should we confine our expectations of relevance to
his private life and personal friendships, excluding that public life
of which the historians tell us?[4] The abundant counsel on the
control of the passions and the contempt of fortune, the precepts
on friendship and generosity, certainly have their principal
sphere of application in private life. Yet there are features of
Seneca's philosophical works that render this restriction unsatis-

---

and Musonius Rufus discoursed and was recorded in Greek. It is hard to agree
with the view of Abel (*Bauformen*, p. 147) that the healing of souls was the whole
aim of Seneca's writing to the exclusion of any interest in literary style itself. Of
course, he held that words should be the servant, but his lengthy discussions
of the proper style for philosophers (e.g. *Ep.* 40; 100) confirm the interest that his
own practice suggests. He knew that an effective style was necessary to the moral
instructor and guide: *Ep.* 38. 1; 108. 8–12 (to convert beginners); *Ep.* 82. 8 ff.;
87. 40–1 (against the natural fear of death and the passion of greed).

[1] *Fin.* 1. 4 ff.; *Acad.* 1. 10 ff.

[2] Quintilian 10. 1, 130 implies that Seneca's subordination of subject-matter
to rhetorical effect lost him the respect of the *eruditi* which a sober Latin style
would have captured, but Quintilian's inordinate respect for Cicero's style and
contempt for philosophers render his diagnosis untrustworthy. Fronto's disapproval of Seneca's style was also conjoined with a dislike of philosophy, but
his influence may partly explain why his philosophical pupil Marcus never
mentions Seneca though Fronto's letter (van den Hout, pp. 149, 9–151, 2) suggests
he had read and originally admired him.

[3] *Ep.* 75. 4. Cf. *Ep.* 24. 19; 52. 8; 108. 36; Haase, frag. IX (18).

[4] Diepenbrock, *L. Annaei Senecae philosophi . . . Vita*, proposed this solution
on p. 42.

factory. First, there is the frequent emphasis on aspects of behaviour that are not strictly private, even where such a line can
be drawn: free speech at court; anger in a judge or a *princeps*;
abstention and withdrawal from public life; the generosity of
the powerful. It was not only his critics who maintained that
his philosophy carried implications for his relations with Nero:
Seneca himself sought to demonstrate that Stoicism was a fit
source of advice for *principes*.[1] Then there is Seneca's preference
for Roman *exempla*, and, among them, for the public figures of
the late Republic and the Empire. His frequent remarks about
Augustus, Tiberius, Gaius, and Claudius are by no means confined to their private lives: he judges them as *principes*, and has
his own conception of the proper imperial attitude towards
Senate and *equites*, conspirators and *amici*.[2] Finally, Seneca chose
to address these discussions to men engaged in public affairs.
His brother Novatus (later Gallio) was a senator and so was Maximus; Pompeius Paulinus, Annaeus Serenus, and Lucilius Junior
were in the equestrian service; Polybius was an imperial
freedman.[3] Cicero, who dedicated his works to statesmen and
used them as participants in his dialogues, had applied Greek
philosophy to some of the problems of public life, notably in
De Re Publica and *De Officiis*. Is it not reasonable to expect that
Seneca would sometimes do the same?

We can then reasonably expect the work of the philosopher to
shed some light on the private and public life of the author. But
the relation between the two is far from obvious. We have
already mentioned some of the hazards in assuming the nature
of the connection. A review and critique of the assumptions
commonly made will make this even clearer and, in itself,
justify a more open-minded approach to the problem.

[1] Tacitus, *Ann.* 13. 42, 4; *Clem.* 2. 5, 2.

[2] See below, pp. 210 ff.

[3] For the addressees of Seneca's extant works see the Chronological Table,
Appendix A1. Of the lost or fragmentary ones, Gallio received *De Remediis
Fortuitorum*, Maximus some letters (Martial 7. 45).

Snares and Delusions

The types of connection that have been proposed can be classified roughly as follows:

I. The doctrines preached in the philosophical works may incorporate (a) Seneca's policy as a statesman; (b) his thoughts on his own way of life.

II. The works may, in whole or in part, be designed, principally or secondarily, to serve some end outside their avowed purpose as didactic literature: (a) certain passages may contain concealed comments on contemporaries; (b) whole works may serve some personal or political purpose.

To bring out the difficulty of our inquiry, let us review some suggestions that have been made in each category and the weaknesses they reveal on examination.

I (a). The most important cases concern Seneca's advice to the Princeps. It would be perverse to deny that Seneca's direct exhortations to Nero in *De Clementia* represent the advice he actually offered in private to the Emperor, especially when Nero's exhibitions of clemency in the early years are amply attested in Tacitus and Suetonius.[1] But it is hard to feel as confident about his implementation as imperial adviser of ideas contained in his other works, when we recall the charges made in his lifetime that he did not practise what he preached, and his own statement that even the *sapiens* will sacrifice means to ends and accommodate himself to circumstances.[2] Even when we know of measures taken in his period of power that fit the opinions in his essays, we may justifiably hesitate to draw the obvious conclusion that Seneca effected them, because of the number of things done in those same years that appear to conflict with his teaching, e.g. the increase in scope of the harsh SC *Silanianum* affecting slaves, and its implementation in 61;[3] the

---

[1] See below, pp. 123-4; 125 ff.

[2] Haase, frag. IX (19): 'Facit sapiens etiam quae non probabit, ut etiam ad maiora transitum inveniat, nec relinquet bonos mores set tempori aptabit, et quibus alii utuntur in gloriam aut voluptatem, utetur agendae rei causa.'

[3] See below, pp. 272; 280.

failure to chastise corrupt governors, and the sudden recall of loans that caused hardship in Britain.[1] Yet, on one point, we seem to reach safe ground: Nero's somewhat indiscriminate bounty could well have been inspired by Seneca's advice, accurately reflected in *De Beneficiis*, that the *princeps* should not contaminate his generosity with censure.[2]

But there is a really serious danger involved in assuming that what Seneca wrote must be mirrored in what he did as a statesman, namely, the temptation to simplify what Seneca wrote and what actually happened. Thus it has been argued that Seneca's condemnation of luxury shows his responsibility for Nero's sumptuary legislation, regardless of the fact that the only indication of date we have for that legislation puts it after his period of power.[3] Similarly, we are told that Seneca's condemnation of cruelty and corruption in provincial government was reflected in the excellent record of the early reign,[4] whereas the record of the early reign in the sphere of provincial administration is far from unmixed, and Seneca's views on the subject far from striking when compared with those of some philosophical Romans.[5] The influence of Seneca's ideas on the humane treatment of slaves and freedmen has been traced in a situation where it is unattested by the historian and was probably unvoiced, and also in measures improbably dated to Nero's reign merely on the ground that Seneca was his adviser.[6] Even where proper caution has been shown, the actual implications for legal action of Seneca's really rather complex views on slavery have not been thoroughly examined.[7]

I (*b*). That the record of Seneca's self-examination and inner moods is to be found in his philosophical works is a view that no one would now hold without serious qualifications.[8] Apart

---

[1] See below, pp. 246–7; 232 ff.   [2] See below, pp. 124–5; 301–2.
[3] F. Stella Maranca, *RAL* 32 (1923), 291, citing Suet. *Nero* 16. 2. Dio 62. 14 dates one of these measures to 62 after the death of Burrus. Cf. p. 218.
[4] J. Crook, *Consilium Principis*, Cambridge, 1955, pp. 119–20.
[5] See below, pp. 237 ff.   [6] See below, pp. 275–6; 280–1.
[7] See below, pp. 276 ff.
[8] Its most extreme exponent was E. Köstermann, *Sitzungsberichte der preuss. Akad. d. Wiss.* 22 (1934), 684–750. M. Pohlenz, *Philosophie und Erlebnis in Senecas Dialogen*, NGG no. 6, 1941, exhibits strong elements of this approach.

from the question of sincerity (a quality hard to assume in a man frequently accused of hypocrisy), Seneca's claims to be dispensing spiritual medicine makes it unlikely that he would concentrate on his own problems to the neglect of those of his addressee and his audience at large: 'aliter enim cum alio agendum est', he wrote.[1]

The inadequacy of this view is most clearly revealed in its application: contradictions from work to work, such as we have noted on the subject of his exile, have to be explained as changes of opinion explicable by changes in his own situation. This can necessitate, on the subject of wealth, a most wilful chronology of his works.[2] Then the terms in which Seneca sets problems for discussion have to be related to his own circumstances at some point in his career, which is not always possible. Chapter 10 will show that some of the favourite candidates for this approach, namely the works in which Seneca discusses the claims of public life against those of philosophy, resist an autobiographical interpretation in this narrow sense of mirroring decisions and opinions immediate relevant to the author's situation at the time of writing.[3]

II (a). If it seems that Seneca only rarely makes overt comments on the contemporary scene, some have thought that his readers enjoyed remarks all the more telling for being concealed. Were they not meant to recognize Nero in the description of the beast leaping up from its lair to prowl, or a known governor of Lower Germany in a discussion of silver used at banquets, or Claudius in a condemnation of antiquarianism?[4] We have already illustrated the difficulties involved in pinning down these allusions

[1] *Cons. Marc.* 2. 1. Hambüchen, *Die Datierung von Senecas Schrift Ad Paulinum De Brevitate Vitae*, pp. 11 ff., rightly emphasizes the necessity of allowing for three factors in Seneca's work: his inner state, the commonplace, the situation of the addressee. Under the third, one should also consider his general audience, to whom were directed his purple patches on luxury, his instructions on the true nature of Stoicism in *De Clementia* 2. 5, 2–3, and his advice on political acquiescence in *Ep.* 73, to give but a few examples.

[2] See below, pp. 304–5.

[3] I. Lana, *Lucio Anneo Seneca*, Turin, 1955, pp. 247 ff., 259 ff., gives an apologetic interpretation of these works, which runs into the same difficulty.

[4] *Clem.* 1. 3, 3; *Brev. Vit.* 12. 5 (cf. Pliny, *NH* 33. 143); 13.

when we suspect them.[1] These are so considerable that we may justifiably wonder if the allusions are there at all. There is, of course, no way of proving that Seneca never concealed a precise topical comment behind a general remark, but a consideration of Seneca's literary models, I believe, suggests that these cases would be isolated rather than a regular feature of the genre or something his readers would be expecting to occur frequently. Some account of these models must now be attempted.

What tradition did Seneca look to in writing his prose works? Little help is offered by the title *dialogi* attached to the ten works in the Codex Ambrosianus. That is most plausibly interpreted as an allusion to a rhetorical device common in Seneca's works, the introduction of remarks contributed by an imaginary speaker, rather than as the name of a definite literary genre, the most popular candidate being διατριβή.[2] But in rejecting the idea that the name *dialogi* means διατριβαί, we have not thereby dismissed the related and even more prevalent notion that these works of Seneca are in fact examples of a literary genre called διατριβή. A discovery of German scholars at the end of the last century,[3] the diatribe was defined as a popular philosophical discourse invented by Bion the Borysthenite, devoted usually to a single moral theme and aimed at a wider circle than school philosophy, being loose in structure and characterized by a pointed style, vivid imagery, and colloquialisms. H. Weber and others[4] were able to point to stylistic features of Seneca's works that were prominent in the remains of Bion, as preserved, in the main, by Teles: colloquialisms, deliberate coarseness, paradox, prosopopoeia, the indefinite interlocutor, and certain characteristic similes.

The whole conception of the genre has come under attack in this century, principally from German scholars themselves who

---

[1] See p. 5.   [2] See Appendix B2.

[3] H. Usener was the inventor in *Epicurea*, Leipzig, 1887, p. lxix; P. Wendland one of its principal developers (e.g. *Die hellenistisch-römische Kultur in ihren Beziehungen zu Judentum u. Christentum*[2], Tübingen, 1907, pp. 75 ff.). For the history of the idea and of criticism of it see *Der Kleine Pauly* 2 (1967), Nachträge, 1577–8.

[4] H. Weber, *De Senecae philosophi dicendi genere Bioneo*, Marburg, 1895; Wendland, ibid., p. 79.

have pointed out that these stylistic features are by no means restricted to works actually called διατριβαί[1] or to authors on whom Bion and Teles could plausibly be said to have had any influence. διατριβή is not the name of an important ancient literary genre; it denotes one of the many types of popular philosophical discourse current in the Hellenistic period.[2]

Now Seneca can certainly not be said to have been influenced directly by Bion or Teles.[3] Weber, in fact, thought that Seneca derived the 'diatribic' features of his style from Stoic writers,[4] among them Chrysippus, for whom there is evidence of such stylistic habits but not of the composition of διατριβαί. Seneca's works cannot then be assigned to an ancient literary genre called διατριβή. But it is fair to admit that Seneca's *dialogi* owe a great deal to a long tradition of popular philosophical writing, for whose characteristic style and themes we can reasonably retain the term Diatribe. Yet, it is important to note that his works, though often non-technical and practical, are not 'popular' like the harangues of street philosophers, being, as they are, more learned and intentionally narrower in appeal than even the discourses of Epictetus or Musonius Rufus.[5] It is even more

[1] Hirzel, *Der Dialog*, I, p. 374 and n. 5, maintained that the διατριβαί of Bion (D.L. 2. 77) were not philosophical discourses but a report of the conversations of other philosophers (like Arrian's record of Epictetus' teaching), since our only fragment of them is an anecdote about Aristippus. Teles' own work is nowhere called διατριβή.

[2] D.L. 7. 34 and the late definition of Hermogenes (*Math.* 5): βραχέος διανοήματος ἠθικοῦ ἔκστασις count against Hirzel's idea that the term was restricted to reports of other philosophers' teachings (see note above) and Halbauer's that they are records by a pupil of his teacher's instruction or lecture material, the term indicating, not the form of the work, but its use in teaching (O. Halbauer, *De Diatribis Epicteti*, Leipzig, 1911, pp. 3 ff.).

[3] Seneca does not mention Teles and has only the most fragmentary knowledge of Bion, all of which could have come from collections of his remarks.

[4] *De Senecae philosophi dicendi genere Bioneo*, pp. 54 ff.

[5] Seneca criticizes the Cynics 'qui libertate promiscua usi sunt et obvios ⟨quosque⟩ monuerunt . . . Hoc . . . non existimo magno viro faciendum: diluitur eius auctoritas . . .' (*Ep.* 29. 1–3). According to Tacitus (*Hist.* 3. 81) even Musonius Rufus, though a Stoic, was a purveyor of 'intempestiva sapientia', cf. Epict. 2. 12, 17ff. In his Preface to the collection of Stoic fragments, von Arnim (I. xvii–xviii) classes Musonius Rufus, Epictetus, and Marcus Aurelius as popular Stoics who preserve little of earlier Stoic views. Seneca, however, although despising scholarly investigation for its own sake, was very learned in the work

essential to our inquiry to note that Seneca's principal stylistic models were not ordinary Stoic philosophers, ancient or modern. Seneca sometimes imitates their dry, hair-splitting style, but more often he condemns it in terms strikingly reminiscent of Cicero.[1] Hirzel long ago advanced the view that Seneca's dialogues were not direct descendants of Cynic Diatribe but an individual blend of philosophical and rhetorical techniques.[2] Even Wendland, who thought Seneca's style could be traced back to Hellenistic diatribe, admitted that there was no direct link and that school rhetoric was an importance influence.[3] Others in Rome had already experimented with such a mixture. Cicero, after all, had praised Cato for enlivening Stoic doctrine with rhetorical ornament and set as his own aim in the *Paradoxa Stoicorum*: 'ea quae dicuntur in scholis θετικῶς ad nostrum hoc oratorium transfero dicendi genus.'[4] Seneca's hero in philosophical exposition was Papirius Fabianus, a trained declaimer as well as a philosopher, whose similar aversion to dry disputation he records.[5] In fact, many of the Diatribe techniques had become

of his Stoic predecessors and is a valuable source of citations. Cf. the attitude of Epictetus 2. 19.

[1] Cicero complains often (e.g. *Tusc.* 3. 13; *Fin.* 4. 3 ff.; *Brutus* 114; *De Orat.* 3. 66) of the starkness ('exilitas') of Stoic style and describes the sect as one 'quae nullum sequitur florem orationis neque dilatat argumentum sed minutis interrogatiunculis quasi punctis quod proposuit efficit' (*Parad. St.* pref. 2). That Cicero is not simply comparing his own style with a pointed style, such as Seneca's own, is clear from the very similar terms in which Seneca criticizes Stoic writing: *Ben.* 1. 4, cf. Cicero, *Fin.* 4. 3; *Epp.* 82. 8–9; 113. 1, cf. Cicero, *Fin.* 4. 52. In *De Ira* 2. 1 he warns his readers that a dry passage is coming, and the terms in which he describes it make it clear that it is in the style he criticized in Stoic works. He justifies it as a necessary preliminary to something more lofty. This is not, of course to deny that Seneca's *dialogi* owe much in content and thought to Stoic treatises, such as Chrysippus' περὶ Χαρίτων.

[2] *Der Dialog*, II, pp. 29 ff. In the Introduction to his edition of *De Constantia Sapientis*, Paris, 1953, P. Grimal has presented a similar idea, but his account seems to me imprecise, particularly as regards the differences between Seneca and the Stoics.

[3] Above, p. 13 n. 3.   [4] Pref. 5.

[5] *Ep.* 100 discusses Fabianus' style. He was a follower of Q. Sextius who had already eschewed dry disputation in his philosophical works written in Greek (*Ep.* 64. 2–3). In *Brev. Vit.* 10. 1 Fabianus is credited with the remark: 'contra adfectus impetu non subtilitate pugnandum, nec minutis vulneribus sed incursu avertendam aciem . . . contundi debere, non vellicari.'

part of the training of the rhetorical schools in the early Empire.[1] In so far as Seneca followed anyone, his literary models were probably Roman, namely Cicero's *Paradoxa Stoicorum*, Horace's *Sermones*, the Sextii, and Papirius Fabianus.[2]

It is time now to apply these suggestions about Seneca's models to the question of concealed comment. There are two principal ways in which Seneca has been thought to allude covertly to living contemporaries: (1) by concealing references to individuals behind general descriptions of the folly of men; (2) by giving his indefinite interlocutor a recognizable personality or attitude. Do our conclusions about Seneca's models help us to determine the likelihood of his using these means?

1. Though Seneca preaches forgiveness and tolerance of others,[3] his essays and letters are rich in mockery of human beings generally and in satirical passages attacking particular types, e.g. antiquarians, devotees of vocal training, fanciers of mullets, reciters and captive audiences, night-birds, and *grammatici*.[4] Many of these are recognizable commonplaces,[5] and where we know of parallels we do not feel tempted to attach the description to particular people. This should lead us to be careful in cases where we have no striking parallels and happen to stumble on a similar criticism of some individual. The point of philosophical teaching was to cure the common weaknesses of mankind, not to concentrate on individual idiosyncrasies. These general attacks are characteristic of Diatribe, and declamation.[6]

It is particularly important to note the practice of Cicero in the

---

[1] This is clearly demonstrated by A. Oltramare, *Les origines de la diatribe romaine*, Lausanne, 1926, who concentrates on the continuity of stock themes.

[2] This conclusion holds as well for the Letters which are like the *dialogi* in style (e.g. the use of 'inquit'), though a certain air of casualness and intimacy has been added (see Appendix B4). The similarity to the *dialogi* is most noticeable in the lengthy letters common in the latter half of the collection.

[3] *Ira* 3. 25; *NQ* 1, pref. 5.

[4] *Brev. Vit.* 13; 12. 4; *NQ* 3. 17–18; *Epp.* 95. 2; 122; 88. 5–8.

[5] See the remarks of W. C. Summers, *Select Letters of Seneca*, London, 1910, on *Ep.* 122 (p. 351) and on *Ep.* 88 (p. 306). For the parallels between passages in Seneca and the declaimers see Ch. Favez in the Introduction to his edition of *Consolatio ad Helviam*, Lausanne, 1918.

[6] Weber, op. cit., p. 28.

Paradoxa Stoicorum written in the spring of 46 B.C. The fifth (sixth) of these, after the standard attacks on those who covet marble houses, silver plate, and Corinthian bronzes, and on legacy-hunters, ridicules those ambitious for offices and commands, referring explicitly to the patronage of Praecia and Cethegus. Is Cicero, as is often thought, attacking Lucullus here? Caution is necessary, for although Plutarch connects Lucullus with Praecia and Cethegus, he also notes that Cethegus had control of almost all patronage at the time.[1] Cicero's attack could be general. But if it is inspired by the most notorious of Cethegus' intrigues, that concerning Lucullus' Cilician command, it is certainly not an attack on a living contemporary: Lucullus had been dead for ten years.

In the sixth (seventh) Paradox, the shadowy victim of Cicero's attack is often thought to be Marcus Crassus who had also been dead for some time. It is true that many features of the *quaestuosus* as portrayed in this Paradox are derived from Crassus (e.g. the remark that no man is rich who cannot support an army),[2] or at least fit in well with what is known of him (e.g. his profits from the Sullan proscriptions, his use of bribery in the courts).[3] On the other hand, Cicero does not mention the notorious profits Crassus derived from the frequent fires in Rome[4] and does mention practices such as usury in the provinces and the absorption of neighbouring estates that are nowhere attributed to Crassus.[5] The portrait of the *sumptuosus* in the second part of the Paradox (49 ff.) is clearly a generalized figure familiar from the standard attacks on luxury. The first-person character in this Paradox is not the real Cicero but a fictional character who is never in debt (cf. Cicero, *Att.* 2. 1, 11; 7. 8, 5; 13. 46, 4) and has an income from his *praedia* of only 100,000 HS.[6]

---

[1] Plutarch, *Lucullus* 5–6.

[2] Cf. Cicero, *Off.* 1. 25; Pliny, *NH* 33. 134.

[3] Plut. *Crassus* 2; Cicero, *Att.* 1. 16, 5.

[4] Plut. *Crassus* 2. 4.

[5] He lent money without interest to his friends, according to Plutarch, *Crassus* 3. 1.

[6] By 45 and probably earlier, the income from Cicero's *insulae* alone came to 80,000 HS or 100,000 HS (*Att.* 12. 32, 2; 15. 17, 1; 16. 1, 5).

If Cicero is any guide to Seneca, it is likely that his satirical sketches were given vividness by details taken from real individuals, but that their purport was general. In any case, Cicero certainly lends no support to the idea that they frequently concealed attacks on the living.

2. Polemic is characteristic of Bion and Teles, of Cicero in the *Paradoxa Stoicorum*, and of declamation. It is therefore to be expected in Seneca. The usual form is an attack on some anonymous example of vicious behaviour addressed in the second person, as in Cicero's last Paradox or in Seneca's *De Ira* 3. 35, 1–4. But sometimes the interlocutor assumes a more definite personality and is allowed an extended attack on the author. Seneca usually attaches these speeches to his addressee,[1] but in *De Vita Beata* 17 ff. he is berated by an anonymous speaker. Cicero may have a lesson for us here as well. In the fourth (fifth) Paradox, the author attacks an opponent who only utters one sentence but whose attitude to the author is made clear. In this figure, one is clearly meant to recognize Clodius.[2] He had been dead six years when the piece was written. As in the case of the pieces that bring Crassus and perhaps Lucullus to mind, there is no warrant for suggesting that this Paradox was really written when Clodius was alive.[3] Their relevance to their date of composition is probably of a different kind: they reflect Cicero's brooding on the position of the Optimates after the defeat of Pompey. In letters of the same period, he thinks about his friends in exile and speaks of the sufficiency of virtue for happiness, or he thinks of himself and says that real exile is life in a state where there is no law.[4] Or he thinks of the corruption that helped to bring down the Republic. Cicero's attack in this Paradox is not aimed at the living, but is, none the less, related to the contemporary situation.

[1] e.g. Serenus in *De Const. Sap.* 3. 1–2; *Tranq.* 1 (where it is not an attack, but a request for advice); the addressee in *De Otio* 1. 4–5. In *Ep.* 27. 1 objections are attributed to Lucilius.

[2] Particularly in 29–30 and 32.

[3] See the objections to this idea by A. G. Lee, *Paradoxa Stoicorum*, London, 1953, Introduction, pp. xviii–xix.

[4] This conception of their contemporary relevance was convincingly set out by K. Kumaniecki, *Philologus* 101 (1957), 113–14.

This Paradox has an obvious relevance to chapters 17 ff. of the dialogue *De Vita Beata* which are generally thought to be a counter-attack by Seneca on Suillius Rufus. Here the accuser is not so definitely characterized as in Cicero's Paradox, but many of the charges he makes, particularly those concerning Seneca's wealth, are reminiscent of those Suillius actually aimed at Seneca in 58;[1] others reflect things we happen to know about Seneca.[2] Furthermore, Seneca often seems to be talking in his own person, for instance when he says: 'De virtute non de me loquor, et cum vitiis convicium facio in primis meis facio' (18. 1) or elsewhere when the subject is nominally Socrates (27. 3) or the wise man (26. 5). Is this Seneca's speech in his own defence? Cicero's example makes us wary of attaching the work to its most obvious context, and Seneca expressly denies that the first person is to be referred to himself. 'Haec non pro me loquor (ego enim in alto vitiorum omnium sum) sed pro illo cui aliquid acti est', he says of his promise to add to the criticisms of himself and of his excuse 'Non sum sapiens' (17. 3–4). The general tone is set at the start—'Si quis itaque ex istis, qui philosophiam collatrant, quod solent dixerit' (17. 1)—and continued later on with references to the charges that famous philosophers have suffered (18–19). The autobiographical note is somewhat unclear in other ways. A taste for old wine is alleged, but Seneca drank sparingly;[3] an allusion is made to gout, but that does not feature among the ailments that Seneca so freely describes elsewhere.[4]

The problem is complex. First, it is unclear whether or not

---

[1] Wealth 17. 1–2; 21. 1 and sexual vices 27. 5 (cf. Tacitus, *Ann.* 13. 42, 3–4; Dio 61. 10, 4); expensive furniture 17. 2 (cf. Dio 61. 10, 5); deference to superiors 17. 1 (cf. Dio 61. 10, 2). The use of Dio's criticisms of Seneca as evidence for Suillius' attack is justified in Appendix C4, p. 431 n. 2.

[2] Softness in bearing the death of a friend 17. 1 (cf. *Ep.* 63); 'malignis sermonibus tangeris' 17. 1 (cf. Seneca's revenge on Suillius); hypochondria 21, 1 (cf. pp. 41 ff.); attitude to exile 21. 1 (cf. *Ad Polybium*); use of flattery 17. 1 (cf. the *Apocolocyntosis* and *NQ* 6. 8, 3; 7. 17, 2; 7. 21, 3 for flattery of Nero).

[3] 17. 2; cf. *Ep.* 108. 16.

[4] 17. 4. If gout is what Tacitus means by 'aeger nervis' (*Ann.* 15. 45, 3) he believed Seneca pretended to have the disease in 64. But Seneca may have had gout even earlier and deliberately failed to mention it because it was believed to be caused by debauchery (*Ep.* 95. 16, 21).

Seneca has a specific opponent in mind as Cicero had Clodius. Perhaps he is a type like the *quaestuosus* in Cicero's other Paradox, with features borrowed from Suillius. Then, even if Seneca is thinking of Suillius, it is uncertain whether or not we should attach the dialogue to the period of that attack. As with Cicero, the construction of a lengthy polemical discussion by Seneca would seem to indicate his concern with that problem at the moment of composition, but there must have been many occasions after 58 when Seneca felt challenged in the same way. There are in fact other reasons for regarding *De Vita Beata* as an *apologia*,[1] but the way in which Seneca has generalized both the accuser and the accused suggests that it is not an immediate counterblast to Suillius' attack, but a general answer, based on his own experience but perhaps written later, to attacks commonly made on the Stoics, attacks that, in Seneca's view, rested on a misunderstanding of the doctrine.

Our investigation of Seneca's models, then, gives no support to the assumption that Seneca frequently makes concealed comments on his living contemporaries. Of course, one cannot prove that he did not choose to do so on isolated occasions, but they would have to be made quite clear, as his readers would not be expecting them to occur regularly. Seneca was concerned with the moral condition of humanity in general. The literary form he chose for his philosophy, despite its rhetoric and satire, would not have tempted him to a more than occasional introduction of contemporary allusions—such as could occur in more sober forms of philosophical writing.[2] For Romans interested in criticizing individuals, history and tragedy were the normal literary forms, though, of course, a sensitive emperor, might take even eulogy amiss.[3]

II (*b*). In referring to *De Vita Beata* as an *apologia* we have already passed on to the question of works written with some personal or political aim. No one would maintain that the Consolation to

---

[1] See below, pp. 306 ff.

[2] Thus Cicero introduced into *De Officiis* barbed references to Antony (1. 139) and Caesar's debt laws (2. 84) that Antony upheld.

[3] Pliny, *Pan.* 3. 4; cf. Dio 59. 19, 2–3.

Polybius was designed solely to cheer up Polybius.[1] Seneca makes a clear plea for recall from Corsica and appropriately addresses his appeal to Polybius who was *a libellis*,[2] garnishing it with flamboyant flattery of Emperor and freedman.[3]

It is equally clear that *De Clementia* is not merely a mirror of Nero's virtues, but an ideal presented to the Princeps with stern admonitions, and to the general public with vigorous self-justification.[4]

An apologetic purpose has recently been proposed for the *Consolatio ad Helviam Matrem*. According to K. Abel, Seneca was not only comforting his mother and himself, but asserting his innocence of the charge of adultery for which he had been relegated, and attempting thereby to rehabilitate the reputation of his family.[5] Abel shows that the consolatory arguments pre-suppose Seneca's innocence: change of place does not matter to the man armed with virtue; the misfortune of a great man carries no disgrace.[6] Unable to offer a straight defence which might be interpreted as defiance of the Emperor, Seneca, we are told, used the more subtle means of showing that unchastity was repugnant to him and alien to his family.[7] This last argument is rather weak, as Seneca's concern with *impudicitia* in this work is matched by his concern with *luxuria*, which is not related to Seneca's crime.[8] If Seneca praised chastity highly among his

---

[1] Abel, *Bauformen*, pp. 70 ff., shows how Seneca works his personal purpose into the avowed one.

[2] The request for recall is clearest in 13. 2–4. At 2. 1 and 18. 9 Seneca seeks to arouse pity for his plight. 6. 5 makes it clear that Polybius was *a libellis*, but Seneca seems to allude in 5. 2 to his post as *a studiis*, a post attested for him in Suet. *Cl.* 28. He could have held both positions at this time, perhaps marking an interruption in the career of Callistus who may have been out of favour at first with Claudius because of his part in the plot to murder Gaius (Jos. *AJ* 19. 64; cf. *Ann.* 11. 29, 2) and who held the post *a libellis* later under Claudius (Dio 60. 30, 6b) before Polybius' death. F. Millar, *JRS* 57 (1967), 16–17, expresses doubts about Polybius' being *a libellis*, but admits *Cons. Polyb.* 6. 5 describes official duties which involved arranging *libelli* for the Emperor. But that is as close as Seneca ever comes to describing a contemporary's post (cf. *Clem.* 2. 1, 2; *Brev. Vit.* 18–19; *Ben.* 3. 22, 3).

[3] See Appendix B3.   [4] See Chapter 4.

[5] *Bauformen*, pp. 47 ff.   [6] *Cons. Helv.* 8; 9; 13. 8.

[7] Ibid. 13. 3; 16. 3–4; 19. 4.

[8] Ibid. 10; 16. 3 (in the praise of his mother); 19. 7 (in the praise of her step-sister).

mother's virtues, that was after all a standard thing to praise in a
woman, particularly if there was little else remarkable to record of
her. Seneca celebrated *pudicitia* elsewhere, and it dominates Roman
epitaphs of the period.[1] Another scholar has perceived a different
purpose concealed in the work: Seneca emphasizes his indifference
to worldly ambition and his devotion to literature and philosophy
in order to convince the Emperor that there could be no danger
in recalling him; he reviews the tragedies of his family to arouse
sympathy.[2] One fact, at least, is clear: if Seneca merely wished
to console his mother or himself, he could not have published
the Consolation at the time. But it is hard to believe that he did
not publish it then, since his final recall from exile, according
to Tacitus, was expected to be popular because of his already
considerable literary reputation.[3] The works written in exile
must be partly responsible for that reputation: Seneca had not
allowed himself to be forgotten.[4] When he displayed his skill in
handling a new type of consolation,[5] he would naturally present
an attractive portrait of the artist as innocent, brave, and philosophical in exile. How can we decide which aim was primary and
which secondary in Seneca's mind?

I have suggested elsewhere and will discuss again in this study
the possibility that *De Brevitate Vitae* was written with the
secondary purpose of presenting an official version of the retirement of Seneca's father-in-law (the addressee) from his imperial
post, and of Seneca's role in that retirement. This thesis can be
defended as the best explanation of certain oddities in the structure
and argument of the work.[6] Nevertheless, it cannot be demonstrated with the certainty that an ulterior purpose for the *Ad
Polybium* can, for the date cannot be fixed independently of the
theory.

Suspicions have also lighted on the *Consolatio ad Marciam*.

---

[1] See the fragments of Seneca's *De Matrimonio* in E. Bickel, *Diatribe in Senecae
philosophi fragmenta*, Leipzig, 1915, pp. 382–94; R. Lattimore, *Themes in Greek
and Latin Epitaphs*, Illinois, 1942, p. 296.

[2] C. Ferrill, *CP* 61 (1966), pp. 253 ff.   [3] *Ann.* 12. 8.

[4] That Seneca was trying through the *Cons. Helv.* to keep his memory alive
at Rome was suggested by R. Waltz, *La vie politique de Sénèque*, Paris, 1909, p. 110.

[5] *Cons. Helv.* 1. 2–3.   [6] See Appendix A2.

Writing under Gaius, Seneca here offers a Consolation on the death of her son over two years ago, to a prominent woman, the daughter of a political victim of Sejanus, whose works she had republished with the sanction of the new Emperor. The Seneca family had friends and relations connected with Sejanus. The only attack on the Prefect that Seneca makes occurs in this work, which also contains his most favourable view of Tiberius. Now Gaius, in 39, reversed his previous tolerance towards the Senate, reviled them as previous satellites of Sejanus, and cleared Tiberius of responsibility for the persecutions of his reign. Dio reports that in 39 Seneca was a near-victim of Gaius' wrath. From these facts, Z. Stewart constructed a theory: in 39 or 40 Seneca, fearing the effects of his previous connections with Sejanus, tried to demonstrate that he had friends who had suffered during his ascendancy.[1] It is an attractive view, but again can hardly be proved since the date of composition cannot be independently fixed after 39 (Appendix A1). Abel's analysis of the work has led him to the conclusion that it is a pure consolation.[2]

A later examination of Seneca's ideas on wealth (Chapter 9) will suggest that *De Vita Beata* is an *apologia* by showing that Seneca there adopts a view of the moral value of wealth unique in his works. This point and the similar problem we have noted in the Consolation to Marcia indicate that detailed examination of Seneca's views on a prominent subject from work to work may contribute to our understanding of the purpose of individual works. But that is not the only reason for embarking on detailed studies of particular topics in Seneca. Such studies are also the means to a direct comparison of Seneca's behaviour with his written opinions—the problem with which we began.

A Possible Approach

We have now seen that the usual general preconceptions of the connections between Seneca's life and work are, at worst,

[1] Z. Stewart, *AJP* 74 (1953), 70 ff., on which see Chapter 2. For Seneca's assessment of Tiberius, see below, pp. 215 ff.
[2] *Bauformen*, p. 19.

erroneous, at best, insecure. It is time to confront the problem of that connection directly. We must set the facts of Seneca's life, recoverable from outside sources and from the concrete details he gives us, beside his written opinions at different periods of his life, and see if we can understand, or suggest ways of understanding, the man who incorporates both. There are enough works assignable to definite dates, enough assignable to manageable periods to make a start.

This study is intended as a limited exercise in this approach. I have concentrated on Seneca's political career and on his period of power because there is the most copious and most reliable information for his activities at that period, and because it is the most interesting for the historian. Part One is an attempt to construct an account of Seneca's career using only outside sources and concrete details from his own works. Apart from these details, two complete works have been included in this account because they are avowedly political in purpose: the *De Clementia* and the *Apocolocyntosis*. This political biography seemed a task worth attempting in its own right, since the last serious attempt at a political biography, René Waltz's *La vie politique de Sénèque* (Paris, 1909),[1] is now over sixty years old and embodies ideas of the workings of the Empire that we no longer accept. Furthermore the decision not to use Seneca's works as a whole in reconstructing his biography might be expected to remove some errors. But this is not as complete a biography as Waltz wrote, although Seneca's early life and background are included in order to make his political career intelligible. The main purpose of the study has also caused it to be a less continuous biography, for Seneca's activity in some spheres has been deferred for separate treatment to Part Two, where it could be directly compared with his views on the relevant subjects.

This political biography is followed in Part Two by studies of Seneca's treatment, in his prose works,[2] of certain subjects of

[1] I. Lana, *Lucio Anneo Seneca*, deals with Seneca's whole career but concentrates on his ideology and spiritual biography rather than a detailed analysis of his career in politics.

[2] I have not considered the dramatic works in this study. There, one is faced with the additional problem that what is said in a play need not be intended as

political significance which occur frequently in his works of all periods. I have taken 'political significance' in a broad sense, selecting subjects that must have come up in his works as adviser to Nero or in his decisions about his own career and position. In the former category, I have studied his views on the Republic and the Principate, on slavery, and on provincial policy. In the latter category, I have chosen the topic of wealth, the issue of political participation *v*. philosophical leisure, and the problem of suicide. Seneca's complex views are expounded as clearly and completely[1] as I have found possible, with due allowance for their context, and due indication of variations in time where they are traceable within the broad chronological limits for his works that are certain. To clarify Seneca's views, some discussion of the history of the question in the Stoa and at Rome has often been given. I have tried not to prejudge the issue, and the comparison of Seneca's views on each of these subjects with what can be known of his actions has yielded different results from subject to subject. His views have often on examination proved to be more subtle and complex than is often supposed and their relation to Seneca's actions rarely a case of simple coincidence or contradiction. It is too often forgotten that, as was natural when applying a philosophical doctrine with a long and varied history to practical problems, Seneca and his readers liked and were adept at casuistry. They were acutely aware of the difficulty of deciding what particular action here and now actually followed from a general philosophical dogma,[2] what remedies for the soul were appropriate on each occasion.[3] We shall, therefore, find

the author's view at all. Seneca's prose works are massive enough to be studied profitably on their own in an investigation of his opinions, and the views expressed in them can be confidently taken as Seneca's (in some sense at least), when one is confronting his life with his words.

[1] I do not claim completeness for the collection of references to wealth that forms the basis of Chapter 9, though I believe that they are representative: in particular, I have not noted there the references in the fragments, as they add no new points and are even harder to date than the dialogues.

[2] *Ep.* 70. 11: 'Non possis itaque de re in universum pronuntiare, cum mortem vis externa denuntiat, occupanda sit an expectanda; multa enim sunt quae in utramque partem trahere possunt'; 71. 1: 'Consilia enim rebus aptantur'; cf. 95. 5. 　　　　　　　　　　　　　　　　　　　　　　　　　　[3] *Ep.* 64. 8–9.

instances of consistency and of conflict, but also of irrelevance. More important will be the discovery that the connection of Seneca's philosophy with Seneca's political life often lies, not in the realm of his own conduct, but in the problems and pre-occupations that he shared with his readers.

PART ONE

2

THE FIRST FIFTY YEARS

Background

'EGONE equestri et provinciali loco ortus proceribus civitatis adnumeror?' In these words Tacitus' Seneca expresses, at the moment when he was about to lose his great power and position, his amazement at what he had achieved.[1] By comparison, his start as the son of a wealthy gentleman and scholar of Corduba in Spain seemed modest indeed.

In his *De Vita Patris*,[2] Seneca himself had probably described his family origins. Since that biography is lost, our knowledge of the *domus Annaeana* must be recovered principally from the works of the elder Lucius Annaeus Seneca and those of his son and namesake.[3]

Spain was the oldest of the great military provinces of the Roman Empire. Although the conquest took over two centuries to complete, from the end of the third century B.C. to early in the reign of Augustus, the assimilation of Roman manners and culture began very early and went very deep. The presence of a large standing army meant veteran settlers and an influx of Italian traders, and to the numbers of these Italian immigrants were added political exiles and speculators who exploited the famous Spanish mines. The assimilation of the native populations was promoted by the enlistment of Spanish auxiliaries, the inclusion of natives in Roman settlements, and the miscegenation which was the inevitable result of large-scale immigration. Apart from the Roman government's exclusive use of Latin as the

[1] *Ann.* 14. 53.
[2] Haase, frag. XV (98–9).
[3] The discussion that follows (pp. 29–34) is based on 'The Elder Seneca and Spain', *JRS* 62 (1972), 1 ff., and does not repeat detailed substantiation given there.

language of administration, and its encouragement of urban settlement as the most effective aid to pacification, there was no policy of Romanization. It was not necessary. Although local languages were not repressed, Latin gained ground. By Strabo's time, the people living along the Guadalquivir, then the Baetis river, had largely forgotten their native dialect.[1] The Guadalquivir is the high road of Andalusia, a region already pacified by the second half of the second century B.C. Its pre-eminently civilized character was recognized, probably soon after the final conquest of Spain in 19 B.C., by its separation from the rest of Hispania Ulterior as the province of Baetica, to be governed by proconsuls chosen by the Senate.[2] Along the river from which the province derived its name lay some of its largest towns, including Corduba which Augustus made the capital of one of the four judicial *conventus* and honoured by sending veterans there and by giving it the status of a Roman colony to be called Colonia Patricia.[3]

By the time of Corduba's imperial elevation, the Elder Seneca was already studying in Rome, but, even at his birth in about 50 B.C.,[4] the town had been for a century the regular military and administrative headquarters of Hispania Ulterior. Corduba had been founded as a *conventus* of Italians and Roman citizens by M. Claudius Marcellus in his second consulship in 152 B.C. According to Strabo, he invited into the settlement certain select natives. The town's mixed character was still reflected in the Elder Seneca's day in the nomenclature of the inhabitants. The *nomen* of his close friend Clodius Turrinus, being that of one of the great Roman *gentes* (Claudii), indicates an enfranchised native or a descendant of one; another eloquent townsman, Statorius

---

[1] Strabo 3. 2, 15.

[2] Dio 53. 12 dates the transfer of Baetica to the senate to 27 B.C. but warns that some items in the passage are anachronistic. The *terminus ante quem* is Agrippa's survey (Pliny, *NH* 3. 16–17) which was probably finished shortly after 7 B.C. (Dio 55. 8), certainly before the boundary change completed by 2 B.C. (*ILS* 102). The Princeps was concerned with organization in Spain in 16–13 B.C. (Dio 54. 23, 7).

[3] Polybius 35. 2, 2; Cicero, *Fam.* 10. 31–3; *Bell. Hisp.* 3. 1; Pliny, *NH* 3. 10.

[4] He could have heard Cicero declaim in 44 B.C. (*Contr.* 1, pref. 11; Suet. *Rhet.* 1; Cicero, *Att.* 14. 12, 2).

Victor, could probably claim Etruria as his *ultima origo*. That same part of Italy or the area further east towards Illyria probably produced the Annaei, but there is no way of telling when the family came to Spain.

A certain social prestige attached to being *Hispaniensis* (Spanish only in domicile) rather than *Hispanus* (Spanish by blood)[1]— unreal as miscegenation must often have made the distinction. In any case, both made one *provincialis*, in contrast with residents of Italy,[2] and, culturally, the difference in civilized areas was non-existent. The educated friends of the Elder Seneca included both types, to judge from their names: in the front rank of declaimers stood *Hispani* like Porcius Latro and Junius Gallio who was also a senator; his friend Gavius Silo of Tarraco can be added to the *Hispanienses* of Corduba mentioned above. Confirmation comes in the scientific works of two writers from the Punic southern coast of Baetica: the *Res Rusticae* of L. Junius Moderatus Columella, whose name suggests descent from a native enfranchised by a Roman Junius, reveals neither a lower level of Latinity nor a lesser degree of identification with Rome than the *De Chorographia* of his older contemporary Pomponius Mela who is probably *Hispaniensis*.[3]

Corduba, like the rest of southern Spain, was deeply involved in the Civil War. Both the Caesarian and the Pompeian sides had supporters there, and the town, trying to protect its possessions, inevitably made enemies of both.[4] There is no telling what side the Seneca family took. Like Clodius Turrinus,[5] they may have suffered material losses, but the war probably brought them one gain, namely, the friendship of Asinius Pollio who spent much

---

[1] Charisius, *Gramm. Lat.*, ed. Keil, I, p. 106; Vell. Pat. 2. 51, 3.

[2] Pliny, *Ep.* 9. 23, 2. Dio (68. 4, 1) (preserved by Xiphilinus) appears to be drawing this contrast when he says of Trajan that he was Ἴβηρ, glossing it οὐκ Ἰταλὸς οὐδ᾿ Ἰταλιώτης, but he then implies that Ἴβηρ means *Hispanus* by saying Trajan was ἀλλοεθνής.

[3] For Columella's attitude to Rome see *JRS* 62 (1972), 17; for Mela's origin see *Choro.* 2. 96 'Tingitera unde nos sumus', and for his identification with Rome linguistically see 3. 15; 3. 30; geographically 1. 19; 2. 121.

[4] Caesar, *BC* 2. 19; *Bell. Alex.* 58; 60; *Bell. Hisp.* 34; no. 18 of the epigrams attributed to Seneca in C. Prato's edition (Rome, 1964).

[5] *Contr.* 10, pref. 16.

of 43 B.C., while in charge of Hispania Ulterior, engaged in literary pursuits at Corduba. For it is striking that when the seas were finally clear enough, after 36 B.C., for Seneca *père* to move on from his studies with a *grammaticus* in Corduba to rhetorical training in Rome, he is immediately found attending the private declamations of the great *triumphator*.[1]

From the mid thirties on, the Elder Seneca spent much of his life in Rome, listening to the various professional and amateur declaimers and joining the literary discussions and gossip in some of the best circles.[2] It was on this first long visit to Rome that he stored in his prodigious memory most of the *sententiae*, *divisiones*, and *colores* that he was to record for his sons, half a century later, in the works we call the *Controversiae* and *Suasoriae*.[3] Around 8 B.C. he returned to Spain. It was probably there that he married Helvia, for the second of their three sons, the younger Seneca, was certainly born in Spain[4] and a poem of Statius suggests that the same was true of the oldest, Annaeus Novatus.[5] By A.D. 5, in time to hear the aged Pollio instructing his grandson,[6] he had returned to Rome to supervise the education of his sons, leaving his wife Helvia in charge of the family estates[7]—another reason for thinking that she had been brought up in Spain.

Father Seneca was about ninety when he died in Spain in

---

[1] *Contr.* 4, pref. 2–4. [2] e.g. *Suas.* 3. 6.

[3] *Contr.* 10, pref. 1. Thorough and helpful discussions of this work can be found in H. Bornecque, *Les déclamations et les déclamateurs d'après Sénèque le père*, Lille, 1902; W. A. Edward, *The Suasoriae of the Elder Seneca*, Cambridge, 1928; S. F. Bonner, *Roman Declamation*, Liverpool, 1959.

[4] Seneca, *Cons. Helv.* 19. 2.

[5] Statius *Silvae*, 2. 7, 30–2 (addressing Baetica):

> Lucanum potes imputare terris.
> hoc plus quam Senecam dedisse mundo
> aut dulcem generasse Gallionem.

The epithet 'dulcis' and the order of names suggest that the Gallio here is not the old declaimer but his adoptive son, Seneca's elder brother (for 'dulcis' applied to him see Seneca *NQ* 4, pref. 11). Statius' words could relate to *patria*, not birthplace, but, as we happen to know that Seneca and Lucan (Vacca Life) were born in Baetica, it is reasonable to take him to mean the same for Gallio. On his adoption see p. 48 n. 2.

[6] *Contr.* 4, pref. 2–4. Pollio died *c*. A.D. 5: *PIR*² A 1241.

[7] *Cons. Helv.* 14. 3.

A.D. 39 or 40. The major part, if not all, of the *Controversiae* and *Suasoriae* was written after Tiberius' death in A.D. 37 and he probably realized his intention to publish them himself. Although it amused the old man to recall the studies of his youth, he did not regard these *commentarii* as a *seria res.*[1] What he counted on to give him lasting fame was a work described in his son's biography as 'historiae ab initio bellorum civilium unde primum veritas retro abiit, paene usque ad mortis suae diem',[2] from which we can infer that it began with the great Civil Wars, taking as its opening date 49 B.C., or perhaps the death of Caesar in 44, and ended with the death of Tiberius. It was clearly a life's work, finished but not published when he died. There are no certain fragments of this history: all that we know of it comes from the few sentences of *De Vita Patris*, where Seneca indicated that he had not yet published his father's work but intended to do so. Probably he never did. The republication of the works of Cremutius Cordus under Gaius[3] and the subsequent elevation to the throne of still another author of historical works covering at least part of the period of his father's history[4] may have made its publication seem an unpromising venture.

Seneca *père* had devoted his life to his sons and his literary pursuits. Perhaps he had practised his oratory on occasion. But he does not seem to have taught rhetoric or to have played any role in municipal or imperial administration. In his work on the declaimers, he confesses to a youthful ambition to be a Roman senator, an ambition that was only to be fulfilled by his two sons. His wealth and his connections in Rome had not proved sufficient. He had been born at the wrong time: too late for the liberal adlections of Caesar and the Triumvirs; too early for the generosity of Augustus in his last years and that of Tiberius in his first. But the Elder Seneca did not become bitter. In the preface to Book 2 of the *Controversiae*, he contrasts the zeal with which he had encouraged his first two sons to become orators and senators

---

[1] *Contr.* 1, pref. 10; 10, pref. 1.

[2] Haase, frag. XV (98–9).

[3] Suet. *Gaius* 16. For Cremutius' *veritas*, Tacitus, *Ann.* 4. 34–5; it was still there in the second edition, though toned down (Quintilian 10. 1, 104).

[4] Suet. *Claudius* 41. 2.

with his happy acceptance of Mela's desire to study philosophy 'paterno contentus ordine'. Only let him study rhetoric as well, an important preparation for all the arts. He adds: 'do not suspect me of a plot to turn you into an orator by introducing you to a study at which you are bound to excel; you are the most gifted of all my sons, but as the others are launched on their noble but dangerous voyage, I will keep you in harbour.'

Something of the pressure he had put on his elder sons can be inferred from that disclaimer about plots. As for the rest, did the last years of Tiberius leave the old man with doubts about the wisdom of choosing a public career? Perhaps he simply enjoyed indulging in his youngest child tastes and attitudes that he had opposed in the others.

Birth and Education

The evidence for Seneca's life before his exile in 41 is so slight, and the potential interest of these years, for social history as well as for biography, is so great, that few writers on Seneca have resisted the temptation to eke out knowledge with imagination. Thus we are let into the details of his conflict with his father over the relative merits of rhetoric and philosophy;[1] of his early acquisition of land in Egypt;[2] of the psychological shock he suffered as a witness to his uncle's death at sea;[3] of his matrimonial unhappiness.[4] While speculation furnishes details of his personal life, the outline of his public career has been supplied from a rigid conception of what a senatorial *cursus* must be: he must have been one of the *xxviri*, and a military tribune before his quaestorship.[5] But more deference is due to the richness of possibilities in the career of a man who later moved from exile to the court of the emperor. A bare outline of what we know plus an adumbration of the possibilities will be sufficient to recommend caution.

---

[1] Waltz, *Vie politique*, pp. 28 ff.

[2] P. Faider, *Bulletin de l'institut français d'archéologie orientale du Caire* 30 (1930), 83-7.

[3] L. Cantarelli, *Aegyptus* 8 (1927), 89-96.

[4] O. Rossbach in *R-E* I, col. 2243.   [5] Waltz, *Vie politique*, p. 53.

Seneca's date of birth must be inferred from three passages in his own works, from which we learn that he could remember Asinius Pollio who probably died in A.D. 5;[1] that he had seen the prodigies at the death of Augustus;[2] and that his 'iuventae tempus' fell early in Tiberius' reign, the year A.D. 19 being clearly indicated.[3] From these scraps, scholars have inferred birth-dates of 8 B.C.,[4] 4 B.C.,[5] and 1 B.C.[6]

Seneca says that he was carried to Rome in the arms of his mother's stepsister.[7] With all due allowance for rhetorical exaggeration, it is fair to conclude that Seneca was in Rome as a very small boy,[8] and thus could have had the great Pollio pointed out to him by his father, so as to retain the memory, even at the age of five. As for the third piece of evidence, the term *iuvenis* in Seneca as elsewhere is very vague,[9] and compatible with any of the alternative dates mentioned above.

In A.D. 62, Tacitus makes Nero say to Seneca, 'verum et tibi valida aetas rebusque et fructui rerum sufficiens', which might

---

[1] *Tranq.* 17. 7; *PIR²* A 1241.   [2] *NQ* 1. 1, 3.

[3] *Ep.* 108. 22: 'in primum Tiberii Caesaris principatum'. Buecheler inserted 'primum' between 'in' and 'principatum', where the manuscripts read '.i.' or nothing. The reading is universally accepted. Seneca is specifically thinking of the year A.D. 19 when, according to Tacitus (*Ann.* 2. 85, 4), foreign cults were expelled. The word 'calumnia' shows (*pace* Préchac in the Budé edition) that the time of persecution is meant, so that 'movebantur' cannot mean 'were being celebrated' but must either be construed as equivalent to, or be amended to, 'amovebantur' or 'removebantur'.

[4] H. Lehmann, *Philologus* 8 (1853), 310.

[5] O. Rossbach, *R-E* I, col. 2240; Waltz, *Vie politique*, p. 22; Lana, *Lucio Anneo Seneca*, p. 75 (6–4 B.C.).

[6] Cantarelli, *Aegyptus* 8 (1927), 89 ff.; F. Préchac, *REL* 12 (1934), 360–75, with additional arguments in *REL* 15 (1937), 66–7.

[7] *Cons. Helv.* 19. 2. For the relationship, *JRS* 62 (1972), 7 n. 81.

[8] Lucan, according to the Vacca Life, was brought to Rome at the age of eight months.

[9] In *Ep.* 49. 2, Seneca calls himself a *puer* at the same period of study. Préchac's attempt to fix Seneca's limits for *iuventus* as 14–21 (above, n. 6) only succeeds in showing how loose his usage is. Certainly nothing suggests that Seneca put the start of *iuventa* as early as 14 (the age Préchac thinks is indicated in *Ep.* 108. 22): in *Ben.* 4. 6, 6, the last tooth, which was expected to appear at about 19 (Pliny, *NH* 11. 166), marks the end of *surgens iuventa*, the start of *iuventa* proper. Cf. *Cons. Polyb.* 15. 4, where 21 is described as 'circa primos iuventae suae annos'.

suggest that Tacitus thought Seneca in his early, rather than his late, sixties.[1] The latter passage and the evidence of Letters 12, 19, and 26 have been used with effect by Préchac who argues that Seneca seems to regard the point of real *senectus* to have been reached between late 63 (*Ep.* 12; 19) and the spring of 64 (*Ep.* 26), and that the sixty-third year, widely regarded as the *climacter* for old men, is the precise point he means.[2] If Préchac were right, 1 B.C. would be established as the best candidate for Seneca's date of birth. But Seneca refers to his age as *senectus* in the Letters before 26 as well,[3] and there is, in addition, no proof that the commencement of old age coincides with the *climacter*.[4]

We must be content with establishing reasonable limits for Seneca's birth. If he was at least five years old when he saw Pollio and under sixty-five when he asked to retire, he must have been born between 4 and 1 B.C.

Seneca was in Rome by A.D. 5. His aunt brought him from Corduba, but his father, perhaps from the start, was in Rome as well. He was sent to a *grammaticus*[5] and after that, we may assume, to one or more teachers of rhetoric, for, though his main interest

---

[1] *Ann.* 14. 56, 1. *Brev. Vit.* 20. 4 shows that senators were excused from attending the senate at 60. *Contr.* 1. 8, 4 seems to show that the age was 65 in the Elder Seneca's day.

[2] *REL* 12 (1934), 360 ff. For the date of these Letters see Appendix A1.

[3] *Ep.* 12: 'quocumque me verti, argumenta senectutis meae video'; *Ep.* 19: 'incipiamus vasa in senectute colligere.' In *Ep.* 26 Seneca writes: 'modo dicebam tibi in conspectu esse me senectutis: iam vereor ne senectutem post me reliquerim', but goes on to reveal that it is really his criteria, in terms of physical decrepitude, for the use of the word *senectus* that have changed. In any case, *modo* has a very vague temporal sense in Seneca; see Lana, *Seneca*, p. 75.

[4] According to Gellius, *NA* 3. 10, 9, and Censorinus 14. 9, these danger points occur every seven years, while Gellius, *NA* 15. 7, 3, shows that the crucial point for *seniores* was 63. There is, however, no direct evidence that these danger points were directly connected with the onset of different life-periods, despite the role the number seven also played in fixing these periods (*Ben.* 7. 1, 5). *Ep.* 83. 4 in which Seneca says that he and his *puer* are at the same *crisis* because they are both losing their teeth does not help to establish Seneca's age, though the early life-periods were associated with stages of dental development (*Ben.* 4. 6, 6): the loss of teeth here *is* the biological turning-point or *crisis*. The joke does not require that Seneca be at the onset of a new life-period. Nor can *crisis* be assumed to mean *climacter* here or elsewhere.   [5] *Ep.* 58. 5.

was philosophy, the two studies were by no means incompatible.
Cicero had described the close connection of *dialectica* and
eloquentia,[1] and Seneca, in a sour mood,[2] puts them together
as examples of useless training. One of his teachers, Papirius
Fabianus, earned equal praise in declamation and disputation and
continued to study rhetoric after his philosophical studies were
well advanced—an example the Elder Seneca recommended to
his youngest son, Annaeus Mela.[3] Seneca probably did not intend,
at this date, any practical outcome of his rhetorical training: only
later did he decide to plead in the forum, as a natural accom-
paniment of a political career.[4] His concentration on philosophy
probably accounts for a rather curious fact of his life: he does not
seem to have gone to Greece.[5] For a person interested in oratory
this would be very odd: the Elder Seneca's work is ample evidence that many of the orators of the previous generation had
studied in Greece;[6] later Seneca's nephew Lucan was to go to
Athens.[7] Although ill health may have played a part in Seneca's
decision, his main reason was probably a belief that the centre of
philosophy had moved from Greece to Rome,[8] for he was
attracted by the school of the Sextii, the only philosophical school
Rome had ever produced, now a generation old and highly
influential. Seneca was too late to hear the founder Q. Sextius,
but he was deeply moved by the exhortations of his followers,
Papirius Fabianus and Sotion.[9] Even in the last year of his life,
he still found Sextius' writings deeply moving,[10] and bitterly

---

[1] *Brutus* 309.   [2] *Ep.* 20. 2.   [3] *Contr.* 2, pref. 1, 4.

[4] *Contr.* 2, pref. 4. When this passage was written, shortly after the death of
Tiberius, Seneca and his elder brother were *preparing* for the forum.

[5] The scholiast on Juvenal 5. 109 reports that in 49, when recalled from exile,
Seneca wanted to go to Athens. Is this just the result of speculation on why
Seneca did not go, or does it go back to a lost letter? In any case, the 'simul
praeturam impetrat' of Tacitus (*Ann.* 12. 8) proves that he did not go then.

[6] *Contr.* 1. 2, 23 (Mam. Aemilius Scaurus); 1. 7, 14 (Arellius Fuscus); 1. 8, 15
(Munatius Plancus); 9. 6, 16 (Albucius Silus). But cf. Strabo 4. 181C for the
importance of Marseilles.

[7] Suet. *Lucanus* 11.

[8] On the move see M. Pohlenz, *Die Stoa*[2] I, p. 280.

[9] Jerome, *Chron.* 171b ff. H., gives A.D. 13 as Sotion's *floruit*, which is not at
variance with Seneca's information.

[10] *Ep.* 64. 2 ff.

lamented the premature death of this 'nova et Romani roboris
secta'.[1]

Q. Sextius, apparently of equestrian or lower senatorial origin,
was offered a senatorial career by Caesar and refused it for the
sake of philosophy.[2] He went to Athens,[3] presumably to study,
and, later in the triumviral period, began to write in Greek a
Roman type of philosophy,[4] pragmatic in approach and eclectic
in doctrine. Seneca says that Sextius was really a Stoic, though
he denied the label—probably an allusion to Sextius' moral
austerity. The interest in natural science evinced by his disciples[5]
was certainly in keeping with Stoicism, but Sextius' denial, which
was a claim to found a Roman sect, could be justified by his scorn
of dialectic,[6] his vegetarianism,[7] and a less well-attested conception of the soul as immaterial.[8]

There probably were Pythagorean strains in Sextius' philosophy, although they did not include the more esoteric doctrines,
and he was not regarded as a member of the sect.[9] Thus Seneca

[1] NQ 7. 32, 2.

[2] Ep. 98. 13: 'honores reppulit pater Sextius, qui ita natus, ut rempublicam
deberet capessere, latum clavum divo Iulio dante non recepit. intellegebat enim,
quod dari posset, et eripi posse.' The motive here given is clearly invented for
the argument of the letter. Plut. Mor. 77 E–F tells of Sextius' spiritual struggle
after making the decision.   [3] Pliny, NH 18. 274.

[4] Ep. 59. 7: 'virum acrem, Graecis verbis, Romanis moribus philosophantem.'
For the date Suet. Gram. 18 mentions a teacher of Iullus Antonius converted
to the sect. That could be as early as 30 B.C. Jerome, Chron. 169g H., puts Sextius'
floruit at A.D. 1. In fact he probably died soon after that date, as Seneca clearly
only knew his views from his books and his disciples.

[5] Ep. 64. 2: 'magni, si quid mihi credis, viri et, licet neget, Stoici.' A. Oltramare, Les origines de la diatribe romaine, Lausanne, 1926, devotes chapter 8 to the
Sextii, whom he is eager to claim for 'Cynic diatribe'.

[6] Reflected in his practice (Ep. 64. 3) and proclaimed by his pupil, Papirius
Fabianus (Brev. Vitae 10. 1).

[7] Ep. 108. 17–18. For Plutarch in De Esu Carnium 995D, 999 the Stoics form
the opposition to the vegetarians.

[8] Claudianus Mamertus, De Statu Animae, 2, 8, a fifth-century writer, attributes
to the Sextii the view that the soul is 'incorporalis' and 'illocalis'—not the best
evidence, but the objections of Oltramare, Diatribe romaine, p. 161, seem to me
unconvincing, especially as Oltramare seems to regard the attributed doctrine
as Stoic. Von Arnim in R-E IIA, 2041 attaches the label 'Platonic–Pythagorean'
which is certainly closer.

[9] In NQ 7. 32, 2 Seneca lists philosophical schools that have died out, putting
'Pythagorica illa invidiosa turbae schola' as a distinct entry before the Sextii.

claimed the example of Sextius in submitting each night the acts
of that day to the judgement of his conscience[1]—a custom that
Cicero labelled Pythagorean, although it need not at this date
have been exclusive to them.[2] More significant is Sextius' belief
in vegetarianism. Though he rested his case, according to Seneca,
not on Pythagorean metempsychosis, but on the grounds of
frugality, good health, and the view that flesh-eating was unnatural and established the habit of cruelty,[3] Sextius probably
did not deny the classic Pythagorean arguments, and those he
preferred were now also ascribed to that sage.[4] His follower
Sotion cited the two types of argument, urging his hearers to
follow the practice for whichever reasons they could accept.[5]
One of his more susceptible listeners was Seneca who gave up
eating meat for a whole year. In his old age, Seneca credited his
conversion to both types of argument, still held the medical
one true, but described his experience as 'falling in love with
Pythagoras'.[6] It is more than likely that Sextius' vegetarianism
passed for a sign of Pythagoreanism in his own day.

Sotion had come from Alexandria,[7] but Sextius attracted
disciples in Italy as well: his own son Sextius Niger, a grammarian from Tarentum called Lucius Crassicius, the encyclopedist
Cornelius Celsus, and Papirius Fabianus.[8] The last made a great

---

[1] *Ira* 3. 36, 1.

[2] *Cato Maior* 38: 'Pythagoreorum more, exercendae memoriae gratia, quid
quoque die dixerim, audierim, egerim, commemoro vesperi.' Oltramare,
Diatribe romaine, p. 163, is wrong to infer from this passage that the practice
in traditional Pythagoreanism was an exercise for the memory. The context
shows that Cato is giving his own reason for imitating the practice.

[3] *Ep.* 108, 17–18.

[4] Ovid, *Metamorph.* 15. 60ff. According to Plutarch, *De Esu Carnium*, this
mixed doctrine was contrasted with the Cynic and Stoic attitudes (995D, 999).

[5] Oltramare, *Diatribe romaine*, p. 166, denies that Sotion was a disciple. It
is true that Sotion, having given both sets of reasons ('dissimilis utrique causa
erat, seu utrique magnifica'), accepted the Pythagorean argument (20), but he
does not cite Sextius merely to refute him. He believes his arguments too and
ends with a Sextian argument: 'alimenta tibi leonum et vulturum eripio' (21).

[6] *Ep.* 108. 22: 'His ego instinctus abstinere animalibus coepi . . . Agitatiorem
mihi animum esse credebam nec tibi hodie adfirmaverim an fuerit.' 17: 'quem
mihi amorem Pythagoras iniecerit.'

[7] Jerome, *Chron.* 171b H.

[8] Suet. *Gram.* 18; Quintilian 10. 1, 124; Elder Seneca, *Contr.* 2, pr. 4.

impression on the Senecas, father and son. Both testify to his combination of rhetorical and philosophical talents,[1] though we hear more of the former from the father. Probably by 10 B.C., at the age of twenty,[2] he had become a Sextian. From then on, declamation was just a preparation for disputation and a vehicle for *convicium saeculi*.[3] The young Seneca came under his spell, for Fabianus' sincerity and encouraging attitude made his philosophical discourse very appealing to the young.[4] He wrote voluminously—more philosophical works than Cicero. Books on natural science and political philosophy are mentioned.[5]

Although Seneca used the scientific works,[6] and had certainly read the others,[7] he reports Fabianus' philosophical views only once and that on a point of method: Fabianus, like Sextius, was against sophistry and subtlety, favouring instead a moving and forceful appeal.[8] Otherwise, Seneca is wholly concerned with his style and the way he used Latin to present philosophy:[9] there were not, after all, many reputable models for writing philosophy in Latin. Yet Seneca, like his father, is rather defensive about Fabianus' style.[10]

Fabianus' influence on Seneca was certainly lasting. More fragile was Seneca's vegetarianism, which lasted a year until, in A.D. 19, when Egyptian and Jewish rites were being prohibited in Rome, his father persuaded him to give up a practice which was being used as an *argumentum superstitionis*.[11] Yet, from his

---

[1] *Contr.* 2. pref. 1; 5, 18; *Ep.* 40. 12.

[2] *JRS* 62 (1972), 169 n. 175.

[3] e.g. *Suas.* 1. 9; *Contr.* 2. pref. 2; 1, 10 ff., 6. 2.   [4] *Ep.* 100. 12.

[5] Ibid. 9. Note the discussion in Oltramare, *Diatribe romaine*, pp. 159–60. Lucilius was reading *Libri civilium*. *Libri Causarum Naturalium* are mentioned by Charisius (*Gramm. Lat.*, ed. Keil, I, p. 106) and were used by Pliny the Elder.

[6] *N.Q.* 3. 27, 3 quotes Fabianus on the final flood that will destroy humanity.

[7] *Ep.* 100. 12. They were not fresh in his memory in 64 but had made a very strong impression.

[8] Above, p. 15 n. 5.

[9] In *Ep.* 58. 6 he claims Fabianus' support for translating οὐσία as *essentia*.

[10] See *JRS* 62 (1972), 16.

[11] Vegetarianism, if interpreted as abstinence from pork, could be taken to indicate adherence to Judaism or the cult of Isis. It was the Jews, including converts, who were severely punished at this time. (Tacitus' reference in *Ann.*

Sextian days, Seneca retained throughout his life the habit of examining his conscience every night, and his great interest in medicine may have received its first impulse then.[1] Sextius had given medical reasons for abstaining from meat. His son, Sextius Niger,[2] like Celsus, an adherent of the medical school of Asclepiades, wrote, in Greek, a work about plants and the remedies to be derived from them. Even Fabianus offered his views on the healthiest position for sleep.[3] It would be a mistake, of course, to trace Seneca's interest in remedies solely or even principally to this acquaintance with medical studies. His own poor health gave him many opportunities to learn of the remedies currently recommended,[4] and a resultant hypochondria, at least in old age, kept his interest alive.[5] Sometimes he found that a precept of philosophy coincided with a current fad in medicine. Seneca was taught by the Stoic Attalus to despise heated bathing as *delicatum*,[6] but the idea of cold-water baths was a medical remedy in the time of Augustus[7] and by the reign of Nero had become a craze.[8] His interest in medicine as a progressive science gave new content to the traditional parallel of soul-healing and body-healing. He compares the two sciences with full details of the progress of medicine,[9] explaining that just as medicine has had to develop because luxury has increased the number of diseases, so moral philosophy must develop to cope with new vices. Perhaps his acquaintance with medicine also lies behind his picture of

2. 85, 4 to the 4000 'ea superstitione infecta' supports Josephus (*AJ* 18. 84; Suet· *Tib.* 36; Dio 57. 18, 5a) for it must refer to the Jewish rites, the immediate antecedent.) E. Mary Smallwood, *Latomus* 15 (1956), 314 ff., argues that Tiberius' severity was provoked by Jewish proselytizing among the upper classes. The 'conversion' of a relative of the prefect of Egypt, the son of a man with senatorial friends, would certainly reach the Emperor's ears.

[1] For Pohlenz's tracing of Seneca's interest in προπάθειαι to Sextian influence see p. 180 n. 4.

[2] M. Wellman, *Hermes* 24 (1889), 530.

[3] Pliny, *NH* 28. 54.

[4] *Ep.* 78. 5. In *Epp.* 15. 6–7; 55; 84. 1 Seneca recommends riding out in a litter as medically beneficial: it was a remedy approved by Celsus 2. 15.

[5] *Epp.* 67; 65. 1; 104.

[6] *Ep.* 108. 16, cf. Epictetus 1. 1, 29.

[7] Préchac collects the evidence in his note in the Budé text of *Ep.* 83. 5.

[8] Pliny, *NH* 29. 10.   [9] *Ep.* 95. 15 ff.

philosophy as an art in which each new practitioner had a duty
to introduce new ideas.[1]

Seneca regarded himself as a Stoic. His education in that
doctrine he owed to Attalus,[2] whose teaching also aimed at
asceticism but for purely moral ends.[3] Seneca preserved from
these days certain ascetic habits. He slept on a hard bed, and
refused to eat oysters or mushrooms, to use unguents, to drink
wine, or to take hot baths,[4] although as he grew older he had
to abandon his yearly swim in the Virgo aqueduct for a bath
warmed by the sun.[5]

Seneca supplies two other facts about his youth. One is an
unexplained visit to Pompeii.[6] The other is his poor state of health.
Throughout his life he suffered from various illnesses, culminating
in old age in a kind of attack that he called *suspirium* and which
has been identified with *angina pectoris*, though it might be
cardiac asthma.[7] Although he may sometimes have used ill health
to excuse a retreat from difficult political situations,[8] there is no
reason to doubt that he really had a weak constitution which made
these stories credible. Seneca tells us that as an *adulescens* he at
first tried to ignore the *distillationes* (catarrh) from which he
suffered until he finally succumbed, reduced to an emaciated
condition.[9] The condition was probably consumption.[10] Fear of

[1] *Epp.* 33. 10–11; 80. 1; 64. 7–10 (a letter devoted to a book of the Elder Sextius;
the passage discusses eye remedies).
[2] Elder Seneca, *Suas.* 2. 12 'Attalus Stoicus'; cf. 'ipse regem se esse dicebat',
Seneca, *Ep.* 108. 13—an allusion to the Stoic paradox.
[3] *Ep.* 108. 3 ff., 23.
[4] *Ep.* 108. 15–16. Compare the simple fare he mentions in *Ep.* 83. 6 and the
testimony of Tacitus for his last year (*Ann.* 15. 45, 3).
[5] *Ep.* 83. 5; cf. 67. 1; 53. 3.
[6] *Ep.* 70. 1.
[7] *Ep.* 54. 1–2. K. F. H. Marx, *Abh. der König. Gesellschaft der Wissenschaften
zu Göttingen* 17 (1872), 3 ff. Marx admits at the end of his article that descriptions
of the two ailments are hard to distinguish. Against the diagnosis of angina is
the fact that Seneca uses the technical term *angina* in *Ep.* 101. 3 of someone else's
ailment.
[8] Dio 59. 19; *Ann.* 14. 56; 15. 45.   [9] *Ep.* 78. 1–4.
[10] In *Ep.* 75. 12 we are told that chronic *distillatio* becomes *phthisis*. That was
the disease of which Caligula was told in A.D. 39 that Seneca was dying (Dio
59. 19). Note that his brother Gallio, at least late in life, suffered from it (Pliny,
NH 31. 62).

his father's grief, he says, kept him from committing suicide at this time and he sought comfort in philosophy instead. This may be the same illness through which, Seneca tells us elsewhere,[1] he was nursed by his mother Helvia's stepsister some time before standing for the quaestorship. In that case, his aunt probably nursed him in Egypt, where she lived with her husband, C. Galerius, during his term as prefect from A.D. 16 to 31, the period indicated, by Seneca's age and acquaintance with philosophy, for the illness.[2] The long voyage there[3] and the climate of the country[4] were both reputed to be good for consumption.

How long Seneca was in Egypt we do not know. His excursus on the Nile in the *Natural Questions* need not embody much personal observation[5] and the same was probably true of his work *De Situ et Sacris Aegyptiorum*.[6] At any rate, when he and his aunt returned in 31, survivors of the shipwreck in which his uncle had died,[7] Seneca was past thirty and had not yet been quaestor.

Entry into Politics

Seneca's aunt helped his campaign for the first magistracy,[8] which he cannot therefore have held before 33. Past thirty, he was already at the crucial age for a man aiming at a senatorial career. Yet Seneca's quaestorship cannot be securely fixed before the reign of Gaius when, according to an anecdote in Cassius Dio, narrated under the year 39, he was in the Senate:[9] that much truth can be presumed to underlie a story which, though dubious,

[1] *Cons. Helv.* 19. 2.

[2] Ibid. 19. 6; *PIR²* G 25. Though the thought of his father's distress stayed Seneca's hand, there is no indication in *Ep.* 78 that Seneca's father was with him in his illness.

[3] Pliny, *NH* 31. 62. Seneca states in *Ep.* 78. 5 that sailing was a standard remedy for *distillationes*, along with *viscerum iactatio* which he certainly practised (*Ep.* 55. 2).

[4] Younger Pliny, *Ep.* 5. 19, 6.

[5] In *NQ* 4. 2, 3 Philae and Meroe are confused. See the note ad loc. by P. Oltramare in the Budé edition.

[6] Haase, frag. VII (12).

[7] *Cons. Helv.* 19. 4.

[8] Ibid. 19. 2.

[9] Dio 59. 19. See pp. 53 ff.

was plausible. Some have tried to establish that Seneca entered the Senate under Tiberius, by adducing *Ep.* 11. 4: 'Fabianus cum in senatum testis esset inductus, erubuisse memini et hic illum mire pudor decuit.'[1] That incident should probably be dated earlier than 37, since the Elder Seneca speaks of Fabianus as if he were dead.[2] But the tense of the infinitive prevents us from assuming that Seneca is reporting something he actually witnessed.[3] In fact there is no definite eyewitness account of a senatorial incident that need be dated before the reign of Gaius.[4] There is therefore no obstacle to the inference one would naturally draw from the fact that Seneca had not reached the praetorship by the time of his exile in 41,[5] namely, that he had only just embarked on the *cursus* when Tiberius died. Confirmation comes from the statement of his father, written shortly after 37,[6] that his elder sons 'foro . . . se et honoribus parant'. To judge by Tacitean usage, that description could fit aspiring quaestors[7]

---

[1] Waltz, *Vie politique*, p. 58, following F. Jonas, *De ordine librorum L. Annaei Senecae philosophi*, Diss. Berlin, 1870, p. 12.

[2] *Contr.* 2, preface. For the date of composition of the Elder Seneca's work, see p. 33.

[3] Madvig, *Latin Grammar*, para. 408, obs. 2. Oltramare, *Diatribe romaine*, p. 177, suggested that Seneca remembered a Sextian work he had read mentioning this fact. Even if this is an eyewitness account, it does not prove that Seneca was a member of the Senate: he could have been called to give evidence as well.

[4] *Const. Sap.* 17 is an eyewitness account that is hard to place, because it is not clear which 'Corbulo' insulted Ovid's son-in-law, the father or the son (the famous general). As Seneca rarely mentions the living, one would normally assume that he meant the father, who could be dead when the dialogue was written between 47 and 62, for he was an ex-praetor of some age in A.D. 21 (Tac. *Ann.* 3. 31, 4). On the other hand, the only way in which a reference to 'Corbulo' could be unambiguous at that date would be if the father was dead and Seneca was referring to the only living 'Corbulo', the son. In either case, the incident need not be dated before Gaius' reign. For the son, the candidate favoured by Syme, *JRS* 60 (1970), 36, was a consular in 47, therefore already in Gaius' Senate, and the father, even if he was over 40 in A.D. 21, could still have been there 17 years later, as the retirement age was 65 (p. 36 n. 1). The Corbulo who was consul in 39 in Dio 59. 15, 5 must be the younger, but the road commissioner there could be the father (as argued by Syme, op. cit., pp. 29–30).

[5] Tac. *Ann.* 12. 8.

[6] Above, p. 33.

[7] *Ann.* 13. 25: 'Iulius Montanus senatorii ordinis sed qui nondum honorem capessisset' with *ILS* 978 which shows that he was *quaestor destinatus*.

or (what suits the case better here) ex-quaestors aiming at higher office, the tribunate or aedileship.[1] Another important fact is revealed by this remark: Seneca's elder brother Novatus had also not progressed beyond quaestorship by the end of Tiberius' reign. They were both then around forty years old.

To explain Seneca's slow start, Waltz suggested that, after serving as one of the *xxviri* and as military tribune early in Tiberius' reign, he was discouraged from entering politics by the Piso affair and then by the rise of Sejanus. But if Seneca had intended to enter on a senatorial career from the start, no time could have been more propitious for him. Through his mother, he was related to the prefect of Egypt, the man at the very top of the equestrian service from A.D. 16 to 31, while his father was a friend and compatriot of Junius Gallio, a senator in favour with Sejanus.[2] Seneca and his brothers had gone with their father more than once to hear Mamercus Aemilius Scaurus declaim,[3] a consular whose high nobility did not make him ashamed of friendship with Sejanus.[4] Finally, Seneca's friendship with C. Sallustius Passienus Crispus, consul suffect in 27, may go back into the reign of Tiberius: Seneca's father had been a friend of the declaimer Passienus, the grandfather of Seneca's friend.[5]

As we have seen, Seneca's father wished him to take advantage of these opportunities. His opposition to Seneca's philosophical studies[6] was probably based on ambition for his son: later he did not try to dissuade the youngest brother, Mela, from his interest

---

[1] *Ann.* 13. 45, with Suet. *Nero* 35: 'honorem nondum functum' of an ex-quaestor; *Hist.* 2. 1, 1 of Titus who had been quaestor and legionary legate. Though, in theory, their two first magistracies can be fitted into Gaius' reign, it suits Dio's evidence (pp. 64 ff.) that Seneca was not in favour after 39 to put their quaestorships under Tiberius.

[2] *PIR*² I 756. The Elder Seneca calls him 'Gallio noster', e.g. *Suas* 3. 6. See below, p. 48.

[3] *Contr.* 10, pref. 2–3.

[4] *Ann.* 6. 29, 3. Cf. his fellow accusers in 3. 66 and his fellow accused in 6. 9.

[5] Seneca attests to his acquaintance with Crispus in *NQ* 4, pref. 6. *Epig.* 14 and 53 Prato (which, even if not genuine, may have been composed with knowledge of Seneca's life) describe Passienus Crispus as a powerful and loyal friend. In *Contr.* 3, pref. 10, the Elder Seneca refers to the grandfather as 'Passienus noster'.

[6] *Ep.* 108. 22.

in philosophy because he was content for him to remain an *eques*.[1] This man of *antiquus rigor* would have felt, with Agricola's mother, that such absorption in philosophy went beyond what was respectable for a Roman senator, especially as Seneca's preference for other-worldly ascetic teachers made it unlikely that he was studying 'quo firmior adversus fortuita rem publicam capesseret'.[2]

Nothing then compels us to believe that Seneca had early political ambitions that were interrupted. Nor is Waltz's assumption of a military tribunate and post in the vigintivirate acceptable. If he had not held a military tribunate before he went to Egypt, he may, on his return, have held it only as a one-year sinecure[3] or have omitted it altogether, simply obtaining the *latus clavus* from the Princeps,[4] perhaps through his aunt's favour. From there he may have moved straight to the quaestorship, as *equites* were not always obliged to hold one of these minor posts and many, in fact, omitted them.[5]

Seneca's failure to enter politics in youth should probably be traced to simple disinclination. There had always been a fair proportion of the equestrian class in the Republic who preferred *quies* to the *molestia* of public life.[6] Their imperial counterparts were not lured by the offer of the *latus clavus* nor, in many cases, by jury duty or the new administrative functions entrusted to their class.[7] In Seneca's case, chronic ill health and a passion for philosophy and natural science may have reinforced his disinclination.[8] This latter enthusiasm, which he shared with his

[1] Above, p. 34. [2] Tac. *Agric.* 4; *Hist.* 4. 5.

[3] Millar, *JRS* 53 (1963), 196.

[4] Seneca's age and the rank of his deceased uncle might have justified such an exception. For the acquisition of the *latus clavus* late, without any post before or after except the quaestorship, see D. McAlindon, *JRS* 47 (1957), 192. M. Raecius Taurus Gallus, in the generation after Seneca and from another part of Spain, may still (as in *PIR*[2] G 64, based on the then-current misreading of the inscription) provide an example, if J. Reynolds is right to cast doubt on his military tribunate (*JRS* 61 (1971), 144).

[5] McAlindon, op. cit., pp. 191–3.

[6] Cicero, *Rab. Post.* 16; *Clu.* 152 ff. Atticus is the prize example, Nepos, *Atticus* 6.

[7] See below, pp. 345–6.

[8] Cf. Ovid, *Tristia* 4. 10, 37: 'nec patiens corpus, nec mens fuit apta labori.'

teacher, Papirius Fabianus,[1] remained with him until old age: it was not just the typical infatuation of young philosophers with an ambitious subject that conferred repute.[2] The founder of the Sextian school provided a precedent for refusing a public career in order to study philosophy, but perhaps too much stress should not be laid on philosophical zeal as a motive: Novatus was similarly disinclined towards politics and there is no sign that he was a philosopher.[3] He shared with Seneca rather the tendency to consumption and, according to his brother, he was of a gentle disposition with a distaste for flattery.[4]

For Seneca's continued political inactivity after his return from Egypt, presumably in better health, reasons apart from distaste can be adduced, though none can be established. Stewart[5] has made the interesting suggestion that the slow progress of Novatus[6] and Seneca after 31 resulted from the family's unfortunate connection with Lucius Aelius Seianus.

Seneca's uncle C. Galerius, was the successor of Seius Strabo in Egypt. He was not a very good governor,[7] and his sixteen years in office may well be explained by the favour of Sejanus,

---

[1] Sextius had also apparently been interested in astronomy, demonstrating his understanding of its application to agriculture by making a killing on the oil market (Pliny, NH 18. 274).

[2] Plut. Mor. 78E. As a iuvenis, Seneca wrote a treatise on earthquakes (NQ 6. 4, 2). Though iuvenis is a vague word (cf. p. 35 n. 9), it is natural to connect this statement with Seneca's characterization of himself as a iuvenis early in Tiberius' reign (Ep. 108. 22). We do not know when he wrote De Lapidum Natura, De Situ Indiae, or De Situ et Sacris Aegyptiorum (Haase, frags. IV, VI, VII). De Piscium Natura (Haase, frag. V) could be dated before 46, and therefore before his exile, if it were certain Seneca actually witnessed the death of the sixty-year-old fish that had belonged to Vedius Pollio (who died in 15 B.C.). The Natural Questions belongs to Seneca's last years (see Appendix A1).

[3] Lana, Seneca, pp. 61–72, exaggerates the influence of Sextian doctrine on Seneca's late start, failing to note that Novatus' career followed a similar course.

[4] Pliny, NH 31. 62; NQ 4, pref. 10ff.

[5] Z. Stewart, AJP 74 (1953), 70.

[6] In Cons. Helv. 18. 1 (written during Seneca's exile) Seneca says of Novatus 'honores industria consecutus est'—that need only indicate the first two steps of the cursus honorum. The praetorian post Novatus held in 51/2 may have been his first after a praetorship achieved after 49 through his brother's influence with Agrippina (see p. 83).

[7] P. Brunt, Historia 10 (1961), 211 and n. 63.

especially since he was recalled in 31, the year the prefect fell, and probably in haste, as there was disorder in Egypt afterwards.[1] Another link with Sejanus was the senator L. Junius Gallio, a close friend of the Elder Seneca, who later adopted his eldest son in his will.[2] Gallio's attempt to flatter Tiberius in 32 was interpreted by the Emperor as a seditious proposal typical of a *satelles Seiani*. It brought Gallio loss of his senatorial rank and exile, later changed to arrest at Rome.[3]

According to Stewart, Seneca was, in fact, associated with a number of the most prominent friends of Sejanus. What is the evidence? Seneca tells a story about a poetry recitation in the later reign of Tiberius that was much enlivened by the remarks of Pinarius Natta and of a knight called Varus, 'M. Vinicii comes'.[4] Pinarius Natta is known from Tacitus as a client of Sejanus who accused the historian Cremutius Cordus.[5] Vinicius' affiliations can be inferred from the eulogy of Sejanus that Velleius Paterculus included in a history written in Vinicius' honour. But what degree of friendship need be involved in attending the same recitation?[6] An obscene anecdote links Annius Pollio and Mamercus

[1] Stewart, op. cit., pp. 78–9, thinks the freedman Hiberus may have been the interim replacement for Galerius until Avillius Flaccus arrived.

[2] Novatus' new name, L. Junius Gallio Annaeanus, indicates the adoption. It is attested by 52 (*PIR*[2] I 757, below, p. 83 n. 5) and came after the death of Gaius, for *De Ira*, written after that event, is addressed to him as Novatus. At the death of Gaius, L. Junius Gallio was at least 70. H. de La Ville de Mirmont, *BH* 12 (1910) 255, puts his birth at *c.* 43, but Gallio was still in the senate in 32, so probably not born earlier than 33 B.C. (see p. 36 n. 1). A testamentary adoption is therefore likely.

[3] Tac. *Ann.* 6. 3.

[4] *Ep.* 122. 10–13. Seneca there remarks on the number of *lucifugae* active at the same period, which, he makes clear, is the reign of Tiberius, probably the later part, for the Sex. Papinius mentioned (15) must be the son of the consul of 36, an unfortunate young man whose debauchery was encouraged by his mother as a preparation for incest and who committed suicide in 37 (Tac. *Ann.* 6. 49).   [5] *Ann.* 4. 34.

[6] Stewart, *AJP* 74 (1953), 71, attached great significance to the fact that in the *Consolatio ad Marciam* Seneca speaks of only one of the two accusers, Satrius Secundus. But friendship with Pinarius Natta is not the only possible explanation. Satrius Secundus was more detestable as he betrayed Sejanus later on (*Ann.* 6. 47, 2); moreover, he was dead before Seneca wrote the work (*Ann.* 6. 8, 5 and 6. 47, 2 refer to him as dead), while Pinarius may well have survived the terror (see n. 4 above).

Aemilius Scaurus: Seneca heard the story bandied about and then praised in front of Scaurus.[1] Now Annius Pollio was probably related to Marcus Vinicius by marriage,[2] and in 32 he was accused of *maiestas* along with Scaurus and other prominent *nobiles*—perhaps as part of the aftermath of Sejanus' fall.[3] But there is nothing to connect Seneca with Pollio or even with Vinicius under Tiberius. If familiarity be detected in his reference to Vinicius in a Letter of 64,[4] it is adequately accounted for by Seneca's later acquaintance with his wife Julia Livilla.[5] As for Scaurus, Seneca introduces his anecdote to show how little he deserved the consulship, and his estimate of Scaurus' oratory in the thirties was even lower than his father's.[6]

If Seneca and Novatus suffered from their family connections with Sejanus, they suffered from the fact that those connections, and the influence of their aunt, were not high enough. Everyone had courted Sejanus when he was in favour, but it was the little men—obscure knights and *novi homines*—who perished when he fell.[7] Even the noblest of his relatives survived: his cousin L. Cassius Longinus in fact was married in 33, like Vinicius, to one of the royal princesses.[8] Cn. Cornelius Lentulus Gaetulicus, whose daughter had been engaged to Sejanus' eldest son, not only survived but remained in command of Upper Germany

[1] *Ben.* 4. 31, 3: 'Referam tibi dictum eius in se quod circumferri memini et ipso praesente laudari.' The context of the passage, on a strict interpretation, would indicate a date for the incident before Scaurus became consul in A.D. 21 (31, 5 in particular).

[2] *PIR*² A 677—a natural inference from the name of Pollio's son, Annius Vinicianus.

[3] So Stewart, *AJP* 74 (1953) 73.   [4] Ibid. 74.

[5] She was married to Vinicius in 33 (*Ann.* 6. 15, 1). On her connection with Seneca see below, pp. 52, 59. Lana, *Seneca*, p. 107, suggests that the Elder Seneca was already familiar with the Vinicii, but his numerous references to P. and L. Vinicius show that he heard them declaim, and no more.

[6] *Contr.* 10, pref. 3. But Father Seneca had no use for Scaurus' accuser of A.D. 34 (*Suas.* 2. 22).

[7] e.g. *Ann.* 4. 71; 6. 3; 6. 4; 6. 7; 6. 10; 6. 14. See Syme, *Tacitus*, pp. 384–5; 406.

[8] *Ann.* 6. 15. The relationship of the Cassii Longini to Sejanus through their mother, a daughter of Q. Aelius Tubero (Pomp. *Dig.* 1. 2, 51), is acceptable no matter what view is taken of the precise way in which Seius Tubero, certainly one of the *consulares fratres* in Vell. Pat. 2. 127, 3, was related to the two families. (See F. Adams, *AJP* 76 (1955), 70–6; G. V. Sumner, *Phoenix* 19 (1965), 134 ff.)

from 30 until 39; his father-in-law L. Apronius similarly governed Lower Germany from at least 28 to at least 34.[1] Despite an accusation in that year on grounds of his connection with Sejanus, Gaetulicus and his family remained in Tiberius' confidence. His father, Cossus Cornelius Lentulus, became prefect of the city in 33: a man whose drinking did not impair his discretion, according to Seneca.[2] The dropping of *maiestas* charges in 32 against Annius Pollio, Annius Vinicianus, and Calvisius Sabinus, who may have been married to Gaetulicus' sister,[3] belongs to the same pattern. The facts are plain, whatever the explanation—that those very *nobiles* who had co-operated with Sejanus, though resentful of his ambitions, finally persuaded Tiberius to depose him,[4] or that Tiberius, who suddenly awoke to the bitter truth that Sejanus had acted from ambition rather than loyalty, 'was able to destroy his minister without imperilling the fabric of government',[5] knowing that these *nobiles* could not ever have preferred Sejanus to the Julio-Claudians. Had Seneca returned from Egypt to pick up existing connections with these noble *Seianiani*, his failure to reach a praetorship before his exile would be harder, not easier, to explain.

Why then did Seneca and Novatus only enter the Senate in the very last days of Tiberius? If not seriously suspect on political grounds, despite their connection with Galerius and Gallio, or even more reluctant to try public life after the political turmoil and terror of 31, they may simply have suffered from a kind of sluggishness in the latter part of Tiberius' reign. With the Emperor away from Rome permanently, it would be hard for an aspiring *eques* to secure his favour. In 38 Gaius had to revise the roll of *equites* and give a large number of them the *latus clavus*, probably to catch up on Tiberius' omissions.[6] Yet some provincials had

[1] On Gaetulicus, *PIR²* C 1390. Tacitus is wrong in saying (*Ann.* 6. 30, 4) that he alone of Sejanus' *adfines* survived (see p. 49 n. 8). On Apronius, *PIR²* A 971.

[2] *Ep.* 83. 15. Cf. *Ann.* 6. 10; 6. 27. *PIR²* C 1380. He was probably the author of a proposal, before Sejanus' fall in 31, designed to protect L. Arruntius, one of the prefect's enemies (Dio 58. 8, 3; *Dig.* 48. 2, 12; *PIR²* A 1130).

[3] So Groag in *PIR²* C 354.

[4] The suggestion of A. Boddington, *AJP* 84 (1963), esp. pp. 12 ff.

[5] Syme, *Tacitus*, p. 385.

[6] Dio 59. 9, 5 (cf. Suet. *Tib.* 41, and *ILS* 206 'absentia pertinaci'). The false

managed to enter the Senate at that time, for example, Julius Graecinus from Forum Julii—a man Seneca admired for his wit as well as his virtue.[1]

By the time the influence of his aunt had helped him to secure his first magistracy, Seneca's rhetorical skill had probably already attracted attention. Soon after 37 his father had described him and his brother as preparing for the forum:[2] in the reign of Gaius he was already well known.[3] Can we find among the numerous names he preserves clues to those who at last helped his ambitions?

The powerful in the last years of Tiberius were a curious mixture. Friends and enemies of Sejanus had been hard to distinguish.[4] Even the instrument of his destruction, Naevius Sutorius Macro, had been *praefectus vigilum* while Sejanus was in power;[5] his friend Avillius Flaccus, who became prefect of Egypt in 32, had testified against Agrippina in 29 along with many a client of Sejanus.[6] The *nobiles*, as we have seen, went on. It would be surprising if they had allowed Sejanus to dictate their friendships posthumously, and there is proof that they did not. When the conspiracy of Lentulus Gaetulicus was discovered in 39, Gaius' sisters, Agrippina and Livilla, were punished as associates. An attempt to determine whether the intended replacement for Gaius, M. Aemilius Lepidus, should be termed a *Seianianus* or the reverse would be a study in ambiguity.[7]

statement he makes that previously knights had not been granted the *latus clavus* (cf. Ovid, *Tr.* 4. 10, 29 ff.; Suet. *Aug.* 38. 2, shows that senators' sons were the only ones to wear the stripe *automatically*) is Dio's own explanation of something which must have caused comment. Perhaps the oddity lay in the numbers involved.

[1] *PIR²* I 344. He entered the Senate directly through the tribunate (*AE* 1946, no. 94). *Ep.* 29. 6; *Ben.* 2. 21, 5.

[2] *Contr.* 2, pref. 4.

[3] Suet. *Gaius* 53: 'tum maxime placens'.

[4] Note that P. Vitellius and P. Pomponius Secundus had brothers loyal enough to serve as their custodians (*Ann.* 5. 8).

[5] *AE* 1957, no. 250. He used the night watch to great effect. Presumably Graecinius Laco who helped Macro (now promoted to praetorian prefect) in the crisis only became *praefectus vigilum* (Dio 58. 9, 3) at that moment. Thus Tiberius ensured the loyalty of the praetorians and the night watch at once.

[6] Philo, *Flacc.* 9, 11.

[7] If he was brother to Aemilia Lepida (as advanced by Groag, *PIR²* A 371),

Passienus Crispus, like Gaius' sisters, was made to accompany Gaius north to unmask Gaeticulus: he may have been suspect.[1]

That Seneca may have been able to call on the services of this group in the early stages of his career is an attractive suggestion.[2] It is always tempting to invoke the help of Passienus Crispus, the faithful friend of the Epigrams. But his services to Seneca's biographers may have been greater than those to Seneca's career: he had been prominent on the scene since his consulate of 27 with little effect on Seneca; later, despite his second consulate of 44, Seneca remained in exile until after his death. Julia Livilla may have been more useful, for Seneca certainly was known to be on terms of social intimacy with her by 41 when a charge of immoral relations with her was at least plausible.[3] A remark of Tacitus might reveal that Agrippina too had done Seneca a favour at some time before his return from exile.[4] Finally Seneca himself, in praising the loyalty of Lucilius to himself at the time of his exile, notes also his friend's loyalty to Gaetulicus in his hour of peril.[5] It would not be surprising if these friendships went back to the period when Seneca was entering public life. Gaetulicus was a writer of history and poetry[6] whose patronage Lucilius and Seneca might have courted.

then he had a sister who was an agent of Sejanus in attacking her husband Drusus, son of Germanicus (Dio 58. 3, 8), but a father who was regarded as loyal till his death (*Ann.* 6. 40, 3). He was a friend of Avillius Flaccus (Philo, *Flacc.* 151, 181), and of Annius Vinicianus (Jos. *AJ* 19, 20).

[1] As J. P. V. D. Balsdon implies, *The Emperor Gaius*, Oxford, 1934, p. 73.

[2] Made by Stewart, who insists on regarding them as a continuous group of *Seianiani* enduring through the assassination of Gaius, esp. p. 77. Lana, *Seneca*, pp. 106–10, 115 (who does not mention Stewart's discussion), more plausibly regards the group as a circle centred on Gaius' sisters.

[3] Dio 60. 8, 5–6; Schol. Juv. 5. 109.

[4] *Ann.* 12. 8, 2: (year 49) 'quia Seneca fidus in Agrippinam memoria beneficii et infensus Claudio dolore iniuriae credebatur.' The most natural way of taking this sentence would be to construe the *beneficium*, like the *iniuria*, as an event of the past that Tacitus mentioned in the lost books, as is pointed out by G. W. Clarke, 'Seneca the Younger under Caligula', *Latomus* 24 (1965), 62. But the *beneficium* could be connected with Seneca's sentence in 41, rather than, as Clarke thinks, with his previous career; see below, p. 60.

[5] *NQ* 4, pref. 15.

[6] Suet. *Gaius* 8; Pliny, *Ep.* 5. 3, 5; Sid. Apoll. *Ep.* 2. 10, 6. See Balsdon, *Gaius*, p. 74. Lana, *Seneca*, p. 108, suggests that the Caesennia to whom, according to

Confirmation of these possible early connections has been sought in the only outside evidence we have for Seneca's life in the reign of Gaius: a well-chewed anecdote in Cassius Dio. In the year 39, Gaius declared war on the Senate: he reversed his previous adverse judgement on Tiberius, upheld his condemnations, and blamed the Senate for the innocent deaths in his reign. The *maiestas* charge was revived and, among those tried, Dio records a pair who nearly died for paradoxical reasons and were saved by astonishing means. One was Domitius Afer, charged for a laudatory dedication to Gaius which the Emperor misunderstood, and saved by pretending to be overwhelmed by Gaius' rhetoric in the prosecution speech. The other was Seneca, ordered to commit suicide for nothing more than pleading well before the Senate in the Emperor's presence, and saved by a mistress of Gaius who reported that he would soon be dead of consumption in any case.[1]

This tale has been rejected by many as an invention of Seneca,[2] or of someone else.[3] As opposed to the story of Domitius, it lacks substance and plausibility. Domitius was accused before the Senate, but who could have witnessed the death order to Seneca, afterwards revoked? The anger of Gaius in Domitius' case is explained by the orator's past as an accuser of Agrippina's associates under Tiberius. But could Gaius have been provoked to a death sentence by mere envy of Seneca's oratory? Domitius' escape is given an additional explanation in the influence of Callistus whom he had courted. Seneca's redeemer has no name, and she told a tale that must have seemed very feeble in the light of Seneca's recent rhetorical triumph. Admittedly, two facts in the anecdote have outside confirmation: Seneca's consumption in

---

Sidonius, he wrote poems was related to Seneca's friend Caesennius Maximus. But his refutation of E. Groag, *Wien. Stud.* 25 (1903), 320; *PIR*² A 976, identifying her with the daughter of L. Apronius (*Ann.* 6. 30), whose name might have been Caesia or Caesiana (cf. her brother Caesianus), is unconvincing and, as he admits, Martial might be right to call Seneca's friend Caesonius (*Ep.* 7. 44, cf. Tacitus *Ann.* 15. 71, 5: Caesennius).

[1] Dio 59. 19.   [2] Balsdon, *Gaius*, pp. 55–6.

[3] C. Marchesi, *Seneca*, Milan, 1944, p. 11; Stewart, *AJP* 74 (1953) 81, and others.

youth is known from a letter; and his oratorical success in these years and Gaius' dislike of it are known from Suetonius.[1] In addition, Seneca shows unrelieved hostility to Gaius in his works and mentions a renunciation of pleading cases.[2] But these facts may help to explain the invention of the anecdote, rather than confirm its truth. Another passage from Seneca is often cited in this connection. In Letter 78. 6, discussing what makes illness terrible to us, Seneca mentions the fear that we will die and challenges our association of disease and death with a paradox: 'multorum mortem distulit morbus et saluti illis fuit videri perire.' Even if this sentence refers, as is often thought, to a political escape, it need not be a reference to Seneca's own past, for the trick had probably been tried before, as it certainly was later.[3] In fact this political interpretation has been doubted on the grounds that Seneca is really making reference to a simple medical fact:[4] that men have finally been cured by an exceptionally severe attack of illness. This is surely the correct meaning, for Seneca refers to the phenomenon in similar language, but more explicitly, elsewhere.[5]

If Seneca's narrow escape from the tyrant is a fiction, it is much more likely to be the work of some apologist than of Seneca himself. For Seneca's writings betray no tendency to inflate his past dangers or to pose as heroic. What could be less so than the story of his abandonment of asceticism at the request of his father when superstition was being persecuted? Seneca there admits how easily he was persuaded to live comfortably

---

[1] *Ep.* 78; Suet. *Gaius* 53: 'lenius comptiusque scribendi genus adeo contemnere, ut Senecam tum maxime placentem "commissiones meras" componere et "harenam esse sine calce" diceret.' Of course, Gaius might have been moved by taste, not jealousy, when he said this.

[2] *Ep.* 49. 2: 'modo causas agere coepi, modo desii velle agere, modo desii posse.'

[3] Plut. *Galba* 17: Tigellinus' illness was meant to count as a reason for leaving him unpunished. It is not clear if Galba believed in it himself.

[4] Clarke, *Latomus* 24 (1965) 64. The Loeb translation by Basore implies that interpretation.

[5] *Ira* 1. 12, 6: 'nam et febres quaedam genera valetudinis levant nec ideo non ex toto illis caruisse melius est: abominandum remedii genus est sanitatem debere morbo.' St. Aug. *Conf.* 6. 1 *fin.* calls such an attack the *critica*.

again and mentions no actual threat made to him.[1] His exile
under Claudius is only once referred to in the works we have
from after the return, and then only indirectly in a story about
Lucilius' loyalty to men in trouble.[2] Similarly Seneca refers only
generally to Gaius' habit of insulting men[3] though we know
from Suetonius that he made cutting remarks about his style.

The alternative to explaining away Dio's story as a fiction—
probably concocted from the facts of Gaius' criticism and
Seneca's illness, intended perhaps to explain his abandonment of
oratory and his animus against Gaius in his works—is to rewrite
the story, giving it the kind of substance that Dio gave to the
companion tale of Domitius Afer in which he was clearly more
interested. A rescue by Agrippina has been suggested, the *beneficium* referred to by Tacitus in his account of Seneca's recall.[4]
But Dio could not knowingly have referred to Agrippina
simply as γυναικί τινι ὧν ἐχρῆτο even though he believed in
Gaius' incestuous relations with his sister.[5] We have to suppose
his use of some source that deliberately concealed her name.[6]
But for what reason? As Seneca is introduced with honorific
epithets in the story, we might suppose that Dio, elsewhere
often hostile to Seneca, is using an apologist source here, but the
story even as it stands—a rescue by a woman on grounds of
illness—is no credit to Seneca. Besides, it was no secret that
Seneca owed Agrippina gratitude, for his later recall if nothing
else. What could be gained by concealing this instance?

A more radical treatment has been accorded the passage by
Stewart, who prunes away the romantic details and replaces
them with politics. If Domitius had a past, so did Seneca, and he
may have had a present as well, if he was already well acquainted
with some of the participants in the conspiracy of Lepidus and
Gaetulicus that was unmasked by Gaius in 39.[7] Dio's placing of

---

[1] *Ep.* 108. 22.   [2] *NQ* 4, pref. 15; below, p. 61.   [3] *Const. Sap.* 18.
[4] See above, p. 52.   [5] Dio 59. 22, 6; cf. Suet. *Gaius* 24.
[6] Clarke, *Latomus* 24 (1965), 69, suggests a 'studious duplicity' on the part
of the historian Fabius Rusticus, known to be biased towards Seneca, who sought
to explain Seneca's delayed career under Caligula.
[7] Before Stewart, Marchesi, *Seneca*, p. 11 n. 18, suggested that Seneca's
danger in 39 was linked with the exile (after the conspiracy of Gaetulicus) of

the incident in the first part of the year, before Domitius Afer's consulship, might seem to rule out this interpretation, for it was only later on, some time in September, that Gaius suddenly marched north to deal with Gaetulicus, leaving Domitius behind as consul.[1] But the placing of Seneca's adventure in Dio need not be chronologically precise. Apart from the strong possibility of error,[2] Dio may have included the incident here because of the interesting parallel it made with the case of Domitius. Or it could be argued that Gaius' suspicion of Gaetulicus' friends might well go back at least to the indictment of Calvisius Sabinus which preceded the attack on Domitius.[3] Seneca's old family connections with Sejanus and the notorious past of Domitius and Gaetulicus could have provoked Gaius' hostility towards them early in the year, if Suetonius is right in saying that Gaius' volte-face about Tiberius shifted the guilt to the Senate as 'Seiani clientes'.[4]

To this political diagnosis of Seneca's danger, we might add a conjecture about the speech that offended Gaius—perhaps too favourable to someone accused, or a speech better than one the Emperor wrote[5]—and about Seneca's rescue—another chance to invoke Passienus Crispus.[6] This is an elegant construction but it is highly dubious. Even Domitius cannot have been suspect principally on political grounds or he would not have been left behind as consul.[7] And then there is Dio's insistence that no other cause than the one he gives was involved, which accords well with the unanimous ancient tradition of Gaius' irrationality in the later part of his reign.

Julia Livilla who was probably already associated with Seneca. Lana, *Seneca*, pp. 106-10, 115, regards the real cause of Seneca's danger as his connection with Gaius' sisters who were suspected of complicity in the conspiracy.

[1] Dio 59. 20-1; Balsdon, *Gaius*, p. 71.

[2] This part of Dio's account includes other examples of predating: 59. 8, 4—the death of Silanus belongs in 38, not 37; 59. 8, 7—the banishment of Piso came after the spring of 40, not in 37.

[3] Balsdon, *Gaius*, p. 71.

[4] Suet. *Gaius* 30. 2; cf. Dio 59. 16, 4.

[5] Cf. Suet. *Gaius* 53. 2.

[6] As does Stewart, *AJP* 74 (1953), 83.

[7] Even if, as Stewart surmises, p. 77, he 'gave information to Gaius'.

Apart from this story all that we know of Seneca's public life[1] under Gaius is that the Emperor made adverse comments on his oratory and that, perhaps partly because of this, the orator gave up speaking.[2] Of his literary life, we know that he wrote the *Consolation to Marcia*,[3] a lady of senatorial family, by origin and by marriage, who might be expected to enjoy fine writing: her father was the historian Cremutius Cordus and her husband may have been the Metilius Rufus to whom Dionysius of Halicarnassus had dedicated his work *De Compositione Verborum*.[4] Of his private life, two details are provided by the Consolation addressed to his mother from exile: he lost his father, and he was married, for, less than a month before his exile, he had lost a young son.[5]

Whether or not this wife was the Pompeia Paulina known from the Letters and historians as the wife of Seneca's latter years is a question on which too much energy has already been lavished.[6] Giancotti, after a careful review of all the relevant passages,

---

[1] The vague sentence in *Cons. Helv.* 2. 5 'Transeo tot pericula, tot metus, . . .' is taken by Stewart, p. 81, to refer to Seneca's danger under Gaius, but its most natural reference is fears for losses in the family. Seneca might be alluding to his own poor health or, more likely, be trying to make Helvia's past calamities seem more numerous.

[2] *Ep.* 49. 2 (cited p. 54 n. 2). The 'desii posse agere' could refer to the facts of exile or ill health. The 'desii velle' must refer to some period before the exile and after a period of popularity under Gaius.

[3] For the date see Appendix A1. For the view that it had a political purpose see above, pp. 22–3.

[4] On her father, the senator and historian Cremutius Cordus who wrote on the Civil Wars with *eloquentia* and *libertas*, see[2] PIR C 1565. Her husband, presumably a Metilius (*Cons. Marc.* 16. 8), may be the Metilius Rufus in Dionysius' dedication, *Comp. Verb.* 1. He was probably proconsul of Achaea in the later part of Augustus' reign (Groag, *Die römischen Reichsbeamten von Achaia bis auf Diokletian*, Vienna, 1939, p. 14 and n. 60). Seneca mentions *magni et adfines viri* (1. 6) which may mark a connection with some noble Marcii. Seneca notes her influence in obtaining an early priesthood for her son (24. 3) and her friendship with Livia (4. 2). She had republished her father's works when Gaius permitted it (Suet. *Gaius* 16. 1) at the beginning of his reign and had some literary interests of her own (*Cons. Marc.* 1. 6 'studia, hereditarium et paternum bonum').

[5] *Cons. Helv.* 2. 5.

[6] Full discussions in A. Bourgery, *REL* 14 (1936), 90–4; H. W. Kamp, *CJ* 32 (1937), 529; Giancotti, *RAL* 8th Ser. 8 (1953), 58; Giancotti, *Cronologia*, pp. 111 ff.

decided the question could not be answered. His verdict was just, and the discussion should have lapsed. But since then it has been argued that the two surviving grandchildren that Seneca mentions to his mother in 18. 4–8, Marcus and Novatilla, are Seneca's own children, in accordance with a theme common in consolation, that the child is the replacement for the parent. The fact that they are entrusted to Helvia is explained by the death of Seneca's wife, the loss of the mother being supposedly mentioned in the case of Novatilla (18. 8).[1] It seems to me that this interpretation of these chapters misconstrues the clear line of thought in this Consolation, and must be challenged, although the conclusion about Seneca's wife, regardless of this false analysis, may yet be right.

At this point in the work, Seneca turns to Helvia's consolations among the living and finds them in the *domus Annaeana*: first her remaining sons, then her grandsons, then her potential great-grandchildren (expected from her granddaughter Novatilla). Novatilla is mentioned with great tenderness, but the emphasis on the male descendants, through whom the family will survive, is absolutely clear: it is before Novatilla is mentioned, and after the portrait of Marcus, that Seneca inserts his prayer: 'quidquid matri dolendum fuit in me transierit, quidquid aviae, in me. Floreat reliqua in suo statu turba. Nihil de orbitate, nihil de condicione mea querar, fuerim tantum nihil amplius doliturae domus piamentum' (18. 6). The sons and grandsons just mentioned remain the theme. Seneca will take on himself all Helvia's sufferings as a mother or as a grandmother: *condicio* (exile) constitutes the first and his *orbitas* the second. *Orbitas* could refer to the loss of the son mentioned earlier (2. 5), but it is more natural to take it here not of one event, but of a state parallel to *condicio*. More important, in listing the mainstays of the *domus* headed by Helvia, Seneca could not have omitted Marcus Lucanus born in November of 39.[2] He must be the Marcus of 18. 5, well over two years old when Seneca wrote.[3]

---

[1] Abel, *Gnomon* 30 (1958), 610; *RhM* 115 (1972), 325 ff.

[2] Here I agree with Lana, *Seneca*, p. 115.

[3] He was born in November of 39, according to the Vacca Life.

Novatilla can hardly be Seneca's daughter. Her name apart, 18. 7 'quam sic in me transtuleram, sic mihi ascripseram, ut possit videri quod me amisit, quamvis salvo patre pupilla' would require a very peculiar interpretation. Novatilla will be the daughter of the eldest brother, Novatus.

There is no mention of Seneca's wife in the *Ad Helviam*.[1] That in itself is not proof that she was dead: her mother-in-law may have disliked her, or she might have joined Seneca in Corsica. But in the absence of definite evidence to the contrary, the tendency for young women to die in childbirth in antiquity must be given its full weight and the possibility allowed that Seneca lost his wife along with his son (2. 5). In that case, he probably married Pompeia Paulina, daughter of the *praefectus annonae*,[2] soon after his return from Corsica in 49.

Exile and Recall

Seneca must have been a witness to the exciting events of Gaius' murder and Claudius' accession. Yet he betrays no first-hand knowledge or gives the slightest hint of his own participation.[3] In 41 Gaius' two remaining sisters were recalled and their property restored.[4] Probably towards the close of that year,[5] Seneca was relegated to the island of Corsica on a charge of adultery with the younger, Julia Livilla.[6] He was, on his own evidence, tried

---

[1] Given the interpretation of 'quidquid matri . . .' (18. 6) offered above.

[2] On his position and the date of Pompeius Paulinus' tenure, *JRS* 52 (1962), 105, 108.

[3] In *Ira* 1. 20, 8–9, he *speculates* on the motives of the conspirators.

[4] Dio 60. 4, 1.

[5] Dio 60. 8. Enough time must have elapsed since Livilla's recall to give Messallina a case against Seneca. The *terminus post quem* is the end of February, for Livilla was probably recalled through the Senate (Suet. *Claudius* 12) and Seneca was certainly tried there before the Emperor (*Cons. Polyb.* 13. 2), while we know that Claudius did not appear there for a month (Dio 60. 3, 2).

[6] Dio calls the charge adultery. The Schol. on Juvenal 5. 109 uses the expression 'quasi conscius adulteriorum Iuliae'—for the meaning of this 'on a charge of immoral connections' see Stewart, *AJP* 74 (1953), 83 n. 86. Livilla's marriage with Vinicius will have been dissolved by her conviction for adultery under Gaius in 39 (Dio 59. 22, 8; Suet. *Gaius* 24. 3) unless Claudius gave her special dispensation on her return. But that is likely as he must have released

before the Senate, which voted for conviction and the death penalty.[1] Relegation was the normal penalty for adultery,[2] but Augustus himself had set the precedent for exceeding his own *Lex Julia de adulteriis* in punishing the lovers of imperial ladies with exile,[3] and Tiberius had followed suit.[4] Claudius, however, asked that Seneca's life be spared: perhaps it was at this point that Agrippina, a favourite of her uncle,[5] conferred a *beneficium* on Seneca by asking Claudius' mercy.[6]

Was Seneca guilty? Dio portrays Seneca as a victim of charges concocted by Messallina in an effort to get rid of Livilla of whom she was envious.[7] In explaining Agrippina's decision to recall him in 49, Tacitus says of Seneca: 'fidus in Agrippinam memoria beneficii et infensus Claudio dolore iniuriae credebatur.'[8] It is not clear whose view *iniuria* represents—Seneca's, Agrippina's, or Tacitus',[9] but Tacitus does not dissociate himself from the view, and he later discourages belief in Seneca's guilt by putting the reproach 'iustissimum exilium' in the mouth of the abominable Suillius.[10]

Seneca's guilt cannot, at any rate, have been manifest, for the Consolation on his exile addressed to his mother presupposes a claim of innocence;[11] and however insincere Seneca might be,

Agrippina from the provision of the law making marriage with an *adultera* an offence, for she married Passienus Crispus. Note that Dio 60. 27, 4 calls Livilla Vinicius' wife at the time of her death.

[1] *Cons. Polyb.* 13. 2: 'deprecatus est pro me senatum et vitam mihi non tantum dedit sed etiam petit.'

[2] See below, p. 288.

[3] Tac. *Ann.* 3. 24: 'morte aut fuga punivit.' The death meant is that of Iullus Antonius (*Ann.* 4. 44, cf. 1. 10), but his death may only have been the result of his condemnation, not the penalty.

[4] *Ann.* 2. 50.   [5] Dio 60. 31, 6.

[6] Above, p. 52.   [7] Dio 60. 8, 5.

[8] *Ann.* 12. 8, 3.

[9] The same is true of 'at Agrippina ne malis tantum facinoribus notesceret . . .', where it is Agrippina apparently who thinks Seneca's recall will be popular and reckoned as a *bonum facinus*.

[10] *Ann.* 13. 42. Dio 61. 10 contains echoes of these charges.

[11] A point established by Abel, *Bauformen*, pp. 48 ff. The claim is particularly clear in 8; 9, 3; 13. 8. Though Abel may be right in regarding the work as partly apologetic in purpose, I cannot see what, except faith, guarantees that Seneca's claim was true, as Abel insists (pp. 70 ff.).

he would not have chosen to be ludicrous. Moreover, when
Seneca appeals for mercy in the Consolation to Polybius,
although he naturally does not insist on his innocence, he asks
that the Emperor, in reviewing his case, recall him as an exercise
of *iustitia* or *clementia*.[1] The former term implies the belief that
Claudius may have thought him innocent. Seneca's case may
well have been just one more example of the use of charges of
immorality to dispose of enemies. Macro had used it against
Scaurus and others;[2] Messallina was to use it against Valerius
Asiaticus,[3] and Tigellinus tried it out on Faenius Rufus.[4] All that
was required as a basis was a well-known connection with Livilla.
If we may assume that Seneca is including himself in a general
passage about Lucilius' loyalty to enemies of Messallina and
Narcissus, two more facts about his exile are recovered: Narcissus' part as Messallina's ally and the interrogation of Lucilius.[5]
There is no warrant for inventing more in the way of political
motives for Seneca's disgrace.[6]

In the Consolation to Claudius' freedman Polybius, in charge
at that time of literature and of petitions,[7] Seneca asked to be
recalled to witness the British triumph.[8] In the event, other
exiles were invited,[9] but Seneca had to wait for a change of wife.
Among the reasons that moved Agrippina to secure his recall

[1] That this is one purpose of *Ad Polybium* can scarcely be denied. It is especially
clear in 13. 2–4. See now Abel's careful analysis, *Bauformen*, pp. 70ff. If Abel
is right to see a reference to Seneca himself in 13. 4, 'scias licet ea demum fulmina
esse iustissima, quae etiam percussi colunt', he is wrong to take it as an admission
of guilt. It is a redefinition of *iustissima*—the Emperor's kindness to exiles and
their hopes of pardon make them accept their fate as just. Claudius could thus
reverse Seneca's sentence without throwing doubt on the justice of his conviction.
[2] *Ann.* 6. 29, 4; 6. 47–8.
[3] *Ann.* 11. 1–2 (Tacitus says Messallina believed in the charge but was after
Valerius' gardens primarily).
[4] *Ann.* 15. 50, 3.   [5] *NQ* 4, pref. 15 ff.
[6] Cf. Clarke, *Latomus* 24 (1965), 67, who thinks Seneca's conviction with the
wife of M. Vinicius suggests that he was suspected of participation in Gaius'
assassination. But even if Livilla was restored as Vinicius' wife after her return
(p. 59 n. 6), Vinicius at any rate survived her banishment to be cos. II in 45.
The participation of a man from Corduba (Jos. *AJ* 19. 17, 19), Aemilius Regulus
(perhaps a client of Lepidus' family), tells us nothing about Seneca.
[7] See above, p. 21 n. 2.   [8] *Cons. Polyb.* 13. 2.
[9] Suet. *Claudius* 17. 3.

Tacitus mentions her expectation that it would be a popular act 'ob claritudinem studiorum eius'.[1] By this time, Seneca's three Consolations and all or most of *De Ira* had been written. Other lost works, such as the biography of his father, may already have appeared. Writing and reading occupied him during the eight years of his ordeal.[2] He mentions studying the famous works of consolation literature, and pursuing his early interest in natural history. He indirectly reveals acquaintance with Ovid's compositions from exile.[3] No doubt Ovid's eight years on the Black Sea gave Seneca occasion for gloomy thoughts, but Corsica was not Tomis. Seneca analyses the mixed character of the native speech, detecting Greek, Spanish, and Ligurian elements,[4] and he complains of his Latin becoming rusty,[5] but he admits that there were two Roman colonies on the island and other exiles.[6] He may even have had a close friend with him.[7]

When Agrippina, early in 49, persuaded Claudius to recall Seneca, probably with formal senatorial approval,[8] and to commend him for the praetorship, she must have known that Seneca was willing to repay her services. The statement of the scholiast on Juvenal 5. 109 that Seneca really wanted to go to Athens on his recall may reflect a wish he then, or later, expressed to friends or an excuse, on grounds of reluctance, for the terrible scheme in which Agrippina's patronage involved him.[9] But

[1] *Ann.* 12. 8, 2.

[2] *Cons. Helv.* 1. 2.

[3] The end of *Cons. Polyb.* is an echo of such lines as *Tristia* 3. 14, 47; 5. 7, 57–8; *Ex Ponto* 4. 2, 15 ff.

[4] *Cons. Helv.* 7. 9.

[5] *Polyb.* 18. 9: 'non facile latina ei homini verba succurrant.'

[6] *Cons. Helv.* 7. 9.

[7] This fact emerges if we press the parallel in the last lines of Martial, *Epig.* 7. 44, addressed to Ovidius, who accompanied Caesonius Maximus into exile: 'audiet hoc praesens venturaque turba fuisse / illi te, Senecae quod fuit ille suo.' But Martial might simply allude to Seneca's close friendship with Maximus (cf. Seneca, *Ep.* 87) as in the next epigram, 'Facundi Senecae potens amicus / Caro proximus aut prior Sereno'. He later became consul. If he is properly identified with Tacitus' Caesennius Maximus, he was banished in the aftermath of the Pisonian conspiracy (*Ann.* 15. 71).

[8] Suet. *Claudius* 12.

[9] If the story is not simply an attempt to explain why Seneca, *princeps eruditorum*, never went to Athens (see above, p. 37).

when Seneca sailed for home, after eight bitter years, he was committed to teaching Domitius, who was now Claudius' stepson. He can hardly have been innocent before of Agrippina's *spes dominationis*, and he will have been left in little doubt when he began his duties probably towards the end of 49.[1] Towards the end of February of the new year, Domitius was adopted by Claudius and became heir apparent.[2]

What was Seneca supposed to do as *magister* or *praeceptor*?[3] Nero, now twelve years old, was approaching the age when the serious study of rhetoric should begin and, with Agrippina to see that even the assumption of the *toga virilis* was accelerated for him,[4] he was bound to start as early as possible. As for his earlier education,[5] Suetonius mentions the employment of *paedagogi* of scandalous incompetence when he lived with his aunt Domitia Lepida.[6] They can hardly have seriously delayed the progress of their pupil, who was three years old, especially as the arrangement cannot have lasted more than a year.[7] To the period after Agrippina's return must belong the instruction, presumably in Greek, of the παιδαγωγός Beryllus[8] and of the freedman Anicetus, 'pueritiae Neronis educator'.[9]

'Ratione consilio praeceptis pueritiam, dein iuventam meam fovisti', Nero says in reply to Seneca's request for retirement.[10] Tacitus includes a hint as to the nature of these *praecepta*: Nero

---

[1] For the date see Appendix C1.

[2] *Ann.* 12. 25; *CIL* 6. 1. 2040, 2041; the Arval Brethren sacrificed on 25 Feb.

[3] *Ann.* 12. 8, 2; 15. 62, 2. The term *educator* = παιδαγωγός used in the latter passage is doubtless meant to heighten the pathos of Seneca's suicide-order. On what Seneca taught see Giancotti, *RAL* 8th Ser. 8 (1953), 114ff. *Praeceptor* is regularly used of a teacher of rhetoric (Quint. 10. 5, 19), a private tutor (Pliny, *Ep.* 3. 3, 4), or an instructor in a school (Pliny, *Ep.* 2. 18; 4. 13).

[4] Tacitus, *Ann.* 12. 41: 'virilis toga Neroni maturata.' That was in A.D. 51 when Nero was just thirteen. (For his birth-date see Appendix A3.)

[5] On Nero's education, E. J. Parker, *AJP* 67 (1946), 44 ff.

[6] Suet. *Nero* 6. 3.

[7] His father died when he was three, so probably at the end of 40; his mother was recalled in 41. For a clear chronology, R. M. Geer, *TAPA* 62 (1931), 57 ff.

[8] Josephus, *AJ* 20. 183. See p. 68 n. 3 against the emendation to Βοῦρρον.

[9] *Ann.* 14. 3; Suet. *Nero* 35. 2, calls him *paedagogus*.

[10] *Ann.* 14. 55, 3.

learned to speak extemporaneously. Seneca tried to teach him *eloquentia* and was still training him after his accession, according to Tacitus.[1] Suetonius remarks that Seneca kept Nero from reading the early orators in order to keep his pupil's admiration for his own style[2]—as if Seneca could prevent Nero from reading what he chose! The genesis of this story is probably to be found in the reservations Seneca expressed about Cicero's style, for although Seneca was in general an admirer of Cicero's oratory,[3] the criticisms he did express were greeted in the Antonine period with the indignation due to heresy.[4]

Nero practised and performed: we hear of two declamations before his accession and one in the first year of his reign.[5] When he assumed the *toga virilis*, he thanked Claudius before the Senate where he subsequently displayed his skill in Greek and Latin, speaking in support of privileges and concessions to various cities.[6]

But Nero had many artistic and athletic interests which prevented him from reaching the proficiency necessary for the major speeches of a *princeps*. These Seneca continued to write for him.[7] After his accession, he seems to have added two more passions: music, of which he already knew the rudiments,[8] and philosophy, which, according to Suetonius, Agrippina had banned from his course of study.[9] We hear of a Peripatetic philosopher Ἀλέξανδρος Αἰγαῖος and a certain Χαιρήμων who taught 'king Nero': perhaps they are to be found among the *sapientiae doctores* whose controversies Nero enjoyed over dinner, at least after his mother's death.[10]

---

[1] *Ann.* 13. 2.

[2] Suet. *Nero* 52. Cf. Quint. 10. 1. 126.

[3] e.g. *Ep.* 40. 11; and the fragment of a lost letter to Lucilius (XVII (111) Haase) preserved in Gellius, *NA* 12. 2, 5: 'summus orator'.

[4] An example of criticism in *Ep.* 114. 16. See the way Gellius cites others in *NA* 12. 2, 6–9.

[5] Suet. *Rhet.* 1. 6–7.

[6] *Ann.* 12. 58, 1 where Tacitus records them under 53. Suet. *Nero* 7 states that Claudius was consul at the time—hence 51, perhaps because the earlier speech of thanks on coming of age was in that year.

[7] *Ann.* 13. 3.   [8] Suet. *Nero* 20.   [9] Ibid. 52.

[10] Suda s.v. Ἀλέξανδρος; Tac. *Ann.* 14. 16, 2.

To have a senator as *praeceptor* was unusual even for a prince, but it was not entirely unprecedented. None other than M. Aemilius Lepidus, the consul of A.D. 6, was a *praeceptor* of Germanicus' son Nero.[1] In the Republic distinguished senatorial orators discussed oratory with young aspirants, and the custom of completing one's oratorical education by joining the entourage of a noted speaker is attested in the Empire.[2] But although Tacitus makes his spokesman for the superiority of the past call these Republican orators *praeceptores*,[3] it is clear that they never supplied the rudiments of rhetoric to their followers, who were, on the whole, several years older than Seneca's pupil.[4]

Tacitus tells us that Seneca was also there to give advice: in practical politics, according to Agrippina's intentions,[5] and probably also in morals, as was usually expected.[6] Seneca was a man of charm, wit, and eloquence who could give the crown prince polish: that may have been Agrippina's idea. Naturally, he would have applied the principles of education and behaviour in which he believed, but, as he assured his readers in *De Clementia*, Stoicism, according to his conception, was not a harsh doctrine unsuitable for *principes*.[7] And flexibility will have been necessary for, if his pupil in *De Clementia* is likened to Augustus, teaching him must, in practice, have been more like teaching

---

[1] Elder Seneca, *Contr.* 2. 3, 23. The *praeceptor* is more likely to be this Lepidus than M'. Lepidus, *cos.* A.D. 11 (see *PIR*² A 363, 372), for M. Lepidus' daughter was married to Nero's younger brother (*Ann.* 6. 40). Lana, *Seneca*, pp. 113–14, tries to answer Groag's doubts (*PIR*² A 363) about a *praeceptor* of such elevated social status. The passage is not discussed in Syme, *JRS* 45 (1955), 22 ff. = *Ten Studies in Tacitus*, pp. 30 ff.

[2] Quintilian, 10. 5, 19; 12. 11, 5.

[3] *Dial.* 34. 5, 6.

[4] Cicero (*De Or.* 2. 2) was quite young when he heard Crassus at his home, but Crassus only encouraged and recommended teachers.

[5] *Ann.* 12. 8, 2.

[6] *Ann.* 14. 55, 3–4. The description of Seneca and Burrus as 'rectores imperatoriae iuventae' seeking to control the 'lubricam principis aetatem' is strikingly like Pliny's remarks on the role of a *rhetor Latinus* (*Ep.* 3. 3, 4): 'in hoc lubrico aetatis non praeceptor modo sed custos etiam rectorque quaerendus est.' Plut. *Mor.* 461B ff., tells a story illustrating the good effect on Nero of Seneca's moral instruction. As for politics, Agrippina blamed Britannicus' teachers for his lack of proper respect for Nero's adoption (*Ann.* 12. 41, 3).

[7] *Clem.* 2. 5, 2.

Gaius.[1] In this situation, restrained indulgence was the nearest one could come to moral discipline: the *libertas* Seneca claimed to have used in his treatment of Nero must often have been no more than *honesta comitas*.[2]

[1] Cf. the story of Seneca's dream in Suet. *Nero* 7.
[2] Tacitus, *Ann.* 15. 61, 1; cf. *Clem.* 2. 2, 2; *Ann.* 13. 2.

3

THE 'MINISTER' OF NERO

Two of our principal sources for the reign of Nero credit Seneca
and Burrus with the excellence of the early years. Tacitus and
Cassius Dio differ somewhat in defining the temporal limits of
their ascendancy,[1] but both agree that, for a period, they effectively controlled Nero and exercised their control in the interest
of good government.[2] The lack of prominence accorded them
by our third main source, Suetonius' *Nero*, is not contrary
evidence but merely reflects the biographer's natural tendency
to portray his subject as the focus of activity.

When Nero acceded to the throne, Burrus was praetorian
prefect; Seneca's position was unofficial.[3] In Tacitus he is always
referred to as Nero's *amicus* or *magister*. On receipt of a suicide-
order in 65, the historian has him remark that Nero was adding
to his earlier crimes 'educatoris praeceptorisque necem',[4] a phrase
echoed in Suetonius' account[5] and clearly designed to underline
Nero's lack of *pietas* as strongly as possible. Elsewhere in Tacitus,
this description is always applied by his detractors, who wish to
disparage the regime of a mere youth and his tutor[6] or to shame
Nero into breaking with his old mentor.[7] Those who do not
disparage him refer to him as a senior *amicus* of Nero, the

---

[1] See Appendix C2.

[2] Dio 61. 4; Tacitus, *Ann.* 13. 2; 13. 4–5 (cf. 13. 3, 3); 14. 52, 1.

[3] The suggestion of A. Gercke, 'Seneca-Studien', *Fleck. Jahr. Kl. Phil.* Suppl.
22 (1895), 298–9, that Seneca took on the post *ab epistulis* after Narcissus' death
rests on a manipulation of Josephus *AJ* 20. 183 as emended by Hudson who
read Βοῦρρον for Βήρυλλον, a man described as a former tutor of Nero, τάξιν
τὴν ἐπὶ τῶν Ἑλληνικῶν ἐπιστολῶν πεπιστευμένος. This correction was rightly
rejected by Niese. See now the summary of points by L. Feldman in the Loeb
Josephus, vol. IX, p. 487, note *h*.

[4] *Ann.* 15. 62, 2.   [5] *Nero* 35. 5.

[6] *Ann.* 13. 6, 2.   [7] Ibid. 14. 52, 4.

description ascribed to Nero and Seneca himself in the crucial retirement dialogue.[1] Tacitus there makes Seneca refer only to his work in educating Nero, but Nero, more generously, lists his services as *ratio*, *consilium*, *praecepta* and asks him to continue his moral guidance. In fact, the transition from being a tutor who was also a friend to being a friend who was also a tutor must have been imperceptible.

The main problem posed by this part of Seneca's career is this: Tacitus and Dio agree that Seneca shared with Burrus the responsibility for Nero's early reign, but neither reports any specific measures he initiated. Seneca's detractors, the *deteriores*, to whom Nero increasingly gave ear after the death of Burrus, could taunt the Emperor, 'Quem ad finem nihil in re publica clarum fore quod non ab illo reperiri credatur?'[2] But Seneca himself knew that if some credited him with all of Nero's good actions, others would attribute to him all of Nero's crimes.[3] The unofficial and personal character of Seneca's influence made it hard for the public to know just what he did. Does the evidence we have put us in a better position to know than the Roman public?

Modern accounts of Seneca's activities as Nero's 'minister' vary of course, but they all rest on three assumptions:

1. That Dio's picture of the administration of Seneca and Burrus is to be accepted: καὶ ἐκεῖνοι συμφρονήσαντες αὐτοὶ μὲν πολλὰ τὰ μὲν μετερρύθμισαν τῶν καθεστηκότων, τὰ δὲ καὶ παντελῶς κατέλυσαν, ἄλλα τε καινὰ προσενομοθέτησαν (61. 4, 2). Seneca was thus responsible for positive reforms.

2. That we may hold Seneca responsible for edicts of the Princeps because his role of adviser to Nero is attested by our sources and illustrated by Tacitus, for example, in the two crises concerning Agrippina.[4] And since Seneca was also a senator—ex-praetor at the start of the reign, consul suffect in 56[5]—we can assume that he also gave the lead in senatorial decisions.

---

[1] *Ann.* 14. 54, 1; 56, 2.   [2] Ibid. 14. 52.   [3] Ibid. 15. 45.
[4] Ibid. 13. 21; 14. 7.   [5] See below, p. 73 n. 6.

3. That we can often tell *which* edicts and senatorial decrees are of Senecan origin by searching his philosophical writings for his views on the issues involved. Where they agree, he is responsible; where they disagree, Seneca has been over-ruled or forced to yield to political expediency.

Modern accounts vary mostly in the caution or freedom with which they apply these assumptions in supplementing the evidence of the ancient sources. At one extreme, R. Waltz saw Seneca as the agent of collaboration between Emperor, magistrates, and Senate, in which assembly he led a docile majority, while implementing his policies concerning finance, justice, and foreign affairs.[1] At the other extreme, P. Faider warned against the ascription of measures to Seneca and Burrus, when the historians give us no details and the use of Seneca's works as evidence only leads to fantasy and contradiction. Yet even he accepted the view that the financial policy of the new reign represented the execution of Seneca's ideas.[2] An intermediate position has been adopted by J. Crook,[3] basing himself on an article of Stella Maranca.[4] Here Seneca is seen as a member of the Emperor's *consilium* which favoured palliatives and changes of detail rather than far-reaching schemes. Yet the picture given is still substantially Waltz's: Seneca and Burrus as provincials are presumed to have encouraged good provincial administration; Seneca's humane view prevailed in the debate in 56 on the right of patrons to revoke the liberty of ungrateful freedmen; Nero's decision to celebrate the opening of his new amphitheatre in the Campus Martius in 57 by a gladiatorial show in which no one was to be killed is traced to Seneca's humanitarianism.

All of these scholars attempt to answer the question: what did Seneca actually do? But their conclusions are vitiated from the start because the three assumptions on which they rest are highly dubious. About the third of these, enough has already been said (pp. 10–11). It prejudges this whole inquiry into the

[1] *Vie politique*, pp. 233 ff.
[2] *Études sur Sénèque*, Ghent, 1921, pp. 222 ff.
[3] *Consilium Principis*, pp. 119–25.
[4] *RAL* 32 (1923), 282–301.

connection between Seneca's political career and his philosophical works.

The case against the first assumption made by modern accounts
is this: the account of Cassius Dio (as preserved by his epitomators) offers no evidence to support his view of Seneca's role
in the early years of Nero's reign as the formulation of new laws
and measures changing existing institutions. Nor is Dio's statement worth much on its own, for what his epitomators preserve
shows a stark presentation of hostile and favourable references to
Seneca without the creation of a plausible portrait.[1] By contrast,
Tacitus, whose superiority as a source for the period is generally
recognized, gives Seneca and Burrus credit for the excellence of
the early reign, without mentioning either of them in connection with imperial edicts or senatorial decrees, or showing any
enthusiasm for such reforms as were introduced. Waltz, remarking on the lack of legislative activity in Tacitus' picture of
Seneca, blamed Tacitus for keeping Seneca in the background
and suggested that Seneca's contemporaries did not know the details of his existence while official records attributed his measures
to the Emperor.[2] The latter, however true, does not account
for Tacitus' silence, and the former is implausible, because Tacitus
was clearly deeply interested in Seneca;[3] he regarded the death
of Burrus early in 62 and Seneca's consequent loss of power as
the turning-point in the reign: the *bonae artes* in which they had
encouraged Nero are now entirely replaced by the *malae artes*
and *scelera* fostered by Tigellinus.[4] Tacitus' interest, which may
go back to an old family connection,[5] led him to use three
sources which together must have covered Seneca's life thoroughly
and revealed to him more than contemporary outsiders had
known. Pliny the Elder was completing the *militia equestris* in
the early years of Nero, serving in Lower Germany under

---

[1] See Appendix C4.   [2] *Vie politique*, pp. 8–9.
[3] See Appendix C5.

[4] *Ann.* 14. 52, 57. That Tacitus had good reasons for choosing this turning-
point and was not simply moved by a desire to exaggerate Seneca's importance
is argued in Appendix C3.

[5] Seneca knew and admired the philosophical L. Julius Graecinus, the father
of Agricola, Tacitus' father-in-law, *Ben.* 2. 21, 5; *Ep.* 29, 6.

Pompeius Paulinus.[1] He may well have known other friends of
Seneca though he mentions (of those known to us) only Paulinus,
Annaeus Serenus, and Seneca's brother Gallio.[2] A mere list of the
men to whom Seneca addressed his works, Paulinus *père*, Lucilius,
Serenus, probably also Aebutius Liberalis[3], indicates how wide
was his acquaintance with the equestrian circles in which Pliny
moved. Though out of Rome for part of Nero's reign, Pliny
was probably in the city for the crucial first year, and again in
59.[4] Cluvius Rufus was probably a senior consular throughout
the period and could supplement Tacitus' use of the *acta senatus*.[5]
For the details of Seneca's personal life and court activities,
Tacitus could rely on Fabius Rusticus, Seneca's protégé.[6]

Alternatively, the explanation is sought in 'Tacitus' lack of
concern for the normal detail of government',[7] or it is said that
Tacitus is not very helpful in describing Seneca's work in the
civil and judicial administration of the Empire 'not in all likelihood because he did not understand these things adequately or
care about them, but because he did not feel that they could be
made *opus oratorium*'.[8] It may be true that Tacitus would not
regard as worthy of historical record the ordinary transactions
of administrators, but it is certainly not true that he so regarded
major reforms or even all minor changes in rules and laws. Thus
his account of the year 57 opens with the remark 'pauca memoria
digna evenere' and a rejection of the topic of the new amphitheatre as unsuitable for *annales*, but he goes on to discuss the few
worthy items: reinforcements of veteran settlements, *congiaria*,
an imperial contribution to the *aerarium*, remission of a minor

---

[1] The standard account of Pliny's career is still F. Münzer, *Bonner Jahrbücher*
104 (1899), 67–111. See Appendix C4 for problems relating to Pliny's later
career.

[2] Pliny, *NH* 33. 143; 22. 96; 31. 62; 7. 55.

[3] On the last see Appendix D8.

[4] Münzer, op. cit., pp. 81–3. For the impossibility of determining Pliny's
attitude to Seneca see Appendix C4.

[5] On Cluvius' consulship see Syme, *Tacitus*, p. 294. The use of the *acta senatus*
is specifically attested for Nero's reign (*Ann.* 15. 74).

[6] *Ann.* 13. 20, 2.

[7] D. Henry and B. Walker, *Greece and Rome* 10 (1963), 101.

[8] W. H. Alexander, *Univ. of Calif. Publ. in Cl. Phil.* 14 (1952), 274 n. 10.

tax, the imperial edict forbidding provincial governors to give
gladiatorial games.[1] If Tacitus was not unwilling to report minor
measures of Nero, still less was he reluctant to discuss *senatus
consulta*, for he regarded such senatorial activity as proof of the
sincerity of Nero's promises for a good reign.[2]

It is clear, however, that Tacitus did not regard the excellence
of Nero's reign as a matter of reforms. Thus, he reveals his
attitude to that supposed triumph of Senecan moderation, the
quashing by Nero of the Senate's *relatio de fraudibus libertorum*, by
connecting it with Nero's arbitrary interference in a court case
in order to deprive a patron of her freedman and by starting the
next chapter: 'manebat nihilo minus quaedam imago rei publicae.'[3]
The one act of Nero that can be taken to show disapproval of
gladiatorial games on humanitarian grounds is omitted by
Tacitus.[4] Of the financial measures, the curb set on the abuses of
the *publicani* in 58 is said to contain fair but ineffective provisions;
the transfer of the 4 per cent surcharge on slaves to the seller in
57 was a reform 'specie magis quam vi';[5] the change in the
management of the *aerarium* in 56 meets with approval[6] but is
certainly not regarded as a piece of 'radicalism'[7]—a transfer of the
effective financial control over the *aerarium* to the Princeps.[8] For
Tacitus the decision to have imperially appointed *praefecti* arises
from a specific case of mismanagement by a *quaestor aerarii* and

[1] *Ann.* 13. 31.

[2] Ibid. 13. 5: 'Nec defuit fides, multa arbitrio senatus constituta sunt.'

[3] Ibid. 13. 26–8. Tacitus also disliked Nero's solution regarding punishment of
the household of Pedanius Secundus which Seneca did not oppose. See below,
pp. 280–1.

[4] Suet. *Nero* 12.1: at the gladiatorial show celebrating the opening of Nero's
new amphitheatre, Nero ordered that no one was to be killed, but there is no
warrant for thinking Nero made a habit of this mildness. The imperial edict
forbidding provincial governors to give gladiatorial games (*Ann.* 13. 31, 3) was
aimed at the protection of provincials; the decree allowing extra gladiators at
the Syracusan games (ibid. 13. 49) was opposed only by Thrasea Paetus and then,
apparently, because it encouraged extravagance ('ne Syracusis largius ederentur').

[5] *Ann.* 13. 51; 13. 31.

[6] Ibid. 13. 28–9.

[7] So C. H. V. Sutherland, *Coinage in Roman Imperial Policy, 31 B.C.–A.D. 68*,
London, 1951, p. 156.

[8] Waltz, *Vie politique*, pp. 261–2; M. A. Levi, *Nerone e i suoi tempi*, Milan, 1949,
pp. 118–19.

reflects past unhappy solutions: choice by the Senate had led to intrigue; choice by lot to incompetence.[1] Claudius determined on appointment by the Princeps,[2] but his decision to return to the quaestors their traditional Republican function was unfortunate. Nero wisely kept to imperial appointment but chose ex-praetors 'experientia probatos'. Finally, although Tacitus does point with approval to measures designed to check the abuses of provincial governors, he also indicates plainly that the record of the early reign was seriously blemished by lack of such discipline.[3]

It is possible, of course, that Tacitus invented a role for Seneca and a corresponding character for Nero's early reign. But Tacitus' sources and his own closeness to the events make this unlikely.[4] Can we then account for Dio's misconception about the activities of Seneca and Burrus? He may have given his own content to the tradition that Seneca and Burrus were responsible for a period of good government: as an *amicus* of the Severan emperors, Dio lived in an era when basic changes in the imperial system were taking place, and, in the speech attributed to Maecenas in Book 52, he put forth his own detailed proposals (many reactionary) regarding financial, military, and judicial institutions.[5]

We come now to the second assumption underlying modern accounts. Seneca had one formal title—he was a senator and for part of 56 he was suffect consul.[6] The vagueness of the public as

[1] Cf. Dio 60. 10, 3.

[2] Tacitus' 'imposuit' implies as much and inscriptions confirm it: *ILS* 966, one of the first to hold the new post, might have been appointed as an exception but *ILS* 967 cannot be explained away in that way. Nero probably retained the three-year term instituted by Claudius (Syme, *Tacitus*, p. 658).

[3] See below, pp. 246 ff.

[4] Tacitus was approaching the age of 10 when Seneca died. He was able to consult participants in the events of that year (*Ann.* 15. 73, 2.).

[5] Crook, *Consilium Principis*, pp. 126–8; Millar, *A Study of Cassius Dio*, Oxford, 1964, pp. 108 ff. For the possible effect of this idea on Dio's date for Seneca's and Burrus' loss of effective power see Appendix C2.

[6] Seneca is attested as suffect consul with M. Trebellius Maximus in August (*Dig.* 36. 1, 1. Cf. Gaius 2. 253; *CIL* IV 5514) and with P. Palfurius on 3 September (*CIL* IV 3340, xlvi). There is no room for these pairs in the years 57, 58, and 59 and there are more likely candidates for 60 and 61 (see A. Degrassi, *I fasti consolari*, Rome, 1952), while a date early in Nero's reign is indicated by political considerations. Therefore 55 and 56 are the main possibilities. New inscriptions (*AE* 1960, no. 61, no. 62) show that Seneca's brother L. Junius

to his specific acts suggests that he initiated little in the Senate. It is true that Tacitus offers Lucius Vitellius' position under Claudius as a parallel to Seneca's[1] and that one of Vitellius' roles had been that of liaison man between the Emperor and the Senate.[2] But this need not be the aspect Tacitus is considering. No historian mentions any occasion on which Seneca was present in the Senate while Nero was Emperor. Augustus had devised a special type of *consilium* to sound senatorial opinion and avoid blunders in dealing with the Senate as a whole. Tiberius had failed to revive the institution when it lapsed in Augustus' last years, and the failure of communication between him and the Senate is apparent in Tacitus' account. Prompting of the consul designate was not always reliable,[3] but proposals or support from a Vitellius or a Seneca would be understood and followed. The hesitation of the Neronian Senate to make a *relatio* without stopping to consult the Princeps[4] makes it unlikely that Seneca was present, for the imperial opinion would certainly have been known through him. But Seneca might let individual senators know what type of measure or even what specific decision would be favourably viewed by the Emperor and his *amici*. We seem to have an example in the first decree passed by the Neronian senate in 54— the renewal of the Lex Cincia. Four years later it was reported to Seneca that Suillius Rufus, one of the principal targets of the renewal, had attacked him. Tacitus does not tell us what provoked Suillius' outburst at this time, but it seems not to have

Gallio Annaeanus was consul with Cutius Ciltus in 55 or 56, and the month of August is certified by *CIL* IV 3340 xlv. Since, apart from the Annaei, 55 has more suffects than 56, the more likely year for Seneca and his *two* partners is 56. Seneca will thus have allowed his elder brother to precede him, fittingly, in the consulship. (Smallwood, *Historia* 17 (1968), 384, just assumes Degrassi's suggestion of 56 for Seneca's consulship in arriving at 55 for Gallio's.)

[1] *Ann.* 14. 56.
[2] Ibid. 12. 5.
[3] Agrippina's prompting of Barea Soranus in 52 (Pliny, *NH* 35. 201) was successful, for he was a man whose opinion carried weight; Lucius Vitellius used the method with success, for he made sure that the speech of his agent, Mammius Pollio, *cos. des.* in 49, clearly echoed a recent one of his own (*Ann.* 12. 9). But when the consul designate was only Junius Marullus, the Senate might rebel (below, p. 92).
[4] *Ann.* 13. 26, 2; 14. 49, 2–3; 15. 22, 1.

been a charge laid against him under that law.[1] Perhaps Suillius
had waged a continuous attack on the renewal, and in 58, for
some reason, this took the form of an attack on Seneca. Suillius
complained that Seneca was hostile to him as a friend of Claudius.
Apparently, Suillius held Seneca responsible in some sense for
the decree of 54. Yet Tacitus makes no mention of Seneca when
reporting the decree, nor does he here, as in another case,[2] repair
his own omission. Probably, even if Suillius was right, Seneca's
part was not reported in the *acta senatus*. In 54 he was not an
ex-praetor, and so not, in any case, likely to have proposed the
motion. But the charge shows that Seneca was thought to
influence senatorial measures behind the scenes.

None the less, there is no reason to think that Seneca often
sponsored *senatus consulta* even in this indirect fashion.[3] Tacitus
makes it clear that this first meeting of the Senate after Nero's
speech was specially staged to demonstrate the new *libertas
senatus*. Although the meeting was held in the Palatine library[4]
for Agrippina's convenience, she was kept out,[5] and the Senate
was allowed to pass two measures undoing those of Claudius.
The second of these rescinded a SC proposed by the servile
Dolabella[6] requiring quaestors-elect to give gladiatorial games,
a rule that, according to Tacitus, demeaned the quaestorship.

[1] Ibid. 13. 42. The circumstances of this attack were left vague by Tacitus.
It was probably public as a reply to it by Galerius Trachalus seems to be reported
by Quintilian (p. 94 n. 4). But was it made in the Senate (in which case Seneca's
absence at the time is interesting) or in a court of law? In the latter case Tacitus,
like Quintilian, could have read of it in the *acta publica* (cf. Pliny, *Ep.* 7. 33, 3).
The occasion cannot be Suillius' trial, as is often suggested, for that was provoked
by the attack and Suillius' challenge 'crimen periculum omnia potius toleraturum'
(13. 42, 4) shows that he had not yet suffered a charge under the Lex Cincia.

[2] *Ann.* 16. 21, 3, where we first learn that Thrasea was important in the trial
reported in 13. 33, 3.

[3] A senatorial decree changing the legal status of those receiving legacies in
trust so as to encourage implementation of the wishes of testators was passed
when Seneca and Trebellius Maximus were consuls but need not have been
proposed by Seneca: despite the fact that Seneca's name probably appeared first
on the Fasti (so on the amphora *CIL* IV 5514 and in *Digest* 36. 1, 1), the decree
is known to the jurists as the SC *Trebellianum* (Gaius 2. 255; *Digest* 36. 1, 1).

[4] Not in itself so unusual, cf. Suet. *Aug.* 29, 3; *Ann.* 2. 37; *Tabula Hebana* 1.

[5] Nero later boasted of keeping her out (*Ann.* 14. 11, 2).

[6] *Ann.* 11. 22, 3 with Furneaux's note; 13. 5, 1.

Perhaps it also had led to imperial subsidies. The custom was allowed to continue on a voluntary basis.[1] The first measure cancelled an edict of Claudius in which he had emasculated the Senate's proposal to renew the Lex Cincia.[2] This proposal, now put into effect, had been aimed at discouraging those accusers who thrived on the political trials *intra cubiculum*. Seneca's intervention on this occasion would probably have consisted not in a suggested reform but in a go-ahead to the Senate to use its new freedom.

The three assumptions commonly used in constructing a picture of Seneca's role as imperial adviser have been shown up as untrustworthy. We are now free to see what picture actually emerges from Tacitus' detailed account, supplemented by particulars from Suetonius and Dio. After that, we can apply a test of coherence to this picture: Dio's legislating advisers go with his reforming regime; does Tacitus assign to Seneca a role that fits the political character he gives to his period of ascendancy, which lasted, according to Tacitus, until 62?

Seneca as Amicus Principis

In his interview with Nero, Seneca is made to cite the voluntary retirement of Agrippa and of Maecenas as precedents for his own request; Nero illustrates Seneca's prospects by citing the power of Lucius Vitellius.[3] Seneca admired Agrippa for his military prowess and public munificence and thought that his success had contributed to the public good.[4] As for Maecenas, Seneca admitted that he had used power mildly but felt that his lax morals and self-indulgence revealed him as soft rather than clement.[5] In only one passage does Seneca mention their role as *amici principis*: Augustus never replaced them, for he said that they alone told

---

[1] According to the Vacca Life, Lucan 'gessit autem quaesturam, in qua cum collegis more tunc usitato munus gladiatorium edidit.' His quaestorship falls *c.* 60 (A. Rostagni, *Suetonio* 'De Poetis', Turin, 1944, ad loc.) when Lucan was only twenty years old.   [2] *Ann.* 11. 5.   [3] *Ann.* 14. 53, 56.

[4] *Ben.* 3. 32, 4; *Ep.* 94. 46: 'solus ex iis, quos civilia bella claros potentesque fecerunt, felix in publicum fuit.'

[5] *Ep.* 114. 7.

him the truth, they alone would have prevented him from raging in public about his daughter's shamelessness. But, Seneca remarks, had they lived, they too would have kept quiet. 'Regalis ingenii mos est . . . his virtutem dare vera dicendi a quibus iam audiendi periculum non est.'[1] The passage illustrates one role of the *amicus*—to advise the Princeps on his public behaviour and to intervene in his personal affairs where they touch politics— and shows how difficult it was to fulfil the role. The *exemplum* cited by Nero, that of Lucius Vitellius, completes the picture by adding responsibility for concocting an 'official version': Vitellius was called in to advise on the Messallina crisis[2] and later found the formula for justifying Claudius' marriage with Agrippina to the Senate and people.[3]

The role of Seneca and Burrus in managing and glossing over court intrigue is well documented: they devised means of counteracting Agrippina's ambitions, while her son kept up the expected display of piety. Perhaps it was their idea to let her eavesdrop on the meeting of the Senate as the price of her absence from the meeting. Certainly Seneca, with great presence of mind, averted the disgrace of Agrippina's mounting Nero's tribunal at the reception of the Armenian envoys.[4] Seneca deputed his young friend Annaeus Serenus to throw Agrippina off the scent of Nero's intrigue with his freedwoman, Acte.[5] When Britannicus was murdered, Seneca and Burrus were given no choice but to be *inter dissimulantes*, but they duly spoke truth, if only through Acte, when Nero began his incestuous relations with his mother.[6] They were called in to deal with the murder of Agrippina, after the first attempt had failed. Burrus pointed out that the obvious henchmen—the praetorians—could not be used, and the job was left to a freedman. Burrus limited himself to reconciling the praetorians to the murder; Seneca at most to writing Nero's letter to the Senate.[7]

If the *amicus* was expected to help the Princeps in crises, and

---

[1] *Ben.* 6. 32, 2–4.

[2] *Ann.* 11. 33–4. His failure to give Claudius advice was partly responsible for the dominant role of Narcissus in this incident.

[3] Ibid. 12. 5.   [4] Ibid. 13. 5.   [5] Ibid. 13. 13.

[6] Ibid. 14. 2.   [7] Ibid. 14. 7; 10–11.

involve himself in court intrigues, he obviously had to consider the others who would try to give advice. As Vitellius 'ingruentium dominationum provisor' had helped Agrippina to secure her marriage and the adoption of her son, so Seneca and Burrus, who owed their positions to Agrippina, were expected to cooperate with her plans on Nero's accession. Instead, seeing that she wished to continue the Claudian pattern of government, merely eliminating some of the personnel, they determined to combat her influence over the young Nero. An *amicus* had only the force of his personality and his popularity with the public to give him influence over the Princeps whose power was absolute, but Seneca had, in addition, the moral advantage of having been Nero's tutor for five years, and Burrus, as sole prefect of the praetorian guard, had powerful means of persuasion in his control. Yet Agrippina could compete with both: she had the moral influence of a mother and king-maker, and she was the daughter of Germanicus Caesar to whom the praetorians were passionately loyal. There is no need to repeat Tacitus' story of the personal struggle for control of the young Nero. Seneca was more tactful than Agrippina and he knew more about psychology.[1] As long as Agrippina was domineering, humiliating her son by the authority she accorded the arrogant Pallas, and jealously resenting his amours, Seneca and Burrus could seriously weaken her position by showing Nero sympathy and indulgence. Yet the situation was inherently unstable. A thwarted Agrippina could be violently threatening, while Nero's timidity could lead to panic and cruelty: thus the removal of Pallas from his post as *a rationibus* had resulted in the murder of Britannicus. Later in 55 Seneca and Burrus averted a second crisis in the relations of mother and son:[2] it was in their interest to keep Agrippina alive, for Nero would only heed them while he saw them as a refuge from his mother. Once she was gone, the full scope of his power would become clear to him, nor would there ever lack people to remind him of it. Unfortunately, once Agrippina had threatened

---

[1] For instance, note the discussion of how to restrain *ira* in children without blunting their spirit in *De Ira* 2. 20–1; see below, pp. 136–8.

[2] *Ann.* 13. 20–1.

Nero with a rival to the throne, those who protected her to any degree could no longer have his full confidence. Although Burrus did prevail upon Nero to give Agrippina a hearing on the charges of treasonable activity, Nero's distrust of Burrus, whose power originally came from the accused, was shown by the presence of *liberti* listening in on Burrus' interview with Agrippina,[1] and by the fact that some immediately seized on the opportunity to accuse the two protégés of Agrippina, Burrus and Pallas, together of treason.[2] When, in 59, Seneca and Burrus failed to help Nero finish the murder of Agrippina, their influence was seriously impaired;[3] and, as a result of this and the mere removal of Agrippina, from whom they had provided a haven, their ability to keep him to decorous public behaviour waned.

Seneca carried the role of publicity agent and creator of the official version further than anyone before him by writing Nero's speeches: the funeral speech for Claudius,[4] the accession speech to the praetorians and that to the Senate,[5] speeches on *clementia* at the start of 55,[6] and perhaps the letter to the Senate after the murder of Agrippina.[7] The political content of the speech to the Senate and that on *clementia* will be discussed below, but the letter deserves comment here, as it recalls Seneca's story about Agrippa and Maecenas. Augustus regretted that he had made public the licentiousness of his daughter: 'flagitia principalis domus in publicum emisit.' He had let anger run away with him. If indeed, as rumour had it, Seneca wrote the account of Agrippina's crimes, was he acting as he thought best, or was he simply taking orders *inter dissimulantes*? An earlier imperial *amicus*, Sallustius Crispus, had prevented Tiberius from making the assassin of Agrippa Postumus report to the Senate, where

---

[1] Ibid. 13. 21.　　　　　　　　　　　　　　　　　[2] Ibid. 13. 23.

[3] Note Nero's bitterness, ibid. 14. 7, 5.

[4] Ibid. 13. 3.

[5] Dio 61. 3, 1. The failure of Tacitus to credit Seneca with the speech to the praetorians may be due to a desire to withhold full comment on Nero's use of Seneca's eloquence to the first book devoted to his reign. It was unnecessary for him to mention Seneca's authorship of the speech to the Senate as he had just noted (in 13. 3) the general practice.

[6] *Ann.* 13. 11, 2.

[7] Ibid. 14. 11, 3. Quint. 8. 5, 18 states as fact what is rumour in Tacitus.

he would have alleged orders from Augustus.[1] Sallustius had
engineered the secret murder and argued 'ne arcana domus, ne
consilia amicorum, ministeria militum vulgarentur, neve Tiberius
vim principatus resolveret cuncta ad senatum vocando'. The death
of Britannicus was not specially reported to the senate; Nero
simply issued a brief edict to the public excusing the haste with
which the funeral was conducted and expressing his grief.[2] If
Seneca drafted this edict, it accorded well with his and Sallustius'
conception of an *amicus principis*. But the account of Agrippina's
death, so long and unconvincing, may have been demanded by
the terrified Nero. Or perhaps, Nero's Anicetus had already so
bungled the job (the shipwreck attracted spectators who also saw
the guards at the villa)[3] that a long, even if unconvincing, explanation seemed necessary to help avert a combination of Senate and
praetorians against the Emperor.[4] And Seneca's sense of the
appropriate, as the funeral speech showed, was not always very
accurate.[5]

A third role in which Seneca is presented is that of selecting
and dismissing imperial appointees, indirectly of course. Towards
the end of 54, fresh trouble with Parthia was reported in Rome.
Both those hostile and those favourable to the new Princeps,
according to Tacitus, held his *amici*, including Seneca (particularly indicated by the word 'magistros'), responsible for the
choice of commander,[6] and when Corbulo was selected, the
Senate at least rejoiced to see that there was now a 'locus virtutibus

[1] *Ann.* 1. 6.

[2] Ibid. 13. 17, 1. Furneaux, ad loc., assumes that Seneca composed the edict.

[3] Ibid. 14. 8.

[4] D. Diderot, *Essai sur les règnes de Claude et de Néron* (*Œuvres complètes de
Diderot*, Paris, 1875), pp. 113, 165, justified Seneca's composition of this letter
by the need to avoid a popular rising against Nero. In fact the letter, reinforced
by acts of clemency, was directed at the Senate. Burrus took care of the praetorians
and perhaps also of the plebs who seem to have been influenced by someone
(*Ann.* 14. 13). Messages congratulating the Emperor on his escape were even
solicited from the provinces (Quint. 8. 5, 15).

[5] *Ann.* 13. 3 'nemo risui temperare, quamquam oratio a Seneca composita
multum cultus praeferret . . .' This is surely a sufficient answer to the argument of W. H. Alexander, *CP* 49 (1954), 94, that Seneca could not have bungled
so badly and that the author of the letter, in Senecan style, was the pupil Nero.

[6] *Ann.* 13. 6.

patefactus'.[1] In another sphere, Agrippina clearly held Seneca and Burrus partly responsible for the dismissal of Pallas from his post *a rationibus*, although Tacitus is certain that Nero made the decision for personal as well as political reasons.[2] According to Plutarch, it was Seneca who suggested Otho's appointment as governor of Lusitania, thus providing the province with a good governor at the price of some constitutional irregularity: Otho was only twenty-six years old and an ex-quaestor.[3] Fabius Rusticus, the historian, is said by Tacitus to have flourished through Seneca's friendship,[4] but we cannot tell the nature of this patronage as we do not know if Fabius held any governmental posts. Seneca may only have forwarded his literary career. Similar uncertainty surrounds the case of Novius Priscus who suffered exile 'per amicitiam Senecae'; but if he (and not his son) is the legionary legate under Vespasian who went on to be *consul ordinarius* in 78,[5] he may well have started his senatorial career in the period of Seneca's ascendancy.

These cases in which Seneca's patronage is explicitly mentioned make it reasonable to put down to his influence the notable advancement achieved by many of his close relatives and known friends between A.D. 49, when Seneca began to teach Nero, and 64, when he finally withdrew from court (see p. 93). It is also tempting to try to identify other men who must have depended on his favour. If we attach our scarce data to the chronological scheme for Seneca's power provided by Tacitus, some patterns may emerge and, perhaps, more names.

The first part of the story really belongs to Agrippina. In 49 Seneca was recalled through her influence and awarded a praetor-

[1] Ibid. 13. 8, 1.

[2] Ibid. 13. 14. The role of Seneca and Burrus can be inferred from Agrippina's attack on them as her real opponents in 13. 14, 3.

[3] Plut. *Galba* 20. 1; *Otho* 2–3.

[4] *Ann.* 13. 20, 2.

[5] Ibid. 15. 71. This is the identification made by J. F. Gilliam, *BCH* 91 (1967), 269ff., on the basis of an inscription at Corinth published in *BCH* 90 (1966), 119ff., showing a Novius Priscus as commander of VI Victrix in Lower Germany. See now Reynolds, *JRS* 61 (1971), 144. On the nature of the family's connection with Pisidian Antioch, B. Levick, *Roman Colonies in Southern Asia Minor*, Oxford, 1957, pp. 115–16.

ship. That year had opened with her marriage to Claudius, an event which marked the start of her power over the Emperor.[1] In 51 Burrus was appointed sole praetorian prefect. That event, following the betrothal of Domitius to Octavia in 49 and his adoption by Claudius in 50, marked the consolidation of her power. Until 13 October 54, when Nero became Princeps, Seneca and Burrus were dependants of Agrippina and exercised what patronage she permitted them, or could permit them, given that until 52 at least she had to reckon with the rival influence of Narcissus.[2] We have explicit evidence for Agrippina's patronage in this period, ranging from the praetorship with which she favoured Seneca to the appointment of new tutors for Britannicus. She is also credited with the dismissal of centurions and tribunes of the praetorian guard and of the freedmen who pitied Britannicus.[3] She had influence with the consul-elect Barea Soranus and with a legate of the proconsul in Africa, M. Tarquitius Priscus.[4]

But to control Rome she must control the praetorian guard, which was still commanded by Lusius Geta and Rufrius Crispinus, both of whom she believed loyal to Britannicus. In 51 Agrippina persuaded Claudius to appoint a single prefect, Sextus Afranius Burrus, a man, no doubt, well known to him as procurator of the estates of Livia and Tiberius, as well as his own. Though a native of Narbonensis, the new prefect was popular with the praetorians perhaps because of his severe and upright character.[5] The top post, the prefecture of Egypt, however,

---

[1] Suet. *Claudius* 29: 'initio anni'.　　　　[2] *Ann.* 12. 57, 4–5; 65.

[3] Ibid. 12. 41; Dio 60. 32, 5–6.

[4] *Ann.* 12. 53; Pliny, *NH* 35. 201; *Ann.* 12. 59. He may be the Ταρκύνιος whose advice is given during the trial of Isidorus and Lampon (*BGU* 5. 11), perhaps just before his banishment, on 30 April 53, in the presence of Agrippina (H. Musurillo, *Acts of the Pagan Martyrs*, Oxford, 1954, no. 4, p. 12). But *CPJ*, vol. II, p. 72, prefers the date of 41.

[5] *Ann.* 12. 42. Tacitus' phrase 'egregiae militaris famae' has been endlessly discussed. We know from *ILS* 1321 that Burrus was a military tribune and then a procurator of imperial estates. It is hard to believe that he acquired a great reputation in the first post, still remembered forty years later. As procurator of imperial property, he might have used troops to collect debts, like Lucilius Capito (*Ann.* 4. 15; Dio 57. 23, 4) or Herennius Capito (Jos. *AJ* 18. 158—on which see Millar, *JRS* 53 (1963), 33) before him, but this would be neither

went to Lusius Geta. Geta must have been too powerful to drop, despite the distrust of Claudius and Agrippina. At Nero's accession, he was instantly replaced by a safe nonentity.[1] While in office, Geta was carefully watched. Tiberius Claudius Balbillus, the son of an old friend of the Emperor and, by 55, a follower of Agrippina, was probably already in charge of the shrines, museum, and library in Alexandria and Egypt.[2] In the year in which Geta became prefect, C. Caecina Tuscus, the son of Nero's nurse, became *iuridicus*.[3]

Agrippina laboured to win over Claudius' friends—not only his doctor C. Stertinius Xenophon,[4] his freedman secretary M. Antonius Pallas, and higher *equites* like Burrus and Balbillus, but the great Lucius Vitellius three times consul and censor. In her efforts to increase her following, Agrippina was generous to the relatives of her son's new tutor—so we must conclude when we find Seneca's elder brother Iunius Gallio serving as proconsul of Achaea in 51–2,[5] his father-in-law Pompeius Paulinus *praefectus*

popular nor glorious. Pflaum has suggested (*Carr. proc.*, vol. I, no. 13, pp. 30–1) that, as procurator of a neighbouring property, he participated in the conquest of Thrace in 46—all speculation (see Millar, *JRS* 53 (1963), 198). Nor is the phrase proleptic, alluding to Burrus' part in the appointment of Corbulo (W. C. McDermott, *Latomus* 8 (1949), 232), for the phrase in antithesis, 'gnarum tamen cuius sponte praeficeretur', is certainly only relevant to the time of his appointment. I have taken the phrase to signify popularity with the praetorians (cause unknown), which is to give *militaris famae* the same sense as *militum fama* in Tacitus' description of another praetorian prefect (*Ann.* 14. 51, 3).

[1] Mettius Modestus, replaced at the end of 55; see A. Stein, *Die Präfekten von Ägypten*, Bern, 1950, pp. 32–4.

[2] On the difficult problem of Balbillus' career, I accept the solution of Pflaum, *Carr. proc.*, vol. I, no. 15, pp. 34–41, identifying the Balbillus of *AE* 1924, no. 78, with the Prefect of Egypt (*Ann.* 13. 22) and with the grandfather of Julia Balbilla (*SEG* 8. 716). He is the son of the Balbillus of Pap. Lond. 1912.

[3] Pflaum, op. cit. I, no. 16 *bis* (27) pp. 44–6. His mother need not be identified with either of Nero's two Greek nurses whose names are preserved by Suetonius (*Nero* 35. 5; 50). The attempted attribution of *ILS* 8996 to Caecina Tuscus, instead of Seius Strabo (Sumner, *Phoenix* 19 (1965), 134–8), should be rejected: a *nutrix* might not necessarily be a Greek or a freedwoman but she would hardly be a Terentia moving in those circles.

[4] *Ann.* 12. 67; Pflaum, op. cit. I, no. 16, pp. 41–4.

[5] *PIR*² I 757. The Delphic inscription showing the proconsulate (*Fouilles de Delphes* 3. 4, no. 286) has been re-examined by A. Plassart, ibid. and *REG* 80 (1967), 372 ff., whose interpretation dates Gallio's term from *c.* May 51 to

annonae not long after 49,[1] and his brother-in-law suffect consul before 55.[2] It is also possible that Seneca's younger brother Annaeus Mela fulfilled his *praepostera ambitio* to become one of the imperial procurators at this time.[3] Agrippina liked to have loyal friends in the equestrian service, like Burrus and C. Crepereius Gallus.[4]

Burrus' patronage is more obscure, but it is tempting to conjecture his influence on the career of Duvius Avitus,[5] a native of Burrus' own town of Vasio in Narbonensis. Burrus was a patron of Vasio by 54 and seems to have maintained estates there,[6] which argues a continued interest in his birthplace. We know nothing of the start of Avitus' career, but his progress after the praetorship is notable. The headless inscription attributed to him[7] lists, as the first post after his praetorship, that of imperial legate of Aquitania 'splendidae inprimis dignitatis administratione ac spe consulatus'.[8] This was a very promising

---

c. May 52. On the legality of Gallio's refusal to involve himself in Jewish quarrels in Acts 18. 11–17 see Sherwin-White, *Roman Society and Roman Law in the New Testament*, Oxford, 1963, pp. 99–103. Under Claudius the post in Achaea probably had considerable prestige (Suet. *Claud.* 42): Claudius calls Gallio ὁ φ[ίλος] μου on the Delphic inscription.

[1] *JRS* 52 (1962), 105.

[2] *Ann.* 13. 53 shows that Paulinus was already legate of Lower Germany in 55.

[3] Tacitus (*Ann.* 16. 17) implies that Mela simultaneously renounced a senatorial career and decided to be a procurator. This is probably malicious, as his father portrays him in 37, when he must have been close to 30, as averse to public life through devotion to philosophy (*Contr.* 2, pref. 3), and, during his exile, Seneca could contrast Mela's *otium* with Gallio's *dignitas* (*Cons. Helv.* 18. 2). The evidence of Suetonius that Mela lived *ruri* owing to domestic infelicity in the early 50s (*PIR*² A 613) would not rule out a procuratorship. Probably he would not have been put through a long *militia equestris*, perhaps just the military tribunate, like Burrus (for this pattern see E. Birley, *Roman Britain and the Roman Army*, Kendall, 1953, pp. 137–8); but Suet. *Cl.* 25, shows that there could be purely nominal service.

[4] On this procurator from Pisidian Antioch, whose friendship with Agrippina brought him to a gruesome end (*Ann.* 14. 5), see B. Levick and S. Jameson, *JRS* 54 (1964), 98.

[5] Syme, *Tacitus*, p. 591.

[6] *ILS* 1321; McDermott, *Latomus* 8 (1949), 233.

[7] *ILS* 979; *PIR*² D 210.

[8] Tacitus, *Agric.* 9. 1. The career of Galba also illustrates the point (Suet. *Galba* 6. 1).

appointment indeed for a man of Duvius' background, even if our inscription omits some post after the praetorship, as it omits mention of the consulship. Duvius Avitus was suffect consul in November and December of 56, so his governorship of Aquitania fell, most probably, between 53 and 56 or 52 and 55, a period when Burrus would certainly have been in a position to advance his career.

With 13 October, Nero's *dies imperii*, the situation changed. Agrippina and her ally Pallas now had to contend with the determination of Seneca and Burrus to emancipate Nero from her influence, but until her death late in March of 59, Agrippina went on affecting the careers of her friends and enemies.

Our most explicit evidence for Agrippina's patronage after her son's accession is her appointment in 55 of four of her *amici* to three equestrian and one senatorial post.[1] The changes were made where appearances and feelings could easily be saved, but they still reveal clearly Agrippina's determination to recover lost ground. The *cura ludorum qui a Caesare parantur*, an *ad hoc* position through which Agrippina might win popularity, went to one of Patavium's knights, Arruntius Stella.[2] With the rebellion of her protégés, Seneca and Burrus, Agrippina had lost control of the praetorian guard and of the corn supply. She now insisted on making Faenius Rufus *praefectus annonae*: Seneca complied. Pompeius Paulinus was in his sixties anyway and would be satisfied with his son's governorship of Lower Germany; his public dignity and Seneca's reputation were to be preserved by an essay addressed to Paulinus, exhorting Paulinus to leave his tedious occupation for higher things.[3] The prefecture of Egypt, still the top of the service, would compensate her for Burrus'

[1] *Ann.* 13. 22.

[2] *PIR²* A 1150: Patavine origin is attested by Martial for a probable descendant (*PIR²* A 1151). The town did well in this period: an Arruntius Aquila is attested as procurator of Lycia–Pamphylia in 60 (*PIR²* A 1139) and the sons of the scholar Q. Asconius Pedianus were apparently destined for the senate when he wrote his commentaries in 54–7 (Asc. 43c). Perhaps Nero's honoured *tutor* Asconius Labeo (*Ann.* 13. 10) from Patavium (Syme, *AJP* 77 (1956), 269) had influence with Agrippina.

[3] For this view of *De Brevitate Vitae* see *JRS* 52 (1962), 104ff., and below, pp. 319–20.

defection: Mettius Modestus was replaced by Tiberius Claudius Balbillus, now promoted from his cultural duties in Egypt.[1] The choice may well have pleased Seneca who later paid Balbillus a fine compliment when he cited in the *Natural Questions* the prefect's account of a battle between dolphins and crocodiles in the Nile.[2]

Her proposal to make P. Anteius Rufus imperial legate of Syria was not as acceptable, but her reasons are clear. The appointment of Cn. Domitius Corbulo as legate of Cappadocia–Galatia had already proved successful and was bringing credit to Seneca and Burrus. Probably at the time of Corbulo's appointment, the notorious *praefectus castrorum* in Armenia, Caelius Pollio, was replaced by Laelianus, former *praefectus vigilum*.[3] That Pollio had not been replaced before was a disgrace that might well be credited by some to Agrippina. Now C. Ummidius Quadratus, the ageing legate of Syria, was being overshadowed by Corbulo and resented it. Nero's act of appeasement in adding laurel to his *fasces* in honour of the achievements of Quadratus and Corbulo may have been a prelude to an honourable retirement for the old man. For Agrippina, who so far had had no share in this popular venture, the next move was obvious: Quadratus must be replaced by a protégé of hers, a man of real

---

[1] See above, p. 83 n. 2. I accept Pflaum's rejection of the idea that Balbillus was procurator in Asia in between. The inscription at Ephesus calling him ἐπίτροπος could refer to his Egyptian post, and be set up by his home town. Balbillus returned to Rome after Claudius' death, perhaps to assist Agrippina in Rome (Pliny, *NH* 19. 3).

[2] *NQ* 4. 2, 13: 'virorum optimus perfectusque in omni litterarum genere rarissime'.

[3] Dio 61. 6, 6. So, O. Hirschfeld, *Untersuchungen auf dem Gebiete der römischen Verwaltungsgeschichte*, Berlin, 1876, p. 146 n. 3. Recently, Pflaum, *Carr. proc.* I, no. 18, p. 49, reasserted the theory of P. Fabia, *RPh* 22 (1898), 133–45, that the fragment of Dio is misplaced, the name Λαιλιανός there is a corruption of 'Paelignus', and the sending of Λαιλιανός to replace Caelius Pollio in late 54 is an error for the unofficial intervention by Paelignus in Armenia in 51, recounted in *Ann.* 12. 49. This would make Paelignus the successor of Calpurnianus in 48 (Tac. *Ann.* 11. 35, 3) as *praefectus vigilum* until 51. But Boissevain's objections (*Dio*, vol. III, p. 26) to the theory as both unlikely and unnecessary still stand. The retention of the corrupt Pollio by Claudius is all too likely (cf. Junius Chilo, *PIR*² I 744) and his replacement at the time of Corbulo's mission intelligible.

ability who might be a match for Corbulo. The idea was not
acceptable, and various excuses were found for retaining Anteius
in Rome while Quadratus continued to rule Syria until his death
in 60, when Corbulo succeeded him.

We may have a reflection of the delicate balance of power at
this time in the career of Antonius Felix, the procurator of
Judaea in the last years of Claudius. Supported by the influence
of his brother Pallas,[1] Felix continued to rule Judaea after Nero
became Princeps. The date of his recall has been much disputed.
But there seems to be no very good reason to reject the Eusebian
date for his successor's arrival, i.e. the second year of Nero,
late 55/6.[2] One might expect the dismissal of Pallas early in 55
to have led to a decision to replace Felix, and the arrival of Porcius
Festus in 56 would fit in very well. Josephus says that, after the
recall of Felix, the Jews of Caesarea complained of him and would
have received satisfaction had not Pallas μάλιστα δὴ τότε διὰ
τιμῆς ἄγων ἐκεῖνον dissuaded Nero.[3] One cannot ignore the
possibility that Josephus here is merely reporting a rumour
current in Judaea explaining how Felix escaped prosecution.
But it is as least equally possible that the reconciliation of Agrippina and Nero at the end of 55 enabled Pallas not to halt the
replacement of Felix, already arranged, but at least to protect
him from punishment on his return. The accuser Paetus, at any
rate thought that Burrus' role in effecting this reconciliation with
Agrippina meant that he could plausibly be accused of col-
laborating with Pallas.[4]

As part of the same story, Josephus says that the Syrians of
Caesarea succeeded in securing a benefit from Nero by bribing
Nero's *ab epistulis Graecis*, Beryllus, once his tutor.[5] Beryllus is
most probably an appointment of the Princeps himself, though
Agrippina may well have approved. Another old tutor certainly
benefited from Nero's accession without the sanction of Agrippina. That was the freedman Anicetus whose duties as prefect

[1] *Ann.* 12. 54, 1; Josephus, *AJ* 20. 137. On the conflict in these sources see
Appendix D5.
[2] See Appendix D5.
[3] *AJ* 20. 182.   [4] Above, p. 79.
[5] *AJ* 20. 183-4. See p. 67 n. 3.

of the fleet at Misenum until 62 included an attempt on Agrippina's life.[1] In at least one case, Nero's patronage may have extended to the equestrian administration: the successor of Vipsanius Laenas, praesidial procurator of Sardinia condemned for extortion in 56, may well have been T. Julius Pollio, the tribune of the praetorian guard who was Nero's agent in the murder of Britannicus.[2] The actual mixer of the potion, Locusta, received large estates and pardon for past offences; the *potissimi amici* accepted villas and houses.[3] Pollio won an important procuratorship which fortunately removed him *per speciem honoris* from the city where he might spread rumours among the guard or serve as a living reproach to the Emperor.[4]

These appointments, incidentally, suggest that Nero may sometimes have taken the initiative in his early reign and thus support, against Dio's view that Nero ignored government and concentrated on his pleasures,[5] the conception of Tacitus, that, in political matters, Nero was a pupil not a puppet. And other incidents, as we shall see, suggest that he sometimes misapplied his lessons.[6]

Fabius Rusticus, the historian, one of Seneca's youthful admirers, claimed in his history that in 55 Nero, made frantic by the reports of Agrippina's plans to overthrow him, wished to replace her appointee Burrus by C. Caecina Tuscus as praetorian prefect and that only Seneca saved Burrus' position.[7] Tacitus is justly sceptical of the story but it may be, in origin, a rumour that reflects the patronage situation at the time, showing that Nero had some influence over appointments, Seneca a great deal more.

His brother Gallio became suffect consul in 55. His nephew Lucan was recalled from study in Athens to assume the quaestor-

---

[1] Suet. *Nero* 35. 2; *Ann.* 14. 3, 3; 14. 62.

[2] Pflaum, *Carr. proc.* I, no. 29, pp. 69–70; III, p. 961.

[3] Suet. *Nero* 33. 3; *Ann.* 13. 18.

[4] Compare Nero's hatred of Anicetus for this reason, and his choice of Sardinia as the place for his exile (*Ann.* 14. 62, 3–4).

[5] Dio 61. 4, 1. Note that Tacitus attributes to Nero the initiative in the dismissal of Pallas early in 55 (*Ann.* 13. 14; cf. 13. 2).

[6] In his liberality, p. 123, and clemency, p. 171.   [7] *Ann.* 13. 20, 2.

ship five years before the legal age, c. 60.[1] His brother-in-law
Pompeius Paulinus, after a suffect consulship, went in 55 as
imperial legate to Lower Germany. His successor in 57 was
Duvius Avitus, a likely protégé of Burrus.

Seneca's own consulship in August–September 56 he shared
with M. Trebellius Maximus, his own choice one would naturally
suspect.[2] Some confirmation comes from Columella's work *De
Re Rustica*[3] where he mentions 'M. Trebellius noster' and 'Gallio
noster' as friends with whom he discussed his work. This Trebellius must be the legionary legate of 36[4] under whom, as
Cichorius brilliantly argued, the young L. Junius Moderatus
Columella of Gades served as military tribune with the legion
VI Ferrata.[5] If he is also the consul suffect of 56, he would be
about fifty years old, a man who like Seneca might long ago have
given up hope of a consulship.[6] We do not know when the
consulship of Seneca's close friend Caesennius or Caesonius
Maximus fell, only that it was before 65 when he was sent into
exile.[7]

Finally, we can probably include in the period of Seneca's
greatest power the appointment of his close friend Annaeus
Serenus as *praefectus vigilum*. Serenus died during his tenure of
the post, in which he either preceded or succeeded Tigellinus who
held it before becoming praetorian prefect in 62.[8] If, as I think,[9]

[1] See p. 73 n. 6; p. 76 n. 1. Cf. K. Rose, *TAPA* 97 (1966), 394 n. 35, proposing 63.

[2] Cf. *Hist.* 1. 77 where Otho is said to have joined one suffect to another
'praetexto veteris amicitiae'—only a plausible pretext, if common practice.

[3] *RR* 5. 1, 2; 9. 16, 2. But Columella's friends need not have been friendly with
each other; he appears to have dedicated a volume *de cultura vinearum et arborum*
to Eprius Marcellus (Schanz–Hosius, II, p. 787) who is unlikely to have been
a member of Seneca's circle (below, p. 91).

[4] *Ann.* 6. 41.

[5] The military tribunate was revealed in *CIL IX* 235. C. Cichorius, 'Zur
Biographie Columellas', *Römische Studien*, Stuttgart, 1922, pp. 417–22—accepted
in *PIR²* I 779.

[6] See Appendix D2: the consul might be the legate's son.

[7] *PIR²* C 172; above, p. 62 n. 7.

[8] For Seneca's close friendship with Serenus there is the evidence of *Ep.* 63. 14
and Martial 7. 45. Seneca addressed two or three dialogues to him. For Serenus
as prefect, Pliny, *NH* 22. 96; for Tigellinus, *Hist.* 1. 72.

[9] See Appendix D3.

the former is more likely, he could have been the replacement
Seneca and Burrus chose when they sent Laelianus to Armenia
at the end of 54, thereby giving Agrippina one more reason for
trying to control two of the great praefectures in 55.[1]

The influence of Seneca and Burrus went on after the death
of Agrippina. The real end of Seneca's authority was finally
marked by the death, early in 62, of Burrus[2] whose firm hold of
the praetorian cohorts had kept the timid Nero in check, but it
did not come abruptly. According to Tacitus, things had been
getting steadily worse.[3] We have already noted that the behaviour
of Seneca and Burrus in the affair of Agrippina's murder had
jolted Nero's confidence in them. The Princeps now found that
there were men who would encourage him in his chariot-racing,
his singing, his poetry, and his resistance to Seneca and Burrus.
'Nero ad deteriores inclinabat.'

The key figure is, of course, Ofonius Tigellinus. His friendship
with Nero probably went back to the reign of Claudius when
Tigellinus was rearing race-horses in Apulia and Calabria.[4] In
59, after the death of Agrippina, Seneca and Burrus had to give
in on the matter of chariot-racing.[5] Tigellinus now came into
his own: personal influence with Nero could now mean high
position. He probably succeeded Annaeus Serenus as prefect of
the watch, and before 62 his son-in-law, Cossutianus Capito,
was restored to the Senate.[6] To the returning influence of some
who have suffered from Agrippina's displeasure, the Flavii and
Sulpicius Galba,[7] Seneca may not have been averse, but he can
have taken little pleasure in the prominence of men like M.
Cocceius Nerva and P. Petronius Turpilianus, who were to be
honoured for loyalty after the Pisonian conspiracy,[8] or Aulus

---

[1] Above, pp. 85–6.

[2] For the great number of events that Tacitus' narrative crams between the
start of 62 and 9 June, the execution of Octavia, see R. S. Rogers, 'Five Over-
crowded Months: A.D. 62', *St. in honour of B. L. Ullman*, Rome, 1964, I, p. 217.
Rogers, in fact, concludes by doubting the causal relations in Tacitus' account,
but he takes them far too strictly: e.g. we are not meant to think that Burrus'
death undermined Seneca's power from scratch.

[3] *Ann.* 14. 51–2.   [4] Appendix D4.   [5] *Ann.* 14. 14.
[6] Ibid. 14. 48.   [7] See pp. 241 ff.   [8] *Ann.* 15. 72.

Vitellius,[1] or T. Clodius Eprius Marcellus[2] and Nero's *elegantiae arbiter*, T. Petronius Niger,[3] one of whom certainly, the other probably, attained the consulship in the fatal year of Burrus' death.

Meanwhile, Seneca's influence went on, as the clouds gathered. His brother Mela continued as procurator. His old friend Lucilius Junior, only slightly younger than Seneca himself, finally reached one of the lower procuratorships, in Sicily, probably about 62.[4] A self-made *eques*[5] from Pompeii,[6] Lucilius was delighted with his post which he reached after varied service in the *militia equestris*.[7] Here he could write poetry on the beauties of Sicily, and poetry and prose on the truths of Stoicism, while working through Seneca's *Natural Questions* and even lengthier *Moral Letters*.[8]

[1] See pp. 99–100.

[2] *PIR²* E 84 now needs correction in the light of *AE* 1956, no. 186, from Cyprus, certifying a proconsulate of Cyprus after his governorship of Lycia (so after 57) and a legionary legateship before the reign of Claudius, and of evidence fixing his first consulship to late 62 (Degrassi, *I fasti consolari*, 'Aggiunte'). Perhaps it is now time to give up the attribution to him of the acephalous *CIL* XIV 2612 (despite the fact that no other triennial tenure of Asia in this period is so far known), as there is no room in his career now for either the Spanish province which the inscription appears to indicate ('. . .]rem optinui[. . .') or for adlection into the Senate by Claudius which it suggests ('hic lectus est ab divo Claud . . .'). For the latter, the suggestion of T. B. Mitford, *Report Dept. Ant. Cyprus, 1940–8*, is implausible.

[3] For the identification of the Petronius of Tacitus *Ann.* 16. 18 with T. Petronius Niger, suff. cos. *c.* 62 (based on Pliny, *NH* 37. 20, and Plut. *Mor.* 60E) see Syme, *Tacitus*, 387 n. 6, and K. Rose, *Latomus* 20 (1961), 821 ff.

[4] On Lucilius Junior see *PIR²* L 388 and Pflaum, *Carr. proc.* I, no. 30, p. 70; III, pp. 961–2. The preserved works that Seneca dedicated to him are *De Prov.*, *NQ*, and *Ep. Mor.* Lucilius was probably already a friend of Seneca at the time of his exile (p. 61). By the winter of 63/4 (see Appendix A1) he was, like Seneca, already *senex* (*Epp.* 19. 1; 33. 7; 96. 3) but slightly younger (1. 5; 35. 2; 26. 7: 'iuvenior es: quid refert?'—the phrase might be there for the sake of his cognomen Junior (*NQ* 3. 1, 1; 4 pref. 9; *Ep.* 76. 5, probably exaggerating the age difference). The procuratorship was recent but not brand new when Seneca wrote *NQ* 4, pref. 1, 3, between 62 and 64 (Appendix A1).

[5] *Epp.* 44. 2; 19. 5.   [6] Ibid. 49. 1; 53. 1; 70. 1.

[7] Pflaum, *Carr. proc.* I, p. 70; III, pp. 961–2, argues rightly that none of the places mentioned in *Ep.* 31. 9 need signify procuratorships, but only places on route to where Lucilius did military service—the Rhine, the East, and Africa.

[8] Poetry about Sicily: *NQ* 3. 1, 1; *Ep.* 79. 5–7; about philosophy *Ep.* 8. 10;

If our previous conjectures about Trebellius Maximus are right, it might be Seneca who won for him the honour of conducting the Gallic census with Q. Volusius, son of the last *praefectus urbi*, and the noble Sextius Africanus, both of whom scorned him.[1]

One more guess may be hazarded. The consul designate who early in 62, at the Princeps' behest, proposed the death penalty in the first *maiestas* trial of the reign, was a Q. Junius Marullus. He could be the Marullus who, in the autumn of 64, received a consolation letter from Seneca on the death of his young son.[2] He would be at the right age to have a son who could be called *puer*. Seneca sent the letter, he tells Lucilius, because Marullus was said to be showing inadequate fortitude in his grief, though Seneca had previously thought him possessed of sufficient courage even against serious evils.[3] Could Seneca have written like this to and about a man who had agreed to help Nero in a scheme that perverted all Seneca's teaching about *clementia*? Could he have remained a friend of such a man? Seneca had neither practised nor preached the maintenance of uncompromising integrity when dealing with the powerful: 'quorundam contumacia non facit ad aulam', 'sapiens numquam potentium iras provocabit, immo declinabit', he had written.[4] Marullus may have had less support in his ancestry than Barea Soranus for standing up to imperial pressure:[5] he might be Spanish.[6] 'Junius' is one of the most common names the Spaniards acquired from their conquerors,[7] and the cognomen is common in Spain.[8]

24. 19; philosophical prose: *Ep.* 46. For procurators who wrote while in office see Syme, *Tacitus*, p. 608 n. 1, to which add (of special relevance here) the Iccius who took care of Agrippa's estates in Sicily, and read deeply in natural science (Horace, *Ep.* 1. 12).

[1] Above, p. 89; *Ann.* 14. 46, 2.
[2] *Ann.* 14. 48, 2 and Furneaux ad loc.; *Ep.* 99. [3] *Ep.* 99. 1, 3.
[4] *Tranq.* 6. 2; *Ep.* 14. 7. Cf. also *Ep.* 14. 8–11; *Ben.* 2. 18, 6–7: 'vim maiorem et metum excipio, quibus adhibitis electio perit.' Note also Tacitus' sentiments in *Ann.* 14. 14, 3: 'nam et eius flagitium est qui pecuniam ob delicta potius dedit quam ne delinquerent.' Life under tyranny leads to casuistry and lower standards of *libertas*.
[5] Above, p. 74 n. 3.
[6] The possibility is mentioned by Syme in *Tacitus*, App. 80.
[7] See the list in Syme, *Tacitus*, App. 78.
[8] *JRS* 62 (1972), 6 n. 71.

According to Tacitus, Seneca twice requested permission to retire and was twice refused.[1] The first time was early in 62, after the death of Burrus, when he knew that his power and his influence with the Emperor were really gone. From that time he refused his morning visitors, discouraged the trains of clients that usually accompanied him, and, pleading health and engrossment in philosophy, rarely went out when in Rome.[2] The second time was late in 64, after the Great Fire of July, when Nero was having temples in Asia and Achaea ransacked to replace what had been destroyed in the fire. Seneca 'quo invidiam sacrilegii a semet averteret' asked to be allowed to go into retirement far away from Rome, was again refused, and now virtually ceased to leave his chamber.[3] At this time the Emperor accepted, for the sake of rebuilding Rome, some of the money Seneca had offered in 62.[4]

It is often said that Tacitus has carelessly combined two sources, giving two dates for Seneca's retirement. How, asked Gercke, could Seneca have expected to be blamed for what Nero did after he had openly given up political life? Tacitus is in contradiction with himself. A recent scholar suggests that Suetonius' statement that Seneca had often sought retirement is likewise a blurring of two traditions.[5]

But Tacitus does not think that Seneca was allowed to give up his political role openly in 62. He makes Nero say that it would look bad if Seneca retired and indicates that Seneca curtailed his public activities in spite of Nero's answer.[6] The scant evidence

---

[1] *Ann.* 14. 53–6; 15. 45.

[2] In the Letters to Lucilius, Seneca does not portray himself as immured in Rome at this time. He travelled to the Campanian coast (e.g. *Epp.* 49. 1; 77) and to his villa at Nomentum (104; 110). In the former trip he may have been part of the imperial retinue, see p. 359.

[3] This final retirement should follow the last letters we have—see p. 358 n. 1.

[4] Dio 62. 25, 3; cf. *Ann.* 15. 64.

[5] Gercke, 'Seneca-Studien', *Fleck. Jahr. für. Kl. Ph. Suppl.* 22 (1896), 159 ff.; C. Questa, *Studi sulle fonti degli 'Annales' di Tacito*², Rome, 1963, pp. 200–1. Suet. *Nero* 35. 5.

[6] For an elaborate defence of Tacitus' account and a refutation of Gercke see Giancotti, *RAL* 11 (1956), 105–19: he makes no use of the prosopographical evidence.

we have for Seneca's patronage supports Tacitus' suggestion that appearances were duly kept up. Mela continued as an imperial procurator; according to the Letters, Lucilius was still in Sicily in the summer of 64, and from the winter of 63/4 Seneca was expecting *urbana officia* to follow, which might be official in character.[1] Late in 62, after the death of Burrus, Nero appointed a commission of three consulars to explore the *vectigalia publica*, and among them was the younger Pompeius Paulinus.[2] Another senator whose career was at least unhindered by Seneca's retirement was P. Galerius Trachalus, probably a grandson or near relative of Seneca's uncle C. Galerius, the prefect of Egypt.[3] A noted orator, he may have attacked Suillius on Seneca's behalf in the famous trial of 58, according to a difficult passage in Quintilian.[4] By 62 Galerius must at least have been *quaestor* and *tribunus plebis*, perhaps even *praetor*. He went on to become *consul ordinarius* in 68. Not that Galerius needed Seneca's active patronage for that. By 62 he was connected by marriage with Aulus Vitellius,[5] and he had a reputation as an orator. All that his career shows is that Seneca's relatives were not being persecuted nor even retarded yet.

Of course, the fact that protégés continue their careers does not mean that the patron has not fallen. There could always be special reasons, and someone had to administer the Empire. That would be enough to explain how Trebellius Maximus, if he was Seneca's dependant, came to govern Britain in 63. But the combined evidence of the careers of Mela, Lucilius, Paulinus, and Galerius shows that the public was meant to think that, despite Seneca's absorption in philosophy, so vividly portrayed in the Letters to Lucilius, and his abandonment of public appearances, he was still *amicus principis*.

---

[1] *Ep.* 79; 19. 8. For the date of the Letters see Appendix A1.

[2] *Ann.* 15. 18, 3.

[3] Birley in *Gnomon* 23 (1951), 443; *PIR*[2] G 30.

[4] Quint. 12. 5, 5: 'orator eminens inter aequales'. 6. 3, 78: 'ut Trachalus dicenti Suelio: "si hoc ita est, is in exilium", "si non est ita, redis", inquit.'

[5] Vitellius' wife Galeria Fundana, married to him by 62 (Dio 65. 1, 2a), protected Trachalus who had served as Otho's speech-writer (*Hist.* 1. 90; 2. 60)—surely a relative.

None the less, after early 62, Seneca no longer had a hand in the most important appointments, as we know from the explicit evidence about the appointment of the praetorian prefects, Ofonius Tigellinus and Faenius Rufus, and from what can be surmised about the advancement of Nero's foster-brother, Caecina Tuscus, who some time between July of 62 and September of 63 became prefect of Egypt.[1]

Moreover, a trend emerges, clearly traceable to Nero—the prominence of Easterners in the administration.[2] The staffing of the imperial *domus* should not be brought into this discussion as it usually is—most imperial freedmen had always been Greek; it was not their origin but their increased influence that represented a new departure in the latter part of the reign.[3] But in the large equestrian prefectures, the presence of Easterners does deserve note. Tiberius Julius Alexander, the apostate Jew and nephew of Philo, emerged in 63 as 'minister bello (sc. Corbuloni) datus', and went on to succeed Caecina Tuscus as prefect of Egypt in 66;[4] C. Nymphidius Sabinus became praetorian prefect in 65; and Claudius Athenodorus *praefectus annonae* in 62.[5]

---

[1] Stein, *Präfekten von Ägypten*, p. 35. The story of his near-appointment as praetorian prefect (above, p. 88) depends for its plausibility on this son of Nero's nurse and likely protégé of Agrippina having, like Anicetus, grown to hate her, thereby earning Nero's trust. That is credible: he had seen her make his former subordinate, Balbillus, prefect of Egypt in 55.

[2] G. Schumann, *Hellenistische und griechische Elemente in der Regierung Neros*, Leipzig, 1930, pp. 34–59; Pflaum, *Les procurateurs équestres sous le Haut-Empire romain*, Paris, 1950, p. 208. Pflaum on p. 206 argued for an earlier period of Eastern dominance initiated by Agrippina and Pallas in 49, but, apart from Balbillus (prefect of Egypt, 55–9), none are attested in the large prefectures, while three of his so-called Easterners prove not to be (for Caecina Tuscus see p. 83 n. 3); Crepereius Gallus and Proculus from Pisidian Antioch are probably descendants of Italian colonists, Levick, *Roman Colonies in Southern Asia Minor*, pp. 119–20.

[3] See pp. 107–8.   [4] Pflaum, *Carr. proc.* I, no. 17, pp. 46–9.

[5] I retain here the view I took of *CIL* VI. 8470 in *JRS* 52 (1962), 105, except that I acknowledge the correction by P. R. C. Weaver, *Familia Caesaris*, Cambridge, 1972, p. 233 n. 1: Carpus had the *nomen* Claudius, so that he must have been Pallas' slave, not his freedman. Pflaum, *Carr. proc.* III, no. 49 *bis*, pp. 964–5, identifies the *praefectus annonae* Claudius Athenodorus with the procurator in Syria of that name under Domitian, but they might be father and son or two unrelated persons. *CIL* VI. 143 (set up by Athenodorus' *adiutor*, like VI. 8470), when compared with *Ann.* 11. 11, 3, suggests a Neronian date.

To this list we can add Gessius Florus of Clazomenae, the disastrous procurator of Judaea from 64 to 66: he owed his appointment to his wife's friendship with the Empress Poppaea.[1] Clearly,
in Nero's last years, his distrust of and antagonism towards the
governing classes led him to disregard their prejudices in this,
as in other matters.

Using Tacitus' outline of Seneca's rise and fall and the careers of
his known friends and relatives, we have traced a plausible, if
sometimes speculative, picture of Seneca's patronage. Apart from
these and the men like Corbulo and Otho he is explicitly said to
have promoted, it is impossible to ascertain his political col-
laborators. But there is a general point of some importance:
probably because of his late start or his long exile, Seneca did not
fit comfortably into senatorial circles, and though he had senatorial friends, such as Passienus Crispus, Caesennius Maximus,
Novius Priscus, and the later conspirator C. Calpurnius Piso,[2]
most of his close friends, to judge from the men to whom he
dedicated his works, were *equites*. In this context his *concordia*
with Burrus does not seem so remarkable, and it is natural to infer
that higher *equites* played an important part in their government.
Two questions of some importance remain: Seneca's attitude
to the friends of the Princeps who had sent him into exile, and his
relations with those men of principle who later formed the
so-called 'philosophical opposition'.

In his first speech to the senate, Nero proclaimed: 'nulla odia,
nullas iniurias nec cupidinem ultionis adferre'. Like Claudius'
deification, that signified an amnesty. But those who had heard or
read the *Apocolocyntosis* would be sceptical. Tacitus says that when
Seneca was recalled in 49, he was believed to be 'fidus in Agrip-

---

[1] *AJ* 20. 252; *PIR*[2] G 170.
[2] *PIR*[2] C 284. That Seneca had at one time been friendly with Piso is the one
clear thing that emerges from the story spun by Natalis (*Ann.* 15. 60) and Seneca's
answer (15. 61, 1). They were both patrons of literature (Juvenal 5. 108; Martial
12. 36) and there might be a family connection: the name of Piso's son, Calpurnius Galerianus (Tac. *Hist.* 4. 11; 49), suggests some link with Galerii, who, in
this period, are likely to be descendants of Seneca's uncle the Tiberian prefect of
Egypt. Piso may have adopted a Galerius or married a Galeria, in the period
between his marriage to Livia Orestilla and that to Atria Galla.

pinam memoria beneficii et infensus Claudio dolore iniuriae'.[1] The former was certainly disproved after Nero's accession. But in 58, Suillius repeated the latter: 'Senecam increpans infensum amicis Claudii.'[2]

Did public promises or personal feelings prevail? In 54 the Senate felt free to reject a charge of *maiestas* against the knight Julius Densus for his friendship to Britannicus.[3] The accuser, judging by Agrippina's past behaviour and Seneca's reputation, doubtless thought the time propitious, but the Senate rightly believed in Nero's promises. Titus, a close friend of Britannicus who witnessed the prince's death from the next seat, probably served as military tribune under Pompeius Paulinus or Duvius Avitus in Lower Germany.[4]

These examples accord with the treatment of Suillius Rufus himself. Agent of Claudius and Messallina, he had brought many men to their downfall, men with whom Seneca, probably a victim of Messallina and Narcissus,[5] must have felt sympathy, if he was not actually among them. Suillius claimed that Seneca had instigated the renewal of the Lex Cincia in 55 as an attack on him. One son, Suillius Caesoninus, had been exiled with Plautius Lateranus in 48,[6] but was not recalled, though the imperial *clementia* was extended to Lateranus in 55. But Suillius Rufus was not prosecuted under the Lex Cincia, and though he could have been convicted for crimes committed as governor of Asia under Claudius,[7] he was not in fact accused until he openly attacked Seneca. One scholar has suggested, however, that Seneca's vengefulness came out in an attempt to have the son, Suillius Nerullinus, prosecuted as well.[8] Tacitus does not suggest that Seneca was behind this further attempted prosecution, and it is more likely that the accusers just hoped to increase their spoils by taking advantage of Suillius' weak position.[9] Nero's veto here sprang from policy and not from affection—Nerullinus was kept waiting eighteen years, until Nero's death, for his

---

[1] *Ann.* 12. 8, 2.　　　　[2] Ibid. 13. 42.　　　　[3] Ibid. 13. 10, 2.
[4] Suet. *Titus* 2; 4; *Hist.* 2. 77.　　　　　　　　[5] Above, p. 61.
[6] *Ann.* 11. 36; 13. 11, 2.　　　　　　　　[7] *Ann.* 13. 43, 1.
[8] W. H. Alexander, *Univ. of Calif. Pub. in Cl. Phil.* 14 (1952), 322.
[9] *Ann.* 13. 43.

proconsulship of Asia[1]—Nero was following the policy of clemency sponsored by Seneca.

If, as has been argued, Nero had a hostile attitude to the Claudian patriciate,[2] Seneca would have to be held partly responsible for that in the early years. The evidence, however, for the neglect of these men seems to evaporate on close inspection. L. Acilius Strabo, if he was related to the patrician Acilii, had been sent out as an ex-praetor to Cyrene, but did not attain his consulship until 71. Nero had exonerated him of extortion charges, though he did not uphold his decisions, preferring to show generosity to the provincials. At any rate, M'. Acilius Aviola went on to be proconsul of Asia in 65/6 after a normal ten-year interval.[3]

M. Helvius Geminus, after being made a patrician very early then *quaestor Caesaris* and praetor, became a legate assisting a proconsul in Macedonia, then in Asia.[4] At least the last of these posts, more promising than the penultimate one, was held under Nero. He may then have been held back, but it is equally possible that he died before reaching higher office.

P. Plautius Pulcher probably died before the end of Claudius' reign,[5] and Cn. Hosidius Geta became proconsul of Africa probably in 54/5.[6] One Claudian patrician was perhaps too obese to be very active, another died before reaching senatorial age.[7]

[1] *PIR*[1] S 699.

[2] See S. J. De Laet, *De Samenstelling van den romeinschen Senaat*, Antwerp, 1941, pp. 263, 314–15, 255, for the list of patricians. The main ground for his thesis is that no member of these new families entered the Senate or was consul under Nero. The latter is belied by Sextius Africanus, cos. in 59; the former by the future emperor Otho (born in A.D. 32).

[3] De Laet, no. 929, no. 927; *PIR*[2] A 82 (below, p. 114 n. 3); 49.

[4] De Laet, no. 1023; *PIR*[2] H 71.

[5] De Laet, no. 727. In *CIL* XIV. 3607 recording his career, Claudius is not called *divus*, though that is not conclusive evidence of pre-Neronian date.

[6] Birley, *JRS* 52 (1962), 221. De Laet, no. 1170. But *ILS* 971 recording the patriciate might belong to a brother (*PIR*[2] H 216, 217).

[7] L. Apronius Caesianus (no. 1169; *PIR*[2] A 972), if the relevant inscription is rightly attributed to him, is a patrician who became proconsul of Africa under Claudius, for he was made a patrician after his consulship in 39. Perhaps he died after that, or was not very mobile. Pliny, *NH* 11. 213, speaks of a son of L. Apronius the consular who had an operation to remove excess weight, but the identification is rejected in *PIR*[1] (Groag). L. Nonius Quinctilianus, who, the

Other Claudian patricians in fact prospered under Nero. L. Salvius Otho had two sons.[1] The elder, L. Salvius Otho Titianus, consul ordinarius in 52, became proconsul of Asia in 63/4. The younger, the future Emperor, was among Nero's close friends at court, and, when he became the Emperor's rival, was sent to govern Lusitania on Seneca's recommendation.[2] T. Sextius Africanus may have owed his consulship in 59 to Agrippina, but he was later, in 61, one of those in charge of the Gallic census. Q. Veranius, whose abilities Claudius rated as high as had Tiberius, was chosen to initiate the aggressive policy in Britain.[3]

To these Claudian patricians who did well must be added evidence about the fate of other notables under Claudius. L. Volusius Saturninus, *praefectus urbi* under Claudius from 42 on was retained by Nero until his death in 56, when he was honoured by the Senate, on the Emperor's motion (as a new inscription reveals), with a public funeral and other marks of esteem.[4] His successor in that post, Pedanius Secundus, had been the only certified Spaniard to attain the consulship under Claudius. The prefect of Egypt, chosen after Agrippina's death to succeed her appointee Balbillus, was Claudius' special friend L. Julius Vestinus.[5]

There was one prominent *amicus Claudii* who might have suffered from Seneca's ascendancy. Aulus Vitellius, according to Suetonius,[6] was favoured by Nero, as by the Emperors before him, because of his enthusiasm for chariot-racing and dicing, and because of his special service to Nero at the Neronia in 65,[7] when he tactfully insisted that Nero perform on his lyre in answer to popular demand. Yet Vitellius, *consul ordinarius* in 48, was probably not governor of Africa until 62/3 or later in Nero's

office of *salius Palatinus* shows, was a patrician, died at 24 (*R-E* XVII, 1937, n. 45, col. 898).

[1] *PIR*[1] S 107. De Laet, nos. 1104–5.   [2] See p. 81.

[3] E. Birley, 'Britain under Nero, and the significance of Q. Veranius', *Roman Britain and the Roman Army*, p. 5; A. E. Gordon, *Univ. of Calif. Pub. in Cl. Arch.* 2 (1952), 234.

[4] *Ann.* 13. 30; *R-E* Suppl. 9 (1962), no. 17, col. 1861; Reynolds, *JRS* 61 (1971), 143.

[5] Pflaum, *Carr. proc.* I, no. 19, pp. 50–1.

[6] Suet. *Vit.* 4.

[7] Clearly the second Neronia, cf. Suet. *Nero* 21. 1; *Ann.* 16. 4.

reign,[1] and he held no other official post except that of *cura operum publicorum* probably after this.[2] Were it not for strange traces of malice in Seneca's references to his father and relatives a satisfactory explanation would be fear of his horoscope.[3]

It is not easy to give an answer to the vital question: what was the role of the men of principle, the professional independents, 'the philosophical opposition' in the period when Seneca and Burrus guided policy? To maintain their integrity and face at once the possibilities of humiliation and death, some imitated the legendary *severitas* of their Republican ancestors and revered the lost cause of Brutus and Cassius; others relied on Stoic doctrines; others used both. Cassius Longinus, who openly honoured the memory of his ancestor, the tyrannicide,[4] showed his acceptance of the new regime by speaking in the Senate freely and accepting a job as arbitrator. Although Rubellius Plautus, who was said to imitate the ancient Roman virtues and to follow Stoic doctrine,[5] was too suspect, on grounds of ancestry, to be allowed a career in politics, he had friends who were active. Barea Soranus had co-operated with Agrippina as suffect consul and came to no harm in the early years of Nero, though the only office we know he held was that of proconsul of Asia in 61/2.[6] Corbulo was also a friend of Rubellius and perhaps married to a daughter of C. Cassius Longinus.[7]

Thrasea Paetus and his son-in-law Helvidius Priscus both revered Brutus and Cassius[8] and were devoted Stoics.[9] Tacitus links the case of Thrasea in 66 with that of Barea. The connection

---

[1] Appendix D6. That there were factors other than the lot determining the proconsuls of Asia and Africa is well attested (*Ann.* 6. 40; Suet. *Galba* 7. 1; Tacitus, *Agric.* 42).

[2] Suet. *Vit.* 5.

[3] Appendix D7; Suet. *Vit.* 3. 2. His father had been so worried about it that he prevented his son's being given a province while he was alive.

[4] *Ann.* 16. 7.

[5] Ibid. 14. 57.

[6] Later he was accused of friendship with Rubellius Plautus and of trying to stir Asia to revolution (*Ann.* 16. 23.).

[7] Syme, *JRS* 60 (1970), 36–7.

[8] Juvenal 5. 36–7.

[9] *Ann.* 16. 22, 2 and 5; 34.

was more than *virtus*, since the poet Persius, who was related to Thrasea's wife and devoted to him, also revered Servilius Nonianus[1] whose daughter may well be Barea Soranus' wife.[2] Thrasea's cognomen was assumed in honour of his father-in-law Caecina Paetus who had joined a rebellion against Claudius in 42, but we know nothing of his career until the early years of Nero when he was doing well, attaining a major priesthood, a consulship in 56 (with Duvius Avitus), and perhaps a provincial command.[3] His Patavine origins[4] and the progress of his son-in-law in the later years of Claudius[5] might suggest the favour of Agrippina. Thrasea spoke of the need for *libertas senatoria* and he was often critical of the policy of the government,[6] but until 59 he tolerated the adulation he despised and limited his reforming zeal to small matters well within the sphere of the newly encouraged senatorial independence.[7] It is likely that he appreciated what had been done, at least the emphasis on fair jurisdiction. An anecdote in Plutarch shows that he had a reputation as an excellent judge,[8] and his behaviour in the first *maiestas* trial of the reign

[1] Suet. *Vita Persi*.

[2] Syme, *Hermes* 92 (1964), 408 ff. = *Ten Studies in Tacitus*, pp. 91 ff.

[3] *PIR*[2] C 1187. The command is an inference from the statement in the Life of Persius (Probus): '[Persius] decem fere annis summe dilectus a Paeto Thrasea est ita ut peregrinaretur quoque cum eo aliquando.' Thrasea could have been away in 57/8 or 58/9 or 60/1, being attested in Rome in 57 (*Ann.* 16. 21, 3), and 58 (*Ann.* 13. 49), the spring of 59 (*Ann.* 14. 12; 16. 21, 1), and early in 62 (14. 48).

[4] See p. 85 n. 2. If he had been favoured by Agrippina, his violent reaction to the Senate's servile celebrations of her murder (*Ann.* 14. 12, 1) takes on a new dimension.

[5] *PIR*[2] H 59. Quaestor between 44 and 50, this son of a *primus pilus* was, as legionary legate in 51, entrusted with a special mission by the governor of Syria, Ummidius Quadratus (who may have married a woman from Patavium according to Syme, *Historia* 17 (1968), 75–7). Pflaum (*Carr. proc.* I, no. 26, 66–7) inferred Agrippina's favour from the fact that Publius Celer, later Agrippina's agent in murder, was Helvidius' *comes* in his quaestorship.

[6] *Ann.* 13. 49; the criticisms of Thrasea in this passage seem to me to be essentially mockery of his failure to take the more sweeping action that his own remarks about the government entailed (*pace* O. Murray, *Historia* 14 (1965), 54).

[7] *Ann.* 14. 12; 13. 49 where Thrasea opposes a proposal about the Syracusan games; 16. 21, 3: he had already contributed greatly to Cossutianus Capito's conviction in the senate in 57 (13. 33).

[8] *Mor.* 810A. See also Dio 62. 15, 7.

showed that he understood Seneca's treatise *De Clementia* (see p. 171).

In 59 Thrasea walked out of the Senate while elaborate thanks were being given for Nero's delivery from Agrippina's treachery;[1] Seneca probably composed the letter giving the official story to the Senate. In that same year Thrasea appeared conspicuously un-enthusiastic at the Juvenalia which Seneca and Burrus formally countenanced.[2] Yet there was no sharp break in Thrasea's participation in politics. In 62, after bitterly offending Nero over the *maiestas* case at the start of the year, Thrasea took the advice of his earlier critics in one respect: after giving his *sententia*, he added a proposal of his own—to end the sending of missions of thanks by provincial *concilia* to governors. It was not revolution-ary, but the consuls were afraid to put the *relatio*. Nero, however, sanctioned the decree.[3] Yet soon after Thrasea was forbidden to come to Antium with the rest of the Senate to celebrate the birth of Nero's daughter.[4] Then Nero told Seneca he was reconciled with Thrasea.[5] Seneca congratulated Nero, it was said, and Thrasea paid his tribute to Seneca by deferring his final absence from the Senate until Seneca's principal power had been broken by the death of Burrus.[6] He even imitated Seneca's final libation.[7]

It is clear that Thrasea appreciated Seneca's efforts and that Seneca admired him. They shared an enemy in Tigellinus[8] and, perhaps, a willing detractor in Eprius Marcellus who put his eloquence at Nero's service to secure Thrasea's conviction.[9] Yet there was little contact between the two Stoics. Each had a close circle, but Persius, who belonged for ten years to Thrasea's group, met Seneca only towards the end of his life and was not impressed.[10] Difference of temperament can be adduced as a reason,

[1] *Ann.* 14. 12.   [2] Ibid. 16. 21, 1.   [3] Ibid. 15. 20–2.
[4] Ibid. 15. 23.   [5] Ibid. 15. 23, 4.
[6] Ibid. 16. 22.   [7] See below, p. 370.
[8] Thrasea had helped to convict his son-in-law and confederate (*Ann.* 16. 21, 3).

[9] Tacitus makes him refer to Nero's *amicitia* in *Hist.* 4. 8, where he is shown carrying on the campaign against Thrasea's follower, Helvidius Priscus. It might be in the year of Eprius' second consulship, 74, that Helvidius received his order to die.

[10] Life of Persius (Probus).

but not too much can be made of this. If his accusers called
Thrasea 'rigidus, tristis', and marked his 'contumacia', the
younger Pliny calls him 'vir mitissimus' and cites as his maxim
'qui vitia odit, homines odit',[1] while Dio reports that he disapproved of flattery for a very sensible reason: it did not save one's
neck and it spoiled one's reputation.[2] He advised the young not to
take risks for the sake of a gesture.[3] 'Sanctissimus', the epithet his
biographer Arulenus Rusticus applied to him, means no more
than 'upright' or 'high-minded',[8] however offensive it might
be to a suspicious emperor.[5] Pliny calls Seneca and many other
notables, including the Emperor Tiberius, 'sanctissimi' when he
is justifying, by their example, the writing of scurrilous verses.[6]

The distance between Seneca and men like Thrasea and Barea
(and probably Cassius Longinus and Antistius Vetus as well) was
more profound, as will appear. Basing their entire conception of
politics on the Senate, they appreciated and used what *libertas
senatoria* the new regime provided, but they could not accept
Seneca's new ideology for the Principate, framed in terms of
Greek kingship,[7] nor his exclusively moral admiration of Cato
and disapproval of Caesar's murder.[8] Finally, they disagreed on
the kind of Stoic justification to use for political retreat.[9]

The Government during Seneca's Ascendancy

In studying the government from Nero's accession until Seneca's
influence broke in 62, it is natural to start with the first speech of
the new Princeps to the Senate, delivered after Claudius' funeral.
Here Nero noted the source of his power in recognition by the
Senate and soldiers, the models for its exercise provided by his

[1] *Ep.* 8. 22, 3.   [2] Dio 61. 15, 3
[3] *Ann.* 16. 26.
[4] For *sanctus* see Val. Max. 2. 10, 8: it signified certain aspects of Cato's
behaviour, notably his puritanical virtue.
[5] For the tone and fate of Rusticus and his biography, Appendix C3.
[6] *Ep.* 5. 3, 5.   [7] Chapter 4.
[8] Chapter 5. Here, at least, Lucan, the friend of Persius, agreed with them.
See below, pp. 187, 191 ff.
[9] Chapter 10.

advisers and predecessors, notably Augustus,[1] and his own special qualifications—youth and a peaceful accession leaving behind no hatred or need for revenge. There followed what Tacitus regards as the significant portion of the speech: the sketch of the 'formam futuri principatus'. This consisted of a repudiation of the most odious features of the Claudian regime—abuses in jurisdiction and the position of the imperial freedmen—and a general formula for a division of responsibilities between Senate and Princeps.

Neither the occasion of the speech nor its contents were new. In his funeral speech for Tiberius, Gaius had emphasized his own connection with Augustus and Germanicus.[2] He flattered the Senate and promised τήν τε . . . ἀρχὴν κοινώσειν σφίσι καὶ πάνθ' ὅσα ἂν καὶ ἐκείνοις ἀρέσῃ ποιήσειν. He called himself their son and ward. On assuming the consulship in 37, he denounced Tiberius for his most popular acts and made many promises that pleased the Senate.

Similarly, Claudius replied to the envoys from the Senate who found him in the praetorian camp that he understood the Senate's lack of enthusiasm for him because of his predecessors' harshness, but that under him they would experience the fairness of moderate times under a government that would be nominally ruled by one man but would really be shared by all.[3] Like Gaius, Claudius was also fond of citing Augustus as his *exemplum*.[4] Nero was neither the first nor the last Princeps to give such a speech. Plutarch says that men expected from Galba ἕτερον ἡγεμονίας σχῆμα but, as usual, were deceived by these early assurances.[5] Pliny summarizes Trajan's speech on entering the consulship in 100: 'nunc singulos, nunc universos adhortatus es resumere libertatem, capessere quasi communis imperii curas, invigilare publicis utilitatibus et insurgere.' He adds that all emperors before Trajan had said the same things, but Trajan was believed.[6]

It is clear that the abuses each Emperor promised to correct might change from reign to reign, but the promise of partnership

---

[1] *Ann.* 13. 4. Tacitus' 'exempla capessendi egregie imperii' is a less explicit version of Suetonius' 'ex Augusti praescripto imperaturus' (*Nero* 10. 1).

[2] Dio 59. 3, 8; 59. 6, 1; 7.   [3] Josephus, *AJ* 19. 246.

[4] *Ann.* 12. 11; cf. Suet. *Claudius* 11, 2.

[5] *Galba* 15. 1.   [6] *Pan.* 66. 2.

remained much the same. Dio tells us that the Senate, on this occasion, voted to have the Emperor's speech engraved on a silver stele and read every time the new consuls entered office,[1] but not even this enthusiastic response was unusual.[2] It is likely that Tacitus omitted to mention this piece of *foedissima adulatio*[3] because he thought Nero's speech deserved sympathetic presentation, and for an important reason: 'nec defuit fides'—the promises were not new, but they were kept.

We have ample evidence of the correction of Claudian abuses. 'Discretam domum et rem publicam':[4] under Claudius the imperial freedmen secretaries advised the Emperor, dispensed patronage, addressed the legions, and won flattery from the Senate. How the members of that body felt about the power of these freedmen is well known. For Tacitus, the small number of his freedmen ranks as a cardinal item in the excellence of Tiberius' early reign.[5] Pliny reminds Trajan:[6] 'Scis enim praecipuum esse indicium non magni principis magnos libertos' and carefully defines the evil of which Trajan is so free: many *principes* have been slaves of their freedmen; they followed their advice, were approached through them, distributed political and religious offices through them. There had been offenders under Augustus and Tiberius, but none to equal Callistus under Gaius, and Callistus, Polybius, Pallas, and Narcissus under Claudius.[7]

Of Claudius' freedmen, many had been killed before their master,[8] including Polybius, a victim of Messallina.[9] Callistus had died naturally.[10] Agrippina had virtually or actually put Narcissus to death[11] at the time of Nero's accession. Pallas had

[1] 61. 3. 1.   [2] Dio 59. 6, 7; 60. 10, 2; Pliny, *Pan.* 75. 2.
[3] Cf. his remarks in *Ann.* 3. 57, 2.
[4] I find the interpretation of this phrase as a promise to withdraw jurisdiction from procurators of the *res familiaris* (granted by Claudius, *Ann.* 12. 60), the meaning suggested by P. Brunt, *Latomus* 25 (1966), 477, untenable: *domus* must have the same sense here as in the phrase 'intra domum' just before, i.e. the imperial household and palace in Rome.   [5] *Ann.* 4. 6.   [6] *Pan.* 88.
[7] For a collection of evidence see A. M. Duff, *Freedmen in the Early Roman Empire*, Oxford, 1928, pp. 174–9. Even a freedman was scandalized by Narcissus' interrogation of witnesses in the Senate (Dio 60. 16, 4–5).
[8] Seneca, *Apoc.* 13. 5.   [9] Dio 60. 31, 2.
[10] Dio 60. 33, 3a.   [11] *Ann.* 13. 1; Dio 60. 34, 4–6.

been the engineer of Agrippina's rise, and, both on her account and through his own *tristis adrogantia*, offended most. Nero could not touch him until Agrippina's interference in politics and her personal ascendancy over him had been checked. The incident of the Armenian legation achieved one, the romance with Acte the other. Then Nero, sometime in the first two months of 55, dismissed Pallas from his post *a rationibus* in which office, according to Tacitus, he had virtually ruled the Empire.[1]

The reasons for Pallas' dismissal are made quite clear by Tacitus: his known rapacity in discharging his duties[2] is not mentioned; there is no hint of a general financial reorganization.[3] It was his arrogant manner and the unofficial extensions of his power that offended. He was suspected of being Agrippina's lover; he had proposed measures to the Senate,[4] and refused an offer of honours so extravagant that they shocked Pliny and made him wish they had been an ironical gesture. Tacitus portrays him satirically as virtually an *amicus principis* under Claudius.[5] On his dismissal by Nero he is ironically described as a magistrate leaving office, escorted by a crowd of friends. Nero remarked that Pallas was going to take the oath of resignation, but, says Tacitus, the only pledge he had taken was one stipulating 'that his past conduct should not be queried, and that his account with the state should be regarded as balanced'.[6] The last is presumably intended by Tacitus as a parody of the magistrate's usual presentation of accounts—Pallas' balance sheet was the terms of his pact with Nero, squaring his peaceful departure against his profits.

---

[1] *Ann.* 13. 24, 1.

[2] The reason suggested by Levi, *Nerone*, p. 115.

[3] Cf. Sutherland, *Coinage in Roman Imperial Policy*, p. 155. Nor is there any evidence for the view of S. Oost, *AJP* 79 (1958), 113, that Pallas helped Claudius centralize the *fiscus* bureau, as Millar points out, *JRS* 57 (1967), 15.

[4] *Ann.* 12. 53; Pliny, *Ep.* 7. 29; 8. 6.

[5] Narcissus calls the imperial freedmen, Callistus and Pallas, 'in consilium' to discuss Claudius' remarriage, *Ann.* 12. 1.

[6] Any attempt to elicit information about the relations between the *aerarium* and *fiscus* is pointless. Note the solemn interpretation of T. Frank in *ESAR* V, p. 40: 'This remark, made when he was discharged from the office of *a rationibus* in 55, meant that the income of the Aerarium was under the control of the imperial procurators and that the Senate had no jurisdiction in the matter.'

Pallas' dismissal removed the most glaring vestige of the Claudian system. But the real change must not be overestimated. As long as freedmen held the vital offices in the palace, there would be a growing contradiction between their apparent (and original) equivalence to the secretaries in the houses of other great nobles and their real political importance attained by serving the greatest of them all.[1] The only cure for the resentment of the upper orders thereby engendered was the reform finally introduced by Domitian and his successors, following a practice started by Vitellius at a time of emergency, namely the replacement of these freedmen by *equites*. On his dismissal, Pallas retained his wealth,[2] and, if an anecdote in Dio is at all accurate,[3] Doryphorus, the successor of Callistus in the post *a libellis*, received a substantial gift from Nero while Agrippina was still alive. Pallas was still regarded, after his dismissal, as sufficiently significant to be accused of treason.[4] And, according to Josephus, the Syrians in Caesarea were able to secure a letter from Nero abolishing the equal citizen rights of the Jews in the city,[5] by bribing Beryllus, his *ab epistulis Graecis*.[6] This influential man was probably a freedman.

None the less, the verdict of A. M. Duff, that 'the reign of Nero saw no abatement in the power of imperial freedmen'[7] is not entirely fair. Freedmen do not figure scandalously in public affairs in the early part of the reign. Pallas' successor is so inconspicuous that he eludes definite identification.[8] Freedmen were

---

[1] *Ann.* 15. 35, 2 shows the development clearly.

[2] *Ann.* 14. 65.

[3] Dio 61. 5, 4. By A.D. 56/7, he had acquired Narcissus' Egyptian estate, presumably as a gift from Nero (*SEHRE*², II, p. 671 (no. 28)).

[4] *Ann.* 13. 23. On the help he was suspected of giving Felix in 55/6 see p. 87.

[5] Josephus, *AJ* 20. 183–4. What Nero really did was, presumably, to reject the claim of ἴση πολιτεία made by the Jews—a claim as bogus in Caesarea as it was in Alexandria. For the Alexandrian disputes over the claim and Josephus' use of tendentious Jewish literature on the subject see V. A. Tcherikover, *CPJ*, I, pp. 61 ff.

[6] See above, p. 87.   [7] Duff, *Freedmen*, p. 178.

[8] For a review of the candidates see P. R. C. Weaver, *CQ* 15 (1965), 149. Phaon, who was only prominent at the end of Nero's reign (Suet. *Nero* 48. 1; 49. 2; Dio 63. 27, 3) held the post at some time (*CIL* III. 14112, 2).

present at Agrippina's defence of herself in 55[1] because Seneca
and Burrus, originally protégés of Claudius' widow, were not
fully trusted by Nero. But this was a court crisis and well within
the imperial *domus*. Similarly, if the Emperor was going to
murder his mother, it was probably better to use a freedman
rather than a praetorian officer to execute the deed.[2] It was not
until 61, when the good era was on its way out, that Polyclitus
was sent to settle affairs in Britain;[3] not until 64 that Acratus was
sent to despoil Greece;[4] not until 66 that Nero left Helius in
charge of Rome.[5] It may be inferred from the popular demand
that Galba execute Halotus,[6] Narcissus,[7] Polyclitus, Petinus,
and Patrobius[8] that these freedmen had enjoyed great power in
Nero's last years, while Epictetus testifies to the power and wealth
of Epaphroditus, who succeeded Doryphorus in 62 as a *libellis*.[9]

One of the worst Claudian abuses was the increase of the
Emperor's jurisdiction at the expense of the ordinary tribunals
and magistrates. Our sources ridicule Claudius' passion for litiga-
tion which led him to try cases at all hours and at all seasons,[10]
and to sit in on those few trials he left to the magistrates.[11] He
is charged with irregularity in procedure through haste and
folly,[12] and with encouraging the venality of pleaders by making
all cases turn on the influence of advocates with him.[13]

Nero promised: 'Non enim se negotiorum omnium iudicem
fore, ut clausis unam intra domum accusatoribus et reis paucorum
potentia grassaretur.' At first glance, Nero's promise means no

---

[1] *Ann*. 13. 21.   [2] Ibid. 14. 3.

[3] Ibid. 14. 49. According to Pliny, *Ep*. 6. 31, 9, Trajan cited him as an example
of a powerful freedman. Cf. Tac. *Hist*. 2. 95 and his view of Pelag. in *Ann*.14.59.

[4] *Ann*. 15. 45; 16. 23; Dio Chrys. *Or*. 31. 149.

[5] Dio 62. 12, 2.   [6] Suet. *Galba* 15.

[7] Dio 64. 3, 4.

[8] Plut. *Galba* 17; Tac. *Hist*. I. 49. Patrobius was responsible for Nero's games
at Puteoli in 66 (Dio 63. 3, 1).

[9] Millar, *JRS* 55 (1965), 143–4. Cf. also the general remarks in Tac. *Hist*.
I. 7; 37; 2. 95.

[10] Seneca, *Apoc*. 7. 5; 12. 2; 12. 3, v. 23; Dio 60. 4, 1–3; Suet. *Claud*. 14; Tacitus,
Ann. 11. 5.

[11] Dio 60. 4, 4. Suet. *Claud*. 12. 2.

[12] Seneca, *Apoc*. 10. 4; 12. 3, vv. 19ff.; 14. 2. Suet. *Claud*. 15; 29. 1.

[13] *Ann*. 11. 5.

more than the cutting down of all jurisdiction by the Emperor, the phrase 'clausis unam intra domum . . .' being simply an exaggerated description of Claudius' general practice.[1] But secrecy is not one of the charges our sources generally bring against Claudius. Dio shows him on his tribunal in the forum or elsewhere,[2] Suetonius in the forum of Augustus,[3] Seneca before the temple of Hercules at Tibur.[4] And although the emperors usually tried to maintain the republican tradition of public justice,[5] Augustus could be forgiven if when ill he sometimes tried cases 'domi cubans'.[6] The cases that Claudius tried *intra cubiculum* were political ones that could not be tried in public—trials of Senators that, in the Senate's view, should have been held in the Senate or not at all. Thus of the trial of Valerius Asiaticus, witnessed only by Messallina, Suillius, and Lucius Vitellius, Tacitus says, 'neque data senatus copia: intra cubiculum auditur.'[7] Our loss of Tacitus' earlier Claudian books has undoubtedly robbed us of other evidence of cubicular jurisdiction, but it is more than likely that this was the procedure used for some of the other victims of Suillius—Lusius Saturninus, Cornelius Lupus[8]— or consular *amici* of Claudius like Pompeius Pedo and Asinius Celer,[9] perhaps his *consocer* M. Licinius Crassus Frugi.[10]

As was appropriate in a speech to the Senate then, Nero particularly abjured trials of senators on political charges. What of Nero's practice? No trials of *maiestas* or related charges are reported in the early years except for that of Pallas in 55, which the Emperor naturally took himself;[11] against senators there is

---

[1] Calp. Sic. *Ecl.* 1. 11, 69–73: 'iam nec adumbrati faciem mercatus honoris, / nec vacuos tacitus fasces et inane tribunal / accipiet consul; sed legibus omne reductis / ius aderit, moremque fori vultumque priorem / reddet, et afflictum melior deus auferet aevum.' [2] Dio 60. 4, 3.

[3] Suet. *Claud.* 33.

[4] *Apoc.* 7. 4–5. Augustus had also tried cases there (Suet. *Aug.* 72. 2).

[5] Crook, *Consilium Principis*, p. 106.

[6] Suet. *Aug.* 33. The cardinal sin was to try cases without a *consilium*, as Tiberius did, according to Dio 60. 4, 3. Cf. Livy 1. 49 on Tarquin: 'cognitiones capitalium rerum sine consiliis per se solus exercebat.' Cf. Cicero, 2 *Verr.* 5. 23.

[7] *Ann.* 11. 2. [8] *Ann.* 13. 43.

[9] *Apoc.* 13. 5. [10] Ibid. 11. 2, 5.

[11] *Ann.* 13. 23. The charge involved Burrus, but the trial was really of Pallas as Burrus' presence on the *consilium* shows.

none until 62, before the death of Burrus, but when the rot had already begun; the Senate had repudiated two early attempts to bring *maiestas* charges.[1] Antistius Sosianus was the first to be tried on that charge and he was tried in the Senate. The case of Fabricius Veiento was also opened in the Senate; it was only because a charge of selling influence with the Emperor was added that Nero took the case,[2] undoubtedly to the relief of the senators.

Nero also seems to have cut down on his personal jurisdiction generally.[3] Probably one result was an increase in the number of civil appeals coming before the Senate: in 60 Nero tried to discourage irresponsible appeals to the Senate and to stress the equality of their authority with his by requiring the same amount of caution money to be deposited for both.[4] The settlement of a dispute between two Italian communities was left to the Senate. His ruling that cases concerning the *aerarium* were to go to the forum, if it was made after 56, would transfer jurisdiction from the imperially appointed *praefecti aerarii* to the magistrates and *reciperatores*.[5]

Not that Nero totally avoided personal jurisdiction early in his reign.[6] Suetonius in the *Nero* 15. 1 describes his procedure in administering justice, and, though he gives no indication of date, we cannot assume that the early years are excluded because Seneca's *De Clementia*, written in late 55 or 56,[7] is largely con-

---

[1] *Ann.* 13. 10.   [2] Ibid. 14. 48–50.

[3] The promise 'nihil in penatibus suis venale aut ambitioni pervium' goes with the reduced power of freedmen and the decrease of the Emperor's jurisdiction. Tacitus connects the venality of men like Suillius with Claudius' mania for jurisdiction (*Ann.* 11. 5, 1–2). In allowing the renewal of the Lex Cincia and reducing rewards to informers under the Lex Papia Poppaea (Suet. *Nero* 10), Nero tried to curb attacks on the upper classes in another way (cf. *Ann.* 3. 56, 1). But his own clemency could be secured through bribery and intrigue (*Ann.* 13. 52, 1; Suet. *Otho* 2).

[4] *Ann.* 14. 28. For this interpretation see J. Bleicken, *Senatsgericht und Kaisergericht*, Göttingen, 1962, p. 155. On his view that these appeals came from the senatorial provinces, below, p. 113 n. 3.

[5] *Ann.* 14. 17; Suet. *Nero* 17. This transference of jurisdiction did not last. Trials ad aerarium are attested under Domitian (Suet. *Dom.* 9) and later (Pliny, *Ep.* 1. 10, 9–10).

[6] Cf. the view of Sherwin-White, *Roman Society and Roman Law*, pp. 110–11.

[7] See Appendix C3.

cerned with the Princeps' administration of justice. Nor does the signing of warrants described in *De Clementia* 2. 1 and by Suetonius[1] prove that Nero delegated cases more than other emperors. Suetonius' 'ex more' refers not only to Nero's practice, as is shown by his contrasting story of Gaius signing death-sentences and saying 'rationem se purgare'.[2]

When Nero did try a case, he no doubt was correct in his procedure in contrast to the irregular *consilia* he used in the years after Seneca lost influence.[3] But what cases did Nero try himself, in the early years? We have already mentioned the trials of Pallas and of Fabricius Veiento, trials which intimately concerned the imperial *domus*.[4] Probably, like previous emperors, he took select cases, originating in Rome or the provinces, some involving citizens of minor social status.[5] For this, the Princeps' diligence and clemency could be praised.[6]

In one passage, Tacitus seems to imply that Nero tried two proconsuls of Africa for extortion in 58, but, as is generally agreed, the right interpretation of 'absolvit Caesar' here is that Caesar procured their acquittal in a trial before the Senate by giving his *sententia* in their favour.[7] This kind of intervention in senatorial trials is elsewhere attested for Nero, as for previous emperors.[8] Of the trial of P. Celer, Tacitus uses similar language: 'quia absolvere nequibat Caesar, traxit, senecta donec mortem obiret.'[9] It is likely that imperial intervention in the Senate is again meant, as the trial took place in 57 when Nero was consul the

[1] *Nero* 10.2.

[2] Suet. *Gaius* 29. 2.

[3] *Ann.* 14. 62, 4 (A.D. 62); 15. 58, 3; 61. 2.

[4] Precedents for an emperor trying cases which personally concerned him may be found in the case of Ovid (*Tristia* 2. 131–2) and in the clear distinction made by Tiberius in 32 (*Ann.* 6. 10) when he separated from a host of *maiestas* victims tried before the Senate two 'e vetustissimis familiarium' to be tried by himself.

[5] For Augustus' practice see Sherwin-White, *JRS* 53 (1963), 203, rejecting Bleicken's view that Augustus did not try cases himself. For the scope of imperial jurisdiction, P. Garnsey, *Social Status and Legal Privilege in the Roman Empire*, Oxford, 1970, pp. 64–90.

[6] Pliny, *Pan.* 77; 80; Suet. *Aug.* 33. 1.

[7] *Ann.* 13. 52, 1.

[8] Garnsey, *Social Status*, pp. 36–40.   [9] *Ann.* 13. 33, 1.

whole year and would appear there frequently, yet scholars assume that, because Celer was procurator in Asia, he was tried *apud principem*. But despite Tacitus, *Dialogus* 7. 1, 'apud principem ipsos illos libertos et procuratores principum tueri et defendere datur', we cannot assume that this practice was regular before the Flavian period, the dramatic date of the *Dialogus*, especially since Tacitus marks a contrast with the custom of his own day in the case of the procurator Lucilius Capito tried in the Senate under Tiberius: 'patres decrevere, apud quos etiam tum cuncta tractabantur adeo ut procurator Asiae Lucilius Capito accusante provincia causam dixerit.'[1] The case of Celer is the first of three, all of which seem to be part of senatorial activities which Tacitus, in these books, tends to put at the end of the year, and of which the second, the trial of Cossutianus Capito, is specifically stated by Juvenal[2] to have been held before that body. Extortion trials held later of two praesidial procurators and a prefect of the fleet at Ravenna can also be located in the Senate.[3]

These trials before the Senate of imperial procurators and legates governing imperial provinces[4] lead us back to Nero's speech to the Senate. Tacitus summarizes the last part of Nero's description of the 'forma futuri principatus', thus: 'teneret antiqua munia senatus, consulum tribunalibus Italia et publicae provinciae adsisterent: illi patrum aditum praeberent, se mandatis exercitibus consulturum.'

The promise of a partnership with the Senate in ruling the Empire was standard in such speeches, as we have seen. But the

---

[1] *Ann.* 4. 15.

[2] 8. 92. The third was that of Eprius Marcellus, legate of Lycia.

[3] *Ann.* 13. 30, 2, where the trial of a senatorial proconsul of Crete falls between that of a procurator of Sardinia and the prefect of the fleet; ibid. 14. 28, where the trial of the procurator of Mauretania occurs in a senatorial context. Brunt, *Historia* 10 (1961), 201, 226, has these two procurators tried before the Senate, but not Celer. Garnsey, *Social Status*, p. 86 n. 3, is even doubtful about the first two.

[4] Eprius Marcellus, governor of Lycia, and Cossutianus Capito, governor of Cilicia. The status of Cilicia Campestris at this period is unclear. But the only real alternatives are that it was ruled by a subordinate of the legate of Syria, or by a *legatus pro praetore* as under the Flavians. There is no reason at all to think that it was a senatorial province: J. G. C. Anderson, *CR* 45 (1931), 190; Sherwin-White, *Roman Society*, pp. 55–6.

terms of the partnership cannot be pressed to prove a real intention
to institute or restore a dyarchy: the Senate ruling Italy and the
public provinces, Nero the imperial provinces and the army. Dio
considers Augustus' declaration that he would govern only some
of the provinces and restore the rest to the Senate as an attempt to
appear democratic while accepting absolute power.[1] The formula
was more precise than the senatorial phrase 'rem publicam resti-
tuit' or Augustus' own 'ex mea potestate in senatus populique
Romani arbitrium transtuli',[2] but just as inaccurate. The trial of
imperial officials by the Senate was not a sign that the balance of
power in the constitution had changed in favour of the Senate.[3]
The division of responsibility for public and imperial provinces
was not so rigid: the *maius imperium* of the Emperor, the lack of
distinct financial systems,[4] and the military arrangements by
which the legions in the imperial provinces defended the peaceful
senatorial provinces show this inseparability as do the trials. There
was a long tradition behind the *senatus consultum* passed with
imperial approval in 62 and affecting provincial votes of thanks
to governors of both types of province.[5] Conversely, instances of

---

[1] 53. 12, 1–2.   [2] *Fasti Praenestini* 27 B.C.; *Res Gestae* 34.

[3] Bleicken, *Senatsgericht und Kaisergericht*, pp. 154–6, suggests that the considerable increase in the number of civil appeals coming to the Senate (see above,
p. 110 and n. 4) is to be explained by an increased tendency for the senatorial
provinces to regard the Senate as the body responsible for them, in accordance
with Nero's accession speech. But the assumption underlying this view, i.e.
that the division of jurisdiction between Princeps and Senate in the matter of
civil appeals corresponded to the classification of provinces, has no support outside
Nero's promise, which Bleicken himself thinks was largely honoured in the
breach (pp. 150–3). In fact, a more likely division of competence for such cases
would be Italy and the provinces, to judge from the division used in the earlier
Augustan system (Suet. *Aug.* 33). Suet. *Nero* 17: 'cautum . . . ut omnes appella-
tiones a iudicibus ad senatum fierent', if it is not just a garbled version of the
measure reported by Tacitus (*Ann.* 14. 28), might indicate, in its context, that
all appeals on *aerarium* cases went to the Senate.

[4] Millar, *JRS* 53 (1963), 29. Even if the objections of Brunt, *JRS* 56 (1966),
75, were right, and the revenues of the imperial provinces were handled apart
from those of the senatorial provinces, financial decisions regarding both kinds
of provinces proceeded from Senate and Princeps, and the Emperor supported
and made use of both funds (evidence in Brunt, pp. 86 ff.).

[5] *Ann.* 15. 22. For the limited significance of the division of the provinces,
see Millar, *JRS* 56 (1966), 156 ff., who does not, however, discuss the trials of
provincial governors or other judicial arrangements.

'interference' by Nero in the senatorial provinces cannot be used
to convict him of breaking a promise to check a Claudian
development.[1] Instances there certainly are: in 57 Nero issued an
edict forbidding all provincial governors to give gladiatorial
games, and, in the next year, after consultation with prominent
senators, an edict checking the abuses on the *publicani*, both
measures that would affect the senatorial provinces.[2] The next
year, the senatorial province of Cyrene tried to prosecute for
extortion an agent of Nero originally sent out by Claudius to re-
claim public land from squatters. The Senate referred the matter
to the Princeps who justified the legate's decisions, but promised
to concede the land anyway.[3] But this 'interference' was not a
Claudian innovation. Augustus had limited the freedom of the
provincials in all provinces to honour their governors,[4] while
the Cyrene edicts show how much the Princeps interfered in
the senatorial provinces. Tacitus, with his concern for senatorial
freedom, does not criticize these actions of Nero. In fact, he
approves of the prohibition on games and does not censure the
use of an imperial edict to effect it.

[1] This is the judgement of M. Hammond, *The Augustan Principate*, Cambridge,
Mass., 1933, pp. 62–3.

[2] *Ann.* 13. 31; 13. 50–1. Brunt, *JRS* 56 (1966), 86 n. 72, suggests that Nero's
edict in 13. 51 was endorsed by a *senatus consultum*, but, on the interpretation of
'senatores' which he rightly accepts, i.e. individual senators, much of this episode
came from sources other than the *acta*, so there is no reason to assume that Tacitus
found the rest of it there.

[3] *Ann.* 14. 18 (A.D. 59); *SEG* 9. 352 (A.D. 55). On the inscription, Nero calls
L. Acilius Strabo *legatum suum*. Presumably Nero renewed his appointment
originally made by Claudius. Tacitus' 'concedere usurpata' should mean that,
after Strabo's dispositions (some of which are recorded on our inscription—no
doubt his lengthy task continued, after it was set up, in other areas) and the
resulting complaints of the dispossessed, Nero approved Strabo's decisions, but,
generously, said he would let the squatters keep the land. G. Olivieri, *Doc. ant.
dell'Africa italiana*, vol. 2: *Cirenaica*, Bergamo, 1933, pp. 131–2, thinks that Nero
upheld his arrangements, simply remitting the back rents Strabo was exacting,
but his case rests on a comparison of the extravagant Nero with the frugal
Vespasian (the work of whose legate is recorded in *SEG* 9. 165, 360) and a
parallel drawn with the work done, on Nero's advice, by a proconsul in Crete
in 64 who restored public lands—a false parallel, as the lands in question belonged
to the Cretan city of Gortyn (E. M. Smallwood, *Documents of Gaius, Claudius
and Nero*, no. 388: 'procos.' is correct, not 'proc.' as in *AJ* no. 55).

[4] Dio 56. 25, 6.

No shift in constitutional balance appears when we look at finance. The change of *aerarium* clerks, as we have seen,[1] is not presented as politically important by Tacitus.[2] Nero's arrangements preserved the Claudian ideas of imperial appointment and long service. As a result of a trial before the Princeps, the records containing old debts to the *aerarium* were burned, but it was inevitable for the Princeps to 'interfere' with the *aerarium*, as it was the only public treasury[3] and received lavish subsidies from the Emperor's private wealth.[4]

The coinage tells the same story.[5] For ten years, the gold and silver struck at the mint in Rome bore the legend 'ex s.c.',[6] an isolated exception to the convention established by Augustus whereby *aes* coinage bore an 's.c.', gold and silver did not. Clearly, some sort of gesture towards the Senate was intended, but, even on the traditional assumption that this 'ex s.c.' indicates senatorial authorization for the minting of the coins, the coins themselves show that the Senate's control was nominal.[7] Coins of 54 honour Divus Claudius; others of 54 and 55 show Agrippina's portrait and titles along with those of Nero, with her titles on the obverse in the earlier ones. Then from late 55 to 60–1 (*trib. pot.* VII), we have what Sutherland calls the 'constitutional types': a bare-headed portrait of Nero on the obverse with his titles on the reverse around the *corona civica* that had already appeared on the earlier coins. In 60–4 the same obverse is retained, but the oak-wreath is dropped in 60–1 from the reverse and replaced by allegorical figures usually identified as Ceres, Virtus, and Roma. The Senate can hardly be responsible

---

[1] Above, pp. 72–3.

[2] For the humble functions of the *aerarium* officials—who did not fix financial policy—see Millar, *JRS* 54 (1964), esp. pp. 39–40. The significance of Tacitus' lack of hostility here was perceived by O. Hirschfeld, *Die kaiserlichen Verwaltungsbeamten*, Berlin, 1963 (same as edition of 1905), p. 13 n. 5.

[3] A. H. M. Jones, *JRS* 40 (1950), 26; Millar, op. cit., p. 29.

[4] *RG* 17. 1; *Ann.* 13. 31, 2; 15. 18.

[5] E. A. Sydenham, *The Coinage of Nero*, London, 1920. Mattingly–Sydenham, *RIC* I, pp. 137 ff.; Mattingly, *BMC* I, pp. 200 ff.

[6] These coins show *trib. pot.* I to *trib. pot.* X, i.e. 54–64. The day for the change of number was 4 December (Hammond, *MAAR* 15 (1938), 26–32).

[7] Sutherland, *Coinage*, pp. 152–3.

for this pattern, particularly for the honour paid to Agrippina. Kraft offered a powerful challenge to the whole notion that 's.c.' or 'ex s.c.' on coins indicates senatorial authorization and argued that they were to be connected with the type.[1] Thus on the earliest Neronian coins, it would indicate that imperial consecrations and the *corona civica* were conferred by the Senate. Kraft thought that, on the coins of 60–4 with allegorical figures, the 'ex s.c.' was retained as a fossil, but the time seems too short for that process. The 'ex s.c.' on these coins could underline the senatorial sanction of Nero's titles which appear on these coins, exceptionally, on the reverse (with the 'ex s.c.'), instead of on the obverse with the head.[2] As in his speech, Nero was simply emphasizing that his power rested on the *auctoritas patrum*.

Nor is there any reason to believe that the Emperor's control of elections was diminished. It may have been in Nero's reign that *commendatio* was first extended to the consulate.[3] Suetonius attests Nero's refusal of office to men he regarded as undesirable because their fathers were freedmen.[4] In 60 passionate canvassing by fifteen candidates for the twelve praetorships led Nero to reduce the number of candidates to that of places by putting three in charge of legions. Tacitus and Suetonius seem to imply that the excess of candidates over places was unusual, and Tacitus does not regard Nero's move, which took the choice of praetors away from the Senate, as an unusual curtailment of senatorial prerogatives.[5]

[1] K. Kraft, *Jahrbuch für Numismatik und Geldgeschichte* 11 (1962), 7 ff. = *Wege der Forschung* 128 (1969), 336 ff., adding more points (pp. 402–3). Cf. objections raised by H. Mattingly, *NC* 3 (1963), 255. A. Bay, *JRS* 62 (1972), 111 ff., accepts Kraft's arguments against the traditional view, but suggests a different significance for the letters on Augustan *aes* coinage.

[2] The tribunician power, consulship, and the title of *pater patriae* which had great ideological value (Seneca, *Clem.* 1. 14). The argument would be clinched by a vary rare gold quinarius of 55/6 bearing on the reverse a victory and no titles or 'ex s.c.'—thus confirming the connection of the latter with the titles— but this coin is generally considered to be some kind of medallion.

[3] Tacitus, *Hist.* 1. 77. See Mommsen, *Staats.*[3] II, pp. 924–5.

[4] Suet. *Nero* 15. 2.

[5] *Ann.* 14. 28; Suet. *Nero* 15. 2, generalizes this one incident. In A.D. 11 Augustus, in a similar situation, also avoided a free and bitterly contested election by a different solution (Dio 56. 25, 4).

Faced with this evidence of a lack of any division of power or responsibilities with the Senate, scholars have decided that Nero only implemented his promises to a very limited extent,[1] or was insincere in making them.[2] But Tacitus' 'nec defuit fides' stands in direct contradiction to these theories. An even more unlikely suggestion is that Nero was promising a return to the Augustan Principate of fact, not theory, but that the Senate misunderstood him.[3]

Tacitus, in the *Dialogus*, puts into the mouths of Flavian senators an acceptance of the fact that the Principate was essentially government by one man.[4] But this recognition of senatorial impotence had come earlier. It appears in Josephus' account of the futile senatorial efforts to control events after Gaius' murder— an account that must rest on a pre-Flavian Roman source.[5] When Tiberius said that he was not equal to the whole burden of government, but would accept what part the Senate gave him, the offer could not be taken literally. Augustus and Tiberius had shared powers and responsibility in the last years but that was quite different from a real division of duties. Gallus' question at the senatorial debate, 'Which part?' could only show up Tiberius' insincerity; so Gallus hastily pointed out that he really meant to show the impossibility of such a division: 'unum esse rei publicae corpus atque unius animo regendum.'[6] Livy, the *Pompeianus*, may

---

[1] B. W. Henderson, *The Life and Principate of the Emperor Nero*, London, 1903, p. 88.

[2] A. Momigliano, *CAH* X, pp. 706–7.

[3] Levi, *Nerone*, esp. pp. 142–9.   [4] *Dialogus*, 38. 2; 41.

[5] D. Timpe, *Historia* 9 (1960), 474–502, has pointed to the mood of Tacitean resignation to the Principate and sad contempt for the Senate's attempts to assert itself in Josephus' pre-Flavian senatorial source for the accession of Claudius (though he doubts the common identification of the source as Cluvius Rufus).

[6] *Ann.* 1. 12. In Dio's version of the debate (57. 2, 5) with Gallus, in outline the same as Tacitus', Tiberius suggests a tripartite division: Rome and Italy, legions, public provinces. When one tries to imagine a real division of financial, judicial, and even military responsibilities (for the legions stationed in imperial provinces were used to defend senatorial provinces), one can only conclude that the notion was too absurd for Tiberius to have suggested. It could be Dio's elaboration of the remark 'ita quaecumque pars sibi mandaretur eius tutelam suscepturum' in Tacitus or of that in Suetonius, *Tib.* 25. 2: 'quando universae sufficere solus nemo posset nisi cum altero vel etiam cum pluribus.'

already have used the comparison of the Princeps as the soul of the state to illustrate Augustus' position.[1]

But Nero was not being insincere nor did the Senate think so. The Augustan Principate was too complex to be reduced to a formula, but some form of words was necessary to describe the condition of co-operation between Princeps and Senate.[2] Nero's formula was a renunciation of the total power of the Princeps, appropriate after Claudius. The positive form was Augustus' τά τε κοινὰ πᾶσι τοῖς δυναμένοις καὶ εἰδέναι καὶ πράττειν ἐπιτρέπειν[3] and the partnership promises of Gaius and Claudius.[4] Nero's promise meant that he would accord the Senate as much responsibility and show it as much respect as was possible under the system.[5]

The early years of Nero saw the fulfilment of his accession promises: if the tradition of the *quinquennium Neronis* and the poems of Calpurnius Siculus attest public approval, the account of Tacitus indicates, particularly, senatorial approval, declining sharply before the turning-point of 62.[6] We have seen that resignation to the facts of power is not anachronistic when applied to the Neronian Senate. Perhaps more attention should be paid to expressions of approval and disapproval in the ancient sources, for where we are trying to explain satisfaction, the verdicts of authors close to the events or using sources close to the events are not mere adornments to the facts they preserve: they are the facts.

For Tacitus, the proof that Nero kept his promise was that many things were done 'arbitrio senatus'. For Suetonius, the

[1] Florus 4. 3.

[2] When the Principate is described as a compromise between a monarchy and a republic (Dio 56. 43, 4, which might go back to a Tiberian or Claudian source) or between *libertas* and *servitus*, it is being justified rather than misleadingly described. For other justifications see Syme, *Gym.* 59 (1962), 2 44–5 = *Ten Studies in Tacitus*, pp. 121–2.

[3] Dio 56. 33, 4.

[4] See above, p. 104.

[5] Or, as B. H. Warmington puts it, 'government which respected as far as is possible the pretensions of the Senate' (*Nero: Reality and Legend*, London, 1969, p. 34).

[6] See Appendix C3.

promise is of wider application. He fixes on those qualities of the Princeps that all orders revered: *liberalitas*, *clementia*, and *comitas*.[1]

In the first winter, the Armenian situation required a good general. The command would offer scope for military glory. Nero and his advisers chose Cn. Domitius Corbulo, a man whom the Senate believed to have been recalled by Claudius from an offensive in Germany as 'formidulosum paci' and 'ignavo principi praegravem'.[2] The Senate was delighted. Not only had a slight of the hated Claudius been removed; Nero had shown that he was not afraid of military distinction and independence of mind. With the view here ascribed to the Senate we may compare Tacitus' own praise of the early reign of Tiberius when the Princeps 'mandabat . . . honores, nobilitatem maiorum, claritudinem militiae, inlustris domi artes spectando'.[3] The same idea is elaborated by Pliny in the *Panegyricus*,[4] a senatorial manifesto of what the good Princeps should be.[5] Tiberius earns Tacitus' contempt for retaining two able men in Rome after their appointments to Spain and Syria.[6] In 55, after the reconciliation with Agrippina, Nero assigned Syria to Anteius Rufus, 'et variis mox artibus elusus ad postremum in urbe retentus est'.[7] Tacitus does not imply, however, that Nero here betrayed the policy that had yielded Corbulo's appointment, for the trouble with Anteius was not his ability but his close friendship with Agrippina.[8] But Tacitus makes plain his disappointment when he relates how the useful Gallic canal project of L. Antistius Vetus, governor of Upper Germany, was stopped in 55 because of the complaints of the governor of Belgica 'formidulosum id imperatori dictitans, quo plerumque prohibentur conatus honesti'.[9] Nero succumbed to the old fear of a combination of Gallic resources and the Rhine

---

[1] *Nero* 10. 1.   [2] *Ann.* 11. 19, 3.

[3] Ibid. 4. 6.

[4] *Pan.* 44. 6: 'eadem quippe sub principe virtutibus praemia quae in libertate'; cf. 45. 1.

[5] M. Durry, *Panégyrique de Trajan*, Paris, 1938, pp. 21–4.

[6] *Ann.* 1. 80; Suet. *Tib.* 63; *Ann.* 6. 27; *Hist.* 2. 65.

[7] *Ann.* 13. 22, 1.

[8] Ibid. 16. 14.   [9] Ibid. 13. 53.

armies[1] and recalled Antistius,[2] a *nobilis* of independent character whose original appointment must have delighted the Senate. As we shall see later, the record of Nero's early years, as regards the competence of provincial governors, was mixed.[3]

Pietas was valued in an Emperor. Suetonius regards the funeral of Claudius, the honours granted to the memory of Nero's father Domitius, Nero's use of the watchword 'Optima Mater', and his benefits to his birthplace Antium as proofs of this quality.[4] Later Pliny was to praise Trajan for this virtue, which he showed in the deification of Nerva. Pliny disapproved of Nero's insincerity in deifying Claudius, but Nero's respect for his father and tutor[5] could only be praised.

More important than *pietas* to the Senate was the refusal of excessive honours, which proved the Princeps *civilis* or δημοτικός and gave him a chance to discourage senatorial adulation.[6] Nero suitably refused statues and alterations in the calendar to honour him.[7] He refused the title of *pater patriae* at first as being unsuitable to his age, but accepted it in late 55 or 56. This was, by now, customary. Augustus had refused the title until 2 B.C.; Tiberius never accepted it. But Gaius and Claudius had only postponed their acceptance.[8]

When Nero in 55 prevented his colleague in the consulship from taking the oath to his *acta* among those of other *principes*,

---

[1] Cf. *Ann.* 11. 1.

[2] Antistius (*PIR*² A 776) was replaced in 56 by Curtilius Mancia, who seems to have been relieved of his suffect consulship in the last days of December 55 (*PIR*² C 1605; 1391), perhaps in order to replace Antistius right at the start of 56. Antistius, consul in the first six months of 55, was thus in Germany less than a year. He could have been recalled, or have resigned, because of Aelius' complaints—not, however, because of the rumours about Rubellius Plautus who was not yet his son-in-law (*Ann.* 13. 19; 14. 22).

[3] See below, pp. 240 ff.

[4] Suet. *Nero* 9.   [5] *Pan.* 11. 1–2; *Ann.* 13. 10.

[6] Suet. *Tib.* 26; Dio 57. 8, 3; 9; Suet. *Claud.* 12.

[7] *Ann.* 13. 10.

[8] Suet. *Nero* 8. But Suetonius seems to be wrong in recording the acceptance of all other honours. On coins, *p.p.* first is found associated with *trib. pot.* II (Dec. 55–Dec. 56). References to the practice of earlier emperors in Durry, *Panégyrique*, on 21. 1 (p. 181) where Pliny praises Trajan for his modesty in postponing acceptance of the title for less than a year.

the Senate was enthusiastic in its praise.[1] They will have remembered Augustus' claim to be no more than an equal to his colleagues in that office, and Tiberius' refusal throughout his reign to have an oath taken to his *acta*. That was *civilitas*.[2] Not that there was any substance to Nero's gesture: Claudius did the same each time he was consul.[3]

Nero's behaviour towards his colleague also showed respect for the powers of the magistrates. In his praise of Tiberius' early reign, Tacitus notes: 'sua consulibus sua praetoribus species; minorum quoque magistratuum exercita potestas', features noted also by Suetonius and Dio.[4] The Emperor's virtual selection, when the chose, of the magistrates would not detract from the importance of such forms. Suetonius stresses Nero's refusal to appoint a suffect when a consul died on 31 December, because Caesar's appointment of Caninius Rebilus for one day had shown disrespect for the office.[5] Yet, we are told, Nero showed an autocrat's contempt for the supreme magistracy: his rejection of *continui consulatus* in 58 was a refusal to make the consulship the basis of his power.[6] But, for Tacitus, the senate's offer of *continui consulatus*[7] is just one of many extravagant honours—triumphal arches, statues, *festi dies*—offered on the destruction of Artaxata. Domitian was to accept the consulate for ten years,[8] which does not suggest that continuous tenure of the office was a retreat from autocracy. Even if it was intended that Nero give up his other powers—which we cannot assume—there is no reason to think that such a step would have been popular: Augustus' attempt to make the consulship the constitutional basis of his power had

[1] *Ann.* 13. 11.
[2] *RG* 34; *Ann.* 1. 72; Dio 57. 8, 4.
[3] Dio 60. 10, 1.
[4] *Ann.* 4. 6; Suet. *Tib.* 30–1; Dio 57. 11, 3.
[5] Suet. *Nero* 15. 2.
[6] *Ann.* 13. 41, 4. Momigliano, *CAH* X, p. 708; Levi, *Nerone*, p. 131, recognizes that the *nobiles* would dislike the idea, but regards it as a glorious constitutional proposal by the progressives of the Senate.
[7] It was not an offer of the *perpetual* consulship as Momigliano (see previous note) thinks. Cf. Mommsen, *Staats.*[3] II, p. 1097 n. 4. Gaius in his most pro-senatorial mood rejected the consulship for life, which Vitellius later accepted.
[8] Dio 67. 4, 3.

certainly not been.[1] If Nero retained his other powers, the repeated consulships would have been just one more honour for him, and a way of denying eponymous consulships to the *nobiles*, for whom they were reserved in the early years. For the *consules ordinarii* before 61 were, without exception, imperial *nobiles* and many of them were patrician and members of the Republican nobility (particularly those with whom the Emperor held the office). In 61 P. Petronius Turpilianus was the son of a consul, but L. Caesennius Paetus can only owe his honour to his father-in-law, an imperial legate soon to be the prefect of the city, Flavius Sabinus.[2] From then on, there is a clear majority of *novi homines* and provincials. Like Tiberius, Nero grew more cowardly and more careless of forms.

The senatorial criteria of a good Princeps were very subtle. Frequent adulatory speeches gave senators practice in finding the laudable or odious element in any action of any Princeps. Pliny is exhibiting no new skill when he praises Nerva for restoring the pantomime actors and Trajan for expelling them.[3] A good illustration of the subtlety of these standards is furnished by Tacitus' account of the debate in the Senate in 56 between the praetor Vibullius and the tribune Antistius who had interfered with the praetor's *coercitio* as applied to certain actors. The Senate curtailed the jurisdiction of tribunes where it interfered with the powers of consuls and praetors. They also diminished the powers of *aediles*. Tacitus begins his account of the incident: 'manebat nihilo minus quaedam imago rei publicae.'[4] What of the value he attached earlier to the 'minorum quoque magistratuum exercita potestas'?[5] The powers of the magistrates clearly do not matter in themselves. The Emperor must not meddle with these

---

[1] Mommsen, *Staats.*[3] II, pp. 1097–8, stresses the difference between these later repeated consulships and those of Augustus' early years when they were the technical basis of his power.

[2] *PIR*[2] C 173. *ILS* 995 shows that he was married to a Flavia Sabina, who is probably the daughter of the *praefectus urbi* (G. Townend, *JRS* 51 (1961), 54–5). In that case she will be the mother of the children he had before 62. On the career of Flavius Sabinus see Appendix D9.

[3] *Pan.* 46. 1–5.

[4] *Ann.* 13. 28, 1.

[5] Ibid. 4. 6, 2.

powers; but free decisions of the Senate are praiseworthy no matter what their content. Tacitus had envied the historians of the Republic who could report 'discordias consulum adversum tribunos'.[1]

Suetonius glosses Nero's promise to rule 'ex Augusti prae-scripto' as follows: 'neque liberalitatis neque clementiae ne comitatis quidem exhibendae ullam occasionem omisit.'[2] The exercise of these virtues affected all the orders of society. As for generosity, Nero gave congiaria to the plebs, and to the praetor-ians a donative and a monthly allowance of grain.[3] Treasure was declared to be the property of the finder,[4] and veterans were given land.[5] Nero made contributions to the public treasury and attempted some tax relief.[6] His new amphitheatre, erected in 57, and his lavish games (before his experiments on the Greek model) delighted the populace.[7] At one point he went too far and pro-posed the total abolition of indirect taxes. As Tacitus indicates, Nero's motive was vanity and a desire to win gratitude for his magnitudo animi.[8] It was a sweeping gesture like the later liberation of Greece[9]—and just as impractical. The aerarium was chronically in the red as it was.[10]

Clementia would show principally in the exercise of jurisdic-tion. The death-warrants he reluctantly signed would presumably be confirming sentences of the quaestiones or of such officials as

[1] Ibid. 4. 32, 1.

[2] Suet. Nero 10. 1.

[3] Ann. 13. 31; Suet. Nero 10. 1; Ann. 12. 69, 2.

[4] Calpurnius Siculus, Ecl. 4. 117–21, on which see Millar, 'Fiscus', JRS 53 (1963), 36.

[5] Ann. 13. 31; 14. 27. Cf. also his concession to squatters on public land in Cyrene, above, p. 114.

[6] Ann. 13. 31, 2; 15. 18, 3; Suet. Nero 10. 1; Ann. 13. 31; 13. 51.

[7] Calpurnius Siculus, Ecl. 7. 23 ff.

[8] Ann. 13. 50.

[9] Crook, Consilium Principis, p. 120. Syme, Tacitus, pp. 416–17, comparing SIG³ 814: ἡ ἐμὴ μεγαλοφροσύνη. The measure has a true Neronian ring and, even if the reading 'senatores' is kept in Ann. 13. 50, 2 and interpreted as meaning the whole Senate, Nero's advisers should not be credited with it. But 'senatores' could mean his amici of that rank, including Seneca.

[10] Ann. 13. 31, 2 (A.D. 56): a special contribution by Nero to the aerarium; ibid. 15. 18.

the *praefectus urbi* and *praefectus vigilum* where those who were not senators or equestrian officials would normally be tried.[1] Nero's prevention of the punishment of the freedmen of the murdered Pedanius Secundus is another example.[2] Suetonius illustrates Nero's *comitas* by his care in greeting men of all orders from memory.

These qualities affected the Senate as well. Nothing better illustrates how far the Senate accepted the real monarchical power of the Princeps (while insisting on the formal masking of it), than its enthusiasm for his displays of *liberalitas*, *clementia*, and *comitas* towards them.

In the year 58 Nero granted annual subsidies to three *nobiles*: Valerius Messalla, his colleague in the consulship, Aurelius Cotta, and Haterius Antoninus. Though, in the damning portrait of Augustus with which the *Annales* begins, Tacitus disparages such liberality as rewards for servility,[3] his usual view, which finds echoes in Velleius and Dio, applauds contributions to the maintenance of noble houses where poverty has not been caused by extravagance and immorality.[4] Tacitus' disapproval of Nero's generosity to Aurelius Cotta and Haterius, 'quamvis per luxum avitas opes dissipassent',[5] may be increased by his dislike of their ancestors. Cotta's father, 'saevissimae cuiusque sententiae auctor', he presents as the opposite of the admirable Marcus Lepidus and Lucius Arruntius, and he was already 'egens ob luxum'.[6] Haterius had for grandfather the despicable Haterius Agrippa, while his father 'inlustribus viris perniciem inter ganeam ac stupra meditabatur'.[7] These were not the *ingentium virorum nepotes*, the *posteri libertatis*[8] whom the Princeps was supposed

[1] Sherwin-White, *Roman Society*, p. 14; Furneaux's note on *Ann.* 14. 42 'praefectum urbis'.

[2] *Ann.* 14. 45. See pp. 280–1.

[3] *Ann.* 1. 2.

[4] *Ann.* 2. 48, 1; *Vell. Pat.* 2. 129 who adds that Tiberius obtained senatorial consent; Dio 57. 10, 4.

[5] *Ann.* 13. 34.

[6] Ibid. 4. 20; 5. 3; 6. 5; 6. 7. Persius' 'magni Messallae lippa propago' (2. 72) is usually taken to refer to him (*PIR*² A 1488).

[7] *Ann.* 1. 13; 2. 51; 6. 4.

[8] Pliny, *Pan.* 69. 5.

to encourage. Tacitus approves however of Nero's generosity
to Messalla, for although his more immediate ancestor was
unworthy, his great-grandfather received help from Augustus
but preserved a reputation for independence of thought.[1] And
he probably regarded even the less deserved gifts as deterrents
to vice ('pecunia ne delinquerent') and preferable to 'pecunia
ob delicta' paid to senators for appearing on the stage in the
next year.[2]

If the Senate regarded Nero's gifts as somewhat indiscriminate,
he had at least erred on the right side. Refusal of requests was
always liable to the interpretation of meanness. Thus when
Tiberius rightly reproved Hortensius Hortalus, a descendant of
the orator, for disregarding proper senatorial procedure and
trying to blackmail the Emperor into helping him by his shame-
less begging, the Senate was displeased, and Tacitus and Suetonius
share that view.[3] When Tiberius granted the request of an ex-
praetor after checking that his inheritance had been small,
Tacitus is all praise, but he and Seneca disapprove heartily of
Tiberius' efforts to curb such requests by requiring candidates
to justify their needs before the Senate.[4] According to Seneca,
aid on such terms is not *liberalitas*, but *censura*. On this subject
he offers his candid opinion: 'dicam, quid sentiam, ne principi
quidem satis decorum est donare ignominiae causa.'[5] Censorship
by the Princeps was always somewhat resented, though many
recognized its necessity. Nero as a young emperor shunned the
invidia.

Those who awaited the *liberalitas* of the Princeps acknowledged
their dependence on him; so did those who hoped for his *clementia*. An old political concept, *clementia* as used of the emperors
recalled inevitably the policy of Caesar the dictator towards his
defeated political enemies. That did not diminish its value in the

---

[1] *Ann.* 4. 34, 4: 'Messalla Corvinus imperatorem suum Cassium praedicabat.'
On the pliant character of the Neronian consul's grandfather, ibid. 1. 8, 4;
3. 18, 2.   [2] Ibid. 14. 14, 3.
[3] Ibid. 2. 37–8; Suet. *Tib.* 47, who relates the incident so as to discredit Tiberius
completely. Tacitus is fairer but unfavourable.
[4] *Ann.* 1. 75, 4; Suet. *Tib.* 47.
[5] *Ben.* 2. 8. Tiberius' ungraciousness is noted first in 2. 7, 2–3.

eyes of the Senate. For Calpurnius Siculus, the new Emperor's *clementia* immediately suggests new security for the Senate:[1]

> . . . et insanos clementia condidit enses.
> Nulla catenati feralis pompa senatus
> Carnificum lassabit opus, nec carcere pleno
> Infelix raros numerabit curia patres.

Tacitus seems to regard Nero's speeches on *clementia* justifying his recall of Plautius Lateranus as the fulfilment of the Senate's hopes 'ut iuvenilis animus levium quoque rerum gloria sublatus maiores continuaret'.[2] Similarly intervention by the Princeps in political trials before the Senate on the side of clemency was commendable, for the Senate might otherwise be forced through fear to a harsher verdict than they thought just. Hence when, in a *maiestas* case, Tiberius yielded to the prayers of a man pleading for his brother, Tacitus regards this as proof that Tiberius knew the better course and realized the good repute he could win through *clementia*.[3] When Tiberius, as a direct result of the execution of Clutorius Priscus, prompted a senatorial decree requiring a period of grace before senatorial sentences were executed, Tacitus criticizes Tiberius for not using the opportunity he himself had provided for pardons.[4] It would certainly be in this light that the Senate regarded Nero's veto of the attempted prosecutions of Suillius' son.[5]

Nero's part in the acquittal and pardon of corrupt provincial governors probably met with more approval from the majority of the Neronian Senate than from the high-minded Tacitus,[6] but his intervention on behalf of the freedman Paris in a case of *restitutio natalium* brought against his *patrona* gained him *infamia* with both.[7] It was an interference with the cherished rights of patrons and a perversion of justice for personal motives.[8] Far

---

[1] *Ecl.* 1. 59 ff.

[2] *Ann.* 13. 11. The senatorial context suggests that, as Furneaux ad loc. says, Nero asked for senatorial authorization.   [3] *Ann.* 4. 31, 1–2.   [4] Ibid. 3. 51.

[5] Ibid. 13. 43.   [6] See below, pp. 247–8.   [7] *Ann.* 13. 27, 3.

[8] Similar action on behalf of Acte was disliked: two consulars were bribed to swear that she had royal origins (Suet. *Nero* 28). For senatorial attitudes towards patron's rights and the record of Nero's reign as regards freedmen and slaves see pp. 278 ff.

more hateful, however, was his attempt in 62 to stage a display of *clementia* by instigating a charge of insulting the Emperor against a man he intended to save. *Clementia* was laudable when political trials were a fact,[1] but to renew *maiestas* trials in order to demonstrate *clementia* was unforgivable. One might be tempted to think that Tacitus has exaggerated the importance of the incident: for him it is the beginning of the end of good rule under Nero. After one other case, Tacitus can represent the death of Burrus as the culmination 'gravescentibus in dies publicis malis'.[2] Trajan sternly rejected *maiestas* cases,[3] and Pliny makes them a key point in the evaluation of a Princeps.[4] It may be objected that the Senate could not have felt so strongly about them before Domitian. But the promises of Gaius and Claudius[5] to abolish the charge would certainly suggest that they did, and, as we have seen, Nero's promise about trial *intra cubiculum* was concerned with such cases. The trial of Antistius was a great come-down for the Senate that, in 54, had been able simply to reject such a case.[6]

Comitas in an Emperor is the quality which renders his relations with his subjects easy and free of arrogance and coldness.[7] Suetonius gives as an example Nero's response to thanks from the Senate: 'cum meruero'.[8] *Comitas* combined with observance of the various forms signifying respect for the Senate is *civilitas*, one of the highest terms of praise for the Princeps.[9]

Civilitas sums up the character of Nero's early reign, as our analysis has revealed it. It is the quality which Sutherland rightly

---

[1] See *Clem*. I. 2, I: 'nec innocentiae tantum clementia succurrit, sed saepe virtuti, quoniam quidem condicione temporum incidunt quaedam, quae possint laudata puniri.'

[2] *Ann*. 14. 51.   [3] Pliny, *Ep*. 10. 82.

[4] *Pan*. 42; cf. 11 on Tiberius.

[5] Dio 59. 4, 3; 60. 3, 6. For a justification of the Tacitean view that Tiberius' policy regarding senatorial criminal jurisdiction was responsible for his failure as a Princeps see Bleicken, *Senatsgericht*, pp. 59 ff.

[6] *Ann*. 13. 10, 2. See Furneaux ad loc. on the case of Densus.

[7] Particularly illuminating are Suet. *Aug*. 53. 2; 74; 98. 1.

[8] Suet. *Nero* 10. 2.

[9] On *civilitas* see J. Béranger, *Recherches sur l'aspect idéologique du Principat*, Basel, 1953, pp. 151–2. On *civilitas* as a 'light touch' allowing *libertas* see especially Pliny, *Pan*. 87. 1.

suggests is exemplified in the coins of late 55–61, showing, on the obverse, Nero's bare-headed portrait and, on the reverse, his titles around a *corona civica* enclosing the words 'ex s.c.'[1] The coinage of the good period of Nero's reign—from Nero's accession till 59 in the popular view, till 62 in Tacitus'—announces no policy. For Sutherland this represents the Senate's failure to state its constructive policy for fear of giving the Emperor, whose achievements were usually featured on coins, the credit. The explanation is far simpler. The coins celebrate no positive programme of reform because there was none. They celebrate *civilitas*—a return to proper procedure and forms set aside by Claudius. That is the promise of Nero's accession speech and the source of senatorial enthusiasm for Nero's early reign.

The character of the government suits admirably the hints of Seneca's role provided by our sources: not proposals in the Senate or plans for financial reform, but personal influence on the Emperor's public behaviour and pronouncements. Some of Seneca's work as *amicus principis* we have already described. It is time to consider the two works which, taken with Nero's speech to the Senate, show how the Emperor's ideologist and publicity expert expressed the ideas we have seen in practice: they are the *Apocolocyntosis* and *De Clementia*.

[1] Sutherland, *Coinage*, pp. 156–7.

4

IDEOLOGY FOR A NEW REGIME

SENECA'S *Apocolocyntosis*, as all would admit, has its serious political side.[1] Menippean satire, a Hellenistic literary form already imitated by Varro, seems to have been social and general in its approach. Seneca took over the literary form and useful motifs but wrote instead political satire, ridiculing the dead Emperor by name and condemning the specific abuses of his reign.[2] The farce was probably presented to the court and specially favoured senators and knights soon after Claudius' funeral and consecration.[3] For the Romans, who valued dignified behaviour so highly, its complete abandonment on set occasions was the rule:

[1] See M. Coffey, *Lustrum* 6 (1961), for an excellent discussion (with particular reference to work published 1922–58) of the problems of authorship (p. 265) and title (pp. 245–7). All the manuscripts attribute the extant work to Seneca and the character of the work does not make his authorship implausible (see below, p. 133). The title in the best manuscript (Sangallensis 569) 'Divi Claudii apotheosis Annaei Senecae per satiram' is so reminiscent of Dio's description (60. 35, 3) of a work written by Seneca ἀποκολοκύντωσιν αὐτὸ ὥσπερ τινὰ ἀθανάτισιν ὀνομάσας as to make its identification with the extant work highly probable.

[2] O. Weinreich, *Senecas Apocolocyntosis*, Berlin, 1923, pp. 9–11.

[3] For a review and rejection of attempts to date the work later on in Nero's reign see C. Russo, *Divi Claudii Ἀποκολοκύντωσις*[4], Florence, 1964, p. 10 n. 13; Coffey, *Lustrum* 6 (1961), 263–5.

Russo, pp. 45–6, suggests a date within a week of 13 October 54, the day of Claudius' death indicated in *Apoc.* 1. In support he cites *Ann.* 12. 69 to show that *caelestes honores* 'a preludio dell'apoteosi' were decreed that same day. But Furneaux (on *Ann.* 13. 2, 3) rightly notes that the voting of *caelestes honores* and the celebration of the funeral are mentioned proleptically in 12. 69, the real notice coming in 13. 2–3 where 'et mox consecratio' (= *caelestes honores*) indicates an interval before the consecration. For Augustus the funeral was soon after his death but the consecration was decreed a month later. A date for the *Apocolocyntosis* in November then is more likely, perhaps even the Saturnalia in December.

one of these occasions was the funeral of the Emperor; another the Saturnalia which fell less than two months after Claudius' funeral.[1] Seneca took advantage of this mood and of the unrestrained ridicule that Nero encouraged regarding Claudius. The deification had been political in purpose: Nero could now style himself *divi f.*; his *pietas* was demonstrated; perhaps most important, those who had prospered under Claudius were assured that there would be no reprisals. But within the court, Claudius' memory was not sacred. Nero's own jokes were aimed at Claudius' *stultitia* and *saevitia*:[2] he would not have hesitated to sanction Seneca's writing on the same themes.

The criticisms of Claudius include those cited in the speech to the Senate:[3] the power of the freedmen (6. 2; 15. 2), and the venality of the court (9. 4; 12. 2; 12. 3, 28); the monopoly of jurisdiction and neglect of due judicial procedures (7. 5; 12. 3, 19 ff.; 10. 4; 14. 2). The praises of Nero echo the 'forma futuri principatus' there outlined: the emergence of proper legal forms (4. 1, 23–4; 12. 2).

In the preamble of that speech Nero gave his personal quali- fications, named his models, principally Augustus,[4] stressed his freedom from hatred, and forswore revenge. In the *Apocolocyntosis*, Claudius appears as the counter-example: his cruelty and wrath are presented (6. 2; 11. 2), and Augustus is made to veto the deification of the man who claimed him as his model (10. 4), but behaved more like Gaius (11. 2).

No doubt these passages were partly meant to impress on Nero that similar use of his power would earn him hatred and ridicule instead of the popularity he so deeply craved. No doubt the long *laudatio Neronis*, announcing the spirit of the new reign, was meant to flatter him and encourage him in the right path. We may imagine the select audience duly showing its enthusiasm for these sentiments.

Some would go further, seeing in the ridicule of Claudius'

---

[1] Suet. *Vesp.* 19; cf. *Apoc.* 12. 2.

[2] Suet. *Nero* 33. 1.

[3] *Ann.* 13. 4.

[4] Suet. *Nero* 10.

deification a serious attack on Agrippina, organizer and priestess of the cult,[1] or on Britannicus, whose claim to the throne, it is suggested, had unexpectedly profited more than Nero's from his father's divinity.[2] Such interpretations ignore the whole spirit of the work.[3] The very title proclaims it a farce.[4] Nothing here is sacred—except Nero.

History and epic and Claudius' attachment to *novi poetae* are ridiculed, but that does not make Seneca a traditionalist in literature.[5] The quarrels of philosophers are good for a laugh, but that does not show that Seneca hated philosophy or despised philosophical disagreements.[6] Even Augustus' elaborate *Res*

---

[1] Scholars supporting this view are listed in Russo, op. cit., p. 12 n. 15; Coffey, *Lustrum* 6 (1961), 261–2. Against this idea is the fact that Claudius' deification was countenanced by Nero and his advisers as well as by Agrippina and that Seneca in the work upholds the official version of Claudius' death, circulated by Agrippina, in respect of time, circumstances, and cause (R. A. Pack, *CW* 36 (1942), 150–1).

[2] K. Kraft, *Historia* 15 (1966), 96 ff., argues that this situation became clear a few months after the consecration and explains why Seneca attacked Claudius' elevation and stressed Nero's descent from Augustus. Against this idea is the peculiarity already noted by D. Baldwin, *Phoenix* 18 (1964), 39 ff., that, although Messallina's victims are mentioned in the *Apocolocyntosis*, she is not blamed for their fate and is herself named by Augustus as Claudius' victim (11. 5)—which would be odd in a work attacking Britannicus. (The fact itself is best explained by Messallina's being old news in 54.) Furthermore, Nero is still called 'Claud. divi f.' on coins of 55 and a rare gold quinarius of 56; also in the *AFA* for 59 and 60 as well as less official inscriptions. That there never was an official deconsecration was shown by M. P. Charlesworth, *JRS* 27 (1937), 57 ff.

[3] Against taking the work as a serious political tract, see Russo, op. cit., pp. 12–14; Giancotti, *RAL* 8 (1953), 238 ff.; Coffey, *Lustrum* 6 (1961), 261–2.

[4] For the problem of interpreting the title, Coffey, pp. 245–54. In my opinion, Bücheler and Weinreich were right to regard it as a play on the word ἀποθέωσις, pure and simple. This interpretation removes the grounds on which the identification of the extant piece with the work Dio calls the ἀποκολοκύντωσις is commonly doubted, i.e. that in the extant work there is no metamorphosis into a god or a pumpkin. The latter would merely have laboured the joke of the title, while the former would have removed the best joke—that of showing Claudius judged unworthy of the honour he had been given with so much ceremony.

[5] The remarks of Quintilian (10. 1, 125 ff.) and Aulus Gellius (12. 2) would prove that he was not, if it needed witnesses.

[6] Seneca compares Stoic freedom with Epicurean dogmatism: *Ep.* 33. 4; 87. 26–7; 113. 23. Seneca himself quarrels with his own sect: *Ep.* 58. 13; 74. 23; 80. 1; 82. 9; 85. 33; 117. 1.

Gestae and his obsession with his family are laughed at,[1] but that does not show that Seneca did not admire him. Similarly, Claudius is not always ridiculed for serious faults. His voice (5. 3), his walk (5. 2), his antiquarianism (5. 4), and his undignified social behaviour (4. 3) are all paraded. Anything that could be made laughable, like the temple in Britain (8. 3) or the granting of citizenship (3. 3), is mentioned. Seneca does not give us a serious political diagnosis of Claudius. He adopts the 'plain man' attitude commonly used by satirists: blunt, conservative, and philistine.

Nero's praises, for the most part, are the counterpart of the ridicule. They concentrate on his voice and his beauty, summed up in his resemblance to Apollo. No doubt in the popular mind, and even for the governing class, Nero's good looks in contrast with Claudius' grotesque appearance did help his popularity. Later Galba was unfavourably compared with him.[2] The mood of licence and liberty was also one of elation. The poets express this mood in the traditional images of the golden age, the return of Saturn and Themis,[3] his identification with the god Apollo.[4] That Nero seemed a promising patron undoubtedly helped their enthusiasm,[5] but Seneca and his audience shared the general elation that at a later time could touch even a pessimistic historian: 'nunc demum redit animus . . . primo statim beatissimi saeculi ortu . . .'[6]

Seneca must have enjoyed savaging the man who had made him suffer, but there is no warrant for seeing the mood of the work as an outburst of Spanish vengefulness[7] or a release of paranoiac feelings.[8] To release such feelings would have been to

---

[1] Russo, op. cit., p. 97 on 10. 2 and p. 99 on 10. 3.

[2] For the importance of good looks cf. Pliny, *Pan.* 4. 7. On Galba, Tacitus, *Hist.* 1. 7. Note the emphasis on Nero's youth, beauty, and eloquence in Calp. Sic. 4. 85–6 ff., 137; 7. 6; 4. 55 ff.

[3] Calp. Sic. 1. 42 ff.; 4. 5. See Weinreich, *Apoc.*, p. 28.

[4] Calp. Sic. 4. 87; 7. 84.   [5] Note especially Calp. Sic. 4. 157 ff.

[6] Tacitus, *Agricola* 3. Weinreich, *Apoc.*, p. 28, notes the parallel.

[7] Weinreich, *Apoc.*, p. 7, though he allows for a multiplicity of motives. Coffey, *Lustrum* 6 (1961), 263, rightly objects to associating bull-fights with this Italian *émigré*.

[8] H. MacL. Currie, *L'Antiquité Classique* 31 (1962), 91–7.

contradict the admonitions Seneca gave Nero in the *De Clementia* and to substitute a policy of reprisals for one of amnesty. His failure to attack Messallina in the work—the probable architect of his exile—shows he did not do so. Wit and humour were not alien to Seneca's personality and need no ulterior explanations. Tacitus attributes a witty retort to him,[1] and his detractors could charge him, plausibly in Nero's eyes, with mocking the emperor's singing voice.[2] In his philosophical works he satirizes folly and enjoys reporting witty remarks,[3] while Pliny says that he wrote humorous verses.[4] In fact, in the *Apocolocyntosis* Seneca parodies his earlier flattery of Claudius in the Consolation to Polybius[5] and makes his well-known hatred of Claudius the object of one of his best jokes: he takes over from the historians the solemn cliché, 'nihil nec offensae, nec gratiae dabitur.'[6]

II

From the start, Seneca assumed responsibility for promoting the ideology of the new regime. In the first year of Nero's reign, he wrote for the young Princeps the funeral eulogy of Claudius and the accession speeches to the praetorian guard and the Senate. Early in 55 he composed a speech to the Senate on *clementia*. Late in that year, or in the next, Seneca published his only work of political philosophy and dedicated it to the Princeps. The public cannot have viewed *De Clementia*, as they could other of his philosophical works, as a purely literary product unrelated to Seneca's political activities. Nor were they meant to. When the Princeps' adviser addressed him on political subjects in public, that was an official statement.

Given the traditional date of late 55 or 56 for the work, Seneca

---

[1] *Ann.* 15. 23.

[2] Ibid. 14. 52, 3.

[3] e.g. *Ep.* 29. 6; *Ben.* 4. 31, 3–5.   [4] Pliny, *Ep.* 5. 3, 5.

[5] Weinreich, *Apoc.*, pp. 41–2; see below, p. 217 n. 1. But we need not construe *Apocolocyntosis* as a serious palinode.

[6] I. I.

wrote his glowing praises of Nero's innocence—'nullam te toto orbe stillam cruoris humani misisse' (1. 11, 3); 'rarissimam laudem et nulli adhuc principum concessam concupisti, innocentiam' (1. 1, 5)—after the murder of Britannicus early in 55.[1] To avoid this painful conclusion, some scholars have tried to alter the date, by tinkering with the internal evidence on which it is based, but their suggestions are not convincing.[2] One scholar has vainly tried to postpone the death of Britannicus to early 56.[3] But most accept the bitter truth. In fact, a date for De Clementia after the murder of Britannicus is politically intelligible and, perhaps, even morally defensible.[4]

None of our sources doubts that Britannicus was murdered nor how it was done.[5] Their accounts confirm what Josephus states explicitly: that while the murder of Agrippina was virtually public, Britannicus was removed ἀδήλως τοῖς πολλοῖς. Though many of those present at the dinner within the palace did not believe Nero's explanation that Britannicus had had an epileptic fit, and though a rumour of murder had made its way to the public, Dio alone reports that the appearance of the body revealed to spectators at the funeral the unnatural death. This is exaggeration, if not invention, since the funeral was conducted in a driving rain before a small audience, and, according to Tacitus, at night.[6] No full explanation was required, such as would be provided after Agrippina's death; the people could be expected to accept Nero's brief edict excusing the hurried funeral.

---

[1] Tacitus, *Ann.* 13. 15, 1; Suet. *Claudius* 27.

[2] See Appendix A3.

[3] P. Thomas in *Serta Eitremiana*, Oslo, 1942, known to me only through the discussion of Giancotti, *RAL* 9 (1954), 587. According to Tacitus (*Ann.* 13. 15, 1), Britannicus was about to complete his fourteenth year when he died. Thomas argued for a birth date of 13 Feb. 42, rather than 41 (the day is given in Suet. *Claudius* 27), but there is conclusive evidence against this in an Alexandrian coin celebrating his birth in the first year of Claudius' reign (before 29 August 41): Vogt, *Alex. Münzen*, I, pp. 24–5; II, p. 5; Smallwood, *Documents of Gaius, Claudius and Nero*, no. 98a.

[4] The discussion of Giancotti, op. cit., pp. 591 ff., is particularly sensible. I have derived from it the idea that the work has a multiple purpose.

[5] Tacitus, *Ann.* 13. 15–17; Suet. *Nero* 33. 3; Dio 61. 7, 4; Josephus, *BJ* 2. 250; *AJ* 20. 153.   [6] *Ann.* 13. 17, 1.

Seneca and Burrus undoubtedly knew the truth.[1] Tacitus records rewards to the *potissimi amici* who must include these two. The likelihood of Burrus' knowledge is strengthened by Tacitus' evidence that a tribune of the praetorian guard was deeply involved in the transaction.[2] None the less, the murder had been carried out in such a way that the official version was not entirely incredible and one who described Nero as innocent soon after would not necessarily appear insincere or obtuse. And there would be many who would prefer to accept the official version despite private doubts. In his relations with those outside his family, Nero's early months promised fair. An atmosphere of open suspicion and disbelief could only drive him to cruelty and repression.

For Seneca, the choice will have been clear. He had never been a man of rigid principle. He had agreed to give up his vegetarian fad for reasons of safety and was not ashamed to admit it later; he had pretended serious illness to escape Gaius' wrath; in exile he had put his literary talent and philosophical training at the service of adulation in an attempt to return; he had accepted recall on the condition that he would teach Domitius when he could scarcely have been unaware that Agrippina meant him to supplant Britannicus. Now if he broke with Nero and retired, he might be put to death by the Emperor. Even if he survived, he would live to see Nero submit to the influence of Agrippina or worse and practise his savagery on those outside his family. Seneca preferred to go on as if nothing had happened.

Just how soon after Britannicus' murder Seneca wrote *De Clementia* cannot be discovered.[3] At least nine months, at most twenty-one, elapsed. *Clementia* itself was part of the publicity of the new reign from the start. It appears by name in the first poem of Calpurnius Siculus and by implication in the *Apocolocyntosis* and in Nero's first speech to the Senate, as recorded by Tacitus. At the beginning of 55, Nero had made the return of Plautius

---

[1] Tacitus, perhaps following Fabius Rusticus, makes Seneca mention the murder when about to die (*Ann.* 15. 62, 2).   [2] *Ann.* 13. 15, 4–5.

[3] Grimal, *REL* 49 (1971), 214, sees in the references to *vota publica* in *Clem.* I. 1, 7 and 1. 19, 7 evidence that Book I was a speech delivered at the *nuncupatio votorum* on I (? 3) January of 56.

Lateranus an occasion for delivering a speech, written by Seneca, on clemency. Since then tensions within the palace had increased. For political reasons, Seneca and Burrus encouraged Nero's friendships and his love affair with Acte. Agrippina's rigid domineering personality and her total lack of tact made her unequal to the contest for control of Nero. Pallas was dismissed—and her next protégé, Britannicus, was murdered. But a reconciliation was effected: it was not in the interests of the older *amici*, whose power had derived originally from Agrippina and who now provided a refuge from her threats, to have Nero completely liberated from her authority. The reconciliation was effected, however, at the expense of Nero's complete faith in Seneca and Burrus, and his adolescent outbursts in 56 demonstrated his growing mood of liberty.[1]

Yet Nero's political behaviour was still up to the standards of his early promises. His relations with the Senate were good and his public manners not such as to offend popular sentiment.

In this context, the mixture of admonition and eulogy that characterizes *De Clementia* is fully intelligible. The work is addressed to the Princeps and there can be no doubt that its purpose in part was to commit him to the clemency that he had so far shown outside the palace.

According to Suetonius, the weaknesses of Nero's character were revealed to Seneca in a dream on the night after his appointment as Nero's tutor.[2] It is unlikely that such divine intervention was necessary. In *De Clementia* Seneca repeats the commonplace of ancient psychology that only *naturalis bonitas* is lasting: 'ficta cito in naturam suam recidunt' (1. 1, 6). But the natural endowment of an Ahenobarbus could hardly be as promising as Seneca here pretends. Suetonius shows Nero's heritage as anger, cruelty, and violence.[3] In addition, Nero's vanity and latent timidity had already appeared. His thirst for applause will have been evident in his vocal training[4] and can be traced in the effusive praises in the *Apocolocyntosis*. That fear could drive Nero to cruelty had been demonstrated all too recently. The young Princeps presented

---

[1] Above, pp. 78–9; *Ann.* 13. 25.   [2] *Nero* 7.
[3] Ibid. 2–5.   [4] Ibid. 20.

a great challenge to Seneca who was interested in early moral training. In *De Ira*, written some years before Nero's accession,[1] he mentions among the methods of modifying natural tendencies, the judicious use of praise and criticism. Particularly with a nature prone to anger, found most commonly in the wealthy and powerful, he urged care in balancing freedom and restraint: 'We must guide the child between the two extremes, using now the curb, now the spur'[2]—advice which Tacitus thought Seneca and Burrus actually applied.[3]

Seneca's skill in psychology is apparent in *De Clementia*. Praise and admonishment are inextricably combined.[4] That eulogy of itself could be exhortation was fully recognized in theory by Aristotle,[5] demonstrated in practice by Cicero in *Pro Marcello*, and most appropriately stated by Pliny in his Panegyric on Trajan: 'boni principes, quae facerent, recognoscerent, mali, quae facere deberent.'[6] The purpose of *De Clementia*, Seneca states at the outset, is to delight Nero by holding up a mirror to him in which he may view his virtues. Nero himself is then made to declare these virtues, but soon Seneca warns: the trust inspired by your good conduct to date makes your responsibility very great. Virtue is not easy to maintain; people grow dissatisfied and even now, when they admit their happiness, they are concerned that their good fortune should continue (1. 1, 6–7). The eulogy which opens Book 2 ends with a more explicit admonition: Seneca disclaims intention to flatter and names as one of his motives 'quod bene factis dictisque tuis quam familiarissimum esse te cupio, ut quod nunc natura et impetus est, fiat iudicium' (2. 2, 2). Similarly, the title *pater patriae* is said to be, not an honour, but a mandate (1. 14, 2).

[1] See Appendix A1. [2] *De Ira* 2. 21, 3.

[3] *Ann.* 13. 2, 1; 14. 14, 1–2; Seneca and Burrus tried to strike a balance between restraint and encouragement, or, rather, indulgence.

[4] Giancotti, *RAL* 9 (1954), 594 ff.

[5] *Rhet.* 1. 9. 35 ff. (= 1367ᵇ).

[6] *Pan.* 4. 1. Compare the views of the declaimer Cestius (Elder Seneca, *Suas.* 1. 5–6) on giving advice to Alexander: 'non eodem modo in libera civitate dicendam sententiam, quo apud reges, quibus etiam quae prosunt, ita tamen ut delectent, suadenda sunt.' In *Ep.* 94. 39, Seneca includes *laudationes* as a form of *monitiones*.

Seneca skilfully manipulates Nero's weaknesses. Timidity is his most valuable ally: Seneca applies to the Principate the traditional arguments urging kings to abstain from anger and cruelty in the interests of personal security, which is only to be won by their subjects' love (1. 8, 6–1. 13; 1. 19, 5; 1. 26). Nero's vanity is also touched: he can surpass Augustus and the early years of Tiberius (1. 1, 6; 1. 11). Both qualities are the target of the long story of Augustus and the conspirator Cinna: Augustus' clemency saved him from future conspiracies; Nero can surpass that clemency and that security.[1]

But *De Clementia* was not simply an essay addressed to Nero: it was meant to reassure the reading public that the murder of Britannicus and the rumoured tensions at court meant no change in the character of the government. To this end all the blessings of the new reign are retold. Nero is made to proclaim a return to legality from the harsh arbitrariness of Claudius' reign. The return of the *leges* had been celebrated in the *Apocolocyntosis* (4. 1, 23–4) and in the first poem of Calpurnius Siculus (71–2: '. . . sed legibus omne reductis / ius aderit . . .'): their authority traditionally marked off the Republic from the *regnum*[2] and the Principate from *dominatio*.[3] The Roman idea is combined with an allusion to the Stoic idea that monarchy is irresponsible (ἀνυπεύθυνος)[4] in Nero's boast: 'sic me custodio, tamquam legibus, quas ex situ ac tenebris in lucem evocavi, rationem redditurus sim' (1. 1, 4).[5] Then the qualities of the *laetissima*

---

[1] For discussion of the dates involved in 1. 9 see Appendix A3.

[2] Lucretius 5. 1136–44; Cicero, *Clu.* 146; Seneca, *Ben.* 2. 20; *Ep.* 86. 2–3.

[3] Ovid, *Fasti* 2. 141; Vell. Pat. 2. 89; Pliny, *Pan.* 65.

[4] Diogenes Laertius 7. 122 (*SVF* 3. 617).

[5] Ch. Wirszubski, *Libertas as a Political Idea at Rome during the Late Republic*, Cambridge, 1950, pp. 133–4, thinks that Seneca means by *leges* here not Roman laws but the unwritten laws of morality and is alluding to the doctrine of the νόμος ἔμψυχος. But 'evocavi' surely points to a contrast with the illegal behaviour of Claudius, and the parallel passages cited above—where Greek philosophical doctrine is unlikely to be involved—are also against his view. Of the two senses of νόμος ἔμψυχος distinguished by Delatte (see below, p. 144 n. 2), pp. 245 ff., the weaker sense (= guarantor of the laws), found in Musonius Rufus frag. 8 (Hense), does not appear in Seneca, the stronger sense (= incarnation of true justice) is only approached by Seneca here and in 1. 5, 4. Applied to Rome in its full sense (as by Themistius 141; 234; 227. 26), it implies *princeps supra leges*, a

forma rei publicae are extolled: *felicitas, securitas, ius, libertas, clementia* (1. 1, 7–9).

But for the public, as for the Princeps, reassurance is coloured with admonition. Nero is urged to look down 'in hanc immensam multitudinem discordem, seditiosam, inpotentem, in perniciem alienam suamque pariter exultaturam, si hoc iugum fregerit' (1. 1, 1). This idea is developed: *clementia* becomes the king or Princeps because he is the *anima* of the *res publica* which he must spare as his own body (1. 5, 1). This conception of monarchy, says Seneca, explains why men are willing to risk their lives for their ruler: his destruction would mean chaos. So the ruler is indispensable in a monarchical system; but the system itself is indispensable to Rome:

Hic casus Romanae pacis exitium erit, hic tanti fortunam populi in ruinas aget; tam diu ab isto periculo aberit hic populus, quam diu sciet ferre frenos, quos si quando abruperit, vel aliquo casu discussos reponi sibi passus non erit, haec unitas et hic maximi imperii contextus in partes multas dissiliet. . . . olim enim ita se induit rei publicae Caesar, ut seduci alterum non posset sine utriusque pernicie; nam et illi viribus opus est et huic capite. (1. 4, 2–3.)

Seneca has moved here from metaphysical justification of Nero's position in the state, to a historical justification of the Principate.

How real can the tone of warning be, if all but the most stubborn spirits must have been resigned to the system by this time? There was probably no organized conspiracy aimed at the restoration of the Republic after the failure of the Senate to avoid the accession of Claudius.[1] In the discontented atmosphere of the last years of Nero, only one man seems to have been suspected

doctrine inconceivable in Seneca's time (Wirszubski, op. cit., pp. 130–3, on Pliny, *Pan.* 65). Thus the attempt of T. Adam, *Clementia Principis*, Stuttgart, 1970, pp. 45–9, to relate Book 2 to this doctrine seems entirely misguided.

[1] The aims of the *bellum civile* led by L. Arruntius Camillus Scribonianus in 42 are differently reported: Dio 60. 15, 3 makes him promise to restore the Republic; Suet. *Claudius* 13. 2 implies that he was to replace Claudius as Princeps. It is possible that Scribonianus changed his aim to the second when the first became impractical, like the revolutionaries of 41 (Jos. *AJ* 19. 249 ff.; *BJ* 2. 205, telescoping the process), but he might, like Galba in 69, have claimed to be leaving the choice of Princeps to the Senate.

of holding such ideas, Julius Vestinus Atticus, and that earned him the hostility of Piso and the other working conspirators; that of the Emperor came from entirely different causes.[1] Moreover, if Seneca was trying to reassure the public, he would not expound unacceptable views of the Principate.

That follows also from Seneca's obvious eagerness in *De Clementia* to justify his own position as Nero's *amicus*.[2] Tacitus says that Seneca wrote the speech on *clementia* for Nero in early 55 to demonstrate the excellence of his advice or to show off his talent.[3] Tacitus, of course, tends to impute the worst possible motives, but the former of these was probably one reason behind the speech as it certainly was behind the treatise. 'Scio male audire apud imperitos sectam Stoicorum tamquam duram nimis et minime principibus regibusque bonum daturam consilium', writes Seneca, going on to repeat one of the stock charges against Stoics famous from Cicero's *Pro Murena*, 'obicitur illi, quod sapientem negat misereri, negat ignoscere' (2. 5, 2). Before the charge of subversion was attached to Stoicism late in Nero's reign,[4] philosophers in Roman public life were subject to attack on three principal counts. It was said that they neglected or quickly abandoned politics for philosophy[5]—Seneca was exempt from that; secondly, that their political activities or way of life conflicted with their philosophical creed[6]—Seneca suffered increasingly from this charge as Nero added to his wealth; finally, that their philosophical beliefs were unsuitable for active politics[7]

---

[1] *Ann.* 15. 52, 3; 68.

[2] Giancotti, *RAL* 9 (1954), 597.

[3] *Ann.* 13. 11, 2.

[4] In Greece philosophers had often been thought of as political intriguers, but the initial Roman suspicions were more of a social and moral kind (Plut. *Cato Maior* 22–3; Seneca, *Cons. Helv.* 10. 8: 'corruptores iuventutis').

[5] Cicero attacked the Epicureans for this (*Rep.* 1. 4–5), but they were not the only ones: Sextius refused the *latus clavus* (above, p. 38). Tacitus, *Hist.* 4. 5, 1.

[6] For the first, examples are Cicero on Albucius (*Tusc. Disp.* 5. 108), Brutus on Cicero (*Ad Brut.* 1. 17, 5), Tacitus on Publius Celer (*Hist.* 4. 10). For the second, Seneca, *De Vita Beata* 17–19; Dio 61. 10 and 43. 9, 3, attacking Seneca and Sallust. *Anticatones* were rich in this material.

[7] Cicero, *Fin.* 2. 76 (Epicureans); *Mur.* 61–5 (Stoics); cf. Tac. *Hist.* 3. 81: 'intempestiva sapientia'.

—on this count Seneca had been suspect from the first. Probably Agrippina had this in mind when she made him promise not to teach Nero philosophy.[1] To reassure the public and justify his position, Seneca was at pains to soften the image of Stoic philosophy.

III

Since it is obvious that reassurance of the public was a large part of Seneca's aim, we must assume that the view of the Principate set out in *De Clementia* was basically acceptable to the reading public. But the tone of admonition noted above was not completely empty: there is something in Seneca's view that required urging. To see in *De Clementia* essentially the same ideas as in Nero's opening speech to the Senate is to overlook Seneca's adoption of a metaphysical description of the Principate that refuted the partnership with the Senate urged in the speech.[2] More important, it means ignoring the frequent use of the word *rex* in *De Clementia*, not in abstract discussions of the classic forms of constitution (as in Cicero's *De Re Publica*), but in contemporary Roman contexts. It is true that Nero is never called *rex* directly, but Seneca certainly calls him that by implication, most clearly in passages where he addresses Nero directly: e.g. 'grave putas eripi loquendi arbitrium regibus' (1. 8, 1; cf. 1. 17, 3). Elsewhere, Seneca chooses Augustus as an *exemplum* illustrating the statement, 'regia crudelitas auget inimicorum numerum tollendo' (1. 8, 7–9, 1), and he clearly alludes to his own position in rebutting the charge that 'the Stoic school is unlikely to give good advice "principibus regibusque"' (2. 5, 2).

[1] Suet. *Nero* 52. The story, which has been doubted, at least fits with Tacitus' idea of an appropriate taunt for her to make about Seneca's philosophical productions: '[Burrus and Seneca] trunca scilicet manu et professoria lingua generis humani regimen expostulantes' (*Ann.* 13. 14, 3). Cf. Tacitus, *Agric.* 4. 3.

[2] See p. 139 above. F. Weidauer, *Der Prinzipat in Senecas Schrift de Clementia*, Diss. Marburg, 1950, p. 44, notes correctly that *De Clementia* completely ignores the political sovereignty, even the existence, of Senate and people, whereas the Senate had been offered the constitutional view of the Principate they liked.

This is all very surprising. Cicero pointed out[1] that after the expulsion of the last Tarquin, the Romans were not able to bear the *nomen regis*, but used the word, not as the Greeks to mean a good ruler as opposed to a tyrant, but in a bad sense to indicate anyone who wanted absolute power.[2] There is evidence that the feeling survived into the Principate.[3] Augustus was offered the title *dictator*,[4] but no one even suggested *rex*, though Tacitus writes of Augustus' choice of the *tribunicia potestas*: 'id summi fastigii vocabulum Augustus repperit ne regis aut dictatoris nomen adsumeret.'[5] Tacitus probably reflects the feeling of his own time about the word: Pliny praises Trajan for an achievement as great as the expulsion of the kings—he protected Rome from *regnum*.[6] For Seneca's time, we have evidence from his own work that *rex* was still commonly a term of opprobrium. In condemning the human habit of becoming angry when one's will is crossed, he writes: 'regum nobis induimus animos; nam illi quoque . . . occasionem nocendi captant querendo; acceperunt iniuriam ut facerent.'[7] Elsewhere he says, condemning the idea of dividing *amici* into grades, 'consuetudo ista vetus est regibus regesque simulantibus.'[8] Lucan uses the word in bitterness to damn the Principate.[9]

Of course, this feeling would have been strongest in the Senate,

---

[1] *Rep.* 2. 47–9; 52. Note the speech Livy gives Scipio in 27. 19, 4: 'regnum nomen alibi magnum, Romae intolerabile esse'. Cf. Suet. *Aug.* 94. 3.

[2] Cicero himself applied the term to Clodius, Caesar, and Antony and was similarly burdened with the *verbi invidia* by his detractors. See especially *Pro Sulla* 21–5: 'peregrinus rex'.

[3] See the discussion in Wirszubski, *Libertas*, pp. 121–2, of the difference between *principatus* and *regnum* as felt by the Romans.

[4] *Res Gestae* 5. 1.

[5] *Ann.* 3. 56, 2.

[6] *Pan.* 55. 7. Cf. Suetonius' description in *Gaius* 22. 1: 'nec multum afuit quin statim diadema sumeret speciemque principatus in regni formam converteret.'

[7] *Ep.* 47. 20.

[8] *Ben.* 6. 34, 1; cf. 5. 16, 6: 'ne Romanis quidem regibus'. These examples make very implausible the simple explanation of Seneca's use of the word *rex* offered by Ch. Favez in the commentary on *De Clementia* for the *Univ. de Gand R. de tr.* 106 (1950), note on 1. 3, 4: 'Sénèque n'a plus à l'égard de ce mot et de ce qu'il représente l'aversion des Romains des autrefois.'

[9] e.g. 7. 643; 440 ff.

while *De Clementia* was probably designed to reach a wider public. None the less, Seneca reveals considerable self-consciousness about using the word. It first occurs in the phrase 'regem aut principem' (1. 3, 3), a combination repeated in Book 2 (5, 2). Elsewhere, *rex* alternates with *princeps* in the course of a discussion (1. 7, 1; 1. 13; 1. 16, 1). The most striking formula occurs where Seneca is describing the need of Rome for the Principate: 'principes regesque et quocumque alio nomine sunt tutores status publici' (1. 4, 3).

Cicero's discussion of the word suggests one explanation: that Seneca used the word *rex* because he wished to apply to the *princeps* the conception of the βασιλεύς as opposed to the τύραννος.[1] Certainly, *De Clementia*, particularly the first book, owes much to Hellenistic treatises on kingship.[2] Although Seneca's own characterization of this part of the work lies hidden under a textual corruption in 1. 3, 1,[3] the content itself clearly reveals the theme of the book: *clementia* as the virtue particularly becoming, useful, and necessary to rulers. This is already apparent in the introductory chapter where Seneca says that, in writing about *clementia*, he is holding up to Nero a mirror that shows his own qualities which have won him the love of the Roman people. Then, in 3. 2–13, Seneca discusses why *clementia*, the most appropriate virtue for man, is particularly appropriate in a ruler. From chapter 14 to 19 he discusses the *officia* of the ruler of a state in comparison with those appropriate to other ruler–subject relationships, and, from chapter 20 to the end, the reasons why a ruler should not punish harshly. In each section, there appears the contrast between the king and the tyrant, the one being characterized by *clementia*, the other by *crudelitas*.[4]

[1] This, in essence, is the explanation of Weidauer, op. cit., p. 17. Seneca, he says, is following a genre traditional in Stoic political thought and Greek Fürstenspiegel, and, as a courtier, he found it easy. The use of the word *rex* only showed that he saw the Princeps as an absolute ruler. Adam, *Clementia Principis*, p. 90, has the curious idea that Seneca used the word *regnum* in order to avoid *principatus* which suggested illegitimate *de facto* one-man rule.

[2] The point is recently stressed by Adam, *Clementia Principis*, who on pp. 12–20 gives a list of these works and attempts to classify them into two types.

[3] See below, pp. 151–2.

[4] In the divisions given here, I have followed K. Büchner, *Hermes* 98 (1970),

It is reasonable then to expect this first book to contain much material derived from works of the genre περὶ βασιλείας. Most of these, including all of the Stoic ones, are lost, but the affinities of Seneca's work with the type have been traced through comparison with Xenophon's Κύρου παιδεία, Isocrates' πρὸς Νικοκλέα περὶ τοῦ βασιλεύειν ἢ περὶ βασιλείας and the Νικοκλῆς, Ps-Aristotle's περὶ βασιλείας, Plutarch's πρὸς ἡγεμόνα ἀπαίδευτον,[1] and the neo-Pythagorean works of Ecphantus, Diotogenes, and Sthenidas.[2] These remains of Hellenistic political doctrine, plus passages in Cicero's philosophical works, reveal that there were Greek antecedents for the passages, usually highly theoretical, in which the word *rex* appears: *clementia* as the virtue particularly appropriate to rulers;[3] the king's security guaranteed by the love of his subjects, this love being explained by the metaphor of the ruler as the mind of the state;[4] the prohibition

---

203 ff., who rightly rejects the elaborate structure proposed by M. Fuhrmann, *Gym.* 70 (1963), 492 ff. But Büchner himself also rejects the usual view of the theme of Book 1 accepted here. This rejection seems particularly perverse as his own schema for the book clearly reveals that it is more concerned with clemency as it applies to rulers, than with its general function in human society, which he takes to be the theme.

[1] A. Elias, *De Notione Vocis Clementiae apud philosophos veteres et de Fontibus Senecae Librorum de Clementia*, Königsberg, 1912, pp. 53 ff.

[2] L. Delatte, 'Les traités de la royauté d'Ecphante, Diotogène et Sthénidas', *Bibliothèque de la faculté de Philosophie et Lettres de l'Université de Liège*, fasc. 97, 1942, p. 149, and see the index of authors, p. 314.

[3] I. 3, 3. Cf. Xenophon, *Cyr.* 6. 1, 37 (πραότης); Isocrates, *Nic.* 29–32 (δικαιοσύνη including πραότης). In the Letter of Aristeas 265 φιλανθρωπία is the most important quality. Cicero (*Off.* 1. 85–6; 88; cf. *Rep.* 2. 27) emphasizes *iustitia* and *clementia* as essential in statesmen, but there is no evidence for the view of H. Knoellinger, Teubner edition of Cicero *De Virtutibus*, pp. 56–7 (on which see below, p. 167) that Stoics before Seneca stressed the supremacy of *clementia*: even his frag. 6 gives *iustitia* (joined with *clementia*) as the main virtue of rulers.

[4] I. 3, 4–6. For love as the guarantor of a king's safety: Isocrates, *Ad Nic.* 21; Cicero, *Pro Marc.* 21. This love is founded on recognition of the king's superiority in virtue (Isoc. *Nic.* 29) and his care for his subjects (Xen. *Cyr.* 8. 2, 1; Isoc. *Nic.* 56; Cicero, *Rep.* 1. 55). The analogy, ruler : people :: soul : body, is applied to the Principate in Florus 4. 3 and, according to Tacitus (*Ann.* 1. 12, cf. 1. 13, 4) was used in the senatorial debate on Tiberius' accession. (The basic idea is in Isocrates, *Areop.* 14.) In Cicero, *Rep.* 3. 37, the analogy appears in contrast with the Platonic one of reason governing the inferior parts of the soul (which is felt

of anger in rulers;[1] the parallel with the attitude of the gods toward mortals;[2] the necessity for extraordinary self-control in a ruler because his life is public;[3] the greater security of the mild ruler;[4] the comparison of the king and tyrant;[5] the intimate character of a king's concern for his subjects;[6] the comparison of kingship to the political organization of bees.[7] Conversely, the word is not found in more concrete passages on the application of *clementia*, or where Roman institutions or *exempla* are treated.[8] But the usual way of adapting such Greek arguments was to use a vague word, for example ἡγεμών or ἄρχων—*tutor* or *rector* or *praeses civitatis* might have done in Latin—or to give a full list of alternatives.[9] Tacitus uses periphrases to avoid

by Cicero to suit masters of slaves, rather than kings, *v.* Arist. *Pol.* 1. 2 (1254ᵇ5)). Stoic cosmology naturally colours Seneca's version (e.g. Marc. Aur. 4. 40).

[1] 1. 5, 6. Cf. Isoc. *Ad Nic.* 23.

[2] 1. 7. Cf. Isoc. *Ad Nic.* 5; Letter of Aristeas 188; Plut. *Ad Prin. Inerud.* 780F.

[3] 1. 7, 4–8. 5. Cf. Isoc. *Ad Nic.* 31, 33; *Nic.* 37. Seneca's 'nobilem servitutem' (1. 8, 1) is a translation of ἔνδοξον δουλείαν, the description of monarchy favoured by Antigonos (Aelian, *VH* 2. 20) who may have absorbed the views of his Stoic adviser Persaeus, author of a περὶ βασιλείας (D.L. 7. 36), as suggested by Pohlenz, *Die Stoa*² I, p. 25. Cf. Tiberius in Tac. *Ann.* 4. 40, 1. The evidence is insufficient to justify Adam's elaborate attempt (*Clementia Principis*, pp. 27–30) to distinguish Seneca's interpretation of the phrase from Antigonus'.

[4] 1. 8, 6. Cf. Isoc. *Ad Nic.* 23–4; *Nic.* 32–3.

[5] 1. 11, 4–12. Cf. Cic. *Rep.* 2. 47. For the Stoics, the idea of a moral qualification for kingship comes naturally from their view (D.L. 7. 122) that only wise men should be rulers.

[6] 1. 16, 1. Cf. Isoc. *Nic.* 21.

[7] 1. 19, 2–3. Plato, *Rep.* 520 b, had first used the simile, comparing the guardian to the 'king' bee but in *Pol.* 301 b he denied that there could be found among men a king naturally and immediately distinguished from his subjects. Xenophon (*Cyr.* 5. 1, 24) applied the simile to Cyrus. Seneca adds to the king bee's distinctive size and colour the absence of sting (a feature which Aristotle, *Hist. An.* 5. 22 (553ᵇ), denied and Pliny, *NH* 11. 52, regarded as controversial). The importance of their 'king' to the bees is described in Vergil's *Georgics* 4. 212 ff. and Pliny, *NH* 11. 29, 53, 56. Dio Chrysostom has the same comparison as Seneca in *On Kingship* 4. 62–3.

[8] Hence not in the discussion from 1. 20 to the end of Book 1 on the way the Princeps should deal with crimes against himself and against others (1. 21, 1 contains the proverbial use of the word outside the main argument), nor in Book 2 except for the reference to the criticism of Stoic advisers (2. 5, 2).

[9] See the list of alternatives in Plutarch, *Maxime cum principibus philosopho esse disserendum*, 778D: δυνατοί, ἡγεμονικοί, ἄρχων ἀνήρ, ἡγεμόνας ἢ βασιλεῖς ἢ τυράννους; and Cicero, *Rep.* 3. 37. Seneca uses *rector Romano imperio* in

the word *rex*,[1] although he does not hesitate to apply the word tyrant, with the traditional philosophical description of the tyrant, to Tiberius.[2]

Nor is Seneca just being careless, thoughtlessly mingling Greek arguments, where the terms belong, with Roman notions where it is absent. For some of the 'Roman' passages are, in fact, Greek ideas carefully adapted to omit the word. Thus, where Cicero says that the Greeks regard the king as one 'who is as solicitous for the welfare of his people as is a father for his children, and maintains in the best possible conditions of life those over whom he is set',[3] Seneca urges these same aims on Nero by appealing to the imperial title *pater patriae* (1. 14; 1. 16, 2)[4] and the honorary crown *ob cives servatos* (1. 26, 5) which Augustus noted proudly in the *Res Gestae*[5] and which had appeared on Nero's earliest coins. Why then did Seneca not consistently avoid the word *rex*?

There remains the possibility that Seneca is deliberately drawing attention to his application of traditional theories of kingship to the Principate. He wishes to maintain that the task of those advising kings and *principes* is the same; that the qualities and behaviour appropriate to the just king are appropriate to the Princeps. The phrase 'kings and *principes* and by whatever other name guardians of the public order go' will then be a deliberate expression of impatience with those who attach too much im-

---

Polyb. 12. 5 and *praeses legum, rector civitatis* in *De Ira* 1. 6, 3 where his message is similar to that of *De Clementia*.

[1] *Ann.* 4. 33, 1–2.
[2] Ibid. 6. 6, 2.
[3] *Rep.* 2. 47; cf. 1. 55.
[4] 1. 14, 2: 'cetera enim cognomina honori data sunt; Magnos et Felices et Augustos diximus . . . Patrem quidem Patriae appellavimus, ut sciret datam sibi potestatem patriam, quae est temperantissima liberis consulens suaque post illos reponens.' For Seneca's conception of the *princeps* as *pater* see Weidauer, op. cit., pp. 36–46. On pp. 39–40 he argues that, in this passage, Seneca deliberately rejects the original meaning of the title as an honour to the founder or conserver of the state in favour of the later senses that prevailed when it had become a part of the normal titles of the Princeps, i.e. the analogue with *pater familias* (juristic sense); the inspiration to a relationship of love and respect between ruler and subjects (parenetic sense). This last sense, as the Cicero passage shows, was influenced by Greek ideas and can be traced back as far as Xenophon, *Cyr.* 8. 1, 1.   [5] 34. 2.

portance to the *summi fastigii vocabulum*.[1] This kind of impatience
is easy to parallel in Seneca's other works, though his irritation
there is usually directed, in typical Roman fashion, to the hair-
splitting of Greek philosophers,[2] who concentrate on verbal
differences rather than on substantial similarities. But in *De
Beneficiis*, Seneca, disparaging the motives that moved Brutus to
kill Caesar, suggests, first, the fear of the name of king (*nomen
regis*) and objects that Brutus should have known from Stoic doctrine that the best form of state is that governed by a just king.
To Brutus' other motives—hope of *libertas* and the belief that the
Republic could be restored—Seneca replies that Brutus should
have seen that the minds of men were already set on monarchy.[3]
This passage is in the spirit of *De Clementia*: resigned acceptance
of the Principate on historical grounds combined with a frank
attempt to infuse into the institution the qualities of ideal kingship to which all the philosophical schools paid tribute.

The use of the word *rex* then points to a major aim of *De
Clementia*. Having written Nero's speech to the Senate which
culminated in Nero's promise to observe the proper forms in his
relations with the Senate, Seneca in his *De Clementia*, intended
not only for the Senate but for a wider audience as well, recommends concentration on the reality rather than the forms.[4] The

---

[1] I believe Seneca is deliberately making the same point in *Ep.* 73, 1 where he
argues that the position of a philosopher in retirement is that of a protected
and grateful subject, not an opponent 'magistratuum ac regum eorumve, per
quos publica administrantur'. Cicero (*Rep.* 2. 43, 50), by contrast, holds that the
nomen regium itself can influence the balance of political power.

[2] Thus in *De Clementia* (2. 7, 4), after carefully distinguishing *clementia* from
misericordia and *venia* to keep within the Stoic pale, Seneca exclaims: 'de verbo,
ut mea fert opinio, controversia est, de re quidem convenit.' Similarly, he says
of the traditional argument about the *tria genera vitae* 'videamus an haec omnia
ad idem sub alio atque alio titulo perveniant' (*De Otio* 7. 1). Compare the views
of the orator Crassus in Cicero's *De Or.* 1. 47.

[3] *Ben.* 2. 20. See further on this passage pp. 202 ff.

[4] Weidauer, op. cit., pp. 101–2, argues that the treatise was partly meant to
reconcile the nobility in opposition, to the realities of the Principate. In this
'nobility' he includes Helvidius Priscus and Thrasea Paetus! He is right to see
that they had a different conception of the Principate, but he predates their
opposition to the regime. In 55/6 these men were co-operating with Nero and
his advisers who met their wish for a significant role for the Senate to a large
extent, as we saw (pp. 100 ff.).

practice of applying to the Princeps virtues prominent in Hellenistic treatises on kingship was already long-established.[1] Seneca
meant to apply the fundamental doctrine as well: everything
turned not on constitutional forms and legal limitations, but on
the character of the ruler.[2] The power of Caesar was absolute
(1. 1, 2; 1. 8, 5); it was how he exercised that power that made
the difference between good government and bad. It was the task
of the Princeps' advisers to develop virtue in him; it was the
duty of his subjects to remain peaceful and obedient as long as
he looked out for their welfare. From the good character of the
ruler *recti mores* would develop in the state (2. 2, 1). These were
dangerous ideas for the wrong man. When Seneca's influence
failed, and Nero determined to enjoy the absolutism he had
preached without the restraints,[3] it could be said cruelly, but not
without some truth, that Seneca had been a τυραννοδιδάσκαλος.[4]

IV

That Seneca was not lost in the clouds of Greek theory but
concerned with the political education of the Roman governing
class emerges again from a consideration of the peculiar literary
character of the first book, the emphasis throughout the work
on one aspect of *clementia*, and the strong contrast presented by
the two books.

We have already noted the affinities of Book 1 with Hellenistic

[1] M. P. Charlesworth, *PBA* 23 (1937), 112.

[2] I cannot agree with Dorison, *Quid de clementia L. Annaeus Seneca senserit*,
Cadomi, 1892, p. 54 (followed by Giancotti), that 'Egone ex omnibus mortalibus placui electusque sum, qui in terris deorum vice fungerer' (1. 1, 2) is an
allusion to Nero's choice by the Senate and the army (cf. *Octavia* pp. 487–9)
and thus to the source and limitations of his power; 'ex omnibus mortalibus'
and 'deorum vice' surely show that the choice has been made by God, as in
Pliny, *Pan.* 80. 4: 'liber solutusque tantum caelo vacat [mundi parens] postquam
te dedit, qui erga omne hominum genus vice sua fungereris.' Adam, op. cit.,
pp. 49–50, suggests a deliberate ambiguity.

[3] Suet. *Nero* 37. 3: 'negavit quemquam principum scisse quid sibi liceret.'
This is the negation of *De Clementia* 1. 11, 2: 'haec est in maxima potestate
verissima animi temperantia . . . non priorum principum exemplis corruptum,
quantum sibi in cives suos liceat, experiendo temptare, sed hebetare aciem
imperii sui.'   [4] Dio 61. 10, 2.

treatises on ideal kingship. In the opening comparison of his work to a mirror which the author holds up to Nero, Seneca, in fact, skilfully combines the two approaches characteristic of the two principal types that make up the genre: works giving an idealized portrait of a particular ruler and those giving a general theoretical picture of ideal rule.[1] Yet, by taking as his title and subject one virtue, Seneca gives this book a highly original character.[2] For none of the Hellenistic writers on the duties of a monarch had, as far as we know, called his work by the name of one virtue. And, although they had stressed the qualities of φιλανθρωπία, ἐπιείκεια, and πραότης—the nearest Greek equivalents to clementia in its various aspects—they did not even have a single word to cover the concept that Seneca treats.[3] Seneca then did not write a straight περὶ βασιλείας because he wished to stress clementia, and the reason why he wished to stress clementia must be sought in Rome, more precisely, as will emerge, in the Rome of his own day.

A Roman concept, clementia is mentioned in the Republic as one of the qualities of political men, but really achieved political importance with Caesar.[4] Cicero, seeing the relevance of the Hellenistic notions of kingship to Caesar's position, used them freely in the speeches for Marcellus, Ligarius, and Deiotarus. It is a sad tribute to Cicero's genius as an orator that he immediately caught to perfection that mixture of flattery and admonition that had served the Greeks and was to serve the Romans under the Principate. Seneca's debt to these speeches is undoubtedly great.[5]

[1] Adam, op. cit., pp. 18–19.

[2] Elias, De Notione Vocis Clementiae. Since Elias wrote, in 1912, much more has been written on these works: see T. A. Sinclair, A History of Greek Political Thought, London, 1951, pp. 301–2, and the bibliography of Adam, op. cit.

[3] Weidauer, Der Prinzipat in Senecas Schrift de Clementia, discusses these words on pp. 106–9.

[4] J. Hellegouarc'h, Le vocabulaire latin des relations et des partis politiques sous la république, Paris, 1963, pp. 261–2. Adam, op. cit., pp. 82–3. Seneca mentions the clementia of Julius Caesar not in this work but e.g. De Ira 2. 23, 4. For clementia in Roman politics see Wirszubski, Libertas, pp. 150–3.

[5] Weidauer, p. 93 n. 1, collects parallels between De Clementia and Cicero's Caesarean speeches, but hesitates to maintain that Seneca used them. But Cicero was Seneca's authority on philosophical vocabulary. Seneca would naturally look for any help he gave on the matter of clemency.

We find there the idea of quoting the ruler's own words to bind
him to them and the comparison of the ruler's decision to that
of a father exercising his *patria potestas*.[1] Most important, Cicero
furnished the model for wedding the Greek doctrines and tone to
the Roman concept of *clementia*.

Augustus mentioned with pride in the *Res Gestae* the *clupeus
virtutis* on which *clementia* was among the virtues inscribed;
clementia and *moderatio* appear on Tiberius' coins perhaps celebrating a *clupeus virtutis*; later he received an *ara clementiae*.[2]
Gaius too had been praised for the quality by a terrified Senate,[3]
and Claudius on his accession had promised that the Senate would
now finally enjoy it.[4]

Seneca's reasons for stressing *clementia*, on Nero's accession,
and now, after a murder, when the idea needed reasserting, are
obvious: if *clementia* had long been recognized as one of the most
desirable qualities in the Princeps, it was the one most in need of
emphasis for Nero, not only because of his heredity, but because
of the cruelty of his predecessor.

Now cruelty in Claudius went with a contempt for proper
judicial procedure. His judicial abuses constituted one of the two
major evils of his reign that had been repudiated in Nero's first
speech to the Senate and ridiculed in Seneca's *Apocolocyntosis*.[5]
This may explain one of the most curious features of Seneca's
treatment of *clementia*, namely, his concentration on clemency in
the administration of justice. There has recently been considerable
discussion of the prominence of this theme in *De Clementia*:[6] at

---

[1] *Lig.* 33; *Lig.* 29–31. Compare also *Mar.* 8; *Lig.* 38 for parallelism of the ruler's
attitude and that of the gods; *Mar.* 21 for the idea that the ruler's task is to conserve
the citizens; *Mar.* 22 for the dependence of the citizens' safety on Caesar and
Mar. 32 for the promise of protection in return.

[2] *RG* 34. 2; C. H. V. Sutherland, *JRS* 28 (1938), 129 ff.

[3] Dio 59. 16, 10.   [4] Josephus, *AJ* 19. 246 (ἐπιείκεια).

[5] See pp. 108 ff. and 130.

[6] Weidauer, op. cit., pp. 66–73, explained Seneca's emphasis on clemency in
a ruler by the fact that it provided the only check on the increasingly important
imperial jurisdiction which was not bound by law (though he failed to note how
closely Seneca's definitions and account of the workings of clemency mirror
actual Roman practice, see below, pp. 161 ff.), but it was Fuhrmann, *Gym.* 70
(1963), who first elevated the concern with jurisdiction to the main theme of
the work.

one extreme, it is claimed by Adam that the subject of the whole work is Princeps Iudex; at the other extreme, Seneca's *clementia* is said by Büchner to be wholly political, containing no juristic aspect.[1] The first of these views overlooks the great increase in concentration on judgement and penalty from Book 1 to Book 2 and the presence in both books of instances of *clementia* which lie outside the sphere of jurisdiction proper and concern rather the treatment of defeated enemies by the victor (1. 1, 2; 1. 21, 2–3; 2. 7, 2). But the second extreme view is more in error. The emphasis on *iurisdictio* and *poena* is so pervasive throughout the work and so striking in the definitions of *clementia* in Book 2, the concrete examples are so preponderantly of criminal trials of various kinds, that it is only by taking a very narrow view of jurisdiction that Seneca's emphasis on this theme can be denied. Büchner, in fact, was correct to point out that the clemency discussed by Seneca is that of a man who has absolute power and is not bound by law, and to attack the idea of Fuhrmann that Seneca's *clementia* is judicial equity, the adjustment of law to allow for mitigating circumstances in particular cases.[2] But, as we shall see, that does not mean that Seneca was not concerned with criminal jurisdiction, but that he is concerned with a particular form of jurisdiction, one that only brings out more clearly how closely related *De Clementia* is to practical political life.

This emphasis on the administration of justice, which we have connected with the political programme of Nero's early years, helps to explain the most difficult problem presented by *De Clementia*—the very different character of the two books. For the work has an odd structure that has recently been the object of much scholarly study and debate.[3] In Book 1, chapter 3, Seneca announces a threefold plan. The first rubric is hopelessly corrupt in the manuscripts; the second is the nature of *clementia* and how

---

[1] Adam, op. cit., pp. 20–4; Büchner, *Hermes* 98 (1970), 204–8; 221–3.

[2] See below, pp. 159–61.

[3] Giancotti, *RAL* 10 (1955), 36 ff.; Fuhrmann, *Gym.* 70 (1963), 492 ff.; Adam, op. cit., pp. 23 ff.; Büchner, *Hermes* 98 (1970), 209 ff. The differences in style and vocabulary are analysed by B. Mortureux in *Recherches sur le 'De Clementia' de Sénèque*, Coll. *Latomus* 128 (1973), 75 ff., which appeared after the final revision of this chapter.

it is to be distinguished from vices resembling it; the third concerns the development of the virtue in the mind from its introduction to its assimilation by practice. The second heading obviously fits Book 2; Part Three and perhaps some of Part Two are either lost or were never completed.[1]

Although the subject of Book 2 was apparently in Seneca's mind when he wrote Book 1, the tone and even the ideas in the two books are very different—one scholar has even suggested that Book 2 is the remnant of a first edition, Book 1 the start of a second.[2] The first book, with its precepts and exhortations, exhibits rhetorical *impetus*; the second, with its dry definitions, Stoic *subtilitas*. There are conflicts in terminology, e.g. in Book 1, *misericordia*, *venia*, and *ignoscere* occur as respectable synonyms for *clementia*;[3] in Book 2 they are carefully distinguished from it.[4] In Book 1, *severitas* is opposed to *clementia* and regarded as un-

---

[1] Rightly rejected by most scholars is the theory of F. Préchac, expounded fully in his Budé editions of 1921 and 1961, that the work is complete and follows Seneca's scheme if we regard Bk. 2. 1–2 as covering the first topic, 2. 3–end the second, and Book 1. 3, 2–end the third, and that the parts have simply been transmitted in the wrong order. Arguments against the theory are most conveniently found in Favez, *Clem.*, pp. 128–9, and Giancotti, *RAL* 9 (1954), 597–603. The failure of Book 1 to correspond to Seneca's third rubric is conclusive and Préchac's conjectures in the first rubric (*manu mitissimi Neronis* in Introd., p. xcviii; *humanissimi Neronis* in the text, for the manuscripts' *manumissionis*), designed to make it fit 2. 1–2, are grotesque. (Büchner's suggestion, 'humanae condicionis' (op. cit., p. 220), reflects his erroneous view of the subject of Book 1 (above, p. 143 n. 4).)

A support to the view that the work was never completed is the difficulty of imagining how Seneca would have managed the subject of the third part. On the analogy of *De Ira* one would expect detailed advice on friends, advisers, education, and a multitude of *exempla* presumably of kings. How one could tactfully relate this to Nero is beyond conjecture. If Seneca did leave the work unfinished, either he published it himself, letting the neglected scheme stand as in *De Ira* (where none of the schemes in 2. 18, 3. 1, or 3. 5, 2 is fully carried out), or someone else published it not long after his death, for it may have been used by Pliny in the *Panegyricus* (Durry, *Panégyrique de Trajan*, Introd., p. 31). I regard the first alternative as far more likely, since Seneca, who wrote speeches for Nero on the theme, would not have wasted the great effort he expended on the work, and after Nero's later career, who would have published it?

[2] This ingenious theory of M. Vallette, *Mélanges P. Thomas*, Bruges, 1930, pp. 687–700, has not found favour.

[3] *Misericordia* 1. 1, 4; *venia* 1. 6, 2; *ignoscere* 1. 2, 2; 1. 9, 6; 1. 10, 1 and 4; 1. 24, 1.

[4] *Misericordia* 2. 4, 4; 2. 5–6; *venia* and *ignoscere* 2. 7.

desirable;[1] in Book 2, Seneca emphasizes that *severitas*, being a virtue, cannot be contrary to *clementia* as the *imperiti* think.[2]

None the less, there is no fundamental difference of doctrine.[3] Instead, we have a conflict between 'common usage' and technical philosophical vocabulary.[4] Various explanations have been offered for the lack of harmony between the two books: some have looked for the answer in Seneca's psychological difficulties caused by the murder of Britannicus;[5] others in the stages through which his conception of *clementia* passed in the course of writing;[6] still others in a deliberate division by Seneca of his subject-matter according to two distinct concepts of *clementia*, or two different approaches to its analysis.[7]

Not enough attention has been paid to the double literary character of the work: a kind of περὶ βασιλείας (Book 1), combined with a philosophical dialogue defining and analysing the particular virtue of *clementia* (Book 2), on the model of *De Constantia Sapientis* or (for a particular vice) *De Ira*. Seneca's decision to write a treatise on *clementia* dictated the inclusion of this second element somewhere, but his concern with the theme

---

[1] 1. 1, 4; 1. 6, 1; 1. 22, 2.

[2] 2. 4, 1.

[3] In Book 1 Seneca is careless with his terms but the substantial features of *clementia* are given: *clementia* is opposed to *crudelitas* (1. 25–6); *moderatio, modus, temperamentum* characterize *clementia* which must not be practised without discrimination (1. 2, 2); *clementia* exceeds the demands of justice (1. 20; 2. 7, 3). The grounds for *clementia* stressed in 2. 7 are given in 1. 2, 2; 15, 7. In both books the treatment of subjects and defeated enemies is regarded as the same in principle (1. 21; 2. 7, 2).

[4] Favez in the commentary *ad* 2. 4, 3; p. 143. *Ep.* 59. 1–4 shows Seneca's interest in the difference between 'verba publica' and 'significatio Stoica'. He was not prepared to condemn the first on all occasions—nor had Panaetius been (Cicero, *Off.* 2. 35).

[5] W. Richter, *RhM* 108 (1965), 169.

[6] Giancotti, *RAL* 10 (1955), 50–2: Seneca had not yet thought out the definitions in Book 2 when he wrote, perhaps even published, Book 1.

[7] Fuhrmann, *Gym.* 70 (1963), 506, thinks that we have the political concept in the first book, the legal one in the second: the first concept designed for the Roman Principate, the second defined with the tools of Greek philosophy for any system. Adam, op. cit., follows Fuhrmann, but thinks the two concepts conflicting: Seneca, unable to harmonize them, left the work incomplete (p. 10 n. 2; p. 23). Büchner, *Hermes* 98 (1970), 209, thinks the difference lies in the methods of approach.

of the good ruler meant that it was postponed until Book 2. The bridge between the two parts is furnished by the introduction to Book 2 which relates a story illustrating Nero's reluctance to sign death-warrants. Some contrast between the two books is thus inevitable: in the first, Seneca wished to capture the kind of rhetorical effect produced by Isocrates' essays or Cicero's Caesarean speeches, or the later discourses on kingship by Dio Chrysostom, while the second book was bound to contain some dry analysis in the dry Stoic style. In fact, Seneca's emphasis on the juristic aspect of *clementia* made the second book especially dry, producing the conflict in terminology noted above. For this aspect of *clementia* was the hardest to reconcile with Stoic doctrine and therefore involved Seneca in sophistic reasoning and cavilling distinctions. Yet the reconciliation was important, principally because the chief moral influence on the Princeps was a Stoic and known to be one, but also because Stoicism provided the moral support and the ethical vocabulary for the most politically critical of the governing class.

It is time to see what difficulties Stoicism presented for Seneca's conception and how he attempted to solve them. In 1912, Elias remarked that the definitions of *clementia* offered by Seneca appeared to be new.[1] Others before and after him have simply assumed that Seneca derived his definitions from earlier Stoics though no traces survive.[2] More recently, intermediate views have been put forth: that Seneca's originality consists in his application of Stoic doctrine to his immediate situation,[3] or that Seneca is following recent moderate Stoics against older more orthodox ones.[4] This diversity of opinion reflects a central problem: Seneca is not usually an originator of the philosophical doctrines he preaches,[5] but the evidence we have of Stoic views

[1] *De Notione Vocis Clementiae*, p. 53.
[2] Dorison, op. cit., p. 5 n. 1; Préchac, op. cit., pp. lxxvi–lxxvii.
[3] Giancotti, *RAL* 10 (1955), 51–2; Adam, *Clementia Principis*, p. 19.
[4] Fuhrmann, *Gym.* 70 (1963), 514.
[5] Though he regards some divergence of belief as possible within Stoicism, and often asserts the right to express his own opinion (above, p. 131 n. 6), his intervention seems to be on specific points where he improves arguments or chooses between versions, and his real originality was in the application of Stoic doctrine to the problem of moral improvement (*Ep.* 64. 7 ff.).

on this subject is not wholly reconcilable with Seneca's definitions or with his ideas on the place of *clementia* in the exercise of justice. Unless we have been very unfortunate in our Stoic fragments, it begins to look as if Seneca really was, as he said, caught between the *imperiti* (2. 4, 1; 5, 2) with their unsympathetic view of Stoicism, and the rigorous Stoics (2. 3, 2; perhaps 1. 2, 1) who would scorn Seneca's adaptations of their philosophy.

Early in Book 1, Seneca claims that it follows from Stoicism, and from Epicureanism as well,[1] that *clementia* of all the virtues most befits man: it is the quality through which man as a social animal fulfils his function of helping society (1. 3, 2). This is the Stoic φιλανθρωπία, more directly referred to later as 'humani generis amor'.[2] Appearing commonly in the remains of Hellenistic treatises on kingship, it was probably included by the Stoics Persaeus, Sphaerus, and Cleanthes in their works on the subject.[3]

The type of *clementia* that Caesar had advertised—willingness to overlook injuries to oneself and to spare the enemy in foreign or civil war—is also prominent in Seneca's treatise.[4] It easily fitted the picture of the *sapiens*, the only true king in the Stoic view,[5] for the *sapiens* does not regard most 'injuries' as such, and avenges only those essential to his safety. Nor is he moved by anger against an offender. Cicero's definition of *clementia* in *De Inventione* is based on this idea.[6] This quality is πραότης which

---

[1] The Epicurean Philodemus speaks of ἐπιείκεια, πραότης, and ἡμερότης but, according to O. Murray, 'Philodemus on the Good King according to Homer', *JRS* 55 (1965), 168, neither this nor Seneca proves that these were Epicurean notions. Yet Philodemus περὶ ὀργῆς, especially col. 24, 17–36 (ed. Wilkes, 1913), seems to be adapting Stoic insistence on φιλανθρωπία etc. to Epicurean doctrine.

[2] 1. 11, 2: this at least can be extracted from a very corrupt passage. Cf. *SVF* 3. 292.

[3] M. E. Reesor, *The Political Theory of the Old and Middle Stoa*, New York, 1951, pp. 18–19, thinks that we have some indication of what was said in the Stoic treatises in the terminology used by Cleanthes and Chrysippus of the gods. The latter called the gods φιλάνθρωποι.

[4] 1. 9–10. Also 1. 5, 5; 2. 2, and especially 1. 20, 2: 'nunc illum [principem] hortamur, ut manifeste laesus animum in potestate habeat et poenam, si tuto poterit, donet, si minus temperet . . .'

[5] *SVF* 3. 617. On the *sapiens*' reluctance to avenge, Seneca, *Ep.* 81. 7.

'*Inv.* 2. 164 (a subdivision of *temperantia*): 'Clementia per quam animi

the *sapiens* possesses by virtue of extirpating the dangerous πάθος of *ira*.[1] The opposition of *clementia* and *ira* is found in Seneca's treatise (1. 5, 6), but it is *ira* in the form of *crudelitas* that is technically opposed to *clementia*.[2]

In Seneca and the men of the Late Stoa this negative notion of πραότης was coloured by the other Stoic notion of love for humanity and given more positive psychological content. In one of Seneca's letters *clementia* is described as the virtue 'quae alieno sanguini tamquam suo parcit et scit homini non esse homine prodige utendum'.[3] But orthodox Stoicism allowed one little in this direction. Later in Epictetus, Musonius Rufus, and Marcus Aurelius we find τὸ πρᾶον in company with τὸ ἐπιεικές and συγγνώμη, and, in the latter, with some embarrassment, ἔλεος.[4] These natural combinations had appeared in Hellenistic treatises and in Cicero's speeches.[5] Similarly, Seneca used *misericordia*, *ignoscere*, and *clementia* as synonyms in the first book, but when he came to giving definitions of *clementia* he distinguished it sharply, like Cicero in the philosophical works,[6] from *misericordia*. The objection to *misericordia* was that it was a form of *aegritudo* which, being a πάθος, must not occur in the *sapiens*. *Clementia*, then, in its psychological aspect, still had to be defined in negative terms.[7]

temere in odium alicuius iniectionis concitati comitate retinentur.' Cf. *SVF* 3. 632.

[1] πραότης was opposed to anger by Plato, defined by Aristotle as a mean with regard to anger inclining towards the negative side. For the Stoics (*SVF* 3. 443–4), *ira* demanded complete extirpation. See Elias, *De Notione Vocis Clementiae*, pp. 4–13; 19–25.

[2] 2. 4, 1–3. *Crudelitas* is here distinguished from *feritas* on the same grounds as, in *De Ira* 2. 5, 2, *ira* is distinguished from *feritas* (which there includes *crudelitas*). Perhaps Seneca here had in mind the view that Sallust attributes to Caesar: 'quae apud alios iracundia dicitur ea in imperio superbia atque crudelitas' (*BC* 51. 14).

[3] *Ep.* 88. 30.

[4] Elias, op. cit., pp. 22–33. Marcus' reserve shows in 2. 13, but the reservation is omitted in 7. 26.

[5] e.g. *Mar.* 12; *Lig.* 15.   [6] *Tusc.* 3. 20–1.

[7] A papyrus fragment, dated a century after *De Clementia*, seems to show that the Stoa was still identified with a view of φιλανθρωπία that excluded the notion of συμπάθεια. Critics replied that this reduced φιλανθρωπία to social courtesy. See D. Comparetti, 'Frammento filosofico da un papiro greco-egizio', *Festschrift Theodor Gomperz*, Vienna, 1902, pp. 80 ff.

Seneca gives four definitions:

(1) CLEMENTIA EST TEMPERANTIA ANIMI IN POTESTATE ULCISCENDI VEL LENITAS SUPERIORIS ADVERSUS INFERIOREM IN CONSTI-TUENDIS POENIS.

Plura proponere tutius est, ne una finitio parum rem com-prehendat et, ut ita dicam, formula excidat; itaque dici potest et

(2) INCLINATIO ANIMI AD LENITATEM IN POENA EXIGENDA.

Illa finitio contradictiones inveniet, quamvis maxime ad verum accedat, si dixerimus

(3) CLEMENTIAM ESSE MODERATIONEM ALIQUID EX MERITA AC DEBITA POENA REMITTENTEM:

reclamabitur nullam virtutem cuiquam minus debito facere. Atqui hoc omnes intellegunt

(4) CLEMENTIAM ESSE, QUAE SE FLECTIT CITRA ID, QUOD MERITO CONSTITUI POSSET. (2. 3.)

Temperantia animi, in the first, and *moderatio*, in the third, give the negative psychological aspect with which *crudelitas* as *intemperantia animi* (2. 4, 2) is contrasted. From this psychological point of view, *severitas*, also a virtue, accords with *clementia* and is not, as the *imperiti* think, its opposite: that role is assigned to *crudelitas*.[1]

There is another criterion, not completely distinguished by Seneca from the psychological one, by which *clementia* and *severitas* stand together, and by which *severitas* is distinguish-able from *crudelitas*. This is the application of *ratio*, which I shall call the behavioural criterion.[2] *Clementia* and *severitas* are both virtues, and virtue, to a Stoic, is the exercise of reason. Seneca uses the words *temperamentum*, *modus*, and *moderatio*; his examples

[1] 2. 4, 1–3. Unfortunately, in what we have of the treatise, Seneca has not discussed *severitas* fully enough for us to grasp his meaning securely. For one aspect of it see below, p. 164 n. 1.

[2] These two aspects of *clementia* correspond to two of Seneca's three divisions of ethics in *Ep*. 89. 14: *de impetu, de actionibus*.

show he is thinking of the process of arriving at a decision based on reasons.[1] By this criterion, *clementia* is distinguished from *venia* which performs what it believes unjustified (2. 7).

The four definitions which Seneca intends to be complementary gradually make more explicit the sphere of operation of *clementia* and its external result—the obvious hallmark of the virtue in common usage. The 'in constituendis poenis' of the first and the 'in poena exigenda' of the second simply give the sphere of operation; the third (which Seneca introduces as controversial) reduces the psychological aspect in favour of 'behaviour' and external result: 'the moderation that remits something from the punishment that is deserved and due'. The last repeats this with an alteration we shall have to return to: 'which *could* have been deservedly imposed'.

Now, by stressing, in his definitions, the place of *clementia* in jurisdiction, Seneca has defined his way into at least apparent contradiction with his school. The Stoic conception of justice, taken over from Aristotle, was practical wisdom in things to be assigned,[2] more concretely, as a distribution to each of what was κατ' ἀξίαν.[3] How one arrived at what was deserved is made clear in a fragment from Stobaeus. In the case of punishment, it was what was fixed by law: 'They say that the good man is not lenient (ἐπιεικῆ), for the lenient man is critical of the deserved punishment (τῆς κατ' ἀξίαν κολάσεως), and it is the same to be lenient and to assume that the punishments fixed by law are too harsh for wrongdoers and to think that the law-giver distributes punishments against desert. They say that the law is good, being right reason (λόγον ὀρθόν).'[4] Similarly, Diogenes Laertius says the Stoic wise men 'are not pitiful and make

---

[1] e.g. I. 22.

[2] Zeno's conception of justice, clearly from Aristotle, was practical wisdom in things to be assigned (*SVF* I. 200).

[3] In a fragment of Ariston justice is a distribution to each of that κατὰ ἀξίαν (*SVF* I. 374). *SVF* 3. 289 shows that Chrysippus too held this view. Finally the same view is found in Musonius Rufus 8 (Hense, p. 33): προσήκει μὲν τῷ βασιλεῖ . . . τὰ δίκαια βραβεύειν τοῖς ὑπηκόοις, ὡς μήτε πλέον ἔχειν μήτε ἐλαττοῦσθαι μηδένα παρὰ τὴν ἀξίαν, ἀλλὰ καὶ τιμῆς καὶ τιμωρίας τυγχάνειν τοὺς ἀξίους; and attributed to Lucilius by Seneca in *Ep.* 81. 7.

[4] *SVF* 3. 640, 613.

no allowance for anyone; they never relax the penalties fixed by the laws, since indulgence (τό γε εἴκειν) and pity (ἔλεος) and even equitable consideration (ἡ ἐπιείκεια) are marks of a weak mind, which affects kindness in place of chastising. Nor do they deem punishments too severe.'[1] The wise man is, in fact, a *iudex severus*.[2] A precious chapter in Aulus Gellius[3] suggests that the view goes back as far as Chrysippus who represented justice as a virgin, pure, inflexible towards wrongdoers and towards τοὺς ἐπιεικεῖς λόγους.

Stoic doctrine then seems to have ruled out precisely that mitigation of penalties which forms the main content of Seneca's *clementia*, on two grounds: first, that one is apt to modify penalties under the influence of emotion; second, that one must not modify the penalties κατ' ἀξίαν laid down by ὀρθὸς λόγος as just.

We have already considered Seneca's handling of the first objection: *clementia*, as opposed to *misericordia*, represents a control of the passions; in this the clement judge affords no contrast with the severe one. Seneca's answer to the second seems to be first the notion of rationality: the fact that *clementia* leads to a rationally justified remission of penalties. But he also suggests, in his modification of 'merita ac debita poena' to 'quod merito constitui posset', that justice may lay down a range of penalties, the most lenient of which would be selected by *clementia*, without violating justice.

A mitigation of penalties that does not offend the demands of justice but rather fulfils them may well suggest the Aristotelian theory of ἐπιείκεια, and it has, in fact, been proposed by Fuhrmann[4] that Seneca's *clementia* is this Aristotelian equity, whose nature is to be a correction of law where its universality makes it imperfect, a kind of justice going beyond the written

---

[1] D.L. 7. 123 (*SVF* 3. 641).

[2] *SVF* 3. 639. The equivalence of αὐστηρός here with *severus* was suggested to me by Professor Brunt. Hence Seneca's eagerness to show that his *clementia* is not the opposite of *severitas*.

[3] *NA* 14. 4 (not in *SVF*). Cf. Plut. *Cato Minor* 4. 1.

[4] *Gym.* 70 (1963), 512–13. His view is accepted by Adam, *Clementia Principis*, pp. 36 ff.; 90.

law.[1] The original Stoic doctrine of justice, outlined above, sounds, from its emphasis on statutory penalties, as if it had been formulated in direct opposition to Aristotle's theory. Yet it is not difficult to see how Aristotle's concept could have been adapted so as to avoid conflict with Stoic beliefs, while giving their system greater flexibility. Seneca could have argued, as Cicero in *De Legibus*, that there is often a disparity between the dictates of *recta ratio* and the provisions of human law, and that *clementia* was needed to correct the penalties of written law so as to conform with the justice laid down by *recta ratio*.[2]

But Seneca has not done this. His theory is clearly not a borrowing from Aristotle, for it lacks all the distinctive features of his ἐπιείκεια. One of Aristotle's most original conceptions was the functional aspect of equity, defined by one lawyer thus: 'Equity constitutes legal dynamics as against legal statics and discharges the function of correction, completion, or adaptation where there is a gap or a defect in the formulation of the law.'[3] This function is exercised not only by the law courts, but also by the legislative assembly through ψηφίσματα.[4] Seneca's *clementia*, by contrast, does not possess the functional aspect at all, and its operation, where it applies to government, is limited to criminal jurisdiction.

Furthermore, so far from being a correction of law, Seneca's *clementia* bears a very ambiguous relation to law. At one point, Seneca has Nero say that, in practising *clementia*, he acts as if he were about to account for his actions to the laws he has rescued

---

[1] *EN* 5. 10 (1137ᵇ26); *Rhet.* 1. 13 (1374ᵃ26). The reason for the Stoic position is not recoverable. It might stem from their distrust of the people who actually exercised jurisdiction in the Greek cities they knew. Aristotle himself not only disapproved of the Ephors in Sparta (*Pol.* 2. 6, 16 (1270ᵇ30)) and Cosmi in Crete (*Pol.* 2. 7, 6 (1272ᵃ38)) judging without the guidance of a written law code, but admitted that where, as in Athens, the citizens heard lawsuits and supplemented and modified the law by their judgements in particular cases, it was difficult to ensure their doing this properly (*Pol.* 3. 10, 5–6 (1286ᵃ)). The Athenian dicasts were unlikely to include a majority of *sapientes*. Under Athenian law, since many penalties were not fixed by statute, the dicasts frequently imposed the penalty after hearing the proposals of plaintiff and defendant.

[2] *SVF* 3. 315–21.

[3] M. Hamburger, *Morals and Law, the Growth of Aristotle's Legal Theory*, New Haven, Conn., 1951, p. 101.

[4] *EN* 5. 10, 7 (1137ᵇ29).

from oblivion (1. 1, 4).[1] This suggests that *clementia* is in accordance with the laws (though the Princeps is not obliged to obey them). But elsewhere Nero is given the striking epigram: 'occidere contra legem nemo non potest, servare nemo praeter me' (1. 5, 4). The norm according to which we recognize *clementia* and *severitas* is not law. Seneca's clemency like Aristotle's equity claims full justice for its actions which follow the *aequum et bonum* (1. 18, 1; 2. 7, 3; 2. 1, 4). But whereas equity is juster than the just defined as existing law, clemency acts relative to a norm itself vaguely described as *aequum, merita ac debita poena, quod merito constitui posset*.[2] The *merita ac debita poena* is clearly here some standard outside the mind of the judge.[3] It is what traditional Stoicism would call the just penalty—as indeed does Musonius Rufus writing after Seneca.[4] But Seneca completely ignores the usual Stoic identification of the just penalty with the statutory penalty.

Finally, although Aristotle did bow to the traditional connotations of ἐπιείκεια and spoke only of correcting the law in the direction of mildness, his definition could cover stiffening of the law as well.[5] Seneca, however, limits *clementia* in his definitions to mitigation of the penalty; it is *severitas* that covers rational adjustments in the other direction.[6]

Aristotle's ἐπιείκεια then cannot shed light on how Seneca envisaged the operation of his *clementia*, but some clarification of his doctrine is offered, I believe, in the historical sources, where they report instances of jurisdiction by the Emperor or the Senate. The type of procedure involved here is *cognitio* and one major respect in which it differed from the regular forms of civil procedure before *praetor* and *iudex* and from the late Republican

---

[1] See above, p. 138 n. 5.

[2] Giancotti, *RAL* 10 (1955), 53–5, points out the problem, but seems to assume that the norm of legally fixed penalties is in Seneca's mind.

[3] As opposed to that in the definition of *venia* as 'poenae meritae remissio' where, as Seneca makes clear, the judge is not imposing the penalty he thinks is deserved (2. 7, 1 and 3). Giancotti, op. cit., p. 53, is certainly right here as against Favez, op. cit., p. 141 (note on 2. 7, 1).

[4] Above, p. 158 n. 3.

[5] Hamburger, *Morals and Law*, pp. 90–1; 94; 99.

[6] See below, p. 164 n. 1.

quaestio system for major criminal cases was in the freedom of the judge to fix the penalty. Even where the case was covered by existing law, the imperial and senatorial courts were not bound to apply the legal penalty, although it served as a respected precedent.[1] As Pliny was to say: 'senatui licet et mitigare leges et intendere.'[2]

Two cases in Tacitus' *Annales* before the Senate are particularly relevant here as they include discussion of the penalty. In 21 Clutorius Priscus was charged with writing a poem during Drusus' illness, in which he anticipated his death.[3] In Tacitus' account no legally defined charge is named, but for the purposes of a senatorial trial the formulation of the charge could be loose as cases did not have to be brought under an existing law. The consul designate proposed the death penalty. Marcus Lepidus argued instead for *interdictio aqua et igni*, 'quod perinde censeo ac si lege maiestatis teneretur'. He said that if the crime itself were considered, no penalty could be too harsh, but that the *moderatio* of the Princeps as well as ancient and modern precedents suggested a way of avoiding both *severitas* and *clementia*. Clutorius' life could be saved without endangering the state, while his death would provide no lesson. *Moderatio* here is the favoured word, while *clementia* (which would result in acquittal) designates excessive leniency. *Severitas* is the course supported by the consul designate which, according to Lepidus, was not undeserved. In Seneca's language, the death penalty was 'quod merito constitui posset'; the statutory penalty was what *clementia* dictated. The arguments through which Lepidus justified applying the legal penalty cover the last two of the three purposes Seneca recommends to the Princeps in punishing injuries to others: 'aut ut eum, quem punit, emendet, aut ut poena eius ceteros meliores reddat, aut ut sublatis malis securiores ceteri vivant' (1. 22, 1).

In 62 the first case of *maiestas* since Nero's accession came before the Senate, and the consul designate proposed a particularly brutal form of the death penalty. This time Thrasea Paetus objected,

---

[1] A full account of the system is given in E. Levy, *Bull. dell'Ist. di Diritto Romano* 45 (1938), 57 ff.

[2] *Ep.* 4. 9, 17.

[3] *Ann.* 3. 49–50.

proposing the penalty of banishment prescribed by law. He argued that the defendant deserved the worst, but that the Senate was not bound to inflict 'quidquid nocens reus pati mereretur'. Application of the legal penalty here counts as *clementia*. In his reply, Nero called it *moderatio* and the original proposal *severitas*, but the Emperor held that the *clementia* should have been left to him; the Senate should have fixed the 'pro magnitudine delicti poena'.[1]

Suetonius records instances of Augustus' clemency in imposing light penalties.[2] In one case the standard by which the Princeps' *lenitas* is measured is the legal penalty—that of the *Lex Cornelia de falsis*, and *ratio* is certainly involved in remitting the penalty.[3] Similarly, Claudius 'nec semper praescripta legum secutus duritiam lenitatemve multarum ex bono et aequo, perinde ut adficeretur, moderatus est'. The example of *lenitas* offered is from civil law; that of *duritia* from criminal—Claudius condemned men to the beasts.[4]

Here in imperial and senatorial *cognitio* we have the situation for which Seneca's recommendations are designed. The Stoic rule about keeping to the penalties prescribed by law was becoming useless in a system where, increasingly, it was legal for the judge to decide the penalties and where for many charges handled no precisely appropriate law existed. Nor was it obvious what the penalty κατ' ἀξίαν was when *cognitio* applied, not a standard fixed by law, but the precedent of the legal penalty, plus moral considerations of desert, deterrence, reform, and security, each case being liable for consideration in the light of the basic principles of punishment. In a provocative tone, Seneca describes *clementia* as a lessening of the 'merita ac debita

---

[1] *Ann.* 14. 48–9. Compare the case of the household of the murdered Pedanius Secundus (*Ann.* 14. 42–5), where the Senate is free to decide, in the matter of punishment, between *misericordia* which would mitigate the *mos antiquus*, the application of the *vetus mos*, or *saevitia* which would sharpen the established penalties (45. 2). Tacitus calls the precedent *vetus mos*; Cassius Longinus appeals to the Augustan *SC Silanianum*. But there is no error, as the Senate is not bound by the *SC*, which acts only as a precedent. Hence Cassius has recourse to the deterrent argument. In a similar case Augustus, apparently personally trying the case, refused to punish the slaves (Seneca, *NQ* 1. 16, 1).

[2] *Aug.* 51.   [3] Ibid. 33. 2.   [4] *Claudius* 14.

poena'—presumably the penalty which, in a particular case, is justifiably advocated as deserved—but in his final definition he alters this to 'quod merito constitui posset'. The Stoic demand for justice without its inflexibility could be met within the framework of *cognitio* by conceiving the penalty to be mitigated as the harshest of a range of penalties that could justly be imposed. *Clementia* is relative to the harshest penalties justifiable in the case, i.e. not to a fixed norm but to *severitas*.[1] Both are compatible with justice and both are virtues in that they give proper reasons for their different proposals. 'Clementia hoc primum praestat ut quos dimittit nihil aliud illos pati debuisse pronuntiet' (2. 7, 3).

Further confirmation that Roman procedure, not Aristotle, is in Seneca's mind comes from the grounds on which the decision to remit penalties is to be based. Leaving aside the vexed question of whether or not the indubitable appearance of the Aristotelian notions of equity in Roman oratory and rhetorical works from the late Republic actually reflects the workings of Roman law,[2] we can see that the grounds Seneca cites include, but go beyond, the equitable in Aristotle's sense. Aristotelian in inspiration are pleas like compulsion from outside (which diminished responsibility) and timid action signifying reluctance (1. 15, 7); or that the defendant was deceived or misled by wine (diminished responsibility); or that his aim was morally good: 'si honestis causis pro fide, pro foedere, pro libertate in bellum acciti sunt' (2. 7, 2). *Clementia* can spare the innocent when 'fortuna pro culpa est' (1. 2, 1), the Aristotelian ἀτύχημα.[3]

But the reasons for *clementia* most emphasized by Seneca—curability and particularly youth as an argument for curability (1. 2, 2; 2. 7, 1); age; *dignitas* (1. 1, 4); the glory that will accrue to the Emperor if he spares those who wish to harm him (1. 20, 2–21)—do not belong to Aristotelian equity. We find them, in the rhetorical writers, among the arguments used in *deprecatio*.[4]

---

[1] Lipsius' explanation of 'quod merito constitui posset' is still the clearest: 'potuisse merito fieri et non potuisse; utrumque cum modo et sine culpa. Illud severitas fuisset, at hoc clementia.'

[2] Hamburger, *Morals and Law*, p. 108, has a useful summary of the controversy.

[3] The fullest exposition of Aristotelian equity is in *Rhet.* 1. 13 (1374 a 26 ff.).

[4] Naturally, arguments used in *deprecatio* include the 'Aristotelian' type as well.

Cicero, listing these in *De Inventione*,[1] says they were not properly used *in iudicio* except as supporting arguments, but were appropriate in the Senate debating about foreign enemies or on the *consilium* of Opimius when he made his inquiry under the *SC ultimum*. In *Pro Ligario*, Cicero used arguments of this type—the glory to be gained through *clementia*, the *dignitas* of Tubero—but said that they were appropriate not to a trial before *iudices* but before a father.[2] Quintilian agrees with Cicero that such arguments cannot be other than supporting ones *in iudiciis* but adds that *deprecatio* is appropriate before the Senate, the people (presumably a reference to the old *iudicia populi* where political arguments had been freely used), and the Princeps.[3] Mommsen's list of grounds on which imperial judges fixed penalties under the Empire shows the same combination of 'Aristotelian' and non-Aristotelian reasons.[4]

[1] 2. 104 ff.; curability 2. 106; *dignitas* 2. 107. Definition of *deprecatio* in 1. 15: 'deprecatio est, cum et peccasse et consulto peccasse reus se confitetur et tamen, ut ignoscatur, postulat.'

[2] *Lig.* 29–30.

[3] 7. 4, 18–19. We find here the arguments of curability, *dignitas*, the glory of the judge. The importance of this passage to the understanding of *cognitio* is discussed in Levy, op. cit., p. 84. Note an example of such pleading before the Princeps in Quint. 5. 13, 5. That age and birth were often grounds for mild punishment in the senatorial court is shown by Garnsey, *Social Status and Legal Privilege*, p. 35.

[4] *Strafrecht*, pp. 1042–4: 1, 2, and 15 are of the non-Aristotelian *deprecatio* type. The freedom of this procedure naturally allowed for the kind of considerations that figured in decisions outside the sphere of jurisdiction proper. Hence Tacitus, who knew how trials before the Senate were conducted, could borrow from the famous Sallustian account of the debate on the punishment of the Catilinarian conspirators, though that action by the Senate under the *SC ultimum* was not technically a trial (cf. Cicero, *Inv.* 2. 110, justifying the use of 'aliquod exemplum . . . quod in senatu agatur' to illustrate pleading in *iuridiciales causae*).

R. S. Rogers, *Stud. presented to D. M. Robinson*, II (1953), p. 711, suggests that Tacitus' account of Antistius' trial in 62 is suspiciously like that of Clutorius Priscus and that both are written to the pattern of the debate in Sallust—a pattern that had passed into the rhetorical schools. His further point, that Tacitus' whole account of the Antistius trial can be dismissed as fiction designed to glorify Thrasea, does not necessarily follow from this first point and is not convincingly argued (see the objections of Allison and Cloud, *Latomus* 21 (1962), 728 n. 1). The resemblance to the argumentation of Caesar in Sallust is certainly striking. Roman senators were probably familiar with the debate, but Tacitus or a literary source could have constructed the speeches on a Sallustian model. The word

When did the concept of *clementia* found in Seneca arise? Hellenistic kingship treatises offer little help: φιλανθρωπία and ἐπιείκεια each occur in conjunction with δικαιοσύνη,[1] and a softening of penalties is recommended here and there,[2] but we have no indication that they anticipated Seneca's complicated mechanism. Whatever the other Stoics said about the king as judge, the view of Chrysippus and his successors on punishment became established as that of the Stoa, and Seneca's formulation results from his struggle with that view.

Fuhrmann has suggested that the Middle Stoa may have modified the Stoic view of *clementia* in the direction of Seneca's theory.[3] In *De Officiis*, much of which depends on Panaetius, Cicero recommends *placabilitas* and *clementia* provided that *severitas* is used in administering the state. The proper attitude in punishing, he says, omits scorn and anger, and aims at the interests of the state only.[4] So far we have nothing more than the standard Stoic praise of πραότης as applied to the judge, with their views on αὐστηρία preserved. But embedded in the passage are some more specific recommendations: that the penalty should not be greater than the crime; and that one should not overlook some and punish other instances of the same crime. Finally, a search for the mean in punishment is enjoined. That φιλανθρωπία stands behind these ideas is suggested by another passage (2. 18) where the punishment to be inflicted on those attempting to injure us is laid down as 'quantam aequitas humanitasque patitur'. *Aequitas* elsewhere (1. 29–30) is roughly equivalent to *iustitia*, and Cicero's *humanitas* here is clearly not envisaging less than a just penalty, but is concerned with the attitude of the punisher.

clementia does not occur in Caesar's speech. It would be interesting to know if Thrasea actually used it in a way so like Seneca's use, or if Tacitus himself introduced the word into his account.

[1] Adam, op. cit., pp. 36–8.

[2] Isocrates, *Ad Nic.* 23; *Letter of Aristeas* 187, cf. 191; Philo (*Jos.* 22) and Diotogenes (Stob. *Anth.* 269. 1) advocate ἐπιείκεια as a softening of penalties.

[3] Fuhrmann, *Gym.* 70 (1963), 514 n. 34.

[4] 1. 88. Weidauer, pp. 88, 106 ff., thinks *placabilitas* and *clementia* translate φιλανθρωπία and ἐπιείκεια respectively. But πραότης must have figured in Cicero's source, since it is the opposite of anger which is prominent in the discussion. Is *placabilitas* πραότης and *clementia* φιλανθρωπία?

The recommendations in the first *De Officiis* passage belong, for Seneca, to justice, not *clementia*,[1] and they are not specifically limited to judges, although it is notable that *clementia* is applied by Cicero to a man who can fix penalties in administering justice. Even at the end of the Republic when the *quaestio* system flourished, rare offences and minor crimes were probably left to the summary jurisdiction of the magistrates, and, even more important, the jurisdiction of provincial governors over *peregrini* and citizens in non-capital cases, and even sometimes in capital cases, was of the *cognitio* type.[2] Cicero's sermon to Quintus on the evils of *ira* in a governor partly concerned jurisdiction.[3] Have we a remnant in this part of *De Officiis* of Panaetius' thought on the subject of magistrates?[4]

If Knoellinger's reconstruction of Cicero's treatise *De Virtutibus* from a fifteenth-century French work could be accepted with confidence,[5] it would provide evidence that before Seneca, the Stoics, whose doctrines clearly infuse the material, had accepted *clementia* as a virtue distinguished from *misericordia*, and had admitted it into the administration of justice with the definition:

[1] These ideas, together with that of keeping the mean, occur in *De Ira* (1. 17, 5–18, 2) as part of the behaviour of the judge who relies on *ratio* rather than *ira*, and in company with the notions of devotion to the truth and concern for the defendant which, in *De Clementia* (1. 20, 2), are specifically assigned to *iustitia* rather than *clementia*.

[2] Garnsey, *JRS* 58 (1968), 55 ff.

[3] *Q.F.* 1. 2, 4–7. Note in *Att.* 6. 2, 5 Cicero speaks of himself as *clemens* in his jurisdiction over provincials.

[4] He wrote about them, in a practical vein: Cicero, *Leg.* 3. 14. My remarks here will make it clear that I do not agree with Murray, *JRS* 55 (1965), 176–7, who thinks that Philodemus and Panaetius deliberately omitted a 'traditional' exhortation of the absolute ruler to be lenient even to the point of disregarding the law, because it would not suit the position of a republican magistrate. His only evidence for this 'traditional' argument is Seneca's *De Clementia*. In fact, (1) Seneca does not make clear the relation of *clementia* to law: in 1. 1, 4 it seems to be in accordance with law. Cf., in the *Letter of Aristeas*, the combination of advice to remit penalties and to obey the law (187; 191 with 279; 140, on which see Murray, *JTS* 18 (1967), 355–6, where he retracts (p. 356 n. 2) his earlier view that the Aristotelian doctrine of equity became a standard view). (2) As I have noted in the text, there were areas in the Republic in which such a 'traditional' argument could have been applied, had it existed.

[5] His Teubner edition (1908) has been adopted by Atzert and Ax. For a reminder of its very doubtful nature see Watt, *JRS* 41 (1951), 200.

'iustitia humane et liberaliter exercitata'.[1] It is opposed to justice exercised in a spirit of anger and cruelty and more severely than the sinner expects. But we have still not gone beyond the negative conception: psychologically, the absence of anger; practically, the absence of arbitrariness and immoderation introduced by anger into punishment.

In his earlier dialogue *De Ira*, Seneca shows how the rational judge, free of anger, actually decides on penalties.[2] We find here already the idea of returning to the principles of punishment in deciding individual cases. The purpose most emphasized is reform, and Seneca shows the judge's estimate of the culprit's curability determining the penalty (1. 16; 1. 19, 5). Concern for the security of the state (1. 6, 4; 2. 31, 8) and for the creation of a deterrent appear as well as the usual considerations of equity: intention or inadvertence, premeditation or momentary weakness (1. 19, 2; 6–7). The notion of *severitas* is associated with the imposition of harsher penalties (1. 16, 5), but *clementia* does not appear, and *misericordia* seems to stand for it in one place (1. 16, 3) but to mean the despised passion, ungoverned by *ratio*, in another (1. 17, 4). Though the only example given is a case of military jurisdiction, Seneca clearly has the Roman magistrate in mind (1. 16, 5).

Seneca's sources in *De Ira* include Posidonius and Sotion.[3] Posidonius could have worked out this view with magisterial and provincial models in mind, or Sotion may have done so with the Empire in mind. And the possibility cannot be discounted that Seneca is analysing for himself a type of jurisdiction familiar to him.

Consonant with its title, *De Clementia* develops the positive content of the notion further. Of the rational modes of determining punishments, *clementia* is now thoroughly preferred to *severitas*. Seneca now insists that most men can be reformed (1. 2, 1–2). This leads him to justify *clementia* not simply as a

---

[1] Fr. 8 (Atzert). On the Stoic inspiration of the work see Knoellinger's edition, pp. 54 ff.

[2] See p. 167 n. 1.

[3] Pohlenz, *Die Stoa*[2], I, p. 311. There were many authors before them whom Seneca might have consulted (Cicero, *Q.F.* 1. 1, 37).

legitimate course in particular cases, but as a policy to be followed
generally in administering justice. Though reform is his main
interest, Seneca tries to show that clemency best fulfils the other
aims of punishment as well: deterrence and general security. In
De Ira, Seneca had accepted the idea of destroying a family
dangerous to the state (1. 19, 2) or of killing a man as an *exemplum* (1. 6, 4). Now he argues that *severitas* is not the best means
of discouraging crime since constant revelations of crime make
people regard it more lightly. Men are more obedient to a mild
ruler (1. 22–4). The development of Seneca's ideas between the
composition of *De Ira* and that of *De Clementia* is the strongest
argument for the developed doctrine being an invention of
Seneca himself.

Seneca is mainly concerned with justice by the Princeps, but he
expects the Emperor's *mansuetudo* to infect the whole Empire.[1]
Perhaps Seneca is thinking not merely of a general growth of
recti mores but, more precisely, of a similar exercise of jurisdiction by provincial governors, prefects in Rome, and the Senate.[2]
With the strict guidance of law removed for the most serious
crimes, many senators will have been troubled by the difficulty
of deciding on just penalties. Those with Stoic leanings will have
received little guidance from that philosophy as it stood, and the
simple notion of desert, which was left when that of conformity
to law became irrelevant, could lead to extreme harshness, as
we have seen. Seneca, perhaps in company with some contemporary Stoics, tried to provide some practical guidance within

---

[1] 2. 2, 1. For the idea, a *topos* of Greek political theory (Weidauer, p. 71),
cf. Cicero, *Fam*. 1. 9, 12, and, applied to the Principate, Tacitus, *Ann*. 3. 55 of
Vespasian: 'obsequium inde in principem et aemulandi amor validior quam poena
ex legibus et metus.'

[2] Jones, *Studies in Roman Government and Law*, Oxford, 1960, pp. 55 ff., and
Sherwin-White, *Roman Society and Roman Law*, pp. 16, 61–2, argued that by
the last three years of Nero's reign, provincial governors had won the right to
try citizens by *cognitio* for certain capital crimes without appeal. That would mean
an increase in the number of vital decisions about penalties made by individual senators and *equites*. But Garnsey, *JRS* 56 (1966), 167 ff. and *Social Status*,
pp. 75 ff., suggests that governors were never under legal obligation to refer
capital charges of citizens nor, until the Severan period, limited in their capacity
to pass capital sentences.

the framework of Stoicism. At the same time as he presented a mild image of the Stoic *amicus principis*, he sought to change the image of the *sapiens* as judge from a rigid dispenser of penalties according to law or desert, to a dispenser of remedies, serene but devoted to the conservation of human life.

Seneca's originality in defining *clementia*, like his provocativeness in using *rex*, had its source in political realism which led him to reject both philosophical rigidity and political hypocrisy. The character of those who governed, not the law, now determined how men were ruled. Humanity and respect for the dignity of his subjects could still be claimed for Nero before the public even after the death of Britannicus. Reassertion of the principles of the new reign might still prove useful for admonition and reassurance.

Nero applied Seneca's ideas of clemency; he cancelled the expulsion of Plautius Lateranus from the Senate; vetoed charges against Suillius' son; vetoed the punishment of the *liberti* of Pedanius Secundus (murdered by his slaves); intervened on behalf of ex-governors faced with extortion charges; and interceded for one of the culprits charged under the *Lex Cornelia de falsis*, on grounds of his *dignitas*.[1] He encouraged free decisions by reviving the Augustan practice[2] whereby the Emperor's *consilium* submitted their verdicts in writing.[3] Seneca had pointed out the virtue of that practice in *De Clementia* (1. 15, 4).

---

[1] Above, pp. 111, 124–6, Tacitus, *Ann.* 14. 40.

[2] Suet. *Aug.* 33. 2; *Clem.* 1. 15, 4. Crook, *Consilium Principis*, pp. 111–12, regards Claudius' own pronouncements *ex tabella* (Suet. *Claudius* 15. 3) as an example of the same practice, but it is clear from *Nero* 15. 1 that Suetonius regarded the form in which the Princeps finally produced his verdict as independent of the form in which his advisers gave their views.

[3] Suet. *Nero* 15. He unfortunately offers no indication of date for the practices there described. Nero's reluctance to render decisions on the spur of the moment when his emotions might not be in control could reflect the spirit of Seneca's treatise. Even his less popular tendency of making the final decision alone, according to his conscience, could be seen as a consequence of Seneca's notions. It seems to be the latter that Suetonius marks as an innovation; note that in *De Clementia* 1. 15, 4 Augustus apparently reads out the votes before the *consilium*. Suetonius clearly dislikes Nero's innovation, but the speech Dio attributes to Maecenas offers a creditable motive for the practice (Dio 52. 33, 4). The passage in *Apoc.* 7 is too vague to be taken, as it is by Crook, as an indication of Senecan responsibility for the other innovation recorded by Suetonius: the conduct of the case point for point rather than by continuous *actio*.

But Nero could no more grasp the spirit of Seneca's *clementia* than he could his ideal of being *rex*. In 62 he engineered a case of *maiestas* before the Senate so that he could veto the severe but 'deserved' punishment. Thrasea Paetus was not willing to allow such a perversion of the principles of the early reign. He claimed the opportunity for the Senate and *publica clementia*. Soon Thrasea gave up attendance at the Senate, and Nero's parody of *clementia* had become customary by 64[1]—the year when Seneca withdrew entirely from public life.

[1] *Ann.* 15. 35, 3: 'ex more'.

PART TWO

INTRODUCTION

THE purpose of Part Two of this study is to examine Seneca's views on certain topics relevant to political life and to compare them with what can be ascertained about his behaviour. It is therefore not our task to survey Seneca's philosophical system as a whole. This would, in fact, be very difficult to do, as the surviving works include little systematic exposition of dogma. Seneca, for the most part, takes for granted the basic Stoic doctrines and is even content not to resolve or choose between conflicting alternative Stoic tenets where they are not directly relevant to his main preoccupation: practical moral exhortation and instruction.[1] Furthermore, although Seneca accepts the traditional division of philosophy into ethics, physics, and logic (*Ep.* 89. 9), his interest was by no means catholic, and the only division of which he even intended to give a complete account was the *pars moralis*.[2] For the rhetoric and dialectic included in the *pars rationalis* he had nothing but contempt, and even the epistemology is simply accepted without argument. By contrast, Seneca's interest in physics was intense. Unlike other later Stoics, he was concerned not only with theology, but with terrestrial phenomena and this interest, as we have seen, developed early and continued throughout his life.[3] But even here, Seneca concentrated on particular topics that interested him, omitting subjects relevant to ethics, such as free will and determinism, and, except for brief allusions, the whole problem of the composition of the soul, even remaining content with an optimistic agnosticism on the question of its survival after death (e.g. *Ep.* 102. 2).

Finally, even if it were possible to give a convincing systematic account of Seneca's philosophy, it would not suit our purpose

[1] For an excellent account of Seneca's therapeutic purpose and of its effect on his interests as a whole see I. Hadot, *Seneca und die griechisch-römische Tradition der Seelenleitung*, Berlin, 1969, especially pp. 79–95; 170 ff.

[2] These *libri* 'continentes totam moralem philosophiae partem' are lost: see Haase frags. XVIII (116–25).

[3] Above, pp. 46–7.

here, as it would only tempt us into hypothetical supplementation of Seneca's actual pronouncements on the topics we are investigating. I have, therefore, limited myself, on the whole, to analysing in depth what Seneca actually said, relating his views to what is known of the views of other Stoics on these topics. If no general picture of his thought emerges thereby, at least Seneca's stand on certain central questions of Stoic philosophy will be discussed— the sufficiency of the *summum bonum*, virtue, for happiness; the distinction between true good and evil and the *indifferentia*; the determination of the individual's *officia*.

None the less, there are some general points about Seneca's thinking that are highly relevant to this study. For just as it will become clear from these separate studies that the evaluation and even understanding of Seneca's statements require a knowledge of how usual or unusual for him are the views they express, so it is important to this study as a whole to know (1) how prominent the topics considered here are in Seneca's work generally and (2) how typical his views on these topics are of his general viewpoint: if, for example, what Seneca says about slavery were to prove out of harmony with his views on related subjects, it would require some special explanation and pose additional problems about the connection of his life and work.

As to the first question, the material of Chapters 5 and 6 consists largely of Roman *exempla* drawn from the late Republic and early Empire which, as a glance at any *index rerum* to Seneca's works will show, predominate over early Roman and foreign examples. Seneca himself states explicitly the great importance he attached to *exempla* in teaching, notably in *Ep.* 95. 72 ff.,[1] where, having explained his view that both the dogmatic and parenetic parts of philosophy are essential for the attainment of wisdom,[2] Seneca adds that descriptions of good men of the past are as valuable as descriptions of how the good man ought to be. Of the other topics considered, no reader of Seneca can be in any doubt about the prominence of wealth (treated in Chapter 9)

---

[1] Cf. also *Ep.* 6. 5; 83. 13.

[2] Seneca's view accords with that of Cleanthes (*Ep.* 94. 4) and Chrysippus (*SVF* 3. 474).

and death (Chapter 11) in his writings as a whole, while the question of whether or not to participate in politics (Chapter 10) is the subject of two whole dialogues and of large parts of a third and of the Letters to Lucilius. The same claim cannot be made for the sentiments collected together to give Seneca's views on the provinces (Chapter 7). This is a fabricated subject, prompted by assertions of Seneca's concern for good provincial government made by modern scholars, but the material canvassed does include themes important in Stoicism, like the metaphysical community of gods and men, even if they are not central to Seneca. Finally, it can hardly be claimed that slavery is one of Seneca's most common themes, but as we shall see (in Chapter 8), the emphasis he gives it is considerable relative to the attention it seems to have received from other Stoic theorists.

The second question, whether his opinions on each of the subjects we shall be exploring fit with Seneca's general viewpoint, is more difficult to treat. If one were asked to characterize as briefly as possible the distinctive Senecan outlook, one would probably point to his morbid asceticism and his realistic humanity —qualities that at first appear irreconcilable, but in fact only reflect, albeit in an individual way, the schizophrenia endemic in Stoic philosophy, with its vision of the *sapiens* and its code of behaviour for the *imperfectus*. The cast of mind that leads Seneca to describe over and over again, with loving and horrifying detail, the suffering by which the wise man's virtue is tested[1] is explicitly acknowledged in Letter 66, where Seneca confesses to an unorthodox preference for the virtue shown in overcoming adversity over that manifested in moderating prosperity.[2] This side of Seneca's thought is well represented in Chapter 9 (wealth) and Chapter 11 (death). How deep his rigorist feeling went is clear when we remember that it was a combination of ill health and the attractions of ascetic preachers that first drew Seneca to philosophy.

---

[1] The principal works concerned are *De Ira*, *De Constantia Sapientis*, *De Providentia*, and many of the Letters.

[2] *Ep.* 66. 49 ff. See Hadot, op. cit., pp. 118, 180 n. 2, who explains this by the Roman military tradition.

By Seneca's humanity is usually meant something far broader than the qualities he denotes by the word *humanitas*. That is a word that, by contrast with Cicero, he uses very rarely[1] and mostly as a term for a minor virtue that can scarcely claim much prominence in his thought.[2] But the few cases in which Seneca does use it already tie together some of the ingredients we think of as constituting his humanity: a sympathy for his fellow men based on the Stoic notion of the link that exists between god and men because of their share in the cosmic λόγος;[3] his insistence on kindness, leniency, and the control of anger and arrogance in our dealings with all men, especially the less fortunate.[4] The most striking ways in which Seneca applies such ideas are his advocacy of good treatment for slaves (Chapter 8), and his abhorrence of gladiatorial shows (*Ep.* 90. 45; 95. 33) and of the slaughter of criminals in the arena (*Ep.* 7. 3 ff.). We have already met these ideas in considering *De Clementia*[5] and shall again when considering Seneca's views on provincial government. It is an attitude whose most famous expression is the line of Terence: 'homo sum, humani nihil a me alienum puto' (*Heaut.* 77), which Seneca himself allows to stand as the mnemonic formulation of his more metaphysically grounded conception.[6]

There is no reason to credit any one particular Stoic with the development of the nearest Greek equivalent to *humanitas*, the notion of φιλανθρωπία which is common in later Stoics, though not confined to that school. But some ingredients of what we call Seneca's humanity do seem traceable to the innovations of

[1] Also, by contrast with Cicero, Seneca's *humanitas* is purely moral, as was typical in the imperial period. The broad notion of Cicero's time (but not exclusive to him, cf. Varro, *RR* 1. 17, 4) which included cultural achievements suffered a contraction, as Gellius, *NA* 13. 17, demonstrates. Seneca, in fact, explicitly denies that *liberalia studia* engender *humanitas* (*Ep.* 88. 30).

[2] *Ep.* 88. 30; 115. 3. It is not one of the four cardinal virtues.

[3] *Ep.* 5. 4.

[4] *Ep.* 88. 30; 81. 26; *NQ* 4, pref. 18 (see below, p. 259 n. 1).

[5] *Ep.* 81. 6–7 where the *sapiens* behaves like a *remissior iudex* and 81. 26 where judicial language is again used suggest that *humanitas* here is equivalent to *clementia* in the treatise: Cicero used *humanitas* of this kind of φιλανθρωπία (above, p. 166). But, since Caesar, *clementia* seemed particularly appropriate when the virtue was exercised by a ruler.

[6] *Ep.* 95. 53; cf. also the echo in *Ep.* 88. 30: 'nullum alienum malum putat.'

Panaetius.[1] How has Panaetius fallen! Once credited with introducing the distinctive Ciceronian notion of *humanitas* to Rome,
he has been stripped of his glory by students of the Stoa[2] and
of 'the Scipionic circle'.[3] Now his creation of the Middle Stoa
seems doomed to succumb to the prevailing belief in the Stoa's
unity. Yet there still remain some attitudes that seem irreducibly
Panaetian,[4] among them three that contribute greatly to Seneca's
humanity:

1. The realistic interest in the *imperfectus* whose improvement
   can only be gained by a long process of therapy allowing, in
   the early stages, for his weakness:[5] thus Seneca would have the
   imperfectus avoid circumstances that stimulate his ill-disciplined
   passions.[6]
2. The awareness that a lack of material advantages can make the
   attainment of happiness more difficult. The exact form of
   Panaetius' idea is disputed,[7] but, as will be argued in chapter 9,
   something of the kind lies behind the view of wealth adopted
   by Seneca in *De Vita Beata*, which is exceptional for him and,
   in fact, confined entirely to that one work. It stands in complete contradiction to the rigorist inclination mentioned above.
3. Panaetius' redefinition of the traditional Stoic formula of life
   according to nature, as life in accordance with the starting-
   points (ἀφορμαί) given to us by nature. Panaetius went on to
   work out how not only general human nature, but our particular natural gifts, and finally our varying circumstances and our
   choice of profession determine what behaviour is appropriate

---

[1] It is curious that in *Ep.* 116. 5, Seneca attributes to him a use of the word in
a derivative vulgar sense (meaning 'condescension') found elsewhere in Seneca,
Ep. 4. 10. Seneca cannot have thought of him as the refiner of *humanitas* as a
philosophical concept.

[2] Pohlenz, *Antikes Führertum*, Leipzig, 1934, pp. 139–40.

[3] A. E. Astin, *Scipio Aemilianus*, Oxford, 1967, Appendix 6.

[4] The moderate views of Panaetius' radicalism taken by J. M. Rist, *Stoic
Philosophy*, Cambridge, 1969, pp. 173 ff., and A. A. Long, *Hellenistic Philosophy*,
London, 1974, pp. 211–16, seem to be the most nearly correct.

[5] *Ep.* 116. 5 where Seneca declares his absolute sympathy with Panaetius' view.

[6] *Ep.* 28. 6; 56. 15; *Cons. Marc.* 1. 1; cf. *Ep.* 13. 4; 63. 1.

[7] See below, p. 296 n. 5.

for us as individuals.[1] His doctrine of τὸ πρέπον and of the four *personae* that help to fix what is fitting for each of us can be recovered in outline from Cicero's discussion of *decorum* in *De Officiis* 1. 93–151.[2] The subject of political participation (Chapter 10) is the point at which these ideas have most affected Seneca's thinking.[3]

Finally, we must mention an idea that, whatever its origins,[4] certainly receives a notable prominence in Seneca and is highly relevant to his humanity. This is the psychological theory of the προπάθειαι (*ictus animi*), emotional reactions which not even the *sapiens* can avoid, though he can prevent them from developing into full-blown πάθη (*affectus*). For Seneca, this means that not only such trivial reactions as blushing (*Ep.* 11. 1–7), panic claustrophobia, fainting at the sight of blood (*Ep.* 57. 3–6) are

---

[1] Frag. 96 van Straaten. Rist, op. cit., pp. 186 ff., like Hadot, op. cit., pp. 32–3 nn. 134–5, thinks that Chrysippus already allowed the individual's nature to play a part in determining his conduct, but the principal distinction in D.L. 7. 88–9 seems to be between cosmic and generic φύσις, which, however, is realized in individuals. According to Panaetius' view, given in Cicero, *Off.* 1. 107 (see next note), *communis natura* (generic human nature) is opposed to *propria natura* (individual nature); as *universa natura* in *Off.* 1. 100 seems to be identical with *communis natura*, cosmic nature was apparently not mentioned by Panaetius in this context.

[2] Cicero names Panaetius as his principal source in *Off.* 2. 60; 3. 7 ff.; *Att.* 16. 11, 4. We may therefore assume that he used him except for the topics treated in 1. 152 ff.; 2. 88 ff.; and Book 3, which Cicero notes were not covered in Panaetius' περὶ τοῦ καθήκοντος (see van Straaten, *Panétius*, pp. 276–83). For a brief discussion of the Panaetian concept of τὸ πρέπον, see Rist, op. cit., pp. 190–1, citing the older and fuller treatments.

[3] Hadot, op. cit., pp. 33 n. 135; 153–4. See below, pp. 341–2.

[4] A. Gellius (*NA* 19. 1, 13 ff.) mentions a Stoic philosopher who traced the doctrine back to 'conditores sectae Stoicae', but the only evidence he adduced was the discourses of Epictetus. Rist, op. cit., pp. 37–42, rightly rejects this as evidence for the doctrine of the original Stoa on the grounds that it presupposes the psychology of Posidonius. Nor does the remark of Zeno quoted in Seneca's *De Ira* 1. 16, 7, cited by Abel, *Bauformen*, p. 57 n. 2, as supporting evidence for the antiquity of the idea, help the case, as it refers not to προπάθειαι but to scars left on a soul that has experienced full-blown passions. Pohlenz, *Die Stoa*,[2] I, pp. 307–8; II, p. 154, thought that Sotion was the originator of the doctrine, but it seems to be mentioned already by Cicero in *Tusc. Disp.* 3. 83, as pointed out by Hadot, op. cit., p. 133 n. 45. She thinks the form in which the doctrine appears in Seneca owes much to his own thinking.

rooted in human nature, but even the first impulses to anger (*De Ira* 2. 2, 5; 2. 4 ff.), the first reactions of grief to the loss of relatives and friends (*Ep.* 63. 1; 74. 31; 99. 18 ff.), and the fear of death itself (*Ep.* 82). Not to feel these, says Seneca, would be *inhumanitas*, not *virtus* (*Ep.* 99. 15).

This last notion is touched on only briefly in Chapter 11, but, as the preceding survey will have made abundantly clear, the picture of Seneca's thinking that will emerge in the following chapters is, on the whole, characteristic, both because the topics studied are prominent throughout his writings and because his ideas on them include the basic attitudes that inform his work. The following chapters must help us to decide how Seneca's opinions and his conduct are related to one another, but there is one respect in which a man's writing is indisputably connected with his life, that is in its revelation of his general cast of mind. That the two sides of Seneca's thinking—morbid asceticism and realistic humanity—are the sides of his personality is clear from Tacitus' account of him: the *comitas*[1] that characterized his friendships and the *constantia* with which he met his end. Seneca's was a philosophy of adversity or, as he himself is made to call it, 'meditata ratio adversum imminentia' (*Ann.* 15. 62).

[1] In *Ep.* 88. 30, Seneca says 'humanitas comem se facilemque omnibus praestat'.

5

SENECA ON THE FALL OF
THE REPUBLIC

SENECA wrote only one work on political theory and one other work essentially political in content. These two pieces, the *De Clementia* and the *Apocolocyntosis*, belong to Seneca's role as minister and courtier. In them the philosopher was at the service of the statesman.

Our present concern is with the philosopher. Do we find in his other prose works any clearly defined attitude, consistent or changing, to the Principate? Any political views he reveals in these works are bound to be incidental to his moral argument and his rhetorical purpose. The inquiry is thus very hazardous.

I

In the early Empire, any attitude towards the Principate tended to involve strong views on the last years of the Republic and the Civil Wars. Seneca, who had in youth little interest in history[1] and continued to regard it, with all the other liberal arts, as entirely subordinate to philosophy,[2] was quite content to rely for his earlier historical material largely on collections of *exempla* which he would borrow, errors and bias included.[3] But Seneca's *exempla* from the last years of the Republic, and later, become fuller and clearer. He tends to digress, adding ideas irrelevant to

---

[1] Elder Seneca, *Suas.* 6. 16.

[2] F. J. Kühnen, *Seneca und die römische Geschichte*, Diss. Köln, 1962, pp. 18–28.

[3] Ibid., pp. 49–51, 54, 59. Seneca was obviously not concerned with adopting a consistent attitude towards such figures as the Elder Scipio, whose military exploits are differently assessed in *Ben.* 3. 33, 3 and *Ep.* 86. 1, and, more strikingly, Livius Drusus who receives sympathetic treatment in *Cons. Marc.* 16. 4, hostile in *Brev. Vit.* 6. 1 (passages discussed by I. Haug, *WJA* 2 (1947), 137–8).

his point,[1] and to revel in lengthy treatments of the same situation in different contexts.[2] Seneca no longer appears to be expressing whatever view of these figures suits the particular moral argument.

Seneca's references to Caesar, Pompey, and Cato have been collected and analysed, not always with the same result. One scholar has argued that Seneca's views conformed to the official version of the Augustan regime: hostility to Caesar, the destroyer of the Republic; sympathy for Pompey, its defender; worship for Cato, its incarnation.[3] Another has found that Seneca's judgements on both Pompey and Caesar grew harsher with age, but that, in the case of Caesar, his verdict was moral not political.[4] Both agree that Seneca's judgement on Cato was primarily moral.

With the last point no one would be prepared to argue.[5] But the other disagreements point to ambiguity and complexity in Seneca's view of Pompey and Caesar. A review of his references to them, according to the (very rough) chronological groups to which the dialogues can safely be assigned,[6] may repay the effort. We have the views of Lucan for comparison and some hints of what other contemporaries thought.

Cato was the best example of the *sapiens*, perhaps surpassing the ideal itself,[7] but praise of Cato did not entail for Seneca complete condemnation of Caesar and Pompey. If Seneca did not believe that the general level of virtue was better in the late Republic than in his own day,[8] he did believe that the age that produced

---

[1] e.g. *Cons. Marc.* 14. 3; *Ira* 3. 30, 4; *Ben.* 2. 20, 1; *Ep.* 14. 13.

[2] In the Letters the courage of Cato as Caesar marched on Rome is repeatedly stressed. See below, pp. 192–3.

[3] W. H. Alexander in *Trans. Royal Soc. of Canada*, 3rd Ser. 35, Sec. 2 (1941), 15–28; 40, Sec. 2 (1946), 59–74; 42, Sec. 2 (1949), 13–29. In the first of these, on Caesar, Alexander's view is distorted by taking *Ben.* 2. 12 to refer to Julius Caesar when Caligula is clearly meant.

[4] Kühnen, *Seneca und die römische Geschichte*, pp. 61–8.

[5] For a treatment of Cato in Seneca as part of the story of Cato's *Nachleben*, see P. Pecchiura, *La figura di Catone Uticense nella letteratura latina*, Turin, 1965, pp. 59 ff., who comes to the same conclusion.

[6] See Appendix A1.

[7] *Const. Sap.* 2. 2–3; 7. 1.

[8] *Ep.* 97. 8–9 with the exaggeration: 'longe enim frugalior haec iuventus est quam ille.' The general point about vice maintaining a constant level is made in *Ben.* 1. 10. In *Ep.* 95. 29 the moral decline is clearly not recent, the

one *sapiens* was particularly rich in good men as well as villains.[1]
Pompey, Cicero, and Caesar[2] in the first category and Vatinius
and Clodius[3] in the second served to challenge and highlight
Cato's virtue.

Seneca never indulges in the passionate denunciations of
Caesar that we find in his nephew Lucan. Notably missing from
his portrait[4] is the pathological *ira*—the cardinal Stoic vice—so
prominent in Lucan's Caesar.[5] Even in the later works, where
the more hostile references are generally found, Seneca is still
capable of neutral allusions[6]—but this contrast with Lucan could
be more a matter of temperament than politics.

There is no sign that Seneca completely changed his mind
about Caesar in the quarter of a century spanned by the dialogues
and Letters, although the earlier works depict Caesar's more
commendable features while the later ones show up the blacker
aspects. In the Consolations to Marcia and his mother Helvia,
Seneca regards Caesar's foreign conquests as a contribution to the
community and the Empire.[7] References to these victories then
cease except for the charge in *De Beneficiis* that Caesar brought
against Rome the armies entrusted to him for war in Gaul and
Germany. Yet Seneca's view of the conquests may not have
changed, for in Letter 94, giving Caesar and Pompey as examples
of men driven by personal ambition, Seneca mentions the conquests of Pompey's earlier career, but illustrates Caesar's ambition
with the civil wars alone.[8]

In writing to Marcia, Seneca shows sympathy for Caesar,
whose conquests were being sabotaged by Pompey's selfishness,

contrast being made with the men of old, but in NQ 7. 31–2 Seneca complains
of growing *nequitia*. For a comparison with Tacitus' freedom from 'idle fancies
about the steady decline of Roman morality from century to century', see Syme,
Tacitus, pp. 564–5.

[1] *Tranq.* 7. 5–6.   [2] Ibid. 16. 1; *Ep.* 97. 8.
[3] *Const. Sap.* 2. 1–2; *Ep.* 97.
[4] Caesar moderate in anger and glad to avoid it: *Ira* 2. 23, 4. In *Ben.* 5. 24,
Caesar is pictured as *subiratus*, but still perfectly capable of listening to reason.
[5] e.g. 1. 146 ff.; 7. 797 ff.
[6] *Ben.* 3. 24; 5. 24; *NQ* 7. 17, 2; *Ep.* 97. 8; 98. 13.
[7] *Cons. Marc.* 14. 3; *Helv.* 9. 7.
[8] *Ben.* 5. 15, 4–6; 16. 5 (anonymous but obviously Caesar); *Ep.* 94. 65.

and regards Bibulus' opposition in 59 as a case of impotent envy.[1]
But in *De Constantia Sapientis* Cato the martyr is pitted against
the immense ambition of the coalition of Pompey, Crassus, and
Caesar,[2] while, in *De Beneficiis* and the Letters, we are repeatedly
shown Caesar at the moment of the march on Rome, unable to
bear a superior, willing to set himself above Rome. Seneca there
condemns his defiance of the Senate, sneers at his *partes* as 'plebem
et omnem erectum ad res novas vulgum', and castigates the
hypocrisy of 'ille plebicola, ille popularis' who could invade his
city like an enemy.[3] In fact, he approaches Lucan's view of Caesar
as the aggressor in the Civil War and the enemy of the Senate
which was the heart of the Republic.[4]

Seneca's attitude to Caesar's dictatorship undergoes a similar
modulation. In *De Ira*, Caesar is an example of clemency. While
Seneca alludes once to popular fear and dislike of the dictator,[5] he
praises at length his self-restraint in destroying Pompey's letters,[6]
and, more significantly, traces the murder of *divus Iulius* to the
unreasonable ambitions of his friends: 'The deified Julius was
killed by more friends than enemies, friends whose insatiable
hopes he had not satisfied. He wanted to satisfy them (for no one
used victory more generously, reserving for himself nothing but
the power of giving), but how could he satisfy such excessive
desires, when everyone wanted what only one could have?'[7]
In *De Beneficiis*, Seneca has not changed his disapproval of the
assassination, but he now disapproves on grounds of practical
politics.[8] He alludes to a common topic for disputation about
Marcus Brutus: 'an debuerit accipere ab divo Iulio vitam, cum
occidendum eum iudicaret'. Seneca's answer is that Brutus was
justified in accepting clemency because the preservation of life is
not a *beneficium* when the power to do so has been obtained by

---

[1] *Cons. Marc.* 14. 2.
[2] 2; also *Ep.* 104. 29.
[3] *Ep.* 94. 65; 104. 31; *Ben.* 5. 16, 5; 5. 15, 6.
[4] e.g. 1. 183 ff.; 2. 519–21; 5. 12–14.
[5] 2. 11, 3.   [6] 2. 23, 4.
[7] 3. 30, 4.
[8] But he can still blame Antony (*Ben.* 5. 16, 6) as ungrateful in condoning
the assassination and giving the killers provinces.

iniuria.[1] But Seneca adds his personal opinion that Brutus was wrong to kill Caesar: either Brutus objected, against the teachings of the Stoa, to monarchy as a constitution, or he wrongly thought freedom could be restored to a state that had lost its ancient morality and to men who were willing to fight for the privilege of servitude. And elsewhere, in the same work, Seneca cites Caesar and Pompey as examples of ingratitude to one's country, maintaining that Caesar's clemency was not worth his determination to retain power and implying that Sulla's abdication after bloodshed was preferable.[2]

Finally, in the Letters, the focus is almost always on Cato when Caesar is mentioned, and the dictator's victory is equated with servitude and the end of freedom.[3] But here again the Letters merely emphasize a view that Seneca held earlier, for in the Consolation to Marcia, he laments that Cato, a man born for personal and public liberty, had to flee from Caesar.[4]

Why did Seneca stress the darker side of Caesar's dictatorship in the later works, and why did he modify his judgement on Caesar's clemency and assassination? To say that Cato was stressed increasingly[5] is only to ask the question in another form, for Seneca need not have concentrated so heavily on the political significance of Cato's opposition, and, as we shall see, did not do so consistently. In any case, Cato is irrelevant to Caesar's assassination. One might invoke family background as the source of Seneca's original favourable view of Caesar, for, as we have seen, the Annaei of Corduba were not necessarily *Pompeiani*. Or the events of January 41 may have left their impression on his earlier

---

[1] *Ben.* 2. 20. Cf. Plut. *Cato Minor* 66. 2, where a similar view of Caesar's right to pardon is ascribed to Cato who concludes that he himself should not ask for mercy though others may.

[2] *Ben.* 5. 16, 5: 'ceteri arma cruentius exercuerunt, satiata tamen aliquando abiecerunt; hic gladium cito condidit, numquam posuit.' Seneca shared the usual hostile view of Sulla, Kühnen, *Seneca und die römische Geschichte*, p. 59.

[3] *Ep.* 71. 9; 94. 65; 95. 70.

[4] *Cons. Marc.* 20. 6. This is unlikely to be said just to please Marcia, the daughter of Cremutius Cordus who wrote of Caesar and Augustus in his history without enthusiasm (Dio 57. 24, 3), for, elsewhere in this work, Seneca contrasts Caesar favourably with Bibulus and Pompey (14. 2–3).

[5] The view of Kühnen, *Seneca und die römische Geschichte*, p. 67.

works in the form of cynicism about the cause and the motives
of high-minded murderers. The direction of Seneca's change, if
not its cause, is clear enough.[1] The view of Caesar expressed by
Seneca came to resemble more closely that found in its extreme
form in Lucan, and held in varying strengths by those who
observed the cult of Brutus and Cassius from Asinius Pollio and
Messalla Corvinus in Seneca's infancy to Cremutius Cordus in
his youth[2] to Thrasea Paetus and Helvidius Priscus who celebrated
the birthdays of Brutus and Cassius in Nero's time.[3] This reverence for the heroes of the Republic, among whom Cato was
always the chief saint,[4] could be called the religion of the Senate,
despite the atheism of some senators in this respect, and the
orthodoxy of many non-senators who identified with the order.[5]
It was not usually a creed of opposition to the Principate as such,
although Caesar's assassination was the natural comparison to
make in justifying the murder of Gaius in 41[6], and the cult was
often associated with a determination that the power and dignity
of the Senate should approximate as closely as possible to what
it had been under the Republic.[7] On the whole, the Princeps, as a
senator, understood and accepted the cult. Indeed Augustus had
encouraged the eclipse of Caesar and done little to discourage the
worship of his enemies.[8] But a nervous emperor could be persuaded that the attitude was subversive.[9]

[1] For other suggestions see below, pp. 193–4.

[2] Tacitus, *Ann.* 4. 34.

[3] Juvenal 5. 36–7. Cf. also the remark attributed by Tacitus to Eprius Marcellus
in *Hist.* 4. 8: 'constantia fortitudine Catonibus et Brutis aequaretur Helvidius.'

[4] Note the religious imagery in Lucan 9. 600 and Seneca, *Ep.* 67. 12.

[5] Like the equestrian official, Titinius Capito (Pliny, *Ep.* 1. 17).

[6] Jos. *AJ* 19. 184.

[7] See Wirszubski, *Libertas*, pp. 126–7; R. MacMullen, *Enemies of the Roman
Order*, Cambridge, Mass., 1967, pp. 32–3.

[8] Dio 53. 32, 4; *Ann.* 4. 34; Macrobius, *Sat.* 2. 4, 18. But cf. Suet. *Aug.* 85. 1,
recording 'Rescripta Bruto de Catone' recited in old age by Augustus. Syme,
The Roman Revolution, Oxford, 1938, p. 506, followed by Pecchiura, *La figura
di Catone Uticense*, p. 38, suggests that Augustus did not attack Cato in this work
but opposed Brutus' use of Cato as the inspiration of tyrannicide. That view
fits the assumption of a date late in Augustus' reign for the composition of the
work, but it might be a composition of the Triumviral period that Augustus
recited in old age.

[9] Under Tiberius, the images of Brutus and Cassius were cautiously omitted

Yet Seneca's increasing harshness towards Caesar's later career only brings out more plainly his persistent lack of admiration for the 'tyrannicides'. Cassius receives no mention at all, and Brutus is rarely mentioned and then without much enthusiasm. Writing from exile, Seneca cites a philosophical argument of Brutus without commendation;[1] in the last work we have he mentions Brutus' book περὶ καθήκοντος as an example of the pointless type of philosophy that gives precepts without explaining their relevance to a final moral aim.[2] Seneca always accepted Brutus as a man of moral stature, 'vir magnus', a man even Cato had to admire,[3] but the one act for which posterity honoured him Seneca condemned. In De Ira—where Caesar receives favourable treatment—Seneca does not exclude Brutus in speaking of the friends who killed Caesar because he could not satisfy their unreasonable ambitions. That Caesar was unjustly and ungratefully murdered is an idea frequently expressed by supporters of the imperial power in the days of Tiberius and later;[4] Lucan[5] tells us that there were those who called Brutus' deed 'nefas'. In De Beneficiis, however, Seneca absolved Brutus from one charge of ingratitude—that based on the fact that Caesar had saved his life.[6] There remained the other grounds for the charge—the acceptance of a province and the promise of a consulship, but Seneca's sympathy for the victim had, by now, declined and he was more interested in destroying the political than the moral hero.

from Junia's funeral procession (*Ann.* 3. 76); soon after, Tiberius was persuaded by Sejanus to allow the prosecution of Cremutius Cordus for his praise of Brutus and Cassius in his history (*Ann.* 4. 34; *Cons. Marc.* 1. 2–3, cf. 22. 4–5 suggesting that he also admired Pompey and showing that Sejanus had personal grounds for disliking him). After Seneca's death, Nero was frightened into making reverence for Cassius a charge against his descendant (*Ann.* 16. 7; cf. also 16. 22).

[1] *Cons. Helv.* 8. 1.   [2] *Ep.* 95. 45.

[3] *Cons. Helv.* 9. 5.

[4] Under Tiberius: Vell. Pat. 2. 56 (who, like Seneca, regards Brutus as a great man in other respects, 2. 72); Val. Max. 1. 5, 7; 1. 8, 8; 1. 6, 13; *Ann.* 4. 34, 3. Later: e.g. Dio 44. 1–2; Appian, *BC* 4. 134.

[5] 8. 608–10. Cf. Petronius 120. 64: 'Iulius ingratam perfudit sanguine Romam', and the *Octavia* where the view is attributed to Nero (498 ff.) but Seneca is made to approve the punishment of Caesar's murderers by Augustus (481).

[6] Above, pp. 185–6. Plut. *Comp. Dion. et Brut.* 3. 3 mentions this as the gravest charge against Brutus.

The same distance between Seneca's views and the cult of the Republic appears in his treatment of Pompey. It was, of course, not easy to make a saint of Pompey, as Lucan's poem makes very clear: the portrait of Pompey there benefits from the blackening of Caesar and improves as the fortunes of his party decline.[1] At no time did Seneca make the effort. His conception of Pompey is consistent throughout: he acknowledges his supreme position and military ability,[2] attributes to him both generosity[3] and modesty,[4] and ranks him with Cicero and Caesar as one of the good men of the period.[5] Pompey was in these respects a great man and Seneca accordingly laments, indignantly and conventionally, his pathetic death.[6] He is also less unfavourable than most sources to Pompey's son Sextus whom he spares for the sake of the father.[7]

None the less, Pompey's faults, in Seneca's portrait, more than outweigh his merits: Pompey's pride was reflected in the empty boast of his cognomen; he was wavering in his friendship for Cicero; his conquests were motivated by an insane passion for false greatness.[8] On the relative ambition of the two rivals, Seneca judged as Lucan: Caesar could not bear one man ahead of him; Pompey could not endure that anyone else should become 'great' in Rome.[9] But the most damning of Seneca's strictures on Pompey occurs in De Beneficiis, where, despite his condemnation of

[1] J. Brisset, Les idées politiques de Lucain, Paris, 1964, pp. 109–26, noting that Cato gives Lucan's final verdict in 9. 190 ff.

[2] Cons. Marc. 20. 4; 22. 5; Brev. Vit. 13. 6; Ben. 4. 30; Ep. 51. 11; 104. 30 'satis unus adversus omnia' is surely Pompey pace Alexander in TRSC 3rd Ser. 42, sec. 2 (1949), p. 23.

[3] Brev. Vit. 13. 6: on the interpretation of 'bonitas' here see Alexander, op. cit., pp. 21–2.

[4] Ep. 11. 4.   [5] Above, p. 184.

[6] Cons. Marc. 20. 4; De Ira 2. 2, 3; Tranq. 16. 1; Brev. Vit. 13. 7; Ep. 4. 7.

[7] Seneca probably reflects the views of Claudius in Cons. Polyb. 15. 1, for the Emperor's son-in-law was a descendant of Sextus, but, even in Ben. 4. 30, Seneca admits that Pompey's sons and descendants deserve honour for the sake of their great ancestor.

[8] Brev. Vit. 13. 6; 5. 1; Ep. 94. 64.

[9] Lucan 1. 125–6; Ep. 94. 65 has the first half of the remark; Cons. Marc. 14. 3 the second half which originated with Caesar (BC 1. 4, 4). Syme, Roman Revolution, p. 42 n. 1, thinks the judgement on Caesar went back to Pollio.

Caesar's march on Rome, Seneca blames Pompey for originating
the fatal coalition of 60 B.C., in order to divide by three the *invidia*
that otherwise would have fallen to him alone: in return for all
the honours his country had given him, Pompey devised extraordinary commands for himself and others, doled out the
Republic to three *domini*, and reduced the Roman people to a
condition in which its safety could only be secured through
servitude.[1] This is a severe political indictment and forms a sharp
contrast with Lucan's final verdict on Pompey:[2]

> . . . salva
> Libertate potens et solus plebe parata
> Privatus servire sibi rectorque senatus,
> Sed regnantis, erat. Nil belli iure poposcit,
> Quaeque dari voluit, voluit sibi posse negari.
>
> (9. 192–6.)

Cato is, throughout Seneca's works, the Stoic sage, a man who
showed himself independent of fortune. Reference is made to his
attitude towards wealth and luxury, the popular respect for his
modesty,[3] and Seneca defends Cato against the standard criticisms
by remarking that nothing in Cato could be a fault: 'facilius
efficient crimen honestum quam turpem Catonem.'[4] But what
makes Cato the great *exemplum* for Seneca is his immovable
courage in the face of insult,[5] political defeat,[6] physical hardship,[7] and finally death. As Alexander has pointed out,[8] Seneca is
not interested in Cato's biography and just gives enough detail
to evoke for the reader the well-known incidents, particularly
the suicide. Cato's death was the perfect act: it was voluntary,[9]

---

[1] *Ben.* 5. 16, 4.

[2] Even Alexander, who holds that Seneca followed the Augustan line in
glorifying Pompey, notes Seneca's coldness to Pompey and remarks that Lucan's
portrait may have rested on a 'counter-sympathy developed in him by his uncle's
relative indifference to the Senate's champion', *TRSC* 42, sec. 2, p. 22.

[3] *Vit. Beat.* 21. 3; *Ep.* 51. 12; 97. 8.

[4] *Tranq.* 17. 4, 9; cf. *Vit. Beat.* 18. 3.

[5] *Ira* 2. 32, 2; 3. 38, 2; *Const. Sap.* 2. 1; 14. 3; *Ep.* 79. 14.

[6] *Cons. Helv.* 13. 5–6; *Const. Sap.* 2. 3; *Ep.* 71. 8; 104. 33; 118. 4; *Prov.* 3. 14.

[7] *Ep.* 104. 33.

[8] *TRSC* 40, sec. 2, pp. 60–1; pp. 65–7.   [9] *Cons. Marc.* 22. 3.

fearless,[1] performed without outside help,[2] and chosen by Cato when he could no longer serve his state or his fellow man.[3] Cato's suicide was one of the most popular subjects in the rhetorical schools,[4] but Seneca could still write of it with great feeling.

The last part of Cato's career, the political context of the suicide, becomes increasingly prominent in those works which probably belong after Seneca's return from exile.[5] The value of Cato's actions in Seneca is always moral, but the descriptions of these actions presuppose certain political views. Cato's cause was good[6]—that was axiomatic; and Cato's cause was *publica libertas*, that is to say, the Republic.[7]

Seneca repeats the long-range explanation of the fall of the Republic that was by now a cliché: the state was degenerate and could no longer support its own weight.[8] Cato alone tried to halt the process and to oppose the immediate cause of destruction— the coalition of 60.[9]

The actual end of the Republic and of *libertas* came with the death of Cato.[10] Brutus was a fool to think that, after Caesar's dictatorship, one could return to the Republic: the old way of life had been lost; and he should have realized that another would arise to take Caesar's place.[11]

The fact that the contest between Pompey and Caesar was one for personal domination created difficulties in explaining Cato's participation on Pompey's side. After Pompey's death Cato could be said to have fought and died for the freedom of his

[1] *Ep.* 24. 6; 67. 7, 13; *Prov.* 2. 10 ff.

[2] *Ep.* 82. 12; 95. 71; 104. 33.

[3] *Const. Sap.* 2; *Ep.* 24. 6; *Prov.* 2. 10.

[4] *Ep.* 24. 6; cf. Persius 3. 44.

[5] See the following footnotes with Appendix A1. The uncertain dating of *De Constantia Sapientis* and *De Providentia* is a serious problem. Thus Pecchiura, *La figura di Catone Uticense*, pp. 69–71, states that Seneca's exaltation of Cato as the martyr of political liberty is not to be found in the works dating from his period in power, a view which depends on his dating of these two works to the period of his exile.

[6] *Prov.* 3. 14.

[7] *Cons. Marc.* 20. 6; *Const. Sap.* 2. 2; *Ep.* 24. 6; 95. 70; *Prov.* 2. 10.

[8] *Const. Sap.* 2. 3. Cf., e.g., Horace, *Epodes* 16. 2; Livy, pref. 4; Petronius 120. 82 ff.   [9] *Const. Sap.* 2. 1–2.

[10] *Tranq.* 16. 1; *Const. Sap.* 2. 3; *Ep.* 24. 7.   [11] *Ben.* 2. 20, 2.

country,[1] but it was a terrible misfortune that forced Cato both to flee Caesar and to follow Pompey.[2] Seneca mentions as a possible theme for disputation whether it was right for the *sapiens* to engage in politics at the time of the Civil War.[3] It was an actual subject in the schools, and Lucan gives a particularly brilliant version in Book 2 of his poem. There Brutus urges Cato to stay out of the struggle, describing Pompey as a *dux privatus*, and claiming that the only way to fight for freedom is to oppose the eventual victor.[4] Lucan's Cato justifies his participation in two ways: his principal argument transcends practical politics, for he admits that *regna saeva* is the expected result but wishes to share the agony of Rome and to follow freedom to the grave; but, more practically, he adds that, as one of the victors, he may prevent Pompey from thinking the victory is only for himself.[5]

Seneca consistently admires Cato's firm stand when Caesar threatened Rome and the freedom of the state—Cato's own freedom was, of course, beyond any threat.[6] In one Letter, Seneca appears to admit Lucan's practical justification of Cato's action. He imagines a possible objection to the Stoic view that everything, except virtue and vice, is morally indifferent: 'Does it make no difference whether Cato is conquered or conquers at Pharsalia? Is the good of being invincible when his party is vanquished equivalent to the good of returning to his country victorious and of re-establishing peace?'[7] Seneca does not quarrel with the statement of historical alternatives here, and thus seems to admit that a victory for Pompey at Pharsalia would have given Cato a large role in reconstruction. But this is an exceptional view for Seneca. His favourite picture of the situation has Cato leading his own battle: he alone fought for the Republic;[8] between

---

[1] *Prov.* 2. 10; *Ep.* 24. 7.

[2] *Cons. Marc.* 20. 6: 'annorum adiectio paucissimorum virum libertati non suae tantum sed rei publicae natum coegit Caesarem fugere Pompeium sequi.'

[3] *Ep.* 14. 13. It is common, but unjustifiable, to assume that the view introduced by 'potest aliquis disputare' is Seneca's own. Inverted commas should be placed around 'Quid tibi vis . . . vicerit'. See *CQ* 18 (1968), 373 ff., and below, p. 336.   [4] 2. 277–84.   [5] 2. 319–23.

[6] *Ep.* 95. 71.   [7] *Ep.* 71. 8.   [8] *Ep.* 95. 70.

Caesar with his *plebs* and Pompey with his Senate, stood the Republic and Cato. He condemned both leaders: he said he would die if Caesar won and go into exile if Pompey did.[1] Cato fought (as in Lucan's first justification) so as to perish along with freedom, 'neque enim Cato post libertatem vixit nec libertas post Catonem.'[2] Perhaps Seneca never thought out the political aspects of Cato's decision. That interested his nephew, but for Seneca the final justification for Cato was the way he conducted himself: his vigour and courage in the midst of popular panic; his fearless confrontation of the powerful and of death itself.[3]

Implicit in Seneca's descriptions of the last heroes of the Republic is the view characteristic of the Roman governing class, including most of the *principes*: the fall of the Republic was the end of political freedom and an irreversible disaster. In *De Beneficiis*, written towards the end of Seneca's period of power or at the start of his unofficial retirement, and in the Letters, written in retirement, Seneca shows his greatest sympathy with this view, condemning Caesar, preferring Pompey's cause, and stressing Cato's role in the Civil War. It is possible that the loss of some of his works is responsible for this pattern but the amount we have makes it unlikely. How shall we explain this tendency? Seneca may have fallen in this period under strong literary influences: the poem of Lucan[4] and the biography of Cato by Thrasea Paetus which, to judge from the Life Plutarch based on it, dealt in detail with Cato's political career.[5] Or perhaps when Seneca's political position increasingly suggested that his life might end

[1] *Ep.* 104. 31, 32.   [2] *Const. Sap.* 2. 2.   [3] *Ep.* 95. 71; 104. 33.

[4] A. Lintott, *CQ* 21 (1971), 495, suggests that Lucan's view of Cato as a fighter, not for Pompey, but for the Republic (9. 18 and 256) was influenced by the Letters in the preceding note. This is difficult as Seneca's later Letters were probably not published until after the dramatic date of the last in late 64 and Lucan died in April 65. But, if the Vacca Life of Lucan is right in stating that the first three books of the *Bellum Civile* were published separately between 60 and 65, they could have led Seneca, in composing these Letters, to think more of Cato's political role in the Civil War. But, of course, exchanging of work in progress between uncle and nephew cannot be ruled out, and traces of literary influence have been claimed in both directions.

[5] H. Peter, *HRR* 2, 1906, p. cxxx, regards Thrasea's biography as Plutarch's main source. The fragments are given on p. 99. We do not know, of course, when Thrasea's work was written.

in suicide, he brooded on Cato's death and found, as Cicero had,[1] that it was not easy to separate Cato's moral qualities from his political convictions. Disillusionment with Nero may have played a part in increasing his nostalgia for the Republic, and, in the Letters, a certain desire to conciliate his senatorial readers for whom he had a serious message cannot be overlooked.[2]

In *De Clementia* Seneca gave a philosophical justification of monarchy and insisted on applying the term *rex* to the Princeps. In that work, Seneca deliberately emphasized the optimistic side of his thought, but in his other philosophical works Seneca increasingly showed his regret for the Republic and portrayed the system as a necessary evil.[3] In this he spoke more like a senator, and less like a political theorist, but he consistently avoided the extreme position of the senatorial idealists. He did not admire Pompey or the tyrannicides, and, even in thinking about Cato, he never approached the degree of interest in the political struggles and ideas of the late Republic that was felt by his nephew Lucan or by Thrasea Paetus and his friends.

II

Hidden in the Institutes of Lactantius is an elegant outline of the history of Rome from the Kingdom to the Principate, in which the new system finds the same grudging and regretful acceptance that Seneca and many other senators expressed. The passage,

[1] *Att.* 12. 4, 2.

[2] In *Ep.* 73 the didactic note is particularly clear. See below, pp. 361–2.

[3] Weidauer, *Der Prinzipat in Senecas Schrift de Clementia*, pp. 9–10, finds the view of the Principate the same in *De Clementia* as in Seneca's other works—the fall of the Republic was inevitable but disastrous, leading to servitude (*Clem.* 1. 1, 1 'iugum'; 1. 4, 2 'frenos ferre')—with only one optimistic note at 1. 1, 8: 'laetissima forma rei publicae, cui ad summam libertatem nihil deest nisi pereundi licentia', which is a deliberate hyperbole serving Seneca's parenetic purpose. In fact, Seneca avoids mentioning in *De Clementia* that the Principate arose as a necessary evil after the fall of the Republic, though he gives a historical reason for its continuation at 1. 3, 3. As was suggested in Chapter 4, Seneca's attempt to apply in that work doctrines of ideal kingship to the system is aimed at making the Principate look like something better than the negation of the Republic.

attributed by Lactantius to 'Seneca', likens the ages of Rome to the six ages of man:

Non inscite Seneca Romanae urbis tempora distribuit in aetates: primam enim dixit infantiam sub rege Romulo fuisse, a quo et genita et quasi educata sit Roma, deinde pueritiam sub ceteris regibus, a quibus et aucta sit et disciplinis pluribus institutisque formata. At vero Tarquinio regnante, cum iam quasi adulta esse coepisset, servitium non tulisse et reiecto superbae dominationis iugo maluisse legibus obtemperare quam regibus, cumque esset adulescentia eius fine Punici belli terminata, tum denique confirmatis viribus coepisse iuvenescere. Sublata enim Carthagine, quae diu aemula imperii fuit, manus suas in totum orbem terra marique porrexit: donec regibus cunctis et nationibus imperio subiugatis cum iam bellorum materia deficeret, viribus suis male uteretur, quibus se ipsa confecit. Haec fuit prima eius senectus, cum bellis lacerata civilibus atque intestino malo pressa rursus ad regimen singularis imperii recidit quasi ad alteram infantiam revoluta. Amissa enim libertate, quam Bruto duce et auctore defenderat, ita consenuit tamquam sustentare se ipsa non valeret, nisi adminiculo regentium niteretur. (7. 15, 14.)

This attractive passage has been discussed frequently and from many points of view. In particular, scholars remain divided on the question of authorship—is this from the historical work of the Elder Seneca, or a historical digression in one of the many lost works of the philosopher? No conclusive arguments, in my opinion,[1] have been produced against the natural assumption that when Lactantius wrote 'Seneca' he meant the philosopher whose works he knew so well.[2] An analysis of the principal themes of the passage here cannot be expected to establish the case for authorship by the younger Seneca—there is probably no thought in it that was not already current by the Triumviral or early Augustan period[3]—but it can show how the passage fits with

---

[1] I have reviewed the main points of the debate in *JRS* 62 (1972), 19.

[2] For Lactantius' knowledge of Seneca's work see Faider, *Études sur Sénèque*, pp. 87 ff. For the influence on Lactantius of Seneca's style, L. Castiglioni, *Riv. di fil.* N.S. 6 (1928), 470–3.

[3] Indeed A. Klotz, in *RhM* N.F. 56 (1901), 429 ff., suggested an Augustan archetype for this passage and the similar sketches in Florus I pref. 4 and Ammianus Marcellinus (14. 6, 4).

Seneca's thought and, for those who accept the philosopher as the author, add to our knowledge of Seneca's political attitudes.

The notion of likening the history of Rome to the ages of man may have been a commonplace by the Empire. Cicero, in *De Re Publica*, applied the metaphor to Rome under the kings,[1] and found it natural in a letter to call the breakdown of Republican institutions a sign 'senescentis magis civitatis quam adquiescentis'.[2] Cicero's use of the image did not lead him to the idea that Rome had eventually to die, any more than it did Seneca; it was left to Lactantius to draw the conclusion: 'quodsi haec ita sunt, quid restat nisi ut sequatur interitus senectutem?'[3] Polybius had used the image of growth as one of his tools for interpreting Roman history, in the bare form: αὔξησις, ἀκμή, φθίσις, and put Rome's ἀκμή at the defeat of Carthage.[4] It has been plausibly suggested[5] that Varro in his work *De Vita Populi Romani* gave the metaphor the systematic form it has in the Lactantius fragment and its different versions elsewhere.[6] But the fragments of that work do not reveal the use of the metaphor, though they do show that Varro divided his history into four books, putting the onset of decadence with the legacy of Attalus and the Gracchi, and that he compared the growing ambition and greed to a gangrene spreading through the *body* of the state (fr. 123).[7] Varro's notion of an internal source of decline (cf. 'intestino malo pressa') is certainly present in our fragment, but there is more Sallust than Varro in the way it puts the turning-point at the destruction of Carthage and lays stress on the misuse of the resources of peace.

Before considering these themes, let us return, briefly, to the basic metaphor, and note what it does *not* imply. First, there is

---

[1] 2. 3; 2. 21. Cf. also Livy 2. 1: at the expulsion of the kings, Rome was 'maturis iam viribus'.

[2] *Q.Fr.* 2. 13, 5 pointed out by F. Vittinghoff, *Historische Zeitschrift* 198 (1964), 558. Cf. Livy 1. 22: 'senescere igitur civitatem otio ratus.'

[3] Cf. Cicero, *Rep.* 3. 34: 'itaque nullus interitus est rei publicae naturalis ut hominis.'

[4] 6. 51.

[5] By B. Riposati, *M. Terenti Varronis De Vita Populi Romani*, Milan, 1939, p. 258; Vittinghoff, *Hist. Zeit.* 198 (1964), 558 n. 3.

[6] See above, p. 195 n. 3. Also a version in SHA, *Vita Cari* 2. 1.

[7] As arranged by Riposati (above, n. 5).

no reason to see in the passage a theory of biological determinism in history.[1] The metaphor does not *explain* what happened to Rome; it merely imposes a striking description on a process whose historical causes are duly noted, e.g. development of tyranny and its rejection, misuse of an access of national power, and confidence after the defeat of a rival. Second, the notion of a return to infancy marked by reversion to one-man rule is not related to Polybius' theory of anacyclosis,[2] except that they both share the common idea of a cycle. For, apart from kingship, the traditional types of constitution, simple or mixed, do not occur and the characteristic analysis of constitutions in terms of classes of society does not appear at all. The metaphor is not found elsewhere in Seneca's works but he does compare the length of human life with the 'urbium saecula',[3] and he never tires of enumerating the stages of life, regarding their predictable succession as an important sign of divine providence.[4] He nowhere gives six stages, the number in the Lactantius fragment, but each of the five main stages there appears somewhere in his different lists.[5] Finally, the proverbial notion of old age as second childhood was used by Seneca in his lost work on moral philosophy.[6]

It is generally agreed that there are Sallustian echoes in the fragment, particularly the phrase 'aemula imperi Romani' from the *Bellum Catilinae* 10.[7] Some have suggested that Lactantius brought in these verbal echoes,[8] but this is unlikely, since the *thought* of the passage from 'sublata enim Carthagine' to 'uteretur'

[1] Vittinghoff, *Hist. Zeit.* 198 (1964), 559 n. 5, is justly critical of this view.

[2] *Contra* A. Garzetti, *Athenaeum* 42 (1964), 148–9.

[3] *Cons. Marc.* 21. 1.   [4] *Ben.* 4. 6, 6.

[5] e.g. *Cons. Marc.* 21. 7; *Ben.* 7. 28, 1; *Ep.* 124. 12. The division of *senectus* can be paralleled in Varro (Censorinus, *De Die Nat.* 14. 2) and Ovid, *Met.* 15. 209–11.

[6] Haase frag. XVIII (121): 'bis pueri sumus', though the actual phrase 'ad alteram infantiam revoluta' may be Lactantian as W. Hartke, *Römische Kinderkaiser*, Berlin, 1951, p. 396, argues. See also Kühnen, *Seneca und die römische Geschichte*, p. 81 n. 1.

[7] Already noted by S. Brandt in his edition of 1890, ad loc. There are parallels also with *BC* 6. 7 and 53. 2–5. Not all those noted by W. Richter in *Gym.* 68 (1961), 310 n. 5, are convincing.

[8] Brandt, op. cit. (with Seneca as an alternative source), and Hartke, *Römische Kinderkaiser*, p. 395.

is basically Sallustian. 'Seneca' also stresses the misuse of the resources acquired through war after the pressure is off, but reverses Sallust's order in putting the conquest of kings and nations *after* Carthage's destruction, so that the misuse of resources now describes the period of Civil War instead of, as in Sallust, the preceding century. The lame idea that opportunities for war were failing is now imported to do the work of the destruction of Carthage in Sallust.[1] This is deliberate adaptation of Sallust and inseparable from the thought of the author. Both Seneca and his father were interested in Sallust and knew his works at first hand.[2]

The view of the Principate implicit in the fragment coincides with that sketched above from Seneca's works. *Libertas* perished with the Republican constitution, indeed was identical with it; the Republic had died of internal moral decay; after the dictatorship was established there was no turning back,[3] the state could no longer be secure without one-man rule.[4]

The comparison of the Principate to the old monarchy was a natural one: it had once been suggested that Augustus be called Romulus.[5] Seneca, it is true, mentions the kings of Rome very rarely,[6] but once he compares Caesar and his successors to them, arguing that the persistence of autocratic rule, after Caesar's assassination, could be predicted from the history of Rome, 'cum Tarquinius esset inventus post tot reges ferro ac fulminibus occisos'.[7] In the Lactantius fragment the word *rex* is not used of the dictatorship or the Principate; more neutral expressions are preferred. That suits the attitude of the passage, for those who regretted the Republic could only accept the Principate

---

[1] The phrase 'viribus suis . . . quibus se ipsa confecit' is a cliché going back at least to Horace (*Epodes* 7 and 16), but in Horace and Lucan (1. 20–2) the suicide is insane because there were other wars to be fought.

[2] Kühnen, *Seneca und die römische Geschichte*, p. 30.

[3] The Brutus in the fragment is Lucius Brutus, the founder of the Republic, not the tyrannicide: see *JRS* 62 (1972), 19.

[4] *Ben.* 5. 16, 4. In *De Clementia* 1. 3, 3 Seneca gives a similar argument for the continuation, but not the establishment, of the Principate.

[5] Suet. *Aug.* 7. 2.

[6] *Cons. Helv.* 9. 3; *Ben.* 2. 20; *Ep.* 108. 30 and Haase, frag. XII (33), are the only passages known to me.

[7] *Ben.* 2. 20, 2.

as the closest alternative. As Augustus knew, unrepublican terminology was best avoided. Seneca showed his dislike of this traditional attitude in *De Clementia*, but even there he respected it by not calling Nero *rex* directly. In his other works, though Seneca clearly thinks of *principes* and *reges* as belonging to the same category for most purposes, he avoids explicit identification.[1]

In *De Re Publica*, Cicero had already described the regal period as the childhood and youth of Rome, and represented the kings as inventing and obeying laws. In the Lactantius fragment, Rome is said to have been 'disciplinis pluribus institutisque formata' by the kings before Tarquin, but *leges* are characteristic of the Republic at whose foundation Rome is said 'maluisse legibus obtemperare quam regibus'. This is a jingle that might well please the Roman rhetorical taste,[2] and we find it used before and after this passage was written to describe the same political event. Cicero says in *De Officiis* that the Romans established kings of good character to ensure justice and would have been content had a single just and good man continued to guarantee equal rights. *Leges* were invented when the system broke down: 'eademque constituendarum legum fuit causa, quae regum.'[3] Cicero is here sacrificing to the striking formula the traditional view of the kings, which he had himself earlier expounded.[4] Livy ostentatiously avoids the jingle by characterizing the new Republic: 'imperia legum potentiora quam hominum' (not *regum*).[5] This phrase also shows what qualification the doctrine needed to fit Roman history: although there were *leges* under the kings, the

---

[1] He comes closest to identification in *Ben.* 5. 4, 2 but even here we are not explicitly told, as in *De Clementia*, that the only difference is the *nomen*.

[2] *Rhetor ad Herennium* 2. 40 gives as an example of inappropriateness: 'si quis potens dixerit: "satius est uti regibus quam uti malis legibus."' This is cited by Castiglioni, *Riv. di fil.* 6 (1928), 466, who suggests a rhetorical origin for the phrase in the Lactantius fragment.

[3] *Off.* 2. 41–2.

[4] In *De Re Publica*. For the traditional view of Romulus as lawgiver see Furneaux's note on Tacitus, *Ann.* 3. 26, 5. K. von Fritz, *The Theory of the Mixed Constitution in Antiquity*, New York, 1954, pp. 124 ff., discusses the extent to which Polybius' lost account is behind Cicero's account.

[5] 2. 1. In 2. 3 the young conspirators contrast the inexorability of *leges* with the comfortable partiality of a king.

will of the king was more powerful. Tacitus shows himself concerned to preserve the traditional version, but he betrays none the less the influence of the *leges–reges* antithesis.[1] Discussing the development of law, he imagines a stage without government where men were pure and needed no restraints, followed by one of moral decline in which 'dominationes' developed. He adds: 'quidam statim aut postquam regum pertaesum, leges maluerunt.' Athens is cited, presumably to exemplify the latter. Rome is among the former. Romulus represents the original *dominatio* and is followed immediately by law-giving kings. This odd version of history and the ambiguity of his formula[2] suggest that Tacitus has made a compromise between traditional Roman history and a formula that put the development of law subsequent to a period of monarchy. In the Lactantius fragment, the beginning of law in Rome comes after the expulsion of the king-become-tyrant (as in *De Officiis*), but the Roman tradition about the kings is preserved by speaking of *disciplinae* and *instituta*.

Have Cicero, 'Seneca', and Tacitus accommodated history to a mere rhetorical device or did they have in mind a doctrine that, in Latin, could be expressed in a neat antithesis? Probability is with the latter as Cicero may be drawing on Panaetius in the *De Officiis* passage[3] and a similar idea is found in Lucretius, without exploitation of the rhetorical antithesis;[4] Seneca, moreover, preserves and attributes to Posidonius a view that could be one version of the doctrine.[5] Posidonius held that the first generation of men lived according to nature and were ruled by the best man who was at once *dux* and *lex*. In this golden age the kings were *sapientes*, preserving harmony in their flocks and teaching them what was beneficial to them. But after vices developed and the kingship became tyranny, *leges* became necessary. The examples given are all Greek: the laws of Solon, Lycurgus, Zaleucus, and

---

[1] *Ann.* 3. 26.

[2] For those who acted *statim*, *leges* are an alternative to *dominationes*; for the others, they are an alternative to *reges*.

[3] *Off.* 2. 41–2 is included as no. 120 of van Straaten's collection, *Panaetii Rhodii Fragmenta*³, Leiden, 1962.

[4] 5. 1105–44.

[5] *Ep.* 90. 4–6.

Charondas.[1] Seneca says that he agrees with this theory, and a hint of how he would have applied it to Rome can be found in the description of Solon as the man 'qui Athenas aequo iure fundavit', for Seneca elsewhere indicates that *aequalitas civilis iuris* and *leges* were the essence of the Republic.[2] The relation of Tacitus' exposition to Seneca's citation from Posidonius has been remarked, but in fact, Tacitus' discussion is not nearly as close to it as the Lactantius fragment, which is a perfect application of the theory to Roman history. Tacitus' anarchic golden age and his ascription of *leges* to kings do not mar the Posidonian pattern here where history opens with Romulus and the introduction of *leges* is reserved until after the expulsion of the tyrant.

There is no need to assume, of course, that the author of the Lactantius fragment used Posidonius and not some earlier Greek or a Roman treatment of the theory. But the treatment of this theme, like that of the others in the fragment, shows that Seneca the philosopher *could* have been the author. For those of us who believe that he was, the passage shows Seneca neatly blending Greek theory with traditional Roman ideas about the regal period and the decline and fall of the Republic—unless, of course, he took over the blend from some Latin predecessor.

[1] These conventional examples do not really fit the doctrine: Zaleucus and Charondas were starting from scratch, not replacing a tyranny, Lycurgus did not *replace* monarchy by laws, and Solon did not follow immediately on the end of a monarchy. But perhaps the doctrine was *a priori*, confirmed by a deliberately rough conception of Athenian history. Cf. the discussion by von Fritz, *Mixed Constitution*, of Herodotus 3. 80–3 (pp. 69–70) and Polybius 6. 7–9 (pp. 73–4).

[2] *Ben.* 2. 20, 2; *Ep.* 86. 2–3.

6

THE PHILOSOPHER ON THE
PRINCIPATE

I

WHAT Seneca says of the last years of the Republic shows that he lamented its demise but regarded the change to the Principate as irrevocable. What was lost with the Republic was *libertas* and the rule of law; what was gained was peace and security. Seneca does not compare the two constitutions. Did he approve of the Principate as a form of government?

It is a common view that the Stoics of the first century A.D. can have had, on philosophical grounds, only sympathy for the Principate as they favoured monarchy as a constitution. One of the main texts cited in support of this view is Seneca's condemnation of Brutus for failing to behave 'ex institutione Stoica': Caesar's assassin feared the name of king 'cum optimus civitatis status sub rege iusto sit'.[1]

If Seneca means literally that, to the Stoics, monarchy was the best form of government, he is guilty of an anachronism in attributing to Brutus' contemporaries the Stoic opinions of his own day. For if the representatives of the Middle Stoa pronounced at all on the relative merits of constitutions, they put the mixed constitution first. There is no reason to doubt that Panaetius, an active politician in the paternalistic aristocracy of Rhodes, shared, if he did not originate, the views on this subject that Scipio is said to have discussed with him and Polybius, in Cicero's *De*

---

[1] *Ben.* 2. 20. Brutus, of course, was not technically a Stoic but a follower of the Old Academy of Antiochus of Ascalon (Cicero, *Fin.* 5. 8). No doubt the adoption of his uncle as a Stoic saint made the mistake inevitable, and Antiochus himself was 'si perpauca mutavisset, germanissimus Stoicus', according to Cicero, *Acad.* 2. 132.

Re Publica. Cicero, who thus associated Panaetius with the prime
defender of the mixed constitution,[1] tells us also that the works of
Panaetius were full of citations from earlier philosophers including
Dicaearchus, the man who worked out in detail the application
of the mixed constitution to Sparta.[2]

The view may in fact have been the traditional Stoic one as
well.[3] Aristotle described how the doctrine of the mixed constitution, already popular earlier, was applied to Sparta in various
ways.[4] The Early Stoa probably adopted this analysis of Spartan
government as one proof of its excellence,[5] for Diogenes Laertius,
discussing the views of Zeno and Chrysippus on government,
says that the Stoics hold the best form of government to be a
mixture of democracy, kingship, and aristocracy,[6] while two of
Zeno's disciples wrote works on the Spartan constitution. Of
Persaeus we have only trivial fragments, but we do know that
Sphaerus' treatise at least contained a discussion of the number of
γέροντες in the Spartan constitution.[7] None the less, Sphaerus'
interest in the Spartan constitution probably centred not on the
form of the whole but on the characteristic institutions—the
ἀγωγή, the gymnastics, and συσσιτία—which he helped King
Cleomenes to restore to proper 'Lycurgan' form.[8] The Stoics
generally were probably not so much interested in the Spartan

---

[1] *Rep.* 1. 34. Von Fritz, *The Theory of the Mixed Constitution*, underestimates
the Stoic influence on Polybius. Cf. M. E. Reesor, *The Political Theory of the
Old and Middle Stoa*, p. 33; J. Kargl, *Die Lehre der Stoiker vom Staat*, Erlangen,
1913, p. 69. Von Fritz, pp. 54 ff., draws a sharp distinction between Polybius'
view that weakness and necessity are the origins of society, and the Stoic emphasis
on the natural gregariousness of men. But it is a matter of emphasis. As he admits,
Off. 1. 11–12 (from Panaetius) combines the two motifs (cf. the Old Academy's
'communicatio utilitatum et ipsa caritas generis humani', *Fin.* 5. 65). Cicero
preferred to stress the second (*Off.* 1. 158).

[2] *Fin.* 4. 79. In *Leg.* 3. 15–6 Cicero may be presenting the view of Panaetius'
teacher Diogenes (cf. 3. 13): the power of the king must be limited. Note the
Spartan example.

[3] So F. W. Walbank, *Polybius*, I, p. 641; D. R. Dudley, *A History of Cynicism*,
London, 1937, p. 129; J. Kargl, pp. 63–9. Against: Reesor, *Political Theory of the
Old and Middle Stoa*, p. 20, and von Fritz, p. 82, who regard Diogenes Laertius'
evidence as isolated (below, n. 6).

[4] *Pol.* 2. 1265ᵇ.

[5] Kargl, *Die Lehre der Stoiker vom Staat*, pp. 63–9.

[6] 7. 131.   [7] Plut. *Lyc.* 5.   [8] Plut. *Cleom.* 11.

government as in their way of life—communal ownership, simple food, lack of coinage, training in self-control, features which Zeno and Chrysippus[1] borrowed for their ideal states.[2] The fragments show that these ideal states were not models for the practical statesman. Descriptions of a natural community of men living under the divine law, imbued with the full complement of Stoic virtues and unhampered by social conventions, these πολιτεῖαι were not recipes for a real state, not even a world state. That is why, despite the many titles of political works credited to the early Stoics, Cicero could maintain that the second-century Stoics, Diogenes and Panaetius, were the first to deal with politics in a detailed and useful way.[3]

The primarily moral concerns of their political theory enabled the Stoics, despite their theoretical preference for the mixed constitution, to come to terms with the dominant contemporary form of government—monarchy. Cleanthes, Persaeus, and Sphaerus, who admired Sparta, also wrote treatises περὶ βασιλείας. Of these nothing remains, but Sphaerus' could have been relevant to Cleomenes whose zeal for the πάτριος πολιτεία did not exclude a vigorous defence of the powers of monarchy.[4] Persaeus was for a long period at the court of Antigonus Gonatas, fought in his wars, and influenced his policies.[5] Pohlenz has suggested that he taught Antigonus the definition of kingship as ἔνδοξος δουλεία.[6]

There is no reason to posit a distinctive Stoic theory of kingship.[7] Like other philosophical schools, the Stoics will have stressed the necessity for the highest virtue in the king and his

---

[1] Chrysippus probably differed from Zeno (D.L. 7. 33) in admitting private property (Cicero, Fin. 3. 67).

[2] See the discussion in Kargl, Die Lehre der Stoiker vom Staat, pp. 40, 64; H. C. Baldry, The Unity of Mankind in Greek Thought, Cambridge, 1965, pp. 156 ff.

[3] Leg. 3. 14: 'nam veteres verbo tenus acute illi quidem, sed non ad hunc usum popularem atque civilem de re publica disserebant.'

[4] Plut. Cleom. 7–11.

[5] SVF I, no. 4. 439 ff., pp. 97 ff.

[6] See above, p. 145 n. 3.

[7] E. Goodenough, Yale Classical Studies I (1928), 55 ff., firmly denied a Stoic origin for the more metaphysical views of kingship; followed now by Adam, Clementia Principis, pp. 12–18.

duty to care for his subjects and earn their love.[1] The wise man could be a king, or advise a king who had the capacity for virtue even if he had not yet achieved it.[2] Many Stoic doctrines lent themselves admirably to such application. If the wise man was a king, so the king should be a wise man.[3] If the cosmos could be likened to an organism, so could the state,[4] and the mind of that organism was the king.[5] No doubt some Stoic treatises pronounced kingship the best form of government on the ground that it was the most natural: traces of that argument survive in references to kingship as the natural type of organization among animals[6] and primitive men.[7]

The ultimate proof of nature's intentions was the organization of the cosmos under the rule of a just God.[8]

In the late Republic, Stoic admirers of Rome probably concentrated on analysing Rome as a contemporary model of the mixed constitution. But their interest in the political works of Plato and Aristotle makes it likely that they combined with this their view that, of the simple forms, kingship was the best, while holding it inferior to the mixed constitution by reason of its tendency to

[1] e.g. Posidonius in Seneca, *Ep.* 90. 4–6, on the first kings; Musonius Rufus, frag. 8 Hense, with the discussion of A. C. van Geytenbeek, *Musonius Rufus and Greek Diatribe*, Assen, 1962, pp. 127 ff.

[2] *SVF* 3. 690, 691.

[3] Musonius Rufus, frag. 8 Hense. The paradox was maintained by Seneca's teacher, Attalus (*Ep.* 108. 13).

[4] Seneca, *Ep.* 95. 52; Epictetus 2. 5, 25–6.

[5] See above, p. 144 n. 4.

[6] Seneca, *Ep.* 90. 4 (Posidonius); Dio Chrysostom, *On Kingship* 3. 50, where he appends to his comparison of monarchy, aristocracy, and democracy in 41 ff. (giving Socrates' followers as his authority for views found in Plato), the view that the organization of cattle and bees shows that the rule of the strong over his inferiors is the natural form for man. Plato is unlikely to be the source of that view as *Pol.* 267 d ff.; 301 b shows.

[7] On this argument see J. Béranger, *Recherches sur l'aspect idéologique du Principat*, pp. 241–2, citing Plato (*Leg.* 3. 690 a–c), Polybius (6. 4, 2), and Seneca, *Ep.* 90. 4; *Clem.* 1. 19, 2. None of these authors explicitly draws the conclusion that monarchy is the best form.

[8] A stock argument: Isoc. *Nic.* 26; Dio Chrys. 36. 31–2 where it is presented as Stoic; 3. 51–2 with the idea of *pronoia* dear to the Stoics. Cf. also Musonius' ζηλωτὴς τοῦ Διός (frag. 8 Hense). 'Deorum exemplum sequi' was a basic Stoic tenet (*Ben.* 4. 25, 1), at least in the later period.

degenerate.[1] This is the view attributed to Scipio in Cicero's *De Re Publica* where the formulations 'singulorum dominatus, si modo iusti sint, esse optimos' and 'cum rex iniustus esse coepit, perit [regnum], et est idem ille tyrannus, deterrimum genus et finitimum optimo'[2] are strikingly similar to Seneca's 'optimus civitatis status sub rege iusto'. It seems to me entirely possible that Seneca is merely recalling here, as a weapon against Brutus, the view of the Stoa in Brutus' day, that kingship was the best of the *simple* forms of government. In that case, he is guilty of sophistry rather than anachronism.[3]

With the fall of the Republic, interest in the doctrine of the mixed constitution naturally disappeared for practical men at Rome. Tacitus expresses what was probably a general disillusionment with the doctrine: 'delecta ex iis et consociata rei publicae forma laudari facilius quam evenire, vel si evenit, haud diuturna esse potest.'[4] It was not necessary to revive the ideas of the old Stoa about monarchy: they had never wholly disappeared. All that was necessary was to describe the government of Rome according to one Stoic doctrine rather than another.

For this application of Stoicism to the Principate of the Julio-Claudians, *De Clementia* is our most important document. As was argued earlier, Seneca there reveals clearly enough that the identification of *princeps* and *rex* might not be easily accepted by all his readers. Ambitious to inspire Nero and to educate his public according to Greek doctrine, Seneca still carefully avoided actually calling Nero *rex*. He showed the same tact in omitting praise of kingship. Seneca did not explicitly identify the 'laetissima forma rei publicae' as *regnum*, and though he used the traditional psychological, cosmological, and zoological analogies for monarchy, he did not use them to demonstrate the superiority of that constitution over others. A *rex* or *princeps*, he wrote, is the *mens*

---

[1] Plato, *Pol.* 302 e ff.; Arist. *Pol.* 3. 12, 1 (1288ᵃ) (monarchy or aristocracy best). Degeneration: Cicero, *Rep.* 1. 69; Seneca, *Ep.* 90. 6 (Posidonius).

[2] 1. 61, 65.

[3] This seems preferable to the view of Adam, *Clementia Principis*, pp. 65–6, that Seneca here exaggerates the Old Stoic acceptance of monarchy in order to justify his own support of Nero's absolutism.

[4] *Ann.* 4. 33.

of the political *corpus*—which explains why Nero is indispensable to Rome once the system exists (1. 3, 5-4, 3). Nero is described as God's chosen representative on earth (1. 1, 2), but in order to indicate, not to justify, his power and responsibility. The merciful rule of the gods is an example to be followed (1. 5, 7; 7. 1-3). Seneca alludes once to the doctrine that kingship is natural (1. 19, 2): 'Natura enim commenta est regem, quod et ex aliis animalibus licet cognoscere et ex apibus', but the point he makes is not that kingship is the perfect form of government, but that there is a *lex naturae* ordaining the correct character and behaviour of the king: the 'king' of the bees has no sting.[1]

Of course, tact alone does not account for Seneca's failure to exploit here all the resources of Stoic argument. His interest was in the moral quality of the ruler—that is what mattered to Rome. If the mixed constitution had failed, why should any other constitution be, in itself, a guarantee? And, strictly speaking, the Stoics themselves could only approve of monarchy under the rule of a *sapiens*.

Our present subject, however, is not Seneca the minister and propagandist, but Seneca the writer of philosophy. How did the philosopher view the Principate? He made no pronouncements on the form of government—unless we take his rebuke in *De Beneficiis* to the 'Stoic' Brutus for un-Stoic fears of Caesar's regal ambitions to be serious approbation by the Stoic Seneca of the regal system of the Caesars.

Outside of *De Clementia*, in fact, Seneca's use of the term *rex* exhibits all the ambiguity one would expect of the philosophical Roman. Greek philosophy brought with it general maxims and examples of the moral behaviour of kings and their dependants.[2]

---

[1] H. Dahlmann, *Akad. d. Wiss. und d. Literatur in Mainz* 10 (1954), 547 ff., argues that Seneca is probably inspired here by Virgil's *Georgics* 4, where the bees' life is to be understood as a paradigm for man, but the analogy was traditional (above, p. 145 n. 7). Dahlmann argues that Virgil implies what, according to him, Seneca expressly states—that monarchy is the *natural* form of government, and that Virgil is using Stoicism to justify the rule of Octavian. But no Roman would advocate the Oriental form of kingship that Virgil attributes to the bees (G. 4. 210-11), cf. Seneca's attitude, below, p. 209.

[2] e.g. *Ira* 2. 23, 3; 2. 33, 2; 3. 14, 6; 3. 30, 5; *Brev. Vit.* 17. 1; *Ben.* 4. 37, 2; *Ep.* 94. 14.

Seneca found it quite natural to apply these precepts to the *princeps* and his *cives*, and to draw from them added examples. For supreme power in any form requires restraint on anger and punishment, and complicates the normal workings of obligation and benefit. Thus general advice about life in a king's court is illustrated by the behaviour of Gaius Caesar and Achilles and Lysimachus.[1] The need of the powerful for frank advice is illustrated by the troubles of Augustus and Xerxes.[2] The paradox that the 'sapiens omnia habet' is explained, in the traditional way, by comparison with the king and, for variation, with the similar condition of the Princeps: Caesar, like the *optimus rex*, has everything in his power, but not in his possession.[3]

Though the point is never made as obviously as in *De Clementia*, Seneca sometimes appears to insist on the similarity in other words. Rejecting the common view that it is shameful to be outdone in benefits, Seneca points out that the view rules out accepting favours from *praepotentes viri*, 'a principibus dico, a regibus'. But, he objects, it is possible to help *reges* and *principes* whose overriding power depends on the consent and services of their inferiors.[4] In Letter 73, Seneca talks about the particular gratitude philosophers owe to rulers who provide them with the necessary *otium*. Here 'magistratus, reges, ei per quos publica administrantur' is picked up by the term *principes* and allusions to *curia* and *forum*, which lead back to *rex*. These passages do not occur in works of political theory: Seneca is discussing personal ethics, specifically *beneficia*,[5] and treating both the constant problem, for the upper orders, of acceptance and repayment of imperial favour, and the particular problem current in 63 and 64 of political withdrawal, intended or construed as a form of protest against the regime. But the model proposed is that of king and inferior: the man with supreme power performs unrepayable services, but he can be supported and served. His greatest benefit is national peace and private leisure, to which open gratitude is

---

[1] *Ira* 2. 33; *Tranq.* 14. 3 ff.
[2] *Ben.* 6. 30, 3–32, 4.   [3] Ibid. 7. 5, 1; 6, 2.
[4] Ibid. 5. 4, 2–3.
[5] *Ep.* 73. 6–9 covers the same ground as *Ben.* 6. 18–24.

the proper return.¹ Here, as in *De Clementia*, there are lessons for both sides.

None the less, the Roman connotations of *rex* are not forgotten. Like Lucan, Seneca can use the word to condemn a Princeps. Augustus praised the frankness of Agrippa and Maecenas and claimed that he could not replace them. 'Regalis ingenii mos est', says Seneca, 'in praesentium contumeliam amissa laudare et his virtutem dare vera dicendi, a quibus iam audiendi periculum non est.'² He shares also the Roman (and the Greek) scorn for Oriental monarchy with its obeisance and other signs of servitude. Antony, says Seneca, showed his ingratitude to his country by threatening her 'ne Romanis quidem regibus'.³ Gaius Caesar, who forced a consular to kiss his gold slipper—the left one at that —was a man destined 'ut mores liberae civitatis Persica servitute mutaret'.⁴ His attempt to build a bridge of boats across Puteoli bay is condemned as imitation of a foreign king.⁵

Seneca the philosopher, then, wrote of the Principate in terms similar to those used by Seneca the statesman in *De Clementia*, but he was not so insistent on regarding the Princeps as *rex*, and his thoughts on the system had their darker side. His regret for the Republic we have marked before, but there is also Roman resentment of a king and fear of the Oriental model.

In his other works, as in *De Clementia*, Seneca regards the power of the Princeps as absolute and sees the state as an organism.⁶

¹ *Ep.* 73. 9.
² *Ben.* 6. 32, 4. The condemnation of *primae* and *secundae admissiones* in *Ben.* 6. 34, 1 (above, p. 142) applies probably to rich Romans outside the imperial house but certainly includes the Princeps and imperial ladies (cf. the formal salutations of Livia (Dio 57. 12) and Agrippina (60. 33, 1)).
³ *Ben.* 5. 16, 6.
⁴ *Ben.* 2. 12, 1–2. 'Libera' does not, of course, mean that Seneca really believed that the Principate was the restored Republic. The point of *libertas* here is behaviour worthy of a free man, not a slave. Cf. *Ira* 3. 17, 1—Alexander killed Clitus 'parum adulantem et pigre ex Macedone ac libero in Persicam servitutem transeuntem'.
⁵ *Brev. Vit.* 18. 5.
⁶ *Ben.* 7. 6, 2; *Brev. Vit.* 4. 4 of Augustus: 'qui omnia videbat ex se uno pendentia'. The date Seneca has in mind is perhaps 27 B.C. (Dio 53. 9, 1) or later (cf. 4. 5); ibid. 4. 6: 'velut grave multo sanguine corpus parte semper aliqua rumpebatur'.

But the glowing optimistic tone of that work appears only in his earlier adulation of Claudius in the Consolation to Polybius. Here we find mention of the noble burden of rule: 'Caesari quoque ipsi, cui omnia licent, propter hoc ipsum multa non licent', and praise of the ruler's supreme virtue, *clementia*.[1] This praise, of course, suits Seneca's plea for return from exile, but, as Momigliano has written, 'Language that, after the manner of the time, might be thought no more than ordinary courtier's flattery is transformed by the tendency to moralize ingrained in Seneca's nature.'[2] Claudius is told to hold the Empire more by benefits than by arms and is warned against Gaius' cruelty and his taste for dice.[3] The resemblance to the model held up to Nero in *De Clementia* shows that if Seneca flattered Claudius, he at least portrayed him as he really thought he should be.

II

Seneca says far more about the men than about the system. A recent student of historical examples in Seneca has found with disappointment that Seneca the statesman shows in them little sign of a political point of view. Even in his portraits of the *principes* where he had personal experience to guide him, says the critic, all judgements are moral and the examples supply the needs of the context.[4] Anecdotes about the Caesars do, it is true, fit the context in Seneca, but that does not prevent them from indicating Seneca's opinions. If they are not contradictory or unrelated to each other, but reveal a consistent point of view, we may fairly regard them as conveying the philosopher's judgement, especially since the rhetorical schools cannot already have developed all of his examples about Gaius and Claudius. Seneca's own experience must often be the source. That the imperial *exempla* are, like his other *exempla*, essentially moral is also true.

---

[1] *Cons. Polyb.* 7. 2; 13. 2 ff.

[2] A. Momigliano, *Claudius*, Oxford, 1934, pp. 74–6, but I do not share his view that the moralizing consists in deliberate caricature, see Appendix B3.

[3] 13. 3, 17. 4. The taste for dice was shared by Claudius before and after becoming Princeps (Suet. *Cl.* 5. 33; *Apoc.* 12. 3; 14. 4; 15. 1).

[4] Kühnen, *Seneca und die römische Geschichte*, p. 75.

But did Seneca have a political view of the Principate as distinct from his moral view of the Princeps? The reader of *De Clementia* may fairly wonder.

Seneca's life spanned the reigns of four men. Two of these appear twice as often as the others in his works: Augustus and Gaius, white and black—though Augustus is not completely white. In *De Clementia*, Augustus was offered to Nero as the model of the good Princeps.[1] That corresponded with what Nero had already said in public, and with the common hope at his accession.[2] More than a decade earlier, Seneca had held up Augustus as a model to Claudius—which agreed with that Emperor's pronouncements.[3]

Augustus' main quality for Seneca, even outside these works, was his clemency. This was part of his general self-control by which he restrained his grief and his anger.[4] To this there was one exception: he lost his temper and detailed his daughter's scandalous adultery to the Senate.[5] Augustus had good judgement and equal generosity in bestowing benefits.[6] His judgement of men was often excellent,[7] especially in choosing Agrippa,[8] but Seneca expresses his own disapproval of Maecenas at great length. This is not mere literary and moral censure; Maecenas was a political mistake. He cut a deplorable figure as the Princeps' representative: 'nam etiam cum absentis Caesaris partibus fungeretur, signum a discincto petebatur.'[9]

In *De Clementia*, Seneca's Augustus adds to his clemency a proper concern for the freedom of thought of others.[10] The picture is not so rosy in *De Beneficiis* where Seneca says of Augustus' rule (in contrast to that of Tiberius): 'nondum hominibus verba sua periculosa erant, iam molesta.'[11] None the less, the example he gives shows Augustus forgiving and generous towards a man who confessed his hostile remarks to the Emperor. Seneca

---

[1] 1. 9 ff.; 1. 16. [2] Suet. *Nero* 10. 1; *Clem.* 1. 1, 6.
[3] *Cons. Polyb.* 12. 5; Suet. *Cl.* 11. 2.
[4] *Cons. Marc.* 15. 2; *Cons. Polyb.* 15. 3; *Ira* 3. 23, 4; 3. 40; *Ben.* 2. 25, 1; 3. 27.
[5] *Ben.* 6. 32. [6] *Ibid.* 1. 15, 5; 2. 27, 2; 3. 27, 4.
[7] *Cons. Marc.* 2. 3; *NQ* 1. 16, 1; *Ep.* 83. 14.
[8] *Ep.* 94. 46; *Ben.* 3. 32. [9] *Ep.* 114. 6.
[10] *Clem.* 1. 15, 4–6; 1. 10, 3. [11] *Ben.* 3. 27.

saves his bitterness for the lack of freedom accorded to Augustus' *amici*.[1] Seneca preaches at length the value to rulers of men who speak the truth, but notes that it is not easy to avoid servitude in advising a king, and that Augustus, in this respect, behaved like one.

These reservations about Augustus cover various periods of his reign. In *De Clementia*, however, for purposes of comparison with Nero, the cruel Octavian of the Civil Wars and proscriptions was sharply contrasted with the later perfect Augustus. *De Brevitate Vitae*, written about the same time, shows a similar repugnance for the Civil Wars but Seneca here speaks of the burden of rule and represents Augustus as 'coactus'.[2] And although Seneca goes on to speak of the armies of Augustus as exhausted with Roman slaughter, he condones their dispatch to foreign wars by describing them as wars of pacification and defence.[3] Again, in *De Clementia*, Nero was told that, although Augustus had to rule men who had not yet been tamed, his *clementia* made him popular and secure, so that after the conspiracy of Cinna (which Seneca clearly places *c*. 16 B.C.) there were no more plots.[4] (The adultery of Julia is noted in a different context.)[5] In *De Brevitate Vitae*, however, Seneca notes the scandal of Augustus' daughter as one of many political conspiracies which were symptoms of disease in the body politic.[6] The picture in *De Brevitate Vitae* is clearly in line with that of Seneca's other works; the contradictions with *De Clementia* are intelligible. It is the fact that Seneca casts Augustus in that work as a model for Nero, but a model whom Nero will surpass by a better start,

---

[1] *Ben.* 6. 32, 4; cf. above, p. 209.

[2] *Brev. Vit.* 4. 5. In the *Octavia* (477 ff.), Seneca is made to praise Augustus' clemency and to regard the early wars as a misfortune: it is Nero (504 ff.) who takes over the idea in *De Clementia* and goes on to depict the whole reign as based on fear.

[3] *Brev. Vit.* 4. 5. P. Jal, *REL* 35 (1957), 249–50, seems to me in error in thinking that this passage is primarily hostile. Cf. also *Ben.* 3. 32 where Octavian is admired 'post debellata arma civilia . . . securae paci praesidentem', and Agrippa is praised for the naval crown he won in the civil struggle at Naulochus.

[4] 1. 9, 12; 10, 2. (For the date of Cinna's conspiracy see Appendix A3.)

[5] 1. 10, 3.

[6] J. Basore in the Loeb ed., *Seneca Moral Essays*, II, pp. 298–9, n. *c*, remarks that Seneca's medical language here 'is reminiscent of Augustus' own characterization of Julia and his two grandchildren in Suetonius, *Aug.* 65. 5'.

that has dictated the unrealistic dichotomy of the reign into a very bad and a very good part.

The *Apocolocyntosis* ridicules everyone, even Augustus. There is a clear poke at the *Res Gestae* and Augustus fills his maiden speech in the Council of the Gods with laments about his relatives.[1] Yet there is no serious criticism of the first Princeps here.

Gaius Caesar, for Seneca, is consistently a monster. He is a disgrace to humanity, demented, and suffering from every vice: cruelty, anger, greed, luxury, pride, and deceit.[2] With such qualities, a ruler could hardly be other than a tyrant. His rule was a *clades* for the human race, and nearly destroyed the Empire completely,[3] as Gaius ate the tribute of three provinces and neglected the corn supply of Rome.[4] Finally, Seneca condemns Gaius by characteristically Roman criticisms: he could not grieve or rejoice *principaliter* and his mode of self-consolation was no example for a Roman.[5] He tried to introduce Persian servitude; his cruelty was the more appalling because it was directed against senators and knights.[6]

In the light of Seneca's constant use of Gaius as an *exemplum*, his failure to appear in *De Clementia* may well be significant, unless he appeared in the part of the work that is lost. Perhaps Seneca did not think it wise to remind Nero or the public of the vices of Nero's uncle to whose tastes the Emperor already inclined.

It is natural to look to Seneca's life for an explanation of why he refers so often, and so bitterly, to the reign of Gaius. Seneca was then attracting notice for his merits as an orator, which the Emperor did not appreciate, and he had perhaps been in serious danger. Perhaps he avenged himself posthumously for this and for the loss of friends who appear in his works as victims of

---

[1] Above, p. 132 n. 1. The *Res Gestae* is also the butt of *Brev. Vit.* 4. 5. See commentary of P. Grimal, Paris, 1959, ad loc.

[2] *Cons. Polyb.* 17. 3; *Ira* 1. 20, 9; *Ira* 2. 33; *Const. Sap.* 8. 1; *Tranq.* 14. 4–10; *Ben.* 4. 31, 2; *NQ* 4, pref. 15; *Ira* 3. 21, 5; *Tranq.* 11. 10; *Cons. Helv.* 10. 4; *Brev. Vit.* 18. 5; *Ben.* 2. 12, 1; *Tranq.* 11. 12.

[3] *Cons. Polyb.* 13. 1—Claudius said this in public (Jos. *AJ* 19. 284).

[4] *Cons. Helv.* 10. 4; *Brev. Vit.* 18. 5.

[5] *Cons. Polyb.* 17. 4, 6.

[6] *Const. Sap.* 18. 2: 'non dico consulari . . .'; *Ira* 3. 19: senators treated like *mancipia*.

Gaius: Lentulus Gaetulicus, the patron of his friend Lucilius,[1] Julius Graecinus, who died 'quod melior vir erat quam esse quemquam tyranno expedit';[2] Valerius Asiaticus, one of Gaius' *primi amici*, who was brutally insulted; Julius Canus, whose heroic death scene, recorded in great detail,[3] foreshadowed Seneca's in solemnity and Petronius' in bravado. But Seneca had literary reasons as well: Gaius was a flamboyant Princeps who met a satisfactorily violent end, thus an ideal subject for a moralist. Moreover, Seneca generally eschewed living examples, but liked recent ones, so that he relied heavily on his experience as a senator of the reign of Gaius, when writing the bulk of his extant works under Claudius and Nero. Hence, most of the references to men he had known come from the days of Gaius: the aged Turranius, so tenacious of his post; the contemptible consulars, Fabius Persicus and Caninius Rebilus; Passienus Crispus and M. Vinicius, husbands of Gaius' sisters.[4]

Many of Seneca's friends, like Lucilius and the Cynic philosopher, Demetrius, could help him remember the period: his consular colleague, Trebellius Maximus (or his father) had come forth in the Senate to remove a ring with Gaius' image from the finger of the consul who was hailing that Emperor's assassination as the cue for the restoration of the Republic.[5] It is not then surprising that Seneca reverts three times to that bloody event.[6] The cause—Gaius' *superbia* and his intolerable insults—Seneca apparently regards as legitimate, and of course, as a tyrant, Gaius counted among those madmen who may justifiably be killed for their own good.[7] If Seneca was present in the theatre or the Senate during that memorable crisis, he betrays no involvement and claims no first-hand information.[8] In discussing the murder, he

[1] *NQ* 4, pref. 15.

[2] See above, p. 70 n. 5; below, p. 290.

[3] *Const. Sap.* 18. 2; *Tranq.* 14. 4 ff.

[4] *Brev. Vit.* 20. 3; *Ben.* 2. 21, 5–6; 4. 30, 2; 1. 15, 5; *NQ* 4, pref. 6; *Ep.* 122. 12.

[5] See Appendix D2. On Demetrius see below, pp. 297 n. 2; 311–12.

[6] *Ira* 1. 20, 9; *Const. Sap.* 18; *Ep.* 4. 7.

[7] *Ben.* 7. 20, 3.

[8] See especially *Ira* 1. 20, 9: 'non puto parum momenti hanc eius vocem ad incitandas coniuratorum mentes addidisse'—as if their motive was a matter of airy speculation to a senator of Seneca's connections!

notes that even if we have abstained from personal revenge, there is consolation in the thought that someone will come to punish the insolence of the man who has insulted us because he is bound to have offended others.[1] Perhaps this is a reference to Seneca's own insulting treatment and his passive role in 41, but Seneca does not go out of his way to enlighten us biographically.

In sharp contrast to his treatment of Gaius, Seneca rarely conveys any judgement in his references to Tiberius. His most favourable portrait occurs in the Consolation to Marcia where Tiberius serves as a model of fraternal piety and courage in the face of grief.[2] No doubt the fact that Livia had been a friend of Marcia largely explains this enthusiasm, which had official backing from Gaius after 39.[3] In the Consolation to Polybius, Claudius is made to speak similarly of Tiberius, but the passage forms part of Claudius' eulogy of all his relatives,[4] except Gaius, and no doubt reflects Claudius' official view. Seneca has two main charges against Tiberius. The first is that he was lacking in the generosity becoming to a Princeps: he helped impoverished senators only after humiliating them.[5] But Seneca is capable of appreciating Tiberius' wit on these occasions: once, he says, Tiberius remarked to a habitual late sleeper who confessed to an exhausted patrimony: 'sero experrectus es.'[6] The second charge against Tiberius is that he allowed free reign to a judicial terror worse than civil war.[7] Except in De Clementia,[8] Seneca fails to endorse the popular view that Tiberius' early reign was good. He tells, in De Beneficiis, of a man who reminded Tiberius soon after his accession of their previous friendship. 'I do not remember what I was', replied the

---

[1] *Const. Sap.* 18. 5. The example of Gaius was introduced to prove this general point: it is not an obvious personal outburst.

[2] 4. 2; 15. 3.

[3] See above, pp. 23, 57 n. 4; Appendix A1, note A.

[4] 15. 5.

[5] *Ben.* 2. 7, 2–8: the episode belongs very early in the reign, before A.D. 17 (Tac. *Ann.* 2. 48).

[6] *Ep.* 122. 10. Cf. the story of the mullet in *Ep.* 95. 42 where Tiberius' meanness is manifest but sympathetically treated.

[7] *Ben.* 3. 26, 1: 'accusandi frequens et paene publica rabies quae omni civili bello gravius togatam civitatem confecit'.

[8] 1. 1, 6.

Emperor—a remark which could be favourably interpreted as a declaration of impartiality, or a rejection of favouritism on taking office. But for Seneca, the explanation is ingratitude and pride.[1]

It is possible that Seneca's low view even of the early reign has been coloured by his own experience of threatened persecution,[2] but on the whole, Seneca shows far less animus towards Tiberius than one might expect. His teacher in youth, Attalus the Stoic, was exiled through Sejanus' machinations;[3] his uncle, the prefect of Egypt, had been recalled when Sejanus fell. Seneca's own career may have been held up in the last years of Tiberius' reign.[4] None the less, Seneca shows no personal hatred for the man. Unfortunately, there is no psychological understanding either. Tiberius was not a fruitful subject for *exempla* and Seneca lost interest except for his two criticisms.

The treatment of Claudius in the philosophical works is even more surprising. The criticism of Claudius' penal policy in *De Clementia*[5] shows that there was no need to be outstandingly polite about Divus Claudius even in public, and after the death of Agrippina, Nero just stopped short of revoking his apotheosis.[6] Yet, after the extravagant praise of the *Ad Polybium* and the coarse ridicule of the *Apocolocyntosis*, Seneca seems to have lost all interest in him. We have a reference to Claudius' lack of judgement,[7] and the rest is neutral. Although Seneca apparently blamed his exile on Narcissus and Messallina,[8] he felt no need to savage them either. It is unlikely that so striking a pattern would be reversed by the recovery of more works. The patronage policy of the minister[9] seems to be perfectly reflected in the writings of the philosopher. If Seneca was a man of great Spanish vindictiveness, as some have claimed, either the *Apocolocyntosis* satisfied his needs, or he repressed his feelings to avoid damaging the spirit of concord proclaimed by Claudius' deification. More likely, his literary ingenuity on that subject was exhausted: in *Ad Polybium* and again in the funeral speech he wrote for Nero, Seneca had said

---

[1] *Ben.* 5. 25, 2.   [2] *Ep.* 108. 22.
[3] Elder Seneca, *Suas.* 2. 12.   [4] Above, pp. 47–50.
[5] 1. 23, 1.   [6] Charlesworth, *JRS* 27 (1937), 57–8.
[7] *Ben.* 1. 15, 5.   [8] See above, p. 61.   [9] Above, pp. 96 ff.

what could be said in favour of an Emperor who, at least, was not Gaius and was sensitive to the example of Augustus; in the satire he had ridiculed the Emperor and indulged in literary self-parody.[1]

In explaining what Seneca says about different *principes*, his personal experiences have offered some help, literary considerations somewhat more. It remains now to compare what he wrote in his philosophical works about the right behaviour of the *princeps* with his official statement in *De Clementia* and the policies he advocated as adviser. We shall also note measures of Nero relevant to Seneca's suggestions, though a connection between the two is by no means clear in most cases.

Seneca's references to the *principes* are moral in that they concentrate on the virtues and vices of the men, not on 'policies'. This is like Seneca's picture in his political propaganda, and, I have tried to show, very like his principal aims as a statesman. In these works, as in *De Clementia*, clemency and liberality are proper for a *princeps*, virtues that, we have seen, Nero exhibited in the years of Seneca's power.[2] But the more 'senatorial' attitudes are also in evidence: tactful and respectful treatment of the upper orders is essential; Roman dress, Roman self-control must mark off the Roman *princeps* from an Oriental king. Though bitterly opposed to political prosecution, Seneca, realistically, lays little stress on encouraging free speech except for the *amici principis*, for in their frank advice lies the only hope of sane government. He claimed to speak freely to Nero.[3] Equally realistic and related to his own experiences is his approval of the judicious use of dissimulation before the public. Of the behaviour of the Elder Julia, Seneca remarks 'haec tam vindicanda principi quam tacenda'[4]— Nero had followed that precept in dealing with Britannicus but

[1] Weinreich, *Sen. Apocol.*, p. 102 n. 1; Russo, *Divi Claudii Ἀποκολοκύντωσις*[4], p. 99: Claudius in *Cons. Polyb.* lists the bereavements of members of the imperial house. In the *Apoc.* Augustus blames Claudius for such *domestica mala*. In *Cons. Polyb.* the thought of Gaius provokes Claudius' 'pro pudor imperii!' (17.4); in *Apoc.* 10. 2 the thought of Claudius moves Augustus to say 'pudet imperii'. Seneca enjoyed literary parody, above, p. 213 n. 1.

[2] Above, pp. 123 ff., 170–1.

[3] *Clem.* 2. 2, 2. Cf. *Ann.* 15. 61, 1. [4] *Ben.* 6. 32.

failed to apply it to the murder of Agrippina;[1] Seneca praised
the corn officials under Gaius who concealed the desperate grain
shortage from the people.[2] Nero used the same approach in 62.[3]

In *De Ira*, as in *De Clementia*, Seneca describes the *princeps* as
a moral doctor who tries to heal with words before he employs
punishment.[4] One method he had in mind is suggested by a letter
in which he argues for the moral efficacy of laws which 'not only
command but teach' and upholds against Posidonius the value of
prologues to laws.[5] Seneca does not, however, advocate diligent
prosecution under laws.[6] This view accords with Nero's introduction of sumptuary laws while reducing fines under the Lex
Papia Poppaea—measures unfortunately without date.[7] It also fits
with Nero's speech on clemency before recalling Plautius Lateranus. But no Roman needed a philosopher to inspire faith in
sumptuary laws, despite their invariable failure; and no Princeps
needed a philosopher to suggest he deliver moral speeches.

Finally, Seneca's attitude to adoption and the imperial cult, in
so far as it can be extracted from his sparse remarks, can be briefly
outlined. It is now generally recognized that philosophers under
the Principate did not advocate adoption over succession by birth.
This view is fully supported by Seneca's writings. For him,
adoption into the imperial house is a mournful expedient when

---

[1] Above, pp. 79–80.   [2] *Brev. Vit.* 18. 6.   [3] *Ann.* 15. 18.

[4] *Ira* 1. 6, 3; *Clem.* 1. 17, 2; cf. also *Cons. Polyb.* 13. 1. On the basis in Greek
philosophy, and Stoicism in particular, for this analogy, see Weidauer, *Der Prinzipat in Senecas Schrift de Clementia*, pp. 30–4.

[5] *Ep.* 94. 38.

[6] *Clem.* 1. 23: parricide increased with its prosecution. Seneca cannot mean
literally that the crime was 'sine lege' before Claudius.

[7] Suet. *Nero* 10; 16. 2. At least part of the sumptuary legislation dates from 62,
after the death of Burrus (Dio 62. 14). T. Birt, 'Seneca', *Preuss. Jahrb.* 144 (1911),
306, suggested that Seneca sympathized with Augustus' legislation to protect
marriage, citing *Ben.* 6. 32, 1 and frag. 87. The first passage mentions but does not
assess the adultery law, and P. Frassinetti, *RIL* 88 (1955), 182 ff., was able to
argue from frag. 87, adducing also frag. 119, that Seneca was opposed to legislative interference in these matters. But frag. 119 is just a comic allusion to the
Lex Papia Poppaea as it stood before Claudius' relaxation of the provisions for
men over 60 (Suet. *Cl.* 23, cf. Ulpian, *Reg.* XVI. 3–4), and frag. 87, while it
shows that Seneca disapproved of marriages contracted 'ad eludendas leges',
does not show that he disapproved of the law as a moral lead. What it does
suggest is a dislike of its strict enforcement.

the Emperor's direct descendants die.[1] One of Seneca's wishes for Claudius, in his Consolation to Polybius, is that his son may succeed him. Yet, where there is no direct successor and several ties of blood exist, the *princeps* can be praised for a wise choice.[2]

Ultimately, any *princeps* must be accepted cheerfully, for, by his elevation, the gods may be acknowledging the merits of his ancestors, or descendants: in this, the gods share the values of the Roman people who justly elect degenerate nobles to the consulship because of their worthy ancestors.[3] Seneca had seen two Emperors for whom Rome might well reproach the gods,[4] and he probably had reason when he wrote this to fear that Nero would go the same way.

Seneca's main references to worship of the dead *principes* occur in works lauding or deriding them. In *Ad Polybium* Seneca speaks of Augustus as a god, and Claudius as destined to be one after death.[5] In *De Clementia* we find the justification for Augustus' deification in his clemency. Because of this virtue, 'deum esse non tamquam iussi credimus' (1. 10, 3). This is an application of the general idea that the virtues and benefits of the *princeps* earn his deification.[6] The negative form of the notion is found in the *Apocolocyntosis*. There, Janus, wishing to avoid a personal insult to Claudius, proposes that *no* mortal shall again be a god, but Augustus, who has the last word, forbids Claudius to enter Olympus on the grounds of his vices and crimes.[7]

This view of imperial deifications was common among educated Romans from their introduction. Possibly Stoic in origin,[8] it at least suits the emphasis that Stoics put on *providentia*,

---

[1] *Cons. Marc.* 15. 2–3. In *Brev. Vit.* 15. 3 Seneca rates adoption into the family of *sapientes* as superior to birth into a family chosen by fortune, but he makes it clear that worldly adoption is also inferior.

[2] *Cons. Marc.* 2. 3.   [3] *Ben.* 4. 30–2.

[4] Gaius is an example (*Ben.* 4. 31, 2), and Claudius (anonymously in 4. 32, 3).

[5] 15. 3; 12.5.   [6] Implied in *Ep.* 73. 10.   [7] 9. 3; 11. 5.

[8] Weidauer, *Der Prinzipat in Senecas Schrift de Clementia*, pp. 54–5, says that Seneca actually rejected the vulgar form of imperial apotheosis and offered a new morally grounded form, founded on Stoic philosophy. But the *Apocolocyntosis* is not a serious criticism of anything, and, in any case, is aimed at *Claudius'* deification in particular. Cicero, *Nat. Deor.* 2. 62, does present the idea that deification is an expression of gratitude for benefits conferred as Stoic, but in

maintaining that our very names for the gods refer to their *munera*.[1] It also fits with the Stoic belief that men and gods are related and that the highest element in man is divine. Seneca states frequently that the *sapiens*, through virtue, is the equal of the gods.[2] Through philosophy, men reach the gods, or rather God enters man,[3] for the *bonus animus* is a god residing in a human body.[4] The *sapiens* is inferior to the gods only in his mortality[5] and consequent lack of time and means with which to exercise virtue. He is not inferior in virtue and indeed can be said to surpass the gods in that he achieves by his own efforts what is natural and inevitable for them.[6]

Such views, of course, would rule out automatically the worship of an evil Princeps like Gaius,[7] but they accord as well with the worship of the living virtuous Emperor as with deification of a dead one. Yet Seneca, though prepared to flatter Claudius in the *Ad Polybium* by calling him a *numen* and referring to his 'divinae manus' and 'divina auctoritas',[8] makes it quite clear that when Augustus was alive he was a man.[9] Most significant is *De Clementia* in which Nero is pictured as god's elect, endowed with divine *potentia*, but is told that the ruler 'qui se ex deorum natura gerit' holds a place *next to* the gods whose mildness is a model to the 'hominem hominibus praepositum'.[10] The distinction Seneca makes between worship of dead and living Emperors rests not on philosophy but on Roman sentiment.[11] Ample evidence of his

---

Rep. 1. 25; 2. 17, and *Leg.* 2. 27 its philosophical pedigree is not clear, and its occurrence in Cicero's speeches on his return from exile to the Senate (30) and to the people (25) shows it was a generally familiar notion. The evidence of Horace, *Odes* 3. 5, 1–4, suggests that the idea was applied, at least by the educated, to imperial apotheosis from the start, as it certainly was later (Pliny, *NH* 2. 18; Younger Pliny, *Pan.* 35. 4).

[1] *Ben.* 4. 7-8.
[2] On the doctrine of the θεῖος ἀνήρ as explaining Seneca's attitude to ruler cult see M. Altman, *CP* 33 (1938), 198 ff.
[3] *Ep.* 73. 15–16.   [4] *Const. Sap.* 8. 2; *Ep.* 31. 11.
[5] *Ep.* 73. 13.   [6] *Ep.* 53. 11; 73. 14.
[7] *Tranq.* 14. 9 where 'Caesari deo nostro' is ironic.
[8] 12.5 ; 13. 2; 14. 2.
[9] 15. 3.   [10] 1. 19, 9; 1. 7, 1–2; 1. 1, 2; 1. 26, 5.
[11] Note that Cicero, in praising Caesar the Dictator, says cautiously that a man who has displayed great virtues is 'simillimum deo' (*Marc.* 8; cf. *Lig.* 38).

respect for Roman tradition has already been adduced, and Seneca expressly stated that, in the sphere of religion, the *sapiens* would observe *leges* and *mores*.[1] In this he followed the spirit of the Middle Stoa.[2]

It it noteworthy that, in the first year of his reign, Nero's tactful handling of the Senate included the refusal of silver and gold statues of himself, which were probably regarded as divine honours.[3] Even after Seneca's death he refused a temple to *divus Nero* in Rome.[4] Tacitus gives Nero's motive as superstitious fear; it could have been fear of outraging sentiment. In any case, he did not have to learn that from Seneca.

[1] In *De Superstitione*, Haase frag. XII (38–40), preserved by St. Augustine who castigates Seneca for compromising with his philosophical convictions about *civilis theologia* because he was a Roman senator.

[2] Cf. Hecato in Cicero, *Off.* 3. 63: 'sapientis esse nihil contra mores, leges, instituta facientem habere rationem rei familiaris'. Seneca certainly practised the latter advice.

[3] *Ann.* 13. 10. See K. Scott, *TAPA* 62 (1931), 101 ff. The effigy of himself that he allowed to be put in the temple of Mars Ultor in 54 (*Ann.* 13. 8) was an honour to the god, not an object of *cultus*: A. D. Nock, *HSCP* 41 (1930), 31–4. Tacitus does not say that the statue of himself accepted in 59 (*Ann.* 14. 12) was gold, though the statue of Minerva, that was to stand next to it, was.

[4] *Ann.* 15. 74, 3–4.

7

THE PROVINCIAL ON THE PROVINCES

As a Spaniard and a Stoic, Seneca had two good reasons for being interested in the Empire and subjects of Rome. Spain was the oldest of Rome's major provinces; Stoicism preached commitment to human society and had boasted among its adherents many champions of just rule over the provinces.[1] Against such a background, the paucity and poverty of Seneca's thoughts on the subject stand out all too clearly. Worse still, even these thoughts, as will appear, played little part in the foreign policy and provincial administration of his years of influence.

Imperial Policy

Seneca condemns war and military imperialism in general as violations of human nature which normally seeks, through love and mutual help,[2] a *concordia* of the human race.[3] He denounces war as a product of the passions: anger, cruelty, greed, ambition.[4] To conquer these is a greater victory.[5] None the less, conquest in the selfless spirit of pacification, defence of the good, defeat of the wicked, are exempt from these strictures: the great model is

[1] Q. Mucius Scaevola (cos. 95), Rutilius Rufus, and the younger Cato were Republican Stoics famed for their integrity in dealing with provincials. For Seneca's own period see below, pp. 248–9.

[2] *Ira* 3. 5, 6. Man behaves worse than the animals: *Ira* 2. 8, 2; *NQ* 5. 18, 9; *Ep.* 95. 31; he puts himself on a level with natural disasters: *Clem.* 1. 26, 5; *NQ* 3, pref. 5.

[3] *Ben.* 6. 30, 5; *Ep.* 90. 26; 95. 31.

[4] *Ira* 3. 5, 6; *Ben.* 6. 30, 5; *NQ* 5. 18, 9; *Ep.* 95. 30–1; *Ira* 3. 33, 1; *Ben.* 7. 3, 1; 7. 10, 2; *NQ* 5. 18, 10; *Ep.* 94. 61. With Hannibal, war became an end in itself (*NQ* 3, pref. 6).

[5] *Cons. Polyb.* 15. 3; *NQ* 3, pref. 10; *Ben.* 7. 3, 2–3; *Ep.* 113. 28–30.

Hercules.[1] These standards are reflected consistently in Seneca's references to Roman empire-builders, though certain concessions to traditional Roman ideas are made, either through patriotism or for the sake of argument. Thus the military exploits of the Elder Scipio, Agrippa, Augustus, and Claudius receive loud praise, though even here the aims of defence and pacification and the need for high moral standards are stressed.[2] The Roman military conception of *virtus* is occasionally admitted,[3] but the Stoic conception dominates: ambition spoiled the victories of Marius, Pompey, and Caesar; greed stained the efforts of Crassus.[4]

Seneca never doubts that the Empire was acquired through Roman virtue and is worth preserving and that the 'victor pacatorque gentium populus' deserved something better than civil war.[5] But after victory, though full control should remain with the victors,[6] *ira* must change to *amicitia*: the mixing of victor and vanquished, the conversion of *hostes* into *socii* had made the Empire great; to parade excessive spoils is to incite their recapture.[7] Every excuse must be seized for the exercise of clemency.[8]

These views, rooted in old Roman tradition,[9] strengthened by Stoic ideas—the natural bond of rational beings,[10] the wickedness of the passions—were common enough. Did Seneca implement them as *amicus principis*?

In order to assess the role of Seneca and his collaborator Burrus in the formation of imperial policy, we have to assume that their attested role in influencing appointments meant that they had a hand in the framing of the policies these appointees were to implement. This is a large assumption and, despite the interest of

---

[1] *Ben.* 1. 13, 3.

[2] *Ben.* 3. 33, 3; *Ep.* 86. 1; *Ben.* 3. 32, 3; *Cons. Polyb.* 15. 3; *Brev. Vit.* 14. 5; *Ben.* 3. 32, 5; *Cons. Polyb.* 12. 3.

[3] *Ben.* 3. 33, 3; *Ep.* 94. 66.

[4] *Ep.* 94. 64; *NQ* 5. 18, 10.

[5] *Ep.* 87. 41; *Ira* 2. 34, 4; *Clem.* 1. 4, 2; *Ben.* 5. 15, 6.

[6] In Haase frag. 42, Seneca says, indignantly, of the maintenance and spread of Jewish customs: 'victi victoribus leges dederunt.'

[7] *Ira* 2. 34, 4; *Ep.* 87. 41.   [8] *Clem.* 2. 7, 2.

[9] The notion of a *iustum bellum* belongs to fetial law, cf. *Res Gestae* 26. 3; for the acceptance of the defeated as clients, *Off.* 1. 35–6, cf. Caesar, *BG* 2. 32.

[10] *SVF* 3. 333; 340, and Panaetius' conception of positive justice in *Off.* 1. 20.

checking Seneca's ideas against his presumed actions, the resulting conjectures might not be worth making, were it not that others have already made suggestions that require examination.

There were three areas that achieved particular importance in the reign of Nero: Armenia, Britain, and Judaea. For the Armenian story, I accept the standard chronology,[1] according to which four of the five episodes into which Tacitus (our main source) divides his account are related under the terminal year of the episode which may cover a number of preceding years.[2] The exception is the first episode which, as Tacitus explicitly notes, covers events after the year under which it is narrated.[3] Dio's account is of no help in determining dates.

On this chronology, Corbulo was appointed at the end of 54, reached Cappadocia in 55, and trained his troops there until the winter of 57/8 when he kept them under canvas in Armenia.[4] The first campaign, in the spring of 58, ended in the capture of Artaxata. Corbulo then, presumably, spent the winter of 58/9 (not mentioned by Tacitus) in Armenia, took Tigranocerta in late summer 59, and held on to Armenia, expelling Tiridates, the brother of the Parthian king (in 59 or the spring of 60), and installing Tigranes as client king (in 60), and finally going to replace Quadratus as governor of Syria. In 61 Tigranes invaded Adiabene. Corbulo then, or (more probably) before, had asked Rome for a separate commander for Armenia. He now sent half-hearted help to Tigranes, but finally made an agreement with Vologeses, the Parthian king (at the end of 61) to carry out a mutual evacuation of Armenia. Vologeses was to send envoys to Nero. In 62 Caesennius Paetus arrived from Rome, and Parthia renewed the

[1] This scheme is set forth in full by H. Furneaux, *The Annals of Tacitus*[2], Oxford, 1907, vol. II, Introd., pp. 107–26; M. Hammond, *HSCP* 45 (1934), 81 ff.; J. G. C. Anderson in *CAH* 10, pp. 758 ff.; and followed by K.-H. Ziegler, *Die Beziehungen zwischen Rom und dem Partherreich*, Wiesbaden, 1964, p. 67, giving a bibliography in n. 167.

[2] *Ann.* 13. 6–9 (A.D. 54); 13. 34–41 (A.D. 58); 14. 23–6 (A.D. 60); 15. 1–17 (A.D. 62); 15. 24–31 (A.D. 63).

[3] *Ann.* 13. 9, 3. The fifth episode is dated 'veris principio' of 63 (*Ann.* 15. 24, 1) and narrated under that year, but the events in it probably ended, as they began, under that year.

[4] He was also negotiating with Parthia, see p. 226.

war, after her envoys returned with an unfavourable answer from Rome. Paetus ravaged Armenia and towards the winter of 62/3 withdrew to his winter quarters in Rhandeia[1] but was followed and defeated by the Parthians. Corbulo, who had answered an earlier appeal from Paetus without enthusiasm, now came to the rescue only to find that Paetus had already surrendered. Paetus withdrew to Cappadocia, while the triumphant Vologeses wrote to Nero demanding control of Armenia without offering any concessions. In the spring of 63 Vologeses' envoys reached Rome, whereupon Nero recalled Paetus and gave Corbulo a *maius imperium* in the East. Corbulo now made a strong display of force and, as a result, Vologeses finally agreed to allow Tiridates, his candidate, to accept the Armenian crown from Nero at Rome.

That Roman policy regarding Armenia fluctuated in the nine years between the appointment of Corbulo and the final settlement has been generally recognized. Furneaux saw a conflict developing between Corbulo and 'the home government'.[2] Momigliano saw a difference in aim from the start between Corbulo and 'the Senate'.[3] Hammond reverted to Furneaux's notion of a developing conflict but gave the parties to it as Corbulo and Nero whose views changed as he gradually shed the influence of Seneca and Burrus.[4]

What were Corbulo's orders when he was first sent out by Nero? Tacitus says he was in charge 'retinendae Armeniae',[5] which is too vague to indicate anything more definite than a mission to expel the Parthian from Armenia and resume some form of Roman control. Vologeses, who had already withdrawn at the first sign of Roman action, gave hostages as a token of his desire to keep the peace.[6] But, later on, Tacitus says that Vologeses (some time before the winter of 57/8) preferred to fight rather than see Tiridates lose the Armenian crown or retain it as a gift from Rome, while Corbulo, on the other hand, thought

---

[1] Dio 62. 21, 2. [2] Above, p. 224 n. 1.

[3] Momigliano, 'Corbulone e la politica verso i Parti', *Atti del II Congresso Nazionale di Studi Romani* (1931), I. 368 ff. (referred to hereafter in this chapter as 'Momigliano').

[4] Above, p. 224 n. 1 (hereafter called 'Hammond').

[5] *Ann.* 13. 8, 1. [6] Ibid. 13. 7.

the dignity of Rome demanded the recovery of Armenia.[1] Presumably then, in negotiations between the Roman commander and the Parthian king, Corbulo had told Vologeses to give up all claim to Armenia or to accept a compromise, i.e. the acknowledgement by Tiridates of the sovereignty of Rome. There seems no reason to doubt that Corbulo was authorized to offer this compromise solution,[2] and that his reply to its refusal expressed the government's determination to recover some form of control over Armenia. Corbulo's subsequent establishment of a camp in Armenia illustrated that determination.

Tiridates responded by attacking Rome's supporters in Armenia, but when hard pressed complained of a violation of the peace of 55 by Corbulo, thereby overlooking the later offer of recognition by Rome. Corbulo advised him to appeal to Nero for recognition of his rule.[3] Clearly, Corbulo hoped that, after his military successes against Tiridates, the latter and Vologeses, who was having his own troubles with the Hyrcanians,[4] would now accept what they had recently refused. But Tiridates did not even turn up for the preliminary negotiations with Corbulo. Again there is no reason to doubt that Corbulo's offer was in complete accord with government policy.[5]

Corbulo now launched a serious campaign[6] culminating in his march on Artaxata which drove Tiridates, after a feeble resistance, to seek refuge in Media Atropatene.[7] Corbulo drove the lesson home with the destruction of Artaxata and, in the next summer (59), the capture of Tigranocerta. He also set up cordial relations

[1] *Ann.* 13. 34, 2.

[2] Momigliano, p. 369, thinks that Corbulo opened negotiations, sincerely hoping for a settlement, but that the Senate, intending the negotiations as a mere device to gain time to train the army, had him demand maintenance of the *status quo* (evacuation of Armenia by Parthia) which made war inevitable (*Ann.* 13. 34). Afterwards, Corbulo offered the compromise solution on his own (13. 37). But *Ann.* 13. 34 seems to show that Corbulo's earlier offer, and Vologeses' refusal, concerned the compromise solution.

[3] *Ann.* 13. 37.   [4] Ibid. 13. 37, 5.

[5] Momigliano, p. 370, thinks Corbulo made this offer on his own, and that envoys may have been sent by Parthia, only to meet with senatorial intransigence, but that Corbulo omitted this insult to himself in the memoirs that Tacitus relied on as a source.

[6] *Ann.* 13. 39.   [7] Ibid. 13. 41; 14. 26, 1.

with the Hyrcanians whose defection had been absorbing Parthian energies since 57.[1]

These successes and the departure of Tiridates (who had proved so recalcitrant) must inevitably have encouraged the home government to think of the solution for Armenia, more traditional than successful, first applied by Augustus: the appointment of a Roman nominee to the throne of Armenia. Corbulo, accordingly, repulsed an invasion by Tiridates, and held on to Armenia until Nero's nominee, Tigranes, arrived. Corbulo left the new king reinforcements and departed to Syria, which had been assigned to him as a province on the death of Ummidius Quadratus.[2]

What Corbulo's attitude was to this change of policy is difficult to determine. In the next year, 61, when Tigranes' invasion of Adiabene provoked the Parthians to serious action, Corbulo is certainly represented, in Tacitus' account, as reluctant to help Tigranes,[3] and, in fact, eager to resign responsibility for Armenia: he had written to Nero asking for a separate commander for Armenia, preferring to look after Syria himself.[4] None the less, it is not clear whether it was the policy or Tigranes himself that Corbulo disliked: he may have realized, from his knowledge of Armenian politics, that Tigranes' life as a hostage in Rome had fitted him neither for rule and favour in Armenia, nor for respect in Parthia, and that he could only be maintained by a Roman garrison which Rome could not afford. As for the Syrian command, Tacitus' account would indicate that Corbulo had reliable information ('certis nuntiis') about Vologeses' intention to threaten the Roman provinces,[5] and may simply have wanted to command where he thought the principal ground of battle would now be. But his arrangement of a truce with Vologeses (just before the winter of 61/2) that involved the evacuation of Roman

[1] Ibid. 14. 25.

[2] Ibid. 14. 26, 2.

[3] The motive Tacitus here attributes to Corbulo shows his typical cynicism and is implausible in this case. Why should Corbulo have thought that effective help of Tigranes would end the war with Parthia? The Parthians would hardly acquiescè so early in Tigranes' rule.

[4] *Ann.* 15. 3, 1.

[5] Ibid. 15. 2–3, 1.

troops and hence the removal of support from Tigranes,[1] can only be construed as a move against the imposition of Tigranes. Corbulo in fact, in sending some help to Tigranes and fortifying the Euphrates, had used the Parthian attack on Tigranes as another opportunity to impress on them the wisdom of accepting nominal Roman control. This time Vologeses listened.[2]

The Princeps, however, did not.[3] Corbulo's critics, according to Tacitus, said that Corbulo merely wanted to postpone war with Parthia and leave the struggle to Caesennius Paetus who was rumoured to be on his way to the Armenian command.[4] This is what those in Rome might think who knew that the government had no intention of retreating from its more aggressive policy into an acceptance of nominal suzerainty over Tiridates. But Corbulo may have been sufficiently out of touch with feeling at Rome to think that he could persuade Nero to be content with the withdrawal of Vologeses, and to regard it as a Roman victory achieved by dire threats.[5]

Caesennius Paetus arrived probably in the spring of 62 in a militant frame of mind, which was shared by the government, as the summary rejection of Vologeses' envoys shows.[6] Paetus impugned Corbulo's successes and threatened to impose real Roman control on Armenia, presumably reducing it to a province.[7] But his campaign, though fairly successful at first, and described in glowing terms in dispatches home, ended in disaster and ignominious surrender.

As in defending Tigranes, Corbulo had done his duty regarding Paetus but no more: he had not moved quickly to Paetus' rescue,[8] and he refused to help him avenge his defeat. Paetus retired to Cappadocia for the winter (62/3) and Corbulo again negotiated

---

[1] Tacitus does not explain how Tigranes came to withdraw from Armenia. Corbulo's critics inferred, from the withdrawal of Roman troops from Armenia, a pact with Vologeses to get rid of Tigranes (15. 6, 1–2). This weighs in favour of Momigliano's hypothesis (p. 373), that Tigranes withdrew himself because he could not hold Armenia without Roman arms, rather than Hammond's (p. 93), that Corbulo somehow eliminated him.

[2] *Ann.* 15. 5, 4.   [3] Ibid. 15. 7, 1.   [4] Ibid. 15. 6.

[5] According to Tacitus (*Ann.* 15. 6, 1), most people did see Vologeses' withdrawal in this favourable light.

[6] *Ann.* 15. 7.   [7] Ibid. 15. 6, 4.   [8] Ibid. 15. 10, 4.

Vologeses' withdrawal from Armenia: this time it was not Tigranes but his aggressive forts on the Euphrates that he sacrificed, as his part of the bargain.

Early in the spring of 63, envoys from Vologeses again came to Rome, but this time Vologeses condescendingly offered to have Tiridates accept his diadem, not at Rome, but before the Emperor's image at a legionary camp.[1] It was clear now that the new aggressive policy assigned to Paetus had failed, and the government decided on a war to be conducted by Corbulo, making it clear by this appointment and the gifts sent to Parthia, that willingness on the part of Tiridates to accept recognition at Rome would now be welcome. By this time, Vologeses knew what Corbulo could do, and a mere display of force by the general led him to negotiate for peace.[2] Tiridates now agreed to accept his diadem from Nero at Rome and the struggle was over.

If the sketch above is accurate, it would seem that at the time of Corbulo's appointment Nero and his advisers, among whom Seneca and Burrus were the most prominent, would have accepted the recovery of Armenia in the sense of nominal sovereignty over the Parthian candidate, Tiridates.[3] As a sign that Rome accepted Parthian interest in Armenia as legitimate, the recognition of a member of the Parthian royal house as king of Armenia went even beyond its nearest precedent, Augustus' acquiescence in nominal suzerainty over an Armenian king picked by Parthia.[4] But Tiridates was too proud to accept even this solution and could not be easily frightened into it. The flight of Tiridates from Armenia and Corbulo's successes now made natural the adoption of the old Augustan policy of supporting Roman nominees. The choice was poor, and seemed especially so to the man on the spot, Corbulo, but that is no reason to deny that Seneca and Burrus originated or at least approved the decision.[5]

What is harder to explain, and to assign, is the decision, after

[1] Ibid. 15. 24.   [2] Ibid. 15. 27.   [3] So Hammond, p. 88.
[4] RG 27. 2, cf. Dio 55. 10, 20. A. Oltramare, REL 16 (1938), 318 ff., discusses the significance of this concession, which he believes is a Senecan inspiration.
[5] As does Hammond, p. 94.

Tigranes had stirred up Parthia by invading Adiabene, to pursue an even more aggressive policy and to appoint the optimistic and precipitate Caesennius Paetus, in the latter part of 61, in answer to Corbulo's request for a separate commander in Armenia. It is difficult to assign responsibility for this change to Nero alone or to particular advisers. Seneca's and Burrus' influence had shrunk somewhat after Agrippina's death and they had more rivals to contend with. For reasons described elsewhere,[1] it is likely that they disapproved of the ordinary consulship of Caesennius Paetus in 61, a position he probably owed to the now rising influence of his son-in-law, Flavius Sabinus, and perhaps that of Vespasian himself, emerging from ignominious retirement after the death of Agrippina.[2] But Seneca would still be on the Emperor's *consilium* until 62 and, as late as 64, was still widely regarded as his adviser.

Even if we cannot name the originators of the new policy with confidence, can we make the policy intelligible? By the time the home government had decided on the appointment of Caesennius Paetus (whose arrival was rumoured by winter 61/2) to implement the new aggressive policy, a drastic change of commander and policy had taken place in the other major sphere of early Neronian operations—Britain. The two changes might be connected: an examination of the British policy is the next step.

Suetonius asserts that Nero once thought of withdrawing the army from Britain and changed his purpose only because he was ashamed to seem to belittle the glory of his adoptive father.[3] Those who do not simply reject this story as evidence[4] usually fix this decision of Nero's in the early years before the forward drive in the governorship of Q. Veranius.[5] But it is more likely to

---

[1] Above, p. 122.   [2] Below, pp. 241–2.

[3] *Nero* 18.

[4] As does Syme, *Tacitus*, p. 490 n. 6, who thinks the passage reflects Hadrianic deliberations.

[5] C. E. Stevens, *CR* 65 (1951), 4, puts the idea before Veranius' will; E. Birley, 'Britain under Nero: the Significance of Q. Veranius', *Roman Britain and the Roman Army*, p. 7, before the appointment of Veranius; followed by D. R. Dudley and G. Webster, *The Rebellion of Boudicca*, London, 1962, p. 46 (hereafter referred to as 'Dudley and Webster').

be an anecdote about Nero's despair at the revolt in Britain.[1] In any case, nothing is less likely than that Nero contemplated undoing the most popular and solid achievement of Claudius' reign.[2]

That Nero retained the safe but unadventurous Didius Gallus as governor is not hard to explain. On Nero's accession, Armenia was the immediate problem; in 55 peace seemed temporarily established there and Corbulo went out to effect a solution. But nothing much happened, as the Parthian king was occupied with internal and external problems and Corbulo spent his time training his troops. There was time to give one's attention to a new area. Probably in 57, possibly on the advice of Seneca and Burrus who had organized the Armenian policy, Q. Veranius was dispatched to subdue Wales.[3] When he died within his first year of office, a worthy rival to Corbulo, Suetonius Paulinus, was appointed to pursue the same mission. For two years he was successful but in the third the eastern portions of the province revolted behind his back.[4] The summer of 60 is the most likely date for the outbreak, despite Tacitus' date of 61 for the *clades*.[5] For it is impossible to accept that one year could contain the outbreak, Suetonius' advance, victory, revenge, the imperial commission, and Suetonius' prolonged period of office, after which Tacitus says[6] he was ordered to hand the army over to 'Petronio Turpiliano qui iam consulatu abierat'. Petronius was *consul ordinarius* in 61. If annual consulships were still the rule, this could be an elegant temporal note comparable to the common 'quae in alios consules egressa coniunxi' and we would be in 62, but with suffects the rule, we must assume that Tacitus is merely indicating a later portion of 61.[7]

---

[1] The view preferred by S. Frere, *Britannia*, London, 1967, p. 85.

[2] Claudius' achievements in foreign policy were taken seriously even after his death (*Ann.* 13. 3, 1).

[3] Birley (op. cit.), pp. 5–6.   [4] Tacitus, *Agric.* 14. 4.

[5] *Ann.* 14. 29. See Syme, *Tacitus*, App. 69, citing previous authorities. Dudley and Webster, App. 3, add nothing, and their arguments about triennial governorships, if anything, detract from the case: Petronius only served for two years (he was *curator aquarum* in 63/4) and there is no evidence for what Suetonius' tenure would have been: Didius Gallus had been there for five years.

[6] *Ann.* 14. 39, 3.

[7] There were probably suffect consuls in 61 (Degrassi, *I Fasti Consolari*, p. 17).

The causes of the rebellion are clearly indicated in Tacitus. The annexation of the former client kingdom of the Iceni had been left by the governor to the unspeakable procurator Catus Decianus aided by some legionary officers.[1] The example then given of rapacity and cruelty made the Iceni fear the worst from the census and taxation that were to follow.[2] The Trinobantes were induced by them to rebel because of their grievances concerning the colonists of Camulodunum. Dio, if he can be trusted, indicates that there was a financial crisis at this time.[3] The Roman money-lenders, on whom the costly process of Romanization hinged, decided (moved by the imposition of taxes on the Iceni or the prospect of widespread military opera-tions)[4] to call in their debts at once. According to Dio, Seneca was the main offender although the example had been set by the procurator who called in Claudius' gifts, alleging that they were loans. Here as elsewhere in his account of Seneca, Dio may be repeating charge as fact[5]—a charge Tacitus deliberately omits. Nero had, it is true, given Seneca capital which he let out at interest,[6] and there is nothing impossible in the idea that, like other money-lenders, he made advances to chiefs of the Iceni and perhaps the priests of Claudius. But the idea that Seneca alone caused the panic and that, as Dio says, he forced the Britons to take the money, is clearly slander and may derive from the

[1] *Ann.* 14. 31. The presence of the centurions is an argument against the suggestion of C. M. Bulst, *Historia* 10 (1961), 496–7, that Prasutagus died while Suetonius was away and that the procurator proceeded to take action on the will without orders. Suetonius must have left or dispatched the centurions to help the procurator; cf. *Agric.* 15. 2 (of the legate and the procurator) 'alterius manum centuriones, alterius servos', the parallel situation in Josephus, *BJ* 2. 41, and Pliny's caution in giving ordinary soldiers to a procurator in *Ep.* 10. 27.

[2] Syme, *Tacitus*, App. 69, p. 764.

[3] Dio 62. 2, 1.

[4] See the ingenious explanation of Dudley and Webster, pp. 50–1. M. F. Gyles, 'Effects of Roman Capital Investment in Britain under Nero', *Laudatores Temporis Acti—Studies in Memory of W. E. Caldwell*, Chapel Hill, N.C., 1946, p. 104, argues that the recall of moneys by the procurator and private money-lenders was really a preparation for Nero's currency reform in 64 (when he reduced the silver content); but four years seems a long time to leave a province without silver, especially if the Iceni were soon to start paying tribute.

[5] See Appendix C4.

[6] *Ann.* 14. 53, 5.

general condemnation of Seneca's and Burrus' policy after the rebellion.

Suetonius Paulinus, having defeated Boudicca, set out to take revenge and subdue the province by force. But the new procurator, Julius Classicianus,[1] reported home that a long and stubborn resistance was imminent unless more diplomatic methods were employed by a new governor. By the spring of 61 an imperial agent was dispatched to report on the situation—the freedman Polyclitus.[2] This marked the first open violation of the promise Nero had made to the Senate in his accession speech,[3] that imperial freedmen would have nothing to do with affairs outside the palace. This was even worse than Narcissus exhorting the legions that first invaded Britain under Claudius.[4] It therefore appears certain that his mission was neither authorized nor approved by Seneca and Burrus. Some confirmation comes from the name of Paulinus' successor, probably the son of that Petronius ridiculed in the *Apocolocyntosis* and a relative of the Vitellii whom Seneca disliked.[5] Of course, that is not to say that Seneca and Burrus would not have recommended conciliation at this point, but only that the agents of their choice would have been different.

If this is correct, the idea that the new policy in Armenia, decided on soon after,[6] was the work of Nero and *deteriores* becomes more plausible, especially when it is seen that the two policies are related. Schur once tried to relate the two changes of policy strategically,[7] arguing that the return to a quiet policy in Britain was necessitated by plans for a more active war with Parthia and that the government did not want to fight on two fronts. But there is no evidence for any plans to move British

[1] On his background and his wife, Frere, *Britannia*, p. 92.

[2] *Ann.* 14. 39. [3] Above, pp. 107–8. [4] Dio, 60. 19, 2–3.

[5] Above, pp. 99–100, and Appendix D7.

[6] On the chronology used here, the home government decided on a new British policy by the summer of 61; on a new Armenian one, only after the news of Tigranes' aggression and Corbulo's request for a new commander—probably late in 61. Cf. Dudley and Webster, p. 83, who date both decisions to the winter 60/1, which is surely too early for Armenia.

[7] W. Schur, 'Die Orientpolitik des Kaisers Nero', *Klio*, Beih. 15 (1923), 16–24. Hammond, pp. 95–7, disagrees on chronological grounds.

legions east—plans which would be endangered by a two-front war—and, more important, it is clear that the British policy, not the Parthian one, was forced on the government. There is, however, a psychological relation between the two policies. Nero accepted the need for conciliation and consolidation in Britain and the substitution of the loyal and dogged Petronius Turpilianus for the dashing Suetonius Paulinus who had caught the popular imagination. Nero's natural flamboyance and thirst for praise would lead him to dramatic moves elsewhere: hence he was amenable to the proposals of those who engineered the dispatch of Caesennius Paetus, even if it was not actually his own idea.

It remains to evaluate the success of Nero's policy in Armenia and Britain. The early policy in Britain made military sense, but the combination of a severe governor interested only in warfare and a corrupt procurator ruined the plan. The later policy, to judge by the fact that no rebellions broke out during the Flavian advance in Britain, was a success.[1] The final solution in Armenia, that approved by Corbulo and, initially, by Seneca and Burrus, was imaginative in its acceptance of Parthian interest in Armenia, but has often been overrated as a practical solution. The serious count against it is not that the vaunted fifty-year peace was not continuous: about 75, when the elder Trajan was governor of Syria, he won *triumphalia ornamenta*, and a Parthian laurel was received at the capitol.[2] In transactions with Parthia, resounding Roman dangers and successes had often had little behind them.[3] More important is the absence of any indication that Corbulo or the home government saw that the Armenian solution required the transformation of Cappadocia perma-

---

[1] See the evaluation of Frere, *Britannia*, pp. 92–5.

[2] Pliny, *Pan.* 14 and 16; Victor, *De Caes.* 9. 10; *Epit. de Caes.* 9. 12. A. W. Braithwaite, *C. Suetoni Tranquilli Divus Vespasianus*, Oxford, 1927, p. 48, stresses this.

[3] See Syme, *Tacitus*, pp. 30–1. If Victor and the Epitomator are referring to this incident, the success would certainly seem to have been diplomatic, but Braithwaite (above, n. 2) doubts if they are. The Parthians also supported two false Neros against Vespasian. For deteriorating relations between Parthia and Rome under the Flavians see Ziegler, *Die Beziehungen zwischen Rom und dem Partherreich*, pp. 78–81.

nently into a military province. Vespasian indeed drew this conclusion but the retention of legions there by Nero in the three years before the Jewish revolt had a special offensive aim and—as the drainage of legions from the Danube provinces shows—was not yet a permanent part of the defences of the Empire.[1]

Vespasian's rational conception of the eastern frontier included the conversion of Judaea into an armed province under a praetorian governor. That change is a measure of the seriousness of the Great Rebellion of 66 whose roots lay in the fundamentally unsatisfactory compromise arrived at by Augustus, whereby Judaea proper was ruled by a Roman procurator without legionary support, while the other parts of Palestine were shared out among Herodian kings. At the beginning of his reign, Claudius had reverted to the earlier Augustan arrangement of uniting Palestine under one Jewish client king,[2] but on the death, in 44, of Agrippa I, a close friend who had proved an extravagant and often difficult subordinate, Claudius reverted to the procuratorial system, though he eventually made Agrippa II ruler of a large but scattered and mostly pagan kingdom in the north of Palestine bordering on Syria.

Claudius' procurators had no more success than the Augustan and Tiberian ones. The end of home rule was a bitter disappointment to the Jews and religious nationalism flourished. In addition, famines and brigandage were on the increase.[3] None the less, Nero and his advisers made no change in the system except for the increase, in the first year of the new reign, of Agrippa II's kingdom. The reason for the grant of territory is certainly to be sought outside any plans for Palestine itself, for the additions, though considerable,[4] only made that kingdom more scattered

---

[1] Note the judgement of Momigliano, p. 375, that the new policy linked Rome and Parthia by an interested friendship, but there were no guarantees. See Appendix F.

[2] The kingdoms of Herod the Great and Agrippa I were of roughly equal size, but not identical in composition (see A. H. M. Jones, *The Herods of Judaea*, Oxford, 1938, p. 208). [3] Ibid., pp. 222–3.

[4] Agrippa II gained the toparchies of Abila and Julias in the Peraea, Tiberias and Taricheae in Galilee.

and, by increasing the Jewish portions, the subjects more mixed. Agrippa II benefited, in fact, from the government's decision to recover Armenia, a policy that involved the co-operation of loyal client kings. Aristobulus, the son of Herod of Chalcis and cousin of Agrippa II, was given Armenia Minor,[1] and he and Antiochus of Commagene and Agrippa II were expected to prepare troops for incursions into Parthian territory.[2]

Nothing suggests that the imperial policy of Nero's early reign, just reviewed, would have been any different, had one of the chief *amici principis* not been a philosopher. The Armenian problem was inherited from Claudius. Although Seneca echoes in passing the view that the defeat of Crassus still required revenge,[3] the only solutions that might plausibly have had Seneca's support—a client king sanctioned by or imposed by Rome on Armenia—follow in a direct line from the facts of the situation at Nero's accession and from the Augustan view of the problem. The same holds for Britain. Although, before the western push in Britain, a purely defensive policy was implemented by Didius Gallus, a permanent halt could never have been considered by anyone. Ostorius Scapula, it was believed, had said that the Silures would have to be exterminated, and they had not been quiet under Didius Gallus.[4] The attack on the Druids by Suetonius Paulinus is in line with Roman recognition, from Augustus on, that the Druids had to be robbed of their enormous power as a focus of resistance.[5] Even the disaster in Judaea is ultimately traceable to the continuation of Augustan policy.

[1] Perhaps some idea of compensation was also involved in this grant, for his father's kingdom had gone to Agrippa II. In 60 Aristobulus received a piece of Armenia Maior in return for support for the new king Tigranes (Tacitus, *Ann.* 14. 26, 2).

[2] *Ann.* 13. 7.

[3] *Cons. Helv.* 10. 3.

[4] *Ann.* 12. 39, 2; 40, 1.

[5] For Roman measures against the Druids, H. Last, *JRS* 39 (1949), 1 ff. Against his idea that the Romans had no political motive for the persecution see the evidence in I. A. Richmond, *JRS* 44 (1954), 48 (cf. also Frere, *Britannia*, p. 60).

Provincial Administration

After conquest, says Seneca, there must be *amicitia*: obedience is
to be won by benefits rather than arms.[1] He devotes in all two
sentences to this idea; far more energy is spent on the demand
that governors exercise clemency and restrain their greed. These
ideas too, professed by the conquerors before they were reinforced by philosophy,[2] were anything but new. What might be
expected of a philosopher is a deepening of them, a development
of them in accordance with philosophical doctrine. But Seneca
adds nothing new. He bases his demand for a benevolent Empire
on Roman self-interest, but Cicero had already worked the
example of the Roman Empire into Panaetius' argument that
benevolence is the best way of winning over men for one's own
advantage.[3] He treats the subject of provincial government
within the general condemnation of the passions, for anger,
cruelty, and corruption were standard temptations to which
governors, and their wives, succumbed.[4] But Cato had already
brought Stoic virtue into political life by preaching and, according
to Cicero, practising self-control in running the provinces.[5] Cato's
correspondence with Cicero shows that he rated moral victory
above military victory and believed that no traditional military

---

[1] *Cons. Polyb.* 12. 3.

[2] Early exponents include the Elder Scipio and Flamininus (Polybius 15. 17, 4;
18. 20, 7) and the Elder Cato arguing against showing cruelty to Rhodes in 167
(*ORF²*, p. 62, frag. 163). There is now wide agreement on this: e.g. L. Wickert,
Klio 36 (1944), 12; F. W. Walbank, *JRS* 55 (1965), 9; 15. H. Strasburger, ibid.,
p. 51, wrongly credits Posidonius with reversing a traditional Roman practice
of regarding enemies as criminals. *Res Gestae* 3. 1–2 reiterates the traditional
attitude.

[3] *Off.* 2. 26; cf. Cicero's claim to have achieved this in Cilicia in *Fam.* 15. 4, 14.
Philosophical statesmen like Scipio Nasica (Posidonius, *FGH* no. 87, frag. 112)
and Gaius Gracchus (*ORF²*, p. 180, frag. 22, cf. 23, 26, 27) expressed the idea
even earlier.

[4] *Ira* 1. 19, 3; 2. 5, 5; *Ben.* 1. 9, 4. With *Helv.* 19. 6–7, compare a debate in the
senate in A.D. 21 on the evil practices of governors' wives (*Ann.* 3. 33–4).

[5] *Fam.* 15. 4, 16. Cf. *Att.* 6. 1, 7; 6. 2, 8. Cicero tells his brother that his philosophical education should help his self-control as governor of Asia (*Q.Fr.* 1. 1, 7;
22; 27).

honours could compare with a public acknowledgement that a governor had exercised *mansuetudo, innocentia, diligentia*.[1]

Seneca not only failed to add, he ignored existing philosophical doctrines that were relevant to the administration of an empire. It does not, at first, seem odd that a Stoic, believing in natural equality,[2] should ignore the view famous from Cicero's *De Re Publica* (3. 37) that, for some, it is most advantageous to be ruled by their natural superiors. But since Seneca accepted Posidonius' notion that the original and natural form of human society was the rule of the inferior by their superior in virtue, might we not expect some application of this view to the Empire? Seneca does not apply it, but neither had Posidonius, though he allowed that voluntary submission might be better for particular peoples too weak to rule themselves.[3] In fact, the idea of justifying the Roman Empire by the natural superiority of the Romans had probably come to them without philosophy and quickly became a standard view.[4] Tacitus puts the view, by then a cliché, into the mouth of the governor of Lower Germany in Seneca's period of power: 'patienda meliorum imperia; id dis quos implorarent placitum, ut arbitrium penes Romanos maneret quid darent quid adimerent.'[5] Duvius Avitus may have benefited by the patronage of Burrus,[6] but he did not take his arguments from Seneca. That philosopher never bothered to justify Roman rule at all.

It is more disappointing to find that Seneca failed to apply to the government of the Roman Empire the Stoic idea of a natural human community requiring the mutual help of its members. Cicero's *De Officiis* shows that this interpretation of the Roman Empire as the *societas hominum* had been made, perhaps by Posidonius, with the Cynic–Stoic hero Hercules offered as a model for imitation: human obligations are not limited to *cives*; we owe

---

[1] *Fam.* 15. 4, 15; *Fam.* 15. 5, 4. But Cicero blames Cato in *Off.* 3. 88 for ignoring Roman obligations to the *socii* when the interests of the *aerarium* were at stake.   [2] e.g. *Cons. Marc.* 20.2.

[3] *Ep.* 90. 4. Strasburger, *JRS* 55 (1965), 46–8.

[4] Ibid., p. 45; E. Badian, *Roman Imperialism in the Late Republic*[2], Oxford, 1968, p. 93 n. 1.

[5] *Ann.* 13. 56, 1.   [6] Above, pp. 84–5.

beneficentia, liberalitas, bonitas, and *iustitia* to *externi.*[1] The only trace of this notion in Seneca is his insistence that *clementia* be shown towards all men, an obligation that springs from this natural bond.[2] Seneca includes a reference to the Stoic doctrine in the self-diagnosis of Serenus which opens *De Tranquillitate Animi:* 'placet honores fascisque non scilicet purpura aut virgis abductum capessere, sed ut amicis propinquisque et omnibus civibus, omnibus mortalibus paratior utiliorque sim.'[3] But he never applies it to the administration of the provinces, although his Letters to the procurator Lucilius provided ample opportunity. When he speaks of Lucilius' duties, it is to lament the time they take from philosophy and to warn him, for the good of his own soul, not to be corrupted by the perquisites of power or to take his office too seriously.[4] In the tribute to Lucilius' virtues in the *Natural Questions,* those he would exercise as procurator come last and receive least elaboration: freedom from greed, frugality, 'adversus minores humanitatem, adversus maiores reverentiam'.[5]

Seneca imagines the traditional Stoic community of men and gods as a *maior res publica* offering wider opportunities for the exercise of virtue than the ordinary *patria.* He used this concept to extend the notion of public service to include work in other countries,[6] or, further, to philosophical teaching and writing for the benefit of all men and posterity.[7] Neither he nor other Stoics suggested that this community was other than a metaphysical conception. Therefore we cannot expect him to plead for its realization in the Roman Empire, but he might have seen that the Empire increased the opportunities for fulfilling our obligations to all men.

What was Seneca's record as an imperial adviser? The programme of the new regime, as recoverable from Nero's speech

---

[1] *Off.* 3. 25; 28. On Posidonius' belief in the humane treatment of subject peoples see Strasburger, *JRS* 55, p. 48 ff., who discusses these passages on pp. 51–2 n. 88.

[2] *Ira* 2. 31, 7–8; note the definition in *Ep.* 88. 30: '[clementia quae] scit homini non esse homine prodige utendum'.

[3] *Tranq.* 1. 10.

[4] Especially *NQ* 4, pref. 1–13; 21–2. [5] *NQ* 4, pref. 18.

[6] *Tranq.* 4. 4. [7] *Otio* 4; *Ep.* 68. 2.

to the Senate in Tacitus and the *laus Neronis* in the *Apocolocynto-sis*, did not stress the welfare of the provinces. In practice too, other considerations often took priority.

In his study of Nero's fall, Brunt remarked: 'Even the early part of the reign hardly deserved the praise sometimes bestowed on its provincial administration.'[1] He based this judgement on two points: first that, despite Corbulo's appointment, governors 'at best incompetent' were retained and initiative was not appreciated; second, that an analysis of the reported trials of the period shows that it was not easy for provincials to gain redress.

As examples of incompetent governors, Brunt cited Antonius Felix, Ummidius Quadratus, and Didius Gallus. Now Josephus and Tacitus both give hostile reports of the rule of Antonius Felix, Pallas' brother, who became procurator of Judaea in 52.[2] Both have strong prejudices involved: for Tacitus, the senatorial resentment at the appointment of a freedman to high office;[3] for Josephus, the Jewish resentment of the Roman who married a Jewish princess without conversion.[4] But even if we allow that the way that Felix handled the terrible problem of Judaea was no worse than that of his predecessors,[5] the rule of his successor, Porcius Festus, showed clearly that a better man could be found. More important, the Jewish resentment of Felix' marriage—which, according to Josephus, took place before Claudius' death—should have been reason enough to replace him at the earliest possible opportunity. For the decision to continue (or rather the lack of decision to change) the unpopular Claudian arrangements for Palestine made the choice of procurators crucial in preserving the peace of the province. While Agrippina and Pallas were still powerful at court that was impossible, but the dismissal of Pallas, marking a great triumph

---

[1] Brunt, *Latomus* 18 (1959), 554–5.

[2] *Hist.* 5. 9: 'Antonius Felix per omnem saevitiam ac libidinem ius regium servili ingenio exercuit'; *Ann.* 12. 54; Jos., *AJ* 20. 162–6.

[3] And at Felix' marriage to Antony's granddaughter Drusilla. (Tacitus may have confused the Jewish Drusilla with that one. But Suet. *Cl.* 28 does say he married three queens.)

[4] *AJ* 20. 141–3.

[5] So Jones, *Herods of Judaea*, pp. 227–30.

for Seneca and Burrus over Agrippina, provided the opportunity. Unfortunately, there is doubt as to whether or not it was taken. On the usual chronology, Felix was not replaced until *c.* 60, but an alternative chronology—the Eusebian chronology, which is difficult but not insuperably so—would put the replacement in 55/6, with the spring or summer of 56 fitting the other evidence best.[1]

The retention of Quadratus, on the other hand, should not be condemned. Given the natural reluctance of the government to give Corbulo a *maius imperium* at the start, the appointment of a strong governor, such as Anteius Rufus was clearly expected to be, in Syria at the same time would only have made more difficult that co-operation which to Corbulo meant his own domination. Nor would it have suited the atmosphere of harmony deliberately cultivated at Nero's accession to make a clean sweep of Claudian governors, particularly those whose prominence went back to the early years of Claudius. An early retirement for Quadratus was probably planned, but when Agrippina tried to achieve a share of the Armenian glory by putting in a strong protégé, Quadratus was naturally retained.[2] As for A. Didius Gallus, admittedly an elderly and inactive governor, he was left safely to hold the position in Britain while Nero was launching the Armenian campaign: he managed to repel the Silures, capture a few forts, and protect Rome's client Queen Cartimandua of the Brigantes.[3]

It is more serious that able men were kept out of governorships in these early years. As with the retention of Felix and Quadratus, rival court influences are again largely to blame. Suetonius specifically ascribes to Agrippina's influence the interruption in the career of the future Emperor T. Flavius Vespasianus.[4] Narcissus had smiled on Vespasian, who, after

[1] Above, p. 87; Appendix D5.
[2] Above, pp. 86–7.
[3] Tacitus, *Agric.* 14. 3; *Ann.* 12. 40. See the judgement of Birley, op. cit., p. 7: '. . . at least he had a long and reputable record as a commander in the field and an administrator.' He had been legate of Moesia in 45–6 where he won *triumphalia ornamenta.*
[4] Suet. *Vesp.* 4. 2.

distinguishing himself in the British campaign and attaining
two priesthoods, became consul for the last two months of 51.
But then, according to Suetonius, Vespasian went into retirement
until his proconsulship of Africa, through fear of Agrippina
who was hostile to the friends of the dead Narcissus. It is not
always easy to believe in the stories of Vespasian's suffering from
the enmity of the great. His inglorious early career does not suggest that he was regarded as very promising anyway, while later
imperial propaganda demanded that he should have fallen foul
of Nero.[1] Moreover, no shadow fell on the career of his brother,
T. Flavius Sabinus, who is found serving as legate of Moesia
from 53 to 60.[2] Vespasian's son Titus was brought up at court
with Britannicus, and, although Agrippina may have disliked
his attachment to her son's rival, Titus continued to live at court
and was seated beside Britannicus in February 55 when he died.[3]
When Agrippina died, Titus was already doing his military
service.[4] None the less, some explanation does seem to be required for the fact that Vespasian, who had already shown
military talent, remained unemployed after his consulship in 51
until he went out to govern Africa probably in one of the years
61 or 62.[5] Perhaps Agrippina felt that his son's relations with
Britannicus, added to this military ability, made him too dangerous to govern a military province, or perhaps she indulged a personal grudge, remembering how Vespasian had flattered Gaius
for his suppression of Gaetulicus' conspiracy while she was on
her way to the Pontian Islands.[6]

It is hazardous to guess at a man's support simply from the
chronology of his career. Not all men who first emerge when

[1] Note the story of Vespasian's dangerous slumbers in *Ann.* 16. 5, 3 and
(with a different date) Suet. *Vesp.* 4 and Dio 66. 11, 2.

[2] On the chronological problems of his career see Appendix D9.

[3] Suet. *Titus* 2. Suetonius' testimony to Titus' loyalty to Britannicus' memory
was thought to be confirmed by a coin, see H. Mattingly, *NC* 5th Ser. 10 (1930),
330–2. But J. Babelon, *Hommages à Léon Herrmann*, Brussels, 1960, p. 127, argues
that the coin is not a posthumous honour to Britannicus issued by Titus as
Princeps, but a late Claudian issue. M. Grant concurs (*Nero*, London, 1970,
p. 258, chap. 1, n. 10).

[4] See Appendix C4, p. 438.   [5] See Appendix D6.

[6] Suet. *Vesp.* 2. 3; Dio 59. 22, 5–9.

Agrippina's influence was fading can be counted as victims of
her displeasure. We cannot divine why C. Suetonius Paulinus,
Corbulo's rival, had to wait about fifteen years after his consulship to govern a province in 58.[1] Nor can we be certain that
L. Julius Vestinus, the *amicus* of Claudius, was kept idle until
he became prefect of Egypt in 59.[2] But the evidence is suggestive
in the case of another future Emperor, Ser. Sulpicius Galba.
Until 48, Galba had a career as distinguished as his birth, marriage,
and connection with Livia would have led one to expect. Quaestor
before the legal age, he moved on to a praetorship and the
coveted legateship of Aquitania. He held the consulship in 33
at the instance of Livia.[3] He then governed Upper Germany with
distinction, accompanied Claudius to Britain, and held Africa
for two years *electus extra sortem*,[4] probably from 45 to 47.
Though known for his integrity in governing Africa, Galba was
then in retirement until 60 when he was appointed legate of
Hispania Tarraconensis which he proceeded to govern with
equal justice.[5] Possibly Galba was just enjoying city life in the
late 40s and 50s, but his acceptance of the important Spanish
command so late suggests great ambition. It is better to suppose
that something held him back, and Suetonius helps to complete
the picture. Probably in 42, after Agrippina's return from exile
and his own triumphal return from Germany, Galba rejected her
advances in circumstances very humiliating to the future wife
and mother of emperors.[6] Perhaps Agrippina used her influence
with her husband Claudius and then with her son to ensure that
Galba would have no more opportunities for fame.

[1] *PIR*[1] S 694.

[2] So Pflaum, *Carr. proc.* I, no. 19, pp. 50–1, but the evidence does not prove
a gap between his service as procurator to Claudius attested in 48 (*ILS* 212)
and the Egyptian prefecture. Pflaum credits Seneca and Burrus with his appointment to that post; Nero, who was friendly with his son (*Ann.* 15. 68), probably
agreed.   [3] Suet. *Galba* 6; Plut. *Galba* 3. 2.

[4] Suet. *Galba* 7. 1. For the years see B. E. Thomasson, *Die Statthalter der
römischen Provinze Nordafrikas von Augustus bis Diocletianus*, Lund, 1960, II,
pp. 32–3.

[5] *Hist.* 1. 49. Suetonius, *Galba* 9–10, shows that he was severe but popular
enough to win widespread support in Spain.

[6] Suet. *Galba* 5. 1.

The career of one member of the younger line of the Plautii exhibits a pattern reminiscent of those of Galba and Vespasian. Agrippina feared most, and taught her son to fear, those who had some claim to the throne. Since the Princeps was in theory a kind of super-senator, he could hardly contract marriage with members of foreign dynasties, but was forced to marry within the Roman governing class, thus creating possible rivals, whose numbers increased as the dynasty went on. Apart from descendants of Augustus, like the Junii Silani and Rubellius Plautus, there were those whose relation to Claudius made them serious rivals to his adopted son: not only Britannicus and Cornelius Sulla, the husband of Claudius' daughter Antonia, but the Plautii, the family of Claudius' first wife, who were held in great honour by Claudius even after his divorce from Plautia Urgulanilla.[1]

Her brother, P. Plautius Pulcher, was made a patrician in 48 and thereafter *curator viarum sternendarum*. He may already have been proconsul of Sicily before the death of Claudius.[2] Even after the participation of Plautius Lateranus in the Messallina–Silius affair, and his consequent expulsion from the Senate, Claudius remained partial to the family because of his uncle, the head of the elder line and conqueror of Britain, A. Plautius Silvanus.[3] Another brother of Urgulanilla, M. Plautius Silvanus, had, before his suicide in A.D. 24, adopted one of the Aelii Lamiae who now called himself Ti. Plautius M. f. Silvanus Aelianus.[4] In the light of hislater achievements, it is fairto demand an explanation of his failure to achieve a military command after his consulship in 45, until 60. The fact that Claudius was not vengeful towards the Plautii and that Plautius Lateranus was restored to the Senate on Nero's accession, as a demonstration of clemency, makes the date of 60 for his emergence as

---

[1] On the Plautii see the stemma in *PIR*[1] P 361. L. R. Taylor, *MAAR* 24 (1956), 26 ff., is an admirable correction to the very inadequate account in *R-E* 21, nos. 38–48. She discusses the divorce of Urgulanilla on p. 28.

[2] Above, p. 98 n. 5. Yet he failed to achieve a consulship, though quaestor as early as 31.

[3] *Ann.* 11. 36, 4. His daughter or sister was married to Claudius' friend P. Petronius (Appendix D7).

[4] Taylor (above, n. 1), p. 29 n. 42, rightly criticizing the account in *R-E* 21, no. 47.

governor of Moesia point to the baneful influence of Agrippina. The safe proconsulship of Asia he had achieved, after a normal interval of ten years in 56.[1] In his last years, Nero reverted to Agrippina's policy. Plautius was legate of Moesia from 60 to 67, in which time he relieved a corn crisis in the city and made considerable progress on the Danube—all without any reward except survival.[2] Vespasian made it up to him, and reproached Nero by implication.[3]

Even in the early part of his reign, Nero had his own enemies: it may have been the ability of Agrippina's favourite, Anteius Rufus, that made the Emperor retain him in Rome after Agrippina's death and even after the decision to give Corbulo an active partner in the Eastern command had been taken.[4] Seneca mentions once that provinces were among the *beneficia* bestowed by the powerful,[5] and his patronage was not the only influence at work. But it is probably Seneca who must take the blame for postponing Vitellius' governorship of Africa, a post in which he eventually distinguished himself through his integrity.[6] (Yet who could have predicted that Vitellius would do well?) Nor can we credit him with the appointment of all of the governors noted for justice, moderation, and honesty, such as T. Vinius in Narbonensis and Petronius in Bithynia, whose appointments could fall within his period of influence.[7] Seneca's relatives, Junius Gallio and Pompeius Paulinus, were competent governors;[8]

---

[1] On the normal intervals see Thomasson, *Statthalter der Nordafrikas*, I, pp. 21 ff. For Plautius' career the main evidence is *ILS* 986.

[2] The dates are those of A. Stein, *Die Legaten von Moesien*, Budapest, 1940, pp. 29–31, accepted by Taylor (above, p. 244 n. 1), p. 29. They depend on the terminal date for the command of Flavius Sabinus in Moesia, on which see Appendix D9. For his achievements see D. M. Pippidi, *Epigr. Beiträge zur Ges. Histrias*, Berlin, 1962, pp. 106 ff.

[3] *ILS* 986.

[4] He was still idle in 66 (*Ann.* 16. 14).

[5] *Ben.* 1. 5, 1.

[6] Suet. *Vit.* 5; Tacitus, *Hist.* 2. 97; above, pp. 99–100; Appendix D6.

[7] Tacitus, *Hist.* 1. 48; *Ann.* 16. 18. On Petronius, above, p. 91 n. 3.

[8] In the one incident preserved of his governorship of Achaea, Acts 18: 12–17, Gallio exercised his judicial powers correctly and refused to be drawn into religious squabbles (above p. 83 n. 5). Tacitus praises Paulinus' engineering project (*Ann.* 13. 53).

presumably Seneca could not have praised Lucilius' humanity and honesty if he were a complete scoundrel. But no excessive degree of cynicism is required to make one wonder how much their qualities influenced their dispatch. For where the evidence for Seneca's responsibility is clearest, he is seen to have considered city politics at least as much as provincial welfare. Otho is said to have been sent to Lusitania in 58 at Seneca's suggestion: he proved an excellent governor, but it was his absence from Rome that was the aim of the appointment.[1] The appointment of the great Corbulo, which was credited to Seneca and Burrus, meant the recognition of military ability, and was also a demonstration to the Senate that Claudius' fears of such ability were not shared by his successor.[2] Both these considerations counted more with Seneca than the character of Corbulo who already had a reputation for great severity.[3] Similar motives probably underlie the appointment of the independent Antistius Vetus in 55 to Upper Germany[4] and of the two able governors of Britain, Q. Veranius and Suetonius Paulinus. Suetonius certainly was not inclined to clemency and was so absorbed in his military plans that he entrusted the annexation of a client kingdom to a rapacious procurator. Seneca and the other money-lenders who called in their loans at the same time probably acted from prudence, not malice, but they clearly put self-interest before the contentment of Rome's subjects.

None the less, the appointments, though not all worthy, were better than the control exercised on the governors once they went out. In Tacitus' judgement, the most striking exception to the excellence of the first years of Nero's reign was the laxness in punishing bad provincial governors. Nero was involved in some of these cases: he used indirect means to save Publius Celer from condemnation; he was responsible for the acquittal of two proconsuls of Africa, and it was probably the Emperor who, under Tigellinus' influence, restored Cossutianus Capito

---

[1] Plut. *Galba* 20. 1; *Ann.* 13. 46; Suet. *Otho* 3. 2.
[2] Above, p. 119.
[3] *Ann.* 11. 18, 2–3.
[4] Above, pp. 119–20.

to the Senate within four years of his conviction.[1] Tacitus marks
the injustice of these moves. The treatment of Celer who had
poisoned Junius Silanus, and of Capito who had a reputation
similar to that of Suillius Rufus,[2] will not have been popular with
the Senate. Nor would they have liked Nero's protection of
Antonius Felix from prosecution, under pressure from Agrippina
and Pallas.[3] But the acquittal of the two proconsuls is in perfect
harmony with the Senate's own slackness in pursuing delinquent
governors. Of the governors they convicted from Nero's accession to 61, one was really punished for an unpopular political prosecution under Claudius,[4] and one had his sentence
diminished through his powerful brother's influence.[5] Tacitus
avers that Eprius Marcellus was unjustly acquitted, even securing
revenge on his accusers.[6] Although the Senate did not have to
wait for provincials to prosecute, one of the proconsuls of Africa,
tried in 58, at least must have avoided prosecution for some years,
while Suillius Rufus, as Seneca knew, was guilty of extortion in
his tenure of Asia under Claudius. Yet Seneca made no move
for four years and then relied on charges that would produce
a quick conviction rather than start a lengthy extortion trial.[7]
At tu victrix provincia ploras.

This is not to say that neither the Emperor nor the Senate had
any conscience. Nero's edict of 57 prohibiting provincial governors from giving games was intended to protect the provincials.[8]
In 60 he showed generosity to the Cyreneans, as, four years later,
to the people of Lugdunum.[9] Even the mad proposal to abolish
indirect taxes at least resulted in tax relief and more protection
against the *publicani*. This edict resulted from consultation with
prominent senators, doubtless including Seneca. But it is notable
that the reforms were prompted by complaints of people in
Rome and were not primarily designed to relieve provincials,
though they were included.[10] As for the Senate, Tacitus says

---

[1] *Ann.* 13. 52; 14. 48. Nero's intervention for acquittal is recorded neutrally
in *Ann.* 14. 18. Cf. also Suet. *Otho* 2. 2. On the method, above, pp. 111–12.

[2] *Ann.* 11. 6. [3] Above, p. 87. [4] *Ann.* 14. 46.

[5] Ibid. 14. 28. [6] Ibid. 13. 33. [7] Ibid. 13. 43.

[8] Ibid. 13. 31. [9] Ibid. 14. 18 (above, p. 114); ibid. 16. 13, 3.

[10] Ibid. 13. 50–1; above, pp. 114, 123.

that they applauded Thrasea Paetus when he proposed a check on provincial deputations praising governors in 62.[1] Thrasea's argument turned on two points: that Roman governors were demeaned by courting provincial eulogies, and that the government of the man who sought cheap popularity often deteriorated. The second is the same idea that, earlier on, had inspired Nero's edict about gladiatorial games. Nero now approved a senatorial decree prohibiting votes of thanks in a provincial *concilium* or embassiet to convey them to Rome.[2] Seneca may well have approved of this proposal, for his relations with Thrasea were reputed to be good at this time.[3] No conflict with his policy of co-operation with the Senate would thereby be involved, for the Senate was prepared to forgo eulogies even if it did not welcome prosecutions.

Tacitus was active himself in prosecuting a particularly corrupt governor, but extortion trials were probably not popular even with the more upright senators. To issue regulations that would help to maintain a high standard was not the same as voting penalties to one's peers on the evidence of one's subjects.[4] Thrasea's speech reveals a preference, his own or at least that of his senatorial audience, for a situation in which provincials fear and court governors over one in which the governors want to be judged by the standards of provincials.[5] As for the Emperor's role, we know that Domitian was hated for instigating prosecutions of provincial governors.[6]

Both in theory and in practice, Seneca compares unfavourably

---

[1] Tac. *Ann.* 15. 22.

[2] Brunt, *Historia* 10 (1961), 216, n. 82c, raises the question of the effectiveness of this decree and says that the existence of eulogies passed by cities—which could be what is described in Pliny, *Pan.* 70—is technically compatible with Tacitus' description referring to *concilia*, but he regards it as unlikely that the decree remained in force.

[3] *Ann.* 15. 23.

[4] Brunt, op. cit., 216, notes that *SIG*[3] 783 (Augustan) shows that a mission of prosecution was not something a man wanted to be praised for, probably because the Senate disliked them. Note Pliny, *Ep.* 9. 13, 21; *Pan.* 70.

[5] Brunt, loc. cit., argues plausibly that Thrasea Paetus in the interest of true reform used this clever appeal to senatorial pride. The real point of his speech was 'laus falsa et precibus expressa'.

[6] H. W. Pleket, *Mnemosyne* 14 (1961), 300 ff.

with his contemporary Stoics, Thrasea Paetus and Barea Soranus. Before Thrasea made his speech against provincial eulogies, appealing to Roman pride and the need for individual self-respect but also pleading for the protection of Rome's subjects, he had helped the Cilicians to obtain a conviction in the extortion trial of Cossutianus Capito.[1] Barea Soranus governed Asia in the great tradition of Q. Mucius Scaevola and Rutilius Rufus, taking thought for their material welfare and taking their part against the exactions of the Emperor's agents:[2] Tacitus makes Barea's accuser deny that his motive was *utilitas communis*[3] —which was presumably a familiar slogan of Barea's. Is Tacitus giving his own estimate of Seneca's attitude even during his years of influence when he makes him object, not to the general provincial hardship resulting from Nero's exactions in 64, but, specifically, to the sacrilege involved in stripping temples?[4] Or is it rather that Seneca, responsible for general government policy and entangled in court rivalries, was not as free as Thrasea and Barea to follow the dictates of his conscience?

Assimilation

Seneca's native land had known many instances of Rome's generosity in granting the citizenship. He was one of a long line of senators coming out of that province. As a Stoic, he believed that all men belonged to one state. But, in common with the rest of his school, he did not see in the spread of the Roman citizenship or in the acceptance of provincials into the Roman Senate a means of realizing such a state or even of fulfilling the obligation to benefit the human race. Seneca's writings, in fact, betray little interest in these remarkable features of the Roman Empire.

There seem to be only three references to extensions of the citizenship. One is neutral: if the Princeps gives citizenship to all Gauls, immunity to all Spaniards, in what sense has each individual

[1] Tac. *Ann.* 13. 33, cf. 16. 21, 3.
[2] Ibid. 16. 23.
[3] Ibid. 16. 30; cf. Cicero, *Off.* 3. 24 ff. (see pp. 238–9 above).
[4] *Ann.* 15. 45, 3.

received a benefit?[1] One is apparently hostile: that is the famous passage in the *Apocolocyntosis* where Seneca attributes to Claudius a plan of extending the citizenship to all remaining *peregrini*: 'constituerat enim omnes Graecos, Gallos, Hispanos, Britannos togatos videre.'[2] Given the determination of the author here to ridicule Claudius, we cannot take this as a serious statement of Seneca's views, especially as the passage is clearly not a criticism of any actual Claudian programme, but of the famous speech preserved on the Lyons tablet in which Claudius, wishing to grant the request of some Gallic chieftains for adlection into the Senate, amassed evidence for innovation in Roman history. His discussion of the extension of the citizenship is now lost, but Tacitus probably preserves some details from it.[3] That Seneca is here caricaturing the Emperor's argument is supported by another passage of the *Apocolocyntosis* where Claudius' allusions, first to men from Vienne and then to senators from Lugdunum (a lame joke about his own birthplace) are reflected in the reference to Claudius' birth at Lugdunum (where the exact distance from Vienna is given) and the description of Claudius as 'Gallus Germanus'.[4] Seneca, in fact, could write in the liberal Claudian vein when he chose. In *De Ira*, preaching the conversion of anger into love, he cites the happy experience of Rome: 'quos populus Romanus fideliores habet socios quam quos habuit pertinacissimos hostes: quod hodie esset imperium, nisi salubris providentia victos permiscuisset victoribus?'[5] The passage could have been written any time in the reign of Claudius before 51/2: perhaps an echo of Claudius' speech, but, more likely, a standard view acceptable both to the philosopher and to the Emperor.[6]

---

[1] *Ben.* 6. 19, 2. Sherwin-White, *The Roman Citizenship*[2], Oxford, 1973, p. 243, suggests that this shows it was fashionable to discuss such magnificent possibilities. No doubt the example of Gaul was suggested by Claudius' action as censor, but the reason for the 'magnificence' of the conception here is clearly Seneca's desire to make the point that, even if one receives a benefit as one member of a *very large* group, one still must feel grateful.

[2] *Apoc.* 3. 3.

[3] Note at the end of col. I (*ILS* 212): 'civitatem . . .'. Cf. *Ann.* 11. 24, 2–4.

[4] Col. II, 9–29; *Apoc.* 6. 1.

[5] *Ira* 2. 34, 4.

[6] Col. II, 8; 35; Tac. *Ann.* 11. 24, 1–4, cf. Dion. Hal. *Ant. Rom.* 2. 17–18.

It is therefore not surprising to find that grants of citizenship under Nero are modest and follow traditional patterns. Two chieftains of the Frisii, sent on an embassy to Rome, received citizenship from the Emperor—a recognition of virtue or a means of buying loyalty while refusing substantial requests.[1] The extension of Latin rights to the Maritime Alps, perhaps the Cottian Alps as well, in 63 when Seneca's power was already diminished, simply continues the extensions of Claudius in the borderlands of Italy.[2]

Something more substantial, however, has been claimed for Nero's reign and for Seneca's influence as regards the recruitment of provincials into government service. This was, of course, a continuous process—once started no Emperor could really stop it and none tried—but it was a process that could be promoted or retarded or given different directions. Seneca and Burrus have been credited with promoting it, and particularly in favour of the western provinces, notably Gaul and Spain.[3]

Statistics have been published, showing three Spaniards and three Gauls from Narbonensis entering the Senate under Claudius, and no fewer than twelve Spaniards and ten Gauls under Nero—figures which must be pruned, for even reasonable accuracy, to three Spaniards and three Gauls under Claudius and nine Spaniards and eight Gauls (one from Aquitania; the rest from Narbonensis) under Nero.[4] Of the latter, one of the Gauls

---

[1] *Ann.* 13. 54, 4. Compare the bribe of land offered to the chiefs of the Ampsivarii (*Ann.* 13. 56) whose tribe was refused land.

[2] *Ann.* 15. 32; Suet. *Nero* 18; Pliny, *NH* 3. 133; *R-E* 16 ('municipium'), col. 599; Sherwin-White, *Roman Citizenship*[2], pp. 242, 252 n. 1.

[3] De Laet, *De Samenstelling van den romeinschen Senaat*, p. 318; Syme, *Tacitus*, pp. 590–2.

[4] De Laet, pp. 318, 279 ff. For Claudius: Gallio (no. 1030) probably did not first enter the Senate under Claudius (above, p. 45). For Nero: no. 1513 (Pomponius), and no. 1643'bis (P. Licinius Caecina), of the Spaniards, could be Galba's men, as argued by Syme, *HSCP* 73 (1968), 217, 228–9; of the Gauls, no. 1302 (M. Antonius Primus) could have entered under Claudius and no. 1607 (M. Aper) could have entered after Nero. The Spaniard no. 1552, listed as a Neronian entry, should be called M. Raecius Tauri f. Gallus (*AE* 1932, no. 84 corrected in *AE* 1966, no. 189) and was a discovery of Galba. His adoptive father, M. Raecius Taurus, is attested as a senator in 49 and is possibly also from Tarraconensis (Syme, op. cit., p. 229). I have counted him in the text as Claudius' third Spaniard.

started his career after Seneca's effective influence was past.[1] The low standard of certainty and completeness in these figures makes them useless for comparing the policies of the two Emperors. That there were all together six Gauls in Claudius' senate, as the same study suggests, is rendered most unlikely by the measure of 49 allowing senators from that province to visit their estates there without imperial permission:[2] it would hardly have been worth it for six. Entry to the Senate is difficult to document, as one rarely hears of the submerged majority in that body. Four of the seventeen names on the Neronian list happen to be known to us, or their origins are known to us, from accounts of the extraordinary year 69.

Consulships are more significant. In the period of the Principate before Nero, Narbonensis advanced faster than the Spanish provinces: three Gauls, perhaps four, as against one Spaniard.[3] Under Nero, there are certainly two Gauls and three Spaniards who reach the consulship,[4] and a possibility of twice that number, with the Spaniards again having a small lead.[5] If the de-Italianization of the senate was inevitable, an emperor could still decide which provincials to have. It is at least clear that Nero, in the period of Seneca's influence, and afterwards, allowed Spain to match, if not to surpass, the dignity of Gaul. The prominence of Spain and Gaul in the period of Seneca's power

[1] Cn. Julius Agricola (no. 1422) was quaestor in 63/4. But Seneca would be pleased as he thought highly of his father, Julius Graecinus (*Ben*. 2. 21, 5; *Ep*. 29. 6).

[2] *Ann*. 12. 23, 1. Cf. *ILS* 212, col. 2: Claudius says Vienna had been contributing senators for a long time.

[3] Syme, *Tacitus*, p. 590; App. 82: Domitius Afer (cos. 39); Valerius Asiaticus (35, 46); Pompeius Paulinus (53 or 54) for Gaul; L. Pedanius Secundus (43) is the Spaniard. But this list may not be complete: for example, Syme suggests that Memmius Regulus, cos. 31, came from Narbonensis.

[4] Ibid. Gauls: L. Duvius Avitus of Vasio in 56; M. Julius Vestinus Atticus of Vienne in 65. Spaniards: L. Junius Gallio Annaeanus of Corduba in 55; L. Annaeus Seneca in 56; Cn. Pedanius Salinator of Barcino in 60 or 61.

[5] Possibly from Gaul: Trebellius Maximus (56), see Appendix D2; P. Marius Celsus (62)—see Syme, App. 32; C. Memmius Regulus (63). Possibly from Spain: Q. Junius Marullus (above, p. 92); M. Aponius Saturninus (Neronian); Q. Fabius Barbarus Antonius Macer (*c*. 64). On these see Syme, App. 82, where others who could be Spanish or Gallic are adduced.

shows also in the four great equestrian prefectures. Apart from Burrus', two are held by a Gaul and a Spaniard between 54 and 62.[1] Perhaps most impressive of all is the post of *praefectus urbi*, held by the Spanish consular L. Pedanius Secundus from 56 to 61.[2]

What does the evidence mean in terms of Seneca's loyalties and prejudices? Since his written views do not point to a belief in the assimilation of Rome's subjects in general, should we rather assume that Seneca and Burrus, the two most powerful *amici principis*, promoted the advance of their fellow Spaniards and Gauls in the governmental hierarchy? Seneca's choice of wife and friends certainly shows that he never attempted to repudiate his provincial origins. His wife's family, the Pompeii Paulini, came from Arelate in Narbonensis,[3] and he may have chosen to share his consulship with another man from that province.[4] The friend to whom he dedicated *De Beneficiis* came from the Roman colony of Lugdunum, at once more provincial and less.[5] Like his father, Seneca had many friends from his native Spain.[6] Annaeus Serenus may be fairly assumed a distant relative and Spaniard; the poet Valerius Martialis of Bilbilis notes Seneca's generosity to him;[7] the historian Fabius Rusticus, the suffect consul Junius Marullus, and the agricultural expert Junius Moderatus Columella, might be other young Spaniards who naturally sought out Seneca when they came to Rome.[8] Of these, the two Pompeii Paulini and Annaeus Serenus probably received their government posts

---

[1] Annaeus Serenus was prefect of the watch in this period (see Appendix D3). Pompeius Paulinus was *praefectus annonae* until 55; Julius Vestinus was prefect of Egypt from 59 until between July 62 and September 63.

[2] See Appendix D9.

[3] Pliny, *NH* 33. 143.

[4] Above, p. 89; Appendix D2.

[5] Seneca, *Ep.* 91, cf. *Ben.* 3. 1, 1. On Lugdunum see Syme, *Tacitus*, p. 460.

[6] On these, *JRS* 62 (1972), 12; 15–16.

[7] *Epig.* 12. 36, 8–10; cf. 4. 40, 1.

[8] The evidence is not conclusive for Rusticus' origin: Syme, *Tacitus*, p. 179. For Columella see below, p. 291 n. 2. The poet Calpurnius Siculus thanks his patron 'Meliboeus' in *Ecl.* 4. 29 ff. for rescuing him from life in the wilds of Spain. His cognomen, however, makes a Spanish origin unlikely, and the lines to which we have referred about Spain are regarded as literary commonplace by E. Cesareo, *La poesia di Calpurnio Siculo*, Palermo, 1931, pp. 172–3, who also justly remarks (p. 160 and n. 2) that we cannot identify 'Meliboeus'.

through Seneca's patronage, and we must not forget Seneca's two brothers whose careers prospered while he was in power.[1] Nor would it be altogether absurd to suggest that the high-ranking centurion found serving in Dalmatia some time between 63 and 69, Q. Aebutius Liberalis (whose name recalls the addressee of *De Beneficiis*) was Seneca's friend or a relative who received his *ordines* through Seneca's recommendation. He served under Ducenius Geminus who had been on the financial commission of 62 with Pompeius Paulinus.[2]

The admixture of Gauls alone in this list dispels the notion of an exclusive attachment to Spain, and Seneca's allusions to his native land suggest a detachment greater even than that of his sophisticated father. If comparison with Martial's interest in Spain prompts an explanation based on Seneca's ultimate Italian origins, an examination of the writings of the detached Columella, whose *nomen* suggests a native origin too, acts as a corrective.[3] In fact, in his Consolation to his mother, who was living on the family estates in Spain, Seneca can note that people have come to Rome 'ex municipiis et coloniis suis, ex toto denique orbe terrarum' to fulfil ambitions or become educated, without mentioning the experience of his own family. When we consider that this work of Seneca's is comparatively rich in autobiographical detail, it is hard not to diagnose deracination.[4]

The most we can infer then from the statistics about Spanish and Gallic recruits to the administration is that Seneca, and probably Burrus,[5] were hospitable and kind to hopefuls from their homelands who sought them out, and that Seneca was not ashamed of his provincial background or snobbish about his own Italian origins when confronted with Junii and Fabii.[6] But the inference

[1] Above, pp. 83–5, 88–9.

[2] See Appendix D8.

[3] *JRS* 62 (1972), 12–17, where the allusions to Spain in the works of both Senecas are discussed.

[4] *Cons. Helv.* 6–7. Haase frags. 98–9 and 88 show, however, that the deracination was not total.

[5] For Burrus' probable advancement of a friend from his native Vasio, above, pp. 84–5.

[6] His father's attitude was the same in this respect, above, p. 31.

should not be too confidently accepted. Apart from his known relatives and friends, Seneca may not have played an important role in the rising fortunes of men from the Spanish provinces. The number of provincials in government was bound to increase, and if Spaniards do seem to fare particularly well under Nero, some credit is probably due to the strong influence of one early Claudian consul, Pedanius Secundus, who rose to be prefect of the city and saw one of his relatives consul.[1]

Seneca's behaviour, in so far as we can discover it, does not reveal anything that runs counter to what his writings, even more than those of his father, suggest: the unimportance of national feeling in the civilized western provinces of the Roman Empire.

[1] Above, p. 252 nn. 3 and 4.

8

SENECA ON SLAVERY

I

SENECA pleaded a powerful case for the humane treatment of slaves. He was not the first philosopher to discuss in detail the proper relations of master and slave: he himself refers to the standard topic *de usu servorum*[1] that, among the Stoics, was included, along with advice on the treatment of wives and children, in their casuistical discussions of justice.[2] These discussions are lost, but, as will appear, they probably did not contain suggestions as practical or attitudes as positive as we find in Seneca's lengthy treatments of the problem.[3] For Seneca does not merely condemn cruelty. He asks that slaves be regarded as individuals with different moral capacities, as potential friends whose relations with the master are based on love or respect rather than fear, generosity on one side being matched by loyalty on the other. The slave should find in the home, not only a master, but a society with responsibilities, honours, and a sense of community.

Seneca's conclusions can be divided for discussion into those deduced from philosophical principles (A) and those deduced from considerations of expediency (B). For each argument, I shall indicate, as far as can be surmised, the relation of Seneca's view to both earlier and contemporary philosophical doctrine and to

---

[1] *Ep.* 47. 11.

[2] *Ep.* 94. 1: 'Eam partem [praeceptivam] philosophiae quae dat propria cuique personae praecepta nec in universum componit hominem sed marito suadet quomodo se gerat adversus uxorem, patri quomodo educet liberos, domino quomodo servos regat.' Cf. *Ben.* 3. 21–2. This topic appears to be included under justice in Cicero, *Off.* 1. 41.

[3] His fullest discussions are in *Ben.* 3. 18–28 and *Ep.* 47, but Seneca mentions the problem often, notably in *De Ira* and the Letters to Lucilius. It is not possible to discern a development in his view, see Appendix E1.

general contemporary attitudes and practice—for the significance of his ideas cannot otherwise be judged. To fill out the
picture, I shall review the attitude in Seneca's purely passing
references to slavery (c), and outline the contemporary attitude
revealed in legislation (D).

It is important to note at the outset that some of the arguments
in categories (A) and (B) could have led Seneca and others who
used them to more unpalatable conclusions: the abolition of
slavery or wholesale manumission of worthy slaves. That these
conclusions were deliberately avoided,[1] even in theory, should
make us cautious when we come to argue what conclusions in
terms of action a man of Seneca's views would draw.

A

The principal philosophical dogma in Seneca's thought on slavery
is that there are no natural slaves: all men share in the divine
reason and thus may claim the gods as ancestors;[2] servitude, like
all social ranks, 'nomina ex ambitione aut iniuria nata', is the
work of fortune which 'aeguo iure genitos alium alii donauit'.[3]

The idea itself goes back to the sophists, some of whom drew
the conclusion that the unnatural institution should be abolished.[4] That slavery was not natural was the only view consistent
with Stoic physics, and it is indirectly attested for the Old Stoa
and was probably retained by the Middle Stoa.[5] Long before
Seneca's day, it had become a cliché, part of the mental baggage
of the educated, or, like Trimalchio, the would-be educated.[6]

The Stoic philosophers seem to have deduced from this doctrine only the most minimal principles of humane treatment.

[1] In Tranq. 8. 8–9 and Ep. 47. 18.
[2] Ben. 3. 28, 1; Ep. 44; 47. 10.   [3] Cons. Marc. 20. 2; Ep. 31. 11.
[4] For a summary history of this idea see W. Richter, Gym. 65 (1958), 206–10.
Aristotle opposed it in Politics 1. 2 ($1253^{b}18$ ff.).
[5] See Appendix E2.
[6] The Elder Seneca had already written of the declaimer Albucius Silus
(Contr. 7. 6, 18): 'Albucius et philosophatus est: dixit neminem natura liberum
esse, neminem servum; haec postea nomina singulis imposuisse Fortuna . . .';
Petronius 71. Juvenal 14. 15 ff. shows the view as a commonplace of parental
instruction; the wife in 6. 222 is tired of the view.

Chrysippus' description of a slave as *perpetuus mercennarius*[1] seems to lie behind the cold formula of those philosophers, surely including Panaetius, whose view Cicero quotes in *De Officiis*: 'ita iubent uti, ut mercennariis: operam exigendam, iusta praebenda.'[2] In Rome such a view would hardly enhance the dignity of slaves, as Cicero rates manual labour so low as to be comparable with servitude.[3] Panaetius seems to have regarded cruelty as a justifiable way of controlling slaves, if other means were insufficient.[4] His pupil Hecato rated the humanity of slaves so low as to deny that a slave could deserve his master's gratitude[5] or that a master was obliged to ruin himself by continuing to feed his slaves when the price of grain was exorbitant:[6] *utilitas* here prevails over *humanitas*. Hecato's contemporary Rutilius Rufus, however, paid his slaves for fish they caught just as he did free men, which acknowledges in practice the view of Chrysippus that one could have obligations and debts to slaves.[7] This poor harvest from the doctrine of the natural equality of man was not improved even in the Stoic writers after Seneca. Epictetus notes the doctrine as a reason for not losing one's temper with one's slaves, while Marcus Aurelius lists slaves along with wives, parents, etc., as a class of persons to whom one has obligations, but only to demand justice, in the negative sense, in our relations with all rational creatures.[8]

Seneca, however, goes further, regarding the slave as entitled to everything covered by man's duty to man. Not only must he be spared physical punishment, which is appropriate only to animals; he must not be insulted.[9] The virtues of *humanitas* and *clementia* should govern our relations with slaves as with other

---

[1] *Ben.* 3. 22, 1.

[2] Cicero, *Off.* 1. 41. On this, M. Pohlenz, *Antikes Führertum*, Leipzig, 1934, pp. 34, 136.

[3] *Off.* 1. 150.   [4] Ibid. 2. 24.   [5] *Ben.* 3. 18.

[6] *Off.* 3. 89. Although Cicero does not say, Hecato presumably gave a similar answer to the question: 'si in mari iactura facienda sit, equine pretiosi potius iacturam faciat an servoli vilis?' Compare St. Augustine, *De Sermone Domini in Monte* 1. 59, who argues against comparingt he value of a horse and a slave.

[7] Athenaeus 6. 274C–D, on which H. Strasburger, *JRS* 55 (1965), 49.

[8] Epictetus 1. 13; Marcus Aurelius 5. 31.

[9] *Ep.* 47. 14, 19.

men,[1] and generosity to slaves and freedmen counts as fulfilment of the obligation to help other men.[2] Finally, the slave can be treated as a social equal, admitted to conversation, asked for advice, and invited to the master's table regularly, not just on the Saturnalia.[3]

Seneca's portrayal of the reaction of the *delicati* to his views: 'nihil hac re humilius, nihil turpius',[4] should not mislead us into thinking that he alone accepted these implications in the doctrine of natural equality. We know, for example, that the Elder Cato often dined with his slaves and other frugal masters may have done so.[5] Letter 47 itself, the fullest treatment of slavery, depicts Lucilius as a man who punishes his slaves verbally and has friendly relations with them.[6] In another Letter, Seneca cites the advice of a Stoic friend to a master who has decided to commit suicide: 'Show your humanity. Just as after a feast the remains are distributed to the slaves standing around, so now give something to those who have served you all your life.'[7] The most eloquent testimony to the acceptance of these standards is that of the satirists who show how much lip-service men bothered to pay them. There is the master who, believing that the bodies and souls of slaves are made of the same stuff as our own, preaches mildness but revels in flogging and tortures;[8] the husband who believes that the death of a slave requires as much justification as any capital punishment, but allows his cruel wife to gratify her whim to have a slave crucified.[9] Finally, there is the ex-slave who at the close of the banquet allows his 'putidissimi servi' to sit down with the guests and indulges himself in philosophical monologue: 'amici, et servi homines sunt et aeque unum lactem biberunt, etiam si illos malus fatus oppresserit.' Then, to earn gratitude for his benevolence without actually incurring loss, he

---

[1] For *humanitas* and *clementia* as owed to men in general, *Ep.* 88. 30; *clementia* advised towards slaves in *Clem.* I. 18, 1; *Ep.* 47. 13. The idea of *humanitas* is specifically connected with slaves only in the speech given to a Stoic in *Ep.* 77. 8, though they are surely to be included in the 'adversus minores humanitatem' recommended in *NQ* 4, pref. 18.

[2] *Vit. Beat.* 24. 3.   [3] *Ep.* 47. 13.   [4] Ibid.
[5] Plut., *Cato Maior* 3.   [6] *Ep.* 47. I, 19.   [7] Ibid. 77. 8.
[8] Juvenal 14. 15 ff.   [9] Ibid. 6. 219 ff.

has his will read out showing his intention to manumit his slaves and reward them, when he is dead.[1]

Another Stoic tenet carrying important implications for the treatment of slaves said that the only significant differences between men lie in virtue, whose acquisition is within anyone's control:[2] the social condition of slavery touches only the body, not the mind.[3] Thus it is in the power of the slave, like the free-man, to achieve true liberty, i.e. spiritual independence of for-tune, or to opt for true slavery, i.e. voluntary submission to worldly pleasure and desire.[4] These ideas, current in Euripides and New Comedy, preached by Cynics and Stoics,[5] were offered to slaves, or to anyone who found himself in the power of another. They form part of the teaching of resignation and acceptance in Seneca and Epictetus: the slave should concentrate on his spiritual development, cultivate a willing attitude, and suppress indignation at his lot.[6] But for Seneca they also carry implications for the master's behaviour: by the exercise of his virtue a slave can benefit his master and put him under obligation;[7] if slaves, like other men, differ morally and these differences alone matter, then we must consider them as individuals and choose friends among them on the basis of character.[8]

---

[1] Petronius 34; 71. Some Scholars, e.g. Trillitzsch (*Seneca im literarischen Urteil*, p. 54), regard this as a serious attack on philosophical views or on Seneca's in particular. But it seems to be rather a hit at the ex-slave who has learned all too well to play the master. Trimalchio is only pompous, ridiculous (cf. the place at table 'libertini locus' when all the guests are freedmen), and mildly hypo-critical. Real ex-slaves could be worse. Note the arrogance of Pallas (*Ann.* 12. 53, 13. 23) and the cruelty of Larcius Macedo 'qui servisse patrem suum parum immo nimium meminisset' (Pliny, *Ep.* 3. 14).

[2] *Ep.* 31. 11.

[3] *Ben.* 3. 20, 1–2; a Platonic view already brought into Stoicism by Posidonius, Richter, *Gym.* 65 (1958), 203.

[4] *Brev. Vit.* 2. 1; *Ben.* 3. 28. 1, 4; *NQ* 3, pref. 16–17; *Ep.* 47. 15–17; *Ep.* 77. 14.

[5] Richter, *Gym.* 65 (1958), 208–10.

[6] *Ep.* 61. 3; *Ira* 3. 16, 1; *Epict.* 1. 9, 20–30; 3. 24, 77; 4. 1, 33. Seneca's remarks are more general and could be applied to any situation in which one man is in the power of another. A further consolation to the slave is the idea that all men are slaves to fortune and share the common refuge of suicide (*Cons. Marc.* 20. 2–3; *Cons. Polyb.* 6. 5; *Ep.* 26. 10; 47. 1; 61. 3; 70. 19 ff.; 77. 14; 80. 4–5).

[7] *Ben.* 3. 18; 3. 21, 22.

[8] *Ep.* 47. 15. That Seneca gave a deeper significance to the *exempla* of loyalty

These ideas are not found in Epictetus or Marcus Aurelius, but, here again, if the philosophers seem to lag behind Seneca,[1] the ideas and practice of his time did not: Cicero before him and Pliny after him express their affection, admiration, and friendship for individual slaves.[2] Feelings of this kind tended naturally to develop between masters and educated slaves—doctors, teachers, readers, or nurses, whose personal services involved intimacy.[3] Seneca is making harder demands on the master's humanity when he urges that for the selection of worthy slaves as friends the proper criterion is character, not functions: 'erras si existimas me quosdam quasi sordidioris operae reiecturum, ut puta illum mulionem et illum bubulcum.' But Columella, Seneca's contemporary, claims to have chatted and joked with rustic slaves even more than with urban ones and to have consulted them on problems of the farm in order to study their individual abilities.[4]

The Stoic doctrine of the wickedness of all passions was naturally applied to that relationship which most of all encouraged anger and licentiousness.[5] In De Ira, Seneca draws some of his most vivid examples from this area of life, showing that the slave narrows his yoke by succumbing to angry feelings,[6] and that the master who punishes his slave in anger has not made sure that there is sufficient cause or estimated the appropriate degree of punishment. He urges masters to admit and even seek out reasons for clemency,[7] a constant preoccupation of Seneca. This

in slaves found in non-philosophical writers is noted by J. Vogt, *Sklaverei und Humanität*, 1965, pp. 90–1.

[1] It is notable that the contemporary Stoic poet, Persius, has only two references to slaves altogether. In one, possession of Cappadocian slaves is a sign of greed (6. 76); in the other (5. 73) true freedom is contrasted with manumission and a worthless manumitted slave portrayed.

[2] Cicero, *Fam.* 16. 1–15; *Att.* 1. 12, 4; Pliny, *Ep.* 5. 19.

[3] On this see Vogt, *Sklaverei und Humanität*, pp. 69 ff.

[4] *Ep.* 47. 15; Columella, *RR* 1. 8, 15.

[5] *Ep.* 47. 19–20; Elder Seneca, *Contr.* 4, pref. 10: 'inpudicitia in ingenuo crimen est, in servo necessitas, in liberto officium'.

[6] *Ira* 3. 16, 1. For examples of anger in slaves, *Ep.* 18. 15; 4. 8.

[7] *Ira* 3. 12, 5; 3. 32, 1; 3. 29 (note that the mitigating circumstance Seneca mentions here—difficult adjustment of an urban slave to field work—arises

kind of advice, of course, is concerned with the moral well-being of the master, not the treatment of the slave, as is particularly clear when it is handled by Epictetus and Musonius Rufus.[1] The doctrine of ἀπάθεια could justify a callous attitude for which the Stoics were criticized.[2] Therefore Pliny may have Stoics particularly in mind when he says that there were men who regarded the loss of a slave as a mere *damnum* and took this attitude to show that they were *sapientes*.[3] This view, combining the Stoic prohibition on grief with the non-philosophical idea that a slave was only a possession, has left its trace in some passages of Seneca.[4]

The institution of slavery was recognized as a hindrance to other moral aims endorsed by the Stoics. Slaves decreased the master's self-sufficiency: for this reason, it was said, Diogenes had not pursued his runaway slave, while Zeno did without one entirely.[5] Further, slaves formed a major item in the wealth and luxury that made devotion to philosophy more difficult[6] and their control wasted the master's time.[7] Though not humanitarian reasons, these were possible grounds for deploring the institution as such, but Seneca only went so far as to advocate decreasing the size of *familiae*.[8]

B

When we turn to Seneca's arguments from expediency, we find him acutely conscious of the more practical disadvantages of the institution to masters. Seneca describes, often with sympathy, the troubles of the slave-owner: he relies on lazy and unwilling labour, he is likely to be robbed, his slaves are expensive to keep

from a custom of masters condemned by Columella I pref. 12; 8. 1–2; 3. 34–5; 3. 24, 1); *Clem.* I. 18, 1.

[1] Epict. 4. 1, 119 ff. In frag. 12 (Hense, p. 66), Musonius is advising chastity in marriage. He admits that adultery with a slave-girl is not injustice, but condemns it as ἀκρασία.

[2] *Clem.* 2. 5, 2.

[3] Pliny, *Ep.* 8. 16, 3. Cicero (*Att.* 1. 12, 4) and Martial (5. 37, 20) testify to the influence of the view.

[4] *Tranq.* 11. 3; *Ben.* 6. 2, 3.

[5] *Cons. Helv.* 12. 4; *Tranq.* 8. 7–8.   [6] *Cons. Helv.* 11. 3; *Ep.* 17. 3; 31. 10.

[7] *Brev. Vit.* 3. 2; 12. 2.   [8] *Tranq.* 8. 8–9.

and likely to run away.[1] But a lofty indifference, not abolition, is the remedy he favours.

The most fruitful of the arguments from prudence are those concerned with the security of the master and of society. Over and over again, Seneca insists that cruelty to slaves may lead not only to financial loss through their flight or death[2] but to brutal revenge in the form of accusation or murder:[3] his answer to the proverb 'totidem hostes quot servos' is 'non habemus illos hostes, sed facimus'.[4] He also points out how productive of loyalty is good treatment.[5] Seneca here follows in a long tradition not only of Greek thought[6] but of practical Roman thought and practice. The agricultural writers, starting with the Elder Cato, are more concerned than Seneca with the positive results of good treatment, for their job is to teach how to get the best work from agricultural slaves. In pursuit of this aim, Cato can advise curtailment of rations to sick slaves and the sale of old and sick ones, while insisting that the *familia* must be kept adequately clothed and fed, that punishments must be in proportion to the fault, and gratitude shown for *beneficia* to encourage good behaviour in the others.[7]

In Varro, the problem of incentive receives more attention. The foremen are to be made more eager by rewards, more dependable by being allowed mates and some property to farm.[8] Workers can be given greater interest in their work and encouraged to feel loyal to their masters by being consulted, by being treated more liberally in the matter of food, clothing, and leisure, and by being given cattle to graze. Verbal punishment is recommended, though flogging is permitted if necessary, and the

---

[1] *Ira* 3. 34, 1; *Tranq.* 8. 7–8; *Ep.* 17. 3; 107. 1, 5.

[2] *Ira* 3. 5, 4. As slaves were scarcer in the Empire than in the Republic, it is perhaps surprising that Seneca is not more concerned with this point.

[3] *NQ* 1. 16, 1; *Ep.* 4. 8; 47. 2–9; 107. 5. Seneca regards hatred as the usual feeling of slaves for masters: *Ben.* 3. 19, 4; 3. 25, 1.

[4] *Ep.* 47. 5.

[5] *Ep.* 47. 4.

[6] Traceable in e.g. Plato, *Laws* 777; Xen. *Hell.* 5. 3, 7.

[7] *De Agricultura* 2. 4, 7; 5. 2.

[8] *RR* 1. 17, 5. Here Varro follows a translation of Mago, made a generation before.

need of some harsh punishment is clearly envisaged.[1] The practical bent of Varro's 'humanity' shows up in his acceptance of the Aristotelian view of a slave as a special kind of tool.[2]

Columella, Seneca's contemporary, claims that he has tried with success the methods he recommends: casual talk and consultation with rustic slaves make them work more willingly; care in making just allowances of food and clothing, in following up complaints of cruel treatment, in rewarding hard work and fertility in women, pays off: 'haec et iustitia et cura patris familiae multum confert augendo patrimonio.'[3] In Columella the concern with security that we find in Seneca appears more than in either of his predecessors. The *vilicus* is to be neither too lax nor too cruel and must favour the better slaves but spare the worse 'ut potius timeant eius severitatem quam crudelitatem detestentur'.[4] Those slaves who have been punished and imprisoned, though they are not to be unchained without the master's orders, must be treated generously and moderately because the more resentful they are, the more dangerous.[5]

The agricultural writers adopt the standpoint of the individual master, but similar conclusions about the necessity of mild treatment followed from considerations of public safety. The public danger of rustic slaves hardly needs illustration: the Late Republic experienced dramatic slave revolts, and, despite greater vigilance under the Empire,[6] brigandage was still a problem.[7] Although we have no trace of Posidonius' views on slavery as a philosopher,[8] his analysis of the Sicilian slave revolt in his history shows him

---

[1] *RR.* 1. 17, 6–7. Varro's views are not ahead of his time, e.g. 1. 2, 17; 19. 3; 2. 10, 5.

[2] Ibid. 1. 17, 1. Cf. 19. 1; Arist. *Pol.* 1. 2 (1253ᵇ 23 ff.): ὄργανον or κτῆμα ἔμψυχον. According to Plutarch, Crassus, a Peripatetic (*Crassus* 3. 3), drew from Aristotle's definition the conclusion that a master's chief duty was to train and care for his slaves and made a fortune in doing so (ibid. 2. 6). Cf. also the use to which the jurist Gaius put the Aristotelian view, below, p. 274 n. 2.

[3] *RR* 1. 8, 15–19.   [4] Ibid. 1. 8, 10.

[5] Ibid. 1. 8, 16–17; Pliny the Elder, *NH* 18. 21, concluded that the use of criminal slaves was unprofitable.

[6] Suet. *Aug.* 32.   [7] *Ann.* 4. 27; 12. 45.

[8] See Appendix E2. Cicero, *Off.* 2. 24, suggests that his teacher Panaetius thought benevolence the proper way to control slaves, cruelty being used as a last resort.

a powerful exponent of clemency for social reasons. His account reveals abhorrence of the cruelty and injustice of the Sicilian slave-owners. But his conclusion—that power in private life, as in political life, must be exercised with clemency over those whom fortune has placed in subjection—is justified on practical grounds: arrogance and harshness produce civil strife in cities, and, in private houses, servile plots against the master and revolts that threaten whole cities.[1] This proposed parallel between relationships in the household and those in the state finds an important place in Seneca's thought on slavery. Seneca imagines an objection to his view that love and respect must underlie the slave–master relationship: 'Colant tamquam clientes, tamquam salutatores?'[2] But to take seriously the doctrine that slaves are men opens the way for comparisons with other human relationships: the master as *pater familias* ruling his wife, his clients, his freedmen, or the *domus* as a miniature *res publica*.[3]

The latter was a more fruitful analogy than Posidonius' of master and ruler. Not all types of political rule represented an improvement on the *dominus*,[4] while the immediate model, the Princeps, needed to be carefully distinguished from a master of slaves.[5] The view of the *domus* as a *res publica* put the emphasis on the rights of slaves and their opportunities in the household for self-government, responsibility, dignity, and even some power— even if all depended on the master's forbearance. In the old days, says Seneca, masters permitted their slaves to hold office in the home, to administer justice:[6] some must have observed that the imperial *res publica* provided a closer parallel than that of *maiores nostri*. Seneca might here seem to be indulging a philosopher's dream, but, in fact, his words reflect the current practice of enlightened or prudent masters. Inscriptions reveal, not only among

[1] *FGH*, no. 87, frag. 108C.
[2] *Ep.* 47. 18.
[3] *Ira* 3. 35, 1; *Ep.* 47. 14.
[4] Note the reproach to masters: 'regum nobis induimus animos' (*Ep.* 47. 20). In *Ben.* 3. 18, 3 Seneca asserts that the king and general have power as unlimited as that of the master.
[5] e.g. Suet. *Tiberius* 27.
[6] *Ep.* 47. 14.

the vast numbers of imperial slaves, but within the richer private homes as well, *collegia* of slaves and freedmen with magistrates bearing the proud names *aedilis, pro magistro iure dicundo, decurio*. The *externa sacra* of foreign slaves were offset by the cult of the master's genius.[1] Trimalchio is made to carry all of this to ludicrous lengths. The guests are treated to his domestic accounts, a miniature version of the *acta diurna* reporting a trial of his steward by his valets, the relegation of a doorman, edicts of the (house) *aediles*, and the wills of his bailiffs.[2] Pliny actually explains his practice of respecting the legacies of slaves (which had, of course, no legal standing) by the principle, familiar from Seneca, 'servis res publica quaedam et quasi civitas domus est.'[3]

C

We have already produced ample evidence that Seneca's views on slavery were not strikingly in advance of the views of his time. He lends support to this, not only by his portrait of Lucilius, but by his statement that cruel masters were regarded with scorn and contempt throughout the city,[4] and by his inclusion, among the disadvantages of the institution, of the great amount spent on keeping slaves.[5] But Seneca's works also illuminate the other side of the picture: they show how resistant social attitudes proved to philosophical notions. As a means of conciliating his readers by starting from common assumptions,[6] or perhaps sometimes as an expression of personal ambivalence, Seneca reflects, except when the treatment of slaves is his topic of discussion, ordinary social prejudice. Slaves count as a type of wealth along with other

---

[1] Evidence and discussion in E. M. Schtajerman, *Die Krise der Sklavenhalterordnung*, Moscow, 1957 (trans., Berlin, 1964), pp. 60 ff. Note *AE* 1912, no. 221: a servile *collegium* for the cult of 'heroi Corbulonis et Longinae'.

[2] Petronius 53.   [3] Pliny, *Ep.* 8. 16, 2.   [4] *Clem.* 1. 18, 3.

[5] *Ep.* 17. 3; *Tranq.* 8. 7–8. If the 5 *modii* mentioned in *Ep.* 80. 7 is a normal ration, it represents an improvement on Cato's recommendation of 3 to 4½ (*de Agric.* 56), and the slave receives pay as well.

[6] For this habit in Seneca, Oltramare, *Diatribe romaine*, p. 256; Abel, *Bauformen*, p. 130, discussing the attitude to slaves in *Const. Sap.* 14. 1.

possessions,[1] or a form of domestic animal,[2] expensive to keep;[3] as men, they represent the lowest category, whose insults are the most negligible of all,[4] whose practical inventions and services only show how banausic these achievements are,[5] whose suicides show how easy it is to leave life,[6] and whose crimes are expected to earn harsher punishments than free men suffer.[7] Seneca's harsh assertions about criminal slaves are surely to be connected with his frequent references to the dangers of masters. He paints a sympathetic picture of the fear in which wealthy slave-owners lived: 'Once in the Senate a proposal was made to have slaves wear a distinctive dress; then it became clear what great danger would threaten us if our slaves should start to count us.'[8] The number of references to masters being murdered by their slaves is remarkable, and some make it hard to believe that servile plots were as rare occurrences as we are usually assured they were.[9] Seneca, of course, knew that some masters deserved what they suffered,[10] but the story of the senate proposal quoted above shows that fear and insecurity infected all slave-owners. The attitude is clearly paralleled in Pliny's letter on the murder of an ex-praetor by his slaves. Pliny, a humane master, knew that the victim had been arrogant and cruel, but the conclusion he draws is the insecurity of all masters: 'Vides quot periculis, quot contumeliis, quot ludibriis simus obnoxii; nec est, quod quisquam possit esse

---

[1] *Tranq.* 11. 1; *Ben.* 6. 2, 3; 7. 5, 3; *Ep.* 31. 10; 110. 14 (the view here attributed to the Stoic Attalus); 119. 11.

[2] *Ep.* 77. 6.

[3] *Tranq.* 8. 7–8.

[4] *Ira* 3. 37, 2; *Const. Sap.* 14. 1. It is instructive to note Seneca's attention to the different functions of slaves and their corresponding social rank: in *Ira* 3. 37, 2, *ostiarius* is *extremum mancipium*, an attitude counter to the view in *Ep.* 47. 15.

[5] *Ep.* 15. 3; 90. 25.

[6] Ibid. 70. 19, 22; 25.

[7] *Ira* 3. 19, 2; *Ep.* 86. 10.

[8] *Clem.* 1. 24, 1.

[9] Above, p. 263 n. 3. Note especially *NQ* 2. 39, 3 citing A. Caecina, the late Republican authority on Etruscan lore, on the different kinds of thunderclaps: the *monitorium* warns us 'ut cum timemus ignem, fraudem a proximis, insidias a servis'. Cf. also the continuous legal concern with the problem, below, pp. 271 ff.

[10] *Clem.* 1. 26, 1; *NQ* 1. 16, 1.

securus, quia sit remissus et mitis: non enim iudicio domini sed scelere perimuntur.'[1]

D

To complete our picture of the contemporary setting of Seneca's views, we must consider the direction of legislation on slavery. For even in an autocratic system, if the autocrat aims at conciliating opinion, the law usually follows average sentiment.

The effect of legislation in the early Empire was to bring the slave increasingly under public control and protection, diminishing the power and responsibility of the master.[2] Jurists stated that by *ius gentium* the master had power of life and death over his slave,[3] and the Emperor Antoninus Pius reaffirmed the principle even while abridging it.[4] The exact steps in the curtailment of this power are not easy to make out, but Claudius' edict freeing sick slaves who had been exposed by their masters provided that a master who killed such a slave instead of exposing him was liable for homicide, thus putting the killing of one's own slave under the murder law.[5] But the real developments belong after Seneca's time. Hadrian perhaps instructed masters to hand over slaves they suspected of public crimes for trial instead of administering the death penalty themselves,[6] and with Antoninus Pius the killing of one's own slave *sine causa* entailed liability under the *Lex Cornelia de sicariis*.[7] Of course, the significance of the

---

[1] *Ep.* 3. 14, 5.

[2] Thus slaves suspected of public crimes were now tried in court, not just left to the master to punish. An *SC* of A.D. 20 laid down the same procedure for slaves charged in the public courts as for freemen (*Dig.* 48. 2, 12, 3).

[3] Gaius, *Inst.* 1. 52.   [4] *Dig.* 1. 6, 2; *Institutes* 1. 8, 2; *Coll.* 3. 3, 1.

[5] Suet. *Claud.* 25. Mommsen, *Strafrecht*, p. 116, accepts this clause, which was necessary to stop an obvious loophole, as Claudian. But W. W. Buckland, *The Roman Law of Slavery*, Cambridge, 1908, p. 37, regards it as a later addition.

[6] Our only evidence for this is SHA *Hadr.* 18 which says 'servos a dominis occidi vetuit eosque iussit damnari per iudices.' That Hadrian banned the master's exercise of the death penalty is impossible: the measures of Pius were clearly regarded by the jurists as establishing the prohibition, which, in any case, was not as complete as this. The interpretation of Hadrian's measure here adopted is that of Mommsen, *Straf.*, p. 617, n. 2.

[7] Gaius 1. 53; *Dig.* 1. 6, 1, 2; *Inst.* 1. 8, 2.

measure is hard to judge without knowing how the clause *sine causa* was applied.[1] By the time of Constantine, the intentional killing of a slave was normally regarded as homicide,[2] though even afterwards there seem to be some cases in which a master could put his slave to death.[3] Without knowing who could accuse the master, it is difficult to estimate the effectiveness of these measures.

Under the Empire, the law stepped in to prevent excessive cruelty to slaves. We have already noted the measure of Claudius protecting sick slaves. Under Nero, if not already under Tiberius, a *Lex Petronia* forbade masters to sell their slaves to fight in the arena without the order of a magistrate.[4] From Hadrian's time on, slaves were protected against further specific kinds of mal-treatment,[5] and, more significantly, the Emperor actually rele-gated a mistress for cruelty to her maidservants.[6]

The most significant development was the provision of machinery whereby slaves themselves could obtain relief—a development that is very difficult to date. According to our legal texts, Antoninus Pius instructed provincial governors to listen to the complaints of slaves who sought asylum at shrines or the Emperor's statue and to sell the slaves if the cruelty they alleged was found to have been 'intolerabilis'.[7] Ulpian in his summary of the duties of the *praefectus urbi*, based on a letter of Septimius Severus to his prefect, includes the hearing of complaints by

[1] Mommsen, *Straf.* pp. 616–17, imagined that the grounds judged sufficient would be much wider than those required for the death penalty in public law: perhaps the judgement of a house court.

[2] Inferable from *Cod.* 9. 14, 1; *C.Th.* 9. 12, 1–2. Perhaps by the time of Paulus who says (*Sent.* 5. 23, 6) that a master is not liable for homicide if his slave dies in the course of a beating—which at least shows that a normal cause for beating would not be regarded as a legitimate reason for killing outright (*Inst.* 1. 8, 2). Perhaps the interpolation 'sine causa *legibus constituta*' in Pius' constitution (made after Gaius, above, p. 268 n. 7) indicates some further limitation.

[3] e.g. *Dig.* 29. 5, 6, 3, where the *SC Silanianum* is said to be inapplicable to *attempted* murder of the master: 'ipse enim in familiam suam potest animad-vertere.'   [4] *Dig.* 48. 8, 11, 1–2. See below, pp. 278–9.

[5] Castration, sale to gladiatorial entrepreneurs *sine causa. Dig.* 48. 8, 3, 4; SHA *Hadr.* 18.   [6] *Dig.* 1. 6, 2.

[7] Gaius 1. 53; *Dig.* 1. 6, 2; *Inst.* 1. 8, 2; *Coll.* 3. 3, 2–3.

slaves who have fled to statues of the Princeps or have saved up to buy their freedom.[1] The complaints are not to be regarded as accusations (slaves were only permitted exceptionally to accuse their masters) and no particular form of redress is mentioned, though it is reasonable to assume that at least one solution would be that recommended to governors by Pius. Now it would be surprising if a procedure existed for slaves in the provinces and not for those in Rome. Either the existence of the procedure described by Ulpian,[2] or some other arrangement such as direct intervention by the Emperor,[3] should go back at least to Pius. In fact, Seneca himself provides evidence that Ulpian's procedure existed in his own day: 'de iniuriis dominorum in servos qui audiat positus est, qui et saevitiam et libidinem et in praebendis ad victum necessariis avaritiam compescat.'[4] The *iniuriae* mentioned are the same and it is hard to see what official is meant if not the prefect of the city[5] who, from the creation of the office by Augustus, was charged with keeping slaves under control and maintaining public order.[6] The prefect's role will have developed naturally: in punishing slaves brought to him as sources of disturbance, he would be certain to hear of injuries to the slaves[7] and to realize that mistreatment could be a source of public disorder. As the masters guilty of mistreatment do not seem to be punished (except perhaps by the loss of the slave) in Ulpian's account, the prefect could have started very quickly to listen to the complaints of slaves taking asylum from mistreatment, without clearly extending his jurisdictional powers.[8]

[1] *Dig.* I. 12, 1, 8. For additional points, see Appendix E3.

[2] Even if Ulpian relied exclusively on Severus' letter, which is not clear, there is no reason to think that all the functions described in the letter were first given to the prefect by Severus. See the remarks of T. J. Cadoux, *JRS* 49 (1959), 158–9.   [3] Cf. the action of Hadrian, p. 269.   [4] *Ben.* 3. 22, 3.

[5] As was already noted by Lipsius. P. E. Vigneaux, *Essai sur l'histoire de la Praefectura Urbis à Rome*, Paris, 1896, p. 182, noted the significance of the passage but, to my knowledge, works on the office since have neglected it.

[6] Tacitus, *Ann.* 6. 11.

[7] Josephus, *AJ* 18. 169, shows a *libertus* being complained of to the prefect under Tiberius. Note the praise of the prefect Rutilius Gallicus under Domitian by Statius, *Silvae* I. 4, 46: 'Dignarique manus humiles, et verba precantum'.

[8] See Appendix E3 for criticism of the view that the prefect only acquired this responsibility in Nero's reign through Seneca's initiative.

The law regarding slaves was not, however, increasingly humane in all spheres. Just as Seneca's sympathy for slaves seems to diminish sharply where malefactors are concerned, so the law retained harsher penalties for slaves than for free men and grew steadily harsher in the case of servile murder of the master. In the Republic, the punishment of the household had been left to the family in these cases,[1] though Sulla's murder law seems to have provided the machinery for dealing with those manumitted in the victim's will and rewards for accusers who produced slaves who ran away before the investigation.[2] The *SC Silanianum* of A.D. 10 made the customary procedure a legal and public one: the whole family remaining *sub eodem tecto* (variously defined) was questioned by torture and executed.[3] The purpose of the measure was, of course, to protect the master by providing the strongest possible incentive to his household to protect his life.[4] To ensure that the heir, through reluctance to diminish the estate, did not fail in his duty to investigate the murder,[5] the praetor's edict and the *SC* laid down that the will, if there was one, was not to be opened before the investigation. This ruling, of course, created a difficulty about those slaves who were given their freedom in the will. Were they, like the other slaves, to suffer execution, whether guilty or innocent? Apparently, they were,[6] but those who fled before the investigation, and were

[1] Tac. *Ann.* 14. 42 ('vetere ex more'); cf. Cicero, *Fam.* 4. 12, 3; Appian, *BC* 1. 20.

[2] *Dig.* 29. 5, 25.

[3] *Ann.* 14. 42–3; *Dig.* 29. 5, 1, 1; 29. 5, 1, 1; 26 and 29. 5, 3, 17 make it clear that execution followed the investigation.

[4] Thus Ulpian in *Dig.* 29. 5, 1, 1.

[5] *Dig.* 29. 5. 3, 29. The heir's connivance with the slaves was also a possibility reckoned with, 29. 5, 13.

[6] The provision in Paulus, *Sent.* 3. 5, 6, and *Dig.* 29. 5, 3, 16, must go back to the *SC Silanianum* because that measure prohibited opening of the will before the investigation and punishment (*Dig.* 29. 5, 13) so that the status of these men would not be known in time. But Duff, *Freedmen*, pp. 63–4, suggested that this was the innovation of A.D. 57, recorded in Tacitus, *Ann.* 13. 32: 'ii quoque, qui testamento manu missi sub eodem tecto mansissent, inter servos supplicia penderent.' The latter change is better related to *Dig.* 29. 5, 3, 17, for the fugitives recaptured after the will had been opened could previously, under the *SC Silanianum*, have been treated differently from the slaves, as their status was known.

found to be free when the will was opened, had to be tried on capture, as before the *SC Silanianum*, by the *Lex Cornelia de sicariis* and executed only if convicted.[1] But under Nero, the lot of these testamentary freedmen was assimilated to that of the slaves: the *SC Claudianum* of A.D. 57 provided that, when recaptured, they were to be investigated and punished on their recovery as the slaves had been.[2] At the same time, the *SC Silanianum* was broadened to cover slaves of the victim's spouse.[3] The process continued: with Trajan *liberti* manumitted in the master's lifetime were examined;[4] Hadrian made it clear that the slave was obliged to protect his master even at the risk of his life.[5] Around

---

[1] *Dig.* 29. 5, 25. Presumably, before the *SC Silanianum*, the will was opened before any punishment was inflicted, as seems to be implied by *Ad Herennium* 1. 24 (though Mommsen, *Straf.*, p. 649, n. 1, assumed that the prohibition in the praetor's edict on opening the will obtained in the Republic and that, therefore, accusation under the *Lex Cornelia* was the only means available to the heir). The heir could punish the slaves, now his own, but not the testamentary *liberti*: those he suspected of participation in the murder he could presumably accuse under the *Lex Cornelia*. That law also provided rewards to accusers who caught and prosecuted fugitive slaves and testamentary freedmen. Only these clauses of those concerning the murder of a master were quoted from the *Lex Cornelia* by later jurists because they remained in useful operation. The above reconstruction is conjectural but it seems preferable to the interpretation of *Dig.* 29, 5, 25 offered by Sherwin-White, *The Letters of Pliny*, p. 463: 'This [the Sullan murder law] seems to have excepted from the general punishment slaves manumitted in the dead man's will, unless they showed guilt by running away.'

[2] This interpretation of *Ann.* 13. 32 (see p. 271 n. 6) makes the best sense of *Ann.* 14. 42–5 where there is no reference made to the recent *SC* of 57, although a proposal to punish the resident *liberti* is discussed. Duff, *Freedmen*, pp. 63–4, assumed that the special class of slaves covered by the *SC* of 57 was simply executed in 61 along with the rest, but there may not have been any if the *SC* changed the fate, not of all those manumitted in the will, but only of those who were caught after the will had been opened. Syme, *Tacitus*, p. 744, takes Tacitus' lack of clarity here as one of the signs that the Neronian books are incomplete.

[3] Paulus, *Sent.* 3. 5, 5, gives this as a *SC Neronianum* which could be the same as the *SC Claudianum* in the title of *Dig.* 29. 5, as 29. 5, 1, 15 contains the provisions. Problems concerning the sale of a slave thus affected were treated in a *SC Pisonianum* (*Dig.* 29. 5, 8) presumably also of A.D. 57.

[4] *Dig.* 29. 5, 10, the motion supported by Pliny against two harsher ones (*Ep.* 8. 14), see below, p. 281.

[5] *Dig.* 29. 5, 1, 28. The unreliable SHA *Hadr.* 18 credits Hadrian with restricting 'sub eodem tecto' to the area in which the slave could hear what was going on, but *Dig.* 29. 5, 1, 27 indicates that this may not have been a new definition.

the same time, exceptions were made to the prohibition on punishing minors.[1]

There is only one way to reconcile these two apparently opposite tendencies in the law: they must be seen as two ways of dealing with the danger to individuals and society created by the institution. We have already given evidence of the general fear in the slave-owning classes. Antoninus Pius introduced his humane measure by statements about security: 'sed dominorum interest, ne auxilium contra saevitiam vel famem vel intolerabilem iniuriam denegetur his qui iuste deprecantur';[2] and 'ne quid tumultuosius contra accedat'.[3] Clearly the state increasingly felt slavery to be too important a social problem for control to be left any longer with individuals.

It is possible that the security problem actually increased in some respects: absentee landlordism may have led to crueller treatment by overseers with a resultant increase in the dangers of revolt;[4] household slaves in Rome may have appeared more threatening as, not their total numbers, but their concentration in individual luxurious homes increased, and the ratio of free to slave in the city decreased.[5] On the other hand, the imperial system, with its proliferation of governmental officials, was increasingly able and likely to intervene in social problems.[6] In any case, the 'humane' legislation is the fruit of that utilitarian stream

---

[1] *Dig.* 29. 5, 14.

[2] *Inst.* 1. 8, 2.

[3] *Coll.* 3. 3, 2, 6. See the remarks of P. Brunt, *JRS* 48 (1958), 169.

[4] Columella, who is more concerned than Cato or Varro with security, dilates on absentee landlords (1, pref. 3 ff.). Shtajerman, *Die Krise der Sklavenhalterordnung*, pp. 46 ff., who rightly urges a utilitarian interpretation of the legal developments, is not convincing in her explanation of them as answers to the increasing resistance of slaves caused by more thorough exploitation brought about by the difficulty in increasing production implicit in the use of slave labour. There is no evidence for this more thorough exploitation and it is hard to believe that conditions could have been worse than those in Sicily which Posidonius described.

[5] Cf. *Ann.* 4. 27, 2.

[6] Cf. Suet. *Aug.* 32; *Tib.* 8; 37. 1; *ILS* 961; *Ann.* 12. 65: though here the charge of insufficient supervision of slaves is a pretext, there probably were genuine cases. The increasing tendency with the Flavians and later to intervene in internal problems in cities is another manifestation.

of thought about slavery, whose most brilliant exponent was the historian Posidonius.

Seneca, as we have seen, gives strong advice in this vein. Shtajerman draws the Marxist conclusion that these ideas, because they reflect the economic and social crisis of his society, constitute the *real* motive for advocating kind treatment: his humane arguments are a veneer.[1] It is very difficult to separate layers of thought in this way, and the possibility exists that Seneca, like many civilized masters and some Emperors, was really more interested in humanity but relied on arguments from prudence to recommend his views to hard-headed masters.[2] At any rate, what originality Seneca shows was on the philosophical side. His arguments from expediency add nothing to Posidonius and Roman tradition; his standards for treatment were advanced but not shocking to his contemporaries; his philosophical principles were already clichés. But he may well have been ahead of the Stoic philosophers in showing what positive conclusions followed from such ideas as the natural equality of man and, in Letter 47, he combined philosophical and utilitarian ideas in a clear doctrine which, despite the diverse origins of its components, he tried to stamp as the proper Stoic attitude.

II

A word must be said now about Seneca's views on ex-slaves. He was clearly not as interested in them and left no discussion of their proper treatment comparable to Letter 47. The same philosophical doctrines of natural equality,[3] overriding importance of moral differences,[4] and the evils of anger[5] are incidentally applied to *liberti*, but the only practical conclusions expressly extended to

---

[1] *Die Krise der Sklavenhalterordnung*, pp. 56–9.

[2] Note the justification in Aristotelian terms offered by Gaius or an interpolator for Pius' measure: 'male enim nostro iure uti non debemus; qua ratione et prodigis interdicatur bonorum suorum administratio', on which see A. M. Honoré, *Gaius*, Oxford, 1962, p. 105.

[3] *Ben.* 3. 28, 3; *Ep.* 31. 11.

[4] *Ep.* 31. 11; 44. 6.

[5] *Ira* 3. 35, 1.

them are the need for generosity and tolerance of free speech.[1]
There are no arguments from expediency and the echoes of
common social prejudice are louder and more frequent:[2] in
particular, resentment of the wealth[3] and power of some
freedmen with allegations of vulgarity and low methods.[4] The
parallels to these remarks are too well known to need citing. In
contrast to his concern with the social problems arising from
slavery, Seneca shows no interest in those concerning *liberti*,
although general awareness of these problems is clearly reflected in
the law. By virtue of their duties to their patrons, freedmen often
remained in close contact, if not in the same house, with their
former masters and had opportunities for plotting and gathering
information that could be used against him. These dangers were
met by the extensions of the *SC Silanianum* already mentioned
and by the ever harsher penalties that faced the freedman whom
his patron accused of ingratitude.[5] On the other hand, whether
out of humanity or a desire to prevent discontent, the opportunities for Junian Latins to attain full citizenship steadily increased, until the category itself was abolished under Justinian,[6]
and the old principle of *favor libertatis* was more liberally applied.[7]

III

Seneca's pronouncements on slavery are justly admired. It is the
one subject on which he has remained immune from charges of
hypocrisy or dereliction of duty: Seneca, it is maintained, applied
his principles, in this case, to his life, preventing the Senate from
making manumission revocable,[8] opposing, though in vain, the

---

[1] *Ira* 3. 35, 1; *Vit. Beat.* 24. 3.

[2] e.g. *Clem.* 1. 9, 10.

[3] *Ben.* 2. 27, 1; *NQ* 1. 17, 9; *Ep.* 27. 5; 86. 7.

[4] *NQ* 4, pref. 7; *Ep.* 27. 5.

[5] Duff, *Freedmen*, pp. 37 ff.   [6] Ibid., chapter 5.

[7] F. Schulz, *Principles of Roman Law*, Oxford, 1936, pp. 220–1. His interpretation of Augustus' limitations on manumission as a gross breach of this
principle seems to miss the point of those measures, cf. Brunt, *JRS* 48 (1958),
164.

[8] Waltz, *La vie politique de Sénèque*, p. 305; Stella Maranca, *RAL* 5th Ser.
(1923), 290. Crook, *Consilium Principis*, p. 120.

execution of a large household of slaves.[1] Some have thought him responsible for including protection of slaves among the duties of the prefect of the city,[2] and for a law requiring masters to obtain the order of a magistrate before selling a slave to the arena.[3] If these hypotheses could be proved, we should have valuable information for understanding the relation, in one important case, of Seneca's philosophy to his political life. But they are more than doubtful, as will appear.

What would Seneca's views, if carried out consistently, lead to in terms of action? His energy is directed towards the conversion of the individual master and patron, urging him to love his slave, to control his anger, to recognize the claims of absolute justice: the *aequi bonique natura, ius humanum, eadem omnibus origo*.[4] Here are attitudes and sanctions that cannot be enforced by law: Seneca's consistency would best be tested in his behaviour as a master and patron, but we have not sufficient information to test it. Cruelty to slaves is not found among the ancient charges of hypocrisy, but positive evidence outside Seneca's works is very thin. His slaves are mentioned only by Tacitus as assisting in his suicide. Their manumission by will appears imminent[5] but there is no reference to the liberality traditional on these occasions[6]— perhaps Seneca was not permitted to part with the money Nero coveted, just as he was not permitted to change his will. Tacitus mentions a freedman Cleonicus who, according to some authorities, was instructed by Nero to poison Seneca:[7] the story reveals only that some thought it possible for a freedman of Seneca to betray the Emperor out of loyalty to his patron, while others

---

[1] Crook, op. cit., p. 121; *contra* Waltz, op. cit., p. 304.

[2] Waltz admits the possibility, as do Vigneaux (above, p. 270 n. 5) and Stella Maranca, op. cit., p. 291. Préchac, edition of *De Benef.* I., p. ii, no. 8, is even more definite about it. See Appendix E3.

[3] Stella Maranca, op. cit., p. 291 n. 3, stating that if not the law itself, at least the 'senatus consulta ad eam legem pertinentia' are due to Seneca.

[4] *Clem.* 1. 18, 1; *Ben.* 3. 18; 3. 28, 1.

[5] *Ann.* 15. 64, 4. The point of the 'libation' to Jupiter Liberator was principally philosophical (see below, pp. 370–1), but the sprinkling of the slaves could be meant to include them in the liberation in a more ordinary sense.

[6] Note the suicide scene in *Ep.* 77. 8 and the death of Petronius in *Ann.* 16. 19.

[7] *Ann.* 15. 45, 3.

thought Seneca distrusted his freedman. The doctor Statius Annaeus 'diu sibi amicitia fide et arte medicinae probatus' might be a freedman, to judge by his name, or just one of the *modici amici* to whom Juvenal tells us Seneca was so generous.[1]

Speaking in the first person in his dialogues and letters, Seneca tells us a lot about himself as a master—or appears to, for Seneca's 'I' and 'we' cannot be trusted to be autobiographical.[2] In the dialogues he includes himself in generalizations about masters: their delight in insolent young slaves, their tendency to inflict capital punishments for mild misdemeanours, the dangers they all face from their slaves.[3] Clearly there are no personal revelations here: Seneca casts himself always as the *imperfectus*, not as the *sapiens*, to make his sermons more palatable. The same consideration applies to the Letters to Lucilius, though here Seneca sometimes supplies names and details that do convince the reader. We meet here the diligent Aegialus who, Seneca omits to mention, was a freedman,[4] the charming gymnastic trainer Pharius, 'puer amabilis', who teases his master about his age,[5] the *vilicus* of Seneca's suburban villa who defends himself successfully when his master accuses him of negligence, and the doorkeeper Felicio who does not hesitate to remind his irritated master that he was his favourite as a child.[6] These slaves must have existed, but did the scenes described really take place? Seneca pictures himself here neglectful of his property and slaves to the point of not recognizing a slave he knew as a child. He admits to seizing a pretext for venting his anger at a slave—exactly the behaviour he condemned in Letter 47. It is a portrait of a kind, but not a perfect master. Could he have hoped to convince, if he had been a notoriously cruel one?

When we turn to consider what action Seneca's views imply

---

[1] Ibid. 15. 64, 3; Juv. 5. 108.

[2] Cf. Appendix D8, n. 3.

[3] *Const. Sap.* 11. 3; *Ira* 3. 32, 2; *Clem.* 1. 24.

[4] *Ep.* 86. 14 ff.; his status is revealed by Pliny, *NH* 14. 49.

[5] *Ep.* 83. 4. Cf. the generalization in *Const. Sap.* 11. 3. In *Ep.* 15. 3 Seneca expresses contempt for the 'mancipia pessimae notae' who concern themselves with oil, wine, and sweat.

[6] *Ep.* 12. 1–3.

in the public sphere, we find the issue very complex. The Stoic concentration on individual morality and resignation in the face of external circumstances did not provide great impulses to legislation. On the other hand, Seneca believed to a certain extent in the moral benefits of legislation[1] and thought that corruption at least could only be controlled by instruction and compulsion. Seneca does not advocate the abolition of slavery or even large-scale manumission, so that if he took steps as a statesman to implement his views, what we should expect are measures to enforce humane treatment. But Seneca was also well aware of the dangers of the institution: if he could recommend humane treatment on grounds of expediency, he could perhaps see a case for harshness in other cases on the same grounds. Roman legal developments showed that combination.

The record of Nero's reign in this respect is not remarkable. We have already argued that the *praefectus urbi* is unlikely to have acquired fresh powers to protect slaves. A *Lex Petronia* prevented masters from selling their slaves to fight with beasts unless a magistrate deemed it a just penalty for the slave's misdemeanour: seller and buyer were liable under the *Lex Cornelia de sicariis*.[2] The date of the *Lex Petronia* is unknown,[3] and most scholars are divided between a Tiberian date identifying the law with a *Lex Junia Petronia* (A.D. 19) which prescribed a verdict of free when the jury was divided in a *causa liberalis*, and a Neronian date, usually 61, when the consul, Petronius Turpilianus, was an active legislator.[4] Bagnani has argued that the law precedes the *Satyricon* of Petronius, where we find a master putting his steward into the arena because he has caught him in adultery with his wife.[5] But

---

[1] *Ep.* 94. 38; he disagrees with Posidonius in thinking that prologues to laws have value (above, p. 218): Antoninus Pius provided these for his rescripts on slaves.   [2] *Dig.* 48. 8, 11, 1–2.

[3] The *Lex Petronia* mentioned in an inscription at Pompeii is clearly different —G. Bagnani, 'Arbiter of Elegance', *Phoenix*, Suppl. 2 (1954), 17.

[4] On the different dates see the entry in G. Rotondi, *Leges Publicae Populi Romani*, Milan, 1912, under the year 61. The *Lex Junia Petronia* is in *Dig.* 40. 1, 24.

[5] 45. Bagnani argues (*Phoenix*, Suppl. 2 (1954), 14 ff.) that the master could not have secured approval without prosecuting his wife. But we are not told when the adultery took place: the wife may have been protected by time (*Dig.* 48. 5, 30), if Petronius considered with these legal niceties. Furthermore, we do not

his argument that the picture Petronius presents makes it impossible to imagine that the approval of a magistrate had been secured first is to read Petronius as a historical source, and his view that the law is a device to close a loophole in Claudius' edict about sick slaves is untenable: can we believe that slaves were regularly being bought for exhibition at the games, who were too feeble to be of any use to their masters? An early date has in its favour that *leges*, though still passed up to Nerva's time, were not used for social and criminal legislation after Tiberius,[1] but no decision is really possible because we do not know the point of the law. Why was this particular form of cruel treatment banned? The law did not *per se* restrict the *vitae necisque potestas*: the Lex Aelia Sentia clearly envisaged the survival of some of these slaves.[2] Nor was fighting with beasts the cruellest form of treatment: there were slaves who ran away to fight in the arena rather than endure punishment for stealing.[3] Perhaps the provision of the *Lex Aelia Sentia* placing slaves who had suffered such punishment under terrible disabilities if they were ever manumitted made it seem necessary to have some check on the use of this punishment. But there is no telling when it was devised.[4]

Freedmen were saved in 56, by Nero's decision, from a senatorial proposal to allow patrons to revoke the manumission of ungrateful freedmen. Nero recommended that no such blanket power should be given to patrons, but that, in individual cases, and after charges by patrons, the Senate could allow re-enslavement.[5] It should be noted that even Nero's proposal worsened

know how strictly the law was observed. Divi Fratres found it necessary to lay down that not even *criminosi servi* could be sold in this way (*Dig.* 18. 1, 42). Buckland, p. 36, suggested that previously slaves of manifest guilt were not covered by the law, but the rescript might only reflect that the law had not been strictly enforced.

[1] Mommsen, *Staatsrecht*[3] III, p. 346. Identification with the *Lex Junia Petronia* is not necessary. A.D. 19 and A.D. 25 show Petronii as consuls.

[2] Gaius 1. 13.

[3] *Dig.* 11. 4, 5.

[4] According to the unreliable SHA *Hadr.* 18, it was left to Hadrian to extend the law to the selling of slaves to gladiatorial schools, though they suffered the same disabilities on manumission.

[5] For this interpretation of Tacitus' very obscure account in *Ann.* 13. 26–7 see

the position of freedmen: it only seems kind by comparison. The extensions of the *SC Silanianum* in 57 have already been noted (pp. 272–3). Then in 61, the majority of the Senate, supported by the Emperor, voted to carry out the execution of the slaves of Pedanius Secundus, the murdered *praefectus urbi*, despite popular protests which found their echo in the *curia*. Nero vetoed a proposal to exile freedmen who had remained in the household.[1] Finally, in 64, Junian Latins were promised full citizenship in return for building a house of a certain value in Rome[2]—a measure to help the rebuilding of the city after the fire.

Of these measures the last belongs to a period when Seneca sought to dissociate himself from the regime.[3] The *Lex Petronia* —even if Neronian—could be the work of a man whose relations with Seneca were probably poor.[4] Tacitus records no opposition to the extensions of the *SC Silanianum* in 57, and, given the known reluctance of the consuls to put through senatorial decrees when disapproval by the Emperor and his *consilium* was even suspected,[5] it seems safe to assume that no objections were raised in that quarter.

But what stand did Seneca take in the debate following the murder of Pedanius Secundus? Tacitus gives us very little help here, indicating only that there were some senators who sympathized with the *plebs* in regarding the proposed execution of the household of four hundred as excessively severe. Presumably, the attitude of the mob is what occasioned the senatorial debate and some speaker before Cassius Longinus opposed the execution. After Cassius spoke, no one did. It is possible that Seneca was on the losing side—his influence had started to fade in 61. But two considerations make this unlikely: first, the stand taken by Nero is very much in the spirit of *De Clementia*, which did

Duff, *Freedmen*, pp. 41–2. Tacitus only implies that the Senate was to have jurisdiction in these cases.

[1] *Ann.* 14. 45.
[2] Gaius 1. 33, cf. *Ann.* 15. 43, 2.
[3] *Ann.* 15. 45, 3.
[4] P. Petronius Turpilianus, cos. A.D. 61, see pp. 90, 233 and Appendix D7. Petronii were also consuls in 58 and *c*. 62.
[5] *Ann.* 13. 26, 1; 14. 49, 1.

lay down rules for public life—no pity was to be shown but cruelty must be prevented. The middle course Nero adopted can be compared with the stand taken by Pliny, a man who believed in humane treatment for slaves: he did not oppose the execution of the slaves of a murdered consular, but adopted the mildest of three views about dealing with the freedmen.[1] Seneca could have behaved similarly. Secondly, although Tacitus inclines towards the milder minority,[2] he only provides arguments on one side: they are powerful ones requiring serious rebuttal. Had there been evidence of a speech by Seneca against Cassius, Tacitus would surely have written one for his account.[3] Nor can we be expected to believe that Seneca simply came to the meeting of the Senate and remained part of the inarticulate discontent. Of course, Seneca may have disliked the proceedings and, none the less, advised the emperor not to interfere because of the policy of respect for senatorial independence: but that is still to say that humanitarianism was not an overriding consideration for the *amicus principis*. Seneca's model in politics, Augustus, had prevented the implementation of the law when the debauched Hostius Quadra was murdered by his slaves—but not out of pity for the slaves. He felt that so degenerate a victim did not warrant revenge.[4]

With Nero's quashing of the senatorial proposal about ungrateful freedmen, we are, I believe, on surer ground. In the meeting of the Emperor's *consilium* to discuss the senatorial proposal, there was bitter disagreement. Tacitus presents arguments on the winning side against the Senate that are so false and

[1] Pliny, *Ep.* 8. 14, 12 ff.

[2] *Ann.* 14. 42–5. The motive for the murder is uncomplimentary to the victim; the word 'innoxios' (42. 2) applied to the household seems to give Tacitus' own judgement; Cassius' *severitas* is noted elsewhere (13. 48). See Syme, *Tacitus*, pp. 533, 564.

[3] He was interested in Seneca's speeches: *Ann.* 13. 3; 13. 4; 13. 11; 14. 11 (a letter to the Senate). The speeches in 13. 27 (see p. 282) and 14. 53–4 (see Appendix C5) are creations of Tacitus based on a solid acquaintance with Seneca's work. Even if the speech was too famous to repeat, Tacitus would have alluded to it.

[4] *NQ* 1. 16, 1. Augustus did not accept, any more than Cassius was willing to do, the idea that a master's treatment of his slaves could *justify* his murder: 'et tantum *non* pronuntiavit iure caesum videri', cf. *Ann.* 14. 43 *fin.*

feeble that they must have been designed by Tacitus to discredit the decision,[1] which he clearly disliked.[2] First, we are offered a gross exaggeration of the role of ex-slaves in public life.[3] There follow two arguments that bear strong—if not unmistakable— Senecan characteristics:[4] (1) the segregation of freedmen will only serve to show how few are the free-born: Seneca had argued that to separate slaves by dress would do precisely this, and elsewhere, that prosecutions for ingratitude would only reveal the numbers of the ungrateful.[5] But in Tacitus, the argument is absurd: no public trials or change of dress that would make freedmen publicly conspicuous was being proposed; no doubt freedmen felt themselves set off by their subjection to their patrons, and, for some of them, their Latin status, but those distinctions already existed.[6] (2) That as long as full manumission was irrevocable, it would be granted more sparingly, while informal manumission had always been revocable: Seneca had argued often in De Beneficiis that benefits were given with greater discernment because gratitude was not enforceable by law.[7] But the point about informal manumission is false: since the Lex Junia, passed under Augustus or Tiberius, there had been no 'locus paenitentiae', though there was a 'novo beneficio locus'. Tacitus no doubt regarded himself as justified in giving the winning arguments in the consilium a Senecan flavour—at that date Seneca

---

[1] Ann. 13. 27. For other examples of this Tacitean technique, Syme, Tacitus, p. 624.

[2] Above, p. 72. He deliberately connects this decision with a case of restitutio natalium in which Nero, he says, gained infamia by using his influence on behalf of the freedman Paris against his patron Domitia, and the opening of the next paragraph 'manebat nihilo minus quaedam imago rei publicae' is, as Furneaux ad loc. says, a comment on the whole of the preceding paragraph. Tacitus' belief in the protection of the rights of patrons is made plain elsewhere (Hist. 2. 92; Ann. 15. 54).   [3] Syme, Tacitus, p. 613.

[4] Préchac, Benef. I. p. ix, n. 5–6, recognizes this but assumes that they were actually used by Seneca. But Tacitus can hardly be reporting a consilium debate: at most they are his way of indicating that Seneca took the stand a source said he did.

[5] Clem. 1. 24, 1; Ben. 3. 16, 1.

[6] Junian Latins had 'libertatem minorem' (Inst. 1. 5, 3). The argument given by Tacitus that the maiores recognized only one kind of freedom was used to justify the abolition of Junian Latinity under Justinian.

[7] Ben. 3. 14, 1–2; 16. 1.

would probably have been the strongest *amicus*, or one of his sources may have recorded Seneca's stand on that issue. Tacitus would also have regarded himself as justified in creating such a weak case: Seneca's compositions were not always convincing.[1]

We noted that political motives may have overcome Seneca's humane sentiments in 61; they may also underlie his apparently humane position in 56. Nero had not previously shown himself out of sympathy with the Senate's attitude towards freedmen. As a body, the Senate was socially conservative. Claudius' promise to enrol in the Senate no one who could not claim to be the third free-born generation was popular, and his own violation of the rule in regard to freedmen's sons was mitigated by Nero's rule that such senators could not hold office. Early in his reign, Nero refused to admit such people to that body.[2] But what motive lay behind the senatorial proposal of 56? Increased control over their freedmen could give senatorial patrons a greater share in the wealth that some freedmen acquired,[3] but the Senate's eagerness to increase the patron's control over his freedmen was not just the result of prejudice and greed. Claudius is said by Suetonius to have reduced to slavery freedmen about whom their patrons complained.[4] Dio mentions the punishment as applied to freedmen who had accused their masters and the case cited in the Digest is of this type.[5] Messallina and Narcissus had employed slaves and freedmen as informers against their masters in investigating the revolt of Scribonianus,[6] and *maiestas* cases[7] were the

[1] *Ann.* 13. 3; 14. 11, 3.   [2] Suet. *Claud.* 24. 1; *Nero* 15. 2.

[3] For this motive, note the evasive tactics of freedmen after Vitellius restored rights over them to patrons returning from exile (*Hist.* 2. 92).

[4] Suet. *Claud.* 25. 1.

[5] Dio 60. 13, 2; *Dig.* 37. 14, 5; cf. Dio 64. 3, 4a: Galba handed over to their masters slaves who had acted or spoken against them.

[6] Dio 60. 15, 5.

[7] Dio 60. 3, 6 records the abolition of *maiestas* charges by Claudius at the start of his reign. Tiberius (Dio 57. 17) and Gaius (Dio 59. 4, 3) had made similar promises and broken them, but Dio implies that Claudius' was kept, at least for some time. None the less, the charge of corrupting soldiers (*Ann.* 11. 1–2) made against Valerius Asiaticus sounds like *maiestas* and the trial of the supporters of Scribonianus is likely to be the same. (Tacitus states Claudius' willingness to accept the charge in *Ann.* 12. 42.) Under the *cognitio* process, of course, Claudius could have avoided labelling the charge as such, cf. Pliny, *Ep.* 10. 81–2.

ones in which such information was most likely to be accepted.[1] Is it not likely that the Senate was hoping to reduce this menace by making freedmen who informed liable to summary punishment by their patrons? This explanation would link the measure to the renewal of the *Lex Cincia* as parts of an attempt by the Senate to reinforce that freedom from political trials that Nero had promised.[2] Stronger control by patrons of their freedmen was thus not in the Emperor's interest. In fact, Nero himself was later, in his time of peril in 65, to welcome information from freedmen against their patrons.[3] Tacitus thought Nero's recommendation that, in the interests of justice, individual freedmen should be submitted to judgement was hypocritical: Nero did not care about justice, as his interference with the law in order to deprive his aunt of patronage over one of her freedmen made all too clear. But a more respectable motive might be involved, for the law consistently replaced private control by public in the interests of general safety.

The clearest evidence then for Senecan influence on legislation in this sphere concerns not slaves but freedmen, about whom he wrote less often and less humanely.

If Seneca's views on slavery found little expression in his work as an imperial adviser, that is in keeping with his emphasis on the master's conscience and on acceptance of the *status quo*. If considerations other than philosophy animated his actions, that is in keeping with his responsibility as a statesman. The role of traditional mental habits may also be surmised: law and philosophy were separate activities. Cicero records a disagreement between two jurists and statesmen of the Republic: P. Mucius Scaevola and M. Junius Brutus disputed 'partus ancillae sitne in fructu habendus'.[4] According to our later legal texts, the negative view, which prevailed, rested on the notion that one man cannot be another man's profit because nature has provided all things for man—a Stoic view.[5] But it was P. Mucius Scaevola who can

---

[1] Duff, *Freedmen*, pp. 38–9.

[2] In 54 the Senate had rejected a charge brought by a slave against his master (*Ann.* 13. 10, 2).

[3] Tacitus, *Ann.* 15. 54; 16. 10; 16. 12.   [4] *Fin.* 1. 12.

[5] *Dig.* 22. 1, 28 (Gaius); 7. 1, 68 (Ulpian); cf. Cic. *Fin.* 3. 67.

more reasonably be assumed a Stoic,[1] and he took the positive
view. Moreover, Cicero, reporting the quarrel as an example of
the fine points of law that were accepted as a fit subject for
principes civitatis, argues that, *a fortiori*, it must be all right for a
statesman to discuss the broad issue of philosophy. Cicero therefore did not think the legal discussion involved formal philosophy
at all.[2]

[1] *Off.* 2. 47; cf. 3. 10 and *Brutus* 114.

[2] I cannot agree with the idea of Schulz, *Principles of Roman Law*, p. 218,
that Brutus' view must have been based on Greek philosophy. More acceptable
is the view of A. Watson (*Tulane Law Review* 42 (1968), 291 ff.; *The Law of
Property in the Later Roman Republic*, Oxford, 1968, pp. 215–16) that moral feelings about the dignity of man best explain Brutus' view, though his phrase
'abstract philosophical principle' is unfortunate.

9

SENECA *PRAEDIVES*

In antiquity and ever since, Seneca has been known best, and hated most, for combining philosophy with wealth. The most persistent charges of hypocrisy centred, then as now, on his fortune and its acquisition, for no one excelled this millionaire in singing the praises of poverty. The subject of Seneca's wealth and his pronouncements, however, concerns not only the state of his soul: what he says, regardless of his practice, is bound to be interesting, for it should show where he stood on the fundamental issues of Stoicism, and what view he presented of how the statesman should live. In *De Officiis* in which Cicero set out the proper conduct for the Roman gentleman, especially the public man, the subject of wealth was discussed under three of the four cardinal virtues. Since then government by a Princeps—a magnified *princeps civitatis* whose personal wealth played as large a part in the conduct of the state as his precursors' had in the conduct of their careers—had greatly complicated the questions of generosity and gratitude. Seneca's views should be worth having.

Finally, the philosopher's practice needs to be measured against his words, with an eye not merely to judgement of the man, but to comprehension of the author and of his readers, whose numbers, in his lifetime and after, were considerable.

I

Seneca's family had the equestrian census and probably a good deal more. He describes himself and his brothers as *locupletes* in the period before his exile, a condition they owed to their father, as Helvia, though generous to them, was not wealthy in her own right.¹ Their *patrimonia* in Spain that Seneca says she managed were probably estates largely devoted to vineyards and olive groves.²

Of property owned by Seneca or his father in Rome during Seneca's student days we are told nothing—with one exception. If Seneca is not grossly exaggerating when he describes, in a Letter to Lucilius, the decrepitude of a suburban villa which he had seen built, and the toothlessness of its *ostiarius* who had been his *pupulus* and *delicium*, his possession of this *suburbanum* ought to go back at least to the days when he was listening to Sotion and Attalus.³ It may also have been the scene of his last philosophical discourse.⁴ Of the other two villas that Seneca mentions in the Letters, the Nomentanum was acquired later, but the date of the Albanum is unknown.⁵

Some have assigned to this period the acquisition of the Egyptian estates mentioned years later, in Letter 77, and attested in papyri of the first and second centuries.⁶ They could be the fruit of Seneca's trip to Egypt when his uncle Galerius was in a position to ensure that his nephew got a good bargain.⁷ But Rostovtzeff's assumption that the estates came to Seneca from Nero as a gift to an imperial favourite may well be right. In that case, the Egyptian estates would be the 'agrorum spatia' that Tacitus, in the retirement speech, makes Seneca ascribe to Nero's generosity, while the villas at Nomentum and in the Alban region are then covered in the reference to 'suburbana'.⁸ There is no conclusive

---

¹ *Cons. Helv.* 14. 3; cf. 5. 4.

² See *JRS* 62 (1972), 6.   ³ *Ep.* 12.

⁴ The 'suburbanum' at which Seneca was staying when the suicide order came (Tacitus, *Ann.* 15. 60, 4) was 4 miles from Rome: it cannot be the Albanum which would be *c.* 12 miles or the Nomentanum which was 10 miles away (Pliny, *NH* 14. 49), and not on the way from Campania.

⁵ See below, p. 289 n. 4 and p. 291 n. 5.

⁶ For the evidence see Rostovtzeff, *SEHRE²* II, p. 671, and a new papyrus, dated 25 October A.D. 62, published by G. M. Browne, *Bull. Amer. Soc. Pap.* 5 (1968), 17 ff., and containing the earliest reference to Seneca's property in Egypt. On the evidence of the papyrus see below, p. 293 n. 9.

⁷ This is the view of Cantarelli, *Aegyptus* 8 (1927), 89–96, and Faider, *Bulletin de l'Institut français d'Archéologie orientale du Caire* 30 (1930), 83–7; Trillitzsch, *Seneca im literarischen Urteil*, p. 17.

⁸ *SEHRE²*, pp. 90, 293; 580 n. 25; *Ann.* 15. 53, 5.

evidence either way, but the view that these lands were acquired earlier implies that land in this key province was left in the hands of a senatorial relative of a supporter of Sejanus, a man who had been removed probably for political reasons, and then either retained by Seneca when a political exile or confiscated and returned to him on recall.[1] It is simpler and more reasonable to conclude that Seneca's lands in Egypt were later gifts of Nero.

In 41 Seneca was convicted on a charge of immoral connections or adultery with Julia Livilla and sent to Corsica.[2] The legal penalty under the Lex Julia for adultery was certainly relegation, and the Scholiast on Juvenal 5. 109 attests that Seneca was *relegatus* on this charge. It is likely enough that the penalty for adultery that Paulus describes, i.e. confiscation of half the property of the man condemned,[3] was already customary and was applied to Seneca: Seneca appears to allude to financial loss in the Consolation to his mother.[4] None the less, the reference is not precise (separation from one's fortune, not actual confiscation, could conceivably be meant), and Claudius, who had vetoed the death penalty proposed by the Senate,[5] could conceivably have proposed a milder penalty than that laid down in the Lex Julia. The restriction to a particular island, however, does not suggest exceptional leniency, and it is probably reasonable to assume that Seneca lost half his property in 41, and that all or some of it was restored in 49.[6]

According to Tacitus, Suillius criticized Seneca in 58 for having acquired a vast fortune 'intra quadriennium regiae amicitiae'. The

---

[1] For the Emperors' nervousness about estates in Egypt, ibid., pp. 293–5.

[2] Dio 60. 8. H. W. Kamp, *CJ* 29 (1934), 101, reviews the evidence. For the charge see above, p. 59 n. 6.

[3] *Sent.* 2. 26, 14, discussing the Lex Julia.

[4] 10. 2: 'intellego me non opes sed occupationes perdidisse'; cf. 5. 4. Cf. Trillitzsch, *Seneca*, p. 17, who says the sources provide no evidence of confiscation.

[5] Above, p. 60.

[6] Restoration is not attested but likely: Seneca still owned under Nero a villa he had owned in youth (*Ep.* 12) and estates at Corduba (*NQ* 3, pref. 2, on a strict interpretation of 'patrimonium', but Trillitzsch, *Seneca*, p. 32, refers the remark to the Egyptian estates). Cf. Dio 60. 4, 2 on the restoration of property by Claudius to Gaius' sisters (though he might take a different view of a man under his own sentence).

sources he specifies are inheritance and interest from loans in
Italy and the provinces.¹ Dio preserves the precise version of this
charge which also indicates a Neronian date: Seneca made large
loans to British chieftains.² The acquisition of legacies would be
a natural consequence of Seneca's position as a principal friend
of the Emperor.³ In the resignation speech in 62, Tacitus makes
Seneca refer to the *pecunia* Nero had given him and the lands,
suburban villas, and investments he owed to Nero's liberality. A
Neronian date for the acquisition of at least one such villa, that
at Nomentum, is confirmed by the Elder Pliny.⁴

Suillius' assertion that his favour with Nero had led to substantial increases in Seneca's fortune is then plausible and confirmed.
To some extent Seneca will have been passive in the process of
enrichment: he probably received some of Britannicus' properties
in 55⁵ and may have received other estates in wills. But Tacitus
records criticisms of him leading to his request to retire in 62
that imply a more active role: 'ingentis et privatum modum
evectas opes adhuc augeret.'⁶ The charges about Britain similarly
imply that he invested the money himself, but the most important evidence for his personal interest and industry concerns the
estate at Nomentum. Around 61 or 62 Seneca bought these vineyards, according to the Elder Pliny, from a freedman he despised,
paying four times the price the owner had paid less than ten years
before. Even so, Pliny attests Seneca's good judgement ('minime
utique mirator inanium'), for Remmius Palaemon, in his first

---

¹ *Ann.* 13. 42, 4.

² Dio 62. 2. See above, p. 232. One could hardly expect chieftains to wish to
acquire luxuries from Rome until real pacification started with the founding of
Camulodunum in 50 (*Ann.* 12. 32).

³ Compare the profits of Tigellinus, *Ann.* 16. 17, 5; 19, 3.

⁴ Ibid. 14. 53, 5–6. Pliny, *NH* 14. 49 ff., places the acquisition of the estate by
Remmius Palaemon 'in hisce viginti annis', and Seneca's purchase 'intra decimum
fere curae annum'. Since Pliny's whole work was written between 70 and 77,
the earliest possible date for Seneca's acquisition of the villa is 61. The latest is
64, for it is mentioned in Seneca's *Ep.* 104 and 110 dated to the autumn of that
year. The period 61–2 best suits Columella's quotation of a normal figure for the
yield while Seneca was alive (*RR* 3. 3, 3).

⁵ *Ann.* 13. 18 (not named). Cf. the gifts of *praedia* to Locusta (Suet. *Nero*
33. 3) and others in *Hist.* 1. 20.

⁶ *Ann.* 14. 52.

eight years, had so improved the productivity of the vines that a single crop was sold for two-thirds the price he had paid for the estate. Pliny and Columella attest that, under Seneca's administration, the estate continued its excellent yield.[1] According to Columella, Italian vineyards were profitable only under constant and intelligent care. The story therefore confirms Seneca's description of himself as a 'vinearum diligens fossor'.[2]

Seneca's interest in scientific agriculture is responsible for some of the most spontaneous passages in the Letters to Lucilius: a description of Scipio's former villa leads to criticism of Virgil's advice on sowing as old-fashioned and a technical discussion of the transplantation of olive-trees and vines; Seneca tells how he pointed out to his *vilicus* the symptoms of neglect in his plane trees.[3] This interest has its origin in the family estates, like that of Seneca's contemporary, Julius Graecinus, a practical landowner in Narbonensis, who wrote knowledgeably and elegantly on viticulture.[4] But Seneca's hereditary bent may have been increased by his attachment in youth to the Sextii. The founder of that sect applied the study of the stars to agriculture[5] and one of the disciples was Cornelius Celsus who wrote at length on husbandry.[6]

Seneca maintained his interest in the theory as well as the practice of profitable agriculture, if the flattering notice he receives in the Res Rusticae of Junius Moderatus Columella

[1] Pliny, NH 14. 50–2; Col. RR 3. 3, 3. On the notoriety of Remmius Palaemon and his success with vines cf. Suet. *Gramm.* 23.

[2] NQ 3. 7, 1. Cf. *Ep.* 112. 1 where viticulture is called 'nostrum artificium'.

[3] *Ep.* 86. 14 ff.—a lesson in modern methods from Vetulenus Aegialus, the present owner, whose opinion on the subject was worth having (Pliny, NH 14. 49); *Ep.* 12. 2. C. Magenta, RIL 73 (1940), 244 ff., collects the references showing Seneca's knowledge of agriculture and his reliance on personal observation. But she exaggerates the degree of technical knowledge some of these passages imply: *Ep.* 83. 16 is a specimen of declamation, showing that Seneca was *not* unique in his use of imagery from viticulture; Seneca's use of the same terms as agricultural writers may only show that he talked like a well-informed landowner.

[4] Col. RR 1. 1, 14. PIR² I 344 rightly accepts the view of Pliny, NH 14. 33, taken by André (Budé edition, ad loc.), i.e. that, in reporting a transcription of Celsus made by Graecinus, Pliny is simply giving a confused version of Columella.

[5] Pliny, NH 18. 274.

[6] I do not see how the evidence cited by Oltramare, *Diatribe romaine*, p. 263 n. 2, shows that Graecinus was a disciple of Sextius Niger.

indicates that Seneca, like his brother Gallio,[1] was one of the writer's patrons. Columella may have enjoyed the patronage of Seneca and his brother as a young Spaniard from a farming family of Gades.[2] Another link would be his friend M. Trebellius Maximus, probably his old commander when he served as military tribune in Syria, and the father of Seneca's colleague in the consulship, if not the consul himself. Columella's military service is revealed in a funeral inscription at Tarentum where men of the Syrian legions, including his own VI Ferrata, obtained allotments in Nero's new colony in 60.[3] Perhaps Seneca suggested the employment of the old legionary officer as an agricultural expert.

Returning to Seneca's fortune, we must consider the evidence for the use Seneca made of it. Some of it clearly was devoted to increasing his impressive capital rating: Suillius said it stood at HS 300 million in 58—which put him in the same bracket with the great imperial freedmen.[4] He lent money at interest and he bought land wisely: perhaps the Nomentanum was not the only villa he bought that made a profit. Pliny reports that one could buy suburban villas cheaply and Seneca may have acquired the one at Alba and perhaps others by purchase.[5] Tacitus reports

---

[1] *RR* 3. 3, 3 (see Appendix C4, p. 434). 'Gallio noster' is said to have requested the poem *de cultu hortorum* that forms Book 10 (9. 16, 2).

[2] He reveals his Gaditane origin in 8. 16, 9 and 10. 18, 5. Uncle Marcus (2. 15, 4) in Gades (7. 2, 4) was, according to his nephew, 'diligentissimus agricola Baeticae provinciae' (5. 5, 15).

[3] Columella alludes to a conversation about surveying with 'M. Trebellius noster' in 5. 1, 2. His service as military tribune with the Syrian legion VI Ferrata is revealed in his burial inscription at Tarentum (*ILS* 2923). The biographical reconstruction that dates his service to A.D. 36 under Trebellius is the work of Cichorius, *RS*, pp. 417–22. On the father and son see Appendix D2. For Nero's colony, Tacitus, *Ann*. 14. 27.

[4] *Ann*. 13. 42; Dio 61. 10, 3. Tacitus gives the same figure for Pallas (*Ann*. 12. 53, 3) while Dio gives HS 400 million for Pallas (62. 14, 3) and Narcissus (60. 34, 4). On the suspicious character of these figures see S. I. Oost in *AJP* 79 (1958), 128 n. 37, who suggests that myriad myriads is the Greek round number for huge wealth as *ter milies* is the Latin. But cf. Seneca, *Ben*. 2. 27, 1, who gives 400 million for Lentulus Augur.

[5] Pliny, *NH* 14. 50 ff.; the Alban villa is mentioned in Letter 123. It could have been presented by Nero in 55, or Seneca might have bought it hoping to make money out of it as at Nomentum. Seneca's visits to Campania in the

charges that Seneca used his wealth to adorn his villas and gardens in a manner impressive to the public. That he lived up to the role of senior *amicus principis* is not to be doubted—at least until 62 when, the historian tells us, he abandoned the entourage of clients and dependants who had greeted and escorted him in his days of power.[1]

He was truly generous as well. Tacitus shows him trying to correct his will in favour of his friends at his suicide.[2] Juvenal and Martial record with nostalgia the gifts that Seneca used to send his clients, among whom doubtless would be writers like themselves. It is not without significance that he is grouped by both authors with C. Calpurnius Piso the conspirator, among whose good points Tacitus lists his 'largitionem adversum amicos' which won him a large popular following.[3] But Piso was also guilty of luxurious living, as was Aurelius Cotta,[4] whom Juvenal includes in the same tribute. Seneca clearly had at one time been friendly with Piso,[5] and it may not be without significance that Nero made his subventions to Cotta when Seneca's influence was at its height.[6] Seneca may well have found these cultivated literary aristocrats more congenial, and more amusing, than some of the more puritanical philistines who paraded the old Roman virtues.

That Seneca's own style of life was debauched and luxurious

late spring of 64 (as revealed in Letters 49 ff.; see Appendix A1, Note I), and in 65 (*Ann.* 15. 60, 4) naturally make one wonder if he owned property there. He never mentions any and Tacitus only refers to *suburbana*. In 64 he may have been with the imperial entourage (see below, pp. 358–9). It is hard to believe that then or at other times he stayed regularly in bath-houses, despite the amusing Letter 56. Perhaps he relied on friends, or perhaps Campanian villas were not properties he cared to mention while he condemned the luxury of other owners (e.g. *Ep.* 55).

[1] *Ann.* 14. 52; 56, 3.   [2] Ibid. 15. 62, 1.
[3] Ibid. 15. 48, 3. Juvenal 5. 109; Martial 12. 36; *Laus Pisonis* where he is compared to Maecenas. Seneca's attack on Maecenas' style and character in the Letters (especially 114; cf. 19. 9; 92. 35; 101. 12; 120. 19) need not show disillusionment with the idea of imperial patronage he earlier approved (the view of Momigliano, *CQ* 38 (1944), 99 ff.).
[4] Ibid. 13. 34, 1.
[5] That at least seems to emerge from the story spun by Natalis (*Ann.* 15. 60) and Seneca's answer (15. 61, 1).   [6] Above, pp. 124–5.

is alleged only by Dio.[1] The charges of adultery that he makes no doubt go back to Suillius' exaggerations which were based on Seneca's early conviction for adultery and on his influence with Agrippina who was alleged to have dispensed personal favours to all her protégés.[2] As for the tables of citrus wood with ivory legs, a standard feature of luxurious dining and a standard target of criticism,[3] they (perhaps not to the number of 500) probably did feature in grand banquets that fitted Seneca's social position. No doubt he was not teetotal on these occasions, but he attests to certain lifelong ascetic habits in one of the later Letters, and, as he is there admitting how badly he had fallen below the more rigid standards of his early youth, it is hard not to believe him.[4] Tacitus depicts him after his final retirement in 64 living on a simple diet of fruit and water,[5] and this may have been the continuation of habits he had always exercised in private. In the will written at the height of his power and wealth he requested a simple funeral.[6]

Seneca offered to hand his wealth over to Nero in 62, and in 64 actually succeeded in contributing some portion of it to the rebuilding of Rome after the Great Fire.[7] No doubt this was prudence[8] as much as generosity: Nero could always have managed a conviction, or even something more direct, if he wanted his money.[9] It was also realism: after his death, the amount Seneca's family and friends received would depend on

---

[1] Dio 61. 10, 3.

[2] Pallas (*Ann.* 12. 25, 1); Faenius Rufus (*Ann.* 15. 50, 3); and earlier Aemilius Lepidus (Suet. *Gaius* 24. 1). Tacitus certainly believed adultery was one of her political weapons (*Ann.* 12. 7, 3).

[3] e.g. Demetrius' speech in *Ben.* 7. 9, 2.

[4] *Ep.* 108. 15–16; 23. Cf. 83. 5–6.

[5] *Ann.* 15. 45, 3; 15. 63, 3. Cf. *Ep.* 83. 6; 87. 1–5; 123. 3.

[6] *Ann.* 15. 64, 4.

[7] Ibid. 14. 54, 3–4 (62). Tacitus does not mention the return of money in 64 (given by Dio 62. 25, 3) but implies in 15. 64 that his wealth had diminished.

[8] Dio 62. 25, 3 says that the need to rebuild Rome was only a pretext for a surrender of money Seneca wished to make.

[9] Browne (*Bull. Amer. Soc. Pap.* 5 (1968), 17 ff.) claims that a papyrus dated 25 Oct. A.D. 62 and naming a μισθωτὴς Λουκείου Ἀνναίου Σενέκα οὐσίας shows that Seneca's Egyptian property had actually been confiscated by that date, but the claim seems dubious because (1) though confiscated domains often carry

how much Nero wanted anyway, not on Seneca's will, however generous it was to the Emperor.[1] But Seneca's conduct still compares here favourably with that of his younger brother Mela who lost his life because he could not bear to lose the wealth of his dead son Lucan.[2]

II

From the charges of hypocrisy recorded in Tacitus and Dio, the high points of Seneca's teaching emerge as follows: he preached against: (1) the possession of more than a moderate amount of wealth;[3] (2) the acquisition of money through friendship with a *rex* (in the pejorative Roman sense), through the ensnaring of legacies, through usury and extortion in provinces,[4] through acquiescence in crime;[5] (3) the employment of wealth in the service of luxury: magnificent furniture, gardens, etc.[6]

With the addition of some qualifications and refinements, this outline accurately reflects the doctrine we read in Seneca's surviving works. The prevailing tenor of the teaching is negative:

the name of an old owner in the form οὐσία Σενεκιανή or οὐσία Σενέκου, the presence of Seneca's *full* name here without the name of any other owner seems to indicate that he is the owner whose agent is informed of the withdrawal from lease. Perhaps this papyrus is evidence against the idea that μισθωτής always signifies an imperial agent in Egypt (cf. Levick, *Roman Colonies*, p. 225, for Asia Minor). (2) *Ep.* 77. 3 shows that Seneca still had agents and property in Egypt in 64: 'olim iam nec perit quicquam mihi nec adquiritur' refers to his state of mind as *senex*, not to the state of his property. The Egyptian estate probably passed to the Emperor in his will.

[1] That Seneca who was childless left a great part of his money to Nero is likely, in view of the date of his will (when he was *praepotens* and *praedives*, *Ann.* 15. 64, 4) and his wish to change it in favour of his friends just before his death. The armed seizure of his gardens described in Juvenal 10. 16 must follow his suicide-order. (The context 'sed plures nimia congesta pecunia cura / strangulat' and the use of force are against the view of Giancotti, *RAL* ser. 8, 11 (1956), 113 ff. that Juvenal refers to mass confiscations by Nero after the Fire. Dio 62. 25, 3 is quite clear that Seneca volunteered to contribute then, and this is supported by the offer of 62.)   [2] *Ann.* 16. 17, 4.

[3] Ibid. 13. 42, 4: in contrast with Suillius' 'modicam pecuniam'; 14. 53, 'ubi est animus ille modicis contentus?'; Dio 61. 10, 3.

[4] *Ann.* 13. 42, 3–4.

[5] Ibid. 13. 18 (Seneca not actually named).

[6] Dio 61. 10, 3; *Ann.* 14. 53, 5.

wealth is a *causa malorum*. But Seneca's views are not uniform: there are extremes which can be roughly described as Cynic or Middle Stoic in inspiration.

In the Stoic view, virtue was the only good, vice the only evil. But of the ἀδιάφορα or *indifferentia*, those in accordance with nature were allowed some value. Wealth figured, along with health, beauty, fame, etc., among these προηγμένα for which Seneca's word is *commoda*, and poverty among their opposites, the ἀποπροηγμένα or *incommoda*. Though Seneca clearly knows the doctrine and terminology earlier,[1] it is only in the mature works —certainly late in Claudius' reign and probably later—that Seneca discusses the philosophical status of wealth and asserts the self-sufficiency of virtue for happiness.[2] Throughout, the emphasis tends to be on the negative side of the doctrine: riches are not good, and, though not evil in themselves, they are a cause of evil: they lead to civil and national wars;[3] they activate the passions of desire, anger, fear, and grief, and thereby cause unhappiness to the owner;[4] they take time from worthwhile activities,[5] expose the owner to danger,[6] and develop vice in the owner and in others.[7] Sometimes these themes are given a distinctively Roman flavour: *maiores nostri* were happier being poor;[8] the increase of wealth in Rome has impaired her fighting ability and incited ambition and strife at home, and an envy abroad, that might prove fatal.[9]

[1] *Cons. Helv.* 5. 6; 6. 1 (*paupertas* among the *incommoda*).

[2] *Vit. Beat.* 24. 5 (a Neronian date is acceptable for reasons given below, p. 309). *Ep.* 76. 12; 104. 9; 120. 2–3 (riches not goods); 66. 22; 73. 12; 92. 18; 115. 6 (irrelevance of wealth to goodness); *Vit. Beat.* 4. 3; *Ep.* 87. 1; 92. 2–3 (self-sufficiency of virtue for happiness); *Vit. Beat.* 3. 3; 4. 3; 22. 4; 24. 5; *Ben.* I. 11, 5; 5. 13; *Ep.* 87. 36; 120. 2–3 (riches as useful).

[3] *Ira* 3. 33; *Ben.* 6. 3, 2; 7. 10 (an imagined speech by Demetrius the Cynic); *Ep.* 87. 41.

[4] e.g. *Cons. Helv.* 11. 3; *Ira* 2. 21, 7; *Const. Sap.* 13. 3; *Tranq.* 8; *Ep.* 42. 9; 59. 14; 80. 6; 88. 10–11; 119. 6, 9; *Prov.* 4. 10; 6. 1–3.

[5] *Cons. Helv.* 10. 2; *Brev. Vit.* 2. 4; 7. 4, 7; 17. 5.

[6] *Ep.* 84. 11–12; 119. 6.

[7] *Cons. Helv.* 10. 4–5; *Ep.* 87. 31 and 35; 94. 74.

[8] *Cons. Helv.* 10. 7–8; Fabricius (*Prov.* 3. 4; *Ep.* 98. 13; 120. 19) is the favourite Roman example of poverty, Tubero of frugality (95. 72; 98. 13; 120. 19).

[9] *Ira* I. 11, 4; *Ep.* 87. 41.

Sometimes, at one extreme, poverty is assigned a positive value of its own: it is natural, being the condition of the gods and of men at birth;[1] it provides an opportunity for men to win glory;[2] it is the only way to true freedom, and can be regarded as another name for *securitas*.[3] At the other extreme, *De Vita Beata* stresses the opportunities for exercising virtue provided by wealth and its contribution, if not strictly to the happy life, at least to the *laetitia* born of virtue.[4] Though elsewhere the usefulness of wealth is conceded, this dialogue is unique in arguing that even the *sapiens* would prefer some wealth with his virtue.

The poles of Seneca's thought generate different visions of the *sapiens*. Out of the standard image of the man unshaken by whatever fortune bestows or denies, Panaetius and Posidonius had developed the self-confident active man, who prefers to have his virtue thrive in prosperity than in adversity, who excels in the virtuous use of his assets in the interests of the human community, and whose life is generally improved by the addition of wealth.[5] This model had been given a toga by Cicero in *De*

---

[1] *Tranq.* 8. 5; *Prov.* 6. 6.   [2] *Prov.* 4. 5.
[3] *Ben.* 7. 9, 1; *Tranq.* 8. 4.   [4] 22. 3.

[5] That Panaetius and Posidonius allowed external goods to play a larger part than other Stoics in their moral philosophy is generally agreed. But it is unclear to what extent they actually departed from the key Stoic doctrines that virtue is the only good and is sufficient for happiness. Diogenes Laertius asserts (1) that Posidonius included wealth and health among the goods (7. 103) and (2) that both he and Panaetius οὐκ αὐτάρκη λέγουσι τὴν ἀρετήν (sc. πρὸς εὐδαι-μονίαν), and considered health, strength, and financial resources necessary ingredients of happiness (7. 128). Some scholars accept both (van Straaten, *Panétius*, pp. 149, 164, even extends the first to Panaetius); I. Kidd, *Problems in Stoicism* (ed. Long), London, 1971, pp. 159–63, who offers a good summary of the problem, rejects both. (1) is clearly false: it is refuted by Cicero, *Tusc.* 2. 61, and Seneca, *Ep.* 87. 31–2; 35. It is not difficult to see how it arose: even Chrysippus could be quoted out of context to this effect (Plut. *St. Rep.* 1048A) and Posidonius may, like Panaetius, have made concessions to ordinary usage (Cicero, *Fin.* 4. 23; 79). But (2) probably contains considerable truth. Cicero, *Off.* 3. 12, seems to me to leave open the possibility that Panaetius ('cum sit is, qui id solum bonum iudicet, quod honestum sit, quae autem huic repugnent specie quadam utilitatis, eorum neque accessione meliorem vitam fieri nec decessione peiorem') thought truly useful things, i.e. those not in conflict with virtue, could improve life. They were, after all, the medium of virtuous action (*Off.* 1. 17) under three of the four virtues. Rist, *Stoic Philosophy*, pp. 7–10, would go further, suggesting that Panaetius and Posidonius meant that certain external goods are not merely

Officiis, and he clearly is the ideal of *De Vita Beata*.[1] Far more frequent in Seneca, however, is a *sapiens* with clear Cynic features, an ascetic who prefers poverty to wealth, demonstrating in his physical life his spiritual immunity to externals. This ideal Seneca presents in the examples of Diogenes, Stilpo, and, most commonly, of his own contemporary Demetrius the Cynic.[2] There had always been Stoics who leaned towards the Cynic extreme[3] and the way Seneca sees the role of Cynicism within Stoicism is not new with him: the life of the Cynic is the quickest and surest way (not the only way) to the life of virtue;[4] he is a messenger of God, demonstrating how superior to fortune man can be.[5] Like Epictetus' ideal Cynic, Seneca's shows no sign of that lack of *verecundia* that led Panaetius and with him Romans like Cicero to condemn Cynicism.[6] Nothing shows up more clearly

material for the achievement of virtue (as even Chrysippus held, *SVF* 3. 491), but necessary material. This view would gain support, as regards Posidonius, if *Ep.* 88 of Seneca could be taken to show that he thought the *liberales artes* (which required wealth to study) were essential to virtue, as argued by A. Stückelberger, *Senecas 88 Brief*, Heidelberg, 1965, pp. 28–30 and Brunt, *Proc. Camb. Phil. Soc.* 19 (1973), 21 ff. But at para. 31 of the letter, where this is stated, Posidonius is no longer clearly the source (thus Edelstein–Kidd, *Posidonius I: The Fragments*, include only chaps. 21–8 as F 90).

[1] The relation between Seneca's doctrine in *De Vita Beata* and the views of other Stoics is treated by Pohlenz in *Philosophie und Erlebnis in Senecas Dialogen*, *NGG* (1941), no. 6, pp. 59–81. Seneca holds to the traditional self-sufficiency of virtue for happiness (4. 3; 16. 3; 22. 3) but, like Panaetius, he lays great stress on the proper handling of wealth, as an exercise of virtue (cf. *Off.* 1. 16, 68, 92), in 3. 3; 21. 4; 25. 5 ff., and on the positive element of joy in the virtuous life, to which wealth contributes, in 3. 4; 4. 5; 22. 3 (cf. the title of Panaetius' περὶ εὐθυμίας and the joy there associated with the use of wealth as revealed in Plut. περὶ εὐθυμίας 474C, a work which followed Panaetius closely, according to H. Broecker, *Animadversiones ad Plutarchi Libellum . . .* , Bonn, 1954, pp. 158–9).

[2] On Demetrius, see *PIR*² D 39; D. R. Dudley, *A History of Cynicism*, London, 1937, pp. 125 ff. He is called 'Cynicae institutionis doctor' by Tacitus (*Ann.* 16. 34).

[3] Dudley, *Cynicism*, p. 99.

[4] D.L. 6. 104; 7. 121; cf. *Tranq.* 8. 3: 'tolerabilius . . . *faciliusque* non adquirere quam amittere.'

[5] Epictetus 3. 22. Cf. *Ben.* 7. 8, 2–3; *Ep.* 20. 9; 62. 3.

[6] *Off.* 1. 148 (cf. *Fin.* 3. 68); Epictetus 3. 22, 10, 50, 80, 89. Seneca thought Cynics should not beg, *Ben.* 2. 17, 2 (cf. *Vit. Beat.* 18. 3), nor upbraid the public indiscriminately (*Ep.* 29. 1, cf. *Ep.* 62. 3).

the complexity of Seneca's thought than the way two of these
three ideals are offered in *De Tranquillitate Animi*. In chapter 8 the
poverty of the Cynic is held up to the *imperfectus* as the easiest
way of achieving peace of mind, while in chapter 11 the orthodox
sapiens appears: he can receive and return wealth without im-
pairing his serenity.

It will be useful to summarize Seneca's views on the acquisition, proper amount, and uses of wealth. Seneca's advice on acquisition ranges from an imagined refusal of all possessions by
Demetrius[1] to an assertion that Demetrius preached *virtus*, not
egestas.[2] But most of the passages on the subject rest on the
assumption that acquisition in itself is not to be forsworn: they
condemn certain means and certain attitudes to gain. One must
attach no importance to enrichment,[3] nor expend great efforts in
getting wealth: energetic trading, mining, legacy-hunting—even
importunate begging—are signs of avarice.[4] Excessive land-
buying is condemned.[5] Nor must one acquire money shamefully
or at another's expense:[6] judicial corruption, extortion, flattery,
and usury are ruled out.[7] The increase of one's fortune honour-
ably, however, by diligence and parsimony is perfectly respectable,[8] as is passive acceptance—wills, gifts from the powerful[9]—

[1] *Ben.* 7. 8–10; cf. the flattery of Polybius in the Consolation to him (2. 3),
but the point is clearly his honesty.   [2] *Vit. Beat.* 18. 3.

[3] *Const. Sap.* 9. 2; *Ep.* 4. 10–11; 36. 6.

[4] *Ira* 3. 33, 4; *Brev. Vit.* 2. 1; 7. 7; *Const. Sap.* 9. 2; *Ben.* 2. 17, 1–2; 6. 38, 4;
Ep. 4. 10–11.

[5] *Ep.* 89. 20, particularly overseas. Seneca's concern is purely moral, unlike
Pliny's in *NH* 18. 35.

[6] *Vit. Beat.* 23. 1; *Ep.* 76. 18.

[7] *Ben.* 1. 9, 4; 3. 15, 4; 7. 10, 3–4 (Demetrius); *NQ* 4, pref. 7–8. Seneca does
not wholly share Cicero's views on the respectable means of acquisition: *Off.*
1. 151 does not envisage the evils of *latifundia* as does Seneca and accepts trade
if its profits are sufficient and are invested in land (cf. above, nn. 4 and 5).
Usury was at all times despised and practised (Cato in *Off.* 2. 89; Cicero in
1. 150).

[8] *Ira* 1. 10, 2 (*industria* clearly a virtue); *Ben.* 2. 27, 1 and *Ep.* 101. 2 show that
diligent acquisition and careful use are preferable to complete neglect of one's
fortune; *Tranq.* 11. 3; *Vit. Beat.* 23. 2. Cf. the view in *De Officiis* of Panaetius
(1. 92) and Cicero (2. 87): 'res autem familiaris quaeri debet iis rebus, a quibus
abest turpitudo, conservari autem diligentia et parsimonia, eisdem rebus augeri.'

[9] *Ben.* 5. 4, 2–3; 1. 15, 5–6.

except from men of bad character,[1] and even this is excusable under duress.[2] The *sapiens*, in fact, is an expert in gratitude.[3]

Seneca often implies, as a further condition of proper enrichment, that a natural limit should be observed, a limit commensurate with the basic natural needs of the owner. The opposite extreme is found, as usual, in *De Vita Beata* where we are shown a *sapiens* who prefers to have *amplae opes*, even a *domus splendida*.[4] According to the latter conception, the *imperfectus* differs from the *sapiens* in that he *needs* the indulgence of fortune for his happiness while the *sapiens* prefers to have it, but is happy without it.[5] According to the former view, the *imperfectus* would be better off if he gave away his money but is too weak to do without it:[6] Seneca even implies that wealth can help to make life tolerable for those who cannot achieve real happiness.[7] But Seneca's normal attitude is one of indifference to the amount of money: what must be achieved is spiritual independence of one's material circumstances.[8] Not only in *De Vita Beata*, but in several letters as well, Seneca insists that the surrender of wealth is not necessary to achievement of the right attitude,[9] and in Letter 5 he carefully distinguishes frugality and spiritual independence from an ostentatious parade of Cynicism.

None the less the advice Seneca offers to the wealthy man is predominantly negative and cautious in tone. He must be prepared for the worst,[10] practise frugality generally,[11] and, to dispel

---

[1] *Ben.* 2. 18, 5; 2. 21, 5.

[2] Ibid. 2. 18, 7; 5. 6, 7. [3] *Ep.* 81. 14.

[4] *Cons. Helv.* 10. 11; *Tranq.* 8. 3; *Ep.* 2. 6; 4. 10; 16. 7; 25. 4; 94. 23; 119; *Vit. Beat.* 23. 1; 25. 1.

[5] *Vit. Beat.* 16. 3; 17. 1.

[6] *Tranq.* 8.

[7] *Ep.* 92. 28: wealth is not actually mentioned here, but I have assumed that the view of προηγμένα here applied to health, longevity, etc., could be extended to the others. For the *sapiens*, 92. 31.

[8] *Cons. Helv.* 5. 5–6; *Const. Sap.* 19. 4; *Tranq.* 11; *Vit. Beat.* 4. 2; 21. 2; *Ep.* 5. 5–6; 36. 6; 45. 9; 59. 8; 96. 1–3; 110. 14.

[9] *Ep.* 18. 13; 20. 10 ff.

[10] *Cons. Marc.* 9. 2; 10. 1–2; *Cons. Helv.* 5. 4; *Const. Sap.* 9. 4; *Tranq.* 11. 3; *Ep.* 98. 5.

[11] *Tranq.* 9 (with 1. 5–9); *Ep.* 5. 5 (but 'non incompta frugalitas'); 51. 13; 87. 9–10; 108. 15.

the fear of loss, rehearse poverty for a stretch of several days at a time. This practice, borrowed from Epicurus, is properly a spiritual exercise, though Seneca indicates that some indulged in it when bored with wealth.[1] He describes his own practice of it, deliberately, on a journey in a mule cart 'cum paucissimis servis', and again, accidentally, when arriving late at his villa.[2]

The most respectable aspect of wealth to philosophers was, of course, its usefulness to good causes. Among the προηγμένα, wealth was pursued for the sake of something else.[3] Seneca says that the practical, preceptive part of philosophy dealt with the proper use of wealth.[4] One might have expected from him advice for the imperial gentleman along the lines developed by Cicero in *De Officiis*. Panaetius had regarded *liberalitas* and *beneficentia* as prime obligations for the wealthy man,[5] and Cicero had developed these themes with concrete Roman details in his advice and his examples.[6] It is symptomatic of Seneca's whole attitude that the lengthy *De Beneficiis*, despite its debt to Panaetius' pupil Hecato,[7] contains few positive ideas about the use of wealth and includes an eloquent condemnation of material possessions even when used in benefactions.[8]

Most of Seneca's interest lies in the misuse of wealth: I have found only one specific condemnation of meanness[9] to set against the innumerable diatribes against luxury.[10] But Seneca leaves no doubt as to the high value he set on generosity. Contributions to the community are not what he has in mind—though once, in

---

[1] *Ep.* 18. 5–13; 20. 13; *Cons. Helv.* 12. 3; *Ep.* 18. 7.

[2] *Ep.* 87. 1–10; 123.

[3] D.L. 7. 104; *Fin.* 3. 56.   [4] *Ep.* 94. 6, 23.

[5] *Off.* 1. 68: '. . . nihil honestius magnificentiusque quam pecuniam contemnere, si non habeas, si habeas, ad beneficentiam liberalitatemque conferre.'

[6] *Off.* 1. 42–60; 2. 52–85.

[7] He is cited in 1. 3, 9; 2. 21, 4; 3. 18, 1; 6. 37, 1. One of Hecato's works he probably used was the περὶ καθήκοντος addressed to Tubero (*Off.* 3. 63), which Cicero also used. See Pohlenz, *Die Stoa*[2], II, pp. 23–4.

[8] *Ben.* 7. 9, 1 (the imagined sermon of Demetrius): 'quae ne daturus quidem acciperem, quoniam multa video, quae me donare non deceat.'

[9] *Ben.* 2. 27, 1.

[10] Luxury is everywhere condemned as unnatural, time-wasting, and a product of the passions; e.g. *Cons. Helv.* 10. 1; *Ira* 1. 21, 1; *Brev. Vit.* 2. 1; 7. 1; *Ep.* 56. 10; 60. 3–4; 86. 3–13; 89. 21; 95. 18; 122.

a very Roman passage, he praises the public buildings with which Agrippa adorned the city.[1] Generosity to individuals is the work that virtue marks out for the wealthy man:[2] to give is to transmute a sordid loan to oneself from fortune into a virtuous action eternally to the giver's credit. It is also a prudent way of preparing against adversity.[3] This generosity is not done on emotional impulse: it must be a rational act[4] in which what we give is beneficial and appropriate in amount to the recipient and ourselves,[5] while the person to whom we give it is not hopelessly wicked or liable to put it to a wicked or harmful use. The social position of the recipient does not affect the value of the benefit: the *sapiens* gives to the poorest as one man to another, out of the common store.[6]

All this discussion seems strangely abstract, certainly removed from Seneca's own life. There is, for example, no reference to patronage of the arts. Seneca comes the closest to discussing the world around him in *De Beneficiis* when he considers the generosity of the powerful. Though the discussion is often general (e.g. 5. 4) or illustrated with Greek examples (2. 10; 5. 6, 2 ff.), Seneca makes very clear his views on the proper role of the Princeps. Augustus was both generous and discriminating in his gifts (1. 15, 5–6). To show ingratitude by grumbling about his new responsibilities was enough, in Seneca's eyes, to condemn

[1] *Ben.* 3. 32, 4.

[2] *Vit. Beat.* 23. 5–24. 3; *Clem.* 2. 6, 3: 'ubi enim opibus potius utetur aut viribus, quam ad restituenda, quae casus impulit?' In Seneca the Stoic obligation to help one's fellow man is applied to individuals as members of the large human community (*Vit. Beat.* 24. 3: 'Hominibus prodesse natura me iubet'; *Clem.* 2. 6, 3: 'sapiens . . . in commune auxilium natus ac bonum publicum'); special obligations to one's own *res publica* or its members find no mention, in strong contrast to Hecato writing to a Roman (*Off.* 3. 63): 'Neque enim solum nobis divites esse volumus, sed liberis, propinquis, amicis maxumeque rei publicae. Singulorum enim facultates et copiae divitiae sunt civitatis.' Cicero believed in this passionately (*Off.* 2. 52–8).

[3] *Ben.* 6. 3; *Tranq.* 10. 6.

[4] *Clem.* 2. 6, 2; *Vit. Beat.* 24. 1; *Ben.* 2. 16, 1: 'Nihil enim per se quemquam decet; refert, qui det, cui, quando, quare, ubi, et cetera, sine quibus facti ratio non constabit.' This is just an application of the Stoic definition of καθῆκον (D.L. 7. 107) = *officium* (*Fin.* 3. 58) or, strictly, *medium officium* (*Off.* 1. 8). Knowing how to give distinguished the *liberalis* from the *prodigus* (*Ep.* 120. 8).

[5] *Ben.* 2. 14, 3–4; 2. 15, 3.   [6] *Clem.* 2. 6, 2–3; *Vit. Beat.* 23. 5; 24. 3.

the favoured Cn. Cornelius Lentulus Augur (2. 27, 1–2) who earned the admiration of Tacitus and the sympathy of Suetonius.[1] Claudius was more lavish in his gifts but his judgement was poorer: Passienus Crispus said they should be regarded as gifts of fortune (1. 15, 6). But it is Tiberius' grudging largess, designed to discourage further senatorial requests for help, that calls forth Seneca's strongest reaction: 'Et ut in transitu de hac quoque parte dicam, quid sentiam, ne principi quidem satis decorum est donare ignominiae causa . . . non est illud liberalitas, censura est; auxilium est, principale tributum est, beneficium non est, cuius sine rubore meminisse non possum' (2. 8, 1–2).

III

Seneca insisted that a philosopher's words must accord with his life,[2] and he set sincerity and consistency as his own aim—though he did not claim to have achieved it. That was the hallmark of the *sapiens* and he was only an *imperfectus*.[3]

In the complex of ideas we have outlined above, it is clear that

---

[1] On the identity of Cn. Lentulus Augur in *Ben*. 2. 27 and Suetonius' Cn. Lentulus Augur (*Tib*. 49) and Tacitus' Cn. Lentulus of *Ann*. 4. 44 see Groag in *PIR*² C 1379 and Syme, *Tacitus*, App. 63. Suetonius' assertion that Lentulus was driven to death by Tiberius so that he could be his only heir could be an uncharitable conjecture from his will and the accusation that preceded his death by a year (*Ann*. 4. 29).

Tacitus' judgement, 'gloriae fuerat bene tolerata paupertas, dein magnae opes innocenter partae et modeste habitae', does not contradict Seneca's estimate of him as ungrateful, pretentious, untalented, and mean. Tacitus applies different standards to him: 'innocenter partae' could include inherited wealth and gifts from a good Princeps (though Seneca's 'cum omnia incrementa sua divo Augusto deberet' is probably an exaggeration), but Tenney Frank, *ESAR* 5, p. 24, cannot be right to surmise that he could have earned some, for Seneca's 'nihil amplius quam vidit' is quite explicit, nor Groag to suggest that Tacitus' tame phrase could signify booty from Dacia. 'Modeste habitae' could, on the new Flavian standards of parsimony, be what Seneca calls meanness.

R. S. Rogers, *CW* 42 (1948), 91–2, is, of course, right that 'divitiarum maximum exemplum, antequam illum libertini pauperem facerent' is a jaundiced comment on the wealth of imperial freedmen like Pallas, not a report of Lentulus' financial ruin, and he was rich at his death, according to Tacitus.

[2] *Ep*. 24. 19; 52. 8; 108. 36.

[3] *Ep*. 75. 4, 15–16.

the Cynic strain accords least with Seneca's own way of life, while the ideal set out in *De Vita Beata* accords best with it. The predominant middle view does not, on the whole, contradict what Seneca did, but so negative a creed does come oddly from the pen of the well-endowed *amicus principis* who took a personal interest in his profitable vineyards and was renowned for his generosity.

Seneca the hypocrite looms up before the reader scanning the praises of poverty, the description of heroes refusing wealth, the advice to the ordinary man to reduce his possessions. The author's image improves when he condemns greedy acquisition but approves of diligence in tending fortune's gifts: for the reader knows that the bulk of his wealth was inherited or given, and that he carefully tended his investment at Nomentum;[1] or when he teaches spiritual detachment from one's possessions: for Seneca did finally give up a substantial portion of his fortune after two years of trying; or when he preaches frugality: for he himself reports definite ascetic habits which are echoed elsewhere; or when he preaches generosity: for the poets attest that he was liberal to poor dependants and, at the height of Seneca's influence, Nero showed gracious liberality to impoverished nobles.

Even by the standards of this, his usual moderate doctrine, Seneca's record is blemished: he condemned usury and made a fortune by it; he gave luxurious banquets but preached frugality; he condemned wealth that was 'alieno sanguine cruentas' but probably accepted property of Nero's victim, Britannicus. But Tacitus knew well that his works provided an answer to that one, at least: 'Una defensio occurrit quod muneribus tuis obniti non debui', he makes him say.[2] And Seneca also wrote that the aim and manner could justify luxury.[3]

---

[1] Seneca's profits in viticulture were respectable by Roman standards; Cicero, *Off.* 1. 151. Note particularly Volusius' 'praecipuae opes bonis artibus' (*Ann.* 13. 30) whose 'longa parsimonia' (*Ann.* 14. 56) will have preserved what he inherited and made in farming (Col. *RR* 1. 7, 3, where the praenomen is wrong; cf. Tenney Frank, *ESAR* 5, p. 24).

[2] *Ann.* 14. 53, 6; above, p. 299 n. 2.

[3] Haase, frag. IX (20): 'Omnia, quae luxuriosi faciunt quaeque imperiti, faciet et sapiens, sed non eodem modo eodem proposito.'

The doctrine expounded in *De Vita Beata* obviously fits Seneca's own situation best: wealth is desirable and can be an instrument of good; lapses from the high standards set for acquisition and use are excusable in an *imperfectus*, if he is sincerely trying to achieve virtue. Why did Seneca not keep to a doctrine that had the support of the Middle Stoa[1] and suited his own position so well? If, on the other hand, he was a hypocrite, why did he not keep consistently to the high-sounding praises of poverty?

One obvious solution would be to attach Seneca's extreme and moderate negative attitudes to one period of his life and his positive attitude to wealth to another.[2] Our summary of Seneca's views has shown that his negative attitude appears in all of his prose works except for *De Vita Beata*, *De Clementia* (where the topic is only touched on in discussing mercy), and *De Otio* (which does not refer to the subject at all). We would need then a chronological scheme that would leave *De Vita Beata* the sole surviving philosophical work (except for *De Clementia*) between Seneca's return to court in 49 and his offer to return some of his wealth to Nero in 62. Now, the dating of the dialogues is so vague that it is just possible to construct such a scheme.[3] The *Ad Marciam* could express gloom about the life that Seneca saw threatened in 39. *De Ira* could have been written during or just before the exile when Seneca felt insecure. Or it could belong to the period to which *De Brevitate Vitae* is often assigned, i.e. just after Seneca's return from exile, when, according to the scholiast

---

[1] E. Caro, *Quid de beata vita senserit Seneca*, Paris, 1852, pp. 25, 34, realizing that the important contradictions were to be found not between Seneca's life and doctrine but within the doctrine, argued that the lofty principles of Stoicism were too unrealistic, so that Seneca asserted them, but was more realistic in giving detailed advice. But the problem is deeper than that: there was a less ascetic Stoicism to hand (above, p. 296 n. 5) and Seneca adopted its *principles* in *De Vita Beata*. The conflict is also found at the level of concrete advice, e.g. *Tranq.* 8; *Ep.* 92. 14 ff. *v. Epp.* 5; 18.

[2] J. Lichy, *De servorum condicione*, Münster, 1927, pp. 51–5, tried to show that Seneca increasingly despised wealth as he got older. But his own scanty references refute the attempt. The autobiographical interpretation of passages concerning wealth features in many discussions of individual dialogues, e.g. Pohlenz, *Philosophie und Erlebnis*, pp. 94–7; see the criticisms of Köstermann on *De Providentia* by Giancotti, *Cronologia*, pp. 291–3.

[3] For the assignable chronological limits see Appendix A1.

on Juvenal, Seneca wanted to go to Athens. *De Constantia Sapientis*, *De Tranquillitate Animi*, *De Beneficiis*, and *De Providentia* could all be pushed to after 62.[1]

But it is not worth straining one's ingenuity to construct this scheme, which leaves unsolved the problem of *De Tranquillitate Animi*, a work that on a strictly autobiographical interpretation yields contradictory results. Its negative view of wealth fits Seneca's intentions, but not his actual situation, in 62–4; its negative view of political retirement could be made to fit, at best, his situation, but not his intentions, in 62–4.[2] Then there are the insurmountable difficulties of the Letters to Lucilius with their contradictory advice: praise of life at subsistence level;[3] insistence that spiritual independence can be demonstrated by the wealthy as well as the poor.[4] The extant Letters purport to be written in 63–4, after Seneca's offer to surrender part of his wealth; they may all have been composed directly for publication in 64–5, some probably after Seneca's contribution to Rome's rebuilding.[5] It must stand as a warning against the strictly autobiographical approach that Seneca there never advocates actually reducing one's fortune.

The range of views in the Letters also defeats another kind of interpretation: that Seneca tailored his advice on wealth to suit the problems and interests of his different addressees.[6] In any

[1] This dating of the first two would require the abandonment of what I have argued (Appendix D3) is the more likely date for the death of their addressee Annaeus Serenus, i.e. before 62.

[2] In fact, on an autobiographical interpretation, Seneca's views on political retirement accord better with his own position around 60, when he was in difficulties but not yet resolved on complete withdrawal (see below, p. 357)—but this date is incompatible with an autobiographical interpretation of the advice to prune one's *patrimonium*. Thus Pohlenz, *Philosophie und Erlebnis*, pp. 95–7, suggests that in composing the Seneca–Nero debate, set in 62, Tacitus used *De Otio* for ideas on retirement and *De Tranquillitate Animi* (which has inappropriate views on retirement) for the views on wealth: which is virtually to admit that Seneca, to reflect his own position accurately, would have had to write *De Tranquillitate Animi* at two different times.

[3] *Ep.* 4. 10–11; 16. 7 ff.; 119.　　　　[4] *Ep.* 5. 6; 20. 10–11.

[5] See Appendices A1 (Note I) and B4.

[6] H. Dahlmann suggested this way of interpreting Seneca's dialogues in *Gnomon* 13 (1937), 366 ff., and applied it to the chapters on wealth in *Tranq.*, p. 379.

case, this solution would only raise the 'Seneca' question in another form: why should wealthy men like Serenus, Gallio, Lucilius, and Aebutius Liberalis[1] want to be shown Cynic ideals?

Perhaps any attempt at a unitary explanation of Seneca's range of views on wealth is doomed to failure. We might try considering each extreme and the intermediate position separately.

The Cynic extreme often occurs in passages where the reader is being urged not to envy wealth or fear poverty.[2] The Cynic's position is an exaggeration of the Stoic: 'hominis naturam cum Stoicis vincere, cum Cynicis excedere' is the invitation of philosophy, according to Seneca.[3] By exaggerating what was necessary, the Cynic showed what was possible.[4] But even orthodox Stoics believed in the persuasive power of *verbal* exaggeration: Seneca defends those exaggerations which amounted to paradox, on the grounds that they served as encouragement to good conduct.[5] This is the spirit in which we must read his extreme statements on wealth: the insistence on limiting possessions to match the basic needs of nature is an enhanced exhortation to frugality; the praise of Fabricius repudiating wealth is a way of removing the fear of loss;[6] the speech of Demetrius rejecting possessions as hazards to freedom is a way of preaching the right attitude to wealth.

The other extreme, as our summary of Seneca's views made clear, is represented by one dialogue: *De Vita Beata*. In this dialogue, Seneca discusses the central doctrine of the Stoa, the nature of the *summum bonum* and its relation to happiness, and reveals his knowledge of how Stoic doctrine developed in relation to the other schools.[7] After an introduction (chapters 1–2) in which he announces two topics, (1) the definition of the *vita*

[1] On Aebutius' wealth see Appendix D8.

[2] The purpose is avowed in *Ep.* 80. 6; 94. 72; 108. 14, and attested by the denial in *Cons. Helv.* 12. 1.

[3] *Brev. Vit.* 14. 1.

[4] *Ep.* 20. 9: 'non praeceptor veri sed testis sit.'

[5] *Ben.* 2. 35, 2; *Ben.* 7. 22, 1 warns against taking such passages literally.

[6] As Seneca actually says, *Ep.* 98. 12–13.

[7] For an excellent analysis of Seneca's arguments in *De Vita Beata* see Pohlenz, *Philosophie und Erlebnis*, pp. 55–81, to which I am greatly indebted in the description above.

beata and (2) the quickest way to achieve it (the right pace being something we can only determine on the way), Seneca offers several definitions, all clearly Stoic (3–5. 4). The Middle Stoa flavour is already pronounced in the emphasis on the careful use of external advantages and the special *gaudium* or *hilaritas* that springs up in the mind of the virtuous man.[1] The rest of the dialogue falls into two sections: the first distinguishes his position from the Epicurean one which is rejected (5. 4–16. 2); the second discusses the role of the προηγμένα or *commoda* in happiness, first with regard to the *proficiens* for whom some are necessary (16. 3–20), then with regard to the *sapiens* who uses them and prefers to have them but does not need them for his happiness (21–end). In the course of this latter part, the Stoic view of external advantages is carefully distinguished from the Academic–Peripatetic one (25). The first section of the dialogue thus covers the issue that Chrysippus had said was fundamental to the question of the *summum bonum*[2]—the contest of pleasure and virtue; the second echoes the long struggle of the Stoa to answer the criticisms of Theophrastus, of Carneades, and, more generally, of the Peripatetics and the Old Academy.[3]

Perhaps *De Vita Beata* is a product of pure intellectual interest: leaving rhetoric and spiritual therapy aside for once, Seneca set out to define happiness and found in the realistic side of the Stoa a more satisfactory answer than the other school could offer. So it could be argued. But two peculiar features of the dialogue are unexplained on that view. One is the concentration on wealth in the second section, to the substantial eclipse of the other *commoda*. It could be countered here that Seneca is bowing to the colloquial Latin connotation of *beatus*,[4] but one would expect Seneca to do that if he were trying to show how liberal and

---

[1] Above, p. 297 n. 1.

[2] Cicero, *Fin.* 2. 44.

[3] The basic texts for the attacks are Cicero, *Acad.* 2. 134, and *Fin.*, especially 5. 16 ff. The Stoic response is discussed by Pohlenz, *Die Stoa*², I, pp. 172–3; 178; 186–7; 189; van Straaten, *Panétius*, pp. 139 ff., and, as regards Carneades and Antipater, A. Long, *Phronesis* 12 (1967), 59 ff.

[4] Cf. *Ep.* 45. 9: 'beatum non eum esse quem vulgus appellat, ad quem pecunia magna confluxit . . .'

realistic Stoicism could be,[1] not defending its claim to be a
courageous and difficult doctrine. Moreover, when Seneca turns
to treat the subject of *beata vita* in Letter 92 he mentions wealth,
but concentrates on other *commoda*.

The second odd feature of the dialogue is structural. Whereas,
in the first section, the Stoic view is matched against the Epicurean, dialectically, with the use of a fictive interlocutor, in the
second it is not the Stoic theory that is attacked for implausibility
and inconsistency, but Stoic philosophers who are accused of
hypocrisy. Why should Seneca change the form of treatment?[2]
It is important here not to exaggerate the degree to which the
dialogue fails to cohere. The change from debate to personal
defence does not completely destroy continuity. That is maintained by the theme of the dangers of public opinion: popular
views on happiness, which are discussed in the introduction,
present the worst snare when we are defining our goal; but in
making our slow way along the path to virtue—the second topic
listed in the introduction—hostile criticism may well seem the
worst hazard.[3] This could explain why, when the second topic
is considered at the start of the second section (16. 3), a statement
of the Stoic view that the *proficiens* needs some material advantages to be happy is followed by an imaginary attack on the
novice for falling short of his lofty goal. It could be claimed that
this attack is meant to represent the dangerous views of the
vulgar. But with the imagined attack on the *sapiens*, and his
counter-attack (21 ff.), Seneca, though still discussing external
goods and happiness, has returned to the first subject of the proper
goal: to continue the attack–defence form here only obscures the
fact that this is a clarification of the Stoic view of happiness

---

[1] Cf. the demonstration of how Stoicism, popularly thought to be harsh,
could admit clemency in *De Clem*. 2. 5, 2 ff.

[2] Pohlenz, *Phil. und Erlebnis*, p. 69, was right to stress the connection in
theme between the two sections: they both clarify the Stoic aim by distinguishing
it clearly from the views of other schools with which it might be confused or
adversely compared. It is not true, as Abel (*Bauformen*, p. 161) has argued, that only
Seneca's autobiography provides a link between the two sections.

[3] *Ep*. 29. 5 ff. rejects the influence of public opinion in the form of charges
of hypocrisy brought against philosophers.

parallel to the earlier discussion of virtue and pleasure. A brief lapse into the early mode of discussion at 25. 1—'Quare illas non in bonis numerem, et quid praestem in illis aliud quam vos, quoniam inter utrosque convenit habendas, audite'—only brings this out more clearly. The structural oddity of the dialogue cannot be explained away.

There is an explanation of both of these odd features: *De Vita Beata* is in part intended as a justification of the author's prosperous way of life. The structure reflects attacks from which Seneca had suffered; the emphasis on wealth reflects the most telling part of these attacks. According to Tacitus, it was the point on which Suillius chose to stress the incompatibility of Seneca's doctrine and life.[1] The connection of *De Vita Beata* with the criticisms of Suillius has been made many times and its significance for the purpose of the dialogue variously estimated.[2] We have argued earlier[3] that the author's insistence that he is not speaking in the first person, and that the attacks he quotes are general and have been made throughout the ages, are not to be simply dismissed. Study of the literary antecedents of Seneca's dialogues supports the idea that Seneca has not simply described what Suillius said omitting his name: he has generalized, using Suillius' criticisms and probably others he suffered at different times[4] as a core. Further, we cannot tie the dialogue to the period immediately after Suillius' attack. All we can reasonably infer is that, at the time the dialogue was written, Seneca was still concerned with the difficulty of justifying his position, which had not ceased to be one of wealth and at least apparent power.

The positive extreme of Seneca's thought on wealth then seems to have been incited by the criticisms he suffered as *amicus*

[1] *Ann.* 13. 42, 4. Abel, *Bauformen*, p. 161, overlooks the fact that Tacitus perceived: it was Seneca's wealth that conflicted most obviously with his teachings. The sexual slurs have been given more prominence in Dio's version (61. 10, 1), no doubt because they made more exciting reading. Thus the emphasis on wealth is not, as Abel thinks, evidence that the Suillius attack was not primarily in Seneca's mind.

[2] See the summary in Giancotti, *Cronologia*, pp. 326 ff.

[3] See above, pp. 19–20.

[4] Tacitus mentions some in 62 (*Ann.* 14. 52) and hints at others in 55 (13. 18) and 59 (14. 11, 3).

principis. Indeed some special explanation is required for the fact that Seneca, who knew the works of Panaetius and Posidonius well, only in this work followed their ideas on wealth, ideas he ignored even in works like *De Beneficiis* and *De Tranquillitate Animi* where Middle Stoa influence is clear.[1] But once Seneca decided to define the Stoic position on happiness in a way that justified or at least excused his life, he thought seriously about the subject and produced a work about the Stoa's position and difficulties, not just his own.

If this discussion of the extremes of Seneca's thought has made the inconsistencies in Seneca's views seem less inexplicable, we still have not illuminated the central difficulty: why is Seneca's prevailing attitude to wealth negative, why are its dangers and abuses so vivid in his works, while its enrichment of the virtuous life is largely ignored? Perhaps Seneca was simply a hypocrite who wished his readers to think that he sincerely regarded his fortune as more of an encumbrance than an asset. But then what shall we say of his great popularity? Why did men of wealth and position wish to read his praises of frugality? Were they all hypocrites too?

In thinking about Seneca and his readers one obvious fact demands recognition: the literary potential of attack was enormous, and attack was easy, for the declamators had been refining the rhetorical tools for years.[2] It was possible to be 'in philosophia parum diligens, egregius tamen insectator vitiorum'. Seneca was a self-indulgent writer, as Quintilian said,[3] and he could not resist ringing the changes yet again on the evils of luxury, the happiness of frugal old Rome. But this is not the whole story. There are much calmer passages, like the advice in *De Tranquillitate Animi*

---

[1] The work on *officia* preserved in very bare outline (Haase, Teub. III (1872), p. 468) in Bishop Martin's *Formula Vitae Honestae* appears to be Panaetian in conception (Pohlenz, *Die Stoa*[2], p. 310) but omits liberality where one might have expected it, i.e. under *iustitia* where it is treated in Cicero's *De Officiis*.

[2] Seneca's debt to the declaimers has often been discussed, e.g. the commentaries of Ch. Favez on *Ad Helviam Matrem* and *Ad Marciam*. The *Controversiae* preserved by Seneca's father have fine examples of the praises of poverty (e.g. *Contr.* 2. 1, 7; 2. 1, 12), evils of wealth (e.g. 2. 1, 10), the superiority of ancestral Rome because of its poverty (e.g. 1. 6, 4).

[3] 10. 1, 129–31.

to reduce one's property, and duller ones, like the syllogisms concluding 'divitiae ergo non sunt bonum' in Letter 87.

It has often been noted that Stoicism assumes a more Cynic key in the early Empire.[1] As regards wealth, it is not difficult to assemble evidence to show that Seneca's views were neither unusual nor, in the circumstances of imperial life, irrational for a man of his rank. In his insistence on frugality, Seneca puts into philosophical form the attraction asceticism had for the high-living. Seneca himself records the little games of poverty his contemporaries under Claudius and Nero played[2] out of *taedium divitiarum*. Seneca rejected the idea that human vice continually increased: different ones were more prominent at different times, he said.[3] Tacitus tells us that luxury was the prominent one under Claudius and Nero and that Seneca was living on the eve of a revolution in manners: the decline of luxury after 69.[4] Symptomatic is the vogue the Cynic Demetrius enjoyed in the circle of Thrasea Paetus and Barea Soranus, both wealthy men.[5] Seneca may have known him in the reign of Gaius, but all his references to him almost certainly belong to Neronian works.[6] Demetrius probably practised his Cynicism, making some concessions in modesty for Romans like Seneca, who shrank from Cynic dress and behaviour,[7] but Seneca is certainly writing him up a bit when he pictures him as simply leaving wealth to others, rather than proclaiming his contempt for it.[8] In Philostratus he is depicted as the typical ranting Cynic.[9] Seneca gives him a stirring diatribe against worldly goods (*Ben.* 7. 8–10). Perhaps Seneca praised Demetrius partly to appeal to Thrasea's circle

[1] e.g. Dudley, *Cynicism*, pp. 188–9.   [2] *Cons. Helv.* 2. 3; *Ep.* 18. 7.
[3] *Ben.* 1. 10, 1–3.   [4] *Ann.* 3. 55.
[5] For their wealth, Dio 62. 26, 1; their cultivation of Demetrius, *Ann.* 16. 34–5.
[6] Seneca refers to him in De Vita Beata, De Beneficiis, Naturales Quaestiones, Epistulae Morales and De Providentia. But the last cannot be dated (see Appendix A1).
[7] For Seneca's distaste: *Ep.* 5; 18; 29. 1. Demetrius did not beg (*Vita Beata* 18. 3), a Cynic habit Seneca disliked (*Ben.* 2. 17). No doubt Demetrius did not have to.
[8] *Ep.* 62. 3. That is an attitude more appropriate to a Roman senator (Gallio in NQ 4, pref. 10, cf. Thrasea in Pl. *Ep.* 8. 22, 3) than a Cynic philosopher.
[9] *Life of Apollonius*, 4. 42; cf. Seneca, 20. 9 and 62. 3 on his outfit.

with which his relations appear to have been expressive of distant admiration.[1] Or Seneca may have shared the attraction: Demetrius had eloquence.[2]

In the austerity of Rubellius Plautus, Stoicism blended with cultivation of the old Roman virtues.[3] The idea that poverty had made Rome great, while luxury caused decline, was well loved of the Romans at all periods after the Hannibalic wars, and Seneca was no exception.[4] But in Seneca's period the behaviour of Claudius and Nero and their freedmen may well have seemed a fresh argument in support of the thesis. Tacitus notes that the main cause of the change in manners after 69 was the example of Vespasian, a frugal man. The counter-example of Nero should not be ignored. Seneca's description of Caligula's luxurious eating habits shows the feeling such imperial behaviour could engender, but it is still weak next to the revulsion he feels for the vulgarity and wealth of imperial freedmen.[5] The senators who witnessed Barea Soranus begging Pallas, on their behalf, to accept a large sum of money as an honour may not actually have started to despise wealth, but they may well have acquired a taste for hearing it despised.[6]

Another cause of the change in taste noted by Tacitus was the *domestica parsimonia* that men from remote parts of Italy and the provinces brought with them. That was not true of all provincials, not of Seneca nor of his Narbonensian brother-in-law who took his silver with him when sent as governor to the wilds of Germany.[7]

But Seneca suffered personally from another deterrent that Tacitus says discouraged conspicuous consumption: some emperors disliked even the appearance of rivalry.[8] Seneca mentions

[1] See above, pp. 100 ff. For another possible concession, p. 194.

[2] *Ben.* 7. 8, 2. When Tacitus says that Demetrius in 70 (*Hist.* 4. 40) defended the manifestly guilty P. Celer 'ambitiosius quam honestius' he could mean that he hoped to manage a rhetorical *tour de force*.

[3] *Ann.* 14. 57, 3.   [4] *Ira* I. 11, 4; *Ep.* 87. 41.

[5] *Cons. Helv.* 10. 4; see above, pp. 275; 302 n. 1.   [6] *Ann.* 12. 53.

[7] Pliny, *NH* 33. 143. On this 'received opinion' and Tacitus' awareness of some egregious exceptions, Syme, *Tacitus*, pp. 608 ff.; 616.

[8] Tacitus, *Ann.* 3. 55, 3. Such charges prompted Seneca to ask to retire (*Ann.* 14. 52, 2). Compare the fate of Valerius Asiaticus (*Ann.* 11. 1, 1: 'opes principibus

danger among the disadvantages of money.[1] Under Nero, its mere possession, no matter how modest one's habits, became hazardous.[2] Seneca tells how Gaius starved a relative to death to get his money;[3] it was rumoured that Nero used poison on Pallas and his aunt Domitia for the same reason.[4]

Frugality and indifference: those are Seneca's themes. He never ceases urging a lofty detachment from the gifts of fortune, as the only way to avoid the pain of loss. It is even worth while to practise living without them. One source of wealth that features prominently in *De Beneficiis* is the Emperor's largess: those who enjoyed it knew all about the insecurity of possession. For an Emperor who eschewed violence, there was still judicial victimization: under Tiberius the custom became established of claiming for the imperial purse money confiscated from condemned men who had enjoyed the Emperor's generosity.[5]

A man in Seneca's position knew that ultimately most of his wealth would belong to the Emperor.[6] According to Seneca, people suspected emperors of using their judicial influence to secure legacies.[7] Even Augustus expected his favourites' wills to reflect their gratitude. Seneca's own will clearly favoured Nero: even in a man's lifetime, his will might be examined to test his loyalty to the Emperor.[8]

Under Augustus or Tiberius,[9] failure to show proper gratitude in a will would be tolerated, but Gaius had initiated the custom of invalidating the wills of men he thought owed him something

infensas') and later of D. Junius Silanus Torquatus (*Ann.* 15. 35: 'prodigum largitionibus, neque aliam spem quam in rebus novis esse . . .').

[1] *Ep.* 14. 9; 84. 11–12; 119. 6.

[2] *Ann.* 14. 22, 1 (of Rubellius Plautus): 'casta et secreta domo, quantoque metu occultior tanto plus famae adeptus'.

[3] *Tranq.* 11. 10.

[4] *Ann.* 14. 65; Dio 61. 17, 1; Suet. *Nero* 34. 5.

[5] Millar, *JRS* 53 (1963), 36–7, discussing *Ann.* 4. 20; 6. 2; 6. 19, with Dio 58. 22, 3.

[6] Suet. *Aug.* 66. 7; Rogers collects the evidence in *TAPA* 78 (1947), 140; the discussion of J. Gaudamet, *Studi Arangio–Ruiz* III, Naples, 1953, p. 115, is superior.

[7] *Clem.* 1. 15, 4–6.

[8] Suet. *Vit.* 14. 3; Tacitus, *Dial.* 13. 6.

[9] *Ann.* 3. 76; Suet. *Aug.* 66.

if they were disappointing;[1] and, by the time of Seneca's death, it had become the custom for friends of the Emperor, or ex-friends, to protect other legacies, by leaving a large share to the Emperor.[2] Later Nero was to rule that *testamenta ingratorum* were forfeit to the imperial purse.[3] Even if Seneca had been allowed to make his gesture and to change his will in favour of his friends, Nero would have invalidated it. In the event, he supplemented the terms of the will by seizing Seneca's famous gardens.[4]

These evils can be explained: a rudimentary financial system allowed the Emperor's private wealth to become more and more vital in the conduct of the state. The Emperor was under greater pressures than just natural greed, particularly if he tended to extravagance. But for Seneca and his contemporaries the system had to be endured. They can be pardoned for trying to convince themselves at times that things external did not matter.

'Patrimonia, maxima humanarum aerumnarum materia', worse than death, pain, fear, or desire, Seneca wrote in *De Tranquillitate Animi*. His principal source in that work was Panaetius' περὶ εὐθυμίας, but Panaetius had not said that. He had stressed the spiritual detachment and the joy with which the wise man can handle wealth.[5] But Seneca was talking about peace of mind for men like himself, in Rome, under the Julio-Claudians.

---

[1] Suet. *Gaius* 38. 2; Dio 59. 15. Pliny, *Pan.* 43, attests the subsequent development of the practice.

[2] *Ann.* 15. 59; 16. 11; 16. 19; cf. Tac. *Agric.* 43. 4. Agricola, as a client of the Flavian house, would be expected to leave a legacy to the Emperor.

[3] Suet. *Nero* 32. 2.

[4] Above, p. 294 n. 1.

[5] Above, p. 297 n. 1.

IO

THE PHILOSOPHER ON POLITICAL PARTICIPATION

OF all the issues treated in the Greek philosophical schools, none had more appeal for the Romans than the choice between a life of service to the *res publica* and a life of *otium* devoted to philosophy. The thesis 'sitne sapientis ad rem publicam accedere' was in the late Republic and the Empire one of the favourite exercises taken over by the rhetorical schools from the philosophers.[1] The prominence of this theme in Seneca's works and the complexity of his views alone would recommend it for study, but it is particularly relevant to the present inquiry as a theme on which Seneca's work might well be expected to reflect his own political career and friendships, and the political climate of the reign of Nero. But before we can examine the relation of his various works on the subject to the political and personal circumstances in which they were composed (III, IV, V), we must first try to give a clear account of what Seneca actually wrote on the subject (I) and then establish where he stood in relation to Stoic doctrines and Roman attitudes as they had evolved (II).

All the usual difficulties of Senecan scholarship combine against us here: the difficulty of distinguishing Seneca's inconsistency from a genuine change or development in thought; the uncertain chronology of the dialogues; the problem of recognizing when his 'I' and 'you' are biographical and when generic; the assignment of a real or fictional character to the correspondence with Lucilius. The manuscripts too are uncooperative: the beginning and end of *De Otio*, the one work explicitly concerned with the subject, are lost and the name of its addressee, noted only in the

[1] Cicero, *Top.* 82; *De Or.* 3. 112; Quintilian 3. 5, 6.

table of contents of the Codex Ambrosianus, has been rendered virtually illegible by erasure. What remains suggests that it read 'ad Serenum', which, if correct, gives valuable help in dating *De Otio*—but it may not be correct. As a result of these difficulties, there will probably never be general agreement on the relation of Seneca's teaching on this theme to his life.

I

The natural method, and the usual one, for studying what Seneca says on the subject of political participation is to examine the relevant works in chronological order. But what is that order? By the standards appropriate to Senecan chronology, these limits seem safe: the Letters report events of 62–4, or, more likely, 63–4, and their publication came after that of the dialogues in which the theme is prominent. Of these, *De Brevitate Vitae* belongs between late 48 and late 55.[1] The dating of the other three works concerned is much less secure. *De Constantia Sapientis* belongs after 47,[2] and before *De Tranquillitate Animi*. The latter was written before the death of their common addressee, Annaeus Serenus, an event that occurred in Nero's reign, certainly before 64, probably by the start of the year 62.[3] The relative chronology of these two works depends on the philosophical attitudes ascribed to Serenus in each of them. *De Constantia Sapientis*, in which Serenus is an avowed Epicurean scoffing at the Stoics,[4] must precede *De Tranquillitate Animi*, in which he is presented as a follower of the Stoics.[5] *De Otio*, if the addressee is also Serenus, belongs, like *De Tranquillitate Animi*, before 62 and after *De Constantia Sapientis*, since Serenus is now definitely not

[1] See Appendices A1 and A2.
[2] It is unlikely that Valerius Asiaticus, who died in 47 (Tacitus, *Ann.* 11. 3), was alive when Seneca wrote *Const. Sap.* 18. 2.
[3] See Appendix D3.
[4] *Const. Sap.* 15. 4; 3. 2: 'Si negas accepturum iniuriam, id est neminem illi temptaturum facere, omnibus relictis negotiis Stoicus fio.' This makes it clear that Serenus' Stoic phase did not precede the Epicurean one.
[5] *Tranq.* 1. 10.

an admirer of Epicurus and appears to be arguing the orthodox Stoic view against Seneca.[1] His doctrinal dogmatism there cannot, however, be put in a clear temporal relation with his spiritual difficulties in *De Tranquillitate Animi*: the eighth Letter to Lucilius proves that Seneca could portray a man struggling with his own moral imperfections while challenging Seneca's conformity to Stoic principles.[2]

Some scholars, without relying on the assumption that *De Otio* is addressed to Serenus, have dated *De Tranquillitate Animi* before that work by adducing a conflict of doctrine between them on the theme we are here considering, and explaining the alleged conflict in terms of Seneca's changing personal situation.[3] But obviously, we cannot assume the correctness of this view when we are about to re-examine precisely that doctrine and its possible biographical relevance.

De Brevitate Vitae

The title, as Seneca explains at the outset (1. 1), refers to a complaint brought against nature by the majority of men, the 'clari viri' as well as the 'turba et imprudens vulgus'. Seneca argues that the complaint is unjustified: there is enough time if it is not

---

[1] I cannot agree with Giancotti, *Cronologia*, pp. 160–3, that the addressee of *De Otio* is portrayed as having no commitment to Stoicism. The crucial passage is 7. 2 where Seneca mentions the Epicurean theorist 'de quo male existimare consensimus'. This parenthesis would be pointless if it were not meant to refer to the addressee as characterized in 1. 4, rather than a vague fictive interlocutor. The agreement is therefore between proponents of *contemplatio* (Seneca) and those of *actio* (Serenus), which is the orthodox Stoic position (1. 4; cf. below, p. 340): no other major school was strongly associated with this view. It is not essential for this view of Serenus that 'Stoici nostri' of the inferior manuscripts be read at 1. 4 instead of 'Stoici vestri' of the Ambrosianus: if 'vestri' is right, it can easily be construed as polemic in function. On Serenus as the addressee of *De Otio* see also p. 354 n. 2.

[2] As Lucilius does in other Letters too: 13; 16; 75. 15–16.

[3] The discussion of R. Waltz in the Budé edition of the Dialogues, vol. 4, pp. 109–10, offers a particularly clear example of this reasoning. Even H. Dahlmann, in his review of Kostermann (*Gnomon* 13 (1937), 366 ff.), attacking the biographical approach, continued to regard Seneca's personal situation as the key to *De Otio* (pp. 379 ff.).

wasted. The only profitable way of spending our time is on the acquisition and practice of *sapientia*: that is the true *otium*; everything else—political life, literary activity, the pursuit of luxury and pleasure that constitutes the vulgar *otium*—is to be rejected. The starkness of this antithesis is sharpened by Seneca's paradoxical use of language: the normally rather colourless but respectable *occupatio* and *negotium* become the generic terms for all these despised activities, thus allowing *otium* to be purged of its more contemptible aspects. Time spent on chariot-racing, singing, and banquets is not called 'otiosa vita' but 'desidiosa occupatio' (12. 2) and 'iners negotium' (12. 4);[1] *officium* with its honourable connotations is transferred to the study of philosophy, so that *vera officia* (as opposed to the more vulgar *officia* in 7. 4; 14. 3) are coextensive with *otium*: 'hos in veris officiis morari putamus . . . qui Zenonem, qui Pythagoran, cotidie, et Democritum ceterosque antistites bonarum artium, qui Aristotelen et Theophrastum volent habere quam familiarissimos' (14. 5). As this sentence shows, Seneca is not recommending Stoic philosophy in particular,[2] nor does he offer any serious philosophical discussion in the work. If the dialogue must be given a label, then *protrepticus* is the least inept,[3] although it gives no hint of the dominant satirical and in fact apotreptic mood of the work.[4] There is no serious consideration here, as there is elsewhere in Seneca, of the claims of the condemned activities, no admission that they can be pursued for different motives and at different moral levels: their practitioners are all condemned as men driven by passion (2. 1–3), or self-disgust (2. 5), rather than guided by rational decisions (2. 2; 3. 3). We are not shown the men who stand on a moral level between them and the *sapientes*, or near-

---

[1] As J.-M. André, *Recherches sur l'otium romain*, Paris, 1962, pp. 40–1, points out, Seneca maintains the Roman values in characterizing such devotees as the most shameful *occupati* (7. 1; 12).

[2] Cf. also 14. 2. The ideal Seneca proposes has, however, definite Stoic features. K. Abel, *Gym.* 72 (1965), 325, points to 'amor virtutium' in 19. 2; 'profectus animi' (20. 5). Note also the metaphysical assumption in 19. 1.

[3] So H. Dahlmann, *Über die Kürze des Lebens*, Munich, 1949, pp. 18 ff.; P. Grimal, *De Brevitate Vitae*², Paris, 1966, p. 5; K. Abel, op. cit., pp. 318, 324.

[4] A point made by Abel, op. cit., p. 326; André, *L'otium romain*, p. 41.

sapientes, who study metaphysical and moral philosophy and learn how to live and die.[1]

The general argument of the work would naturally lead to an exhortation to everyone to give up, at any time in life, any kind of work but philosophy. Instead, we find an exhortation addressed to Paulinus,[2] including a realistic description of his service as *praefectus annonae*,[3] a more positive evaluation of public activities,[4] and a more conditional justification of political retirement. It is said that Paulinus' post has given scope for *virtus* (18. 1); that unselfish devotion to the state (not mere personal ambition) has been involved (18. 2); that the prefecture, even if more suited to dimmer men than Paulinus, and scarcely compatible with the perfect life, is a 'ministerium honorificum' which 'frugalitatis exactae homines' can justifiably exercise (18. 4). On the other hand, the advice to retire is supported by appeals to Paulinus' right, after years of public service, to time for himself, to the excessive burdens and ignoble aims peculiar to the post he occupies, and to his early training in *liberalia studia* which prepared him for philosophy (18. 4–19. 1).

Even if one ascribes these features to flattery and the wish to strengthen, at any price, the case for retirement, the effect is to present the reader with an addressee whose personality and position are not wholly appropriate to the dialogue's theme, and yet are not wholly irrelevant, as in the case of a mere dedication.[5]

---

[1] In 20. 5 Seneca does allude to the idea of spiritual progress, but the dialogue, in keeping with its satirical tone, portrays only the moral extremes.

[2] 18. 1–19. The *exemplum* (20. 3) of Turranius, the aged *praefectus annonae*, must be taken with it.

[3] This contrasts with the use elsewhere in the work of the usual conventional images for public life, usually the courts, clientship, magistracies, e.g. 7. 7–8; 17. 5; 20. 5.

[4] As compared with the grudging concession in 7. 1: 'ceteri, etiam si vana gloriae imagine teneantur, speciose tamen errant.'

[5] Abel, *Gym.* 72 (1965), 319, falsely compares Paulinus' role with that of Maecenas in Horace's first Satire. But here Paulinus' job and post-retirement activities are described, and he is exhorted, not merely addressed. By contrast, *De Vita Beata* and *De Ira* do seem to be merely dedicated to Seneca's brother. In the light of the character sketch of the brother in *NQ* 4, pref. 10 ff., the reference to his particular fear of anger and request for a treatise on the subject (*Ira* 1. 1, 1) is probably conventional. In some cases, the nasty suspicion arises that

Although Paulinus is not said to be particularly interested in the subject theoretically, and is portrayed by Seneca as a practical functionary, hardly likely to be moved by arguments about the grandeur of philosophy,[1] yet the thesis of the work fits broadly with the exhortation to Paulinus to retire.[2] Clearly Seneca has not created a portrait of Paulinus and his predicament to match his theme, but if the retirement is real, is the exhortation the real means by which it was effected? I have argued elsewhere that this passage was not intended to effect Paulinus' withdrawal but rather to persuade the public that the reasons for the retirement of the *praefectus annonae* were advanced age and a desire to return to liberal studies.[3] The subject of the dialogue perhaps appealed to Seneca anyway, or he may have written this racy, popular work specifically to meet this occasion. In either case, it seems likely that at least a secondary purpose of the work was to save public appearances for Seneca and his father-in-law when the latter had to surrender his post for reasons of court politics. The work is largely irrelevant to Seneca's own position when it was composed, though not incongruous from a tutor or adviser who had considerable time for philosophical reflection.[4]

Despite its more popular character, *De Brevitate Vitae* introduces some of the most important themes of the other two dialogues we shall consider and the Letters. For we shall meet again the redefinitions of honourable words signifying active life,[5] and the purging of the ordinary concept of *otium*[6] to exclude

Seneca's choice of addressee was determined by a name, however appropriate he then made it appear: what could be more apt than to dedicate *De Beneficiis* to a Liberalis, or *De Tranquillitate Animi* to a Serenus?

[1] Abel, op. cit., pp. 318–20, makes this important point which he wrongly thinks conflicts with my interpretation of the dialogue.

[2] Pohlenz, *Philosophie und Erlebnis*, p. 84, perceived and described the sharp break between the general discussion and the precise exhortation, but he took the exhortation as real advice to Paulinus, and the general discussion as a reflection of Seneca's own reluctance to enter active political life on his return from exile.

[3] *JRS* 52 (1962), 104 ff. See Appendix A2.

[4] For its irrelevance to Seneca's position in 49, see *JRS* 52 (1962), 112; as regards 55, see below, pp. 356–7.

[5] Philosophy as *opus* (*Ep.* 8. 2); *officia hominis* (*Tranq.* 4. 3); *labores* (*Ep.* 120. 12); *agere* (*Otio* 6. 4–5; *Ep.* 8. 6; 68. 2, 10).

[6] *Tranq.* 4. 8, cf. 5. 5; *Otio* 3. 4; *Ep.* 14. 15; 55. 4; 82. 2, 3.

all but philosophy. We shall hear again of the evil origin of other pursuits in the passions and external pressures,[1] and of their evil outcome in agitation and inconstancy.[2] The exhortation to Paulinus introduces the idea that only some natures are suited to philosophy and that withdrawal is more justifiable in some circumstances than in others.

De Tranquillitate Animi

This work presents the author as spiritual teacher. It opens with the longest piece of formal dialogue in Seneca's philosophical essays: a description of his ailment by Serenus, the patient, followed by the diagnosis offered by Seneca, the doctor. In contrast to *De Brevitate Vitae*, the work is explicitly Stoic: it is an exercise in applied Stoicism—practical advice aimed at men on various levels of spiritual progress. 'Ad imperfectos et mediocres et male sanos hic meus sermo pertinet, non ad sapientem' (11. 1), Seneca says at one point, and his decision to begin and end with advice to Serenus makes it clear that this is the sort of audience he has in mind throughout. For Serenus introduces himself as a man neither ill nor whole, 'in statu ut non pessimo, ita maxime querulo et moroso positus sum' (1. 2), while the metaphorical descriptions of his condition, as a sailor in sight of shore (1. 17), a patient no longer in need of harsh cures but of self-confidence in his new state of health (2. 1–3), place him, according to Seneca's analysis in the Letters, in the highest grade of *profecti*:[3] those whose passions, though no longer deep-seated nor permanently in control, still stir them.[4] Seneca proposes at the outset to prescribe general remedies among which Serenus will

---

[1] *Tranq.* 1. 11–2; 2. 9–10; *Otio* 1. 1–3; *Ep.* 19. 6; 21. 1; 23. 7–8; 37. 5; 69. 2; 73. 2; 118. 5.

[2] *Tranq.* 2. 9–10; 12; *Otio* 1. 1–3; *Ep.* 36. 6; 55. 4–5.

[3] As noted by O. Hense, *Seneca und Athenodorus*, Univ.-Prog. Freiburg, 1893, p. 12.

[4] *Ep.* 75. 9–11. In this letter, these constitute the first class of *imperfecti*, the classes being given in descending order. By the classification of Letter 72, Serenus is in *genus tertium*, as is shown by the phrase 'in conspectu terrarum laboranti' (1. 17, cf. *Ep.* 72. 10).

find his cure (2. 4), and his final summary shows that he has kept this purpose to the end.[1] But we are not to think that only *imperfecti* at Serenus' high level are addressed: just as Seneca provides glimpses of the sage's mentality (5. 2–3; 8. 4–8; 11; 13. 3), he also considers *pessima ingenia* (2. 11), whose restlessness is more extreme. In this dialogue, we have a sympathetic, constructive treatment of the people so cynically treated in *De Brevitate Vitae*, a more realistic appreciation of the problems of ordinary human life.[2] In both works, the addressee is a superior specimen of this class: Paulinus in having earned philosophical retirement, Serenus in being far advanced in his spiritual convalescence.

The fact most essential to understanding *De Tranquillitate Animi* is that most often overlooked: the subject of the dialogue is not *otium*, but *tranquillitas*.[3] Although Seneca probably expanded the section on political retirement that he found in Panaetius' περὶ εὐθυμίας,[4] inner peace, not outer conduct, is the unifying theme. Serenus names three separate manifestations of his malady, i.e. *sibi displicere*: vacillation between *amor parsimoniae* and *luxuria* (1. 5–9); between the *res publica* (first conceived as *honores*, later as oratory) and *otium* (1. 10–13); between simplicity of expression, with matter dominating style, and a more ambitious eloquence (1. 14–15).[5] Similarly, for well over half of the

---

[1] 'Habes, Serene carissime, quae possint tranquillitatem tueri, quae restituere, quae subrepentibus vitiis resistant.'

[2] So André, *L'otium romain*, pp. 37; 43; 46–7; 49–50.

[3] Giancotti does stress this, *Cronologia*, p. 172, but André, op. cit., p. 49, still goes badly wrong.

[4] Broecker, *Animadversiones ad Plutarchi Libellum* περὶ εὐθυμίας, pp. 204 ff.

[5] Serenus says: 'infirmitas qualis sit non tam semel tibi possum quam per partes ostendere' (1. 4). I cannot agree with André, op. cit., p. 44, that in 1. 5 he describes a continuous series of events, the vacillation between frugality and luxury showing the vacuity of a certain kind of *vita privata* which drives him to public life from which he then retreats into an *otium* 'sedentary, mean, and egoistic'. Nor does it seem to me that the *otium* to which Serenus in his disillusionment with public life turns is meant to seem contemptible. Of the three pairs of contrary states, only the first (*parsimonia* v. *luxuria*) exhibits the contrast of good and bad. In the second and third, the moral shadow falls only on Serenus' inconstancy: *otium* is described (1. 11) in favourable terms similar to those in *De Brev. Vit.*, while the elevated style is treated later on (17. 11) as an instance of the moderate and occasional release of the mind recommended.

work, Seneca gives advice about aspects of life other than participation in politics: the right choice of friends (7); regulation of
wealth (8–9); simplicity and pretence in social behaviour (17.
1–2); mental recreation in the form of games, jokes, and drinking
(17). Two major themes run through this advice: one is that of
moderation and the mean—in wealth (8. 9), social behaviour
(17. 2), drinking (17. 9), even the passions (9. 2; 10. 7; 15. 6). The
second is that one's attitude to fortune is more important than
what fortune brings: one must choose one's course rather than
be pushed by emotion or drift through inertia (2. 6–8; 5. 5;
10. 6; 12. 3); though *consuetudo* and *ratio* make ineluctable difficulties bearable (10. 1–4), one should be prepared for everything
(11. 6 ff.; 13. 2–3); not attempt what is clearly beyond one (12);
not be discouraged by human viciousness or fortune's unfairness
(15–16).[1]

To remember that *res publica* v. *otium* is not the unifying theme
of *De Tranquillitate Animi* offers protection against certain facile
interpretations of Seneca's teachings. Thus the following passage
should not be cited to show that Seneca, in this dialogue, in
contrast with *De Brevitate Vitae*, advocates a return to the traditional Roman idea of equilibrium between *otium* and *negotia*:[2]
'miscenda tamen ista et alternanda sunt, solitudo et frequentia
. . . odium turbae sanabit solitudo, taedium solitudinis turba'
(17. 3). For these words occur not in the discussion of political
retirement, but in a chapter advising the mean in social behaviour:
simplicity as a mean between lack of reserve and simulation;
recreation and leisure (*otium*) as a mean between continuous labour
and complete self-indulgence: *otium* is clearly not a way of life
here, but simply a break from business.[3] In the passage quoted,

---

[1] Broecker, op. cit., pp. 207–8, thinks these were also the main themes of
Panaetius' περὶ εὐθυμίας, as of the two works for which it was the principal
source: Seneca's *De Tranquillitate Animi* and Plutarch's περὶ εὐθυμίας.

[2] As André argues, op. cit., pp. 35, 43.

[3] In *De Officiis* 1. 19; 1. 104, similarly of Panaetian origin (above, p. 180 n.2),
Cicero says that intervals of study are permissible in a life of action. In the same
work, 3. 2–4, Cicero clearly distinguishes the *otium* that is a rest from politics
from that which constitutes retirement from politics. In 2. 4, Cicero says that
when he was totally immersed in politics, philosophy filled his spare time.

then, withdrawal and solitude are not—as they often are in *De Otio* and the Letters[1]—directly connected with retirement as a way of life just as, earlier in the dialogue, the philosopher Athenodorus is made to contrast solitude with the life of philosophical retirement (3. 6–7). What we have in this passage is advice on social conduct, as in Letter 3 where the recommendation to observe a mean between indiscretion about oneself and secretiveness is followed by the precept, 'inter se ista miscenda sunt: et quiescenti agendum et agenti quiescendum est' (3. 5–6).

In analysing the key passages on political participation, we must remember not only the theme of *tranquillitas* but also the realistic way in which Seneca, prescribing for *imperfecti*, accepts the existence of certain natural desires and drives. In his confession, Serenus is made to say that he first decides, in accordance with Stoicism, to enter politics for the right reason, i.e. to help his fellow citizens, but that, discouraged by difficulties, humiliation, or excessive demands on his time, he changes to *otium* (1. 10–11). He continues: 'But when my mind has been aroused by reading of great bravery, and noble examples have applied the spur, I want to rush into the forum, to lend my voice to one; to offer such assistance to another as, even if it will not help, will be an effort to help . . .' (1. 12). Seneca traces this type of dissatisfaction to desires unrepressed but unfulfilled which breed fear and regret (2. 7–8), and says that the condition is aggravated when men take refuge in leisure and solitary studies 'quae pati non potest animus ad civilia erectus agendique cupidus et natura inquies . . .' (2. 9). When Seneca comes to cite the remedy proposed by the philosopher Athenodorus,[2] 'optimum erat et rei

---

[1] *Otio* 1. 1–3; *Ep.* 7, though the verbal similarities of 7. 1 and *Tranq.* 17. 3 are striking. In Letter 8 Lucilius interprets the advice to avoid the crowd as conflicting with Stoic recommendations to a life of action.

[2] Of the two philosophers from Tarsus called Athenodorus, most scholars think Athenodorus Sandonis filius, Strabo's friend and Augustus' adviser, is the one cited here, rather than the older Athenodorus Kordylion. The sensible discussion by Hense, *Seneca und Athenodorus*, pp. 20–6, is expanded by speculation in P. Grimal's 'Auguste et Athénodore', *REA* 47 (1945), 261, and 48 (1946), 62. Without Athenodorus' own writings, we cannot hope to explain how his view given here fitted or failed to fit with his political mission to his native city in old age (Strabo 14. 5, 15; Dio Chrys. 33. 48).

publicae tractatione et officiis civilibus se detinere', he directs it to those preparing for *res civiles*:[1] 'nam cum utilem se efficere civibus mortalibusque propositum habeat, simul et exercetur et proficit, qui in mediis se officiis posuit communia privataque pro facultate administrans' (3. 1). Athenodorus then goes on to order withdrawal because of the corruption of actual political life. Seneca is not as clear in his presentation as he might be, but it seems likely that Athenodorus' advice (at least as presented by Seneca), and Seneca's counter-advice in 4. 8, 'longe itaque optimum est miscere otium rebus, quotiens actuosa vita impedimentis fortuitis aut civitatis condicione prohibebitur', are not categorical imperatives but advice for men with certain natures and purposes. Seneca's later discussion of the way to decide whether or not you are naturally suited to politics accords with this interpretation.[2]

According to Seneca, Athenodorus recommended, in theory, for such men as Serenus, a full share of public responsibilities, but added that the actual conditions of political life—the dangers to simplicity and risk of failure among the ambitious and slanderous —made it imperative to withdraw. The *otium* thus gained should be devoted, he said, not to luxurious solitude, but to the study and teaching of moral philosophy, a pursuit that will prevent self-disgust and profit one's fellow men as much as political duties. The man who can inculcate virtue in the young 'in privato publicum negotium agit'. The affinities of this idea with those in *De Brevitate Vitae* are obvious. Yet Seneca here rejects Athenodorus' advice.

What is the precise nature of Seneca's disagreement with

[1] Seneca here draws a parallel with athletes for whom it is most useful to spend most of their time developing their physical prowess 'cui se uni dicaverunt'. In 'ita vobis animum ad rerum civilium certamen parantibus', 'vobis' is the reading of the Ambrosianus and has been preferred by editors since Haase (except for Waltz in the Budé). The 'nobis' of vulgar editions could mean that the advice suited all Stoics, but there is no reason to accept it.

[2] This interpretation is supported also by 465D–466A of Plutarch's περὶ εὐθυμίας concerning the failure of inactivity to bring peace to certain souls. Even Epicurus, he says, believed that it was right τῇ φύσει χρῆσθαι πολιτευομένους καὶ πράσσοντας τὰ κοινὰ τοὺς φιλοτίμους καὶ φιλοδόξους ὡς μᾶλλον ἀπ' ἀπραγμοσύνης ταράττεσθαι καὶ κακοῦσθαι πεφυκότας. And on the Panaetian doctrine that activities had to suit one's 'propria natura' see below, p. 341.

Athenodorus? Seneca goes on to admit the possibility of with-drawal from public life under the pressure of circumstances, i.e. *impedimenta fortuita* or *civitatis condicio* (4. 8)—even to the extent of reducing one's usefulness to mankind to the mere exemplifica-tion of virtue (4. 7), just as Athenodorus had allowed (3. 6). His objection seems to be to the speed and completeness of the advocated withdrawal.[1] The grounds of Seneca's objection come out clearly. One is directly related to the general theme of the work: constancy in purpose, though not inflexibility (14. 1), is necessary for internal peace; we must not let our course be decided by fortune or personal inertia; we must follow the condition of the state and fortune 'utique movebimus nec alligati metu torpebimus' (5. 4); when political circumstances are not propitious, we can retire to port, but we must leave affairs spontaneously, not be deserted by them (5. 5). A second reason for Seneca's objection to the advice of Athenodorus is an idea that is to recur often: no state is so bad, so devoid of all possibility of improvement, that all *honesta actio* is precluded (4. 8–5. 3), while even a flourishing state contains vices.

The person who has chosen public life should, according to Seneca, fulfil his decision as far as possible. Martyrdom is not expected (5. 4). If full political activity is forbidden or dangerous (4. 3), then such a man must choose of his own accord some more limited *officia* and devote the rest of his time to *otium* and *litterae*, but the condition of the state and the pressures of fortune will never render active life completely impossible. In keeping with this view, Seneca's recommendations for life in retirement differ from Athenodorus', not in substance—both suggest the giving of good advice privately to friends (3. 3; 3. 6; 4. 3) and the setting of good examples (3. 6; 4. 6–7)—but in his gloomy presentation of them not as preferable or even equal alternatives to the life of civic duty, but as an impoverishment of that life.[2]

---

[1] Note the phrases 'nimis cito refugisse' (4. 1) contrasted with 'sensim relato gradu' (4. 1), 'non statim' (4. 2); 'nimis summisisse temporibus' *v.* 'aliquando cedendum salvis signis' (4. 1) and 'parcius se inferat officiis' (4. 2).

[2] André, *L'otium romain*, p. 48, points to Seneca's negative treatment here of the universal *res publica*, which receives such glorious praise in De Otio. In *Tranq.* 4. 3–4, Seneca seems to stress the original negative Cynic strain of the doctrine,

That view of them is dictated by the fact that he is showing how men embarked on political careers can be constant to their original aim, in all circumstances.

Although Seneca will not allow a man who has decided on political life to opt out completely and immediately because of bad political conditions, he does allow in this dialogue for an original decision of abstention from politics. One of the factors contributing to peace of mind is a correct choice of occupation,[1] for which we must consider our own nature, the nature of the occupation, and of those with whom we will be associated through it (6–7. 2). In the first category, certain retiring or contumacious or spontaneous temperaments are regarded as better suited to *quies* than *res civiles*, and men of certain talents are naturally fitted for *otiosum studium* and *contemplatio* rather than active life. Grounds for political abstention could also be found in the second category, in which *negotia* that generate more *negotia* and prevent us from leaving when we choose are condemned.[2]

Seneca's position in *De Tranquillitate Animi* is primarily that of the Middle Stoa, in particular, of Panaetius. But it contains no general treatment on Stoic lines of the problem of political participation: no general defence or prohibition of abstention in itself, no evaluation of the alternatives of *otium* and *res civiles* in the abstract.

---

arguing that we must not feel geographically limited to one state, that political activity in other regions is a possibility: the ideal of spiritual service to humanity as a whole is not mentioned. Pohlenz, *Philosophie und Erlebnis*, p. 90, remarks that *otium* here is the Roman conception, i.e. the opposite of a political career, not the βίος θεωρητικός of *De Otio* and *De Brevitate Vitae*.

[1] The parallel discussion in Plutarch's περὶ εὐθυμίας 471D–473F makes the connection with the title theme more explicit.

[2] The similarities of 6–7. 2 with Cicero's exposition in *Off.* 1. 71 ff. and 1. 110 ff. (on which see below, pp. 341 ff.), together with the resemblance to Plutarch περὶ εὐθυμίας 471D ff., point clearly to a Panaetian origin for these chapters. Cicero presents similar grounds for decision and allows for change of purpose if one finds oneself mistaken. Seneca does not mention this possibility here, but presumably his grounds for decision would serve as grounds for changing one's mind (allowed for in *Ep.* 23. 7–9).

De Otio

It is in this dialogue that we find this theoretical approach, but the incompleteness of the work at start and finish seriously hinders an analysis of its content. At the start there remains an exhortation in general terms to *otium*, which provides internal peace and the opportunity to choose a moral *exemplum* as a model for self-improvement. Similarities to *De Brevitate Vitae* and various letters are striking.[1] The advice, though general, may have been introduced by some question or even, as in *De Tranquillitate Animi*, by a lengthy statement from the addressee. But whereas, in that work, Serenus then silently accepts lengthy advice, drawn from Stoicism, for the *imperfecti*, here the addressee challenges Seneca to justify, as a Stoic, the choice of *otium* over the active life (1. 4–5). From then on, Seneca conducts the discussion as a Stoic theoretician concerned with the conduct of the *sapiens*, rather than as a practical moral teacher.

Seneca promises a twofold proof that, in advocating *otium*, he is not departing from Stoic principles: (1) that it is possible to justify total devotion from youth to the study of philosophy; (2) that one can, after years of service, rightly pass on one's duties to others. The fact that all trace of the second topic has vanished from the work as we have it means that we have nothing to compare directly with the debate between Seneca and Athenodorus in *De Tranquillitate Animi*, which concerns retirement from a political career started or intended, not an initial decision to abstain from politics. It is essential to state this at the outset, since it bears on the common view that, in *De Otio*, Seneca adopts the view of Athenodorus that he rejected in *De Tranquillitate Animi*.

What remains in our manuscripts is a lengthy but incomplete discussion of the first topic. Seneca's challenger has accused him of posing as a Stoic while retailing Epicurean views, on the ground that the Stoics are committed to action in the service of their fellow men until death. Seneca first replies that his

---

[1] For solitude as morally salutary cf., e.g., *Ep.* 7; for consultation of an internal moral exemplar or teacher cf. *Brev. Vit.* 14. 5; *Ep.* 7. 8; 11. 8–9; 25. 5–6; 95. 72; 104. 21; for dependence on external judgements and resulting inconstancy of purpose cf. *Brev. Vit.* 2. 1.

position is consistent, if not with the precepts, at least with the *actions* of the Stoic philosophers, none of whom entered politics.[1] But, he goes on to insist that he can show that neither his teaching nor their actions really conflict with Stoic doctrine (1. 4–2. 1).

To show that it is possible for a Stoic to choose *otium* from the start, Seneca pursues two lines of argument. He starts with the explicit Stoic teaching on the subject, noting that the precept of Zeno, 'accedet ad rem publicam, nisi si quid impedierit', differs from the Epicurean 'non accedet ad rem publicam sapiens, nisi si quid intervenerit' only in that it advocates the same thing by exception (*ex causa*) rather than on principle (*ex proposito*). In fact, argues Seneca, the Stoics accept *causae* so sweeping that they leave the door to *otium* wide open, and he goes on to give three of the traditional *causae*:[2] (1) if the *res publica* is too corrupt to be helped by the *sapiens*; (2) if the *sapiens* has too little influence or vigour and the state refuses his services; (3) if the *sapiens* through ill health is unsuited to a public career. The last two are, of course, in accord with Seneca's rules for choosing one's life-work in *De Tranquillitate Animi*.[3] The first *causa* seems to be behind Athenodorus' view in that work, that the wickedness of political life justifies the potential politician in opting out, a reason Seneca accepted as justifying gradual and partial withdrawal, but not total and immediate retirement.[4] Seneca returns to this first *causa* further on in *De Otio*.

Seneca's other line of argument is to show that *otium* accords with the most basic doctrines of Stoicism: 1. The Stoa lays down that a man must benefit his fellow men and serve the general interest: now, says Seneca, the man who cultivates virtue in *otium* benefits others in that he prepares himself morally to benefit them (3. 5). 2. The Stoa lays down that there are two *res publicae*, the lesser (one's particular country), and the greater (the whole world in which we are fellow citizens with all men and

---

[1] See p. 340.

[2] These grounds are implied in *Ep.* 68. 2: 'nec ad omnem rem publicam mittimus nec semper.'

[3] The second in 6. 2 (*verecundia*) and 6. 3 (*vires*). The third in 6. 2 ('alius infirmum corpus laborioso premit officio').

[4] *Tranq.* 3. 2; 5.

gods): now, says Seneca, some serve both, but some only one or the other, and we can certainly serve the greater *in otio*, by providing God, through our study of moral and natural philosophy, with a witness to his works (4).[1] 3. The Stoa lays down that the *summum bonum* is life according to nature: now, says Seneca, nature has given man the drive to learn new facts about nature and history, a position in the centre of the universe from which he can see it all, a physical structure which enables him to hold his head up to view the heavens, and a mind that naturally passes from consideration of the sensible to the truths beyond.[2] Finally, since nature has given us enormous intellectual ambitions and a limited life-span, to spend a lifetime in contemplating nature will be in accordance with nature (5). 4. The Stoa lays down that nature intended us for action and contemplation:[3] now, says Seneca, *contemplatio* itself includes action. Though there seems to be an allusion here to the Aristotelian doctrine of θεωρία as a form of εὐπραξία and hence πρᾶξίς τις,[4] Seneca mainly relies, in meeting the Stoic condemnation of contemplation unmixed with action, on less theoretical arguments. First he specifies that the *sapiens* will, if possible, test out the fruits of his moral studies (6. 3); then he shows the *sapiens* retiring with the intention of benefiting posterity (6. 4–5), giving as examples Zeno and Chrysippus who passed laws for all humanity instead of for one state and addressed not a few citizens, but all mankind, present and future. Finally, Seneca tries to reduce the whole dispute about the ultimate aim of life to a matter of words, saying that all the schools in fact advocate a mixture of aims with *contemplatio* included by all, and that even the Stoics do not admit *actio* alone, though *contemplatio* is for them an *accessio propositi*, not a *propositum* (7).

---

[1] In *Ep.* 68. 2 this doctrine leads to a similar argument—that we are not outside the greater commonwealth even when we withdraw from the lesser.

[2] Panaetius was the first Stoic to concede that pure knowledge was the object of a natural drive and formed a special sphere of *phronesis*, according to Pohlenz, *Die Stoa*², I, p. 202, and van Straaten, *Panétius*, p. 175, but, as Professor Brunt points out, Cicero, *Fin.* 3. 17; 37; 49, suggests that this is an exaggeration.

[3] Cf. *Ep.* 94. 45: 'in duas partes virtus dividitur, in contemplationem veri et actionem.' That was Panaetius' division (D.L. 7. 92; cf. Cicero, *Off.* 1. 15–17).

[4] 5. 8; Aristotle, *Pol.* 7. 3, 5 (1325ᵇ).

The last argument does not, of course, really help Seneca's proof that *contemplatio on its own* fulfils the basic principles of Stoicism.[1] It is clearly there because Seneca cannot resist bringing in one of his favourite themes: the trivial, purely verbal nature of many philosophical disagreements, particularly between Stoicism and Epicureanism.[2] Seneca has already touched on this theme in chapter 3 of this work where he showed that the pronouncements of the two schools on involvement in public affairs came virtually to the same thing.

The proportions of the extant fragment of *De Otio* show that Seneca prefers to draw inferences from Stoic first principles than to manipulate their explicit precepts about *otium*.[3] But in the final chapter (8), he returns to the *lex Chrysippi*: the *sapiens* will engage in public affairs, unless something prevents him. This chapter, as usually interpreted, provides the most solid basis for the view that Seneca in *De Otio* has changed his mind and accepted the arguments of Athenodorus that he rejected in *De Tranquillitate Animi*.[4] In chapters 3 and 6, Seneca indicated how the orthodox Stoic formula easily *allowed* for *otium* by tolerating

---

[1] André, *L'otium romain*, pp. 51, 59–60, 80, sees in this passage and in chapter 5. 8 proof that Seneca could not bring himself in *De Otio* to preach anything more extreme than a mixture of πρᾶξις and θεωρία. But the total argument of the dialogue, and the context of this passage, are against this.

[2] Similarly, in *Const. Sap.* 16. 3, *Vit. Beat.* 13. 1, he insists on the closeness of the two schools (cf. also *Clem.* 1. 3, 2). None the less, in *Ben.* 4. 2 Seneca argues that the disagreement of the two major schools on the *summum bonum* is not reducible to a mere matter of verbal expression. Seneca's familiarity with Epicurean thought goes back to his youth (R. Schottlaender, *Philologus* 99 (1955), 133 ff.); no development is traceable in Seneca's attitude to Epicureanism: it varies with the problem he is treating (Pohlenz, *Phil. und Erlebnis*, pp. 66–8).

[3] Note that, in this discussion of Zeno's and Chrysippus' abstention from public life, Seneca passes quickly over the justification by exception offered by his interlocutor, 'non fuit illis aut ea fortuna aut ea dignitas quae admitti ad publicarum rerum tractationem solet', preferring to stress the notion that their *quies* was more profitable to men than the activity of others (6. 5).

[4] 8. 3 is particularly stressed by Hense, *Seneca und Athenodorus*, p. 19. The general position, as illustrated by Waltz in his various works; E. de St. Denis, *RPh* 64 (1938), 214; R. Joly, *Le thème philosophique des genres de vie dans l'antiquité classique*, Brussels, 1956, p. 169; Hadot, *Seneca*, p. 141, is that Athenodorus in *De Tranquillitate Animi.* advocates political abstention which Seneca there rejects, but defends in *De Otio*.

a variety of excuses. Now he decides to go further and to show that the formula does not really rule out even a *free* choice of *otium*. The Stoics admit, he says, as an obstacle to public life the corruption of the state, or, putting it negatively, 'negant nostri sapientem ad quamlibet rem publicam accessurum.' But this restriction in practice obliterates the distinction between voluntary and enforced *otium* because no actual state is ever worthy of the *sapiens*. Thus *otium* becomes, in fact, a necessary choice, not merely a possible one, for a Stoic. Our loss of the rest of the work —perhaps as much as half of the original—makes it difficult to imagine how this argument proceeded. It is clear, however, that Seneca cannot simply have adopted the conclusion he extracted from Chrysippus' law as his own, for that would have made it impossible for him to proceed to the second topic announced in chapter 2, i.e. that one can, after years of service, legitimately choose *otium*, passing on 'ad alios actus'. If *otium* is *necessary* for a Stoic, how can any kind of public career or *actio*, whenever terminated, be justified? Moreover, Seneca had set out to prove, even under his first rubric, only that total abstention was possible, and though he suggested at some points in his argument that it might be preferable (4. 2; cf. 6. 4), that would not rule out completely the alternative preferred by his school.

In fact, even in presenting the argument from the low standard of actual states, Seneca indicates his reservations about this Athenodorean approach, for he says that a *res publica* for the *sapiens* 'semper deerit fastidiose quaerentibus' (8. 1). *Fastidiosus* in Seneca often signifies 'arrogantly' or 'fussily'.[1] His use of it here shows that he disliked this particular Stoic *causa*, just as he had in *De Tranquillitate Animi*. But here, he goes further and suggests that the real trouble lies not so much with the *causa* as with the whole orthodox Stoic position on political participation that lies open to this paradoxical interpretation. The Stoic doctrine is, in fact, self-contradictory: 'If someone says that the best life is to

---

[1] Particularly, *Tranq.* 7. 6: 'nunc vero in tanta bonorum egestate minus fastidiosa fiat electio'; cf. *Epp.* 44. 2; 47. 17; 70. 20; 73. 15; also *fastidium* in 24. 26; 66. 25. Pohlenz, *Phil. und Erlebnis*, p. 86, noted the pejorative significance of *fastidiose* and denied that Seneca meant to favour total rejection of political life, but did not see what the point of the argument was.

sail the sea, then says that I must not sail upon a sea where ship-
wrecks commonly occur and there are often sudden storms that
sweep the helmsman in a contrary direction, I conclude that this
man, while he praises sailing, forbids me to weigh anchor.' This
is not the only time that Seneca ridicules an argument of Chrysippus. In *De Matrimonio* he points out that another of his arguments
is self-defeating: 'Chrysippus says that the *sapiens* should take a
wife so as not to offend Jupiter Gamelius and Genethlius—
ludicrously, for it follows that there should be no marriages
among the Latins who have no Jupiter Nuptialis. If, as he thinks,
the names of the gods imply judgements on the life of men, then
the man who sits down offends Jupiter Stator.'[1] In *De Otio*
Seneca appears to be less explicit, although we cannot be sure
that he did not go on to make his criticism more definite. But
since he is primarily concerned to show that his own teaching
does not conflict with the orthodox doctrine, it is more likely
that he went on to say that, if Chrysippus' law could be interpreted as an injunction to *otium*, then, *a fortiori*, it must be all
right for a Stoic to choose *otium* in appropriate circumstances.
From there the transition to his second topic would be easy.

The differences in attitude between *De Tranquillitate Animi* and
De Otio need not in effect be construed as contradiction. If, in the
former, we do not find the positive view of the virtues of *otium*
that marks the latter, neither do we find a condemnation of
initial and complete abstention, nor a recommendation to enter
political life on general Stoic principles.[2] In fact, abstention is
allowed for, given certain *causae*.[3] If, in *De Otio*, Seneca prefers
more general arguments for abstention, the only *causa* that (as
far as we can tell) he directly rejects is that rejected in *De Tranquillitate Animi*, i.e. the condition that the state be worthy of
the *sapiens*. In the missing part of *De Otio*, Seneca may well
have justified complete retirement after public service;[4] in *De*

---

[1] Haase frag. XIII (46) = E. Bickel, *Diatribe in Senecae philosophi fragmenta I.
Fragmenta de matrimonio*, Leipzig, 1915, fr. 2; discussed there on pp. 353 ff.

[2] The elements of such a recommendation are in Cicero, *Rep.* 1. 1–3.

[3] *Tranq.* 6.

[4] Seneca compares the retired public servant to the Vestal Virgins (2. 2) who
turn in old age from active *officia* to teaching (*ad alios actus*). How did he develop

Tranquillitate Animi, a complete change of purpose is condemned, but only the case of the man bullied by circumstances, political danger, or the condition of the state, is considered. Even normal old-age retirement—the case of Paulinus—is omitted. The differences between the two works can all be ascribed to the difference in theme. *De Tranquillitate Animi* offers practical advice on achieving peace of mind for the morally imperfect: hence, as concerns political participation, it concentrates on individual choices of occupation and frustrated purposes. *De Otio*, however, is a theoretical discussion of the proper Stoic line on political participation, in terms of the *sapiens*.

Letters to Lucilius

The *Epistulae Morales* present far more complex problems of analysis than those encountered so far. In them we find, on the theme of *otium*, all the types of approach, all the motifs of the three works we have been discussing. The satirical exaggeration of *De Brevitate Vitae* predominates in Letter 55; the personal therapy of *De Tranquillitate Animi* in 19 and 22; the theoretical exposition of *De Otio* in 68. Though writer and recipient are presented as *proficientes*,[1] the psychology and conduct of the total *imperfectus* and of the *sapiens* are fully treated as well. The result is such a wealth of advice on the subject that it is difficult, if not impossible, to give an account of Seneca's views which, while remaining faithful, would produce a consistent and coherent system.

The call to *otium* in the Letters, though accompanied by conditions, cautions, and justifications, is a categorical imperative.[2]

---

the parallel? He could, like Plutarch (*An seni resp. ger. sit* 795E) have argued that an old man should continue his activities, but in the form of giving advice (as in Cicero, *Off.* 1. 123), or he might have taken the Vestal teaching as a kind of *contemplatio in otio*, conceiving *contemplatio* (as in chapters 5–6) as a kind of *actio*. See p. 336 n. 2.

[1] e.g. 27. 1; 75. 15; 52. 7; 44 (Lucilius); 87. 4–5 (Seneca).

[2] As noted by André, *L'otium romain*, p. 59. But note the curious incidental criticism of Epicureanism in 90. 35: 'non de ea philosophia loquor quae civem extra patriam posuit . . .'

The *sapiens*, or near-sage, we are told, will, if possible, choose *quies*[1] in which he will develop his moral excellence (73. 4), contemplate nature (68. 2; 78. 26), and, by moral teaching (8. 1–2, 6; 14. 14), serve the larger *res publica* (120. 12). He scorns electoral contests and all other competitions for the goods of fortune (98. 13; 118. 3). None the less, if he is enmeshed in *occupationes* or *officia civilia*, he still will not be distracted from philosophizing (56. 11–14; 62; 72. 4; 104. 7), and—it is implied in one letter (118. 11)—can even raise public functions from the level of *indifferentia* to that of *bona* since his exercise of virtue in them makes them 'honeste administrata'.

At the other end of the scale, the total *imperfectus* never finds *tranquillitas*. The only *otium* he knows is a living death (82. 2–4), a shameful devotion to the lower pleasures. His ambitions, though unfulfilled, are still ardent: his retirement is merely a retreat in the face of frustration (55. 5; 56. 6–10, 13 ff.). But active life for him is also terrible, as he is constantly driven by insatiable desires, ambitions, and fears (73. 2–3; 82. 3; 94. 73–4; 104. 9). Outside philosophy there is no salvation.

For the all-important[2] men in-between on the moral scale, *imperfecti* but *proficientes*, the picture is far more complicated. Lucilius, the elderly procurator, is of course the central case considered, but Seneca does indicate that the man starting out in life should choose *otium* from the start (28. 6–8; 36) and devote it to *liberalia studia* and the cultivation of moral perfection. Those who are involved in public life should cut down their *occupationes* as much as possible and avoid assuming any new ones—in order to study philosophy (7. 8 'quantum potes'; 72. 3, 11). Seneca is clearly concentrating here on the value of solitude

---

[1] 28. 6–7. Note that Seneca here discounts the noble picture of Socrates retaining his freedom in the midst of the Thirty Tyrants, a picture he used, in *Tranq.* and *Otio*, to show the value of any appearance of the *sapiens* in an evil state. Here Seneca regards only the psychological freedom of the *sapiens*, not its public demonstration, as valuable.

[2] The doctrine of moral progress, important for Stoicism from the start, receives great prominence in Seneca with his interest in practical advice and personal therapy. Panaetius (Seneca, *Ep.* 116. 5) had already, in teaching, adopted the attitude of one *imperfectus* advising another. Seneca devotes considerable space to the different grades of *proficientes* in *Ep.* 72 and 75.

and study in itself rather than on justifications for choosing *otium*.

There is, in fact, little discussion, considering the prominence of the *otium* theme, of the theory of political participation. Letter 14 is typical: Seneca, in giving advice about avoiding danger from the powerful, recommends an unostentatious, unprovocative devotion to philosophy and finds himself challenged by the counter-example of Cato; he ends by postponing the general question 'an sapienti opera rei publicae danda sit'[1] and considering those Stoics actually excluded from public life. In urging Lucilius to retire, Seneca sometimes speaks as if no special reasons need be produced—the value of *otium* is enough, but elsewhere, in assuring Lucilius that Stoic doctrine provides no obstacle to his withdrawal, Seneca briefly applies to this case some of the arguments used, in *De Otio*,[2] to justify political abstention from the start: that philosophical *otium* can benefit one's fellow men more than political activity (8); that the *sapiens* is never more active than when he is outside his particular *res publica* but surveying the greater commonwealth (68. 1–2); that Stoicism allows for *exceptiones* to its traditional prescription of political participation, 'nec ad omnem rem publicam mittimus nec semper nec sine ullo fine' (68. 2). We have seen that the first exception cited here was discouraged in *De Tranquillitate Animi* and *De Otio*. But this passage is not enough to prove that Seneca changed his mind, as he offers no criticism or support of the Stoic view cited and goes on instead to stress the argument from the greater *res publica*. And it is significant that, in Letter 14, Seneca avoids committing himself to the notion that the wickedness of the state can justify political abstention for the *sapiens*.[3]

There is a longer discussion in Letter 22 of the role of these *causae* in modifying the Stoic insistence on *constantia*:

dicentur tibi ista [turpe est cedere oneri], si operae pretium habebit perseverantia, si nihil indignum bono viro faciendum patiendumve

---

[1] If Madvig's emendation of the corrupt manuscript reading is correct.

[2] This makes it likely that these arguments were applied by Seneca in *De Otio* to the case of retirement as well.

[3] *CQ* 18 (1968), 373–5.

erit; alioqui sordido se et contumelioso labore non conteret nec in negotiis erit negotii causa. Ne illud quidem quod existimas facturum eum faciet, ut ambitiosis rebus implicitus semper aestus earum ferat; sed cum viderit gravia in quibus volutatur, incerta, ancipitia, referet pedem, non vertet terga, sed sensim recedet in tutum. (22. 8.)

These are reminiscent of the arguments used by Athenodorus in *De Tranquillitate Animi* to justify retreat from politics, but Seneca has here stated them in a form that meets the principal objection he raised against Athenodorus: that one must not immediately surrender to circumstances.[1] Here as there, Seneca allows for retreat if it is gradual, and accepts safety as a legitimate reason for it. None the less, Seneca's preoccupations in the Letter are importantly different from those in the section of *De Tranquillitate Animi* just mentioned: here he is not considering the general problem of political activity in adverse conditions, but the specific 'occupationes speciosae et malae' in which Lucilius is embroiled: some of the grounds for withdrawal in this letter in fact are more reminiscent of the grounds for abstention from specific *negotia* offered in that dialogue.[2]

This brings us back to the strain in the Letters that is contrary in spirit to *De Tranquillitate Animi*: Seneca's tendency in some letters to represent *all* political offices as 'speciosa' (98. 13; 118. 3 ff.) and to regard the futility of Lucilius' burdens as *typical* of public life (68. 10–11). Throughout the Letters, in fact, there is tension between the idea that Lucilius should retire simply because of the higher value of *otium* (and the low value of public duties)— the spirit of *De Brevitate Vitae*—and the notion that his special circumstances warrant withdrawal—the spirit of *De Tranquillitate Animi*. In the latter category, we have the portrait of Lucilius as a man who has not rationally chosen his occupation[3] but has

[1] Note the word *sensim* here and in *Tranq.* 4. 1.

[2] (a) 'nihil indignum', cf. *Tranq.* 7. 1: 'hominum utique dilectus habendus est, an digni sint quibus partem vitae nostrae impendamus.'

(b) 'si operae pretium', cf. *Tranq.* 6. 4: 'relinquenda quae latius actu procedunt nec ubi proposueris desinunt' (also 12. 1; *Otio* 3. 3 'non nitet sapiens in supervacuum').

[3] 22. 4: 'impedire te noli; contentus esto negotiis in quae descendisti, vel, quod videri mavis, *incidisti*.'

been lured into it and retained there by ambition and cupidity;[1] his procuratorship in Sicily is the type of job that leads to greater *officia* and never releases its victim;[2] Lucilius is an old man who must hurry if he is to enjoy some real life before death.[3] To the former category belong the pictured delights of *otium*: Lucilius should never have left the obscurity from which he rose (19. 5); only in retirement will he enjoy true friendship (19. 12), achieve moral health (e.g. 37. 4; 53. 9; 94. 69), avoid the most fearful physical dangers 'quae per vim potentioris eveniunt' (14. 3, 7–11). This last—the theme of security, briefly touched on in *De Brevitate Vitae* 15. 1 and in *De Tranquillitate Animi* (4. 3; 6. 2; 12. 7)— becomes very important in the Letters.

Despite a similar enthusiasm for *otium*, the Letters are furthest from the theoretical dialogue *De Otio*, for, in writing to Lucilius, Seneca seems far less interested in the justification of retirement than in the way to achieve and use it. He urges Lucilius to retire at all costs (1; 19. 1; 32. 3; 68. 12), but recommends a gradual change (22) as required by Stoic *constantia*. The first step is to avoid new commitments and to make a firm, rational decision, overcoming one's ambitions and desires for the superficial advantages of power and wealth (22. 9–12). This is only possible through a prior acquaintance with philosophy (37. 3–5); a simple flight from men and affairs, because of the frustration of one's desires, will not bring *tranquillitas animi* (55. 5 ff.; 56. 9–11).[4] Finally, one should retire unostentatiously, to the point of offering excuses of ill health and laziness rather than admitting a deliberate preference for philosophy and peace (68. 1, 3–4).

The retirement itself must be spent on philosophy—moral improvement and the study of nature (53. 9; 68. 8; 78. 26; 82. 3, 5–6); it must be unobtrusive—neither vaunted nor elaborately concealed (19. 2; 68. 5). A moral reason is given for this caution—to boast of retirement is 'iners ambitio' (68. 3)—but more stress is laid on reasons of prudence: one does not want to

---

[1] 19. 6; 21. 1; 22. 9–12. In *Tranq.* 1. 10 Serenus cites the proper Stoic reason for entering public life 'ut amicis propinquis et omnibus civibus, omnibus deinde mortalibus paratior utiliorque sim'.

[2] 19. 5–6; 20. 1. Compare the condemnation of such *negotia* in *Tranq.* 6. 4.

[3] 1; 19. 1; 32. 3; 68. 12.   [4] Cf. *Tranq.* 2. 7–9.

incur the *odium* or *invidia* of anyone (19. 2, 4); it is dangerous to practise philosophy contumaciously, turning our virtue into a reproach of others' vices (103. 5). Seneca seems to have in mind general public hostility, but also the resentment of the government (14. 10–11, 14); he refers to those Stoics who, excluded from public life, retired to instruct mankind 'sine ulla potentioris offensa', and notes that the *sapiens* will be inconspicuous (14. 14); the natural attitude, he says, of the devotee of philosophy to the government is gratitude (73). In this kind of retirement, a man continues to fulfil his private duties to his fellow men (93. 4),[1] and bestows great benefits on mankind generally (8; 68. 10; 120. 12).

What has emerged from this analysis of Seneca's views on political participation is the fact that no clear development can be traced. If Seneca's views are not all easily reconcilable, neither do the conflicting elements fall neatly into different works so as to show a clear development. The Letters, written at the end of his career, combine strong unqualified indictments of public life with recommendations to *otium* qualified as to grounds, pace, and manner. At no point does Seneca's enthusiasm for philosophy and leisure blind him to the contrary claims of public life. In fact, years before any of these crucial works were written, when Seneca was living in the enforced *otium* of exile, he consoled his mother with a picture of his two brothers as embodiments of the different virtues of the βίος πρακτικός and the βίος θεωρητικός: 'alter honores industria consecutus est, alter sapienter contempsit. adquiesce alterius fili dignitate, alterius quiete, utriusque pietate! . . . alter in hoc dignitatem excolit, ut tibi ornamento sit, alter in hoc se ad tranquillam quietamque vitam recepit, ut tibi vacet . . . potes alterius dignitate defendi, alterius otio frui' (*Cons. Helv.* 18. 2).

II

How do Seneca's views compare with those of his Stoic mentors and Roman contemporaries?

[1] Seneca does not make clear how Metronax the philosopher actually fulfilled the 'officia boni civis'.

The Stoa had evaded the traditional choice between the βίος θεωρητικός and the βίος πρακτικός, by advocating a βίος λογικός combining θεωρία and πρᾶξις.[1] But the emphasis was on πρᾶξις and the βίος πολιτικός was held to satisfy the ideal.[2] In the popular imagination, Stoicism stood for participation in politics.[3] But the Stoic position, as indeed that of other philosophical schools,[4] had never been unequivocal on this question. The fact that none of the masters of the Old Stoa had followed their own precepts was, in Seneca's day, a commonplace, providing the occasion for ridicule[5] or complex explanation.[6] More important was the ambiguity of the precepts themselves. Plutarch's account in De Stoicorum Repugnantiis shows how, with a little malice, one could convict the founders of the Stoa, particularly Chrysippus, of innumerable inconsistencies: in the same work, Chrysippus condemned the σχολαστικὸς βίος for philosophers, recommending, instead, life as a ruler or attached to one,[7] but also said that the φρόνιμος would be ἀπράγμων καὶ ὀλιγοπράγμων.[8] Even without malice, it is easy to see that the doctrines of the natural association and mutual service of man could be undermined by Stoic insistence on the pursuit of virtue, from which it followed that participation in a state that is good or making moral progress is preferable and participation in a hopelessly corrupt one unjustified.[9] There was the further difficulty that in imperfect states the wise

[1] D.L. 7. 130 = SVF 3. 687; D.L. 7. 92 (Panaetius), cf. Cicero, Off. 1. 15–17; Seneca, Ep. 94. 45. See Joly, op. cit., pp. 143–7.

[2] SVF 3. 695–7; cf. 622–3.

[3] Ep. 90. 35 gives Seneca's own characterizations of Epicureanism and Stoicism: cf. Horace, Ep. 1. 1, 16–17; Epictetus 3. 7, 21–3; Dio Chrys. 47. 2, and the teaching of Euphrates, a pupil of the Stoic Musonius (Fronto, Ep. 1. 1), in Pliny, Ep. 1. 10, 10.

[4] For a summary of their views see de St. Denis, RPh 64 (1938), 195–204; Joly, op. cit., pp. 143–7.

[5] As in Plutarch, De Stoicorum Repugnantiis 1033B–E. Seneca alludes to their inconsistency in Tranq. 1. 10; Otio 1. 5; Ep. 68. 1.

[6] Otio 6. 5 preserves one justification on Stoic lines. Dio Chrys. 47. 2 gives them a motive appropriate to his own circumstances.

[7] SVF 3. 691; 702.

[8] SVF 3. 703. Perhaps Chrysippus meant what Seneca says Democritus meant: 'ad supervacua scilicet referentem' (Tranq. 13. 1).

[9] SVF 3. 611; Otio 3. 3; 8. 1—the emphasis on the overriding importance of virtue also encouraged indifference to worldly concerns.

man's exclusive competence to rule would not be accepted.[1] The result was a conditional prescription: 'accedet ad rem publicam [sapiens], nisi si quid impedierit.'[2]

With the Middle Stoa, the idea that justice meant not merely the avoidance of *iniuriae* but positive service to human society bolstered the view of political participation as an ideal.[3] But the more practical outlook of a man like Panaetius made the doctrine even more flexible than before. There was more emphasis on the difficulty of determining what actually followed, in particular cases, from these general precepts,[4] and on the importance of our individual natures (as well as general human nature) in determining our duties.

In *De Officiis* 1. 107 ff. we have a development of this latter theme, certainly derived from Panaetius, which shows how it could be used to turn the conditional Stoic recommendations of political life into a recommendation to *otium ex causa*.[5] According to this doctrine, each man has four *personae*: two are furnished by nature. They are the *universa natura* we share with all men, and the *propria natura*—our physical condition, talents, and personality traits. The third *persona*—our social position and material resources—is furnished by fortune. The fourth is the role in life we choose on the basis of these, properly more on the basis of nature than of fortune.[6] Once we have decided on the way of

[1] SVF 3. 694; Otio 3. 3.   [2] Otio 3. 2; D.L. 7. 121.

[3] Cicero, *Off.* 1. 28–9. For Panaetius as the principal source of *De Officiis* see above, p. 180 n. 2.

[4] Cicero discusses this theme as regards the duties imposed by justice, particularly promises, at *Off.* 1. 31 ff.; in 1. 142–4, the notion of εὐκαιρία is related to τὸ πρέπον.

[5] Seneca makes this point in *De Otio* 3. 3 ff.

[6] Brunt, *Proc. Camb. Phil. Soc.* 19 (1973), 20–1; 24–5, points out that the early Stoics had defended the *pars praeceptiva* of philosophy 'quae dat propria cuique personae praecepta'. Traces certainly survive of an analysis of *officia* based on *tempora, loca, personae* (Seneca, *Ep.* 94. 35), the *personae* being the roles of men in society which carry obligations to others, e.g. husband, father, brother, child, pupil, friend, citizen, farmer, master (Seneca, *Ep.* 94. 1, 3, 10, 14–15; Marcus Aurelius, 5. 31; cf. also Seneca, *Ben.* 3. 18; 21–22; 28. 1 (*persona*)). But there is no sign that this kind of analysis in terms of *personae* took account of individual talents or choices which constituted Panaetius' second and fourth *personae*. Furthermore, the old analysis seems to have been particularly connected with the virtue of *iustitia* rather than with *temperantia* as in Panaetius (note in *Ep.* 94. 11: 'quia

life that suits us, we must pursue it with *constantia* unless we realize that we have erred in our choice. In that case, we can change, preferably when circumstances are propitious; otherwise, very gradually. Once we change, our behaviour must show that our decision was right. It is hardly necessary to point out how much Seneca's treatment of the problem owes to these ideas. In *De Tranquillitate Animi*, the sixth chapter on how to choose *negotia* is clearly an application of this doctrine: of the factors to be considered, eloquence,[1] health,[2] *verecundia* and *contumacia*, *ingenium*[3] all belong to the second *persona*; *patrimonium*[4] to the third. As in Cicero's discussion, outstanding talent for philosophy justifies opting out of politics. The temperamental qualities given by Seneca as disqualifications—*contumacia*, *indignatio*, and imprudent uncontrolled *urbanitas*—may be his additions to the doctrine as they are principally relevant to political life at court.[5] But there are indications that Seneca's recommendation to avoid *negotia* that increase of themselves and prove ineluctable belongs to recognized Stoic teaching.[6]

iustum est'; cf. *Off.* 1. 41 on 'adversus infimos iustitia'). Some attempt by Panaetius to incorporate the older distinctions into his analysis of the *officia* pertinent to *decorum* may lie behind the curious transition at *Off.* 1. 122 from the four *personae* which concern one's whole life to precepts relevant to certain portions of our lives: the social roles of *magistratus*, *privatus*, *civis*, *peregrinus* in 1. 124–5 seem to be the old *personae*. A further sign of imperfect cohesion is the difficult sentence in 1. 125: 'Ita fere officia reperientur, cum quaeretur quid deceat et quid aptum sit personis, temporibus, aetatibus.' According to the analysis of L. Labowsky, *Die Ethik des Panaitios*, Leipzig, 1934, pp. 51–2, the term *personae* is here restricted to the four *personae* of 1. 107–21 and *tempora* is used for these social roles, which have some connection with Panaetius' third *persona*. But it may be that 'quid deceat' refers to 107–21, while 'quid aptum sit personis, temporibus, aetatibus' is an allusion to the old classification treated briefly in 122–5.

  [1] Compare *Off.* 1. 121.
  [2] Compare ibid. 1. 71, 121; see also *Otio* 3. 4.
  [3] Compare *Off.* 1. 71.
  [4] Ibid. 1. 73: 'ad rem gerendam autem qui accedet, caveat . . . ut habeat efficiendi facultatem.' The *causa* in *Otio* 3, 3, 'si parum habebit auctoritatis aut virium nec illum erit admissura res publica', clearly also belongs to the third.
  [5] Of *urbanitas*, Cicero is Seneca's prime example (*Const. Sap.* 17. 3), but it was not a generally dangerous quality to be regarded as a disqualification for public life under the Republic.
  [6] *Ep.* 68. 2 in which Seneca summarizes Stoic doctrine: 'nec ad omnem rem publicam mittimus nec semper nec *sine ullo fine*.'

Given all these possible exceptions to the rule of political participation, Stoics could not only justify *certain cases* of abstention or withdrawal,[1] but, by arguing that some of the conditions in fact were always present, advocate *otium in general*. The conditions that lent themselves to this treatment were those concerning political circumstances: the character of the state, the worthiness of the men one would work with and serve. Not everyone accepted these *causae*. We find Cicero in *De Officiis* i. 71, whether on his own or following Panaetius,[2] condemning those who abstain from politics on the grounds that *imperia* and *magistratus* are unworthy of them, for showing insufficient *constantia*: 'videntur labores et molestias, tum offensionum et repulsarum quasi quandam ignominiam timere et infamiam.' Cicero's insistence on giving the facts of nature priority over those of fortune in determining one's work leads to further condemnation of this attitude.[3] Similarly, Seneca set out to counter Athenodorus, a Stoic who argued for retreat from politics on the grounds of the evils of political life. In *De Tranquillitate Animi* he insists that even though one must sometimes yield to unpropitious political conditions, one must not retreat easily nor utterly desert the *res publica* even if it is vicious.

In advocating retreat generally, Athenodorus approached,

---

[1] Epictetus, who discusses the doctrine of *personae* in 1. 2 (the dignity inherent in the second and fourth in Panaetius' scheme) and 3. 23, 4 (first and fourth), uses it in this way in 3. 22 where he argues that the man who has the natural gifts for being a Cynic preacher should abstain from politics so as to fulfil his mission.

[2] Pohlenz, *Antikes Führertum*, pp. 46–7, thought Cicero was true to Panaetius' view in 1. 71–2 and that Panaetius' ideal was political leadership (pp. 140–3). Rist, *Stoic Philosophy*, pp. 193, 200, thinks that Cicero in *Off.* 1. 152–60 (definitely not derived from Panaetius, cf. 1. 10), where he sets one's duties to society firmly above pure knowledge, contradicts the view of Panaetius who did not make the comparison and would have thought the active life superior to the contemplative only under certain conditions. But it is difficult to isolate non-Panaetian elements in 1. 71–2 (see citation below): Panaetius after all belonged to the Rhodian governing class and served on one occasion as ἱεροποιός at Athens organizing a festival (Strabo 14. 655; IG 2. 2. 953); van Straaten, *Panétius*, p. 207 n. 2, notes the problem.

[3] *Off.* 1. 120. Note also 1. 72: 'Sed iis qui habent a natura adiumenta rerum gerendarum, abiecta omni cunctatione, adipiscendi magistratus et gerenda res publica est.'

through the back door, the position of the Epicureans.[1] The Stoic doctrine of *causae* paved the way, for as Seneca pointed out in *De Otio*, the clause 'nisi si quid impedierit' allowed Stoicism to be applied to the same effect as the Epicurean 'non accedet ad rem publicam sapiens, nisi si quid intervenerit'. In making this point, Seneca showed the weakness of the traditional Stoic mode of dealing with political participation, and went on to ridicule, in particular, the exception based on the viciousness of the state, saying that, since all states would be examined by standards by which they would fail, this was in effect to order and forbid political life simultaneously (*De Otio* 8). Seneca shows himself, in the two dialogues and the Letters, willing to apply many of the Stoic exceptions, but he makes it clear that he dislikes that based on the unsatisfactory conditions of states. In this he may have followed Panaetius (or Cicero's adaptation of Panaetius), but he went further in advocating a straightforward justification of *otium* such as the basic principles of Stoicism, in his view, allowed.

As for the standard Roman attitude, Cicero's elaborate explanations and self-justifications alone make it clear that, in his day, politics was regarded as the most honourable way of life, and retirement before old age badly in need of defence for a senator.[2] Though Cicero's language often betrays a willingness to accept in his own case those reasons for voluntary political withdrawal that he continued to the end to condemn,[3] his official account of his retirement after Caesar's victory was that it was forced upon him.[4] The same attitude was still common in Seneca's day and after,[5] but there had been modifications: Sallust had described his

---

[1] As Cicero states it in *Rep.* I. 4–10.

[2] e.g. *Brutus* 7–8; *Off.* 2. 2 ff.; 3. 1–3. Cf. Sallust, *BJ* 4. 3.

[3] Cf. *Rep.* I. 9 with *Off.* 3. 2: 'extincto enim senatu deletisque iudiciis quid est quod dignum nobis aut in curia aut in foro agere possimus?'

[4] *Off.* 2. 2; 3. 3 where the emphasis on *necessitas* shows, contrary to the view of de St. Denis (*RPh* 64 (1938), 195 ff.), that Cicero in *De Officiis* did not simply abandon, because of his own political position, the views of *De Re Publica*. Cf. also *Off.* I. 71 and I. 153, on which see above, p. 343 n. 2.

[5] *Ep.* 36; Epictetus 3. 7, 21; Quintilian 11. 1, 35; 12. 2, 7 attacking with vehemence those who desert politics and rhetoric for philosophy: this work was published under Domitian and could reflect that Emperor's concern with the problem of political abstention (cf. Dio on Herennius Senecio, 67. 13, 2).

political retirement as voluntary, justified by the corruption of contemporary political life,[1] and he and Cicero had shown the way to a Roman defence of *otium* by arguing that history and philosophy were useful to their fellow citizens.[2]

For the end of the Republic saw an increase of political apathy. Under the dictatorship of Caesar, we find not only a reluctance to serve in worthies of the old regime, but an ultimately more important phenomenon: the philosopher Sextius was offered a place in the Senate by Caesar and refused it, either because he preferred leisure to pursue philosophy, or for the philosophical reason that he despised the gifts of fortune.[3] The danger or tedium of senatorial life under the Empire led senators' sons to flee their heritage,[4] and others to avoid elevation to senatorial rank:[5] *studia* and *quies* became a cultural ideal.[6] Seneca's own late début in politics, as we have seen, is probably best explained along these lines. His brother Mela stuck to his decision not to enter the Senate, though, according to the hostile Tacitus, his zeal for philosophy was mixed with enthusiasm for the wealth to be gained through equestrian procuratorships and the power that personal influence could achieve.[7]

With the end of the Republic, decision and justification became more pressing as the emperors sought to create and maintain a hereditary senatorial class, rescuing worthy impoverished

[1] *BJ* 3. 5; 4. 3–4.

[2] *Tusc. Disp.* 1. 5; *Nat. Deor.* 1. 7; *Off.* 2. 5; Sallust, *BJ* 4.

[3] See above, p. 38 n. 2.

[4] Dio 54. 26, 3 ff. shows apathy among descendants of senators under Augustus. Suet. *Aug.* 38. 2 (if 'mallent' is read) could be a reference to the same problem. Cornelius Fuscus, though of senatorial family, preferred the equestrian posts (*Hist.* 2. 86), and Trebellius Rufus seems to have preferred a peaceful life in Athens (Appendix D2).

[5] Ovid is here the prize example (*Tristia* 4. 10, 28 ff.). Lack of enthusiasm for a senatorial career is implied in Augustus' ruling in 12 B.C. (Dio 54. 3, 2) giving knights, drafted as tribunes, the option of returning to the *equester ordo*. Later examples include Minicius Macrinus (Pliny, *Ep.* 1. 14, 5), Arrianus Maturus (Pliny, *Ep.* 2. 11, 1; 3. 2), Terentius Junior (*Ep.* 7. 25, 2).

[6] See A. Grilli, *Il problema della Vita Contemplativa nel mondo greco-romano*, Milan, 1953, pp. 212 ff.

[7] *Ann.* 16. 17. Tacitus takes the same cynical view of Maecenas and C. Sallustius Crispus (*Ann.* 3. 30).

senatorial families and combating apathy in the young *laticlavii*.[1]
Nor were those *equites* who had no wish for a senatorial career
exempt from pressure as under the Republic: apart from the
onerous jury-duties for which it was difficult to find enthusiasts,[2]
the *latus clavus* might be offered.[3]

Seneca's enthusiasm for philosophical *otium* and his concern
with conditions and justifications are in harmony with the
thoughts of his contemporaries, Roman and Stoic. It remains to
be seen if his works on the subject can be more precisely related
to circumstances at the time of their composition.

III

The most obvious way to relate a literary work to the period of
its composition is to find in it reflections of the contemporary
circumstances of its author or the addressee. It has already been
argued that *De Brevitate Vitae* has such a connection with both,
though probably not in the primary sense of giving real advice
or reflecting the author's deliberations about his own case.[4] But
just this kind of direct relevance is customarily claimed for *De
Tranquillitate Animi*, *De Otio*, and the *Epistulae Morales*: are these
claims legitimate?

There are works of Seneca that were undeniably composed to
suit the situation of the addressee:[5] the Consolations and *De
Clementia* are clear examples. Should we not add the Letters to
Lucilius and *De Tranquillitate Animi* where Seneca openly assumes
the role of moral teacher?[6]

---

[1] In 13 B.C. Augustus forced young *senatorii* to assume senatorial rank and
obligations, though he excused the older hardened abstainers (Dio 54. 26, 3;
cf. above, p. 345 n. 4).

[2] Suet. *Aug.* 32. 2; Pliny, *NH* 33. 33. Cf. Nero's concern about equestrian
segnitia in Tacitus, *Ann.* 16. 27.

[3] Claudius punished *equites* who refused senatorial rank by removing equestrian rank as well (Suet. *Claudius* 24).

[4] Above, pp. 319–20.

[5] As persuasively argued by Dahlmann, *Gnomon* 13 (1937), 373–4; 379.

[6] *Ep.* 20. 1; 22. 1–3; 34. 1; *Tranq.* 2. 4–5. Note Seneca's view in *Ep.* 89. 13
that the *sapiens* is 'generis humani paedagogus'—Tacitus makes Agrippina ridicule
that idea by attacking Seneca and Burrus 'generis humani regimen expostulantes'
(*Ann.* 13. 14, 3); cf. *Ep.* 123. 11 for general ridicule of this type.

As for the Letters, the idea that the addressee's circumstances have inspired and shaped Seneca's precepts about political retirement gains substance from the fact that the portrait of Lucilius in the Letters is quite detailed. We are told of his origins, his earlier equestrian posts, his literary activities, his current procuratorship in Sicily, and his prospective *urbana officia*.[1] Seneca's exhortations to literary and philosophical *otium* are persistent and precise. Do they constitute a real exhortation to a real retirement?

In trying to trace Lucilius' circumstances through the Letters, two sources of uncertainty must be noted at the outset. One is that the 'you' and the 'I' of the Letters cannot always be assumed to be biographical:[2] the other is that, given Seneca's deliberate redefinitions of words like *otium*, *occupatio*, and *negotium*, it is often difficult to know just which meaning is intended.[3]

Blurred by these uncertainties, the following story seems to emerge: in the early Letters, as in the Natural Questions, Seneca is urging Lucilius to avoid the crowd and seek spiritual mentors as company,[4] but he envisages Lucilius' devotion to philosophy as compatible with his procuratorial duties in Sicily, if they are kept within proper limits.[5] But in Letters 19–21, Lucilius is urged to extricate himself from his procuratorship altogether. As opposed to the picture in the Natural Questions,[6] Seneca here describes Lucilius as corrupted by his success into desiring the material

[1] See above, pp. 91, 94. *NQ* 4, pref. 1, mentions the Sicilian procuratorship as well and belongs to the same period (62–4).

[2] For an example in *Ben.* see Appendix D8, n. 3; for examples in *Brev. Vit.* see Abel, *Gym.* 72 (1965), 317; in other dialogues and the Letters, see above, p. 277. In *Ep.* 53. 9, 68. 10–11, 88. 41, 104. 9, the occupations and worries mentioned show a general 'you' is meant. These naturally make the reader wonder about less obvious passages.

[3] e.g. 75. 16; in the context (cf. 'praeoccupati sumus') *occupationes* may be vices, not outside activities; in 56 real *quies* and *tranquillitas* are internal; in 49. 8 *otiosus* has the conventional sense of idleness, but in 73 and 82. 2 *otium* is time devoted to philosophy. Seneca changes from the conventional to the special sense in the course of a letter: note *otium* of 55. 3 *v.* that of 55. 4, also in 56. 9–11.

[4] *NQ* 4, pref. 3, 20; *Ep.* 25. 5. But *Ep.* 10. 1 expresses more confidence in Lucilius' ability to profit from total solitude.

[5] *NQ* 4, pref. 1, 21 (mental withdrawal); *Ep.* 1; 7. 8: 'recede in te ipse quantum potes.'

[6] *NQ* 4, pref. 1, 'officium procurationis otiosae'; 'scio quam sis ambitioni alienus.'

perquisites of his position (19. 5–6; 21. 1), and regards the
procuratorship—which he now thinks will lead to new posts—
as incompatible with true friendship, generosity, or peace (19. 8,
11–12). Yet, despite the urgency of his plea, Seneca allows for
some time interval before eventual retirement.[1] In Letter 22 we
find that Lucilius now agrees that he must leave his 'occupationes
speciosae et malae' and in fact excuses, as the effect of chance, his
involvement in them. Asked for advice on how to retire, Seneca
replies that he can only give general guidance as he is not on the
scene and advises a gradual extrication starting with the refusal
to take on anything new. Finally, Seneca assures Lucilius that
Stoic doctrine permits a gradual retirement in his circumstances
and insists that what is holding him back is not theoretical scruples
but the 'occupationum pretia'.

Letter 32 finds Seneca confident that Lucilius will stick to his
decision. He now urges him to hurry (32. 2–3), and in 37 answers
Lucilius' question 'Quomodo ergo me expediam?' with the assurance that, providing he acts on a rational decision and not an
emotional impulse, he will find the right way. Seneca mentions
in Letter 45 that he expects Lucilius soon to secure release from
his post.[2] Letter 53. 8 ff. contains renewed exhortations to abandon
everything for philosophy. In 68 Lucilius' decision is regarded as
firm, and Seneca, after a brief justification of *otium* on Stoic lines,
develops the theme 'ipsum otium absconde', and laments the
lateness of Lucilius' resolve. We are now, on either of the two
possible chronologies, in the early summer of 64.[3] In the very
next letter, Lucilius appears to be in retirement[4] and is warned
against excessive travelling: he must consolidate his *otium*.
Unfortunately, Seneca gives us no details that could put the
implication of Lucilius' actual retirement beyond doubt.[5] The
travelling is inconclusive: Lucilius had travelled earlier when
still procurator[6] and later, in Letter 79, it is still Sicily that he

---

[1] 20. 1: 'si vales et te dignum putas qui *aliquando* fias tuus, gaudeo.'

[2] 45. 2: 'nisi mature te finem officii sperarem impetraturum . . .'

[3] The *ver* of Ep. 67 is always taken to refer to 64; see Appendix A1 (Note I).

[4] Especially 69. 2: 'quies et vitae prioris oblivio'.

[5] As Albertini, *Composition dans Sénèque*, p. 141, rightly notes.

[6] Ep. 28.

tours. After that, there are no further indications that Lucilius is in Sicily. In 82 Lucilius' *otium* is mentioned again with the warning that it will become a living death, if not devoted to philosophy. Letters after this tell Lucilius what type of philosophy to study (e.g. 102. 20 ff.) and how to study it without incurring danger (103. 5). There is certainly nothing in them that definitely tells against his being in retirement.[1]

We return now to the question: do we have in the Letters a real exhortation to a real retirement? The details about Lucilius, furnished in them and in the Natural Questions, put beyond reasonable doubt the existence of a man of that name with those origins and prospects.[2] Since it is inconceivable that a real man would be represented to the public in a work of literature as retired, before he actually was, the retirement also must be real. But what part the Letters played or were meant to play in his decision is a more difficult problem. The Letters in their published form—and Seneca, from the start, intended them to be published[3] —were not meant to convey practical and practicable advice to Lucilius, as the following consideration shows: since there is no reason to suppose that Seneca published less than the first seven books (Letters 1–69) together,[4] the fulfilment of Seneca's exhortation must have appeared in the same volume as the exhortation itself, and, since the retirement was real and predated its description in the Letters, Lucilius was already in retirement when Seneca's advice came before the public, perhaps in the latter part of 64.

But even if the *published* exhortation was not real, could not

---

[1] In *Ep.* 103. 4 Lucilius is told, as in the earliest letters, '*quantum potes autem in philosophiam recede*', but the competition for Lucilius' time here seems to come from ordinary human duties, not official ones. As for '*occupatio publica*' in 88. 41, Seneca could be using the generic 'tu', or describing Lucilius' situation over a lifetime.

[2] But given the problems discussed here, the attempt of Delatte (*Les Études Classiques* 4 (1935), 367 ff.; 546 ff.) to construct a detailed biography of Lucilius from Seneca's Letters seems rash. Compare the scepticism of Maurach, *Der Bau von Senecas Epistulae Morales*, p. 11 n. 1.   [3] *Ep.* 21. 5.

[4] On this point, an exponent of the fictional nature of the correspondence, A. Bourgery, *RPh* 35 (1911), 54 n. 1, and a champion of their genuineness, Albertini, *Composition dans Sénèque*, pp. 196–7, are agreed.

Seneca *actually* have urged retirement on Lucilius in letters that he only published after his advice had been taken? Here we encounter the most difficult question about the correspondence: are these letters, which Seneca intended to publish, a literary correspondence like Pliny's Letters, or a philosophical work in letter form, like the letters of Epicurus? The correct answer, I believe, is the latter: the *Epistulae Morales* are Senecan dialogues with an epistolary veneer inspired by Cicero.[1] It is unlikely that this highly artificial work contains fragments of candid private advice, especially since Seneca continues to discuss the question of political participation in the Letters after the indications of Lucilius' retirement (98. 13; 101; 118).

Why then did Seneca include exhortations to retirement in composing a fictitious correspondence to a man in retirement? The kind of purpose we discerned in *De Brevitate Vitae* is unlikely to be involved: Lucilius' retirement, unlike Paulinus', cannot have been of sufficient political significance to warrant a public explanation.[2] Moreover, the correspondence would be an unnecessarily complicated means to the simple end of explaining Lucilius' *otium*, for many other problems are ascribed to Lucilius and treated there. Though talks about Lucilius' withdrawal may have suggested giving prominence to the theme in the Letters, it is less likely that Lucilius' real predicament generated its treatment than that Seneca's views on this and other problems generated the Lucilius we are shown in the Letters.

This conclusion is reinforced by the conflict, noted by Gercke, between the picture of Lucilius' character drawn in the early Letters and that in the preface to Book 4 of the Natural Questions written about the same time, within a year of their dramatic date.[3] Finally, the synthetic quality of Lucilius' character and problems in the Letters is put beyond reasonable doubt by

[1] See Appendix B4.

[2] Lucilius' Sicilian procuratorship was not a very important post, see Pflaum, *Carr. proc.* I, pp. 72–3.

[3] Gercke, *Seneca-Studien*, pp. 326–7. In *NQ* 4, pref. 1 (the latest section of the work), Lucilius is 'ambitioni alienus', but in *Ep.* 19–22 he has to be cured of ambition. Unfortunately, the dates of neither work can be fixed so precisely as to make the temporal relation clear, see Appendix A1.

the fact that he is given a spiritual development of incredible rapidity.

Seneca is constantly referring to Lucilius' progress, and, despite a certain ambiguity in Seneca's portrayal of the moral distance between author and correspondent, a pattern does emerge. Lucilius is pictured as a man of natural fortitude of mind (13. 1, 15)[1] who, when the correspondence opens, is regarded as having Epicurean sympathies[2] and reading widely in philosophy.[3] He is apparently training himself in Stoicism,[4] and is very concerned to challenge his Stoic friend's inconsistencies.[5]

In Letters 1 and 2 Seneca infers from Lucilius' letters to him a serious employment of his time that promises well. In Letter 16. 2 Seneca remarks on Lucilius' progress, but warns, 'iam de te spem habeo, nondum fiduciam.'[6] By 19 Seneca says that Lucilius' letters 'iam non promittunt de te sed spondent'. With the end of Book 3, a turning-point is reached, marked by a change in the form of the letters, as an early letter of the next book explains. The letters of these first three books are basically tripartite in structure. There is an opening section making contact with the correspondent through a reference to a letter or question of his, or a discussion of his behaviour or some details of Seneca's own life. There follows a general philosophical discussion and then a tag, playfully represented as a debt owed to Lucilius, in the main

---

[1] Just as in NQ 4, pref. 14 ff.

[2] See Schottlaender, *Philologus* 99 (1955), 136–9. The main texts are *Ep.* 23. 9 'Epicuri tui' and 20. 9 where 'invideas licet' seems to show that Lucilius is playfully expected to resent Seneca's use of his own Epicurus against him. Further on (20. 11), even without Beltrami's reading ('Epicuree'), Lucilius is clearly represented as speaking for Epicurus.

[3] As also in NQ 4, pref. 1, 14.

[4] I take it that 'dura vincentibus' in *Ep.* 13. 1 refers to Stoic precepts (cf. *De Const.* 2. 1–2). In this letter, Seneca says he will not teach Lucilius 'Stoica lingua, sed hac summissiore' but by 13. 14 he goes back on this (as again in 24. 1). I agree with Schottlaender, p. 139, that Seneca is here contrasting Epicurean with Stoic remedies.

[5] e.g. 8. 8; 12. 11.

[6] By the categories of *proficientes* Seneca later sets out, Lucilius is lower than Serenus in *Tranq.* (cf. above, p. 321). The description in *Ep.* 16 fits best with the second category in the system of 72. 9. This equals 2 and 3 on the *Ep.* 75 system where Seneca declines to assure Lucilius (para. 16) that he will rise above grade 3.

from Epicurus. Though foreshadowed in the citation of a popular proverb at the end of Letter 1, this practice is really introduced in Letter 2 where Seneca is giving Lucilius advice on how to derive the most profit from philosophical books: Seneca warns him against promiscuous and rapid reading and suggests that he pick out one precept every day and digest it, and illustrates the point by citing an excerpt he has made from Epicurus. The idea, in fact, shows clearly the influence of Epicurus whose philosophical letters were meant to give a brief summary of doctrine that could be easily committed to memory by those who could not read his long treatises.[1] Seneca is happy to exploit Lucilius' Epicurean beliefs while gradually weaning him on to more solid Stoic fare.

But in Letter 33, supposedly answering a query from Lucilius, Seneca explains that he has stopped giving these citations in his letters for two reasons: one, that he cannot properly excerpt from the works of the Stoics, because, unlike Epicurus' works, they are worth reading in full, while, because of the democratic nature of the Stoa, no citations from a particular Stoic can be assumed to represent the school (1–6). The second reason is that Lucilius is now beyond this method of teaching which is suited to 'rudibus adhuc et extrinsecus auscultantibus' and 'pueris' but not to 'certi profectus viro', 'seni aut prospicienti senectutem' (6–7). To learn philosophy, not merely memorize it, Lucilius must teach and write as well as read, and he must not think philosophical invention beyond him (8–11). In Letter 34 Seneca exults in the success of his instruction: 'adsero te mihi; meum opus es'; Lucilius has only to press on now, as he is already in a position to give Seneca encouragement in return.[2] In 36 we hear that he has been giving moral instruction to a young friend. But the path is not always smooth: in 60 Seneca expresses his disappointment at something Lucilius has said; yet by 82 Seneca announces, 'desii iam de te esse sollicitus': Lucilius' soul is safe; but then in 107 Seneca upbraids Lucilius for allowing the flight of his slaves to upset him.

[1] D.L. 10. 35. They were also intended to inspire meditation in more advanced students, ibid. 10. 83; 135. Cf. the κύριαι δόξαι learned off by heart by members of the school.

[2] But note this last is already in *Ep*. 6. 6 where Seneca pauses for a moment to modify his immodest claim to be a living example to Lucilius.

Finally, in the later letters, Lucilius, who once relied on schoolboy maxims, asks a growing number of difficult logical questions and Seneca has to warn him repeatedly not to forget that the practical application of philosophy, and even metaphysical speculation, is more important than theoretical subtleties.[1] But by the last letters preserved, Seneca has clearly made his point, and now has to justify his own indulgence in such subtleties to Lucilius.[2]

The Letters are set in the period winter 62 to autumn 64 or, more probably, winter 63 to autumn 64. This is hardly enough time for the type of spiritual progress Lucilius is supposed to be making,[3] especially since, on either chronology, the first three books of letters (1–29) during which Lucilius comes of age philosophically must cover at the most nine months.[4]

This conclusion will help us in considering the portrait of Annaeus Serenus in Seneca's works. In De Tranquillitate Animi Serenus is characterized so sharply that the work comes closer than all the others to being a real dialogue. But we are in difficulties if we assume that Serenus' plight is the focal point of the dialogue, first because Seneca insists on treating Serenus' malady in general terms (2. 4) and includes features irrelevant to Serenus in his description of it,[5] but also because Seneca fails to include in his portrait of Serenus anything about his actual career. Not only are there no references to his being praefectus vigilum—that post could have been assumed after these works—but there is no

---

[1] Ep. 89. 18; 102. 20; 106. 11–12; 108. 1–2; 109. 17; 111; 113. 1.

[2] Ep. 121. 1; 124. 1.

[3] Cf. Ep. 16. 1 where Lucilius is told how much work is required 'ut proposita custodias'; also 42. 1; 52. 7; 75. 15; 94. 50–1. Guillemin (REL 31 (1953), 218–19) contrasts the conversion Seneca envisages with examples of sudden conversion. Plutarch, Mor. 1057E, in attributing sudden conversion to Stoic teaching, is probably making a deliberate confusion with the change of heart that impels a man to change himself and that can be represented as sudden (Ep. 6. 1); Mor. 75D–76E is similarly tendentious. On this see the discussion of Maurach, op. cit., p. 41 n. 58.

[4] For the detailed chronology of the Letters see Appendix A1. If the spring mentioned in Ep. 23 is the spring of 63 then Ep. 29 can hardly fall later than the summer or autumn of 63. On the more probable one-year chronology, 1–29 cannot cover more than six months. Abel, Bauformen, p. 158, sees the progress but thinks it is the record of Lucilius' actual conversion to Stoicism.

[5] Giancotti, Cronologia, pp. 209–12.

indication that Serenus is embarked on an equestrian public career at all. This is all the stranger when we recall that in *De Tranquillitate Animi* one of the symptoms Serenus describes is his betrayal of his original resolve to enter public life. His political activity is described instead wholly in terms of senatorial *honores* (1. 10) and pleading in the forum (1. 13). Admittedly, these are the terms in which Seneca discusses political participation throughout his works, but in the case of his other equestrian addressees, Paulinus and Lucilius, he does not omit to indicate their real situation.[1] The vividness of Serenus' portrait, then, extends only to his spiritual life: in *De Constantia Sapientis* he is an avowed Epicurean scoffing at the more perverse Stoic doctrines; in *De Tranquillitate Animi* he struggles as an *imperfectus* to follow Stoic doctrines; in *De Otio* (if he is also addressed there)[2] he argues the orthodox Stoic line against his teacher.

In the light of what we have noticed about Lucilius—who is at least given a biography as well as a soul—we may well suspect that these dialogues give us, not a spiritual portrait of the real Serenus, but a literary *persona*, based on Serenus and given his name, but essentially an invention of the author for the purpose of treating certain problems. Serenus may indeed have discussed Stoic paradoxes with Seneca or come to him for spiritual guidance. He may in fact have changed from an Epicurean to a Stoic. All that this view implies is that the dialogues addressed to him are not an actual record of that conversion, each addressed to him when his mental state was that ascribed to the addressee. If so,

---

[1] One cannot rule out the possibility that such a description occurred in the lost parts of *De Otio*, but it is not likely, as very little is probably lost at the start, and the problem is discussed purely theoretically from then on.

[2] Above, pp. 315–17. Most scholars think the addressee is Serenus, for his personality, ardent and stubborn, yet open and honest, suits the portrayal of Serenus in *De Constantia Sapientis* (1. 3; 3. 1; 7. 1) and the opening chapters of *De Tranquillitate Animi*. Hermann's suggestion (see Giancotti, *Cronologia*, p. 237) that Lucilius is addressed in *De Otio* is unlikely: when Lucilius is made to question Seneca's orthodoxy (*Ep.* 8) it is from the viewpoint of an Epicurean sympathizer (see above, p. 351) which the addressee of *De Otio* is not. I have assumed in the following discussion that Serenus is the addressee of *De Otio*, as it does not affect my own interpretation of how these works are relevant to Seneca's life, but does strengthen the other interpretations I attack in III and IV and is usually accepted by their proponents.

even if *De Constantia Sapientis* was published before *De Tran-quillitate Animi* and *De Otio* rather than just placed first in a joint publication, we cannot insist on a number of years between them.[1] And, of course, if the problems of Serenus in *De Tranquillitate Animi* and, perhaps, *De Otio* are creations of Seneca, they cannot be used to explain Seneca's choice of subject or the nature of his recommendations.

IV

The temptation to date and explain the message of these works by connecting them closely with phases in Seneca's own career is a natural one and has rarely been resisted.[2] The Letters, whose dramatic date can be fixed without recourse to this hypothesis, appear to strengthen it: they show Seneca, after he had asked permission to retire and withdrawn as much as possible when the request was refused, describing his *otium* (*Ep.* 8; 68. 8) and exalting philosophical leisure over political life. In the case of *De Tranquillitate Animi* and *De Otio*, the idea that Seneca reverses his position from one to the other has strengthened the theory of a connection with his own decisions, though scholars who hold this theory have not been able to agree on which decision each dialogue explains. But if the two dialogues are not in basic con-tradiction, as I have tried to prove, then, even if they directly reflect Seneca's situation, they need not be assigned to different phases of his life.

The course of Seneca's life certainly goes far towards explaining his great interest in the question of *res publica* v. *otium*. He had to face these fundamental questions about political participation at

---

[1] Giancotti, *Cronologia*, pp. 175–6, refuses to suggest an interval, but on the ground that we cannot tell how long such a spiritual conversion would take.

[2] For a critical summary of these views see Giancotti, *Cronologia*, pp. 197–215; 226–42. Since then, André, *L'otium romain*, p. 50 n. 1, has supported the idea of a time lapse between *Tranq.* and *Otio* on the ground that the latter is announced in *Ep.* 14. 14: 'sed postea videbimus an sapienti opera rei publicae danda sit . . .' But this could refer to a lost letter, or, what is more likely, just be a way of avoiding the question for the moment. Cf. the remarks of Pohlenz, *Phil. und Erlebnis*, p. 102, on similar passages elsewhere in Seneca.

the very start, when he resisted pressure from his father to embark on a senatorial career at the normal age.[1] At last, past the age of thirty, Seneca did decide to enter political life, but exile brought an enforced *otium* for eight years and the need for another decision when he was fifty or more. He decided to resume his position in the Senate and new and dangerous responsibilities as Nero's teacher and Agrippina's tool. That was the most important decision of his life: from it followed his later position as *amicus principis*, his political achievements, and moral compromises. Last of all came the decision which he twice tried to implement, that of extricating himself from a position where he could achieve nothing, and would certainly stain his earlier record.

None the less, the autobiographical approach to these works has been subjected to serious and pertinent criticism: scholars have rightly pointed to Seneca's generic treatment of the problems and to his coverage, within each dialogue, of two related but distinct conditions—initial abstention and retirement. In addition, when we look at the terms in which the problem is set in the dialogues, it is difficult to fit them precisely to Seneca's own case. *De Tranquillitate Animi* and *De Otio*, like *De Brevitate Vitae*, envisage the life of *officia civilia* as full-time activity in public office, the army, or the courts. Now this conception fits the life of the ordinary senator or equestrian official, but it does not fit Seneca's. After his return from exile, though a senator, he rarely, if ever, attended the Senate,[2] and his oratorical career was limited to writing another's speeches. Before Nero's accession, he wrote, on his own account, philosophical works, while his actual duties, though they may have excluded formal philosophical teaching, certainly involved literary instruction and moral and political guidance. After Nero's accession, he continued to write philosophy and provide moral counsel,[3] and, according to Dio,[4] demanded hours of leisure in which to pursue philosophy. Seneca's life, in fact, at the height of his political career, embodied

[1] See above, pp. 34, 45.   [2] See above, pp. 73–6.
[3] Note Agrippina's gibe in *Ann.* 13. 14. Tacitus makes Seneca describe all his services to Nero as springing from his 'studia in umbra educata' (*Ann.* 14. 53, 4).
[4] 61. 10, 5.

precisely that mixture of public functions with *otium* and *litterae* that is recommended in *De Tranquillitate Animi* to the man gradually forced out of political life.[1] But when Seneca felt himself being forced out in 62, he asked, on grounds of age and health, not to be allowed to mix *otium rebus*, but to cease his advisory functions and shed their trappings in order to enjoy complete *otium*. He repeated that request in 64 after the Great Fire.

On an autobiographical interpretation, *De Tranquillitate Animi* must be either a statement of Seneca's own intentions or a justification of his actual position.[2] The likely date for the work is before 62, and it is perfectly possible that some time earlier, after Agrippina's death perhaps, Seneca intended a gradual and partial retreat, or, perhaps better, represented his continued service to Nero, in an effort to excuse it, as the minimum of public service compatible with *constantia*.[3] Yet, on either of these interpretations, we run into conflict with the views on wealth in the dialogue, which have no less claim to being regarded as autobiographical. Seneca's recommendations to prune one's property suit neither his life nor the evidence for his intentions before 62.[4] Seneca was probably not thinking primarily of his own case in writing *De Tranquillitate Animi*: it is worth noting that a natural justification for his own retirement—old age—does not figure at all in the work.[5]

As for *De Otio*, it is impossible to tell if it suited Seneca's own intentions or way of life, as the discussion of retirement has been lost. Certainly, at least half the work dealt with a problem unconnected with his personal situation after 49—that of initial abstention from politics. But it was only after that date that the question of retirement became relevant.

[1] 4. 8; 5. 5.
[2] I have ignored the possibility that Seneca could simply be writing to convince or console himself. The elaboration of style and the fact of publication tell against such an interpretation. On the 'difficult truth that ancient writers think of their work primarily in terms of persuasive presentation' see the remarks of D. Russell, *Plutarch*, London, 1973, p. 162.
[3] The latter is the view of Lana, *Seneca*, pp. 247 ff.
[4] See above, p. 305.
[5] Tacitus naturally stressed it in composing Seneca's resignation scene (*Ann.* 14. 54, 2–3; 56, 1).

The outlook is similarly unsatisfactory when we turn to examine the Letters. All or nearly all the letters we have fall, on either chronology, within 63–4. Seneca's travels in Latium, described in the later letters, fit the period when the arrangements of 62 still held, before retirement to his chamber in the latter part of 64,[1] and there is nothing against the natural assumption that the dramatic date of the various letters roughly matched the actual date at which the reported travels and activities—at least, those based on life—took place. What do they reveal?

Seneca says, in the first letter, that he has stopped wasting time, and, in the eighth, Seneca describes himself as withdrawn from men and affairs in order to profit posterity by his writings (8. 1–2). But in three subsequent letters, 62, 72, and 106, Seneca appears to be involved in some kind of *occupationes*. In the first of these he denies that *negotia* must impede *liberalia studia*, saying that he can always withdraw his mind when busy with friends or involved with people through some 'causa ex officio nata civili'. Here, of course, Seneca is speaking like a *sapiens*:[2] how personal is the first person and how precise the present tense here? In 72 Seneca declines to answer a question from Lucilius on the grounds that it would require 'otium et secretum', but adds 'nihilominus his quoque occupatis diebus agatur aliquid et quidem totis' (72. 1–2). The rest of the letter is an exhortation to make our *occupationes* give place to philosophy. In 106 Seneca could but declines to give the conventional excuse for a tardy reply: 'quia destrictus occupationibus sum'. *Occupationes* is of course too ambiguous to be pressed, but it is given more significance by some outside information we have. Letter 72 belongs to Seneca's travels in Campania and its dramatic date is late

---

[1] See above, pp. 93–4. Tacitus (*Ann.* 15. 45) seems to indicate late 64 (certainly after the July fire) for Seneca's request to be allowed to retire far away in the country and his withdrawal to his room when Nero refused. But in the spring of 65 (*Ann.* 15. 60) Tacitus shows him out of Rome, but in Campania, from which he returned to his suburban villa on the eve of the Pisonian conspiracy. The last letters we have show him at Rome (104. 1), Nomentum (104; 110), and Alba (123) but not in Campania. They probably report events before he took to his room.

[2] As is made clear by *Ep.* 56. 11 ff. Seneca there contrasts his own and Lucilius' state of mind with the *sapiens* who cannot be distracted.

spring of 64.[1] Now we know that before the July fire of that year Nero went to the theatre at Naples to perform,[2] a fact which led Waltz to suggest that Seneca was present in Campania, at the time of Letter 70 and the following ones, as a member of the court.[3] He also noted that the Alexandrian fleet, whose arrival Seneca describes in Letter 77, could be the one that brought the young Alexandrians who delighted Nero with their 'modulatae laudationes', according to Suetonius.[4] The *officium civile* of Letter 62 might be part of the same story for that letter belongs, on the one-year chronology, to *spring* 64,[5] and could be set in Naples to which Seneca is shown returning in Letter 57.

It is hard to believe that Seneca was primarily concerned with explaining or justifying his own retirement through ostensible advice to Lucilius to leave his procuratorship—when Seneca represents himself as giving this advice while still mixing *otium* with court duties. In fact, he was probably still in this half-way position for part of the time of actual publication.[6] But this discrepancy was against his wishes, and Seneca clearly did not expect its revelation to tell against the sincerity of his exhortations, when he revealed it to his readers. Could one therefore say that the emphasis on *otium* in the Letters springs from Seneca's personal situation in a different sense—as an expression of his frustrated longings? Seneca must indeed have been wishing that his request for complete leisure to devote to philosophy had been granted, but such wishes do nothing to explain why his discussions of *otium* are principally in the form of justification and recommendation, or instruction in the proper manner of achieving it inconspicuously.

A more sinister kind of connection with his own life is

[1] 67: 'ver inclinatum in aestatem'. 86. 16: 'Iunius mensis est . . . iam proclivis in Iulium.' His travels in Campania start in *Ep.* 49. 1.

[2] Tacitus, *Ann.* 15. 33–4.

[3] *Vie politique*, pp. 419–20. Tacitus notes that Nero's theatre audience included 'quique Caesarem per honorem aut varios usus sectantur'.

[4] Suet. *Nero* 20. 3; the suggestion is in *Vie politique*, p. 420 n. 4.

[5] Waltz accepted a two-year chronology and thought Letters 58–69 represented the winter of 63–4, but the one-year scheme is preferable—see Appendix A1.

[6] The *terminus post quem* for the start of publication is Lucilius' retirement which Seneca dates to summer of 64 (above, pp. 348–9).

suggested by Waltz for Letter 73 which deals with the natural gratitude felt by philosophers for those who govern and ensure peace and order, namely that it was written to protect Seneca.[1] The idea could be extended to the whole correspondence: was Seneca trying to show Nero how innocent were his preoccupations and intentions by exalting innocent philosophical leisure? This suggestion is undermined by the number of things in the Letters that would irritate rather than soothe the Emperor: first, the references to the necessity of avoiding giving offence to those in power (14. 7; 105); then, the criticism of gymnastics (15. 3);[2] finally, the slight to the Emperor in Letter 76, where Seneca tells how he passes the theatre at Naples every day on his way to hear Metronax the philosopher and remarks bitterly that the theatre was full and the lecture-room empty—a fact which makes him feel ashamed of the human race (76. 4). Nero was performing at the theatre at that time:[3] what did he make of that tribute to his art?[4]

V

The key to Seneca's preoccupation with *otium* does not seem to spring simply from his own career or those of his correspondents. It is more profitable to note where his teachings reflect known features of life around him. Despite his preference for describing political life generally in terms of the senatorial career, Seneca does note, in *De Tranquillitate Animi* (6), the temperamental

---

[1] Waltz, *Vie politique*, p. 418, explaining similarly the flattery of Nero in NQ 1. 5, 6; 6. 8, 3; 7. 21, 3. I do not see why Albertini, *Composition dans Sénèque*, p. 44 n. 1, sees a flattering allusion to the Emperor in *Ep.* 7. 5.

[2] But compare *Ep.* 83 for Seneca's own moderate exercises. Nero tried to make the Greek gymnasium take root in the life of the Roman upper classes. He not only introduced gymnastic contests in public games (the Neronia of 60: Tacitus, *Ann.* 14. 20), but in 61 he included a gymnasium in his new baths and distributed free oil to senators and *equites* (*Ann.* 14. 47; Suet. *Nero* 12. 3). He also maintained a troupe of court wrestlers (Suet. *Nero* 45).

[3] Suet. *Nero* 20 mentions that Nero performed 'saepius et per complures dies'.

[4] K. Heinz, *Das Bild Kaiser Neros*, Bern, 1948, pp. 92–3, finds many other possible criticisms of Nero concealed in the Letters.

qualities necessary for life at court,[1] and imperial conditions are also reflected in the fact that Seneca's addressees on these topics are equestrian officials.[2] Of the qualities mentioned in *De Tranquillitate Animi* as incompatible with life at court, *contumacia* immediately reminds us of the common criticisms of the Stoics in Seneca's day,[3] while the warning about 'periculosi sales' recalls the world of *delatores*. So does the preoccupation in the Letters with avoiding offence to the powerful: the threats from those who have political power are greater than those from poverty and death (14. 4); we must avoid not only giving offence but also appearing to avoid it (14. 8); the political climate of Rome is comparable to the physical climate of the malarial Ardea (105. 1); we must hide our wealth and behave inoffensively in order to avoid *invidia* and *odium* (105. 3).

Seneca's recipe for security in the Letters is philosophical retirement (14. 11), but how one withdraws and how one behaves afterwards are crucial: ostentatious withdrawal will cause offence (19. 2), for to glory *in otio* is *iners ambitio* (68. 3); yet total withdrawal will attract the same attention (19. 2; 68. 5); the best thing is to plead ill health or laziness as the reason, not contempt for ordinary life (68. 3, 8); when studying philosophy one must behave *tranquille modesteque* (14. 11), not *insolenter* and *contumaciter*, curing one's own vices not reproaching others with theirs (103. 5). These warnings clearly reflect in part the anxieties of prominent men living under an immoral and paranoiac Princeps. It was the air of moral disapproval worn by Thrasea Paetus and his *rigidi et tristes satellites* (as Thrasea's accuser was to describe them in 66) that first enraged Nero against this Stoic who would not show enthusiasm at the Iuvenalia.[4]

Particularly significant is Letter 73, where Seneca disputes the

---

[1] This consideration is naturally absent from the comparable discussion in Cicero, *De Officiis* (see above, p. 342).

[2] Note also *Ep.* 101 about the *eques* Cornelius Senecio who died in harness.

[3] e.g. *Ann.* 16. 22, 2, and Seneca's own Letters 73. 1; 103. 5.

[4] *Ann.* 16. 21, 1; 22, 2. Cf. Suet. *Nero* 37. 1: 'tristior et paedagogi vultus'. But Thrasea actually believed in tolerating human weaknesses, according to Pliny, *Ep.* 8. 22, 3.

idea that philosophers are 'contumaces ac refractarios contemptores' of rulers, representing them instead as devoted subjects, grateful for the *tranquillum otium* that governments provide. This combination of a warning to philosophers with an assurance to the government illuminates Seneca's repeated insistence in *De Tranquillitate Animi* and *De Otio* that the condition of the *res publica*, however bad, is not a proper justification for withdrawal from public life. A man who bases his retirement into philosophical leisure on disapproval of the government would rightly be viewed as a political dissenter; Seneca, who acknowledges that the dangers of public life may justify a gradual retreat,[1] condemns initial abstention or hasty withdrawal grounded on the view that the state is unworthy of our services and sets out the proper grounds on which a Stoic may choose *otium*: not merely the more acceptable of Chrysippus' *exceptiones*, but the basic Stoic principles of the natural drive to knowledge and the *maior res publica*. Seneca himself followed these principles: he requested retirement on the basis of ill health and old age, and behaved like an invalid when he finally withdrew late in 64.[2]

By contrast, Thrasea Paetus in walking out of the Senate in protest in 59 had advertised the idea of opposition by political abstention.[3] According to his accuser in 66, Thrasea had been absenting himself from the taking of vows for the Emperor's safety and for the past three years had not attended the Senate.[4] The idea of showing disapproval of the government or of political conditions by withdrawing from public life was not new. It had always been intensely disliked by heads of government: Caesar the Dictator, Augustus, and Tiberius.[5] Nor was this the first time

---

[1] *Tranq.* 4; *Ep.* 22. 8. [2] Tacitus, *Ann.* 15. 45, 3.

[3] If the failure of his son-in-law to rise above the tribunate he held in 56 was deliberate, Thrasea's act was even more menacing (Helvidius Priscus did not reach the praetorship before his exile in 66 (*Ann.* 16. 33, 2) for he held that post in 70 after his return (*Hist.* 4. 4)). Later on, Helvidius' biographer earned Domitian's enmity by refusing to rise above the quaestorship (Dio 67. 13, 2).

[4] Tacitus, *Ann.* 16. 22, 1: though the temporal indication is not to be taken literally, Thrasea's non-cooperation roughly coincides with the last period of Seneca's life when he was composing the Letters.

[5] W. Allen Jr., *CJ* 44 (1948), 203. Examples are Sulpicius Rufus (Cicero, *Att.* 10. 14, 1, 3); Sallust (his story, in any case—*BJ* 3); L. Calpurnius Piso (*Ann.*

that men identifiable as Stoics were found among the real or alleged opponents of emperors.[1]

But if Seneca by 61 was combating the use of Stoicism to justify political withdrawal as a protest against existing political conditions, it may have been because he foresaw a new and terrifying development. It was in 62 that adherence to Stoicism was denounced as a politically dangerous attitude and the long drama, usually called the 'Philosophical Opposition', opened. Perhaps the story of the punishment and expulsion of philosophers both in and out of politics, under Nero and the Flavians, should rather be named the 'Philosophical Persecution' after the feature of these purges that was new: Stoicism became a criminal charge. The idea of frightening Nero with 'Stoicorum adrogantia' was, according to Tacitus, an inspiration of Tigellinus in 62, prompted perhaps by the recent withdrawal of Seneca under a cloud. Rubellius Plautus was the first victim.[2] Soon after, Thrasea Paetus ceased to attend the Senate. Seneca's Letter 73, defending philosophy as peaceful and implicitly warning that defiance would bring philosophy into disrepute and philosophers into danger, was written after this, but Seneca was dead when, in 65, the Stoic Musonius Rufus and, in 66/7, Demetrius the Cynic were expelled for teaching philosophy.[3] In 66 Tigellinus' son-in-law made Stoicism one of the charges he brought against Thrasea.[4] This

---

2. 43); his son (*Ann.* 2. 34). For Caesar's rebuke to Cicero, *Att.* 9. 18, 1; for Tiberius' concern, *Ann.* 6. 27.

[1] e.g. under Gaius: Julius Canus (Seneca, *Tranq.* 14. 4); his ἑταῖρος Rectus (Plut. *Mor.* frag. 211S); Julius Graecinus, *Agric.* 4, cf. *Ep.* 29. 6.

[2] Tacitus indicates his belief that Tigellinus first used philosophical commitment as a charge by leaving all mention of Stoicism out of his account of Plautus' enforced withdrawal in 60 (*Ann.* 14. 22) and making it prominent in Tigellinus' proposal to Nero that he be killed (*Ann.* 14. 57). The Senecan evidence is conclusive in showing that Tacitus has not just read back into the Neronian period the kind of criticisms of Stoics made by men like Aquillius Regulus under Domitian (*pace* Sherwin-White, *Letters of Pliny*, p. 95; the expulsions of philosophers under Nero also tell against this view).

[3] Dio 62. 27, 4; Tacitus, *Ann.* 15. 71 (according to Tacitus, Musonius was banished for his philosophical reputation). For Demetrius, Epict. 1. 25, 22 confirms Philostratus, *Apoll.* 4. 42; 5. 19. Note also *Apoll.* 4. 35-6.

[4] *Ann.* 16. 22: Capito presumably repeated this charge in his speech in the Senate, though Tacitus does not repeat his arguments (16. 28).

pattern continued under the Flavians: Helvidius Priscus was put to death by Vespasian and, at the same time, philosophers, including Demetrius again, were expelled.[1] Finally under Domitian, in 93, a grand expulsion of philosophers accompanied the treason trials of Arulenus Rusticus and Herennius Senecio, biographers of Thrasea and Helvidius.[2] This was the period of the exile of Artemidorus, Epictetus and, possibly, Plutarch.[3] The friendship of Dio Chrysostom with Nerva and Trajan marks the end of a chapter in imperial history.

Cossutianus Capito labelled, as characteristically Stoic, political resistance by way of abstention. In attacking Thrasea, he played on all the possible dangers of such conduct, labelling it secession and rebellion. Then Eprius Marcellus elaborated the charges before the Senate, taking his cue from Nero who lectured the Senate on the evils of neglecting public duties and the bad example men like Thrasea set to the equestrian class.[4] The Princeps grasped the dangers of opposition by abstention. It was the most difficult form to combat. As philosophers, men like Thrasea were committed to regarding death without fear; as senators, they regarded exile as worse, but that penalty they had already imposed on themselves.[5] Tacitus gives Eprius impressive lines: 'requirere se in senatu consularem, in votis sacerdotem, in iure iurando civem, nisi contra instituta et caerimonias maiorum proditorem palam et hostem Thrasea induisset.'

---

[1] Dio 66. 13.
[2] Tacitus, *Agric.* 2; Pliny, *Ep.* 3. 11, 2; Suet. *Dom.* 10; Dio 67. 13, 3.
[3] *PIR²* E 74.　　　　　　　　　　　　　　　　[4] *Ann.* 16. 27–8.
[5] Note *Ann.* 16. 28, 3: 'qui minitarentur exilium suum'. (Cf. Dio Chrys. *Or.* 40. 12 for the idea of self-imposed exile.) Earlier in 63, Thrasea had quietly accepted the order to stay away when the Senate went to Antium, a 'praenuntiam imminentis caedis contumeliam' (*Ann.* 15. 23, 4). The remark quoted in Dio 62. 15, 1ᵃ (Exc. Vat. 58), ἀνδρὶ βουλευτῇ ἐσχάτην εἶναι τιμωρίαν τὴν φυγήν, must, as Boissevain showed (vol. III, p. 54), belong here and should be related to this incident: Thrasea was not afraid of death; being cut off was worse (perhaps Epict. I. 1, 26 should be connected with this). Yet later his loss of faith in the government was so complete that he imposed exile on himself. (Attempts are often made to connect the Dio fragment with Thrasea's stand on the proper penalty for *maiestas* in 62, e.g. A. Sizoo, *REL* 5 (1927), 46; A. R. Birley, *CR* 12 (1962), 197–9, but the preceding Exc. Vat. (Dio 62. 14, 1) already refers to the death of Rubellius Plautus that succeeded that case.) Garnsey, *Social Status*

If it was false, as Tacitus believed, that Thrasea Paetus and his followers plotted revolution, it was true that they meant to show their disapproval of the government. But it is quite clear that the grounds of Thrasea's opposition to Nero's regime did not follow from his Stoicism: for one thing, Seneca had shown in his *De Clementia* how Stoicism could be used to justify and provide a monarchical ideology for the existing system. What Thrasea and Helvidius Priscus wanted was *libertas senatoria*.[1] Later Helvidius was to make the position even more explicit than Thrasea had: he tried to get the Senate in 69 to act on its own without waiting for Vespasian's return from the East, and to undertake to give the new Emperor honest advice through specially elected envoys.[2] Thus Wirszubski[3] was able to maintain that Thrasea Paetus was a Roman with Stoic views, not a Stoic who happened to be a Roman senator, for his aims were not deduced from Stoic doctrine, though Stoicism strengthened his courage to express them[4] and supported his moral disapproval of Nero's extravagant behaviour: the Stoa, like all the philosophical schools, distinguished king from tyrant, not according to the legal basis of their power, but the virtue or vice with which it was exercised. For Toynbee, Stoic moral disapproval was the whole content of Thrasea and his circle's activities under Nero.[5] Now moral censure of the Princeps could be taken to imply the wish to replace him with a better ruler, but the Pisonian conspiracy had shown that such thinking was not restricted to Stoics.[6] Thus, in so far as there was political opposition, it was not philosophical in origin. Why then was the persecution, which alleged political treason, 'philosophical'?

Seneca's evidence strongly suggests that Thrasea Paetus' accusers had at least a pretext for blaming Thrasea's philosophy.

---

and Legal Privilege, p. 105, leaves the date open but gives the same interpretation.

[1] See above, pp. 101–2, 117. [2] Tacitus, *Hist.* 4. 6, 7, 9.

[3] *Libertas as a Political Idea at Rome*, pp. 138 ff. R. MacMullen, *Enemies of the Roman Order*, Cambridge, Mass., 1967, pp. 53 ff., has a similar view.

[4] Cf. Tacitus on Helvidius, *Hist.* 4. 5.

[5] J. M. C. Toynbee, *Greece and Rome* 38 (1944), 43 ff.

[6] Note the attitude of Subrius Flavus, Tacitus, *Ann.* 15. 65, 67.

Seneca seems to be arguing against people who cast their reasons for disapproving of Nero's vices and for abstaining from politics in Stoic terms. The first is confirmed by a story in Epictetus showing that one of Thrasea's satellites, Q. Paconius Agrippinus who was exiled in 66,[1] justified his decision not to attend Nero's games, in terms of Stoic philosophy.[2] The second is confirmed by a passage in Tacitus, probably derived from the biography of Thrasea by his young Stoic friend, Arulenus Rusticus.[3] Thrasea urged this man, then tribune, to consider carefully what course in public life he would adopt *at such a time*. This hint of the relevance of political conditions to one's conduct suggests that Thrasea himself could be responsible for the story in Plutarch's Life of the Younger Cato, that on his death-bed Cato advised his son against entering public life in such political conditions.[4] Stoicism was not then the inspiration for the political opposition that Thrasea expressed by withdrawal, but it provided a formula for justifying abstention once he judged the state evil and corrupt. The use of this formula was enough to give substance to the charges against Stoicism.

Seneca wrote constantly about the problem of political participation because it was a constant preoccupation of the governing class at Rome. His works show clearly that, although late Stoicism was too complex to provide its adherents with definite directives, it did give them a rich supply of terms and arguments to use in analysing different courses and weighing the alternatives. Seneca himself did not disapprove of political abstention or withdrawal as such—perhaps he was insufficiently aware of the danger to Rome of such inactivity. But he regarded it as disastrous that philosophers should use their devotion to wisdom as a political protest and that the government in turn should grow suspicious of philosophy. Instead, he advised unostentatious retreat, and, for Stoics, an *otium* motivated by a real interest in morality and mankind, not by a petulant disapproval of the current Princeps.

---

[1] Tacitus, *Ann.* 16. 28, 1; 33, 2.   [2] Epict. 1. 2, 12.

[3] Tacitus, *Ann.* 16. 26, 4; on the source see Syme, *Tacitus*, p. 298.

[4] Plutarch, *Cato Minor* 66. 3. Thrasea's *Cato* was a major source for Plutarch, ibid. 25; 37—apparently Plutarch knew the account of Cato's contemporary Munatius Rufus, which he mentions in these chapters, through Thrasea's work.

II

MORS DIU MEDITATA

IN the latter part of 64, Seneca, though again refused permission to retire from Rome, surrendered part of his fortune and retreated to his room to lead the life of an invalid.[1] Early in the next year a plot was formed to assassinate Nero and set C. Calpurnius Piso on the throne. On the very day fixed for the murder of the Emperor, probably 19 April 65, Seneca, who had apparently left Rome again to travel in Campania, returned to his villa near the city.[2] Seneca may well have known of the conspirators' plans, but he was probably not a conspirator, unlike his nephew Lucan from whom Seneca differed in temperament and political outlook.[3] Soon after, certainly before 30 April 65,[4] when Lucan committed suicide on imperial instructions, Seneca took his own life.

Seneca's death is clearly relevant to a study of his career in politics, for it was, in its cause, its performance, and its effect, a political act. Ordered by Nero on the pretext that his old tutor and adviser had turned conspirator but really to remove the last goad to his flagging conscience, Seneca's suicide was modelled closely on that of Socrates and, like his, was meant to add weight to the ideals which, he claimed, had brought his destruction: the free expression of the truth which political authority resented.

[1] See above, pp. 93–4; 358 n. 1.

[2] Tacitus, *Ann.* 15. 53; 60, 4. For the date, P. Treves, *Studia Florentina Alexandro Ronconi Sexagenario Oblata*, Rome, 1970, pp. 507 ff.

[3] For arguments in favour of Tacitus' view that Seneca was innocent and on Lucan's part see *Seneca*, ed. Costa, London, 1974, pp. 25–8. On the contrast between Seneca's and Lucan's attitudes see above, pp. 103, 187–90, 192 ff., and W. Rutz, *Hermes* 88 (1960), 472 ff., who contrasts Lucan's view of death as the supreme expression of virtue and means to freedom with Seneca's interest (shown even in the tragedies) in rational decision concerning death and suicide.

[4] Vacca Life of Lucan.

For Tacitus, whose account is the most detailed, Seneca's end was admirable but a shade histrionic; he clearly preferred the panache of Petronius.[1] But at least one senator of the highest moral standing, Thrasea Paetus, judged it worthy of imitation.

The manner of Seneca's death might well be expected to find some reflection in his philosophical works. First, because, like other ancient philosophers, he held that one of the chief tasks of moral philosophy was to teach men how to die. But also because, to judge from what remains, suicide figures more prominently and more passionately in his works than in those of other Stoic philosophers.

Suicide had been a practical problem for him long before A.D. 65. In youth, ill health led him to contemplate ending his life more than once, but, as he tells us, the thought of his father's grief deterred him and philosophy gave him the courage to go on.[2] If, as is likely, philosophy also helped to supply arguments against suicide at that time, we may well expect to find arguments of this type in the extant works. But neither this early attempt, predating by a decade all of the works we have, nor, obviously, the later successful one can be reflected *directly* in what we read: there can be no question here of *apologia* nor, indeed, of hypocrisy. Possible connections between Seneca's behaviour and his words here must be sought first in a comparison of the attitude to suicide implicit in his actions with that expressed in words, and, second, in a search for departures from orthodoxy or peculiarities of emphasis in his doctrine that seem to crave explanation in the events of his own life or in what he observed around him. Thus some have suggested that the very constancy with which he returns to the theme of suicide is to be explained by his own persistent ill health, or by his neurotic psychology, or by the circumstances in which his political position and social class placed him.

[1] *Ann.* 16. 19. Tacitus' admiration is apparent throughout the chapter, and in 2, 'audiebat referentes nihil de immortalitate animae et sapientium placitis', he is clearly comparing Petronius with Seneca to the former's credit, see below, p. 370.

[2] *Ep.* 78. 2–3. The middle of the reign of Tiberius is the period indicated, see above, pp. 42–3.

I

The biographical evidence is quickly rehearsed. For Seneca's early contemplation of suicide we are dependent on his own account in Letter 78. 1–4. Adopting at first an off-hand attitude to the symptoms of tuberculosis, Seneca became, as the disease progressed, discouraged about his prospects of recovery. Expecting to die of the disease eventually, he thought of ending his own life, but the thought of what his father would suffer by his loss made him resolve to live. Seneca regards this contemplated suicide as a brave act, though, in the circumstances, living was braver. The courage required to live, he makes clear, consisted in enduring pain and the fear of pain and death. Presumably, the courage to commit suicide would have consisted in overcoming the fear of death.

For the details of Seneca's death we rely on the sympathetic account of Tacitus and the hostile one of Cassius Dio.[1] Both make it quite clear that Seneca committed suicide only in the purely material sense that he cut his own veins. The moral responsibility for this *caedes*, as Tacitus calls it, lay entirely with Nero: he makes Seneca compare it to the murder of Agrippina and Britannicus. Seneca did not even anticipate the imperial death sentence. The praetorian tribune sent to interrogate him about a reported exchange of messages with the conspirator C. Calpurnius Piso could report no sign that Seneca was preparing a *voluntaria mors* and was sent back to order him to end his life. Tacitus emphasizes Seneca's calm and courage; he makes Seneca himself remind his friends of their philosophical convictions and the long mental preparation they had undergone for meeting just such contingencies. It emerges that he kept a stock of hemlock by him. With this detail, Tacitus shows us what model Seneca had in mind: we are to see his death as a re-enactment of the end of Socrates as written by Plato.[2]

[1] Tacitus, *Ann.* 15. 62–4; Dio 62. 25.

[2] *Ann.* 15. 64: 'orat provisum pridem venenum quo damnati publico Atheniensium iudicio extinguerentur promeret.' Seneca's imitation of Socrates' death inspired the double herm in Berlin (C. Blümel, *Römische Bildnisse, Katalog der Sammlung Antiker Skulpturen*, Berlin, 1933, p. 44 and Tafel 71).

The essential resemblances between the ends of the two philosophers are the death sentences preceding the act of self-destruction, the exhortation to friends to live according to the philosophical doctrines they have discussed together, and the philosophical discourse held in the face of death. Tacitus does not actually tell us that the last words that Seneca dictated (which were well known to his readers) were concerned with death and immortality, but there are reasons for thinking that they were: Tacitus seems to indicate that they were not an indictment of Nero's crimes;[1] Dio probably alludes, however inaccurately, to these same words when he says that Seneca took time to re-vise a βιβλίον he was writing and, by adding that he entrusted others to his friends, Dio implies that the last words were similar to Seneca's other books, hence philosophical;[2] finally, Thrasea Paetus, whose death was a deliberate imitation of Seneca's in its echoes of Socrates' death and in the final libation, was discussing the nature of the soul and the separation of soul and body while waiting for news of the Senate's sentence.[3] Both Seneca and Thrasea poured a symbolic libation to Jupiter Liberator, one in water from the suicidal bath, the other in blood. The idea prob-ably combines the popular philosophical cliché of life as a banquet[4] with an allusion to Socrates' wish in the *Phaedo* to pour a libation to the gods from the lethal cup.[5] The selection of Jupiter Liberator instead of Ζεὺς Σωτήρ, the customary deity honoured at Greek banquets,[6] must have been meant to mark the liberation of the soul from the body, which was celebrated in the *Phaedo*. Per-haps it was also meant to suggest that Seneca had, by his prompt and ready obedience of Nero's order, avoided any possibility of

---

[1] *Ann.* 15. 67, 3: Tacitus says of the last words of Subrius Flavus whose death was after Seneca's 'nihil in illa coniuratione gravius auribus Neronis accidisse constitit, qui ut faciendis sceleribus promptus, ita audiendi quae faceret insolens erat': Nero can hardly then have had his crimes rehearsed by Seneca also (even if he only read his discourse later).

[2] See Appendix B4, p. 418 n. 4.

[3] *Ann.* 16. 34–5.

[4] *SVF* 3. 768 gives a Stoic elaboration of the image as applied to suicide, and Seneca makes a Stoic philosopher allude to it in a suicide context (*Ep.* 77. 8).

[5] *Phaedo* 117 b.

[6] Suda s.v. Κρατήρ (Adler III, p. 182. 4).

violating that *libertas* of which he had just reminded Nero—free speech and free conduct even towards the Emperor.[1]

Socrates had sent the women of his family away before taking the hemlock. Seneca and Thrasea each had to face the problem of a wife who wished to join him in death. Thrasea was to dissuade Arria by noting her obligations to their child; Seneca's wife did follow him but her suicide was forcibly interrupted by Nero's order. Of Seneca's reasons for allowing her attempt we cannot be sure. Dio says that he insisted on her death (against her wish) and that she survived because soldiers had hastened Seneca's death so that he died first. In Tacitus' account, Seneca at first exhorts Paulina to find consolation for her loss in the contemplation of his memory, but, after she announces her intention to die, he is reluctant to deny her the glory of a death which excels his in not being so directly compelled. He is also concerned about what will happen to her if she does survive him. Even the nasty rumour reported by Tacitus—that she was thinking only of the glory and was not sorry to be saved—is no match for Dio's malice. He also differs from Tacitus in making the soldiers hasten Seneca's death: in Tacitus they save Paulina, while Seneca and his doctor carry out his suicide. Tacitus' sources for Seneca's suicide include Seneca's own last words and the history by Seneca's friend Fabius Rusticus whose evidence is cited in this context and who might well have been one of the two friends present at the death.[2] That is sufficient justification for adopting his version of the facts, including the reasons Paulina gave for her decision and Seneca for accepting it.[3] It is important

---

[1] *Ann.* 15. 61. An allusion to the legend 'Iuppiter Liberator' on coins of Nero, suggested by H. Mattingly, *JRS* 10 (1920), 38, is unlikely as the coins were minted after Seneca's and Thrasea's deaths in 66/7 in Greece. For the Stoic view of suicide as a guarantee of freedom see below, pp. 383–4.

[2] *Ann.* 15. 60, 4; 61, 3.

[3] Dio's account is suspect also in that he makes Seneca say that he had taught Paulina not only to despise death (a message that fills his writings) but to wish to die along with him. The extant works do not contain this sentiment, while the fragments of *De Matrimonio* show him praising women who showed their loyalty by not remarrying (frs. 18, 22, 23, 25, 26, 28 in Bickel, *Diatribe in Senecae philosophi fragmenta* I, pp. 382–94), building a monument (fr. 15 Bickel), or risking death to save a husband (Alcestis fr. inc. Bickel) or to bury him (fr. 16

that our acceptance of his version is thus independent of any comparison of the views he attributes to Seneca with those in the philosopher's extant works. For appropriateness of utterance could, in itself, result from Tacitus' construction of a convincing scene based on his own considerable knowledge of Seneca's works,[1] and, if that were the case, our use of Tacitus' account of Seneca's death to check Seneca's consistency in thought and deed would be completely circular.

Finally, it will be illuminating to note the conduct in youth of Seneca's friend Lucilius, to whom those works that have most to say about suicide were later to be dedicated. According to Seneca, Lucilius faced the possibility of torture and death rather than say anything that would involve breaking faith with his friend Gaetulicus, or do anything unworthy of a good man. But he did not seek refuge in suicide.[2] Even if the rationale for Lucilius' conduct here is of Seneca's own invention, the basic facts are probably correct as Seneca, in praising Lucilius, was not defending any particular part of his life, but choosing freely episodes of Lucilius' life that seemed to him particularly creditable.

In comparing Seneca's behaviour with his doctrine, it will be economical to proceed via an examination of orthodox Stoic doctrine concerning suicide, so far as it can be reconstructed. For we shall find that the decisions about suicide taken by Seneca, his

---

Bickel). Of the three examples that show wives dying with their husbands, one is explicitly given as an example of *pudicitia* (the Indian women, fr. inc. Bickel: 'puto quae sic moritur, secundas nuptias non requirit'), one (Laodamia, fr. inc. Bickel) follows two illustrating *pudicitia*, and the third, the only Roman one— 'Brutus Porciam virginem duxit uxorem, Marciam Cato non virginem; sed Marcia inter Hortensium Catonemque discurrit et sine Catone vivere potuit, Porcia sine Bruto non potuit. magis enim se unicis viris adplicant . . .' (fr. 24 Bickel)—contains a historical confusion of fact which editors agree (Bickel, pp. 59, 293; P. Frassinetti, *RIL* 88 (1955), 176) cannot be Seneca's, yet has been so inextricably bound into the anecdote by Jerome as to make it uncertain what the original Senecan point was. Yet Bickel (pp. 333–4), on the basis of these examples, thought that Seneca and Paulina had made a suicide pact which was misrepresented by Tacitus. But the historian's picture of Seneca urging her to remain faithful to his memory is truer to the spirit of the fragments as a whole.

[1] His method in writing the retirement dialogue with Nero (*Ann.* 14. 53–6) and the arguments in *Ann.* 13. 27, see above, p. 281 n. 3; Appendix C5.

[2] *NQ* 4, pref. 15–16.

wife, and his friends are entirely in keeping with it and that
Seneca's views on the subject in his essays and letters[1] are also,
for the most part, faithful reflections of that doctrine. First, the
imitation of Socrates. Seneca, like Epictetus, frequently celebrates
his death.[2] In this they were following Stoic tradition, for the
Phaedo was clearly a basic text on suicide for the founders of the
school. There it was maintained that taking one's own life was
only justified when God sent the necessity upon one: for Socrates,
the death sentence passed in accordance with Athenian law was
that necessity. Zeno and Cleanthes both ended their lives when
ill health came upon them. Tradition held that Zeno after a fall
in which one of his digits was fractured, exclaimed 'I come. Why
do you call me?' and killed himself.[3] Bonhöffer[4] was probably
right to argue that Zeno took this trivial mishap as a hint from
God that his body was no longer capable of life according to
nature, the end that Providence has ordained for man, and that
the same interpretation can be given to the tradition that Cleanthes refused to resume eating after an inflammation of the gums
had led to his abstinence from food for two days.[5] Now Seneca
contrasts Zeno's and Socrates' deaths in an elegant antithesis:
'alter [Socrates] te docebit mori si necesse erit, alter [Zeno]
antequam necesse erit' (*Ep.* 104. 21). According to Rist, in a
recent study of Stoic views on suicide,[6] Seneca here represents
Zeno's suicide as 'an arbitrary act of decision, unconnected with
external pressures or signs'. But Seneca makes clear elsewhere
the meaning that is here obscured by conciseness. Speaking of old
age in Letter 58. 34, he says that if the body is too weak to perform its functions, then the soul can justifiably be freed from it by
suicide: 'et fortasse paulo ante quam debet faciendum est, ne cum
fieri debebit facere non possis.' The anticipation of the obligation

---

[1] A full collection of evidence, including passages in the tragedies, is given
by N. Tadic-Gilloteaux, *Ant. Class.* 32 (1963), 541 ff.

[2] Seneca, *Tranq.* 16. 1–4; *Prov.* 3. 4; *Ep.* 13. 14; 24. 4; 67. 7; 70. 9; 98. 12.
Epictetus 1. 29, 28; 4. 1, 123 and 162–4; *Ench.* 5.

[3] D.L. 7. 28.

[4] A. Bonhöffer, *Die Ethik des Stoikers Epictet*, Stuttgart, 1894, pp. 38–9.

[5] D.L. 7. 176.

[6] Rist, *Stoic Philosophy*, p. 246.

is only a way of ensuring its fulfilment. Again, Seneca remarks in Letter 70. 5 that the *sapiens* will release himself not only 'in necessitate ultima, sed cum primum illi coepit suspecta esse fortuna'. Clearly Seneca meant, in his remark about Zeno and Socrates, that the first acted on a hint from outside before the order became as explicit as the other's divine ἀνάγκη. And that is what, as Rist himself says, the Zeno of the anecdote must have meant.[1]

This slight amplification of the Platonic doctrine by the Stoics makes sense because, for them, the divinity of the world consists in its λόγος, parts of which are present in man as his reason. Therefore, a man's λόγος, at least if it is ὀρθός, will enable him to judge correctly when his departure from life is divinely ordained.[2] Seneca frequently mentions suicide as following properly on a dictate of *ratio*,[3] or on adverse circumstances as assessed by *ratio*. That this is the meaning of such expressions in his works as 'si ita res suadebit' or 'quando res exiget'[4] is made plain in Letter 98. 16 where Seneca's praise of the victim of a painful ulcer who has not taken an easy way out in suicide meets the objection, 'non si suadebit res exibit?' Seneca's reply, 'Why shouldn't he depart, if no one will any longer be able to use his services, if he can attend to nothing but his pain', shows that the 'res' here is a worsening of the disease to a measurable extent. Yet Rist says 'His neglect of the requirement of the divine call is a radical departure.'[5] This is, I believe, an error, but an intelligible one. For Seneca is less explicit than Epictetus about the need for a sign, and such allusions to the doctrine as have just been cited are, although clear, very brief. Even in Letter 117 where, as Rist suggests, it is the *longing* to die (without doing it) that is condemned, not the wish, Seneca actually says, 'doce . . . quomodo ultimum

---

[1] *Stoic Philosophy*, p. 243.

[2] Bonhöffer, *Ethik*, p. 30. As Cicero puts it in *De Finibus* 3. 61, 'Itaque a sapientia praecipitur se ipsam si usus sit sapiens ut relinquat.' Therefore Marcus Aurelius (3. 1, 1), as Prof. Brunt points out, implies that it may be right to make the decision to kill oneself before one's powers of reasoning fail.

[3] *Ep.* 14. 2: 'cum exiget ratio'; 24. 24: 'cum ratio suadet finire'; *Vit. Beat.* 20. 5: 'ratio dimittet'.

[4] *Epp.* 69. 6; 26. 10.   [5] *Stoic Philosophy*, p. 247.

ac necessarium non expectem, sed ipsemet, *cum visum erit*, profugiam': that is, a good reason is here required.[1] We must, after all, remember that Seneca nowhere sets out the basic doctrines of Stoicism as a coherent system. He believed, of course, that a secure grasp of the basic tenets was essential in formulating precepts for practical conduct,[2] but, in the works we have, he takes them for granted or states them, often in epigrammatic form, without full explanation of the system's coherence.[3] His philosophical and erudite readers would have been quicker than we to pick up these allusions to the basic doctrines on which his precepts rest, for they had more Stoic dogmatic works to read than we; his less educated readers would not have been concerned to check his orthodoxy. By virtue of the scrappy remains of Stoic theory, we are often, in fact, in the position of the second type of reader while trying to be the first. This is particularly true of Seneca's teaching on suicide because all of his discussions of this theme are incidental to, or illustrative of, some other subject. As he wrote no work devoted principally to the subject, he is little concerned to present the full Stoic scheme of argument explicitly, but most of what he says fits obviously into that scheme. Sometimes, it is true, he speaks as if what is given by Providence is not a hint in special circumstances but a means to freedom that can be used at will.[4] But, in the light of the traces of the more orthodox doctrine, this sounds like an additional argument invented to counter some Stoics who, as he tells us, drew the conclusion from Stoic doctrine that if we are supposed to live according to nature, we should wait for nature to release us from life.[5] Cato's suicide had, after all, been criticized by Brutus as οὐχ ὅσιον, probably on traditional Academic grounds, to which Cicero's defence of it as a parallel to Socrates is probably an answer.[6] It must also have aroused contention among Stoics

[1] Ibid., p. 250 n. 1; *Ep.* 117. 21.
[2] *Ep.* 95.
[3] The *libri moralis philosophiae*, from Seneca's allusions to it in frs. XVIII (116–18) Haase, contained a systematic exposition.
[4] For example, *Ep.* 70. 14 ff.; *Prov.* 6. 7 ff.
[5] *Ep.* 70. 14.
[6] Plut. *Brutus* 40. 4; Cicero, *Tusc. Disp.* 1. 74.

and given the incentive to fashion fresh arguments. Seneca's contribution here, if original with him, is parallel to his attempt to develop a new Stoic justification for abstention from public life (see Chapter 10).

The circumstances that, according to Stoic doctrine, are rightly interpreted as signals for a rationally justifiable departure—the εὔλογος ἐξαγωγή—are of three types which, no doubt because of their idea that the important thing was to get the moment right, seemed to the Stoics to afford morally comparable reasons for suicide.

One type of situation existed where the balance of the μέσα κατὰ φύσιν was such that the undesirable ones (ἀποπροηγμένα) predominated over the desirable ones (προηγμένα) sufficiently to prevent life in accordance with nature. As life itself was not a good but only one of the προηγμένα, the abandonment of it could in these circumstances be an *officium*:[1] the possession of virtue (the only good) or its lack is irrelevant to this decision.[2] This formula covers cases of severe deprivation of the necessities of life such as food and shelter, of intolerable pain, or incurable disease.

[1] The clearest statement is to be found in Cicero, *Fin.* 3. 60-1 (*SVF* 3. 763); see also *SVF* 3. 759; 761; 764; 766, and Bonhöffer, *Ethik*, pp. 188 ff. Suicide was presumably a καθῆκον περιστατικόν like self-mutilation (D.L. 7. 109 = *SVF* 3. 496): Posidonius dealt with these duties imposed by circumstance (Cicero, *Att.* 16. 11, 4). Normally, of course, self-preservation in accordance with the primary natural impulses was καθῆκον. All καθήκοντα, by definition, have a εὔλογον ἀπολογισμόν (D.L. 7. 107 = *SVF* 3. 493) but justification was bound to be more elaborate for these exceptional duties.

[2] Rist, *Stoic Philosophy*, pp. 240-1, suggests that Chrysippus inclined towards the asymmetrical position that whereas the *sapiens* may *sometimes* be obliged to end his life, the fool should *always* remain alive, principally because *SVF* 3. 761 omits any qualification in the case of the fool. But Chrysippus is there stating his view at its most paradoxical because he is attacking the view of Plato that he who has no hope of learning how to live is better off dead. In any case, Cicero, *Fin.* 3. 61 (*SVF* 3. 763), makes it clear that, for the Stoics he is following, the requirement about the balance of desirable and undesirable *indifferentia* applied to both, and his remark 'cum vitiorum ista vis non sit, ut causam afferant mortis voluntariae, perspicuum est etiam stultorum, qui iidem miseri sint, officium esse manere in vita, si sint in maiore parte rerum earum, quas secundum naturam esse dicimus' suggests, in addition, that these Stoics somehow even accommodated for extreme cases the Cynic doctrine 'either reason or the rope' (i.e. folly itself as a reason for suicide). That would explain traces of the Cynic view in Seneca, *Ep.* 22. 3: 'censeo aut ex ista vita tibi aut e vita exeundum', cf. *Ira* 3. 15, 3 *ad fin.*

Much casuistry was employed in deciding how severe the circumstances had to be and what counted as compensating advantages. They also had to be weighed against the social obligations that the Stoa laid on men. Of the basic doctrine, we find no discussion in Seneca, only an allusion: 'saepe enim et fortiter desinendum est et non ex maximis causis; nam nec eae maximae sunt quae nos tenent.'[1] But the casuistical aspect is well represented in Seneca's works. The pressure of 'necessitates ultimae' caused by extreme poverty justifies suicide, but as nature requires little to live, the lack must be very extreme: Apicius' decision to kill himself because he had only 10 million HS left will not qualify as one based on *ultima fames*.[2] When old age brings complete physical debility, one can start thinking about suicide,[3] but, for his own part, Seneca would not kill himself unless his mind were affected.[4] Similarly, with disease, the criterion for him is not so much the degree of pain as whether or not the disease is curable and potentially damaging to the mind—factors which determine whether the victim will ever again be able to perform those duties, especially those to others, in which the virtuous life consists.[5] Seneca admires a man who prefers to bear the pain of an ulcer that may still be curable, a man who is still of service to his friends;[6] on the other hand, he approves the advice of a Stoic philosopher to another sick friend to take his life, though the disease involved is not incurable but merely long, troublesome, and demanding much attention. The difference between these cases seems to be that the second man is so indolent that his death will not curtail any useful activities.[7] On the other hand,

---

[1] *Ep.* 77. 4 cited in this sense by Bonhöffer, p. 188 n. 1. The causes are trivial in the sense that everything but virtue, all the *indifferentia*, desirable and undesirable, are trivial. Curiously, on p. 53 n. 43, Bonhöffer omits the end of the sentence and misinterprets it as a contradiction of *Ep.* 17. 9.

[2] *Ep.* 17. 9; *Cons. Helv.* 10. 8–10.

[3] *Ep.* 30. 2.   [4] *Ep.* 58. 36.

[5] Ibid.; cf. *Ep.* 60. 4: 'vivit is qui multis usui est, qui se utitur.'

[6] *Ep.* 98. 15–16.

[7] *Ep.* 77. 5–6: the man is described as 'adulescens quietus et cito senex'; his life consists in a round of 'cibus, somnus, libido'. In fact, he sounds like an Epicurean, except for the fact that he is taking advice from a Stoic. For more on this letter, below, pp. 384–5.

if obligations to others can still be performed, reason often dictates continued existence: it is the mark of a great man to continue living, even in pain, and to be prepared to interrupt a suicide attempt when the need of his wife or friend demands it.[1] Seneca even claims that Socrates' wish to serve his friends led him to wait for the hemlock rather than commit suicide in prison.[2]

This last attitude is perfectly illustrated by Seneca's account of how he decided for his father's sake not to commit suicide, though he despaired of being cured. Similarly, in his account of Lucilius' decision to risk torture or execution under Gaius rather than evade the *furor potentium* by suicide, Seneca represents Lucilius as thinking he could do more to show his loyalty to his friends by living than by dying.[3] It is characteristic of Seneca that for him the pain and damage that may be extreme enough to justify suicide are often thought of as springing, not from disease or lack of material necessities, but from punishment by political authorities.[4] This may illuminate the line of thought involved in Paulina's decision to kill herself, for in Tacitus' account Seneca is moved by the *iniuriae* she may suffer if she survives him. Perhaps it was the thought of Nero's cruelty to the defenceless that made her see that the right moment for her death had come.

Seneca makes Lucilius say that he was willing to die if that was the only way of keeping faith with his friends. That fits the second type of situation that, in Stoic theory, can provide a reason for suicide: one in which one's death is called for by one's obligations to friends or country. Just as our social obligations can act as a check on the first type of justification, so they can themselves provide a positive reason for sacrificing one's life.[5]

---

[1] *Ep.* 104. 3.   [2] *Ep.* 70. 9.

[3] *NQ* 4, pref. 15–17.   [4] *Ben.* 1. 11, 2; *Ep.* 14. 4; 70. 15.

[5] A. Bodson, *La morale sociale des derniers Stoïciens*, Paris, 1967, pp. 90 ff., has recently insisted that the suicides approved of and disapproved of by the Stoics fall into the categories invented by Durkheim: namely, altruistic and fatalistic suicides are accepted; egoistic and anomic ones rejected. Bodson is right to emphasize, more than is usually done, the role of social obligations in Stoic thinking on the subject, but the Durkheim labels are inappropriate here. Durkheim himself was distinguishing types of suicide not by the different conscious motives of the agents but by the different social causes of which they were often unaware.

Again, it is characteristic of Seneca that the case he imagines is one in which suicide is a way of avoiding the giving of false evidence under torture.

So far we have discussed the two types of situation justifying the εὔλογος ἐξαγωγή, as they appear in the statement of Stoic doctrine in Diogenes Laertius 7. 130: 'They say that the wise man will make a rational exit from life, either on behalf of his country or for the sake of his friends, or if he suffers intolerable pain or mutilation or incurable disease.' There was a third type of situation attested as one justifying suicide in the Stoic view, namely where one is under compulsion to do or say disgraceful things.[1] There may be an echo of this idea in Seneca's Letter 14. 2 where he speaks of three things that may require the sacrifice of the body: *ratio, dignitas, fides*. If we apply this to suicide as one way in which the sacrifice is made, we can see that *fides* covers the second type of situation justifying suicide described above, while *ratio*, if it does not cover all cases, may here cover that type of situation not covered by the other two words, i.e. unfavourable balance of the ἀδιάφορα. In any case, *dignitas* seems to point to this third route by which Stoic doctrine allowed for suicide. One of the Stoic paradoxes pronounced that only the wise man is free, because he alone is in control of his actions. He has the power of αὐτοπραγία (self-determination) because he cannot be swayed by his passions or compelled or impeded by threats so as to do anything that is not in accordance with virtue.[2] The fullest exposition of the paradox is by Philo, but a citation from

Using these categories as a classification by motive, Bodson combines under 'fatalistic' the suicides we have included under the first type of justification plus suicide for the maintenance of an ideal—which seems quite different. He confines the idea of the divine hint to this latter type, which does not include Socrates! That suicide he further misrepresents, along with Cato's, as 'altruistic' in the sense of fulfilling a duty to society. But, in the *Apology*, Socrates makes it clear that his divine obligations were prior to any demand the state might make (29 d), while it was a common view that Cato was serving a principle, as it was no longer possible for him to serve his country (Seneca, *Ep.* 24. 7).

[1] *SVF* 3. 768 gives as one of the five occasions for suicide compared with five reasons for leaving a banquet: διὰ τοὺς ἐπεισκωμάζοντας τυράννους καὶ ἀναγκάζοντας ἡμᾶς ἢ πράττειν αἰσχρὰ ἢ λέγειν τὰ ἀπόρρητα.

[2] *SVF* 3. 362–3; 544; 355.

Zeno suggests that his treatment goes back in its principal lines to the Old Stoa.[1] It is significant that Cato, according to Plutarch, betrayed his intention of killing himself by the vehemence with which he defended the paradox at dinner on the day he died. For the fact, Plutarch should be believed as his ultimate sources for this Life include Cato's contemporary Munatius Rufus,[2] but we need not accept his suggestion that the relevance of the paradox to Cato's decision lay in the fact that, by suicide, he was freeing himself from his present troubles. This crude interpretation is on a par with other misreadings by Plutarch of Stoic views on suicide.[3] Cato, as is clear from his contemporary Cicero, as indeed from Plutarch, and from Appian's historical account (perhaps based on the history of Asinius Pollio, another contemporary), could have been pardoned by Caesar. What Cato was avoiding was the recognition of Caesar's position that receiving his pardon would have implied.[4] In the development of the paradox by Epictetus, examples of men preferring death to flattering tyrants, holding their tongues before tyrants, or obeying the immoral orders of tyrants are given.[5] According to Seneca, death is preferable to the loss of *libertas*, *pudicitia*, and *mens bona*. Willingness to face death is a way of safeguarding proper conduct: 'bene mori est effugere male vivendi periculum.'[6] That was Cato's concern.

The problem of reconciling this view with basic Stoic doctrine was pointed out clearly by Bonhöffer:[7] if the virtue of the wise man's action lies in its intention, not its result, what danger of disgraceful action can he be said to avoid through suicide? The answer must be that, as life is not a good, one may choose on occasion to reject it, even if what one thereby preserves is a thing less valuable than one's virtue, which is secure. Even the wise man can consider the external character of his actions, and

1 Philo, vol. II, p. 445 Mang. = *SVF* 1. 218, and 1. 219 is in keeping.

2 Plut. *Cato Minor* 25; 37, see above, p. 366 n. 3.

3 Plut. *Cato Minor* 67. 2, cf. *Moralia* 476A and 1076B which Rist justly criticizes in *Stoic Philosophy*, p. 241.

4 Cicero, *Off.* 1. 112; Plut. *Cato Minor* 72; Appian, *BC* 2. 99.

5 Epictetus 4. 1, 58; 68 ff; 132. Cf. *SVF* 1. 219.

6 *Ben.* 1. 11, 4; *Ep.* 70. 6.

7 *Ethik*, p. 35.

avoid inappropriate acts and impediments to the performance
of appropriate ones. He can decide that life is not worth living
if he cannot do this.[1] Presumably, a divine hint can be inferred
in these cases, though, as far as I know, this is not explicitly
stated anywhere. But Cicero, probably in answer to the condemnation by the Academic Brutus of his uncle's suicide, represented Cato's suicide as a response to a *causa iusta* sent by God.[2]

With the Middle Stoic doctrine of *personae*, some highly individual factors came into the assessment of a man's *officium*.[3] Thus
Cicero can say that Cato was right to kill himself after Caesar's
victory in Africa, whereas others would have been wrong to do
so, because Cato's character and way of life had always been
absolutely unbending, so that he could not compromise with his
former attitude to tyranny.[4] The cases that Rist points to in
Epictetus as puzzling for a Stoic and smacking of pride, in fact,
fit in with this line of Stoic thought: the athlete prefers death to
the loss of his genitals because his character (πρόσωπον = *persona*) is to be a man as nature designed him and, being an athlete,
a particularly good physical specimen of one; the philosopher
refuses to part with his beard because it is a part of the role he has
chosen and he must show *constantia* in sticking with it.[5] This is

---

[1] Philo (*SVF* 3. 513) shows that the σοφός can perform τὸ μὴ καθῆκον καθη-
κόντως when he lies to save his country: presumably his act is a κατόρθωμα,
but, in terms of external character, not a καθῆκον. That the same situation obtains
with unseemly acts done or seemly acts omitted under coercion is suggested by
Marcus 8. 47: if a lion is across your path the blame for not performing a sound
action is not yours. But Marcus still allows suicide in such a situation if one feels
life is not worth living with the action left undone. Yet some texts suggest that
the consistent virtue of the wise man is guaranteed precisely by the fact that he
cannot be forced to act against his will (*SVF* 1. 218) so as to perform ἁμαρτήματα
(*SVF* 3. 363)—which include πᾶν τὸ παρὰ τὸ καθῆκον (*SVF* 3. 499)—and he
would instead, in these circumstances, perform the καθῆκον περιστατικόν of
suicide (Marcus 5. 29; 9. 2; 10. 32). [2] *Tusc. Disp.* 1. 74.

[3] For the Panaetian doctrine see above, pp. 327, 341 ff.

[4] Cicero, *Off.* 1. 112. Rist, *Stoic Philosophy*, p. 245, errs in suggesting that
Cicero means that Cato was justified because he was a Stoic wise man: Cicero
indicates (*Off.* 3. 16) that Cato was not *sapiens* in the technical Stoic sense. In any
case 1. 114 shows that even for two *sapientes* different courses of action could be
appropriate on the same occasion.

[5] Epictetus 1. 2, 25 ff. The fourth *persona* according to Cicero, *Off.* 1. 115, is
the profession we have chosen.

the preservation of *dignitas* (to give it a distinctively Roman flavour) that Seneca means in Letter 14. 2.[1]

This way of thinking is richly represented in Seneca's writings. In his earliest preserved work, he speaks of the suicide of Cremutius Cordus in anticipation of sentence: suicide is a way of keeping the soul secure and in control of itself.[2] In *De Ira* he offers suicide as a way out to those in the service of kings who offer Thyestean feasts and commit other atrocities towards their courtiers (3. 15, 3–4). Similarly, in Letter 70. 6, he says that it is better to kill oneself than live and be treated like an animal by a tyrant, in hopes of a change of fortune.

The Stoa's attitude just sketched also explains its approval of martyrdom; for suicide to protect one's freedom to act as one thinks right is only a special case of risking one's life to secure that freedom. Neither for Seneca nor for Epictetus is suicide in these circumstances preferable to martyrdom by execution.[3] In Letter 70, in fact, having explained that the wise man will consider suicide as soon as his circumstances suggest a change for the worse, Seneca goes on to argue that sometimes, even when faced with certain death, the sage will not kill himself. Typically, Seneca has in mind political convictions. All the circumstances of each case must be considered before a decision is made. It is permissible to choose the easier death, but sometimes there is no reason to spare the executioner,[4] which might show fear.

All cases of suicide allowed by the Stoa must, of course, be rational acts. Accordingly, Seneca urges that one must not be moved by a sudden impulse,[5] or driven by one of the passions, i.e. by fear of misfortune or of death itself; by love of death or angry contempt for life.[6]

---

[1] Cf. *Ben.* 2. 16, 2 for the connection of *personae* and *dignitates*. Cicero links *dignitas* with *decorum* in expounding the Panaetian doctrine in *Off.* 1. 94, 106.

[2] *Cons. Marc.* 20. 2.

[3] Rist, *Stoic Philosophy*, p. 248, maintains that it is for Seneca.

[4] The suicide of the condemned of course freed the executioner from the taint of murder (Dio 58. 15; Tacitus, *Ann.* 6. 25). For an actual case of refusal to commit suicide, *Ann.* 16. 9.

[5] *Ep.* 24. 24; 30. 12; *Ira* 2. 36, 5–6.

[6] *Ep.* 4. 4; *Tranq.* 2. 14–15; *Ep.* 24. 25–6; 30. 15.

Seneca's suicide was in harmony with his doctrine. He showed no sign of fear. He did not rush to kill himself when Nero first had him interrogated. He waited for the death sentence, but then, calmly and deliberately, he took his own life. On the other hand, to have killed himself 'cum primum illi coepit suspecta esse fortuna' would also have been in keeping with his teaching, as would waiting for the executioner that Nero would have had to send had he refused to kill himself. We cannot recover Seneca's reasoning. What mattered was that Seneca's demeanour indicated that his was a rational decision made after weighing the circumstances with all the casuistical acumen we see displayed in Letter 70.

II

So far we have seen how Seneca's teaching and behaviour conformed to the standard Stoic ideas about suicide. Yet there are problems. At the least, scholars have accused him of directly contradicting these views at times,[1] or of appearing to do so through his use of rhetoric;[2] recently, he has been charged by Rist with a radical departure from Stoicism. We have already discussed Rist's assertion that Seneca neglects the requirement of the divine call. Other points of unorthodoxy he points to are 'an identification of suicide as a free act, perhaps as the supremely free act', and its celebration as an act 'peculiarly ennobling'.[3] In fact, Rist seems to have mistaken for difference of doctrine the prominence Seneca gives to certain aspects of the Stoic doctrine.

To say that Seneca thinks of suicide as the supremely free act suggests that he was interested in suicide as a vindication of free will. In fact, Seneca shows no interest in the problem of free will: he takes for granted freedom of choice and moral responsibility. One can choose to die but that is no freer than any other rational choice, and, like any other choice, it is not free when moved by fear. What Seneca does say repeatedly is that Providence has given man easy ways to freedom: suicide brings him quickly to

[1] Bonhöffer, *Ethik*, p. 53 n. 43 (see above, p. 377 n. 1).
[2] Tadic-Gilloteaux (above, p. 373 n. 1).
[3] *Stoic Philosophy*, pp. 247–9.

death which is freedom.[1] Now the emphasis on freedom is implicit in the Stoic doctrine we have reviewed: first in its use of the Socratic precedent, for the *Phaedo* celebrated death as the liberation of the soul from the body;[2] then, in its suggestion that the possibility of death guarantees the freedom of the wise man; finally in its tolerance of such reasons as disease and pain for committing suicide. Of course, the Stoic point here was that these circumstances indicated the intention of Providence, but, on a vulgar level—or to make Stoicism more attractive—the doctrine could be preached as giving freedom from troubles. The fact that Seneca does not discuss suicide methodically must not mislead us into taking his non-technical rhetorical discussions as accurate indications of his philosophical convictions. On the other hand, it *is* significant that Seneca so often reverts to this argument and that his examples are more often examples of escape from torture and imprisonment and punishment than from hunger, exposure, or illness.

What more than anything else makes Seneca appear as an apostle of suicide is the frequent appearance in his works of examples of people committing suicide, often from trivial motives. But often these suicides are clearly condemnable by Stoic standards,[3] and, more important, sometimes Seneca himself indicates that they are not admirable acts.[4] If we look at the context, we find, in an overwhelming number of cases, that what concerns Seneca is not suicide *per se* but the fear of death. The German prisoner who chokes himself with a lavatory sponge is supposed to inculcate contempt of death by showing that even 'contemptissimi, perditi, noxiosi' can scorn it; the Spartan boy who kills himself shows that even children can despise death. Of the suicide of Tullius Marcellinus where *fastidium vitae* plays a part (though elsewhere abused as a motive), Seneca says 'saepe enim talia exempla necessitas exigit. Saepe debemus mori nec

[1] *Ira* 3. 15, 3–4; *Prov.* 6. 7–8; *Ep.* 12. 10; 26. 10.
[2] This is the kind of *libertas* meant in *Ep.* 65. 16–22, and is probably uppermost in Seneca's final libation.
[3] *Ep.* 70. 19 ('ingenti impetu', cf. *Ep.* 24. 24); *Ep.* 77. 6 ('mori velle etiam fastidiosus potest', cf. *Tranq.* 2. 14–15).
[4] See particularly *Ep.* 4. 4; 30. 12, cf. Epictetus 4. 1, 172.

volumus, morimur nec volumus.'[1] That is, the example streng-
thens us in the face of death in any form. Most of the celebrations of Socrates' and Cato's suicides are used to illustrate the
sage's contempt of death and misfortune.[2] Rist, in fact, comes
closest to the truth when he remarks that Seneca's wise man is in
love with death, but he mistakes for paeans to suicide what are
really hymns to death and exhortations against its terrors.[3] Seneca
was acutely conscious of the difficulty most men find in overcoming the fear of death: he stresses that this fear has a basis in
nature, if not in reason. In Letter 82, where the theme is developed
at length, he argues that all the techniques of rhetorical persuasion
must be employed to conquer this fear. If, in preaching contempt
for death, Seneca seems morbidly in love with it, that was not
peculiar to him. The dilemma for all the dogmatic Hellenistic
philosophies was that while they sought to make life bearable by
pouring scorn on external goods and worldly ambitions and by
minimizing the terrors of death, they tended to make death seem
more attractive than life. For the Epicureans it was necessary to
claim that suicides motivated by *odium vitae* were in fact caused
by that same fear of death[4] against which their own teaching
might otherwise be too effective.[5] Just as Seneca says that it is
brave spirits that are liable to suicide motivated by *libido moriendi*,
so Epictetus points to these same risks in studying philosophy
when he pictures the ideal student–teacher relationship as one in
which the teacher has to dissuade the student from wishing to
escape life.[6] For Marcus Aurelius, it was self-dramatizing and

---

[1] *Ep.* 77. 16–17; 10.

[2] *Tranq.* 16; *Prov.* 3. 4; *Ep.* 24. 5–6; 71. 14–15.

[3] *Stoic Philosophy*, p. 249; *Ep.* 70 contains a long discussion of suicide as part
of an exhortation not to care whether death comes soon or late (3) and to prepare
oneself mentally for it (17–18; 27).

[4] D.L. 10. 125–6; Lucretius 3. 80.

[5] Their emphasis on pleasure as the aim of life also tended to make pain seem
worse than death. Compare the praise of suicide by the Cyrenaican Hegesias
in Cicero, *Tusc. Disp.* 1. 83. Suicide was allowed as a last resort in case of severe
pain (Cicero, *Fin.* 1. 49; Vat. frag. 9), but Epicurus' own endurance of the
agonies of disease (D.L. 10. 22) was probably the main reason why Epicureans
had a reputation for being against suicide.

[6] Epictetus 1. 9, 12.

glory-seeking through death against which warnings were necessary: even if he mentions the Christians here[1] his concern may well be wider, to judge from Ulpian's recognition of a motive for suicide characteristic of philosophers—*iactatio*.[2]

That the examples and portrayals of suicide in Seneca are aimed at conquering the fear of death rather than at advocating suicide itself is supported particularly well by Letter 30 where a non-suicide scene is treated just as elaborately as the suicide scenes and serves to point the same lesson. The Epicurean Aufidius Bassus preferred to await his natural end than to make his own escape from pain and decrepitude. (This was a justifiable decision even by Stoic standards, for his mind was sound.) Men like him who meet death calmly and cheerfully, says Seneca, give us even greater courage to face death than suicides, because their tranquillity results from a firm conviction brought about by long meditation, whereas suicides sometimes act from madness or anger (30. 12).

As for the notion that Seneca exalted suicide, the truth is more that he exalted martyrdom, i.e. the willingness to face death rather than do what one thinks is wrong. It is sufficient to note Seneca's glorification of the death of Julius Canus who was executed by Gaius: he gives as exalted a description of Canus' gallantry, courage, and philosophical conviction as he does of Cato's suicide.[3] In this he is at one with other imperial writers. Epictetus and Marcus Aurelius put Thrasea Paetus who committed suicide and Helvidius Priscus who was executed in the same class; and Tacitus' 'ambitiosa mors' (or, in an even more bilious mood 'segnis mors') covers cases of both types.[4] Seneca's own death was, after all, only nominally suicide, but it was certainly glorious and courageous.

That Seneca used suicide frequently to preach contempt of death is a piece of social history: by his day suicide to escape disgrace, conviction, or punishment had long been accepted.[5]

---

[1] 11. 3: ὡς οἱ Χριστιανοί has been suspected of being a gloss.

[2] *Dig.* 28. 3, 6, 7.   [3] *Tranq.* 14. 4–10.

[4] Epictetus 1. 1, 26; 1. 2, 19; Marcus 1. 14 (where death is not mentioned); Tacitus, *Agric.* 42. 4; *Ann.* 16. 16.

[5] Apart from the practice of *devotio* and the case of Lucretia, the earliest Roman

The practice of letting upper-class defendants kill themselves[1] is parasitic on the general acceptability of the practice. So is the extension in the early Principate to those who committed suicide of the privileges that previously belonged to those who died naturally in the same circumstances, i.e. termination of criminal proceedings which, by preventing the passing of sentence, protected the property of the accused from confiscation and his body from denial of burial rights.[2] The prominence of suicide in Seneca's work is also a piece of literary history. For the literary fashion for death scenes of famous men[3] gave a special place to suicide because of its dramatic possibilities: the suicide could stage his death effectively, including the lengthy preliminary deliberation and justification that was now traditional. In this latter development, the dominant philosophy of the period with its emphasis on good reasons no doubt played a part; Cato's death and the celebrations of Socrates' end it inspired probably contributed more. In any case, there is some truth in Nock's dictum that suicide was in the first century A.D. 'the Stoic form of martyrdom *par excellence*',[4] while the suicide in the face of severe illness already attained a high literary level in Nepos' biography of Atticus before its eventual triumph in Pliny's Letters.[5]

That disease is so often involved as a cause of natural death or

suicides we hear of are those of military leaders killing themselves to avoid the disgrace of defeat that they believed inevitable (Cicero, *Pro Sestio* 48, Val. Max. 5. 84) and those killing themselves to forestall proscription or condemnation (Cicero, *Nat. Deor.* 2. 7; *Brutus* 103; *Pro Sestio* 48—a mere sample). For a collection of material bearing on ancient practices and attitudes concerning suicide, R. Hirzel, 'Der Selbstmord', *Archiv für Religionswissenschaft* 11 (1908), 75 ff.; 243 ff.; 417 ff.

[1] Already attested for 123 B.C. by Appian, *BC* 1. 26.

[2] Val. Max. 9. 12, 7 would put the practice back in the Republic but Cicero, *Att.* 1. 4, 2 shows that his account of the Licinius Macer case is anachronistic in this respect. The practice certainly existed in Tiberius' day (*pace* R. S. Rogers in *TAPA* 64 (1933), 18 ff.), though that Emperor was not consistent in observing it (Tacitus, *Ann.* 6. 29; Dio 58. 15, 4; Seneca, *Cons. Marc.* 22. 6); see C. W. Chilton, *JRS* 45 (1955), 78–81.

[3] K. Marx, *Philologus* 92, N.F. 46 (1937), 83 ff.; H. Musurillo, *The Acts of the Pagan Martyrs*, Oxford, 1954, pp. 236 ff.

[4] Nock, *Conversion*, p. 197.

[5] Pliny, *Ep.* 1. 12; 1. 22; 2. 7.

suicide in Seneca's works may spring partly from his own frailty and hypochondria. He may have felt himself especially well equipped to preach against the fear of death of this kind because he suffered from a kind of chest or heart attack called *meditatio mortis* which gave him intimations of mortality, frightening but sometimes almost pleasurable.[1] Yet we may wonder if any special explanation is necessary for the prominence in his writing of a type of suicide that was common in his time and, as we have seen, celebrated in literature: the atmosphere was such that even the effete Caninius Rebilus could find the courage to elude a painful old age in this way, counter to general expectation.[2]

The final peculiarity of emphasis that craves explanation, Seneca's frequent allusions to death in the face of torture and imprisonment, may also have roots in his own experience, past anxieties under Gaius and Claudius, grim expectations under Nero. But the number of examples of this kind he was able to collect and the *saeva iussa, continuae accusationes, pernicies innocentium* that fill the pages of Tacitus suggest the inspiration of a wider experience than his own. Seneca wrote for the upper classes, men in politics, men of property, who stood in need of such exhortations. We are reminded of the remark of Thrasea Paetus that deaths like his own could serve as the *constantia exempla* so necessary in his time.[3]

[1] *Ep.* 54. 1–2; 77. 9.   [2] Tacitus, *Ann.* 13. 30.   [3] *Ann.* 16. 35.

CONCLUSION

THE purpose of this study has been to shed some light on the relevance of Seneca's philosophical works to his political life. On the whole, the initial expectation that the word of the philosopher would illuminate the work of the statesman has been justified, but notable exceptions have been found and the links that have been revealed have not always been the most obvious ones.

As regards the idea that Seneca sometimes wrote his essays with political purposes in mind, it has been argued that Seneca did not regularly make covert remarks about contemporary individuals or events. On the other hand, the case for finding an ulterior political purpose in *De Brevitate Vitae* and *De Vita Beata* has been strengthened by considering the structure of these works, and, in the latter case, by noting the uniqueness, in the Senecan corpus, of the views on wealth expressed there.

As regards the relation of Seneca's views in his dialogues and letters to his actions in public life, the first task was to expose the dangers inherent in the facile assumption that what Seneca wrote as a philosopher was reflected in his work as adviser to the Princeps or was generated directly by the events of his own career. The subsequent examination of some topics relevant to public life and prominent in Seneca's works has shown how complex his views are and how the degree and type of relevance to Seneca's life vary with the theme.

Seneca's conception (in works other than the *De Clementia*) of the origin and proper conduct of the Principate suits the imperial adviser who devised a 'senatorial policy' which gave greater independence and dignity to the Senate in its usual sphere, but no real increase in power. He describes the fall of the Republic as an irrevocable disaster and prefers the 'senatorial' side in the Civil War, yet he knows that the Republic had long been decayed morally and admires Cato, not so much for his political judgement, as for his personal virtue. The Principate is seen as a necessity, albeit an evil one, and the murder of Caesar as political folly. Seneca does not pronounce on the Principate as a constitutional system, but clearly regards it as absolute autocracy and accordingly lays great stress on the moral character of individual emperors. Here respectful treatment of the Senate is mentioned, but the only kind of free speech that rouses his enthusiasm is that of the emperor's *amici*, and he accepts that dissimulation is an essential part of the imperial government. Throughout, in his policy and writing, Seneca is less optimistic about the Principate and more traditional in his sentiments than in *De Clementia* where he proposed a new ideology, whereby the Princeps would be accepted, even in theory, as *rex*.

The examination of Seneca's attitude to provincial government and to slavery has shown that, in so far as we can establish what influence Seneca had, his performance in both was disappointing. When we consider the behaviour of other Stoics of the period and his own provincial origin, the standard of provincial government in Seneca's period of power is not impressive. Even the measures taken that did afford some relief to Rome's subjects did not originate with Seneca. But this is not seriously inconsistent with his writings, where the little that is said consists entirely of platitudes. He has little to say even on the participation of provincials in the citizenship and government, though the evidence seems to suggest that he did extend his patronage to aspiring Spaniards, presumably, therefore, not on doctrinaire grounds. Again, as regards the treatment of slaves, no legislative progress can be shown to have taken place in his period of power, nor can he be shown to have resisted decisions where severity prevailed, except for one involving freedmen. Though Seneca's works show less concern for the humane treatment of freedmen than of slaves, on whose behalf he is most eloquent, his views generally cannot be said to be in direct conflict with this record, for it was the conduct of the individual master that was the target of his preaching. Yet it is fair to point out that Seneca did not take the opportunity afforded by his position to mitigate the evils of the system. Commitment to the policy of senatorial independence probably goes a long way towards explaining his record.

The relevance of Seneca's views to his life is greatest where he is concerned with the code of the individual statesman—the acquisition and use of wealth, the decision to participate in or abstain from active political life, the fitting occasion and right reasons for committing suicide. Although the degree of conflict is often exaggerated, this investigation has only confirmed that the largely negative tone of Seneca's teaching about wealth, outside *De Vita Beata*, cannot be reconciled with his conduct. The explanation, it has been suggested, is not to be found in the idea that Seneca tried to pose as something everyone knew he was not, but in the ambivalent attitude he shared with his readers in a period when the socially despised became rich and the socially distinguished found their lives endangered by their wealth. Similarly, it has been shown that Seneca's stress on the theme of political participation and the way he treats it derive less from his own career or the personal problems of his addressees, than from the deep concern with the problem current in the governing class in his time, and his own desire to warn them not to endanger the study of philosophy by lending it a subversive colour.

Finally, we have seen that the degree of emphasis Seneca lays on suicide and the circumstances in which he recommends it reflect the political terrors of the governing classes in the early Empire. Men could learn to die well, even if they could not live as they chose.

It is often observed that whereas, for Cicero, philosophy had a contribution to make to political theory as well as to individual morality, only the latter seems to remain in philosophy's sphere under the Empire.[1] This study suggests that such a view is too simple, at least as regards Seneca: first, because he saw that the new system of government made the personal character of ruler and ruled more important than constitutional legal arrangements; second, because Seneca's interest in individual morality concerns, in great part, the code of behaviour of men of the upper classes at those points where it most affected their political lives.

[1] For example, Hadot, *Seneca*, pp. 80, 83.

APPENDICES

A. CHRONOLOGY

1. Chronological Table of Seneca's Extant Prose Works
2. The Date of *De Brevitate Vitae*
3. The Date of *De Clementia*

B. LITERARY PROBLEMS

1. 'Positivism'
2. Seneca's *dialogi*
3. Flattery in the Consolation to Polybius
4. The Fictional Character of Seneca's Correspondence with Lucilius

C. SENECA'S HISTORIANS

1. When did Seneca start teaching Agrippina's Son?
2. The Period of Seneca's Ascendancy
3. The Turning-Point of Nero's Reign
4. Seneca in the Histories of Cassius Dio and the Elder Pliny
5. Tacitus' Attitude to Seneca

D. PROSOPOGRAPHY

1. Living Contemporaries mentioned by Seneca
2. M. Trebellius Maximus, cos. 56
3. Annaeus Serenus as Prefect of the Watch
4. Ofonius Tigellinus' Early Friendship with Nero
5. The Recall of Antonius Felix
6. The African Proconsulships of T. Flavius Vespasianus and of A. and L. Vitellius
7. Seneca on the Vitellii
8. Aebutius Liberalis
9. The Career of T. Flavius Sabinus

APPENDICES

E. SLAVERY

1. Did Seneca's Attitude to Slavery Change?
2. Did the Old and Middle Stoa hold that there were no Slaves by Nature?
3. Did the City Prefect only start hearing Complaints from Slaves in Nero's Reign?

F. NERO'S PLANS FOR THE EASTERN FRONTIER

A. CHRONOLOGY

1. *Chronological Table of Seneca's Extant Prose Works*

I HAVE not been concerned in this study with the dating of individual works, except incidentally. My subject is Seneca's opinions, and the chronology of his works is, for the most part, simply part of the given. Out of concern for the security of my conclusions, I have naturally preferred to base them on a safe, if vague, chronology, rather than to use a more precise one which might have yielded a clearer picture of the temporal sequence of Seneca's thoughts, at the risk of prejudging the question of the autobiographical relevance of his works.

In the following table, which is the one used in my investigations (except that the conclusions of Chapter 9 about *De Vita Beata* have been incorporated), the extant prose works are arranged in broad but safe chronological groups. For the dating of the ten dialogues of the Codex Ambrosianus, F. Giancotti presented a very thorough review of the evidence and of the conclusions of previous scholars in *Cronologia dei 'Dialoghi' di Seneca* (Turin, 1957) which includes a summary in table form at the end. For the other prose works, E. Albertini's survey in *La composition dans Sénèque* (Paris, 1923) remained the most useful until the recent publication of K. Abel's *Bauformen in Senecas Dialogen* (Heidelberg, 1967). On pages 155–70 of that work, Abel summarizes the evidence for dating all the works and compares his views on the extant prose works with those of Giancotti and Albertini (p. 170). Abel criticizes Giancotti justly in some cases, but in others he is merely less cautious. On the other hand, he is more cautious than Albertini. In the construction of my scheme, I have therefore adopted Giancotti as my main authority. In the table that follows, the dates given without discussion are his. Where a date contradicts his findings or falls outside the scope of his book, I have justified it in a note or referred the reader to a discussion elsewhere in this study. Abel's objections to Giancotti's conclusions are also discussed in the notes.

I. Under Gaius:

    CONSOLATIO AD MARCIAM[A]

II. Under Claudius:

    A. During Seneca's exile (41 to 49):

        CONSOLATIO AD POLYBIUM (not long before the British triumph of 44: 13. 2, cf. Dio 60. 23, 1)

        CONSOLATIO AD HELVIAM MATREM (Seneca has been in exile for some time: 1. 2; 2. 5)[B]

    B. By 52:

        DE IRA to Novatus[C]

III. Under Claudius or Nero:

    A. Between mid-48 and mid-55:

        DE BREVITATE VITAE to Paulinus[D]

    B. Some time before spring of 64 by which time Serenus was dead (*Ep.* 63); probably before 62 (see Appendix D3):

        DE CONSTANTIA SAPIENTIS to Serenus (after 47: 18. 2, cf. Tacitus, *Ann.* 11. 3)[E]

        DE TRANQUILLITATE ANIMI to Serenus (after DE CONSTANTIA SAPIENTIS)[E]

        DE OTIO to ? Serenus (after DE CONSTANTIA SAPIENTIS)[E]

IV. Under Nero before the Retirement in 62:

    APOCOLOCYNTOSIS November or December 54: (see p. 129 n. 3)

    DE CLEMENTIA to Nero (between 15 December of 55 and 14 December of 56: see Appendix A3)

    DE VITA BEATA to Gallio[F]

    DE BENEFICIIS to Aebutius Liberalis (after 56)[G]

V. Under Nero after the Retirement in 62:

    NATURALES QUAESTIONES to Lucilius (Book 6 after the Campanian earthquake of February 62 (or 63); Book 7 before the comet of late 64)[H]

    EPISTULAE MORALES to Lucilius (*dramatic date:* winter 62–autumn 64 or, more probably, winter 63–autumn 64; *date of publicaton:* summer or autumn 64–spring 65)[I]

VI.   DE PROVIDENTIA to Lucilius belongs after the death of Tiberius in March 37 (4. 4), and probably not during the later period of Seneca's exile, but is otherwise undatable.[J]

Note A

Giancotti's date for this work is any time after the accession of Gaius in 37, this limit being provided by the mention of the republication of Cremutius Cordus' works (1. 3) which occurred under Gaius (Suet. *Gaius* 16. 1). But Abel (*Gnomon* 30 (1958), 610, and *Bauformen*, p. 159) has argued correctly that there is internal evidence for a date before Seneca's exile in 41: Seneca's presence in Rome (16. 2) excludes the years 41–9, while Marcia's age makes the years after 49 impossible. The evidence for Marcia's age is as follows: (*a*) 'Iuliae Augustae, quam familiariter coluisti' (Marcia) (4. 1). (*b*) Marcia belongs to the same *saeculum* (2. 2) as Octavia (70–11 B.C.) and Livia (58 B.C.–A.D. 29). (*c*) Marcia's son Metilius has been dead three years (1. 7). When he died he was past 13 (24. 1) but probably not yet 25 as his mother's powerful influence (24. 3) had secured him a priesthood but not yet a quaestorship (12. 3). From (*b*) Abel arrives at 30 B.C. as the latest possible date for Marcia's birth, for he takes *saeculum* as equal to 25 years citing *Ep.* 74. 34 in support. But the period there described as a *saeculum* is clearly 50 years, and a birth date of 30 B.C. for Marcia would have the unlikely consequence of making her father Cremutius Cordus a man of nearly 80 when he made his spirited defence in A.D. 25 (Tacitus, *Ann.* 4. 34): Dio (57. 24, 2) describes him at the time as only ἐν πύλαις ἤδη γήρως. Livia could have had young friends. Still, (*a*) and (*b*) surely make a date for Marcia's birth after 20 B.C. unlikely. Her son should then have been born before A.D. 20. This date combined with (*c*) puts the dialogue before 49. Gaius is not mentioned, although he is the Emperor most frequently mentioned by Seneca and references to him occur in all the complete works before *De Clementia*. (*De Providentia* includes no reference but cannot be dated.) Therefore, this work was probably published during his reign. Abel tries to tie it to 37 by the argument for putting Marcia's birth in 30 B.C. or before, that we have just rejected. In fact, a date after 39 seems to me to be more likely in view of the laudatory references to Tiberius (3. 2; 15. 3) which would not be prudent before 39 (Dio 59. 16, 4; Suet. *Gaius* 30. 2).

Note B

Abel (*Bauformen*, p. 163) has tried to fix the *terminus ante quem* at 42, on the basis of 16. 1 where Helvia is urged to set a limit to her grief and a reference is made to the ten-month period allowed by the *maiores* for mourning in the case of widows. Abel argues that Helvia cannot have been mourning longer than that period when the work was published. It belongs then in the period of ten months after Seneca went into exile. But the ten-month period is only brought in to exemplify the idea of limit and was, in any case, meant for those mourning husbands, not sons (cf. *Ep.* 63. 13 where a limit of a year for female mourning in general is given). Seneca and his contemporaries will not necessarily have demanded of a woman in their day a rigour equal to that of the *maiores*. Note that Helvia who did not follow her son into exile is none the less edified with the example of Rutilia who did (16. 7).

Note C

Abel (*Gnomon* 33 (1961), 164–5; *Bauformen*, p. 159) has accepted the view of Coccia that *De Ira* was written after Gaius' death and just before Seneca's exile in 41, insisting that Junius Gallio whose name the addressee Novatus acquired by 52 (above, p. 48 n. 2) cannot have survived after 49 and that Book 3, the last, was composed when Seneca was in Rome (3. 36 ff.). But a birth date of 30 B.C., the date Abel accepts, would bring Gallio to 78 in 49. Survival to 80 cannot be ruled out, as Giancotti (p. 100) noted. This is especially true in the case of a man who was still attending the Senate when over 60 (*Ann.* 6. 3). Abel also holds that Seneca's disparagement of court life in 3. 15, 3 has no parallels in works after his exile. But compare *Ben.* 5. 6, 6–7. Seneca could, in the same work, praise *magnanimitas*, shown in dignified courage at court, and condemn *contumacia* (*Tranq.* 14. 3–6; 6. 2).

Note D

In mid 48 C. Turranius was still *praefectus annonae* (Tacitus, *Ann.* 11. 31). In 55 Faenius Rufus received the post (*Ann.* 13. 22). I argued for the view that *De Brevitate Vitae* was addressed to Paulinus when he was holding this position in the period between these two, in *JRS* 52 (1962), 105, 108–9, and the point has been accepted even by those who object to the date of 55 for the dialogue, suggested in that article. Therefore, the date of 62, favoured by Giancotti, may safely be abandoned. For a reply to objections to the 55 date see Appendix A2.

Note E

If the addressee of *De Otio*, whose name has been largely erased, is not Serenus, the work is undatable. The relative chronology of this and the other two dialogues addressed to Serenus is discussed on pp. 316–17.

Note F

The name of the addressee puts the work after *De Ira* in which Seneca's brother is still called Novatus. Giancotti's dating followed on the table rests on the idea that this dialogue is, at least in part, a piece of self-defence against criticisms faced by Seneca at the height of his wealth and power. On pp. 306 ff., I have considered the views in the dialogue without this assumption about its autobiographical significance and then shown how the views and the structure of the piece lead inevitably to this view of its purpose.

Note G

Ben. 1. 15, 6 shows that Claudius was dead. In 2. 21, 6 Seneca tells a story about 'Rebilus consularis, homo eiusdem infamiae'—clearly the same as the infamous Caninius Rebilus who died in 56 (Tacitus, *Ann.* 13. 30). Seneca rarely refers to the living (except his correspondents) and certainly not in these terms. Hence the *terminus post quem* of 56, as suggested by Abel, *Bauformen*, p. 165. The *terminus ante quem* is the summer of 64, the date of *Ep.* 81. 3 which mentions *De Beneficiis*. I list the work before the retirement in 62 because the amount of prose that Seneca definitely wrote after that retirement is so great (including the lost *Moralis Philosophia* mentioned as in progress in *Ep.* 106, 108, and 109 and cited by Lactantius: Haase frag. 116–25) that an earlier date for this bulky work is more likely. On the other hand, in the 50s Seneca was partly occupied with tragedies, for that is the most likely date for his discussion with Pomponius Secundus in Quintilian 8. 3, 31.

Note H

I agree here with Abel's limits. The *terminus ante quem* for Book 7, one of the earlier books, is the comet of late 64 (Tacitus, *Ann.* 15. 47, 1) for Seneca refers in that book to the comet of 60 as the only one seen during Nero's reign (7. 21, 3). The *terminus post quem* for the work is the Campanian earthquake mentioned at the start of Book 6 (1. 2), as it is one of the earlier books. Seneca places this upheaval in February of 63 giving the consular date. Tacitus (*Ann.* 15. 22, 2), however, places it in 62. Either date is compatible with Seneca's own references to an earthquake in Greece 'anno priore' (6. 1, 13) of which warning was given by a comet of six months' duration (7. 21, 3) in the second half of 60 (7. 28, 3; *Ann.* 14. 22), for Seneca uses the fact to support his view that a comet can foreshadow events a year away. Abel is confident that the consular date in the Natural Questions is correct and that Tacitus is in error about the date of the Campanian earthquake. But the consular dates in Seneca could clearly be interpolated and I am somewhat attracted by the suggestion of M. Hammond in *MAAR* 15 (1938), 28 ff., that archaeological evidence at Pompeii supports Tacitus' date.

Note I

The dramatic date is given by *Ep.* 91 mentioning the fire at Lugdunum, and seasonal references throughout the series. The chronology is thoroughly discussed by Albertini, pp. 44 ff. Abel in *Bauformen*, p. 168, has now added another strong argument against the longer (62–4) chronology: it would be an odd coincidence if the seasonal references in letters of the first year (62–3) failed to overlap at all with those of the second year (63–4). The short chronology (63–4) is therefore preferable. On that system the Letters run as follows:

1–18: autumn–December 63;
19–23: December 63–early spring 64;
24–67: early spring–late spring 64;
68–86: later spring–end of June 64;
87–91: end of July–fire at Lyons (datable after the Roman fire in mid July 64 from *Ann.* 16. 13, 3);
92–122: late summer or later–autumn 64;
123–4: autumn 64–before Seneca's death in April 65.

For the probable date of publication see pp. 349 and 418 n. 4.

Note J

Giancotti, pp. 308–9, decides that there are no conclusive arguments against assigning *De Providentia* to any period of Seneca's life after the death of Tiberius, though 3. 3 ('Demetrii nostri et haec vox est, a qua *recens* sum. sonat adhuc et vibrat in auribus meis') makes the later period of his exile very unlikely (pp. 269–71). His own preference for the early period of the exile or the period after Seneca's partial surrender of his wealth in 64 presupposes a congruence between Seneca's own circumstances and his written views that could not be assumed in this study and is not borne out by it, particularly on the subject of wealth (see Chapter 9). Abel in *Bauformen*, p. 158, dates *De Providentia* firmly in the last year of Seneca's life because Lucilius is depicted as a Stoic (1. 4), whereas in the early Letters he is an Epicurean. Abel believes that the firm adherence to Stoicism achieved by Lucilius, according to the Letters, in six months marks a real conversion in that time. But if, as I have argued (pp. 350–2), Lucilius' philosophical development in the Letters is a literary fiction, though it may have some basis in the facts of the real Lucilius' life, it is clearly irrelevant to the philosophical attitude, fictional or real, that Lucilius has in *De Providentia*. Note that Seneca was capable of describing Lucilius' attitudes at the same period in conflicting ways in the early Letters and the latter part of the Natural Questions, (see p. 350).

A2. *The Date of* De Brevitate Vitae

In *JRS* 52 (1962), 104 ff., I argued:

A. that the dates usually accepted for the composition of *De Brevitate Vitae*, either 49 or 62, were unacceptable—62 because there was no evidence for it, 49 because chapter 13. 8 of the work, on the interpretation I offered, made it impossible.

B. that the date of 55 was compatible with my interpretation of chapter 13. 8 and provided a plausible context for the composition of the work.

My views have since been examined by Abel (*Gymnasium* 72 (1965), 308 ff.) and B. Hambüchen (*Die Datierung von Senecas Schrift Ad Paulinum De Brevitate Vitae*, Diss. Köln, 1966, especially pp. 26–81; 152–3), both of whom accept my arguments against the year 62 but reject those against 49, and prefer that date to my suggestion of 55. The following remarks constitute a reply to their objections, not a new treatment of the problem in itself.

A. *The argument against 49:*

I argued that Seneca's last citations from an antiquarian lecture which he said he had recently heard (13. 3: 'his diebus audivi quendam referentem') presupposed the Claudian extension of the *pomerium* in 49;

that the lecturer omitted Claudius' extension by way of criticism; that the lecture and Seneca's work therefore belong *after* that extension rather than before.

The relevant passage in Seneca reads:

idem narrabat . . . Sullam ultimum Romanorum protulisse pomerium, quod numquam provinciali sed Italico agro adquisito proferre moris apud antiquos fuit. Hoc scire magis prodest, quam Aventinum montem extra pomerium esse, ut ille adfirmabat, propter alteram ex duabus causis, aut quod plebs eo secessisset, aut quod Remo auspicante illo loco aves non addixissent, alia deinceps innumerabilia quae aut farta sunt mendaciis aut similia?

My argument can be divided into four points, some of which are criticized by Abel, all of which are attacked by Hambüchen:

1. In the clause 'quod numquam provinciali sed Italico agro adquisito', the antiquarian (on my interpretation) contrasted a traditional ground for extension used by Sulla with an illegitimate one not sanctioned by tradition: he claimed that, by ancestral custom, the *pomerium* was moved when Italian territory was added, not provincial. *Provinciali agro adquisito* is equivalent to the justification Claudius put on his *cippi*, *auctis populi Romani finibus* (more loosely phrased by Tacitus in *Annales* 12. 23: 'qui protulere imperium'), by which he meant primarily the addition of Britain to Rome's provincial possessions. *Italico agro adquisito*, correspondingly, refers to the extension of Italy proper. This description would fit the change in the western boundary of Cisalpine Gaul that we know took place and that could, without difficulty, be ascribed to Sulla.

Hambüchen points out (p. 57) that Mommsen originally (in the *History of Rome*, Bk. 4, p. 346) interpreted the clause in the way described above, but later preferred to give a more precise meaning to *agro adquisito*, i.e. 'Bodeneigenthum erwerben' (*Staatsrecht*[3], III, p. 735 n. 1), the acquisition of *ager publicus*. Claudius' justification then lay in the increase of *ager publicus* abroad; Sulla's in the conversion of lands in Italy into *ager publicus* for the foundation of colonies. This view, as Hambüchen points out (pp. 58–9), involves us in inconsistency: *provinciali* applied to the relevant land only after it had been acquired; *Italico* was appropriate to the relevant land before acquisition. Hambüchen prefers (p. 60) to interpret *Italico agro* in a sense strictly parallel to Mommsen's interpretation of *provinciali*, i.e. *ager publicus* acquired by the actual addition of territory to Italy. Such additions, of course, were impossible after Rome completed the conquest of the peninsula to the Alps after the Punic Wars. The clause, on Ham-büchen's view, is thus a harmless parenthesis noting the original reason for extensions, a reason that could not have been used by Sulla, who, in fact, moved the *pomerium* for the reason that Tacitus gives in *Ann.* 12. 23 as 'magnis nationibus subactis': he was among those 'qui protulere imperium'.

Hambüchen's interpretation of Sulla's action is impossible: Sulla did not in fact add any provincial territory to Rome's control. Tacitus is in error here just as he is on the question of Augustus' extension of the *pomerium*.[1] Nor is it plausible to think that the relative clause is irrele-vant to Sulla's extension: the emphatic 'numquam' shows that, in the antiquarian's mind, the two reasons must have been possible alternatives for the *maiores* at some time; Hambüchen's notion that one reason had virtually ceased to operate when the other became possible would require 'nondum'.

I cannot accept Hambüchen's interpretation of 'Italico agro ad-quisito' in this clause. One could defend Mommsen's later interpreta-tion despite its slight internal inconsistency, but I prefer to think that Mommsen would have done better to maintain his original inter-pretation. Of course, the addition of territory in the peninsula under the kings had rather more substance, but Seneca's antiquarian wanted to bring Sulla under a rubric that would fit the earliest extensions. He was probably giving the justification Sulla himself had used: Sulla could hardly have been checked in his interpretation of the proper reason for performing a ritual that had not been performed for cen-turies. Badian, indeed, suggests that Sulla may have changed the boundary for the sole purpose of justifying the *pomerium* ceremony (*Roman Imperialism in the Late Republic*[2], p. 34).

---

[1] There is no need to re-argue the case against an extension by Augustus as Hambüchen and Abel do not disagree on this point. Tacitus' two errors may be connected if, as Syme has suggested (*Tacitus*, II, p. 705), the historian was relying on a speech of Claudius in which he claimed that his extension was justified *more prisco*—Sulla's reason had been the same as his—and credited Augustus, a more respectable precedent, with an extension actually planned by Caesar though perhaps not completed until after his death. (Both Abel and Hambüchen mis-construe Syme's view, stating that he believes in an Augustan extension.) Momi-gliano (*Gnomon* 33 (1961), 56 ff.) does not wish to blame Claudius for the error about Augustus, and Tacitus could, of course, be wrong without help from Claudius, but the notion that Claudius was reluctant to name Caesar gains some support from the way in which he omits Gaius' generosity in granting the *latus clavus* (Dio 59. 9, 5) when citing precedents in his speech on the *primores Galliae* (*ILS* 212, Col. II, 3–5).

2. I argued that 'Sullam ultimum Romanorum protulisse pomerium' is factually incorrect in its denial of an extension by Julius Caesar. The antiquarian, learned in these matters, was unlikely to have been simply ignorant on this point. Since Caesar's extension was based, like Claudius', on a claim of provincial acquisition, the best explanation of his omission is that it is an implied criticism. It is therefore more likely that Claudius too has been omitted by design, than that he had not yet extended the *pomerium* when the antiquarian spoke.

I reviewed the evidence for Caesar's extension on pp. 109–10 of my article. Abel and Hambüchen argue against the fulfilment of Caesar's intention. Abel (pp. 310–11) simply prefers the evidence of Tacitus and Seneca's antiquarian to that of the more reliable Gellius who had read the augur Valerius Messalla Rufus, Caesar's contemporary, on the subject of the *pomerium*.[1] To accept the antiquarian's evidence is to beg the question of our inquiry, while Tacitus' omission of Caesar is hardly to be relied on in view of his other errors about the *pomerium*.[2] Hambüchen (pp. 67–9) maintains that the best literary evidence, Cicero's letters and Gellius, *NA* 13. 14, 4, only confirms that Caesar planned and possibly started an extension, not that he completed one. The archaeological and literary evidence for the building over of the Servian wall near the Esquiline in the triumviral period and later— which Oliver and Labrousse took as evidence of a change in the boundary—he tries to explain away.

The archaeological evidence is less than conclusive because its interpretation rests on hypotheses that have been questioned: the substantial coincidence of the Servian Wall and the *pomerium* at the end of the Republic;[3] the observance of the rule that buildings could not stand on the *pomerium* (Livy 1. 44, 4). Once these are accepted, however, the fact that major encroachments on the Servian Wall near the Esquiline, starting in the triumviral period and extending to the second century A.D., are attested by material remains and literary evidence would seem to show that either Caesar or Augustus must have extended the *pomerium*. Abel and Hambüchen deny that either

[1] Hambüchen (pp. 71–5) rightly accepts the argument of Grimal that the present tense 'sit' in Gellius 13. 14, 4 is to be explained by the influence of Messalla's phrasing. Messalla, though not named until later on in the chapter, was Gellius' source throughout the discussion on the *pomerium*.

[2] See above, p. 403 n. 1. On Syme's view, Tacitus' omission of Caesar is directly connected with his mention of Augustus.

[3] Doubted by Blumental in *R-E* 21. 2. 1873, who does not argue the point in detail.

of them did. Hambüchen (p. 63, cf. p. 68) appears to argue that Augustus could have cleared the wall, but some of the buildings are of Augustan construction with additions of later work.[1] Since neither of them attacks the hypotheses on which the interpretations of the archaeologists rest, possibility and even probability are with those hypotheses and with an extension carried out by Caesar or after his death.

As for the literary evidence, I cannot agree that the completion of Caesar's plans is not implied in Gellius' statement: 'quaesitum est . . . quam ob causam . . . Aventinum solum . . . extra pomerium sit, neque id Servius Tullius rex neque Sulla, qui proferendi pomerii titulum quaesivit, neque postea divus Julius, cum pomerium proferret, intra effatos urbi fines incluserint.' The imperfect tense of 'proferret' is the natural tense to use as the inclusion of the Aventine would be carried out *in the course of* extending the *pomerium*: it certainly does not imply that Caesar never consummated his plans, any more than 'quaesivit titulum' implies that Sulla went no further than to seek justification for an extension. The puzzling fact noted here is the failure of three men who did alter the boundary to alter it in a particular way. What would be puzzling about the failure of a man who effected no change to make a particular sort of change? Finally, if Caesar's change was not carried out, 'incluserint' has a different meaning when taken with its first two subjects than it has with the third one.

3. The statement that the Aventine is not within the *pomerium* can be interpreted in a corresponding manner. The lecturer insisted that the Aventine remained outside the *pomerium* (despite Claudius' claim to have included it) for either of two ancient reasons, one political, one religious.[2] Hambüchen (pp. 72–3) objects that these reasons could only have made the inclusion inadvisable, not invalid once made: the invalidity would follow from the illegitimacy of Claudius' extension. But the antiquarian may have wished to add to his general denial of Claudius' extension a particular denial of the most striking feature of it, because he believed there were strong political and religious reasons against it.

[1] J. H. Oliver, *MAAR* 10 (1932), particularly pp. 164–8. M. Labrousse, *Mél. de l'École française de Rome* 54 (1937), 173.

[2] The remark about the Aventine in Gellius 13. 14, 4 is not to be interpreted polemically in the same way. Here I agree with Hambüchen in his interpretation (see above, p. 404 n. 1) and in his argument that a man who took this conservative line about the Aventine would be unlikely to quote Caesar's example in support.

4. Seneca himself gives us warning that these remarks about the *pomerium* may not be trustworthy.

(*a*) I argued that, in the parenthesis 'ut ille adfirmabat', Seneca dissociates himself from the whole statement about the Aventine. Both Abel (p. 310) and Hambüchen (p. 78) have objected that Seneca's caution can only refer to the *reasons* that the antiquarian gave for the exclusion of the Aventine, since Seneca could hardly express doubt about the actual exclusion without cautioning his readers concerning the preceding statement about the *pomerium*. This objection seems to me to have little weight: Seneca naturally cautions the reader where he might otherwise take the opinion expressed for Seneca's own. The risk of the reader thinking that Seneca has vouched for the opinion is incomparably greater for the remark about the Aventine, which is not ascribed to the lecturer directly, than for the statement about the *pomerium*, which depends on 'idem narrabat'.

(*b*) Seneca ends his citation from the lecture: 'alia deinceps innumerabilia quae aut farta sunt mendaciis aut similia'. Hambüchen (p. 78) admits that this criticism appears to cast doubt on the remarks actually cited previously and cannot be strictly limited to the *alia* that are not cited. His objection that the statements quoted up to the *pomerium* passage are substantially correct when checked by outside evidence only tends to strengthen the natural assumption that the criticism is meant to reflect strongly on the last quotations, i.e. the *pomerium* passage. Nor is it possible to deny, as Hambüchen tries to (p. 80), that *mendacium* has here the meaning of deliberate falsehood. Not only does the next sentence ('nam ut concedas omnia eos *fide bona* dicere') show clearly what Seneca had in mind, but, *pace* Nigidius Figulus (in Gellius 11. 11), this meaning is common in Cicero (e.g. *Pro Murena* 62) and in Seneca (*Ep.* 79. 18; *Ben.* 7. 30, 2).

B. *The date 55:*

I should have made it clearer that my positive suggestion was put forward as a hypothesis for which there was no positive proof. Here I would agree with Hambüchen (p. 152). Given the unacceptability of 49 and the implausibility of 62, the way seemed clear for a new suggestion and I proffered one.

The purpose I suggested is regarded as unproved but possible by Hambüchen (p. 152), who construes it correctly. It is vigorously attacked by Abel, who does not. I did not, as Abel says (p. 317), suggest that Seneca was really trying to persuade Paulinus to retire by addressing this dialogue to him. In fact I stated (p. 106) that a personal letter would have served that purpose better. What *De Brevitate Vitae* was meant to provide, on my view, was an official version: a self-justification for Seneca who allowed his father-in-law to be retired, and a face-saving device for Paulinus.

Nor did I argue that Seneca had *only* this reason for writing the dialogue. He was very interested in the subject of the active *v.* the contemplative life and might have written this lively and satirical work, intended for a wide audience, even without this secondary purpose. Abel himself has since noted in *Bauformen in Senecas Dialogen* the possibility of a secondary purpose in the Consolations to Polybius and Seneca's mother, detecting them partly through oddities of emphasis and argument. *De Brevitate Vitae* exhibits these features as well: the usually neutral *tu*-form, as Abel himself says, is clearly specifically addressed to Paulinus in chapters 18. 1–19. 2. I have argued on pp. 319–20 that this section concerned with a real Paulinus in a real post is relevant to the theme of the dialogue, but does not suit completely the argument of the dialogue as a whole. A secondary purpose seems the best explanation of this peculiarity.

For the purpose of studying Seneca's views on the subjects chosen, I have simply considered *De Brevitate Vitae* as falling in the very broad chronological group in which it appears in the table in Appendix A1. I have not insisted upon my suggestion of 55 because I do not wish to rest my work on a hypothesis, however attractive I find it, or to vitiate my conclusions from the start in the eyes of those who continue to believe in 49 as the date for the composition of the dialogue. In Chapter 10 on political retirement I have had to discuss the date of the work. Except in this chapter, I do not believe that my conclusions would have been different had they been based on a firm date of 49, or 55, for this dialogue.

A3. *The Date of* De Clementia

The traditional date for *De Clementia*—Nero's nineteenth year, i.e. between 15 December 55 and 14 December 56[1]—depends on one

[1] The most explicit evidence for the date of Nero's birth is Suet. *Nero* 6. 1. The day is confirmed by *ILS* 229 (*AFA* for 58). Suetonius' year is confirmed by the details in *Nero* 6. 3 (interpreted correctly by R. M. Geer, *TAPA* 62 (1931), 60–1). Notices in Tacitus (*Ann.* 12. 25; 12. 58; 13. 6) contradict each other; so do those in Dio–Xiph. (61. 3, 1; 63. 29, 3). Suetonius (*Nero* 57) makes Nero's

paragraph (1. 9). No other passages have any independent weight.[1]
The crucial passage is given opposite with Madvig's excellent supplement ⟨clade⟩, and shown punctuated in three different ways.

The structure of the passage seems to me to require the first punctuation, which is the traditional one. Leading up to the comparison of
Nero to Augustus in 1. 11 (in which Nero comes out ahead), Seneca
here contrasts Augustus' early cruelty with his later clemency. The
point is given a double elaboration: (a) Augustus as Princeps v.
Octavian in the civil wars—down to *movit*; (b) (more precisely)
Octavian at 18 (Nero's age) v. Augustus in his forties ('cum hoc aetatis esset . . . sed cum annum quadragensimum . . .'). After this comes
the story of Augustus and the conspirator Cinna, further examples
of Augustus' clemency, and finally the comparison with Nero, introduced by a third version of the above antithesis (1. 11): (c) 'Haec
Augustus senex aut iam in senectutem annis vergentibus; in adulescentia caluit . . .'

The different punctuations and corrections (2 and 3 on p. 409) have
been offered to solve the problem of Seneca's historical inaccuracy
concerning Octavian's career. Between the ages of 18 and 19 (23
Sept. 45 and 22 Sept. 44 B.C.) Octavian had not yet betrayed friends,
nor, strictly speaking, plotted against Antony,[2] nor been a colleague
in the proscriptions. The separation of this time indication from
the *iam* clauses in which these events are contained clears Seneca of
his error. The price, however, is very high.

Punctuation (2) ruins the parallelism of the *cum* clauses and produces
syntactical difficulties as *iam* requires some time indication to which it is
relative. The later *cum* clause is ruled out as it is separated from these
iam clauses by *sed*; the earlier *cum* clause lands us back with the inaccuracy.

age 31 at the time of his death but this is easily explained as an error for 30 fitting
into the pattern of other overstatements of age in Suetonius (Sumner, *Latomus*
26 (1967), 420–1, who, however, on pp. 416–18, wants to accept the passage as
evidence for Nero's birth in 36).

[1] 'Principatus tuus ad gustum exigitur' (1. 1, 6) cannot be pressed for an
earlier date, since the expression is relative to the reigns of Augustus and Tiberius
with whom Nero is being compared, and could thus easily refer even to a two-
year period. The reference to the title *pater patriae* (1. 14, 2) might indicate
Nero's acceptance of the title (late 55 or 56) or the offer at his accession (Suet.
Nero 8. 1). The attempt to find in 1. 3, 3 an allusion to Nero's street brawls in
56 is best forgotten.

[2] Cicero, *Fam.* 12. 23, 2 (after 7 Oct.).

De Clementia 1. 9, 1–2

Divus Augustus fuit mitis princeps si quis illum a principatu suo aestimare incipiat in communi quidem rei publicae ⟨clade⟩ gladium movit cum hoc aetatis esset quod tu nunc es duodevicensimum egressus annum iam pugiones in sinum amicorum absconderat iam insidiis M. Antonii consulis latus petierat iam fuerat collega proscriptionis sed cum annum quadragensimum transisset et in Gallia moraretur delatum est ad eum L. Cinnam . . . insidias ei struere

1. Divus Augustus fuit mitis princeps, si quis illum a principatu suo aestimare incipiat: in communi quidem rei publicae ⟨clade⟩ gladium movit. Cum hoc aetatis esset, quod tu nunc es, duodevicensimum egressus annum, iam pugiones in sinum amicorum absconderat, iam insidiis M. Antonii consulis latus petierat, iam fuerat collega proscriptionis: sed cum annum quadragensimum transisset . . .
   Lipsius *et al.*

2. Divus Augustus fuit mitis princeps, si quis illum a principatu suo aestimare incipiat: in communi quidem rei publicae ⟨clade⟩ gladium movit cum hoc aetatis esset, quod tu nunc es, duodevicensimum egressus annum. Iam pugiones in sinum amicorum absconderat, iam insidiis M. Antonii consulis latus petierat, iam fuerat collega proscriptionis. Sed cum annum quadragensimum transisset . . .
   F. Giancotti, 'Il posto della biografia nella problematica senechiana, IV. 1. Sfondo storico e data del De Clementia', *RAL* 9 (1954), 344.

3. (*a*) Divus Augustus fuit mitis princeps, si quis illum a principatu suo aestimare incipiat; in communi quidem rei publicae ⟨clade⟩ gladium movit, cum hoc aetatis esset, quod tu nunc es, duodevicen⟨simum annum ingressus; vicen⟩simum egressus annum, iam pugiones in sinum amicorum absconderat, iam insidiis M. Antonii consulis latus petierat, iam fuerat collega proscriptionis. Sed cum annum sexagensimum transisset . . .
   F. Préchac, 'Sénèque De La Clémence', Budé, Paris, 1961.

   (*b*) Divus Augustus fuit mitis princeps, si quis illum a principatu suo aestimare incipiat; in communi quidem rei publicae ⟨clade⟩ gladium movit, cum hoc aetatis esset quod tu nunc es; deinde vicensimum egressus annum iam pugiones in sinum amicorum absconderat, iam insidiis M. Antonii consulis latus petierat, iam fuerat collega proscriptionis. Sed cum annum quadragensimum transisset . . .
   W. Richter, 'Das Problem der Datierung . . .', *RhM* 108 (1965), 146 ff.

Of the third solution, it must first be said that neither of the proposed textual corrections really solves the problem, as the proscriptions were not even agreed upon before 23 Sept. 43 when Octavian 'left his twentieth year'. That is minor: either the number could be changed or 'nondum' substituted for 'deinde'.[1] What matters is that this arrangement destroys the structure and central idea of the passage: the contrast between Triumvir and Princeps, between the young man and the old. Instead we are offered a pedantic division of Augustus' career into three stages, with the first two a few years apart and similar in character.

These distortions of the manifest structure of the passage are quite unnecessary. Seneca *is* being inaccurate about Octavian's age. For the sake of the comparison with Nero, he backdates Octavian's crimes to demonstrate that Nero has *already* earned the right to be judged superior to Augustus. That this is Seneca's technique is clear from what he does with Augustus' age in the story of Cinna the conspirator that follows this passage directly. The Cinna incident, illustrating Augustus' conversion to clemency, probably came to Seneca from a historical source to judge from the definite indications of time and place. Augustus was in his forties and in Gaul, probably then 16 B.C.[2] Having described Augustus' nocturnal consultation with Livia and his decision not to punish Cinna but to inflict on him a lengthy lecture and then repay him for listening with a consulship *post hoc* (i.e. A.D. 5!), Seneca notes (1. 10) other instances of Augustus' clemency (some earlier than this) concluding (as we have seen) 'Haec Augustus senex aut iam in senectutem annis vergentibus . . .' (1. 11). The latter phrase is a feeble attempt to justify the term 'senex'. The next phrase shows why it was used: 'comparare nemo mansuetudini tuae audebit divum Augustum, etiam si in certamen iuvenilium annorum deduxerit senectutem plus quam maturam.' Inferior to Nero's innocence, Augustus' clemency

---

[1] The suggestion of H. Fuchs, *RhM* 108 (1965), 378.

[2] M. Adler, *Zeitschr. für die öst. Gym.* 60 (1909), 193 ff., suggested that Seneca took the story from the manuscript of his father's history. Objections have been raised to Seneca's dating of Cinna's conspiracy, by H. R. W. Smith, *Univ. of Calif. Publ. in Class. Arch.* 2. 4 (1953), 133 ff., and R. A. Baumann, *The Crimen Maiestatis in the Roman Republic and Augustan Principate*, Johannesburg, 1967, p. 196. The only substantial one is based on Dio's statement (54. 19, 3) that Augustus' trip to Gaul was rumoured to be a means to carrying on his affair with Terentia away from gossip in Rome: how then could Livia, to whom Seneca and Dio assign a central role in Augustus' treatment of Cinna, have been in Gaul with him? But Dio says that it was city gossip that worried Augustus: Livia was thought to countenance his amours, in contrast to Scribonia (Suet. *Aug.* 71. 1; 69. 1).

was merely 'lassa crudelitas'. Seneca uses the inappropriate term *senex* because he wishes to give the impression that Augustus' conversion to clemency was very late, in order to make Nero's youthful mercy more remarkable. And he succeeded in giving this impression. Dio's account of Augustus' treatment of Cinna (55. 14–22, 1) is clearly derived, directly or indirectly, from Seneca's:[1] his date of A.D. 4 for the incident no doubt results from his knowledge of the date of Cinna's consulship in A.D. 5[2] plus the idea of lateness and old age which came to dominate, in his memory, the precise data of time and place that Seneca had given.

For the third type of punctuation, chronological inaccuracy is only a pretext. The real motive is a refusal to believe that Seneca wrote his glowing praises of Nero's innocence after the murder of Britannicus.

[1] Adler (p. iv n. 1) suggested that Dio's account (55. 14–22, 1) came from Seneca but via a non-historical source; W. Speyer, *RhM* 99 (1956), 278–9, that Dio used *De Clementia* but was misled by 'post hoc detulit ultro consulatum', which was deliberately employed by Seneca to conceal the gap between Augustus' pardon and his display of confidence in Cinna, thus heightening the value of the precedent for Nero. Millar, *A Study of Cassius Dio*, pp. 78–9, thinks Dio may have used *De Clementia*, inaccurately.

[2] Dio has the correct praenomen, Gnaeus, which may have come from the consular list, as Seneca calls him Lucius. The identification of the conspirator with Cn. Cornelius Cinna Magnus, *cos.* A.D. 5, has been doubted by Baumann, op. cit., p. 193, because his birth can be fixed to after 46 B.C. which makes him too young to have fought against Octavian and have his *patrimonium* restored by him, as Seneca says of the conspirator (1. 9, 8). But Sumner (*Phoenix* 25 (1971), 368 n. 57) is probably right to suggest that Seneca has here confusedly attributed facts about L. Cornelius Cinna (*cos.* 32 B.C.), whom he clearly means in *Ben.* 4. 30, 2, to Cn. Cornelius Cinna Magnus, his son (or younger brother).

B. LITERARY PROBLEMS

1. *'Positivism'*

K. ABEL in his *Bauformen in Senecas Dialogen* strongly criticizes 'positivism' (i.e. the explanation of a literary work by its outward circumstances), but he allows for purposes outside Seneca's avowed didactic aim when oddities in the structure and argument seem to require such an explanation. Thus, on pp. 47 ff., 70 ff., he sees in the *Ad Helviam* the effect of Seneca's desire to portray himself in a certain light to the public, and in *Ad Polybium* the influence of his practical aim of securing recall. Even if such suggestions can never be proved, they must be made where there is some internal support for them in the work. It is a pity that Abel failed to see that *De Brevitate Vitae* is a dialogue whose structure and peculiarities of argument do lead to the suggestion of a secondary purpose (see Appendix A2, p. 407).

Abel seems to me to exhibit a weakness for the opposite kind of positivism; i.e. the assumption that the circumstances of writing portrayed in a literary work are the actual ones in which the author and his addressee found themselves. Thus, on pp. 124 ff., Abel argues from the fact that Serenus' challenges in chapters 2, 3, and 7 determine the direction of the arguments in *De Constantia Sapientis* that these challenges were really made to Seneca by Serenus in that form. Similarly, he argues that the way in which Seneca builds the discussion in *De Providentia* around Lucilius' opening request shows that Lucilius really asked the question and that the dialogue was an answer for him (pp. 104–5). Cicero's remark to Varro about the *mos dialogorum* (*Fam.* 9. 8, 1) should serve as a warning against such assumptions. For my quarrel with his belief in Lucilius' conversion to Stoicism in the Letters see pp. 350–3.

B2. *Seneca's* dialogi

The title, attached to the ten works in the Codex Ambrosianus, goes back, if not to Seneca himself,[1] at least to the generation after him,

---

[1] Seneca uses the word twice. He describes some lost works of Livy as 'dialogos quos non magis philosophiae adnumerare possis quam historiae' (*Ep.* 100. 9),

for Quintilian uses it in describing Seneca's output as 'orationes, poemata, epistulae, dialogi'.[1] It was probably applied to all the prose works aside from the letters and speeches—even those not included in the Codex Ambrosianus.[2] But into what category does the description *dialogi* put these works, which have no named characters, no organized conversation, no definite setting? What relation can this use of the word bear to Cicero's, for whom it meant live debate or a type of literary composition exemplified by his own philosophical and rhetorical works?[3] In the early Empire, the word still seems to be used, as it always had been, of philosophical works with named characters and organized debate.[4] The unhappy suggestion has been made, and repeated, that *dialogus* translates the name of some other Greek genre such as διατριβή or διάλεξις. But normal Latin practice would have prescribed the simple transcription of the Greek for the name of a

but as we do not know the form of these works, we cannot tell what Seneca meant by the word here. In *Ben.* 5. 19, 8, Seneca breaks off a long debate with an anonymous objector (whose remarks are introduced by the vague 'inquit') by saying: 'sed ut dialogorum altercatione seposita tamquam iuris consultus respondeam.' This statement does not show that the work as a whole is a *dialogus*, as has been remarked by Giancotti, *Cronologia*, p. 16. It simply likens the shadowy debate that precedes to that characteristic of *dialogi*.

[1] Quintilian 10. 1, 129.

[2] Quintilian appears to apply it in that way. The exclusion of *Ben.*, *NQ*, and *Clem.* from the Codex Ambrosianus probably was not based on the idea that they were not *dialogi*. The lost work *De Superstitione*, also omitted from the Codex A, is described by the grammarian Diomedes as a *dialogus* (Haase, frag. XII (44)). The Codex A represents a selection from the complete corpus of *dialogi* (O. Rossbach, 'De Senecae Dialogis', *Hermes* 17 (1882), 365–76).

[3] *Att.* 2. 9, 1; 4. 16, 2; 5. 5; 13. 42, 1; 13. 19, 3; *Brutus* 218.

[4] Lucian, *Bis Accusatus* 29. 32, and Diogenes Laertius 3. 48 show that in Greek the term διάλογος certainly retained the sense of real dialogue long after Seneca's time. The Latin, according to Pohlenz, *Die Stoa*[2], II, p. 156, had lost by Seneca's time any special significance beyond that of 'philosophical discussion'. He cites in support Suetonius, *Aug.* 89, where we are told that the Princeps listened to 'carmina, historias, orationes, dialogos'. But there is no reason why *dialogi* here should not be a reference to works with named characters and organized discussion. R. Hirzel, *Der Dialog*, II, p. 6, suggested that the word here covers works by Maecenas, who is credited with a *dialogus* by the grammarian Charisius (*GL* 2. 146). We know from Servius (on *Aen.* 8. 310) of a symposium written by Maecenas in which Virgil, Horace, and Messalla Corvinus discussed the power of wine. Suetonius, we should note, uses the term *dialogus* elsewhere (*Tib.* 42) to mean a comic dialogue in the usual sense: 'Asellio Sabino sestertia ducenta donavit pro dialogo in quo boleti et ficedulae et ostreae et turdi certamen induxerat.' Clearly its characters were unorthodox but none the less clearly characterized.

literary form or, as for other words, the use of a genuine Latin equivalent or a paraphrase or a coinage.¹ The use of one borrowed Greek term to translate another is unthinkable.²

The explanation of the title may, in fact, lie more in the sphere of rhetorical technique than in that of literary form. According to Quintilian, some divided the figures he calls προσωποποιίαι into προσωποποιίαι proper (where the speaker is fictional as well as the words) and διάλογοι, i.e. 'sermones hominum assimulatos', for which a common Latin equivalent was sermocinatio.³ A discussion of sermocinatio features in the rhetorical treatise Ad Herennium.⁴ In both writers, the examples given include remarks attributed to speakers characterized in some definite way and those provided only with an indefinite speaker: 'dicat aliquis', or 'nam quid putamus illos dicturos?'⁵ Seneca's works include examples of both types, though the indefinite speaker is more characteristic.⁶ That this feature was part of a Roman orator's equipment is confirmed by the fact that the 'inquis' of Seneca's Letters to Lucilius and the 'inquit' found there and in the dialogi can be paralleled in Cicero's letters and speeches respectively.⁷ The title

---

¹ For διατριβή, Albertini, La composition dans Sénèque, p. 306; Schanz–Hosius, Geschichte der römischen Literatur, Munich, 1935, p. 683. For διάλεξις H. Dahlmann, Über die Kürze des Lebens, p. 14. In fact the Romans were most willing to borrow Greek words when it came to names of disciplines or literary forms. By Gellius' time, the transcription diatriba is found for διατριβή in the meaning of philosophical school (NA 1. 26, 1; 17. 20, 4; 18. 13, 7).

² Dialogus was certainly not felt as a Latin word yet: Cicero still hesitates between the Greek and Latin orthography. Had the Romans perversely wished, in this case, to use one Greek word to translate another, dialogus, which names a literary form in virtue of its characteristic use of dialectic argument, would be far less appropriate as a translation of διατριβή than schola, for σχολή is the nearest synonym of διατριβή in its non-technical sense, i.e. a way of spending time, and in its more technical use for philosophical discussion or school. Cicero uses schola in both the last senses (Tusc. 1. 7–8; Off. 2. 87; Pis. 70); Seneca in the last (Ep. 95. 23; 106. 12). It is possible that Diogenes Laertius means to include the ἠθικαὶ σχολαί of Persaeus mentioned in 7. 28 in the category διατριβαί in 7. 36, but Hirzel, Der Dialog, I, p. 370, disagrees.

³ Quintilian 9. 2, 31.   ⁴ 4. 55, 65.

⁵ The second, Quintilian calls 'incertae personae ficta oratio' (9. 2, 37).

⁶ προσωποποιίαι in the strict sense: Prov. 2. 6. 10; 3. 14; Otio 5. 6. Speeches attributed to definite persons: Cons. Marc. 4. 3–5; Cons. Polyb. 9; Const. Sap. 3. 1; Tranq. 1; Otio 1. 4; Prov. 2. 10; 3. 7; the many instances of 'inquis' in the Letters, e.g. 24. 6. Speeches given to an indefinite speaker: Vit. Beat. 2. 3–4; 17. 1–2; the vague objector who is the subject of the ubiquitous 'inquit', e.g. De Ira 2. 6, 1; 2. 16, even in the Letters: 28. 8; 85. 5; 94. 31.

⁷ 'inquis' in Att. 9. 2a, 1; 'inquit' in Clu. 92; Rab. Post. 12. These are clearly

of Seneca's works could be a transcription of διάλογος (in preference to the Latin equivalent *sermocinatio*), i.e. the name of the rhetorical figure, applied in virtue of the frequent occurrence of that figure in them; or the presence of the figure may simply have rendered easier the assimilation of Seneca's works to the greatest philosophical compositions, the dialogues of Plato and Aristotle.

B3. *Flattery in the Consolation to Polybius*

In a passage reflecting contemporary criticism of Seneca by his enemies, notably Suillius (see App. C4), Dio (as preserved by Exc. Val. 239) says that Seneca composed a βιβλίον flattering Messallina and Claudius' freedmen which he sent to them from exile (61. 10, 2). Is this βιβλίον the same work as the extant Consolation to Polybius? The absence of courtesies towards Messallina and freedmen other than Polybius in the extant work is no obstacle to the identification: they could have been included in the missing opening chapters. But 'Dio' says that Seneca ἀπήλειψε the βιβλίον, which, if we take the verb in its literal sense, should mean that he destroyed it. Yet it is hard to see how one could destroy a work years after its publication: ἀπήλειψε should perhaps be taken in a metaphorical sense, meaning 'repudiated' (as suggested by Giancotti, *Riv. di fil.* 34 (1956), 30), or it might represent an abbreviation by the Excerptor of a statement by Dio to the effect that Seneca tried to destroy the work. Hostile contemporary opinion probably then regarded the Consolation to Polybius as a work of blatant adulation.

Some have asserted that the flattery is so grotesque that it must really be satire (e.g. 6. 1; 12. 3). The speech invented for Claudius (14–16) is then seen as ridicule of his antiquarianism. We know, of course, that Seneca was charged with making fun of Nero's singing-voice (*Ann.* 14. 52, 3) and we have an example of Senecan satire in the *Apocolocyntosis*, but imitations of Nero in private before friends or a savage attack on the defunct Claudius are very different from what we are asked to see in *Ad Polybium*. Abel, *Bauformen*, p. 72, has countered that a satiric purpose is ruled out by its incompatibility with Seneca's hopes of recall. That argument does not hold against the views of A. Momigliano, *Claudius*, pp. 75–6, and W. H. Alexander, *Trans.*

not real quotations, although, in judicial speech, the audience would naturally attach the remark to the accuser.

Royal Soc. Canada, 3rd Ser. 37 (1943), 33–55, who think that the satire was not meant to be perceived by Polybius and Claudius either because it was (Momigliano) in some sense 'unconscious' or (Alexander) intended to be recognized only by Seneca's friends.

The principal objection to these views is that we know of an occasion on which Seneca's flattery was so grotesque that it provoked laughter, i.e. when Nero, reading out Seneca's *laudatio funebris* for Claudius, came to the deceased's *providentia* and *sapientia.* On that occasion Tacitus is quite definite in his indication that the result was not intended by Seneca (*Ann.* 13. 3): 'nemo risui temperare, quamquam oratio a Seneca composita multum cultus praeferret . . .' The only answer to this would be to say that Tacitus misunderstood Seneca's intention. But Tacitus is quick to see irony (cf. *Ann.* 2. 36; 11. 4, 3). It has been suggested that *Ann.* 12. 53—the proposal of honours to Pallas—provides a parallel instance of irony concealed under flattery. If so, Tacitus clearly missed the point there, for he makes clear his disgust with the Senate's decree. But I am inclined to think he was right not to see irony—it was not there. Pliny, *Ep.* 8. 6, 3 and 15, later entertained and rejected the idea that the Senate was being witty on that occasion. Such flattery of imperial favourites was not unusual (e.g. Suet. *Nero* 28. 1, on Acte's origins). Pliny and Tacitus understood the realities of despotism better than to see irony where it was painful to see flattery. Nor could Seneca have hoped to avoid detection in his satire. If anything, emperors were over-suspicious (Pliny, *Pan.* 3. 4).

B4. *The Fictional Character of Seneca's Correspondence with Lucilius*

The works mentioned on p. 349 n. 4 give a thorough treatment of the question from both sides. Sykutris in *R-E* Suppl. 5, 185 ff. (1931), decided (204) in favour of Bourgery's view of a fictional correspondence. Abel, *Bauformen,* p. 167, has since followed Albertini in thinking the correspondence genuine, though he is careful to emphasize that Seneca intended from the start to publish it. Recently, G. Maurach, *Der Bau von Senecas Epistulae Morales,* p. 21 n. 37, has pronounced in support of Bourgery, noting the agreement of H. Cancik in her study of the Letters (*Spudasmata* 18 (1967)).

Many features of the Letters commonly cited in support of their genuineness can equally well be taken as signs of skilful simulation: allusions to seasons given in chronological sequence (see Appendix

A1, p. 400, Note I); allusions to letters from Lucilius without further specification as to contents (40. 1; 48. 1; 59. 1; 71. 1); references to statements, questions, requests, or comments in Lucilius' letters (1. 1 and 2; 2. 1; 3. 1; 27. 1; 28. 1; 39. 1; 44. 1; 45. 1; 76. 7; 88. 1; 89. 1; 95. 1; 100. 1; 114. 1); allusions by Seneca to letters of his own not in the collection (102. 3); allusions to specific incidents in Lucilius' life (24; 36; 40. 2; 78; 107). Other features can be explained on either hypothesis: the absence of proper names might suggest suppression by an editor working with real letters or economy of invention by the author; the references to specific events in Seneca's life could be made either in real letters or in short essays composed after the events; the repetitions and contradictions in Seneca's views appear in the dialogues as well.

The only weighty arguments against genuineness are the traces of faulty simulation. One of these, I have argued (pp. 351–3), is the inadequate space of time allowed for Lucilius' spiritual development. Another is Seneca's failure to maintain a consistent 'tone of voice' in addressing Lucilius. The lack of clarity in the indications of their relative ages already noted (p. 91 n. 4) is only one sign of this. Sometimes he teaches his friend from above (16. 2; 32; 85. 1; cf. 121. 4), even in a patronizing tone (27. 9; 34. 1–2). Yet he frequently describes himself as an *imperfectus* just like Lucilius (52. 7; 68. 9; 75. 1 and 15), who is able to advise him in return (34. 2; 38. 1), and in 27. 1 he states, in reply to a complaint about his preaching, that he is no more than a fellow invalid sharing remedies. It is true that in 34. 2 Seneca seems to regard these two styles of discourse as compatible: 'ego cum vidissem indolem tuam, inieci manum, exhortatus sum, addidi stimulos nec lente ire passus sum sed subinde incitavi; et *nunc idem facio*, sed iam currentem hortor et invicem hortantem.' But the reader is bound to feel that Seneca cannot have addressed real letters to a friend in these different ways at the same time (the two styles are found in the same portions of the correspondence). The difficulty is caused by Seneca's attempt to unite in his therapy the didactic tone of the stirring lecturer with the supporting one of a teacher who is himself learning. The image of his pupil similarly wavers as it is the correlative of that of the author/teacher (on which see p. 5).

A third sign of faulty simulation is the spacing of the Letters in time: Seneca says (3. 1) that the imperial post—the quickest way—was not the only means used by Lucilius for sending his letters, which sometimes could take months to arrive (50). Yet there are stretches of the correspondence where we are expected to believe, as Bourgery calculated,[1] that Seneca, whose practice was apparently similar (cf. 38. 1; 118. 1), sent thirty-two letters in about forty days. We would have to believe, not only that he often failed to wait for a reply before writing (as he does in 118. 1 as a concession), but that he sometimes sent letters, not individually, but in packets.[2] This is to take all meaning out of the phrase 'genuine correspondence'. Finally, if the correspondence was genuine, the letters must have been edited for publication. Now Seneca composed at least two more books of Letters[3] (about 10 to 15 letters on the scale of the latest surviving books) after the autumn of 64, the dramatic date of the last extant ones. How could he have managed to finish editing the correspondence, after sending these, before his death in the spring of 65?[4]

At first glance, there is one powerful objection to the idea of simulation: why should Seneca take the trouble to disguise the character of his work? His main model must surely have been the philosophical letters of Epicurus,[5] and they were, unashamedly, essays in letter form.[6] The answer is to be found in Seneca's literary ambitions. No one writing letters in Latin could escape comparison with Cicero's

---

[1] *RPh* 35 (1911), 43–5.

[2] As even Albertini concedes, *Composition dans Sénèque*, p. 138 n. 1.

[3] Gellius, *NA* 12. 2, 3, refers to Book 22 of the Letters to Lucilius.

[4] Dio (62. 25) says that Seneca, as he died, deposited some books with his friends. If unpublished works are meant, the *moralis philosophia* is the natural candidate. Even if the Letters to Lucilius are meant, they must have been composed much as we have them, for Seneca would not have left to a friend the elaborate job of changing real letters into a literary work. In the same chapter, Dio says that Seneca was writing a book whose correction he completed before he died, but despite Dio's word συνέγραφεν, he is probably alluding here, inaccurately, to Seneca's last words which we know, from Tacitus (*Ann.* 15. 63), were published.

[5] Seneca draws a parallel between his own works and these letters in 21. 5. He cites Epicurus' letters frequently (e.g. 7. 11; 9. 1 and 8; 18. 9; 21. 3 and 7; 22. 5; 79. 15; 92. 25) and admires his style in 46. 1. For Seneca's limitation of subject-matter see above, pp. 3–4. Maurach, op. cit., pp. 182 ff., makes a thorough examination of Seneca's models: the efforts to make the correspondence seem genuine and the idea of a collection of letters addressed to one man are not inspired by Epicurus.

[6] Epicurus clearly states that the letters addressed to Herodotus and Pythocles are summaries of doctrine for public consumption (D.L. 10. 35; 10. 85); the first is probably that called an ἐπιτομὴ τῶν πρὸς τοὺς φυσικούς in D.L. 10. 27. Maurach, op. cit., pp. 186–8, thinks that Epicurus' shorter letters to friends had more influence on Seneca.

correspondence.[1] Seneca himself draws the parallel (118. 1), promising his correspondent the immortality that Cicero conferred on Atticus (21. 4), and in one letter (97) he quotes at length from one of these letters. Seneca the writer felt obliged to embellish the efforts of Seneca the philosopher.

The idea that the *Epistulae Morales* are really dialogues with an epistolary veneer is strengthened by the fact, often remarked,[2] that they are very similar in style to the dialogues. Thus, though the objections of the fictive interlocutor are often introduced by *inquis* and might be taken to come from Lucilius, we also find the *inquit* familiar from the dialogues.[3] Even the difference in length, often cited as a distinguishing mark,[4] becomes less striking in the later letters, which are very long for letters. Seneca himself says that letters should have the carelessness and informality of intimate conversation between two people (*sermo*) in contrast to 'disputationes praeparatae et effusae audiente populo' (*Ep*. 38). In practice, there is a greater air of casualness and a wider range of subject-matter including personal experiences and a mixture of topics in single letters. But the style and method of argument are basically the same.

[1] Pliny also felt the pressure of Cicero's example (*Ep*. 9. 2, 2).
[2] e.g. Albertini, *Composition*, p. 308; Hirzel, *Der Dialog*, II, p. 27.
[3] See Appendix B2, p. 414 n. 6.
[4] Seneca says in 45. 13 that he intended the Letters to be brief.

C. SENECA'S HISTORIANS

1. *When did Seneca start teaching Agrippina's son?*

F. GIANCOTTI in 'Da quando e in che senso Seneca fu maestro di Nerone?' *RAL* 8 (1953), 102–18, has discussed in detail the problem of when Seneca began to teach Nero. Tacitus puts Seneca's recall in 49, Nero's betrothal following it in 49, and Nero's adoption in 50 (*Ann.* 12. 8–9; 12. 25). Seneca's tuition of Nero he dates to 49 (*Ann.* 14. 53). Suetonius (*Nero* 7), however, says: 'undecimo aetatis anno a Claudio adoptatus est Annaeoque Senecae iam tunc senatori in disciplinam traditus.' Nero's age is wrong (there is probably a textual corruption involved),[1] but the dating of Seneca's teaching to after the adoption is clear.

Giancotti is inclined to accept Suetonius' version as correct, because he thinks that Xiphilinus and Zonaras are in accord with it (Dio 60. 32, 2–3, in Boissevain III, pp. 8–9). Xiphilinus and Zonaras do put Nero's training with Seneca after his adoption, but it seems to me that this results from their confused compression of Dio's account, where the temporal indications were somewhat subtle. For Exc. Val. 228 (better evidence for Dio's account) lacks this indication of temporal sequence, while Zonaras agrees with Exc. Val. in reporting under 49 the betrothal (Δομίτιον γαμβρὸν ἀπέδειξεν—which cannot mean, as G. thinks, Agrippina's plans to bring it about) and adding that ὕστερον she achieved his adoption as well—an anticipatory note, clearly. Xiphilinus omits this information, but then all three go on *in the imperfect tense* to talk about Nero's education, Agrippina's collecting money, etc. Thus, in Dio, Nero's training was probably not put in a precise relation with the betrothal but dated, with it, to 49. Then, under 50, Xiphilinus (60. 33, 2, Boissevain III, p. 10) notes Nero's adoption and adds γαμβρὸν ἐποιήσατο which must mean the marriage (not the betrothal, as G. thinks). The marriage has clearly been noted here incorrectly (it took place in 53—*Ann.* 12. 58) because Octavia's transfer of *gens*, necessary to it, occurred in this year. That Dio's account made this hard to understand is clear from Zonaras

---

[1] For Nero's date of birth see Appendix A3.

who mentions the change in *gens* after the adoption, but thinks the betrothal followed it.

G. greatly over-emphasizes the importance of the problem, arguing that Seneca can be deemed overtly hostile to Britannicus only if he began to teach Nero after the adoption. But Seneca would certainly know or surmise Agrippina's plans from the moment of his recall. The significance for the succession of Claudius' termination of his daughter's betrothal to L. Junius Silanus at the end of 48 could hardly have been missed, even if her betrothal to Domitius came after Seneca's duties began. Seneca's moral position is exactly the same whether the adoption had taken place, or was only being plotted.

C2. *The Period of Seneca's Ascendancy*

Though the relevant material in Dio is found in his general survey of Nero's reign rather than in his detailed chronological account (which begins 61. 6, 1) it is clear that he dated the start of Seneca's and Burrus' control to after the incident of the Armenian embassy (61. 3, 3–4), dated by Tacitus to the end of 54 (Furneaux *ad* 13. 5). Dio, in the manner of Suetonius (*Nero* 9), regards Agrippina as still running the government after Claudius' funeral and indeed after Nero's opening speech to the Senate. Tacitus, however, thinks that Seneca and Burrus already outstripped Agrippina in Nero's favour before the day of the funeral and the delivery of the speech (13. 2), and that the Armenian embassy (13. 5, 2) merely marked the termination of the total outward deference to her that had so far been observed (13. 2, 3; 13. 5, 1: the Senate summoned to the Palatine; 13. 6: some critics remarked 'quod subsidium in eo qui a femina regeretur?'). For both, the Acte incident early in 55 marked the crisis in Agrippina's control of Nero's personal affairs (*Ann.* 13. 12; Dio 61. 7, 1).

The difference, whether original with Tacitus and Dio or going back to their sources, clearly reflects no difference of information but different interpretations of the same facts.[1] Tacitus, not unreasonably,

---

[1] So, rightly, K. Heinz, *Das Bild Kaiser Neros*, p. 21. But Giancotti, *RAL* 8 (1953), 238–9, thinks that Dio gives the facts accurately and that Tacitus is not in serious disagreement but is only noting proleptically in 13. 2 the antagonism between Agrippina and Seneca and Burrus that came later. Certainly 12. 69, 3 and 13. 2, 3 show Tacitus' use of prolepsis, but in the case under discussion, Tacitus clearly indicates that Nero and his tutors were hostile to his mother's protégé at the very time when Agrippina was receiving honours

found it impossible to believe that Agrippina's position could still have been as great as her new titles and outward honours (confirmed by the coins of December 54–5) indicated, at the time when Nero gave his speech to the Senate promising to reverse Claudius' methods. He saw Nero as already wise to her before the day of the funeral address (13. 2: 'propalam *tamen* omnes in eam honores cumulabantur'), and explained the change by the work of Seneca and Burrus. He inferred a long-standing annoyance with Pallas on Nero's part from his dismissal early in 55 (13. 14).

Dio's account produces a different and less credible synthesis of the facts. Seneca wrote the speech (whose content is not given), but Agrippina was still in complete control of the government. Pallas was objectionable to Seneca and Burrus, who could deal with him only after the incident of the Armenian embassy when they took control. Nero was only interested in pleasure and scarcely noticed. Against the latter notion, see p. 88.

The question of the terminal date for their ascendancy is much more difficult. For Tacitus, the break in Seneca's real power came in 62 with the death of Burrus, though his final retirement came after the fire in the summer of 64. What is preserved of Dio's account gives us no indication of Seneca's loss of power but indicates a change in the attitude of Seneca and Burrus in 55 after the murder of Britannicus (61. 7, 5) from independence and dedication in governing to a defensive minimal type of government. Something may be due to the epitomators' omissions, but the difference may well be due again to different interpretations of the same facts. Dio describes Seneca as a τυραννοδιδάσκαλος after this (61. 10, 2) and charges him with influencing Nero to kill Agrippina (61. 12, 1). Thus 55 does not mark the end of the personal influence of Seneca and Burrus for Dio any more than for Tacitus who writes of their role in the Agrippina crisis (*Ann.* 14. 7). But Dio, unlike Tacitus, distinguishes sharply between an active stage of control and a passive one (not incompatible with influence in personal affairs). Perhaps, having invented the picture of Seneca and Burrus as legislators (see p. 73), Dio then tried to account for the lack of evidence for such activity by limiting the active period to only one year. The Elder Pliny, speaking of the period around A.D. 61–2

just after the Senate voted Claudius' consecration. As to the correctness of Dio's view, Giancotti himself admits that the *Apocolocyntosis*, which he dates to the same period, incorporates views on which Seneca's antagonism to Agrippina was based.

(see p. 289 n. 4), calls Seneca 'princeps tum eruditorum ac potentia quae nimia ruit super ipsum' (*NH* 14. 51), thus confirming Tacitus' idea that Seneca exercised active political influence as late as 62. Tacitus' view that Seneca was not allowed to retire formally in 62 and that the appearance of his being a prominent *amicus* was maintained is compatible with Suet. *Nero* 35. 5, and with the prosopographical evidence (see pp. 93 ff.).

C3. *The Turning-Point of Nero's Reign*

Tacitus placed the turning-point of Nero's reign from good to bad in 62, at the death of Burrus and Seneca's consequent withdrawal from active participation in the government. The death of Burrus followed on the first *maiestas* trials of the reign: 'sed gravescentibus in dies publicis malis subsidia minuebantur, concessitque vita Burrus' (14. 51, 1). As a result, Seneca's power was broken: 'quia nec bonis artibus idem virium erat altero velut duce amoto' (14. 52, 1). Tigellinus and, with him, 'malae artes' grew daily in strength (14. 57, 1).

In this, the other sources do not agree. Suetonius sees the whole reign as a gradual revelation and strengthening of innate vices, the first indications being events which Tacitus dates to 56 (Suet. *Nero* 26–7; *Ann.* 13. 25). For Dio, Nero began to go wild after the murder of Britannicus (61. 7, 5), but his behaviour took a sharp turn for the worse after the murder of Agrippina in 59 (Dio 61. 11, 1), the year Dio probably chose to begin Book 61.[1] As far as we can tell from what the epitomators have preserved, the year 62 was not explicitly marked as a turning-point.

In fixing the crisis of the reign in 62, has Tacitus perhaps exaggerated Seneca's importance? One of his sources, Fabius Rusticus, certainly tried to introduce Seneca into one incident where Tacitus, agreeing with his other sources, decided that he did not belong (*Ann.* 13. 20). Was Tacitus always able to avoid the influence of this biased source? One must also reckon with the fact that Tacitus himself was interested in the literary politician, the philosopher who did not choose *segne otium* (see Appendix C5).

There was a tradition, known to Tacitus, that put the turning-point in Nero's reign at 59, after Agrippina's murder. It appears in the remark of the praetorian tribune Subrius Flavus, which Tacitus claims to quote verbatim: 'odisse coepi, postquam parricida matris et uxoris,

---

[1] Syme, *Tacitus*, p. 263 n. 8.

auriga et histrio et incendiarius extitisti' (15. 67). Tacitus, like Dio,
allowed that tradition to influence the structure of his work: Book 14
opens with the murder of Agrippina. The idea, originating during
Nero's reign, is clearly the basis of the judgement attributed to Trajan,
'procul distare cunctos principes Neronis quinquennio', in two fourth-
century works, Sextus Aurelius Victor's *Liber de Caesaribus* (5. 1–4)
and the *Epitome de Caesaribus* (5. 1–5).[1] The interpretations of the
remark offered in these works combine two conflicting notions: one
that the quinquennium was the opening years of Nero's reign when he
still displayed moral virtue; the other that Trajan was talking about
Nero's buildings and provincial acquisitions, namely, Pontus annexed
in 64 and the Cottian Alps annexed about 63. Whether these two
authors (perhaps following a common source) added the idea of an
initial virtuous period to a story concerning Nero's buildings and
foreign successes or added the idea of Nero's buildings and foreign
successes to a story concerning his early virtue,[2] they demonstrate
the durability of the conception of an initial good period of five
years.

Thus there was a traditional turning-point still known in Tacitus'
day and later that he deprived of significance, preferring one in 62.
This would be particularly remarkable, if, as has been argued,[3] the
exaggerated version of this idea preserved in these late sources, namely,
that Nero actually surpassed all *principes* (including Augustus) for
five years, was actually accepted by Trajan under whom Tacitus at
least started the Annals, and originally invented by Q. Arulenus
Rusticus in his biography of Thrasea Paetus written under Domitian

[1] That the quinquennium indicated in these sources is the first five years
was demonstrated by F. A. Lepper, *JRS* 47 (1957), 95 ff., and supported by
Murray, *Historia* 14 (1965), 41 ff.

[2] The former alternative is preferred by Syme, *Emperors and Biography*, Oxford,
1971, pp. 106 ff., and J. G. F. Hind, *Historia* 20 (1971), 488 ff., who make the
very attractive suggestion that the ultimate source for the anecdote was the
early third-century biographer Marius Maximus in his Life of Trajan (cf. SHA,
Alex. 65. 4–5). But the latter alternative, favoured by Lepper and Murray (see
preceding note), is more likely: why should these fourth-century writers, in
fitting an anecdote about Trajan into their accounts of Nero, have distorted a
story about Nero's buildings, for which he was chiefly remembered in their
period, into a story about his early virtue which they clearly found difficult to
credit (note the Epitomator's phrase 'iste quinquennio tolerabilis visus')?

[3] By Murray. Hind's suggestion that Trajan made the remark in praise of the
years 60–5 between Nero's two quinquennial games leads to the much more
unpalatable conclusion that Tacitus made no allusion at all to Trajan's view.

and probably used by Tacitus in the Neronian books.[1] But this theory is very unlikely to be true because (1) in Tacitus' account of Thrasea's political behaviour, for which he must have consulted Rusticus' work, there is no sharp break in 59 (see p. 102); (2) Tacitus' picture of the reasonable Thrasea accords, if Pliny is any guide (p. 103), with the Flavian view and is a portrait likely to have been drawn by Rusticus, a man who was prepared to serve as consul under Domitian late in 92. A similar view of Thrasea was known to Dio who contrasts the rigid Helvidius with the reasonable Thrasea (66. 12, 2); (3) we can explain in other ways why Rusticus was attacked by Domitian for his book. A paranoiac Emperor, perhaps already enraged by the biography of the extreme Helvidius written by the extreme Herennius Senecio who had declined to hold the higher magistracies,[2] could have failed to notice the differences in Rusticus' portrait of Thrasea. In any case, to publish a eulogistic biography of a man condemned for treason by Nero would have been enough: Domitian was aware that he was often compared to Nero[3] and he had already executed enough consulars to make the story of Thrasea's death a suggestive parallel. Moreover, Thrasea's condemnation had been part of a policy later continued by Vespasian (pp. 363–4). Plutarch unhelpfully says Domitian punished Rusticus τῇ δόξῃ φθονήσας (Mor. 522E), though he knew the man well.

A different genesis for the remark about an incomparable quinquennium can be suggested. The original anecdote (probably in Marius Maximus) could have been part of a discussion of the bloodlessness of Trajan's accession on which, as Pliny's Panegyricus (5) suggests, Trajan prided himself. Nero's freedom from a bloody past, mentioned in the speech he delivered to the Senate on his accession, had been celebrated by Seneca in De Clementia and it was in that context that Seneca had even been prepared to say 'comparare nemo mansuetudini tuae audebit divum Augustum' (1. 11, 1, cf. 1. 1, 5). Similarly, the author of the anecdote could have made Trajan exaggerate the traditional view of a quinquennium Neronis that was good relative to what followed, so as to suggest that in those five years the

[1] Syme, Tacitus, p. 298.

[2] We do not know the order in which Rusticus' and Senecio's biographies appeared. The order in Tacitus, Agric. 2. 1, with the biography of Thrasea listed first, is not decisive: he might have had in mind that the events of that biography preceded the events recorded in the other.

[3] Pliny, Pan. 53. 4. For the comparison, e.g. Tacitus, Agric. 45; Juvenal 4. 38: Domitian as 'calvus Nero'; Dio 67. 14, 4.

Principate had had its best chance—a young Princeps with a good adviser, good aims, and no enemies outside his family.

To return to Tacitus. The turning-point he chose to play down in the interests of 62 was based on the horror of matricide and the artistic excesses of Nero that followed.[1] Tacitus chose a date that coincided with the first *maiestas* trials of the reign and marked a change of advisers. Tigellinus became one of two praetorian prefects on Burrus' death. It is very likely that the 62 turning-point is Tacitus' own, just as the break in Tiberius' reign in 23 at the death of Drusus and consequent supremacy of Sejanus was probably proposed by Tacitus in preference to the tradition he knew which put the break at the death of Germanicus.[2] Though, in Book 6, he chose to develop the cliché of the release of innate vice as restraints are removed, he contributed the idea that the influence of evil characters like Sejanus and Tigellinus was just as important.

Tacitus' break is better, politically, than 59. There are still things to Nero's credit on senatorial criteria after 59,[3] but in 62 Rubellius Plautus and Cornelius Sulla were murdered, *maiestas* cases started, and Poppaea ousted Octavia. None the less the break was not so sharp, even on Tacitus' evidence: Seneca still exerted some influence until 64 (15. 45; cf. pp. 93 ff.), and there were spots of brightness in Nero's behaviour. Tacitus approves of the Senate's decree against fictitious adoptions,[4] and Thrasea's excellent proposal about votes of thanks to provincial governors was supported by the Emperor, late in 62.[5] Tacitus' solution can be surmised. He did not just mark one turning-point: there were others in the lost books. Again the account of Tiberius is relevant. Book 2 ends with the year of Germanicus' death; Book 4 opens with the death of Drusus and the supremacy of Sejanus; Book 5 opened with the death of Livia and closed with the death of Sejanus in 31 or with a quarrel between the consuls arising from his downfall at the end of that year. All these phases are listed in the

---

[1] *Ann.* 14. 13. Agrippina restrained Nero's *libidines*. After her death 'grates exolvit seque in omnis libidines effudit quas male coercitas qualiscumque matris reverentia tardaverat'.

[2] F. Klingner, 'Tacitus über Augustus und Tiberius' (1954), *Studien*, Zürich, 1964, pp. 651 ff.; C. Questa, *Studi sulle fonti degli Annales di Tacito*[2], pp. 125 ff, 137. They think that Tacitus simply chose the Drusian tradition as opposed to the Germanican. Cf. Syme, *Tacitus*, pp. 254–5.

[3] *Ann.* 14. 28, 2; 42; 46.

[4] Ibid. 15. 19.

[5] Ibid. 15. 22.

summary of Tiberius' reign that closes Book 6.[1] So Tacitus did or would have done with Nero.[2]

Tacitus did not then tailor his account of Nero to a desire to exaggerate Seneca's importance. If he rejected other turning-points, and regarded Seneca's withdrawal as important, he did so because other dates were politically unenlightening, and because of ideas about the development of emperors already formed in dealing with Tiberius. Moreover, the break in 62 probably looked much less dramatic when the work was complete. The death of Agrippina and the Pisonian conspiracy would have counted as well as Seneca's retirement.

C4. *Seneca in the Histories of Cassius Dio and the Elder Pliny*

Seneca has always been an emotional subject for his biographers. The fiery defence of Diderot and the sharp denunciations he countered had their parallels in antiquity. Seneca's style, his morals, and his politics provoked a set of strong but antithetic reactions, both in his contemporaries and in those who wrote about him later on. On the literary side, we know from Quintilian's account (10. 1, 125–31) how popular Seneca's works were in Quintilian's youth and from Suetonius (*Gaius* 53. 2) how savagely Gaius criticized them; for his posthumous reputation, Quintilian's own judgement of his style can be compared with the admiration of the author of the *Octavia* who tried too faithfully to imitate it. Similarly, Seneca's moral and political behaviour were attacked in his lifetime, as we could guess from his own apology in *De Vita Beata* even if we did not have Tacitus' account of the charges of Suillius (*Ann.* 13. 42) and others (14. 52). After his death, the failure of the Stoics Epictetus and Marcus Aurelius to mention him may be a form of criticism.[3] By contrast, Juvenal's question:

> Libera si dentur populo suffragia, quis tam
> Perditus ut dubitet Senecam praeferre Neroni? (8. 21)

and the *Octavia* assure us that in some quarters he was revered after death as a good man and a good imperial adviser. Plutarch (*Mor.* 462A) even attests to his good influence on Nero's moral behaviour, at least on one occasion. As for his lifetime, there was a rumour at the time of the Pisonian conspiracy that certain praetorian officers had joined

---

[1] U. Knoche, *Gym.* 70 (1963), 211 ff.   [2] Questa, op. cit., pp. 224–5.

[3] They may have been critical of him from a literary point of view as well, see p. 8.

only as a means to putting Seneca on the throne (*Ann.* 15. 65) and, of course, he had his disciples.

I

It is natural to find such conflicting estimates of Seneca mirrored in the extant historical accounts. The fragments of Dio's history of the period indicate that it was, on the whole, hostile to Seneca. He is portrayed, in what remains, as a hypocritical sermonizer who urged Nero to murder his mother (61. 12, 1), encouraged his degrading exhibitionism (61. 20, 3), drove the Britons to revolt by suddenly calling in a huge loan (62. 2, 1), and tried to kill his wife also when forced to commit suicide (62. 25, 1).

Tacitus is, in general, sympathetic (cf. Appendix C5), but allows himself some sharp remarks. He reveals that one source he used was definitely partial to Seneca. That was Fabius Rusticus (*Ann.* 13. 20). He does not state the attitude to Seneca of the two other authorities he names, Cluvius Rufus and the Elder Pliny, nor do his rare citations from them reveal it. In any case, Tacitus is so near the events that many of his hostile notices could simply reflect the gossip of Neronian Rome. Tacitus claimed it was his duty to report durable rumours (4. 10). Examples of this material could be: Tacitus' account of the shocking reception accorded Claudius' funeral speech (13. 3), his reference to the vanity that prompted Seneca to write speeches for Nero on clemency (13. 11), his remark 'incertum an ante gnaros' of the two advisers when they heard of Agrippina's supposed accident (14. 7), his report 'Seneca adverso rumore erat' because he was believed to have composed Nero's letter to the Senate justifying an accidental death (14. 11). Others of the historian's more adverse comments (e.g. 14. 14, 3) clearly spring from his own judgement.

Dio's hostile remarks require a different explanation. He is too far from events to be reporting rumours directly, without some written intermediary. Now it has been established that he did not use Tacitus as a major source, and that the resemblances between the authors are rather to be traced to common sources.[1] As regards Seneca, the usual solution adopted is that Dio used a hostile source shared by Tacitus who was, however, more sceptical of it and often preferred the evidence of more favourable ones. Despite sharp words from Syme,[2] the view that the hostile source was the Elder Pliny has remained orthodox

---

[1] See the review of the discussion in Syme, *Tacitus*, App. 36.
[2] Syme, *Tacitus*, p. 292.

doctrine.[1] But a claim has been put in for Cluvius Rufus—'harena sine calce', for there is no proof that Dio even used Cluvius' work.[2]

A strong case can certainly be made out for Dio's use of Pliny's history 'a fine Aufidii Bassi'. Alfred Gercke[3] argued it very plausibly, mainly by amassing parallels between the preserved parts of Dio and historical details of the Claudian and Neronian periods recorded in the Natural Histories, and by pointing to the great number of portents in both (especially, *NH* 2. 199 and 232 where Pliny indicates that these portents were reported in his history). But there is room for scepticism. The frequency of portents in Dio's account could spring from his own interests, not those of any particular source,[4] while the verbal parallels can be given a more simple explanation: Dio could have read the Natural Histories thoroughly. This suggestion by Ciaceri[5] at first appears highly dubious, when one considers that even Pliny's nephew does not seem to have finished Book 9,[6] but Dio's definite interest in natural history[7] raises it to the level of possibility.

[1] E. Ciaceri, 'Claudio e Nerone nelle *Storie* di Plinio', *Proc. pol. e Rel. int.*, Rome, 1918, pp. 387 ff.; P. Faider, *Études sur Sénèque*, pp. 32–3; 35–6; recently, Questa, *Studi sulle fonti degli Annales di Tacito*[2], pp. 84 ff. Trillitzsch, *Seneca*, p. 51, regards the case as unproved but does not examine the problem.

[2] G. Townend, *Hermes*, 89 (1961), 227 ff. Townend alleges that Dio 59. 19, 7, where Seneca is introduced favourably, is not from Cluvius, whereas the damaging passage in Dio 61. 10 'bears the marks of one of Cluvius' unrestrained attacks comparable to that on Caligula'. The argument rests on Townend's view that Cluvius' approach can be recognized through the Greek passages in Suetonius (*Hermes* 88 (1960), 98 ff.), which can be traced to Cluvius as the only Roman historian who (as we know from Josephus, *AJ* 19. 92–3) did not shrink from using Greek. This is a slender thread to hang so much on. The quotation from Homer in Josephus need not derive from Cluvius' history (L. Feldman, *Latomus* 21 (1962), 320 ff., and others). Even if it did, we do not know what stages the verse passed through in reaching Josephus: in his text, it is missing a word. Must we assume Cluvius quoted the Greek, instead of just alluding to the verse? The Greek in Suetonius, on the whole, suggests popular tradition, e.g. *Claudius* 1. 1; or letters to which, as *ab epistulis*, he had access, e.g. *Claudius* 4. 2; or anonymous charges in *occulti libelli* sent to the Emperor (*Nero* 39. 2, cf. *Ann.* 1. 74, 2). Nor is Townend very consistent: the stories of Domitius Afer and Seneca as they appear in Dio 59. 19 are parallel; why should one be traced to Cluvius and the other to Aufidius Bassus?

[3] 'Seneca-Studien', pp. 159 ff.

[4] Dio wrote a pamphlet on dreams and portents foretelling the rule of Severus (72. 23, 1).   [5] Ciaceri, op. cit., pp. 403–4.

[6] As is shown by a comparison of Pliny, *Ep.* 9. 33, with *NH* 9. 26; also cf. Pliny, *Ep.* 7. 29, with *NH* 35. 201.

[7] See Millar, *A Study of Cassius Dio*, pp. 177–8.

Ciaceri none the less admitted that Dio used Pliny's history, but rightly rejected Gercke's assumption that he was Dio's only source.[1] That view is not tenable. Apart from a clear conflict between Pliny (*NH* 7. 58) and Dio (61. 6, 5) in the matter of the murder of Marcus Silanus, there is Dio's own claim to have consulted more than one authority about Seneca: he bolsters his contention that Seneca incited Nero to murder Agrippina with the remark (61. 12, 1): ὡς πολλοῖς καὶ ἀξιοπίστοις ἀνδράσιν εἴρηται.

The problem is more complicated still, for Dio's references to Seneca are by no means uniformly hostile—as indeed Gercke realized though some of his followers do not (Faider, Ciaceri). There are some neutral references:

60. 32, 3 that Agrippina was training Nero for the throne and entrusting his education to Seneca.
60. 35, 3 that Seneca composed a work called the *Apocolocyntosis*.
61. 3, 1 that Seneca wrote Nero's accession speech to the praetorians and to the Senate.

Then there are reports that are definitely favourable. First (Cary's translation in the Loeb Classical Library):

59. 19, 7 'Lucius Annaeus Seneca, who was superior in wisdom to all the Romans of his day and to many others as well, came near being destroyed, though he had neither done any wrong nor had the appearance of doing so, but merely because he pleaded a case well in the senate while the emperor was present.'
60. 8, 5 that Messallina secured Livilla's banishment by 'trumping up various charges against her, including that of adultery (for which Annaeus Seneca was also exiled) . . .'.

These have been explained by Questa as coming from a source used by Dio before he switched to the hostile Pliny, namely, Cluvius Rufus.[2] But it is impossible to dismiss in this way the mixture of favourable and hostile remarks in Dio's account of Seneca's activities under Nero.[3] Thus, under the year 54, we are told (61. 3, 3) how Seneca and Burrus φρονιμώτατοί τε ἅμα καὶ δυνατώτατοι τῶν περὶ τὸν Νέρωνα ἀνδρῶν

---

[1] Ciaceri, op. cit., p. 403.
[2] Questa, op. cit., pp. 90–1.
[3] Trillitzsch, *Seneca*, p. 118, rightly emphasizes the contradictions in Dio's account.

ὄντες cured Agrippina of her taste for ruling, and opened a period of excellent government (61. 4, 1–2), but were inexcusably wrong about the way to control Nero. Under the year 59 (61. 18, 3) we hear that Seneca deterred Nero from committing murders by reminding him that he could not kill his successor, but also that he appeared on stage with Nero, prompting him and leading the applause in a ludicrous manner (61. 20, 3). Under the year 65, Faenius Rufus and Seneca are described as organizing the Pisonian conspiracy (Cary's translation) 'for they could no longer endure his disgraceful behaviour, his licentiousness, and his cruelty' (62. 24, 1)—favourable, I think. Yet not long after, we are given a discreditable version of Seneca's suicide (62. 25), also containing the allegation that Seneca had tried to save himself by giving Nero all his money ostensibly to help his building appeal.

Some scholars have suggested that Dio himself would have reason to regard Seneca unfavourably. According to Syme, Dio, as a Greek, was hostile to the literary glory of Rome and, as a defender of absolutism, was hostile to philosophers.[1] Dio respects genuine philosophers (52. 36, 4; 71. 35, 1–2) and resents their persecution (67. 13), but he thinks that many pretended to be philosophers to gain enrichment and honour (71. 35, 1–2; 77. 19, 1–2) or in order to make subversive political teachings seem innocuous (52. 36, 4; 66. 13 ff.). That he put Seneca in the false category derives some support from the list of misdeeds illustrating the gulf between Seneca's moral teachings and his practice (61. 10) which Dio gives in the context of an attack on Seneca for adultery with Agrippina. This can be explained as a misunderstanding by Dio of a source more accurately reflected in Tacitus (Ann. 13. 42) where the charges are ascribed to Suillius, but it might be a deliberate distortion.[2] We can compare with this Dio's

[1] Tacitus, pp. 550–1.
[2] That Dio 61. 10 is related in this way to Ann. 13. 42 is generally accepted. Giancotti, Cronologia, pp. 334–62, in his discussion of the date of Seneca's De Vita Beata, suggested that Dio's account relates to criticisms of Seneca made earlier than Suillius'—either in 57 or, preferably, in 55 (pp. 336–9; 351–2) after the murder of Britannicus (Ann. 13. 18). Giancotti's main reasons, apart from some differences between the charges listed in Ann. 13. 42 ff. and Dio, are (1) the reference in Dio 61. 10, 6 to Seneca's defence of Pallas and Burrus which he connects with the incident in 55 in Ann. 13. 23; (2) the reference to Doryphorus in the Exc. Val. 239 between αἰτούμενος (at the end of Boissevain's 61. 9, 4) and ὅτι ὁ Σενέκας αἰτίαν ἔσχε in 61. 10, 1, which he connects with Nero's liberality noted in 61. 5, 4 and dates to 54. Giancotti thinks that Dio here introduced

praise of Augustus (56. 44), in substance the same as the meditation ascribed by Tacitus in Book 1 to those present at Augustus' funeral, or his reporting as fact (56. 30, 1) what Tacitus reports as a rumour about Agrippa Postumus (1. 5).

Certainly, other hostile notices seem traceable to his own interpretation of events that may have been differently reported in his sources. Thus (61. 4) the policy followed by Seneca and Burrus of leaving Nero some space for self-indulgence while restraining his more dangerous impulses is harshly criticized as short-sighted. They should have seen, says Dio, that a self-willed character like Nero is only encouraged by laxity. Tacitus reports essentially the same policy (*Ann.* 13. 2) but with sympathy, even though later on (*Ann.* 14. 14) he admits that a particular application of the policy failed, namely allowing Nero to perform in a private circus: 'ceterum evulgatus pudor non satietatem, ut rebantur, sed incitamentum attulit.' Dio may then either have added an independent judgement of the policy or have altered the emphasis in his source. When Dio writes that, after the murder of Britannicus in 55, Seneca and Burrus neglected public business so that 'Nero now openly and without fear of punishment proceeded to gratify all his desires' (61. 7, 5), he could be offering his own explanation of Nero's hooligan antics that seem to have started in 56. The charge of causing the revolt in Britain could have been suggested by one of Suillius' charges (cf. *Ann.* 13. 42: 'Italiam et provincias cum immenso faenore hauriri'). Even his account of Seneca's efforts to kill his wife when he committed suicide (62. 25) could be Dio's interpretation of the fact that her veins were opened and then bound again at the Emperor's orders (see p. 371), and he could also

a flashback of which the charges about Seneca formed a part. As concerns (2), Giancotti's idea is not convincing. The date of the charges against Seneca is fixed firmly to 57 or later by the sequence in Xiphilinus in which the reference to Nero's amphitheatre, opened in 57 (*Ann.* 13. 31), precedes a reference to δικανικοὶ ἀγῶνες dated μετὰ ταῦτα (cf. *Ann.* 13. 33 in 57). Perhaps Suillius' trial, arising from his attack on Seneca, was given as an example. The fragment about ὁ δορυφόρος, if it does refer to the freedman, most likely concerns his receipt, as *a libellis*, of Montanus' apology. As to (1), the passage about Pallas and Burrus could concern charges levelled by Suillius against them as well, but since Pallas would not be important enough to attack after 57, it is better to assume that Suillius blamed them along with Seneca for renewal of the Lex Cincia, or contrasted Seneca's defence of these two with his own honest use of eloquence. As the date of 55 is unacceptable and a date after 57 indicated, it is likely that the traditional interpretation of Dio 61. 10 as derived from Suillius' charges against Seneca is correct.

have given Seneca's contribution to Nero's building programme an evil interpretation.

In fact, however, it is hard to believe that Dio's bias fully accounts for the hostility in his reports. For had he been as bitter as this theory would require, could he have included such sympathetic notices of Seneca? Surely he would have been more systematic in following a strong prejudice. *Quellenforschung* therefore leaves one unable to decide between such alternatives as:

1. that Dio employed a mixture of favourable and hostile sources which he made no attempt to harmonize. If Dio's use of Fabius Rusticus could be established, we would have identified one definitely favourable source. It has been suggested[1] that Dio 61. 7, 5—the remark that Seneca and Burrus gave up their active role in government after the murder of Britannicus in 55—derives from the favourable Fabius. But Dio goes on to say that, as a result, Nero went mad and poisoned people and implies that Seneca and Burrus were bent on self-preservation. So the remark as a whole is hardly favourable. Moreover, Tacitus, *Ann.* 14. 2, shows that Fabius credited the story of Acte's intervention which show that he believed Seneca was still trying to influence Nero some years later. This last is not a conclusive argument against Fabian origin, as Dio was able to combine the two views (Appendix C2).

2. Dio had one or several sources which were 'mixed', that is, they reported events concerning Seneca with qualifications and included reports of rumours which Dio, through carelessness or a desire for rhetorical effect, obscured, leaving a stark mixture of praise and blame. The work of his epitomators has perhaps heightened this effect.

Of course, a careless combination of both techniques may be involved and in either case we cannot exclude the possibility that Dio also, sometimes, added his own comments.

II

Scrutiny of Dio then does not reveal the attitude to Seneca adopted by the Elder Pliny in his history. But the problem is sufficiently interesting to justify further inquiry by other methods: Pliny is, after all, a major source for the two authors on whom we rely in reconstructing Seneca's life.

[1] Murray, *Historia* 14 (1965), 52.

Do Pliny's views in the Natural Histories give any clue to his treatment of Seneca in the lost work? Inferences of this sort from one work
of an author to another are often dubious, but, in this case, there is no
problem of a different audience or of a different time of composition
to consider, for the history was begun before the Natural Histories
but not published until afterwards (*NH*, pref. 20). Moreover, there
was clearly a basic similarity in political attitude between the two
works, for the Flavian bias so apparent in the *NH* (e.g. pref. 4. 11;
2. 18) was maintained in the History (below, p. 436).

1. There are two references to Seneca himself apart from passages
in which he is referred to as a source (*NH* 1 under Books 6, 9, and 36;
6. 60; 9. 167).[1] Pliny, criticizing the fad for cold bathing popularized
under Nero by Charmis of Massilia, says 'videbamus senes consulares
usque in ostentationem rigentes. qua de re etiam exstat Annaei Senecae
adstipulatio' (29. 10). This passage is more notable for what it does
not say than for what it does: Pliny reminds his readers that Seneca
testified to the practice, but he does not point out, maliciously, that
Seneca followed the fad himself (*Ep.* 53. 3; 83. 5). In 14. 51 Pliny
recounts how the grammarian Remmius Palaemon bought vineyards
in Nomentum and vastly increased their yield. People flocked to see
them '. . . novissime Annaeo Seneca, principe tum eruditorum ac
potentia quae postremo nimia ruit super ipsum, minime utique
miratore inanium, tanto praedii eius amore capto ut non puderet
inviso alias et ostentaturo tradere palmam eam.' Seneca bought them
for four times the original value. Pliny goes on to note the continuing
success of the estates, though he does not explicitly give Seneca credit
for it (cf. Columella 3. 33). Scholars have regarded this story as either
complimentary to Seneca,[2] critical of his greed,[3] hostile to the man
ironically described as 'princeps eruditorum',[4] or coolly appreciative.[5]
Of course, Pliny might just be applying high-flown adjectives to the
purchaser in order to impress his readers with the extraordinary quality
of the estate.

Pliny's references to Seneca are ambiguous, certainly not overtly
hostile, and he makes an omission that might show favour: Seneca is
not named among Pliny's examples of men bitten by a mania for

---

[1] The references are collected by Trillitzsch, *Seneca*, II, pp. 331–2, and discussed in I, pp. 49–52.

[2] H. Peter, *HRR*, II, p. clviiii.   [3] Ciaceri, op. cit., p. 418.

[4] Faider, *Études sur Sénèque*, pp. 35–6; cf. Trillitzsch, p. 51.

[5] Gercke, 'Seneca-Studien', p. 268.

citrus tables (*NH* 13. 91 ff.). Yet, according to Dio (61. 10, 3), Seneca was reported to have 500 of them.[1]

2. What of Pliny's remarks in the Natural History about friends and contemporaries of Seneca? Pliny used Papirius Fabianus as a source for Books 2, 11, 14, 17, 18, 23–6, 28, 36, styling him 'naturae rerum peritissimus' (36. 125). But admiration of the teacher need not imply any particular attitude towards the pupil.

Lentulus Gaetulicus had been a close friend of Seneca's friend Lucilius (*NQ* 4, pref. 15) and may well have encouraged Seneca himself.[2] We know from Suetonius (*Gaius* 8. 2) that Pliny charged Gaetulicus with lying about the birthplace of Gaius in his history 'per adulationem'. But Pliny regarded criticism of his predecessors as a routine duty of historians (*NH* 1, pref. 20) and Sallust had made a similar criticism of his predecessor Cornelius Sisenna, of whom he none the less thought very highly (*BJ* 95).

Sallust's attitude is relevant to our inquiry in another way. Pliny called his history, 'A fine Aufidii Bassi'—a compliment to the earlier historian, it might appear. Now Bassus, though an Epicurean, was a close friend of Seneca (*Ep.* 30) who visited him often to discuss philosophy. Did Pliny share Bassus' view of Seneca, whose early career at least must have been covered in Bassus' work? Such an inference would not be safe: Sallust continued the work of Sisenna whose favourable view of Sulla he did not share.

Pliny's references to Seneca's brother Gallio (*NH* 31. 62; 7. 55) are neutral and he betrays no particular attitude towards Seneca's protégé Annaeus Serenus when he relates how he died of eating mushrooms (*NH* 22. 96).[3] On the other hand, Pliny cannot resist a jeer at the pretensions of Seneca's brother-in-law Pompeius Paulinus, who came of Gallic stock ('paterna gente pellitum') but was now so refined that he felt the need for silver plate when in the wilds of Lower Germany (*NH* 33. 143).

The vicissitudes of Seneca's career—minister then victim of Nero, protégé then opponent of Agrippina—make it impossible to infer Pliny's view of Seneca from his undoubted hostility in the Natural Histories to Nero and Agrippina.[4]

A similar difficulty arises if we attempt to reason from the avowed

---

[1] I owe this observation to Mr. Russell Meiggs. [2] See p. 52.
[3] See p. 89; Appendix D3.
[4] For the first, see Gercke, 'Seneca-Studien', pp. 168 ff.; for the second, Ciaceri, op. cit., p. 416, citing *NH* 22. 92; 35. 201; 7. 45.

Flavian bias of Pliny's history (*NH*, pref. 20). What was the official
Flavian view of Seneca? Within the Julio-Claudian dynasty, the new
ruler did not explicitly condemn his predecessor or punish his friends,
though he might pardon his enemies. But with a new dynasty, successful through violence, the problem was different. The seizure of power
had to be justified, the immediate predecessor condemned (Tacitus,
Hist. 3. 86), and the new dynasty glorified at the expense of the old,
particularly its last representative. Though peace and convenience
demanded that many agents of the old regime be protected (*Hist*.
4. 44), those mistreated by the last dynasty were honoured if they
offered no immediate threat. Pliny's hatred of Nero and praise of
Vindex are both in accord with the Flavian official view. What
follows about Seneca? He could be treated as agent or victim of the
tyrant. Dio's account shows traces of the former technique; the death
scene in Tacitus the latter. Or one could portray him as the good
adviser unheeded, as he appears in the *Octavia*. In any case, Pliny's
nephew restricted the period of *servitus* to the last years (*Ep*. 3. 5, 5)
when Seneca was no longer alive.

3. Does the Natural History give us reason to believe that Pliny
would find many of Seneca's views offensive? Pliny appears to accept
a fundamentally Stoic view of nature and providence, but without
displaying rigorous consistency.[1] He expresses indignation about the
high social and financial position attained by many freedmen (*NH*
35. 201), while Seneca promoted the Stoic view that freedmen and
slaves were not to be regarded as inferior because fortune had treated
them unkindly. On the other hand, Seneca's Stoicism did not prevent
him from sharing, or, at least, expressing the prejudices of his own class:
he speaks indignantly of the wealth and influence of freedmen.[2] Pliny
and Seneca express similar views on the growth of luxury and about
the 'good old days', but these are commonplaces.

Natural history, however, was a special concern of both authors.
Here agreement might be significant, and it exists over the question
of progress in the knowledge of natural phenomena. For Seneca
nature is like a shrine which reveals its inner chambers only gradually
from age to age (*NQ* 7. 32, 4). But we make far less progress than we
should because we devote time and energy to making progress in
vice instead. Pliny implies his belief in the possibility of progress
when he contrasts the Greeks, who were able to make great dis-

---

[1] W. Kroll, *R-E* 21. 1 (1951), pp. 409 ff.   [2] See p. 275.

coveries in an unstable world when travel was restricted, with his own contemporaries, who, in a time of peace when travel is easy and the Princeps encouraging, fail to make progress because of their devotion to luxury and profit. He adds bitterly that they even forget things previously discovered (2. 117), a sentiment shared by Seneca (*NQ* 7. 32, 4). But, on its own, this agreement is hardly sufficient to prove a positive attitude towards Seneca in Pliny's lost history.

III

What Pliny has left in writing then does not betray a strong attitude to Seneca. Can we draw any inferences from what we know of Pliny's life?

First, there is the question of Pliny's career. The classic study by F. Münzer ('Die Quelle des Tacitus für die Germanenkriege', *Bonner Jahrbücher* 104 (1899), 66 ff.) combined the evidence of Pliny's nephew (*Ep.* 3. 5) and Suetonius' fragmentary Life attesting 'procurationes quoque splendidissimas et continuas', with some apparently first-hand accounts in the Natural History, to produce this scheme:

47–50:	military service under Corbulo in Lower Germany
50–1:	military service under Pomponius Secundus in Upper Germany
52:	Pliny in Italy
c. 56–7 or 58:	military service with Pompeius Paulinus in Lower Germany (perhaps continued under Duvius Avitus)
30 April 59:	Pliny in Campania to witness the eclipse
Last years of Nero:	Pliny in retirement writing the *Dubii Sermones Octo*
70–1:	procurator in Narbonensis
71–2:	procurator in Africa
73–4:	procurator in Hispania Tarraconensis
74–5 or 6:	procurator in Gallia Belgica
c. 76:	prefect of the fleet at Misenum.

Various points in this scheme have been criticized, notably the procuratorships which are crowded and not all securely attested.[1] What concerns us is Pliny's career under Claudius and Nero.

The military service under Domitius Corbulo and Pomponius

---

[1] See the objections, old and new, reviewed in Sherwin-White, *Letters of Pliny*, pp. 216–23, and the vindication of the main points of Münzer's scheme by Syme in *HSCP* 73 (1968), 201 ff.

Secundus rests on strong evidence: eye-witness accounts of Lower
Germany (NH 12. 98; 17. 47), including a visit to the land of the Chauci
(NH 16. 2–4) where Corbulo made an expedition, and of Upper
Germany (NH 31. 20), and Pliny's well-attested devotion to Pom-
ponius Secundus. There was a later military phase when Pliny was
a *contubernalis* of Titus (NH 1, pref. 3) who served in Germany and
Britain (Tacitus, *Hist.* 2. 77; Suet. *Titus* 4), presumably about 57.
Since there are no eyewitness reports from Britain, and Pliny vouches
personally for the scandalous story of Pompeius Paulinus' silver (NH
33. 143: *scimus*), Münzer's suggestion that Pliny and Titus served under
that governor of Lower Germany (55–8) is likely to be correct.
Münzer's view that Pliny was in retirement in the last years of Nero is
based on his nephew's remarks that Pliny restricted himself as an
author to grammatical work 'sub Nerone novissimis annis, cum omne
studiorum genus paulo liberius et erectius periculosum servitus fecisset'
(*Ep.* 3. 5, 5). A break here in Pliny's career has never been questioned,
but the letter does not prove that Pliny was administratively unemployed, however cautious he had become as an author, while his
nephew's statement that between youthful work as a pleader and his
death 'medium tempus distentum impeditumque qua officiis maximis
qua amicitia principum egisse' runs counter to the idea of a period of
retirement. The plural, *principes*, here could just cover Vespasian and
Titus, but there is no hint that Nero is not included.

Of Münzer's four procuratorships, Spain is certain (Pliny, *Ep.*
3. 5, 17), Africa very likely (eyewitness reports in NH 7. 37; 17. 41
and perhaps 9. 26). The procuratorship in Belgica is less well attested,
while Pliny's first-hand knowledge of Narbonensis could have other
explanations.[1] These two posts, if they belong in Pliny's career at all,
should be the first (Narbonensis) and the last (Belgica) of the series,
according to their importance.

The procuratorship in Spain overlapped with the operations of
Larcius Licinus as *legatus pro praetore* in Hispania Tarraconensis (*Ep.*
3. 5, 17; cf. NH 31. 24; 19. 35). As NH 19. 35 shows that he was an
ex-praetor at the time and concerned with jurisdiction, Syme is surely
right to regard him as *iuridicus* rather than governor of the province
and his suggestion that Pliny's knowledge of the census figures for
73–4 (NH 3. 28) places him in Spain at that date is also attractive.[2]

---

[1] Syme, *Tacitus*, p. 61 n. 2; HSCP 73 (1968), 211–14. Sherwin-White, *Letters of Pliny*, p. 221.

[2] Syme, *Tacitus*, pp. 68 n. 5, 61 n. 7; HSCP 73 (1968), 215–16. According

An early Flavian date for the Spanish procuratorship is therefore very likely.

Suetonius' reference to continuous procuratorships[1] suggests more than two. If Pliny was employed in Narbonensis or Africa, or both, these jobs could have preceded the Spanish procuratorship and belong to the end of Nero's reign. He could have been in Narbonensis before 69[2] (*Hist.* 3. 43 reveals the procurator in 69) or in Africa, even if his procuratorship there is properly tied by Syme to the proconsulate of Tampius Flavianus by a story in *NH* 9. 26, dated 'intra hos annos'. Pliny's time references are vague: he uses *nuper* and *proxime* of the Neronian period (6. 18, 1; 14. 51; 7. 33). A Neronian date for Flavianus' proconsulate has often been proposed.[3]

It cannot be shown, then, that Pliny suffered under Nero. He continued his military service and may have held one or two procuratorships. He may even have been an *amicus* of Nero: his presence in Campania in 59 is suspicious as Nero and the court were there then, Nero not yet daring to return to Rome after the murder of Agrippina (Tacitus, *Ann.* 14. 12). In the early years of Seneca's power, Pliny saw his old commander Domitius Corbulo receive recognition, while Pompeius Paulinus echoed Pliny's admiration for Drusus by completing the canal he had started sixty-three years earlier (*Ann.* 13. 53). But, as we have seen, Pliny had grave reservations about Seneca's brother-in-law, under whom he may have served.

to G. Alföldy, *Fasti Hispanienses*, Wiesbaden, 1969, pp. 70–1, there was an interval in 70 when Spain had no governor, which explains Pliny's inaccurate description of the *iuridicus*.

[1] Sherwin-White, *Letters of Pliny*, p. 222, does not regard this as independent evidence. For him it is an interpretation of Pliny, *Ep.* 3. 5, 7. But that is by no means certain: Sherwin-White himself shows (p. 374) that Suetonius' Life of Pliny the Elder has different information from that provided in Pliny's Letters. It is Sherwin-White's rejection of Suetonius' information that allows him to propose an early Neronian date for the African procuratorship (p. 221) and a possible date after 69 for the Spanish one.

[2] In *NH* 13. 43: 'septem his annis in Narbonensis provinciae Alba Helvia', even if it is an eyewitness account, can be placed late in Nero's reign. In the same book, cf. 14. 51, where 'twenty years ago' refers to a date around 52, see p. 289 n. 4.

[3] Against Syme, *REA* 58 (1956), 236 ff., Thomasson, *Die Statthalter der römischen Provinzen Nordafrikas*, I, pp. 42–4, suggests a date between 62 and 68. As regards Pliny, the procurator Trebonius Garutianus mentioned in Tacitus, *Hist.* 1. 7, need not be the procurator of the province of Africa in 69, but some minor official. Cf. again, Syme, *HSCP* 73 (1968), 215, insisting on the precision of these references.

Pliny's Flavian connections do not imply hostility to Seneca. Though Seneca had some reason to hate Vespasian who, as praetor in 39, had proposed additional penalties for the followers of Gaetulicus (Suet. *Vesp.* 2. 3), Vespasian had no reason to hate Seneca. His career was retarded by Agrippina (Suet. *Vesp.* 4. 2) and, on her death, he received the proconsulate of Africa while Seneca was still in power. His son and his brother flourished throughout the early years of Nero.[1]

Faider adduced Seneca's hatred for Pomponius Secundus as support for his view that Pliny hated Seneca. Pomponius was Pliny's lifelong friend (Pliny, *Ep.* 3. 5; *NH* 13. 83): Pliny wrote a biography of him to celebrate his memory and frequently quoted his opinion on grammatical points (Charisius, pp. 125, 137K). But the evidence for this hatred is painfully thin. Quintilian (8. 3, 31) reports a discussion between the tragedian Pomponius Secundus and the tragedian Seneca 'in praefationibus' about the use of a certain phrase. But as Cichorius noted,[2] this sounds like a friendly literary discussion: Pliny's nephew shows that Pomponius frequently disagreed with his friends on grammatical points (*Ep.* 7. 17, 11).

Pomponius Secundus was a friend of the famous Thrasea Paetus (Charisius, p. 125K) and it is clear from the letters of Pliny's nephew that he, at least, had a long-standing connection with Thrasea's circle. The Elder Pliny might have known them as well: it is perhaps a reflection of his attachment that in *NH* 35. 201 he reports a shameful decree of the Senate prompted by Agrippina but omits the name of the proposer, who, according to Tacitus (*Ann.* 12. 53), was Barea Soranus, Thrasea's associate. But, as we have seen,[3] Thrasea co-operated with Nero's government in the early years and there is evidence for a certain admiration between Seneca and Thrasea, though they moved in different circles and had different ways of approaching politics. Pliny's nephew, who was ever at pains to advertise his friendship with the circle of Thrasea Paetus, mentions Seneca with respect (*Ep.* 5. 3, 5).

This inquiry has a negative conclusion: there is no reason to believe that the Elder Pliny painted a hostile portrait of Seneca in his history. Pliny cannot be blamed for the savage passages in Dio. On the other hand, he was not particularly favourable to Seneca's friends and he was probably not a member of Seneca's circle.

[1] See p. 242.
[2] *Römische Studien*, p. 428.
[3] See pp. 100 ff.

C5. *Tacitus' Attitude to Seneca*

Tacitus' attitude to Seneca has been much discussed. For Diderot, *Essai sur les règnes de Claude et de Néron* (1778), Seneca was Tacitus' hero: the historian was a great support to Diderot's defence. It has been convincingly argued by I. Ryberg, 'Tacitus' Art of Innuendo', *TAPA* 73 (1942), 383 ff., that Tacitus used the technique of innuendo in favour of Seneca: he minimizes criticisms of Seneca by citing justifications, omitting his name (13. 18; 14. 15, 4, cf. Dio 61. 20), or ascribing the charges to figures he has already blackened (13. 14; 13. 42; 14. 51–2); he defends him against the charge of immorality by calling his exile *iniuria* (12. 8); refers to the rumour that Nero tried to poison Seneca (15. 45) later on as fact (15. 60). More directly, Tacitus approves of Seneca's and Burrus' methods of trying to control Nero (13. 2), and regards their failure as a fact (14. 14), rather than an inevitable and foreseeable consequence of their policy (as Dio does, 61. 4, 2). Tacitus' picture of Seneca is considered favourable on the whole by Syme, *Tacitus*, pp. 551 ff., Trillitzsch, *Seneca*, pp. 94 ff., and D. Gillis, *La Parola del Passato* 18 (1963), 5 ff., who defends Tacitus against a charge of hostility to Seneca brought by B. Walker in *The Annals of Tacitus*, Manchester, 1922, p. 222. But F. R. D. Goodyear, *Tacitus* (Greece and Rome New Surveys in the Classics no. 4), Oxford, 1970, p. 40 n. 1, suggests that Tacitus despises Seneca and makes him 'sound as empty as he conceives Seneca to be'.

It is common ground between supporters of these opposing views that Tacitus lavished considerable effort on his portrait of Seneca. In fact the view of D. Henry and B. Walker, *Greece and Rome* 10 (1963), 98 ff., that 'Tacitus shows remarkably little interest in Seneca at all' will startle anyone who merely considers the amount of space devoted to him. As a glance at the *index nominum* to the Annals shows, it is greatly exceeded only by that devoted to the emperors, Germanicus, and Drusus. The space devoted to Agrippina and Sejanus is only slightly greater and Corbulo (who may have figured in later books as Seneca may have in the earlier lost books) earns about the same. Tacitus was certainly interested in them.

This lack of interest resulting in a 'pasteboard figure' (ibid., p. 106) is supposedly indicated by the conventional rhetoric of the lifeless speeches attributed to Seneca and Nero in their confrontation in 62 (*Ann.* 14. 53–6), the banality of Seneca's death scene, and the failure of Tacitus to read deeply in Seneca's works in an effort to grasp his tortured personality. The first two involve judgements of taste. The death scene is meant to compare unfavourably with Petronius' (see p. 368), but that is true also of Thrasea's death scene, and Tacitus was interested in him. We may find Seneca's display of eloquence at the last minute ludicrous, but his last words were widely read, for Tacitus could assume they were better known to his readers than the speech of Claudius on the Gauls (*Ann.* 15. 63).

As for the interview with Nero, not all Tacitus' readers find it dull, but, what is more to the point, its interest derives in part from its echoes of Seneca's works. Syme (*Tacitus*, pp. 335–6), like others before him, has found hints and echoes of the authentic Seneca in the language and style; and the thought is also reminiscent. Most would not go as far as M. Pohlenz, *Philosophie und Erlebnis in Senecas Dialogen*, NGG 1941, p. 225, who thought Tacitus used *De Tranquillitate Animi* as his source for Seneca's speech, but the Senecan echoes are too striking to be accidental. 'Una defensio occurrit quod muneribus tuis obniti non debui' reminds one of *De Benef.* 2. 18, 6–7. The argument from Augustus' practice echoes, as P. Jal (*REL* 35 (1957), 259) points out, Seneca's constant use of that exemplar in advising Nero, while Nero's reply with its emphasis on the warlike youth of Augustus uses Seneca's own criticism of Augustus against him (see the comparison of Nero's youth to Octavian's in *De Clementia* 1. 11). Nero's argument that Seneca's retirement would bring him *infamia* may be repeating the lesson of *De Clementia*: 'principes multa debent etiam famae dare' (*Clem.* 1. 15, 5). Finally, the ending 'Seneca, qui finis omnium cum dominante sermonum, grates agit' is not merely a Tacitean cliché (*Agric.* 42. 3; *Hist.* 2. 71). It occurs in Seneca's dialogue *De Ira* (2. 33, 2) as a recipe for achieving old age at court: 'iniurias accipiendo et gratias agendo'. Its proximity there to the epigram about rulers, 'quos laeserunt, et oderunt', suggests that Tacitus has Seneca's words in mind in describing Agricola's interview with Domitian where the same combination occurs, and 'proprium humani ingenii est odisse quem laeseris' is completed by 'Domitiani vero natura praeceps in *iram*'. In the Annals, Tacitus may be thinking also of the anecdote in *De Tranquillitate Animi* (14. 4–5) where Seneca speculates on the possible motives behind the reply of Julius Canus to Gaius' order for his execution: 'gratias ago, optime princeps' and concludes, 'quidquid est, magno animo respondit.' Tacitus probably intends the same favourable interpretation of Seneca's remark to Nero: Seneca was receiving an injury in not being permitted to retire and his offer to do so was sincere. The similarity of Agricola's behaviour towards Domitian tells us how Tacitus saw Seneca and why he tended to defend him. Less favourable chapters also feature Senecan material (pp. 281-3).

If Tacitus' lack of interest in Seneca is implausible, Henry and Walker still have another explanation for Tacitus' 'colourless and indeterminate' portrayal of Seneca—a literary and psychological one. W. H. Alexander (*Univ. of Calif. Publ. in Cl. Phil.* 14, 8 (1952), 269) had already argued that Tacitus failed to provide us with a judgement on or portrait of Seneca because Seneca eluded him. Tacitus was factually prepared to give us a thumb-nail sketch, but ran into a stylistic difficulty: 'Seneca couldn't be handled as a set character like Nero gradually revealing his innate flaws.' The diagnosis of Henry and Walker is that Tacitus could not fit Seneca into any 'predetermined type-character'. As Syme protests (*Tacitus*, p. 552 n. 1), such views underrate Tacitus, whose favourite characters are in fact complex mixtures of good and bad, like Petronius, Otho, Lucius Vitellius, or flexible characters like Agricola or Marcus Lepidus who sought a compromise between 'abruptam contumaciam' and 'deforme obsequium' (*Ann.* 4. 20). As for the absence of a character-sketch of Seneca, Seneca's personality may not be the cause. We must note that most necrological notices occur in the first six books and that those in the last books are brief and devoted to men not otherwise mentioned (Syme, *Tacitus*, pp. 313, 744). More generally (ibid., p. 313), single portraits are more common in the Histories than in the Annals where, as Syme notes, indirect characterization prevails (ibid., p. 314). The treatment of Seneca is comparable with that accorded Agrippina, Burrus, and Thrasea Paetus, and the notices about Seneca seem to add up to a judgement as much as the account of these.

Tacitus' Seneca is an equestrian of provincial origin (14. 53), popular in the first instance for his writings (12. 8; 13. 3), through which he hopes for glory (13. 11, 2; 15. 63; cf. *Ep.* 21. 4-5 for confirmation). This trait of vanity he shares with Thrasea Paetus (14. 49) and Helvidius Priscus (*Hist.* 4. 6); it is accepted by Tacitus as a fact of human nature, 'etiam sapientibus cupido gloriae novissima exuitur.' The common defect is more than balanced by the rare quality of being able to share power (13. 2) and to co-operate with Burrus in guiding Nero and counteracting the influence of Agrippina. Though Seneca's literary abilities do not always match his aims (13. 4; perhaps 13. 11), and Nero's vices prove in the end a match for his preventive measures (14. 14, 3), Seneca's sincerity and good character are stressed to the end (14. 52–3) and his continued good repute implied (15. 65). The charge that Seneca sought vengeance against Claudius' supporters is made by Suillius (13. 42, 2) and believed by some at the time of his recall from exile (12. 8, 2) but Tacitus nowhere suggests that it was true. Suillius Rufus suffered only when he directly attacked Seneca.

In the closing minutes of his life, Tacitus' Seneca shows himself kind to his friends and wife. And despite his vanity, his will showed genuine modesty: at the height of his power and wealth he had given instructions for simple cremation without ceremony (15. 64).

None the less, for all his sympathy for and curiosity about Seneca the politician and stylist, there is a Seneca in whom Tacitus has no interest: the philosopher Seneca.

D. PROSOPOGRAPHY

1. *Living Contemporaries mentioned by Seneca (not including the addressees of his works)*

(a) *Those known outside Seneca:*

1. Novatus (later Gallio), his elder brother: *NQ* 4, pref. 10; 5. 11, 1; *Ep.* 104. Cf. *PIR²* I 757.
2. (Pompeia) Paulina, his wife: *Ep.* 104. Cf. Tacitus, *Ann.* 15. 60, 4.
3. Marcus (probably the poet Lucan, see p. 58): *Cons. Helv.* 18. 4.
4. Corbulo (perhaps the younger, see p. 44 n. 4): *Const. Sap.* 17. 1. Cf. *PIR²* D 142; the Seneca reference is under D 141 in *PIR²*.
5. Marullus: *Ep.* 99. Q. Junius Marullus, cos. suff. 63, is perhaps the same (*PIR²* I 769 which does not mention this possibility).
6. (Caesennius or Caesonius) Maximus: *Ep.* 87. 2. Cf. *PIR²* C 172.
7. Aufidius Bassus: *Ep.* 30. Cf. *PIR²* A 1381.
8. Aegialus: *Ep.* 86. 14. Cf. Pliny, *NH* 14. 33.
9. Balbillus, ex-prefect of Egypt: *NQ* 4. 2, 13. Cf. *PIR²* C 813.
10. Burrus: *Clem.* 2. 1, 2. Cf. *PIR²* A 441.

(b) *Those not known outside Seneca:*

1. Novatilla, his niece: *Cons. Helv.* 18. 7.
2. Marcellinus: *Ep.* 29.
3. Tullius Marcellinus: *Ep.* 77.
4. Claranus: *Ep.* 66. 1–4.
5. Cornelius Senecio: *Ep.* 101.
6. Flaccus, a friend of Lucilius: *Ep.* 63.
7. Metronax, a philosopher: *Ep.* 76. 4. Cf. 93.
8. Felicio, his *ostiarius*: *Ep.* 12. 3.
9. Pharius, his *progymnastes*: *Ep.* 83. 4.
10. Harpaste, his wife's clown: *Ep.* 50.
11. His mother's stepsister: *Cons. Helv.* 19.

Of these, the deaths of Aufidius Bassus, Tullius Marcellinus, Cornelius Senecio, and Metronax are recorded. For all but the last, this is their only mention in Seneca, so that they do not really count as 'living' contemporaries.

D2. *M. Trebellius Maximus, cos. 56*

The usual view (*PIR*[1] 234, 239; *R-E* 6A (1937), 2265-6 (Stein and Hanslik)) is that there were two men, M. Trebellius Maximus consul in 56 being the son of M. Trebellius, legionary legate in 36. The Trebellius Maximus who in 41 removed a ring bearing the image of Caligula from the finger of the consul Cn. Sentius Saturninus as he harangued the Senate after the murder (Josephus, *AJ* 19. 185) is identified with the son, the cognomen not being attested for the legate.

This would require that the legionary legate be in his forties, which, as Cichorius objected (*Röm. Stud.* p. 420 n. 3), is not likely. It is not, of course, impossible. Titus Vinius was over fifty when serving as Galba's legate (*Hist.* 1. 48), but he had been legionary legate previously under Claudius and his career was interrupted (*PIR*[1] V 450). In favour of one Trebellius, Cichorius cited *Ann.* 14. 46: 'Census per Gallias a Q. Volusio et Sextio Africano Trebellioque Maximo acti sunt, aemulis inter se per nobilitatem Volusio atque Africano: Trebellium dum uterque dedignatur, supra tulere.' C. argued that the son of a legionary legate would not be regarded as a *novus homo*. But next to a descendant of the Republican nobility and a Claudian patrician, Trebellius, with or without such a father, was socially negligible. And there is a possibility that he came from Narbonensis, if he was some older kinsman of the Q. Trebellius Rufus of Tolosa honoured at Athens where he had gone to seek ἡσυχία (probably then an Epicurean) and served as archon between 85/6 and 94/5.[1] This Trebellius Rufus seems to have declined senatorial rank,[2] and the name of his son, Trebellius Rufus Maximus, makes it tempting to connect him with our Trebellius.

Against the monist view is Tacitus' description of the suffect consul of 56, when governing Britain, as 'nullis castrorum experimentis' (*Agric.*16. 3)—unless, as Sir Ronald Syme suggests, Tacitus did not know

[1] *IG* II[2] 4193; J. H. Oliver, *Hesperia* 10 (1941), 72; *AE* 1947, no. 69; Syme, *HSCP* 73 (1968), 222.

[2] Lines 39-40 look as if they contain a reference to the Roman Senate, followed by ἐ]πε[θ]ύμησεν ἡσυχίαν. Perhaps Trebellius could have been a senator had he not opted for *quies*. See Oliver, *Hesperia* 11 (1942), 80; Syme, loc. cit.

of Trebellius' exploit in 36 (*Ann.* 6. 41) when he wrote the *Agricola*. It is uncertain then whether there was one Trebellius or two. If, however, there were two, we could rejuvenate the legionary legate by making him, rather than his son, the senator of 41. That would also mean that the son would be young in 56 when he attained the consulship.

D3. *Annaeus Serenus as Prefect of the Watch*

Among those supporting the view that Annaeus Serenus was *praefectus vigilum* after Tigellinus, one can name O. Hirschfeld, *Untersuchungen auf dem Gebiete der römischen Verwaltungsgeschichte*, p. 146 n. 5, and Albertini, *Composition dans Sénèque*, pp. 40 ff. That Serenus was Tigellinus' predecessor is the view, for example, of Momigliano, in *CAH* X, p. 710, Waltz, *Vie politique*, pp. 214, 384; Lana, *Seneca*, p. 267. Giancotti, *Cronologia*, pp. 153–7, discusses Serenus' career as it bears on the chronology of Seneca's works and finds the evidence inconclusive.

Pliny (*NH* 22. 96) tells us that Serenus died as prefect, and in a letter to Lucilius (63. 14), purporting to be written in 63 or 64, Seneca confesses his immoderate grief at the death of his friend, adding, 'hodie tamen factum meum damno.' This temporal reference is too vague to help us to choose between a date for Serenus' death a year or two before the letter or years earlier. The chronology of the dialogues addressed to Serenus—*De Constantia Sapientis*, *De Tranquillitate Animi*, and probably *De Otio*—cannot help us as their dating is uncertain and largely dependent on the date one accepts for Serenus' death. Equal circularity attends arguments that Seneca could or could not have secured his close friend such a post in 62 after the death of Burrus. Our evidence for Seneca's patronage is not so extensive as to enable us to make deductions of this sort in particular cases, and the argument would be particularly useless here when it is the pattern of Seneca's influence that is under discussion.

But in order to reconstruct Seneca's influence we must make some decision, however tenuous, about Serenus' career. Two facts incline me to the view that Serenus was the successor of Laelianus in 54 rather than of Tigellinus in 62. (1) One is that Serenus was prominent at court in 55, and his presence there was so natural that it was thought he could pretend a liaison with Acte, an imperial *liberta*,[1] without

[1] Dio 61. 7, 1.

appearing specially imported for the role.[1] (2) The other is that in 57 Cossutianus Capito was condemned by the Senate for extortion (*Ann.* 13. 33, 3) but shortly before 62 (*Ann.* 14. 48, 1) he was restored to the Senate by the intercession of Tigellinus, his father-in-law. He then had sufficient confidence, and contact with Nero, when the year 62 opened, to undertake the prosecution in a case of *maiestas* staged by Nero to demonstrate his *clementia*. Tigellinus, a *iuvenis* (Schol. Juv. 1. 155) in Gaius' reign, is more likely to have married his daughter to Cossutianus before 57 than to have arranged a marriage for her with an exile. Why then could he not save Capito in 57? Tigellinus' power came from his personal influence with Nero. In 57 then he did not yet enjoy great influence with the Emperor, or that influence, because of the control of Nero by Seneca and Burrus, meant little. Both alternatives lead to the conclusion that he was not yet *praefectus vigilum*. This one might also suspect from what we have been able to trace about Nero's personal patronage before 59. This leaves a space for a *praefectus vigilum* after Laelianus and before Tigellinus. Of course, one or more unknowns may belong there, but given a space and the evidence in (1), it is very tempting to put Serenus in it. It follows that Serenus died sometime before Tigellinus became praetorian prefect in the early part of 62 after Burrus' death.

D4. *Ofonius Tigellinus' Early Friendship with Nero*

According to the Scholiast on Juvenal 1. 155, Tigellinus, exiled by Gaius in 39 (Dio 59. 23, 9), was allowed to return under Claudius on condition that he kept out of the Emperor's sight. He went to raise horses for chariot-racing in Apulia and Calabria. There he won the friendship of Nero and was the first to incite him to interest in the circus. Tacitus says that Nero's interest in racing began *puerilibus annis* (*Ann.* 13. 3, 3). Tigellinus probably does not deserve all the credit, but the idea would have been absurd if he had not been Nero's friend before his accession. One might guess that Nero met Tigellinus at his aunt's ranch in Calabria (*Ann.* 12. 65, 1). Domitia Lepida's brother, Nero's father, had known Tigellinus before his exile (Schol. ibid.). Nero lived with her while his mother was in exile (when Tigellinus was in Achaea). After, despite his mother's hostility to her, she had

---

[1] *Ann.* 13. 13. That Tacitus makes no reference to Serenus' position is no drawback; Tigellinus was undoubtedly *praefectus vigilum* in early 62 but the post is not mentioned in the Annals (*Ann.* 14. 48, 1; 14. 51, 2–3; cf. *Hist.* 1. 72).

opportunities to lavish her *blandimenta* and *largitiones* on him (*Ann.* 12. 64, 3), among which may have been the company of Tigellinus.

D5. *The Recall of Antonius Felix*

Concerning the date when Antonius Felix was succeeded by Porcius Festus as procurator of Judaea, scholarly opinion is divided between a late chronology locating the event *c.* A.D. 60 and an early chronology fixing it at A.D. 55 or 56. A recent and fairly full review of the rival arguments can be found in G. Ogg, *The Chronology of the Life of Paul*, London, 1968, pp. 146–70 (where the late chronology is favoured).

The Armenian version of Eusebius' chronicle gives the 14th year of Claudius, i.e. 54, as the start of the procuratorship of Porcius Festus. In Jerome's version, Festus succeeds Felix in the second year of Nero, i.e. late 55/6. It is generally recognized that Jerome's date is true to the Eusebian original (cf. *HE* 2. 22, 1—see the discussion by Ogg, p. 152; Lambertz in *R-E* 22. 1 (1953), 220 ff., who favours the Eusebian date), yet it is often rejected in favour of the *c.* A.D. 60 dating—which rests purely on scholarly calculation from the evidence of Josephus, Tacitus, and Acts—for two reasons: (*a*) the Eusebian date is held to be a mere conjecture by Eusebius, not resting on any evidence unavailable to us; (*b*) the difficulties involved in reconciling the early date with statements of the three ancient sources just mentioned are considered insuperable.

(*a*) We do not know how Eusebius arrived at his date, but the idea that he simply inferred a date of 56 from the narrative of Josephus, his main source in this part of his chronicle, is hard to accept. In both the *Jewish War* and the *Antiquities*, the change of procurator is connected with the conflict between the Jewish and Syrian population of Caesarea and their representations to Rome (*BJ* 2. 270–1; 284; *AJ* 20. 173–6; 182–5). In the earlier work, a close connection is made between Nero's decision on this dispute and the outbreak of the Great Revolt in May of A.D. 66! In the *Antiquities*, the connection with the Great Revolt is made more remote, but it is only additional information from Tacitus about Pallas' death in 62 (*Ann.* 14. 65) that enables us to see that Josephus is probably talking about a period before 62 (cf. Feldman in Loeb edition, vol. II, p. 434 n. *a*), and Josephus' postponement of his lengthy narrative of the events of

Felix' procuratorship to after his notice of Nero's first year (AJ 20. 158) would hardly allow any one reading him alone to infer that these all took place in Nero's second year, as is suggested in the Vermes–Millar revision of E. Schürer's *History of the Jewish People*, I, Edinburgh, 1973, p. 465 n. 42. Eusebius must in some way have corrected the impression Josephus' accounts gave. That does not, of course, mean that he used a good source to do so. But the fact that his date, as will appear, fits best with the evidence of Tacitus, *Ann.* 13. 14, gives it some right to be accepted over our own calculations if it can be reconciled with the evidence of the older sources.

(b) The main difficulties that lead to rejection of the Eusebian date are:

1. Josephus in *AJ* gives more information about Felix' term as procurator than Festus'. But if Festus, who died before the autumn of 62 (*BJ* 6. 288), succeeded Felix in late 55/6, he would have a longer term than Felix who was dispatched in 52, or somewhat earlier (see 3), according to *AJ* 20. 137 with Tacitus, *Ann.* 12. 54.

2. Josephus (*Vita* 13) says that, on his visit to Rome in 63/4, he asked for the release of some priests sent to Rome by Felix. If Felix was recalled in late 55/6 these priests had spent at least seven years in detention, though Philo (*Flacc.* 128–9) regards two years as a long period.

3. In Acts 24: 10, Paul says of Felix ἐκ πολλῶν ἐτῶν ὄντα σε κριτὴν τῷ ἔθνει τούτῳ at a time when Felix still had two years of his procuratorship before him (Acts 24: 27: διετίας δὲ πληρωθείσης ἔλαβε διάδοχον ὁ Φῆλιξ Πόρκιον Φῆστον). If he was recalled in late 55/6, Paul would be referring to the two years 52–4 as 'many'.

4. If (as is assumed above) Acts 24: 27 shows that Paul was in prison for two years before Festus' arrival (which is preferable to taking the phrase as a gratuitous note on the length of Felix's governorship), and if Festus arrived in the spring or summer of 56, then the Pentecost on which Paul reached Jerusalem (Acts 20: 16) was that of 54. But after his confrontation with Gallio in the summer of 51 (Plassart, *REG* 80 (1967), 372 ff.), Paul spent some time in Syrian Antioch and then went on the Third Missionary Journey during which, he said, he stayed three years at Ephesus (Acts 20: 31). Pentecost (late May) 54 is thus too early for his arrival in Jerusalem.

5. Josephus, *AJ* 20. 169, places the arrival in Jerusalem of an Egyptian with whom Paul was confused (Acts 21: 38) in the time of Felix, under Nero. That indicates the Pentecost of 55 as the earliest possible

date for Paul's arrival. Felix was in office for two more years (Acts 24: 27) which takes us beyond 56.

6. Josephus, *AJ* 20. 182, credits Pallas with persuading Nero to acquit Felix on his recall from Judaea when he was tried for extortion. But Pallas was dismissed and disgraced by early 55, in fact by February (Tacitus, *Ann.* 13. 14, cf. 15). How could Pallas have used his influence with Nero a year later?

These difficulties can be overcome:

1. Josephus, regardless of the length of their terms of office, would be apt to report the lurid details of Felix' procuratorship in greater detail than the operations of the wise Festus.

2. Even on the traditional chronology, the priests had been detained for three years, so that the circumstances, in any case, were very unusual.

3. Felix may have served in Palestine in some capacity before 52, as many scholars have argued in the attempt to reconcile Josephus' account of Cumanus' procuratorship with Tacitus, *Ann.* 12. 54, where Felix is said to have been procurator of Samaria while Cumanus ruled Galilee. This notion receives some confirmation in Jos. *AJ* 20. 162, where we learn that the high priest Jonathan had requested Felix' appointment, presumably because he had some experience of his rule. The most attractive suggestions are those of Momigliano, *Annali d. R. Scuola norm. sup. di Pisa*, 2nd Ser. 3 (1934), 388–91, and of Small-wood, *Latomus* 18 (1959), 560. Both of these give Felix an interim appointment either as governor of Samaria during Quadratus' investi-gation (Momigliano) or as governor of the whole province after Cumanus' recall for trial (Smallwood). Although Paul's 'many years' is still only three at best, that is enough to make him an experienced judge in Judaea, which is Paul's point.

4. Most of the temporal indications in the section of Acts from 18: 18 to 21: 15 are either of periods too short or too vaguely de-scribed to provide a clear chronology. The most important for the total length of time involved are 19: 8 giving 3 months for Paul's teaching at the synagogue in Ephesus; 19: 10 giving 2 years for his teaching at the school of Tyrannus; and 20: 31 where he refers in retrospect to a period of 3 years (τριετία) when he taught at Ephesus. Considering the amount of travelling he did in Acts 20: 6 to 21: 15 in less than the six weeks from Passover to the Pentecost late in May, we can place the start of his Ephesian ministry (after his visit to Antioch)

in the autumn of 51 and accommodate the 3 months, the 2 years, the χρόνος of 19: 22 before the 3-month visit to Greece (20: 3) and the return to Philippi for the Passover (20: 6) in April. As for the τριετία, that is bound to be as much an exaggeration as Paul's accompanying claim to have taught day and night. Moreover, it is likely that Paul is here meaning the period from his first arrival in Ephesus before the visit to Antioch for he seems to mention it earlier at 20: 18.

5. The story of the Egyptian forms part of an account of a long-term situation in Judaea which, though inserted after the notice of Claudius' death, could cover earlier events in Felix' procuratorship. Paul could then have come to Jerusalem at the Pentecost of 54.

6. As explained on p. 87 above, this rumour, on the Eusebian chronology, fits very well with Tacitus' evidence for the superficial reconciliation of Nero and Agrippina late in 55. The decision to recall Felix could have been made in mid 55 after Pallas' dismissal: the arrival of Festus and the return and trial of Felix could belong in the summer of 56 when Agrippina's improved position could have enabled her and her favourite Pallas to rescue Felix from condemnation. On the traditional chronology, it is necessary to posit an unattested and very unlikely return to power by Pallas in 60 or to reject the story as invention. As the arguments for each chronology are otherwise of equal weight, the Eusebian chronology seems preferable.

C. Saumagne, *Mél. Piganiol*, 1966, III, pp. 1373 ff., also rejects a late recall of Felix but prefers to date his return late in 54, shortly after Nero's accession and before Pallas' dismissal. Aside from the question of Eusebius' authority, this is less satisfactory than 56, because it aggravates difficulties 2, 3, 4, and 5, leading him to take the less acceptable interpretation of Acts 24: 27.

D6. *The African Proconsulships of T. Flavius Vespasianus and of A. and L. Vitellius*

According to B. Thomasson, *Die Statthalter der römischen Provinzen Nordafrikas*, II, p. 42, the most likely dates for Vespasian's proconsulship are 60/1 or 61/2, but his collection of material shows that 62/3, 63/4, and 64/5 are also possible. But the additions of Birley in his review (*JRS* 52 (1962), 221, 223) make 63/4 and 64/5 the most likely for the Vitellii. Thomasson (pp. 39–40) indicated two possible gaps in which the two successive years in which Aulus and Lucius Vitellius

governed Africa could fall (Suet. *Vit.* 5): 54–7 and 63–8. U. Weidemann's attempt in *Gnomon* 37 (1965), 797, to defend 60/1 and 61/2
for the Vitellii runs up against the evidence of Tacitus, *Ann.* 14. 49
(cf. above, p. 90 n. 2), showing Aulus Vitellius (who remained in
Africa as a legate when his brother took over as governor) in Rome
very early in 62, earlier than a full term in 61/2 would have enabled
him to return (cf. T. D. Barnes, *Tertullian*, Oxford, 1971, pp. 260–1,
on the evidence for the proconsular year in Africa): *CIL* 6. 2046 =
AFA, p. lxxxii Henzen, may attest his presence in Rome as early
as January of 62. Birley's addition of Cn. Hosidius Geta (*cos.* 44 or
45) as a contender for a place in the 54–7 gap means that at least two
(Geta and Sulpicius Camerinus), perhaps three (though Curtius
could go later) proconsuls are known for the years 54/5, 55/6, 56/7,
leaving no room for the Vitellii. In the later gap 63–8, 65/6 is excluded because Aulus is attested at the second Neronia (Suet. *Vit.* 4;
cf. *Nero* 21) and Birley has now suggested *c.* 67/8 for the governorship
of Curtilius Mancia. If that is right, the most likely years for the
Vitellii are 62/3 and 63/4, or 63/4 and 64/5.

The *consul ordinarius* of 51, Ser. Cornelius Orfitus, is likely to have
preceded Vespasian, suffect consul in that year, as governor of Africa.
If he belongs in 60/1, that leaves 61/2 or 62/3 as the most likely years
for Vespasian. But 64/5 is also a possibility.

D7. *Seneca on the Vitellii*

The idleness of A. Vitellius during the period of Seneca's ascendancy
(pp. 99–100) craves explanation. Seneca, who is not free with adverse
comments on the ancestors of the living, may, if an emendation is
right, have cited the elder Vitellius as the greatest practitioner of the
art of flattery.[1] Moreover, in the *Apocolocyntosis*, only two such men are
singled out for ridicule. One was M. Crassus Frugi 'tam fatuum ut
etiam regnare posset'[2]—he was a friend, but also a victim, of Claudius.
His son-in-law, consul in 57, was quite active in the early years of
Nero,[3] while his son took the first steps leading to a consulship in 64.[4]
The other butt is P. Petronius, 'vetus convictor eius, homo Claudiana

---

[1] *NQ* 4, pref. 5. 'Villeium' is the manuscript form.
[2] *Apoc.* 11. 2; 11. 5.
[3] L. Calpurnius Piso, *curator aquarum* 60–3, after being *cos.* 57 (*PIR*[2] C 294).
[4] M. Crassus Frugi (*PIR*[2] L 190).

lingua disertus', who alone offers to defend Claudius before Aeacus.[1] A strange target for Seneca's ridicule, for Petronius had shown great courage in resisting Gaius,[2] but, as an old man, he had clearly been a friend of Claudius and had not redeemed himself by becoming a victim. His son-in-law was Aulus Vitellius[3]—a marriage that confirmed an existing tie, for Petronius' mother-in-law was a Vitellia.[4] His son, P. Petronius Turpilianus,[5] despite a consular father, came late to the supreme magistracy,[6] and reached it in 61, a year when the policies of Nero's early reign were being reversed in Britain, in Armenia, and at home in the matter of ordinary consulships. Turpilianus showed his great loyalty to Nero in the Pisonian conspiracy of 65.[7] The other important link of the Petronii, i.e. with the Plautii,[8] who were protected early in the reign, cannot explain this late consulship. Of course, this evidence is not unshakeable: there is Vitellius' horoscope, and Plutarch might be wrong about Turpilianus' age. But the dislike of Seneca and Burrus is a possible explanation. Vitellius' famous father had enjoyed power and flattered Messallina and Narcissus, in the period when their victim Seneca was seeking recall from exile.[9] The son added to his enthusiasm for chariot-racing a voluntary subservience to the Emperor. The subtle morality of those living under absolute rule distinguished sharply between the behaviour of a Barea Soranus or a Marullus who were bullied into making discreditable proposals in the Senate, and that of a Vitellius who, when he could have followed the majority in a courageous decision, preferred to flatter Nero.[10]

[1] *Apoc.* 14. 2.

[2] Jos. *AJ* 18. 261 ff. Petronius succeeded his relative L. Vitellius in Syria whose comprehension of Jewish sentiment he shared.

[3] The marriage of Vitellius and Petronia was dissolved by 62 (above, p. 94 n. 5), leaving bitter feelings and perhaps leading to murder (Suet. *Vit.* 6; *Hist.* 2. 64).

[4] *Ann.* 3. 49, 1.

[5] *PIR¹* P 198 and Hanslik in *R-E* 19. 1, col. 1226, accept the connection. Despite his lack of cognomen, the praenomen of P. Petronius, *cos.* A.D. 19 (surely the man in *Apoc.* 14. 2, *Ann.* 3. 49, and Suet. *Vit.* 6), not associated with any other known Petronii, suggests that the Augustan moneyer P. Petronius Turpilianus is his father, and the Neronian consul his son.

[6] Plutarch, *Galba* 15. 2, notes him as an old man in 69, so hardly in his thirties in 61.   [7] *Ann.* 15. 72.

[8] Syme, *Tacitus*, p. 386 n. 5; *JRS* 60 (1970), 38.

[9] Suet. *Vit.* 2. 4–5.

[10] *Ann.* 14. 49, 1. Compare Pliny, *Ep.* 3. 7, 3, of Silius Italicus: 'credebatur *sponte* accusasse', and the speech of Curtius Montanus in *Hist.* 4. 42.

D8. *Aebutius Liberalis*

Stein (*PIR*² A 111) suggested that Seneca's friend was in some way related to Q. Aebutius Liberalis who, on inscriptions from Dalmatia (*ILS* 5953 and 5953a), appears as one of two centurions instructed by A. Ducenius Geminus the legate of Dalmatia to measure certain boundaries. Ducenius Geminus will have governed the province between 62 and 69 (*PIR*² D 201). The centurion was in the *primi ordines*, being the *hastatus posterior*, the last of the six centurions, of the first cohort (H. M. D. Parker, *The Roman Legions*, Oxford, 1928, p. 201).

The man to whom Seneca dedicated *De Beneficiis*, written after the death of Claudius, and probably after 56 (Appendix A1), was a man of some wealth. This is clear from the subject of the essay which deals largely with material *beneficia* and particularly from 5. 1, 3 where Aebutius is praised for his generosity.[1] He was also a man of considerable education to judge from the many literary references and especially from the knowledge of civil law which Seneca attributes to him.[2] It is reasonable to assume that he was an *eques*.[3]

E. Birley ('Origins of Legionary Centurions', *Roman Britain and the Roman Army*) has shown that many legionary centurions in the early Principate were of provincial origin, and it is well known that many *equites* became centurions.[4] They tended to be promoted rapidly and, if promising, could omit the lowest ranks altogether. There is nothing against the idea then that a close relative of Seneca's friend could be the *hastatus posterior cohortis I* of the inscription. Appointments to the centurionate went largely by personal recommendation. Pliny (*Ep.*

---

[1] Noted by F. Préchac in the Budé edition (1927), p. xl. Seneca is certainly punning here on the name Liberalis, but the temptation to do so cannot have cancelled all considerations of appropriateness.

[2] 6. 5, 4–5. There is no warrant for believing, as does Préchac (loc. cit.), that he was a jurisconsult. Seneca, in fact, makes him say: 'Iuris consultorum istae acutae ineptiae sunt . . .' The subject-matter of the work is largely responsible for the legal terminology and analogies, as is made clear by similar discussion in *Ep.* 81. 3 ff. to Lucilius.

[3] Préchac (loc. cit.) cites 7. 12, 5 concerning *equites* as showing that Aebutius was one. But the *tibi* in 'nam nec equestria, et tamen communia tibi cum ceteris equitibus sunt' is probably not peculiar in its reference any more than the first person in the preceding discussion, e.g. 'Habeo in equestribus locum.' Seneca was not in this period an *eques*.

[4] For example, *ILS* 2654–6: *ex equite Romano* is the phrase used.

6. 25) tells of a fellow townsman for whom he procured a post as centurion. Seneca could have done the same. Ducenius Geminus had served on the financial commission of 62 with Pompeius Paulinus (*Ann.* 15. 18, 3), Seneca's brother-in-law.

The chief motive for relinquishing equestrian rank to become a centurion, besides a desire for military life, was lack of means.[1] Perhaps Aebutius Liberalis suffered financial loss in the fire at Lugdunum. Seneca says the destruction was total and Liberalis' love for his native city made his grief very severe—he would hardly mention anything else in a letter on the unexpected blows of Fortune written in elevated language (*Ep.* 91). Perhaps it was Liberalis himself who asked for Seneca's recommendation.

D9. *The Career of T. Flavius Sabinus*

The central problem in reconstructing Sabinus' career is Tacitus' statement that he served seven years in Moesia and twelve as prefect of the city (*Hist.* 3. 75). Pedanius Secundus was murdered in 61 when prefect (*Ann.* 14. 42), which would leave only seven (or eight) years for his successor Sabinus, who was prefect until Nero's death in 68 and then again in 69 (*Hist.* 1. 14, 46; 3. 64–74). If we accept the text of *Hist.* 3. 75, we have to assume an interruption in Sabinus' tenure in 61 and make him prefect in 56–60 as well, succeeding L. Volusius Saturninus who died in office in 56. Besides the inherent improbability of this (the interruption in 68 during the civil war is hardly comparable), there are two problems about this solution: (1) it gives Sabinus' predecessor in Moesia (which Sabinus held, on this hypothesis, *c.* 48–55) only a year in office, for Tullius Geminus was *cos. suff.* in 46, and gives Sabinus' successor, Ti. Plautius Aelianus, who was succeeded by a *cos. suff.* of 65, a tenure of ten years (evidence in the Horothesia dossier, complete in J. H. Oliver, *Greek, Roman and Byz. Studies* 6 (1965), 143 ff.). (2) We have to suppose that two censuses of Gaul were carried out at an interval of only five years, for Sabinus (*ILS* 984) was [*curator census*] *Gallici* after governing Moesia and before becoming prefect, and *Ann.* 14. 46 mentions a census in 61. Though such an interval was normal for peaceful provinces, it is very unlikely for a difficult

---

[1] Parker, *Roman Legions*, p. 200. *Hist.* 1. 46 indicates one way in which centurions could make money. According to Frontinus, *Strat.* 4. 6, 4, Vespasian disapproved of a well-born young man without military talent becoming a centurion 'angustiarum rei familiaris causa'.

province like Gaul: Augustus took one in 27 B.C., in 13 B.C., then in A.D. 14 (not completed until 16). I therefore prefer to accept one of Borghesi's emendations in *Hist.* 3. 75: *septem* or *totidem*. Sabinus then governed Moesia 53–60, was appointed *curator census Gallici*, but either refused, or, more likely, was replaced when appointed *praefectus urbi* on the death of Pedanius. Among the supporters of the first hypothesis are: A. W. Braithwaite, *Divus Vespasianus*, pp. 20–1; G. Vitucci, *Ricerche sulla Praefectura Urbi*, Rome, 1956; D. M. Pippidi, 'Ti. Plautius Aelianus und Moesien unter Neros Regierung', *Epigr. Beiträge zur Ges. Histrias*, Berlin, 1962, pp. 106 ff. The second had the support of Groag in 1938 (*R-E* 19. 23) and Stein in 1940 (*Die Legaten von Moesien*, pp. 28–9) but they leave the question open in *PIR*² F 352.

E. SLAVERY

1. *Did Seneca's Attitude to Slavery Change?*

J. LICHY, *De servorum condicione quid senserit L. Annaeus Seneca*, argued that Seneca's attitude toward slaves became increasingly liberal between the early and later dialogues. He distinguished two phases (pp. 36–7), the second beginning with *De Beneficiis* and including the *Letters to Lucilius*. This view does not stand up to examination.

(*a*) Lichy's division requires that *De Beneficiis* be definitely later than *De Constantia Sapientis* and *De Tranquillitate Animi* (see the passages he cites on p. 37). But this is by no means clear (see Appendix A1). The latter may be before 61, but *De Beneficiis* must have been completed by the summer of 64, and, given its length, could have overlapped with them in time of composition.

(*b*) Seneca's two lengthy discussions of slavery, in *De Beneficiis* 3 and Letter 47, both occur in the second phase. There is no discussion of the problem as such in the early works. It is difficult to compare incidental remarks with treatments of a subject as such. In particular, the absence of certain ideas in the earlier works is therefore unlikely to be significant: why should Seneca discuss the generosity of slaves to their masters, before the subject arises in *De Beneficiis* (cf. Lichy, p. 24)? Naturally, Seneca will stress the shamefulness of a master's cruelty to a slave, rather than the rights of the slave, when he is discussing the vice of anger (cf. Lichy, pp. 23–4). Of course, it might be significant that Seneca does not discuss slavery in itself until the later works, but the reasons for this are by no means clear: the topic clearly arose in Hecato's work, one of Seneca's sources in *De Beneficiis*, which could explain its appearance in that work; we cannot be sure that the subject did not occur in his lost works, some of which could be early.

(*c*) The differences Lichy alleges are not very convincing:

1. Seneca certainly says that slaves are men (*Clem*. 1. 18, 2) before he enlarges on the view in *Ep*. 47. In fact it is certainly implied by the statement that slaves are 'aequo iure genitos' in his earliest surviving work, *Cons. Marc.* 20. 2. Cf. Lichy, pp. 15–17.

2. It is not only in the earlier works that Seneca urges the master's advantage in advocating humane treatment: *Ep.* 47 appeals to Lucilius' *prudentia* as well as his *sapientia*. Cf. Lichy, pp. 23–4.

3. His sympathy for slave gladiators is by no means unequivocal in the Letters (especially 70. 19 ff.). Cf. Lichy, pp. 28–9.

4. Seneca's echoes of commonly accepted views are not limited to his early works (see above, p. 267 nn. 1–7). Lichy himself (p. 36) recognizes the existence of embarrassing exceptions in the later works, but tries to explain these away as isolated examples of rhetoric. But the idea of a clear progress in Seneca's thought on the subject of slavery is, as I think the above arguments show, not worth saving.

E2. *Did the Old and Middle Stoa hold that there are no Slaves by Nature?*

As regards the Old Stoa, the clearest evidence is *SVF* III, no. 352. But this explicit statement of Philo's, ἄνθρωπος γὰρ ἐκ φύσεως δοῦλος οὐδείς, is regarded as very questionable evidence of Stoic doctrine by Richter, *Gym.* 65 (1958), 205, and by F. H. Colson in the Loeb Philo, vol. VII, pp. 624–5. But the context—the natural subordination of animals to man—is a doctrine of Chrysippus (Cicero, *Fin.* 3. 67). Richter also suggests that Philo's other statement οἱ δὲ δεσπόται τοῖς ἀργυρωνήτοις μὴ ὡς φύσει δούλοις ἀλλ᾽ ὡς μισθωτοῖς προσφέρωνται is his own interpretation of Chrysippus' doctrine 'servus perpetuus mercennarius est' (*Ben.* 3. 22, 1). But the second half of the antithesis actually occurs in Cicero, *De Off.* 1. 41 (probably from Panaetius), and in company with the idea that servitude is a result of fortune. Philo's remark does seem then to be Stoic, probably going back to Chrysippus. A remark in Diogenes Laertius 7. 121 (*SVF* III, no. 355) contrasts political and chattel slavery with real servitude, i.e. the moral servitude of the wicked. Since no Stoic could have held that there were natural differences in men that conflicted with moral ones, this shows that the Old Stoa held that slavery had no basis in nature. It is obscure what φαύλη οὖσα καὶ αὐτή (sc. ἡ δεσποτεία) means: does it express a philosopher's contempt for all worldly, as opposed to moral mastery, or is it a condemnation of the temporal institution of slavery?

As for the Middle Stoa, W. Capelle, *Klio* 25 (1932), 86 ff., argued that the view in Cicero's *De Rep.* 3. 37 that there are natural slaves,

men who need, for their own good, to be ruled forcibly as the passions
by reason, is Panaetian and that Panaetius and Posidonius accepted
that, where it involved such men, slavery was a natural institution.
But Cicero, *Off.* 1. 41 (from Panaetius), seems to imply that fortune
is the regular cause of slavery and that all slaves are to be regarded as
long-term labourers. (*Off.* 2. 24 does present masters as the paradigm
case of those 'qui vi oppressos imperio coercent', which would, of
course, fit the view in *Rep.* 3. 37, but one cannot tell from it if Panaetius
meant only that some actual slave–master relationships were, in fact,
based on force.) On Posidonius see now Strasburger, in *JRS* 55 (1965),
48 ff. Posidonius' views (in Seneca, *Ep.* 90) about the natural rule of
deteriores by *potiores* which, among men, are the more virtuous,
certainly fits the view in *Rep.* 3. 37 (as does the fragment in Athenaeus
6. 263C), but Posidonius' discussion of the Sicilian slave revolt in his
history (*FGH* no. 87, 108C) is in direct contradiction in two ways:
(1) the application of the same precepts to rulers and masters, particularly the advice on how to have willing subjects, contradicts the
Aristotelian distinction in *De Rep.* between the nature of political
and dominical rule; (2) the acceptance as tolerable of the actual
institution of slavery where slaves have lost their freedom through
fortune contradicts the view in *De Rep.* which should render only the
natural form of slavery acceptable and lead to a demand for the
liberation of the superior and enslavement of the inferior. Finally, we
may note that Seneca agrees with the view of Posidonius set out in
the letter (90. 7), but he never dreamed of applying it to slavery.

E3. *Did the City Prefect only start hearing Complaints from Slaves in Nero's Reign?*

P. E. Vigneaux, *Essai sur l'histoire de la Praefectura Urbis à Rome*, p.
182, suggested that this role of the prefect in dealing with complaints
of mistreatment brought by slaves might be an innovation of Nero's
under the influence of Seneca, but admitted that the institution sprang
from the logic of the situation: once it was admitted that the master
could *injure* his own slaves, the intervention of a magistrate followed.
But the idea that a master could injure his slaves is recognized before
Nero: perhaps under the Republic (Mommsen, *Strafr.*, p. 24 n. 1),
certainly under Claudius. The operative factor was probably the existence of an official charged with keeping order (see pp. 269–70 ff.).

Préchac (Budé edition of *De Beneficiis*, I, p. ii) tried to date the practice precisely in Seneca's period of influence with Nero—between *De Clementia* and the debate on the murder of Pedanius Secundus. He argued that Seneca's words in *Clem.* 1. 18, 2, 'cum in servum omnia liceant, est aliquid quod in hominem licere commune ius animantium vetet', show that the slave was then still unprotected by the law. But (1) Seneca's statement is, in any case, an exaggeration as at least Claudius' edict protected old and sick slaves, (2) even after the prefect was heeding complaints, Musonius Rufus gave, without contradicting it, the view that a master can do just what he wants with a slave (frag. 12, Hense, p. 66) and Pius admitted that a master's power ought to remain undiluted (*Coll.* 3. 3, 2). In fact, the limitations in existence in Seneca's day were very slight compared with the master's power, so that moral feelings and the master's self-interest, not legal sanctions, were the only real protection of the slave. In the very discussion in *De Beneficiis* where Seneca mentions the responsibility of the prefect for slaves (the subject being whether or not slaves can confer benefits on their masters), Seneca first uses arguments compatible with the premiss of the slave's rightlessness (*Ben.* 3. 18, 2–20, 1): note especially 3. 19, 1: 'servus non habet negandi potestatem . . . iam sub ista ipsa lege vincam.'

Préchac's *terminus ante* of 61 depends on the argument that Tacitus' account of the Pedanius Secundus debate implies the established existence of the city prefect's special connection with slaves. In fact, there is no hint of this role in the debate: only the victim's *dignitas* as prefect comes in. Tacitus is not concerned to tell us facts about the prefect's jurisdiction, though there was one fact that would have been specially relevant. One reason alleged for the murderer's desperation was that the prefect had refused him manumission though he had saved enough to pay for it: Ulpian tells us that this was one grievance the prefect was supposed to listen to. If he already did in Seneca's day, excellent material for the side advocating mildness lay to hand: but Tacitus was not interested in writing that speech.

F. NERO'S PLANS FOR THE EASTERN FRONTIER

ANY reconstruction of Nero's ultimate plans for the eastern frontier after the Armenian settlement must be highly conjectural. We lack the detailed Tacitean evidence for eastern movements after 63. In addition, it is obvious that when the news of the defeat by the Jews of the Syrian governor on 8 November 66[1] reached Nero in Achaea, the Emperor subordinated whatever previous plans he had made to the need for a consular command with full legionary complement in Judaea. It is therefore events before the end of 66 that are most significant for us.

In 63 Corbulo had been put in charge of the war and made *legatus pro praetore*[2] of Cappadocia–Galatia with control of the military forces in Syria and *imperium maius* over the surrounding provinces. Corbulo took four legions to Cappadocia and left three in Syria.[3] By October 66 we find Cestius Gallus[4] the legate of Syria leading the twelfth legion, which Corbulo had left in the province, and detachments from the sixth, which Corbulo had taken with him.[5] Ritterling[6] argued that this arrangement must postdate the death of Corbulo which must thus fall in August–September 66. Now the date of Corbulo's summons to Greece by Nero and suicide at Cenchreae cannot be precisely determined, as our only source, Xiphilinus' epitome of Dio (63. 17), includes it among the events of Nero's visit to Greece without separating the years 66 and 67 or dating Nero's arrival. Nor does he arrange the events strictly chronologically.[7] But it is none the less clear that Nero was probably not in Greece before early October,[8] so that the arrange-

---

[1] Josephus, *BJ* 2. 555.   [2] *ILS* 232.

[3] *Ann.* 15. 25–6.

[4] He may be the same as 'Citius' (*Ann.* 15. 25, 3) put in charge of Syria in 63, or a successor.

[5] Josephus, *BJ* 2. 500; 544.

[6] *R-E* 12, col. 1257, s.v. 'Legio'.

[7] In Dio 63. 18, 1 is reported the banishment of Caecina Tuscus who had already been succeeded as prefect of Egypt by mid May 66 (*BJ* 2. 309, 315), probably before Nero left for Greece (see next note).

[8] *AFA* (*CIL* 6. 2046) shows his departure on 25 September 66. Helius (Dio 63. 19, 1) made the journey in seven days but the fact is stressed as remarkable

ments with Cestius will have been made before the death of Corbulo, which probably fell late in 66 or early in 67.

Before Corbulo's death then we seem to see the Flavian arrangements basically foreshadowed in that (despite the technical subordination of one to the other) the two military commands, Cappadocia–Galatia and Syria, were retained after the Armenian crisis was settled.

There are, however, some difficulties in the evidence about Cappadocia to be faced before we can accept that these were the provincial arrangements in 66:

(a) Josephus (BJ 2. 368 ff.), in a speech to the Jews attributed to Agrippa II in June of 66, gives the Roman legionary dispositions. He names Cappadocia, along with Pamphylia, Lycia, and the Cilicians, as unarmed. Schur[1] argued that, some time after the settlement of 63, Corbulo had become legate of Galatia and Pontus, which had been annexed in 64–5,[2] instead of Galatia and Cappadocia, and that his reconnaissance expedition to the Caspian Gates in this period after 63[3] shows that Nero intended him to lead the campaign in the north against the 'Albani'.[4] It is not impossible that Nero had at one time such plans for Corbulo,[5] but Pontus, which was probably annexed in connection with plans for the expedition, could have been added to Cappadocia–Galatia as it was later under Vespasian. The speech in Josephus, as is generally agreed, goes back to some good authority, but it is not necessarily completely accurate for 66.[6] The note on Cappadocia might reflect the situation after Vespasian took up his command in 67. For certainly by the first half of 69 Cappadocia was unarmed.[7]

(b) Galba put Galatia and Pamphylia under one praetorian legate.[8]

---

and he was not encumbered with Nero's entourage. But the connection of these *AFA* vows has been doubted by Schumann, *Hellenistische und griechische Elemente*, pp. 65 ff., who thinks Nero's arrival in Greece is to be placed shortly before the closing of the sailing season in early November.

[1] *Klio*, Beih. 15 (1923), 93.

[2] See Anderson, *CAH* X, p. 774.

[3] Pliny, *NH* 6. 40.

[4] Fortunately, the question of Caucasian *v.* Caspian and Alani *v.* Albani is irrelevant to our inquiry here.

[5] See further, p. 465.

[6] It is anachronistic about the German legions, Ritterling, 'Legio', *R-E* 12, cols. 1262–3; Anderson, *CAH* X, p. 776.

[7] *Hist.* 2. 81 (implied in 2. 6). Otho was thinking of doing something about it (1. 78).   [8] *Hist.* 2. 9.

It might be thought that the arrangement went back to Nero, for
Statius (*Silvae* 1. 4, 74 ff.) shows a subordinate of Corbulo active in
Galatia and Pamphylia for nine years after his praetorship in 55 and
before his tenure of Asia in 68 or 69. The natural time for this arrangement would be when Lycia gained her freedom,[1] an act of generosity
that one would naturally ascribe to Nero. Had Corbulo then ceased
to have a military command in Cappadocia? But Syme has argued[2]
that Galba could have freed Lycia, and that we know that the Lycia–
Pamphylia combination persisted some time after 58, as Mucianus
was governor of both.[3] Syme concluded that Statius' geography was
erroneous, and that Nero retained the combinations Cappadocia–
Galatia and Lycia–Pamphylia to the end. Alternatively, Rutilius may
have been conducting operations in Pamphylia under Corbulo's *imperium maius*.

But the notion that Lycia was not freed by Nero is not very attractive.[4] Instead one could hold that Nero freed Lycia, and retained
the Cappadocia–Galatia combine, if Pamphylia was now governed
separately,[5] or was added to Cappadocia–Galatia.[6]

Even if we dispose of the two pieces of contrary evidence in the
above manner, there is no reason to think that Nero regarded this
provincial arrangement as permanent and defensive, in the way Vespasian did. Tacitus reports rumours of Nero's secret plans to visit

[1] The grant was cancelled by Vespasian, Suet. *Vesp.* 8. 4.

[2] In *Klio* 30 (1937), 227 ff. He points to Tacitus' words 'Galatiam ac Pamphy-
liam provincias . . . permiserat [Galba]' (*Hist.* 2. 9) as an indication that the two
were separate before Galba.

[3] *ILS* 8816; *AE* 1915, no. 48, presumably succeeding Eprius Marcellus, who
was governor before prosecution by the Lycians in 57 (*Ann.* 13. 33, 4). Mucianus
may have been with Corbulo on his march to Artaxata in 58 before going there
(Syme, *Tacitus*, App. 84, p. 790).

[4] B. Levick, *Roman Colonies in Southern Asia Minor*, pp. 227–8, inclines towards
the view that Nero gave the Lycians their freedom and that Galatia and Pamphylia were amalgamated some time after 58, Tacitus' use of the plural (above,
n. 2) being a reflection of their separation in his own day.

[5] W. Ramsay in *JRS* 16 (1926), 207, stated that in 68–9 Galatia and Cappadocia
were two separately governed provinces, which would provide a parallel, but he
seems to have rested this view on the notion that a praetorian governor of
Galatia in 68–9 was known, i.e. Sergius Paulus *filius*. There is, however, no reason
to think that this young man governed Galatia at all (R. K. Sherk, *The Legates
of Galatia from Augustus to Diocletian*, Baltimore, Md., 1951, pp. 36–7, following
Groag, *R-E* 4. 2, col. 1718).

[6] In which case Tacitus' use of the plural in *Hist.* 2. 9 is anachronistic (as Levick
suggests, above, n. 4).

eastern provinces,[1] and Dio mentions intended expeditions to Ethiopia and the Caspian Gates.[2] But more conclusive than these is the attested movement of XV Apollinaris (one of Corbulo's legions since 63) to Alexandria by the end of 66,[3] and the presence of Libyan detachments in Alexandria in the summer of 66.[4] These have been plausibly regarded as the start of the enormous troop movements being executed in 67 and 68 for Nero's eastern and northern campaigns. The annexation of Pontus in 63/4 will have been directed towards the latter, and Nero's bringing with him of 6,000 praetorians to Greece also indicates a campaign in the immediate future.[5] Thus, if Cappadocia remained a military province at the expense of the Danube garrisons, that was part of new military plans, not of a new conception of eastern defence.

In Nero's grandiose plans then, Corbulo, a successful and so far trustworthy general, must have played a large part. Yet some time after the Jewish war broke out, he was forced to commit suicide.[6] Schur suggested that Nero changed his mind about Corbulo when Cestius Gallus was defeated by the Jews, and, in his anger[7], blamed Corbulo who must have decided on Gallus' military force, as well as Gallus. But he has to discard the evidence of the Emperor's political suspicions in Tacitus,[8] evidence strengthened by references to a *coniuratio Viniciana*,[9] presumably staged by Corbulo's son-in-law and legate Annius Vinicianus. If Nero changed his mind about Corbulo for political reasons, he may well have thought that Corbulo might decide on rebellion rather than submit to an order to hand over command of his seven legions. This is suggested by Dio's interpretation of Corbulo's dying word: ἄξιος—he was a fool to have replied to Nero's flattering summons, going to Greece without his army. We might even wonder if the famous hostility between Vespasian and Licinius Mucianus was due not merely to envy in command but to the fact that Mucianus

---

[1] *Ann.* 15. 36, 1 (under 64).

[2] 63. 8 (under 66). The idea that Nero's expedition to find the sources of the Nile (Seneca, *NQ* 6. 8, 3—thus earlier than the end of 64 (Appendix A1)) had the motive of preparation for the Ethiopian expedition assigned to it (if he means the same one) by Pliny, *NH* 6. 181, seems to me too difficult chronologically. We cannot be sure of reconnaissance that early. Pliny may be assuming a purpose that fitted with Nero's later activities. Cf. Anderson, *CAH* X, pp. 778–9.

[3] Josephus, *BJ* 2. 494; cf. 3. 8

[4] Ibid. 2. 494.   [5] Schur, op. cit., p. 104.

[6] Ibid., p. 94.   [7] *BJ* 3. 1.   [8] *Hist.* 3. 6.

[9] Suet. *Nero* 36; cf. *AFA* for spring 66.

had served under Corbulo while Vespasian's appointment had been the result and perhaps the aim of the great commander's enforced suicide. The hostility of Mucianus to Arrius Varus, a soldier of Corbulo who informed on his commander, might be a clue, since Domitian did not share his hostility.[1]

[1] *Hist.* 3. 6; 4. 11; 4. 68.

BIBLIOGRAPHY

This list contains only books and articles expressly cited, excluding standard reference works, editions, and collections of ancient literary and material evidence (many of which are listed under Abbreviations).

Seneca's Life (including work on the Historical Sources)

Alexander, W. H., 'The Tacitean "non liquet" on Seneca', *Univ. of Calif. Publ. in Cl. Phil.* 14 (1952), 269 ff.

Birt, T., 'Seneca', *Preuss. Jahrb.* 144 (1911), 282 ff.

Bonner, S. F., *Roman Declamation*, Liverpool, 1949.

Bornecque, H., *Les déclamations et les déclamateurs d'après Sénèque le père*, Lille, 1902.

Bourgery, A., 'Le mariage de Sénèque', *REL* 14 (1936), 90 ff.

Browne, G. M., 'Withdrawal from Lease', *Bulletin of the American Society of Papyrologists* 5 (1968), 17 ff.

Cantarelli, L., 'Per l'amministrazione e la storia dell'Egitto romano, II: Il viaggio di Seneca in Egitto', *Aegyptus* 8 (1927), 89 ff.

Ciaceri, E., 'Claudio e Nerone nelle *Storie* di Plinio', *Processi politici e Relazioni internazionali*, Rome, 1918.

Clarke, G. W., 'Seneca the Younger under Caligula', *Latomus* 24 (1965), 62 ff.

Diderot, D., *Essai sur les règnes de Claude et de Néron* (1778), in *Œuvres complètes de Diderot*, Paris, 1875.

Diepenbrock, A. J. M., *L. Annaei Senecae philosophi Cordubensis vita*, Diss. Amsterdam, 1888.

Edwards, W. A., *The Suasoriae of the Elder Seneca*, Cambridge, 1928.

Faider, P., *Études sur Sénèque*, Ghent, 1921.

—— 'Sénèque en Égypte', *Bulletin de l'Institut français d'Archéologie orientale du Caire*, 30 (1930), 83 ff.

Feldman, L., 'The Sources of Josephus' Antiquities, Book 19', *Latomus* 21 (1962), 320 ff.

Gercke, A., *Seneca-Studien, Fleckeisens Jahrbücher für Classische Philologie*, Suppl. 22 (1896), 1–334.

Giancotti, F., 'Il posto della biografia nella problematica senechiana, I: Dall'esilio al *Ludus de Morte Claudii*', *RAL*, 8th Ser. 8 (1953), 52 ff.

Giancotti, F. (*cont.*):

—— 'Id. II: Da quando e in che senso Seneca fu maestro di Nerone?' ibid. 102 ff.

—— 'Id. III: Seneca antagonista d'Agrippina', ibid. 238 ff.

—— 'Id. IV. 1: Sfondo storico e data dal De Clementia', *RAL*, 8th Ser. 9 (1954), 329 ff.

—— 'Id. IV. 2–4: Il De Clementia', ibid. 587 ff.

—— 'Id. IV. 5: Struttura del De Clementia', *RAL*, 8th Ser. 10 (1955), 36 ff.

—— 'Sopra il ritiro e la ricchezza di Seneca', *RAL*, 8th Ser. 11 (1956), 105 ff.

Gillis, D., 'The Portrait of Afranius Burrus in Tacitus' *Annales*', *La Parola del Passato* 18 (1963), 5 ff.

Goodyear, F. R. D., *Tacitus*, Greece and Rome New Surveys in the Classics no. 4, Oxford, 1970.

Griffin, M. T., 'The Elder Seneca and Spain', *JRS* 62 (1972), 1 ff.

—— 'Imago Vitae Suae', *Seneca*, ed. Costa, London, 1974, pp. 1 ff.

Grimal, P., *Sénèque*², Paris, 1957.

Henry, D., and Walker, B., 'Tacitus and Seneca', *Greece and Rome* 10 (1963), 98 ff.

Kamp, H. W., 'Concerning Seneca's Exile', *CJ* 29 (1934), 101 ff.

—— 'Seneca's Marriage', *CJ* 32 (1937), 529.

Klingner, F., 'Tacitus über Augustus und Tiberius' (1954), *Studien*, Zürich, 1964, pp. 651 ff.

Knoche, U., 'Zur Beurteilung des Kaisers Tiberius durch Tacitus', *Gym.* 70 (1963), 211 ff.

Lana, I., *Lucio Anneo Seneca*, Turin, 1955.

de La Ville de Mirmont, H., 'La date du voyage de Sénèque en Égypte', *RPh* 33 (1909), 163 ff.

Lehmann, H., 'Lucius Annaeus Seneca und seine philosophischen Schriften', *Philologus* 8 (1853), 309 ff.

Marchesi, C., *Seneca*, Milan, 1944.

Marx, K. F. H., 'Das Leiden des Philosophen Lucius Annaeus Seneca', *Abh. der König. Gesellschaft der Wissenschaften zu Göttingen* 17 (1872), 3 ff.

Millar, F., *A Study of Cassius Dio*, Oxford, 1964.

Münzer, F., 'Die Quelle des Tacitus für die Germanenkriege', *Bonner Jahrbücher* 104 (1899), 67 ff.

Oltramare, A., 'Sénèque diplomate', *REL* 16 (1938), 318 ff.

Préchac, F., 'La date de naissance de Sénèque', *REL* 12 (1934), 360 ff.; 15 (1937), 66–7.

Questa, C., *Studi sulle fonti degli Annales di Tacito*², Rome, 1963.

Ryberg, I., 'Tacitus' Art of Innuendo', *TAPA* 73 (1942), 383 ff.

Stella Maranca, F., 'L. Anneo Seneca nel "Consilium principis" ', *RAL* 32 (1923), 282 ff.

Stewart, Z., 'Sejanus, Gaetulicus, and Seneca', *AJP* 74 (1953), 70 ff.

Syme, R., 'Pliny the Procurator', *HSCP* 73 (1968), 201 ff.

Timpe, D., 'Römische Geschichte bei Flavius Josephus', *Historia* 9 (1960), 474 ff.

Townend, G., 'The Source of the Greek in Suetonius', *Hermes* 88 (1960), 98 ff.

—— 'Traces in Dio Cassius of Cluvius, Aufidius, and Pliny', *Hermes* 89 (1961), 227 ff.

Treves, P., 'Il giorno della morte di Seneca', *Studia Florentina Alexandro Ronconi Sexagenario Oblata*, Rome, 1970, pp. 507 ff.

Trillitzsch, W., *Seneca im literarischen Urteil der Antike*, 2 vols., Amsterdam, 1971.

Waltz, R., *La vie politique de Sénèque*, Paris, 1909 (also issued as *La vie de Sénèque*).

Wedeck, H., 'The Question of Seneca's Wealth', *Latomus* 14 (1955), 540–4.

The History of the Period

Adams, F., 'The Consular Brothers of Sejanus', *AJP* 76 (1955), 70 ff.

Alexander, W. H., 'The Communiqué to the Senate on Agrippina's Death', *CP* 49 (1954), 94 ff.

Allison, J. E., and Cloud, J. D., 'The Lex Julia Maiestatis', *Latomus* 21 (1962), 711 ff.

Anderson, J. G. C., Review of Gwatkin, *Cappadocia as a Roman Procuratorial Province*, in *CR* 45 (1931), 190 ff.

Babelon, J., 'Numismatique de Britannicus', *Hommages à Léon Herrmann*, Brussels, 1960, pp. 124 ff.

Balsdon, J. P. V. D., *The Emperor Gaius*, Oxford, 1934.

Baumann, R. A., *The Crimen Maiestatis in the Roman Republic and Augustan Principate*, Johannesburg, 1967.

Bay, A., 'The Letters SC on Augustan *Aes* Coinage', *JRS* 62 (1972), 111 ff.

Birley, A. R., 'The Oath not to put Senators to Death', *CR* 12 (1962), 197–9.

Birley, E., *Roman Britain and the Roman Army*, Kendall, 1953.

—— Review of Stein, *Präfekten von Ägypten*, in *Gnomon* 23 (1951), 440–3.

—— Review of Thomasson (cited below), in *JRS* 52 (1962), 219 ff.

Bleicken, J., *Senatsgericht und Kaisergericht*, Göttingen, 1962.

Boddington, A., 'Sejanus, Whose Conspiracy?' *AJP* 84 (1963), 1 ff.

Boissevain, U. P., *Cassii Dionis Cocceiani Historiarum Romanarum Quae Super-sunt*, 3 vols., Berlin, 1898–1931.

Braithwaite, A. W., *C. Suetoni Tranquilli Divus Vespasianus*, Oxford, 1927.

Brunt, P., 'The Revolt of Vindex and the Fall of Nero', *Latomus* 18 (1959), 531 ff.

—— 'Charges of Provincial Maladministration under the Early Principate', *Historia* 10 (1961), 189 ff.

—— 'The "Fiscus" and its Development', *JRS* 56 (1966), 75 ff.

—— 'Procuratorial Jurisdiction', *Latomus* 25 (1966), 461 ff.

—— Review of W. L. Westermann, *Slave Systems*, *JRS* 48 (1958), 164 ff.

Buckland, W. W., *The Roman Law of Slavery*, Cambridge, 1908.

Bulst, C. M., 'The Revolt of Queen Boudicca in A.D. 60', *Historia* 10 (1961), 496 ff.

Cesareo, E., *La poesia di Calpurnio Siculo*, Palermo, 1931.

Charlesworth, M. P., 'Flaviana', *JRS* 27 (1937), 57 ff.

Chilton, C. W., 'The Roman Law of Treason under the Early Principate', *JRS* 45 (1955), 73 ff.

Chilver, G. E. F., *Cisalpine Gaul*, Oxford, 1941.

Cichorius, C., *Römische Studien*, Stuttgart, 1922.

Crook, J., *Consilium Principis*, Cambridge, 1955.

Degrassi, A., *I Fasti Consolari*, Rome, 1952.

Dudley, D. R. and Webster, G., *The Rebellion of Boudicca*, London, 1962.

Duff, A. M., *Freedmen in the Early Roman Empire*, Oxford, 1928.

Fabia, P., 'Julius Paelignus: Préfet des Vigiles et Procurateur de Cappadoce', *RPh* 22 (1898), 133 ff.

Frere, S., *Britannia*, London, 1967.

Garnsey, P., *Social Status and Legal Privilege in the Roman Empire*, Oxford, 1970.

—— 'The Criminal Jurisdiction of Governors', *JRS* 58 (1968), 51 ff.

Gaudamet, J., 'Testamenta ingrata et pietas Augusti', *Studi Arangio-Ruiz*, Naples, 1953, III, pp. 115 ff.

Geer, R. M., 'Notes on the Early Life of Nero', *TAPA* 62 (1931), 57 ff.

Gilliam, J. F., 'Novius Priscus', *Bulletin de Correspondance Hellénique* 91 (1967), 269 ff.

Gordon, A. E., 'Quintus Veranius Consul A.D. 49', *Univ. of Calif. Publ. in Cl. Arch.* 2. 5 (1952), 231 ff.

Grant, M., *Nero*, London, 1970.

Groag, E., *Die römischen Reichsbeamten von Achaia bis auf Diokletian*, Vienna, 1939.

Gyles, M. F., 'Effects of Roman Capital Investment in Britain under Nero', *Studies in Memory of W. E. Caldwell*, Chapel Hill, N.C., 1964, pp. 104 ff.

Hammond, M., *The Augustan Principate*, Cambridge, Mass., 1933.

—— 'Corbulo and Nero's Eastern Policy', *HSCP* 45 (1934), 81 ff.

—— 'The Tribunician Day during the Early Empire', *MAAR* 15 (1938), 23 ff.

Heinz, K., *Das Bild Kaiser Neros bei Seneca, Tacitus, Sueton u. Cassius Dio*, Diss. Bern, 1948.

Henderson, B. W., *The Life and Principate of the Emperor Nero*, London, 1903.

Hirschfeld, O., *Untersuchungen auf dem Gebiete der römischen Verwaltungsgeschichte*, Berlin, 1876.

—— *Die kaiserlichen Verwaltungsbeamten bis auf Diocletian*[2], Berlin, 1905.

Jones, A. H. M., *The Herods of Judaea*, Oxford, 1938.

—— 'The Aerarium and the Fiscus', *JRS* 40 (1950), 22 ff. (Reprinted in *Studies in Roman Government and Law*, Oxford, 1960.)

Kraft, K., 'S(enatus) C(onsulto)', *Jahrbuch für Numismatik und Geldgeschichte* 12 (1962), 7 ff., reprinted with an Appendix in *Wege der Forschung* 128 (1969), 336 ff.

Labrousse, M., 'Le *Pomerium* de la Rome impériale', *Mél. de l'École française de Rome* 54 (1937), 165 ff.

De Laet, S. J., *De Samenstelling van den romeinschen Senaat gedurende de eerste Eeuw van het Principaat (28 vóór Chr.–68 na Chr.)*, Antwerp, 1941.

Last, H., 'Rome and the Druids: a Note', *JRS* 39 (1949), 1 ff.

Lepper, F., 'Some Reflections on the "Quinquennium Neronis"', *JRS* 47 (1957), 95 ff.

Levi, M. A., *Nerone e i suoi tempi*, Milan, 1949.

Levick, B. M., 'Two Pisidian Colonial Families', *JRS* 48 (1958), 74 ff.

—— *Roman Colonies in Southern Asia Minor*, Oxford, 1967.

—— and Jameson, S., 'C. Crepereius Gallus and his Gens', *JRS* 54 (1964), 98 ff.

Levy, E., 'Gesetz und Richter im kaiserlichen Strafrecht, Erster Teil', *Bull. dell'Ist. di Diritto Romano* 45 (1938), 57 ff.

McAlindon, D., 'Entry to the Senate in the Early Empire', *JRS* 47 (1957), 191 ff.

McDermott, W. C., 'Sextus Afranius Burrus', *Latomus* 8 (1949), 229 ff.

MacMullen, R., *Enemies of the Roman Order*, Cambridge, Mass., 1967.

Marx, K., 'Tacitus und die Literatur der exitus illustrium virorum', *Philologus* 92 (1937), 83 ff.

Mattingly, H., 'Some Historical Coins of the First Century A.D.', *JRS* 10 (1920), 37 ff.

—— 'Britannicus and Titus', *NC* 10 (1930), 330 ff.

Millar, F., 'The Fiscus in the First Two Centuries', *JRS* 53 (1963), 29 ff.

—— 'The Aerarium and its Officials under the Empire', *JRS* 54 (1964), 33 ff.

—— 'Epictetus and the Imperial Court', *JRS* 55 (1965), 141 ff.

—— 'The Emperor, the Senate, and the Provinces', *JRS* 56 (1966), 156 ff.

—— Review of Pflaum, *Carr. proc.*, in *JRS* 53 (1963), 194 ff.

Mitford, T. B., 'Two Roman Inscriptions of New Paphos', in *Report of the Department of Antiquities, Cyprus (1940–48)*, Nicosia, 1958, pp. 1 ff.

Momigliano, A., 'Corbulone e la politica verso i Parti', *Atti del II Congresso Nazionale di Studi Romani*, Rome, 1931, I, pp. 368 ff.

—— 'Ricerche sull'organizzazione della Giudea sotto il dominio romano 63 a.C.–70 d.C.', *Annali della R. Scuola normale superiore di Pisa*, 2nd Ser. 3 (1934), 183 ff.

—— *Claudius*, Oxford, 1934.

Musurillo, H., *The Acts of the Pagan Martyrs*, Oxford, 1954.

Nock, A. D., 'Σύνναος θεός', *HSCP* 41 (1930), 1 ff.

Ogg, G., *The Chronology of the Life of Paul*, London, 1968.

Oliver, J. H., 'The Augustan Pomerium', *MAAR* 10 (1932), 45 ff.

—— 'Greek Inscriptions', *Hesperia* 10 (1941), 72 ff.; 11 (1942), 29 ff.

—— 'Texts A and B of the *Horothesia* Dossier at Istros', *Gk. Rom. and Byz. Studies* 6 (1965), 143 ff.

Olivieri, G., *Documenti antichi dell'Africa italiana*, vol. II: *Cirenaica*, Bergamo, 1933.

Oost, S. I., 'The Career of M. Antonius Pallas', *AJP* 79 (1958), 113 ff.

Parker, E. J., 'Education of Heirs in the Julio-Claudian Family', *AJP* 67 (1946), 44 ff.

Parker, H. M. D., *The Roman Legions*, Oxford, 1928.

Pflaum, H.-G., *Les procurateurs équestres sous le Haut-Empire romain*, Paris, 1950.

—— *Les carrières procuratoriennes équestres sous le Haut-Empire romain*, 4 vols., Paris, 1960–1.

Pippidi, D. M., 'Ti. Plautius Aelianus und Moesien unter Neros Regierung' (1958), *Epigr. Beiträge zur Geschichte Histrias*, Berlin, 1962, pp. 106 ff.

Pistor, H.-H., *Princeps und Patriziat*, Diss. Freiburg, 1965.

Plassart, A., 'L'inscription de Delphes mentionnant le proconsul Gallion', *REG* 80 (1967), 372 ff.

Pleket, H. W., 'Domitian, the Senate and the Provinces', *Mnemosyne* 14 (1961), 300 ff.

Ramsay, W. M., 'Studies in the Roman Province Galatia', *JRS* 16 (1926), 201 ff.

Reynolds, J., 'Roman Inscriptions 1966–1970', *JRS* 61 (1971), 136 ff.

Richmond, I. A., 'Queen Cartimandua', *JRS* 44 (1954), 43 ff.

Rogers, R. S., 'Ignorance of the Law in Tacitus and Dio', *TAPA* 64 (1933), 18 ff.

—— 'The Roman Emperors as Heirs and Legatees', *TAPA* 78 (1947), 140 ff.

—— 'The Tacitean Account of a Neronian Trial', *Studies presented to D. M. Robinson*, 1953, II, pp. 711 ff.

—— 'Five Over-crowded Months: A.D. 62', *St. in Honour of B. L. Ullman*, Rome, 1964, I, pp. 217 ff.

Rose, K., 'The Author of the Satyricon', *Latomus* 20 (1961), 821 ff.

—— 'Problems of Chronology in Lucan's Career', *TAPA* 97 (1966), 379 ff.

Saumagne, C., 'Saint Paul et Félix', *Mél. Piganiol*, 1966, III, pp. 1373 ff.

Schtajerman, E. M., *Die Krise der Sklavenhalterordnung*, Moscow, 1957 (German translation, Berlin, 1964).

Schulz, F., *Principles of Roman Law*, Oxford, 1936.

Schumann, G., *Hellenistische und griechische Elemente in der Regierung Neros*, Leipzig, 1930.

Schur, W., 'Die Orientpolitik des Kaisers Nero', *Klio*, Beiheft 15, 1923.

Schürer, E., *History of the Jewish People in the age of Jesus Christ* (revised by G. Vermes and F. Millar), I, Edinburgh, 1973.

Scott, K., 'The Significance of Statues in Precious Metals in Emperor Worship', *TAPA* 62 (1931), 101 ff.

Sherk, R. K., *The Legates of Galatia from Augustus to Diocletian*, Baltimore, Md., 1951.

Sherwin-White, A. N., *The Roman Citizenship*[2], Oxford, 1973.

—— *Roman Society and Roman Law in the New Testament*, Oxford, 1963.

—— *The Letters of Pliny*, Oxford, 1966.

—— Review of Bleicken, *Senatsgericht*, in *JRS* 53 (1963), 203–5.

Sizoo, A., 'Paetus Thrasea et le Stoïcisme', *REL* 4 (1926), 229 ff.; 5 (1927), 41 ff.

Smallwood, E. M., 'Some Notes on the Jews under Tiberius', *Latomus* 15 (1956), 314 ff.

—— 'Some Comments on Tacitus "Annals" 12. 54', *Latomus* 18 (1959), 560 ff.

—— 'Consules Suffecti of A.D. 55', *Historia* 17 (1968), 384.

Stein, A., *Die Legaten von Moesien*, Budapest, 1940.

—— *Die Präfekten von Ägypten*, Bern, 1950.

Stevens, C. E., 'The Will of Q. Veranius', *CR* 65 (1951), 4 ff.

Sumner, G. V., 'The Family Connections of L. Aelius Seianus', *Phoenix* 19 (1965), 134 ff.

—— 'Germanicus and Drusus Caesar', *Latomus* 26 (1967), 413 ff.

—— 'The Lex Annalis under Caesar', *Phoenix* 25 (1971), 246 ff.; 351 ff.

Sutherland, C. H. V., *Coinage in Roman Imperial Policy, 31 B.C.–A.D. 68*, London, 1951.

Sydenham, E. A., *The Coinage of Nero*, London, 1920.

Syme, R., 'Pamphylia from Augusta to Vespasian', *Klio* 30 (1937), 227 ff.

—— *The Roman Revolution*, Oxford, 1938.

—— 'Marcus Lepidus, *Capax Imperii*', *JRS* 45 (1955), 22 ff. = chap. IV in *Ten Studies in Tacitus*, Oxford, 1970.

—— 'Some Friends of the Caesars', *AJP* 77 (1956), 264 ff.

—— 'Deux proconsulats d'Afrique', *REA* 58 (1956), 236 ff.

—— *Tacitus*, Oxford, 1958.

—— 'Tacitus und seine politische Einstellung', *Gym.* 59 (1962), 244 ff. = chap. X in *Ten Studies in Tacitus*.

—— 'The Historian Servilius Nonianus', *Hermes* 92 (1964), 412 ff. = chap. VIII in *Ten Studies in Tacitus*.

—— 'The Ummidii', *Historia* 17 (1968), 72 ff.

—— 'Domitius Corbulo', *JRS* 60 (1970), 27 ff.

Taylor, L. R., 'Trebula Suffenas and the Plautii Silvani', *MAAR* 24 (1956), 26 ff.

Thomasson, B. E., *Die Statthalter der römischen Provinzen Nordafrikas von Augustus bis Diocletianus*, 2 vols., Lund, 1960.

Townend, G., 'Some Flavian Connections', *JRS* 51 (1961), 54 ff.

Toynbee, J. M. C., 'Dictators and Philosophers in the First Century A.D.', *Greece and Rome*, 13 (1944), 43 ff.

Vigneaux, P. E., *Essai sur l'histoire de la Praefectura Urbis à Rome*, Paris, 1896.

Vitucci, G., *Ricerche sulla Praefectura Urbi in età imperiale*, Rome, 1956.

Warmington, B. H., *Nero: Reality and Legend*, London, 1969.

Weaver, P. R. C., 'The Father of Claudius Etruscus', *CQ* 15 (1965), 145 ff.

—— *Familia Caesaris*, Cambridge, 1972.

Weidemann, U., Review of Thomasson (cited above), in *Gnomon* 37 (1965), 786 ff.

Ziegler, K.-H., *Die Beziehungen zwischen Rom und dem Partherreich*, Wiesbaden, 1964.

Seneca's Prose Works

Abel, K., Review of Giancotti, *Cronologia*, in *Gnomon* 30 (1958), 607 ff.

—— Review of Coccia, *I problemi del De Ira*, in *Gnomon* 33 (1961), 162 ff.

—— 'Seneca de Brevitate Vitae: Datum und Zielsetzung', *Gym.* 72 (1965), 308 ff.

—— *Bauformen in Senecas Dialogen*, Heidelberg, 1967.

—— 'Sen. Dial. 12. 18, 4 ff., ein Zeugnis für die Biographie Lucans?' *Rh M* 115 (1972), 325 ff.

Adam, T., *Clementia Principis*, Stuttgart, 1970.

Adler, M., 'Die Verschwörung des Cn. Cornelius Cinna bei Seneca und Cassius Dio', *Zeitschr. für die österreich-Gymnasien* 60 (1909), 193 ff.

Albertini, E., *La composition dans les ouvrages philosophiques de Sénèque*, Paris, 1923.

Alexander, W. H., 'Julius Caesar in the Pages of Seneca the Philosopher', *Trans. Royal Soc. of Canada*, 3rd Ser. 35, sec. 2 (1941), 15 ff.

—— 'Seneca's *Ad Polybium De Consolatione*, a reappraisal', ibid. 37, sec. 2 (1943), 33 ff.

—— 'Cato of Utica in the Works of Seneca Philosophus', ibid. 40, sec. 2 (1946), 59 ff.

—— 'References to Pompey in Seneca's Prose', ibid. 42, sec. 2 (1949), 13 ff.

Altman, M., 'Ruler Cult in Seneca', *CP* 33 (1938), 198 ff.

André, J.-M., *Recherches sur l'otium romain*, Annales littéraires de l'Université de Besançon, no. 52, Paris, 1962.

Baldwin, D., 'Executions under Claudius: Seneca's *Ludus de Morte Claudii*', *Phoenix* 18 (1964), 39 ff.

Bickel, E., *Diatribe in Senecae philosophi fragmenta*, I: *Fragmenta de matrimonio*, Leipzig, 1915.

Bourgery, A., 'Les lettres à Lucilius sont-elles de vraies letters?' *RPh* 35 (1911), 40 ff.

Büchner, K., 'Aufbau und Sinn von Senecas Schrift über die Clementia', *Hermes* 98 (1970), 203 ff.

Caro, E., *Quid de beata vita senserit Seneca*, Diss. Paris, 1852.

Coffey, M., 'Seneca, Apokolokyntosis 1922–1958', *Lustrum* 6 (1961), 239 ff.

Currie, H. MacL., 'The Purpose of the Apocolocyntosis', *L'Antiquité Classique* 31 (1962), 91 ff.

Dahlmann, H., *Über die Kürze des Lebens*, Munich, 1949.

—— Review of E. Köstermann, *Untersuchungen zu den Dialogschriften Senecas*, in *Gnomon* 13 (1937), 366 ff.

Delatte, Louis, 'Lucilius, l'ami de Sénèque', *Les Études Classiques* 4 (1935), 367 ff.; 546 ff.

Dorison, *Quid de clementia L. Annaeus Seneca senserit*, Diss. Cadomi, 1892.

Elias, A., *De Notione Vocis Clementiae apud philosophos veteres et de Fontibus Senecae Librorum de Clementia*, Diss. Königsberg, 1912.

Faider, P.–Favez, Ch., *Sénèque, De la clémence, II Commentaire*, Univ. de Gand, R. de tr. 106 (1950).

Favez, Ch., *Consolatio ad Helviam*, texte, comm., Lausanne, 1918.

—— *Consolatio ad Marciam*, texte, comm., Paris, 1928.

Ferrill, C., 'Seneca's Exile and the *Ad Helviam*', *CP* 61 (1966), 253 ff.

Frassinetti, P., 'Gli scritti matrimoniali di Seneca e Tertulliano', *RIL* 88 (1955) 151 ff.

Fuchs, H., 'Zu Seneca de Clementia 1. 9, 1', *RhM* 108 (1965), 378.

Fuhrmann, M., 'Die Alleinherrschaft und das Problem der Gerechtigkeit', *Gym.* 70 (1963), 481 ff.

Giancotti, F., 'La consolazione di Seneca a Polibio in Cassio Dione, LXI, 10, 2,' *Riv. di fil.* 34 (1956), 30 ff.

—— *Cronologia dei 'Dialoghi' di Seneca*, Turin, 1957.

Griffin, M. T., '*De Brevitate Vitae*', *JRS* 52 (1962), 104 ff.

—— 'Seneca on Cato's Politics: *Epistle* 14. 12–13', *CQ* 18 (1968), 373 ff.

Grimal, P., 'Est-il possible de dater un traité de Sénèque?', *REL* 27 (1949), 178 ff.

—— 'La composition dans les 'dialogues' de Sénèque. I. *De Constantia Sapientis*', *REA* 51 (1949), 246 ff.

—— *Sénèque De Constantia Sapientis*, comm., Paris, 1953.

—— *L. Annaei Senecae De Brevitate Vitae*[2], Paris, 1966.

—— 'Le *De Clementia* et la royauté solaire de Néron,' *REL* 49 (1971), 205 ff.

Guillemin, A.-M., 'Sénèque directeur d'âmes', *REL* 30 (1952), 202 ff.; 31 (1953), 215 ff.; 32 (1954), 250 ff.

Hadot, I., *Seneca und die griechisch-römische Tradition der Seelenleitung*, Berlin, 1969.

Halbauer, O., *De Diatribis Epicteti*, Leipzig, 1911.

Hambüchen, B., *Die Datierung von Senecas Schrift Ad Paulinum De Brevitate Vitae*, Diss. Köln, 1966.

Hense, O., *Seneca und Athenodorus*, Univ.-Prog. Freiburg, 1893.

Jal, P., 'Images d'Auguste chez Sénèque', *REL* 35 (1957), 242 ff.

Köstermann, E., 'Untersuchungen zu den Dialogschriften Senecas', *Sitzungsberichte der preuss. Akad. d. Wiss.* 22 (1934), 684 ff.

Kraft, K., 'Der politische Hintergrund von Senecas Apocolocyntosis', *Historia* 15 (1966), 96 ff.

Kühnen, F. J., *Seneca und die römische Geschichte*, Diss. Köln, 1962.

Lichy, J., *De servorum condicione quid senserit L. Annaeus Seneca*, Diss. Münster, 1927.

Magenta, C., 'Riflessi di agronomia ed economia agricola in Seneca Filosofo', *RIL* 73 (1940), 244 ff.

Maurach, G., *Der Bau von Senecas Epistulae Morales*, Heidelberg, 1970.

Misch, G., *A History of Autobiography in Antiquity*[3] (English translation), 2 vols., London, 1950.

Mortureux, B., *Recherches sur le 'De Clementia' de Sénèque*, Collection Latomus 128, 1973.

Pack, R. A., 'Seneca's Evidence on the Death of Claudius and Narcissus', *CW* 36 (1942), 150-1.

Richter, W., 'Seneca und die Sklaven', *Gym.* 65 (1958), 196 ff.

—— 'Das Problem der Datierung von Senecas de Clementia', *RhM* 108 (1965), 146 ff.

Rogers, R. S., 'Seneca on Lentulus Augur's Wealth: a Note', *CW* 42 (1948), 91-2.

Rossbach, O., 'De Senecae Dialogis', *Hermes* 17 (1882), 365 ff.

Russo, C., *Divi Claudii Ἀποκολοκύντωσις*[4], Florence, 1964.

Schottlaender, R., 'Epikureisches bei Seneca', *Philologus* 99 (1955), 133 ff.

Smith, H. R. W., 'Problems Historical and Numismatic in the Reign of Augustus', *Univ. of Calif. Publ. in Cl. Arch.* 2. 4 (1953), 133 ff.

Stückelberger, A., *Senecas 88 Brief*, Heidelberg, 1965.

Summers, W. C., *Select Letters of Seneca*, London, 1910.

Tadic-Gilloteaux, N., 'Sénèque face au suicide', *L'Antiquité Classique* 32 (1963), 541 ff.

Valette, P., 'Le De Clementia est-il mutilé ou inachevé?' *Mélanges P. Thomas*, Bruges, 1930, pp. 687 ff.

Weber, H., *De Senecae philosophi dicendi genere Bioneo*, Diss. Marburg, 1895.

Weidauer, F., *Der Prinzipat in Senecas Schrift de Clementia*, Diss. Marburg, 1950.

Weinreich, O., *Senecas Apocolocyntosis*, Berlin, 1923.

Literary, Philosophical, and Ideological Background to Seneca's Works

Allen, W., 'A Minor Type of Opposition to Tiberius', *CJ* 44 (1948), 203 ff.

André, J., *La vie et l'œuvre d'Asinius Pollion*, Paris, 1949.

Astin, A. E., *Scipio Aemilianus*, Oxford, 1967.

Badian, E., *Roman Imperialism in the Late Republic*[2], Oxford, 1968.

Bagnani, G., 'Arbiter of Elegance', *Phoenix*, Suppl. 2 (1954).

Baldry, H. C., *The Unity of Mankind in Greek Thought*, Cambridge, 1965.

Béranger, J., *Recherches sur l'aspect idéologique du Principat*, Basel, 1953.

Bodson, A., *La morale sociale des derniers Stoïciens*, Paris, 1967.

Bonhöffer, A., *Die Ethik des Stoikers Epictet*, Stuttgart, 1894.

Brisset, J., *Les idées politiques de Lucain*, Paris, 1964.

Broecker, H., *Animadversiones ad Plutarchi Libellum* περὶ εὐθυμίας, Bonn, 1954.

Brunt, P. A., 'Aspects of the Social Thought of Dio Chrysostom and of the Stoics', *Proc. Camb. Phil. Soc.* 19 (1973), 9 ff.

Capelle, W., 'Griechische Ethik und römischer Imperialismus', *Klio* 25 (1932), 86 ff.

Charlesworth, M. P., 'The Virtues of a Roman Emperor', *PBA* 23 (1937), 105 ff.

Comparetti, D., 'Frammento filosofico da un papiro greco-egizio', *Festschrift Theodor Gomperz*, Vienna, 1902, pp. 80 ff.

Dahlmann, H., 'Der Bienenstaat in Vergils Georgica', *Akad. d. Wiss. u. d. Literatur in Mainz* 10 (1954), 547 ff.

Delatte, L., 'Les Traités de la Royauté d'Ecphante, Diotogène et Sthénidas', *Bibliothèque de la Faculté de Philosophie et Lettres de l'Université de Liège*, fasc. 97, 1942.

Dudley, D. R., *A History of Cynicism*, London, 1937.

Durry, M., *Panégyrique de Trajan*, Paris, 1938.

Edelstein, L., and Kidd, I., *Posidonius I: The Fragments*, Cambridge, 1972.

von Fritz, K., *The Theory of the Mixed Constitution in Antiquity*, New York, 1954.

van Geytenbeek, A. C., *Musonius Rufus and Greek Diatribe*, Assen, 1962.

Goodenough, E., 'The Political Philosophy of Hellenistic Kingship', *Yale Classical Studies* 1 (1928), 55 ff.

Grilli, A., *Il problema della Vita Contemplativa nel mondo greco-romano*, Milan, 1953.

Grimal, P., 'Auguste et Athénodore', *REA* 47 (1945), 261 ff.; 48 (1946), 62 ff.

Hamburger, M., *Morals and Law, the Growth of Aristotle's Legal Theory*, New Haven, Conn., 1951.

Hartke, W., *Römische Kinderkaiser*, Berlin, 1951.

Haug, I., 'Der römische Bundesgenossenkrieg 91–88 v. Chr. bei Titus Livius', *WJA* 2 (1947), 100 ff.

Heinze, R., 'Horazens Buch der Briefe', *N.J.f.d.kl.Alt.* 43 (1919), 305–15 = *Vom Geist des Römertums*³, 1960, pp. 305 ff.

Hellegouarc'h, J., *Le vocabulaire latin des relations et des partis politiques sous la république*, Paris, 1963.

Hind, J. G. F., 'The Middle Years of Nero's Reign', *Historia* 20 (1971), 488 ff.

Hirzel, R., *Der Dialog*, 2 vols., Leipzig, 1895.

—— 'Der Selbstmord', *Archiv für Religionswissenschaft* 11 (1908), 75 ff.; 243 ff.; 417 ff.

Jal, P., *La guerre civile à Rome*, Paris, 1963.

Joly, R., 'Le thème philosophique des genres de vie dans l'antiquité classique', *Acad. roy. de Belgique Mémoires* 51 (1956), 7 ff.

Kargl, J., *Die Lehre der Stoiker vom Staat*, Diss. Erlangen, 1913.

Kumaniecki, K., 'Ciceros Paradoxa und die römische Wirklichkeit', *Philologus* 101 (1957), 113 ff.

Labowsky, L., *Die Ethik des Panaitios*, Leipzig, 1934.

Lattimore, R., *Themes in Greek and Latin Epitaphs*, Illinois, 1942.

Lee, A. G., *Paradoxa Stoicorum*, London, 1953.

Long, A. A. (ed.), *Problems in Stoicism*, London, 1971.

—— 'Carneades and the Stoic Telos', *Phronesis* 12 (1967), 59 ff.

—— *Hellenistic Philosophy*, London, 1974.

Momigliano, A., 'Literary Chronology of the Neronian Age', *CQ* 38 (1944), 96 ff.

Murray, O., 'The "Quinquennium Neronis" and the Stoics', *Historia* 14 (1965), 41 ff.

—— 'Philodemus on the Good King according to Homer', *JRS* 55 (1965), 161 ff.

—— 'Aristeas and Ptolemaic Kingship', *JTS* 18 (1967), 337 ff.

Nock, A. D., *Conversion*, Oxford, 1933.

Oltramare, A., *Les origines de la diatribe romaine*, Lausanne, 1926.

Pecchiura, P., *La figura di Catone Uticense nella letteratura latina*, Turin, 1965.

Pohlenz, M., *Antikes Führertum: Cicero De officiis und das Lebensideal des Panaetius*, Leipzig, 1934.

—— *Philosophie und Erlebnis in Senecas Dialogen*, NGG no. 6, 1941, pp. 55 ff.

—— *Die Stoa*², 2 vols., Göttingen, 1959.

Reesor, M. E., *The Political Theory of the Old and Middle Stoa*, New York, 1951.

Richter, W., 'Römische Zeitgeschichte und innere Emigration', *Gym.* 68 (1961), 286 ff.

Riposati, B., *M. Terenti Varronis De Vita Populi Romani*, Milan, 1939.

Rist, J. M., *Stoic Philosophy*, Cambridge, 1969.

Rutz, W., 'Amor Mortis', *Hermes* 88 (1960), 462 ff.

de St. Denis, E., 'La théorie cicéronienne de la participation aux affaires publiques', *RPh* 64 (1938), 193 ff.

Sinclair, T. A., *A History of Greek Political Thought*, London, 1951.

van Straaten, M., *Panétius*, Amsterdam, 1946.

Van Straaten, M. (*cont.*):

—— *Panaetii Rhodii Fragmenta*³, Leiden, 1962.

Strasburger, H., 'Poseidonios on Problems of the Roman Empire', *JRS* 55 (1965), 40 ff.

Sutherland, C. H. V., 'Two "Virtues" of Tiberius', *JRS* 28 (1938), 129 ff.

Vittinghoff, F., 'Zum geschichtlichen Selbstverständnis der Spätantike', *Historische Zeitschrift*, 198 (1964), 529 ff.

Vogt, J., 'Sklaverei und Humanität', *Historia Einzelschriften* no. 8 (1965).

Walbank, F. W., *A Historical Commentary on Polybius*, 2 vols., Oxford, 1957–67.

—— 'Political Morality and the Friends of Scipio', *JRS* 55 (1965), 1 ff.

Watson, A., 'Morality, Slavery and Jurists in the Later Roman Republic', *Tulane Law Review* 42 (1968), 289 ff.

—— *The Law of Property in the Later Roman Republic*, Oxford, 1968.

Watt, W. S., Review of the 1949 Teubner edition of Cicero's *De Virtutibus* by W. Ax, *JRS* 41 (1951), 200.

Wellmann, M., 'Sextius Niger', *Hermes* 24 (1889), 530 ff.

Wickert, L., 'Princeps und βασιλεύς', *Klio* 36 (1944), 1 ff.

Wirszubski, C., *Libertas as a Political Idea at Rome during the Late Republic and Early Principate*, Cambridge, 1950.

INDEX

This index is particularly selective as regards the Appendices, for which the reader will find help in the list on pp. 393–4 and in footnote references. In the registering of proper names, a compromise has been made between common usage and technical accuracy.

PASSAGES OF SENECA DISCUSSED

Apocolocyntosis

(Chapters and paragraphs follow C. Russo, *Divi Claudii* Ἀποκολοκύντωσις[4], Florence, 1964)

Dialogi

(Chapters and paragraphs follow the Teubner editions of Hosius (1900), Hermes (1905), and Gercke (1907))

Epistulae Morales

(Paragraphs follow the Oxford Classical Text by L. D. Reynolds (1965))

Fragmenta

(The numbering used is basically that of the 1852 edition by F. Haase. For the fragments of *De Matrimonio* I have given the numbers first according to the later edition of E. Bickel, *Diatribe in Senecae philosophi fragmenta*, Leipzig, 1915, adding the equivalents in Haase's edition where they exist)

Epigrams Attributed to Seneca

(Numbers follow C. Prato, *Gli epigrammi attribuiti a L. Anneo Seneca*, Rome, 1964)